LITERATURA CHI
1965–1995

D0141495

GARLAND REFERENCE LIBRARY OF THE HUMANITIES
VOLUME 1912

Literatura chicana, 1965–1995
An Anthology in Spanish, English, and Caló

Edited by
Manuel de Jesús Hernández-Gutiérrez
and David William Foster

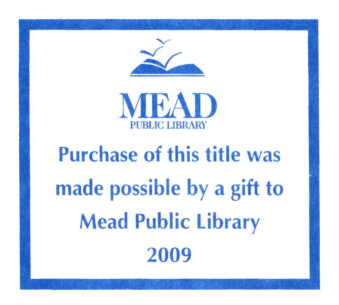

Garland Publishing, Inc.
New York and London
1997

Cover illustration of *Hanna en El Viejo Santo Tomás* by Pauline Reyes-Crewse
(HTTP://www.public.asu.edu/~atfgc/art/gallery.html). Paperback cover design by Karin Badger.

Published in 1997 by
Routledge
Taylor & Francis Group
270 Madison Avenue
New York, NY 10016

© 1997 by Manuel de Jesús Hernández-Gutiérrez and William Foster
Routledge is an imprint of Taylor & Francis Group

Printed in the United States of America on acid-free paper

International Standard Book Number- 0-8151-2080-9 (Softcover)
Library of Congress Card Number 96-24202

Library of Congress Cataloging-in-Publication Data

Literatura chicana, 1965-1995 : an anthology in Spanish, English, and Cálo /
    edited by Manuel de Jesús Hernández-Gutiérrez
        p.   cm. — (Garland reference library of the humanities ; vol. 1912)
    ISBN 0-8153-2077-9 (alk. paper) — ISBN 0-8153-2080-9 (pbk. : alk. paper)
    1. American literature—Mexican American authors. 2. Mexican Americans—Literary collections. 3. Mexican American literature (Spanish). 4. Mexican Americans—Intellectual life. I. Hernández-Gutiérrez, Manuel de Jesús. II. Foster, David William. III. Series.
PS508.M4L58   1997
810.8'086872-dc20   96-24202

Taylor & Francis Group
is the Academic Division of T&F Informa plc.

Visit the Taylor & Francis Web site at
http://www.taylorandfrancis.com

and the Routledge Web site at
http://www.routledge-ny.com

ÍNDICE DE MATERIAS

Ensayo/Essay

Cuento/Short Story

Índice   vii

Teatro/Theater

Novela/Novel

PREFACIO

Tres décadas de literatura chicana contemporánea

> El año 1965 marca el principio del Período Chicano
> Contemporáneo o el Renacimiento Chicano en letras,
> una explosión o un *boom* general en cada y todo
> género literario. (Francisco Lomelí, "An Overview of
> Chicano Letters: From Origins to Resurgence" [1984];
> traducción nuestra.)

*Literatura chicana, 1965-1995: An Anthology in Spanish, English, and
Caló* tiene como proyecto presentar el surgimiento y la evolución de la literatura
chicana contemporánea de 1965 a 1995—tres décadas—alrededor de sus principales temas: la búsqueda de identidad, el feminismo, el conservadurismo, el revisionismo, el homoeroticismo y el internacionalismo. Provenientes del deseo del
sujeto, ya masculino o ya femenino, de crear, estos núcleos temáticos son las
unidades simbolizantes que inscriben en el lenguage ciertas visiones ideológicas
específicas (Hernández-Gutiérrez 51-53). Los seis temas principales han hecho
posible que la producción literaria chicana de los últimos treinta años haya recibido premios nacionales e internacionales, entre ellos, el Premio Anual Quinto
Sol, el Premio Casa de las Américas, el Before Columbus Foundation American
Book Award, el Walt Whitman Award, el Western States Book Award, el Premio Nacional de Literatura José Fuentes y el Western Arts Foundation Award.
Además, el discurso presentado en esta antología incluye textos contestatarios de
fines del siglo XIX y de principios del siglo XX, así como la producción donde
domina o el espacio rural o el espacio urbano. Las escritoras y escritores seleccionados incluyen tres de los cinco—Gloria Anzaldúa, Lorna Dee Cervantes y
Luis Valdez—cuya obra ha sido aceptada por el College Board (la mesa universitaria) en la Recommended Reading List (la lista de lecturas recomendadas) para
el Advanced Placement Exam (el examen avanzado de diagnosis universitario)
del Educational Testing Service (el servicio de exámenes educativos). Valiéndose
de ocho ensayos, dieciséis cuentos, treinta poemas, tres dramas y dos novelas
completas, la colección pretende no sólo llegar a una nueva generación universitaria chicana, sino también al lector general norteamericano, afroamericano,
latinoamericano y peninsular. A lo largo de los textos seleccionados, la expresión
lingüística es diversa: inglés, español y bilingüe (caló).

Al igual que la publicación de un número significativo de antologías de letras mexicoamericanas—bajo el término *chicano*—a fines de los 1960 y a principios de los 1970,[1] la década actual le ofrece al lector un fenómeno similar el cual indica un mayor interés en la literatura mexicoamericana de parte de todos los estadounidenses, empero, esta vez incluye un marcado interés en la escritura de la mujer chicana. Una lectura general de las nuevas antologías revela varios objetivos detrás de su publicación, los cuales van desde celebrar la integración de la escritura chicana a la corriente principal,[2] a documentar las diversas voces de la mujer chicana,[3] a presentar a nuevas escritoras y escritores,[4] a

---

[1]Octavio Romano-V., ed., *Espejo/The Mirror: Selected Mexican American Literature* (Berkeley: Quinto Sol Publications, 1969); Ed Ludwig and James Santibáñez, eds., *The Chicanos: Mexican American Voices* (Baltimore: Penguin Books, 1971); Edward Simmen, ed., *The Chicano: From Caricature to Self-Portrait* (New York: Mentor, 1971); Antonia Castañeda-Shular *et al.*, eds. *Literatura chicana: texto y contexto* (Englewood Cliffs: Prentice Hall, 1972); *Aztlán: An Anthology of Mexican American Literature* (New York: Vintage Books, 1972); Philip D. Ortego, ed., *We Are Chicanos: An Anthology of Mexican-American Literature* (New York: Pocket Books, 1973); y Dorothy E. Harth and Lewis M. Baldwin, eds., *Voices of Aztlán: Chicano Literature of Today* (New York: Mentor Books, 1974).

[2]Charles Tatum, "Introduction", xi-xiv, *New Chicana/Chicano Writing 1*, Charles Tatum, ed. (Tucson: The University of Arizona Press, 1992); Denis Lyn and Daily Heck, eds. *Barrios and Borderlands: Cultures of Latinos and Latinas in the United States* (New York: Routledge, 1994); y Ray González, "Preface", xiii-xiv, *Currents from the Dancing River: Contemporary Latino Fiction, Nonfiction, and Poetry* (1994), editado por Ray González (San Diego: Harcourt Brace Company, 1994).

[3]Tey Diana Rebolledo and Eliana S. Rivero, eds., *Infinite Divisions: An Anthology of Chicana Literature* (Tucson: The University of Arizona Press, 1993); y Roberta Fernández, ed., *In Other Words: Literature by Latinas of the United States* (Houston: Arte Público Press, 1994).

[4]Charles Tatum, ed., *New Chicana/Chicano Writing 2* (Tucson: University of Arizona Press, 1992); y Charles Tatum, ed., *New Chicana/Chicano Writing 3* (Tucson: The University of Arizona Press, 1993).

considerar las letras chicanas como parte de una literatura latinoestadounidense[5] y hasta llegar a los lectores mexicanos y peninsulares.[6] En la década de los 1990, la integración a la corriente principal estadounidense parece ser la afirmación más sonada en la voz de los editores de las antologías (González, Tatum, Augenbraum and Stavans, Lyn and Heck). De hecho, el asiduo lector de la literatura chicana de los últimos treinta y un años ahora encuentra escritoras y escritores desde un pasado como el siglo XVI hasta la década actual en dos antologías recientes de la corriente principal estadounidense: *The Heath Anthology of American Culture I* (1994), editada por Paul Lauter, y *The Norton Anthology of Modern Poetry*, 2a edición (1988), editada por Richard Ellmann y Robert O'Clair.

Sin embargo, las numerosas antologías de los 1990 editadas por editores mexicoamericanos ni la inclusión de unos pocos ejemplos de literatura chicana en las antologías editadas por autores angloamericanos, no ofrecen ni una representación amplia ni una evolución histórica de la literatura mexicoamericana publicada durante los últimos treinta y un años.[7] En reconocimiento que 1995 fue el trigésimo aniversario del inicio de la literatura chicana contemporánea (Lomelí 111; Fernández xxvii), *Literatura chicana, 1965-1995: An Anthology in Spanish, English, and Caló* se planeó y se seleccionaron los textos con la meta

---

[5]Delia Poey and Virgil Suárez, eds., *Iguana Dreams: New Latino Fiction* (New York: HarperCollins, 1992); Denis Lyn and Daily Heck, eds., *Barrios and the Borderlands: Cultures of Latinos and Latinas in the United States* (New York: Routledge, 1994); Ray González, ed., *Currents from the Dancing River: Contemporary Latino Fiction, Nonfiction, and Poetry* (San Diego: Harcourt Brace Company, 1994); y Roberta Fernández, ed., *In Other Words: Literature by Latinas of the United States* (Houston: Arte Público Press, 1994).

[6]María Eugenia Gaona, ed., *Antología de la literatura chicana* (México: Centro de Enseñanza para Extranjeros, 1986); y Manuel M. Martín-Rodríguez, ed., *La voz urgente: antología de literatura chicana en español* (Madrid: Editorial Fundamentos, 1995).

[7]La colección de cuentos, *North of the Rio Grande: The Mexican-American Experience in Short Fiction* (1992), editada por Edward Simmen, representa un esfuezo para lograr tal representación general; sin embargo, el uso de sólo un género literario y la presentación ahistórica limitan su impacto. Véase: Edward Simmen, ed. *North of the Rio Grande: The Mexican-American Experience in Short Fiction* (New York: Mentor, 1992).

de llevar a cabo la necesaria tarea de presentar una antología comprensiva de su producción contemporánea. Las selecciones representan un diálogo interno entre los escritores mexicoamericanos y un descubrimiento para todos los demás norteamericanos (blancos o de color), un diálogo y un descubrimiento que prometen enriquecer el proyecto multicultural y la literatura *American* o estadounidense en general. La amplia representación, y su evolución, de la literatura chicana se desenvuelve a partir de la presencia de los seis temas arriba citados. Mientras que entender el significado de la búsqueda de identidad, el feminismo y el conservadurismo no representa ningún problema, el revisionismo significa un interés en el Sudoeste decimonónico desde la perspectiva de la escritora o escritor contemporáneo; el homoeroticismo incluye tanto la voz lésbica como la gay u homosexual; y el internacionalismo se refiere a textos cuyas acciones principales ocurren fuera de los Estados Unidos pero que son de interés al sujeto chicano, ya sea feminino o masculino. Históricamente evolucionado, el discurso que se presenta en *Literatura chicana, 1965-1995: An Anthology in Spanish, English, and Caló* no se debe ver como un sistema fijo y congelado, sino como orgánico y dialéctico en su relación a la experiencia mexicoamericana de los últimos treinta y un años.

Desde la temprana discusión y los planes preliminares, esta antología se desarrolló con la meta de servir a estudiantes del *community college* o de la universidad que forman parte de varias facultades y programas. Pensamos en estudiantes bilingües y en egresados de programas de lengua en español cuyo nivel es por lo menos tres años de lengua a nivel univesitario y, preferentemente, con una clase de introducción a la crítica literaria con los conceptos de período, género y movimiento. Pensamos en estudiantes de tercer y cuarto año en las facultades de literatura anglo-norteamericana, en programas de estudios étnicos y feministas, y en facultades de ciencias sociales. Para estos estudiantes y para todo lector de *Literatura chicana, 1965-1995: An Anthology in Spanish, English, and Caló*, recomendamos como textos de consulta las siguientes obras: para biografía, *Chicano Authors: Inquiry by Interview* (1980), editado por Juan Bruce Novoa y los volumenes 82 and 122 en el *Dictionary of Literary Biography*, respectivamente intitulados *Chicano Writers: First Series* (1989) and *Chicano Writers: Second Series* (1992), ambos editados por Francisco A. Lomelí y Carl R. Shirley; para novela, *Contemporary Fiction: A Critical Survey* (1986), editado por Vernon E. Lattin, *Chicano Narrative: The Dialectics of Difference* (1990) de Ramón Saldívar y *El colonialismo interno en la narrativa chicana: el barrio, el anti-barrio y el exterior* (1994) de Manuel de Jesús Hernández-Gutiérrez; para drama, *Chicano Theater: Themes and Forms* (1982) de Jorge A. Huerta and *El Teatro Campesino: Theater in the Chicano Movement* (1994) de Yolanda Broyles-González; para poesía, *Chicano Poetry: A Critical Introduction* (1986) de Cordelia Candelaria y *Movements in Chicano Poetry: Against Myths, Against Margins* (1995) de Rafael Pérez-Torres; para escritura de la mujer, *Beyond Stereotypes: The Critical Analysis of Chicana Literature* (1985) de María Herrera-Sobek and *Women Singing in the Snow: A Cultural Analysis of Chicana Literature* (1995) de Tey Diana Rebolledo; para cuento, "Cuentos y cuentistas chicanos: perspectiva temática y producción histórica del género, 1947-1992" (1993) de Rosamel Benavides; para ensayo, *Pain and Promise: The Chicano Today* (1972) editada por Edward Simmen y *Chicano Studies: A Multidisciplinary Approach* (1984) editada por Eugene E. García *et al.*; y para historia, *Occupied America: A History of Chicanos*, 3ra edición (1988) de Rodolfo Acuña y *Roots of Chicano Politics, 1600-1940* (1994) de Juan Gómez-Quiñones. Para entender el vocabulario del español bilingüe, se puede consultar: *El lenguaje de los chicanos: Regional and Social Characteristics of Language Used by Mexican Americans* (1975) de Eduardo Hernández-Chávez *et al.*, *El libro de caló/Pachuco Slang Dictionary* (1983) de Harry Polkinhorn *et al.* y *El diccionario del español chicano/The Dictionary of Chicano Spanish* (1986) de Roberto Galván y Richard V. Teschner.

　　Además de ser fiel al eje histórico de la producción literaria chicana contemporánea y de haber seleccionado textos que son manifestaciones de los núcleos temáticos, esta antología está organizada alrededor de los cinco géneros literarios tradicionales: ensayo, cuento, poesía, drama y novela.

　　La sección dedicada al ensayo exhibe expresiones del historicismo, el conservadurismo, el feminismo, el postmodernismo y la cultura popular. Para resaltar la evolución del pensamiento chicano a través de los últimos treinta y un años, la sección se abre con el ensayo "Chicanology: A Postmodern Analysis of Meshicano Discourse" (1992) de Francisco H. Vázquez el cual representa, en su alineamiento con el pos-modernismo, una dirección de vanguardia en el pensamiento chicano, particularmente por su crítica de los programas de Estudios Chicanos. En seguida regresamos a textos tempranos en su orden de publicación cronológica. "The Evolution of the Mind" (1969) de Ysidro Ramón Macías, un ensayo del *Chicano Renaissance* o Renacimiento Chicano en letras (Ortego 294-96), detalla la diversidad ideológica entre los mexicoamericanos desde un principio de la literatura chicana contemporánea. Siendo originalmente una publicación estudiantil, el ensayo de Macías puede exhibir debilidades de estilo, empero, su resonancia se mantiene alta a veintisiete años de su aparición. "The His-

torical and Intellectual Presence of Mexican Americans" (1969) de Octavio
Ignacio Romano-V. ostenta el indigenismo y el nacionalismo cultural como la
clave al temprano pensamiento chicano militante. "Prologue: Middle-Class Pastoral" (1981) de Richard Rodriguez[8] defiende el derecho de un sujeto chicano
conservador quien desea tomar parte en gobernar a *America* o Estados Unidos—una línea adoptada por otros mexicoamericanos conservadores como Linda
Chávez y Rubén Navarrete, Jr. "La Güera" (1981) de Cherríe Moraga, "La conciencia de la mestiza: Towards a New Consciousness" (1987) de Gloria Anzaldúa
y "Letting La Llorona Go, or, Re/reading History's 'Tender Mercies'" (1993)
de Cordelia Candelaria son una expresión del feminismo de la chicana. Por
último, "Pendejismo" (1993) de José Antonio Burciaga expone a la lectora o
lector a la cultura popular y humorística del chicano.

De 1965 a 1996, el cuento chicano tiene una rica producción dentro de
cuyos practicantes tenemos un gran número de escritoras y escritores. Para *Literatura chicana, 1965-1995: An Anthology in Spanish, English, and Caló*, hemos
seleccionado los trabajos más representativos, algunos de los cuales han recibido
premios nacionales e internacionales. La selección se inicia con "Do You Speak
Pocho...?" (1924) de Jorge Ulica, quien publicó en español desde a fines de los
1910 hasta principios de los 1920 en San Francisco. Este último texto y muchos
otros exhiben un artístico y ameno uso del español chicano del norte de California. En cuanto a la búsqueda de identidad, tenemos "El Hoyo" (1947) de Mario
Suárez. Entre otros, "The Paris Gown" (1975; 1993) de Estela Portillo Trambley
y "The Moths" (1985) de Helena María Viramontes representan el feminismo,
mientras que "Then They'd Watch Comedies" (1984) de Alberto Álvaro Ríos
exhibe la feminización del narrador masculino. El espacio rural es representado
por "Las salamandras" (1972) de Tomás Rivera, mientras que "Looking for
Work" (1985) de Gary Soto representa el espacio urbano. Este último cuento
procede de la colección *Living up the Street*, ganadora del 1985 American Book
Award. Con un enfoque particular en el SIDA, "Fugitive" (1987) de Gloria
Velásquez representa el homoeroticismo. De otras selecciones, "La junta" (1980)
de Jim Sagel y "A Long Walk" (1980; 1996) de Alejandro Murguía representan
la militancia, mientras que "El conejo pionero" (1988) de Sabine Ulibarrí, por
medio de una fábula, se detiene en el conservadurismo clasemediero. "Feliz
cumpleaños E.U.A." (1979) de Rolando R. Hinojosa-Smith, "Huachusey" (1986)

---

[8]Richard Rodriguez insiste en escribir su apellido sin acento.

de Miguel Méndez-M. y "Cumplir mi justa condena..." (1987) de Ricardo Aguilar Melantzón exhiben la expansión espacial del sujeto chicano a través de todo Estados Unidos. Por último, "Coyote emplumado" (1988) de Sergio Elizondo es un texto del realismo mágico.

Por razón de sus veintinueve representantes, tanto hombres como mujeres, la sección de poesía es la más rica y diversa a nivel del punto de vista. Aquí es donde incluimos tres textos contestatarios de fines del siglo XIX: los anónimamente escritos "Corrido de Joaquín Murrieta" (¿1850?) y "Corrido de Gregorio Cortez" (¿1901?), más "El idioma español" (1889) del nuevomexicano Jesús María H. Alarid. La búsqueda de identidad es representada en la sección de poesía por *I Am Joaquín* (1967) de Rodolfo "Corky" Gonzales y "Crisis de identidad, o, Ya no chingues" (1970) de Margarita Cota-Cárdenas. El feminismo se manifiesta en "Notes from a Chicana 'Coed'" (1977) de Bernice Zamora, "Aborto" (1975) de Yolanda Luera y "Beneath the Shadow of the Freeway" (1977) de Lorna Dee Cervantes. "Are You Doing That New Amerikan Thing?" (1983) de Juan Felipe Herrera sobresale como una crítica del conservadurismo. El homoeroticismo se expresa en "Me gusta caminar junto a tu lado" (1991) de Francisco Alarcón. "Barrios of the World" (1971) de Ricardo Sánchez, "Death in Vietnam" (1972) de Luis Omar Salinas, "Nativity: For Two Salvadoran Women, 1986-1987" (1989) de Demetria Martínez, "Kilotons and Then Some" (1985) de Carlos Cumpián y "Trust" (1992) de Alma Luz Villanueva mejor representan el internacionalismo. El espacio rural lo representan "Daybreak" (1977) de Gary Soto y "Pinos Wells" (1984) de Jimmy Santiago Baca. "Tarde sobria" (1971) de Alurista, "El Louie" (1969) de José Montoya, "Barrios of the World" (1971) de Ricardo Sánchez, "Mexicans Begin Jogging" (1981) de Gary Soto, "Padre Nuestro Que Estás en el Banco" (1986) de Reyes Cárdenas y "The Blast Furnace" (1991) de Luis Rodríguez representan el espacio urbano. Una resonante muestra del arte lingüístico bilingüe es "Poema en tres idiomas y caló" (1977) de José Antonio Burciaga, uno de los fundadores del grupo cómico Culture Clash. Por último, la poesía de amor ocupa un espacio en esta antología con "Cómo desnudar a una mujer con un saxofón" (1986) de Rubén Medina, del libro, *Amor de lejos . . . Fools' Love*, el cual ganó en 1986 una mención honorífica en el género de poesía del premio cubano Casa de las Américas; "Comiendo lumbre" (1986) de Gina Valdés; y "Me gusta caminar junto a tu lado" (1991) de Francisco Alarcón. Este último poema se encuentra en *De amor oscuro/Of Dark Love*, el único libro profundo de poesía de amor escrito en los últimos treinta y un años por un poeta heterosexual o homoerótico. Otros poemas de significado histórico son "Los caudillos" (1970) de raúlrsalinas, "Stupid America" (1969) de Abelardo, "Mi abuelo" (1982) de Alberto Álvaro Ríos, "Unción de palabras" (1987) de Tino Villanueva y "Recipe: Chorizo con Huevo Made in the Microwave" (1989) de Bárbara Brinson Curiel.

Del drama chicano, hemos seleccionado dos obras cortas de Luis Valdez, *Las Dos Caras del Patroncito* (1965) y *Los Vendidos* (1967), así como *Giving Up the Ghost* (1986; 1994) de Cherríe Moraga. Además del hecho de que la obra *Las Dos Caras del Patroncito* marca el inicio de la literatura chicana contemporánea, ambas obras de Valdez simbolizan, respectivamente, el espacio rural y el urbano, proyectando de esta manera la transición de la cultura mexicoamericana pastoril a una principalmente moderna y urbanizada. Con sus diversos personajes, *Los Vendidos* también representa la búsqueda de identidad. Respecto a *Giving Up the Ghost*, este drama es un ejemplo marcado del homoeroticismo en su cara lésbica. La obra dramatiza la iniciación personal y la compleja manifestación de un estilo de vida alternativa que vive consciente de su participación subjetiva en la cultura chicana, la femenina o la masculina. En medio de estos textos, y después del último, existe un catálogo fenomenal de dramas que el lector puede investigar y leer.

De las numerosas novelas publicadas durante los últimos treinta años, hemos seleccionado *El diablo en Texas* (1976) del arizonés Aristeo Brito y *There Are No Madmen Here* (1981; 1996) de la californiana Gina Valdés. Una temprana novela del Renacimiento Chicano en letras, *El diablo en Texas* no sólo representa la búsqueda de identidad, sino también anuncia un interés en el revisionismo. Es decir, como en la novela *Not by the Sword* (1982) de Nash Candelaria—ganadora del premio Before Columbus Foundation American Book Award—*El diablo en Texas* tiene lugar principalmente en el siglo XIX. Una de las primeras novelas abiertamente feministas, *There Are No Madmen Here*, como lo implica su título, abre dramáticamente un espacio chicano profundamente feminizado en el que los personajes masculinos son estrictamente secundarios. En esta novela, como simbolizado por un padre violento y solitario, un esposo excéntrico e irresponsable y una generación de hombres jóvenes confundidos, el patriarcado ha fallado en la tarea de mantener la unidad de la familia, dejando tan importante rol a la protagonista, María Portillo Vega. El mismo mensaje se repite una y otra vez en novela tras novela de la mujer chicana como *Trini* (1986) de Estela Portillo Trambley y *So Far from God* (1993) de Ana Castillo.

Damos las gracias a las editoriales y a los autores que nos otorgaron el derecho para reproducir los textos incluidos en esta antología así como a varios estudiantes de posgrado quienes participaron en el proceso: Fabio Correa Uribe, Elizabeth Flores, José María García Sánchez, Loida Gutiérrez, Arthur Hughes y Francisco Manzo-Robledo.

Dirigido por el Dr. Felipe G. Castro, el Hispanic Research Center de Arizona State University contribuyó a esta antología por medio de fondos sustanciales para la preparación del manuscrito.

Manuel de Jesús Hernández-Gutiérrez

Obras citadas

Fernández, Roberta. "Introduction: A Mosaic of Latino Literature of the United States". *In Other Words: Literature by Latinas of the United States*. Ed. Roberta Fernández. Houston: Arte Público Press, 1994. xxv-xxxvii.

Hernández-Gutiérrez, Manuel de Jesús. "El proyecto ideológico: la autorrepresentación chicana en la narrativa". *El colonialismo interno en la narrativa chicana: el barrio, el anti-barrio y el exterior*. Tempe: Bilingual Press /Editorial Bilingüe, 1994. 28-56.

Lomelí, Francisco. "An Overview of Chicano Letters: From Origins to Resurgence". *Chicano Studies: A Multidisciplinary Approach*. Eds. Eugene E. García, Francisco Lomelí, and Isidro D. Ortiz. New York: Teachers College Press, 1984. 103-19.

Ortego, Philip D. "The Chicano Renaissance". *Social Casework* 52.5 (May 1971): 294-307.

PREFACE

Three Decades of Contemporary Chicana/o Literature

> The year 1965 marks the beginning of the Contemporary Chicano Period or Renaissance of Chicano letters, an explosion or general boom in every literary genre. (Francisco Lomelí, "An Overview of Chicano Letters: From Origins to Resurgence" [1984].)

Literatura chicana, 1965-1995: An Anthology in Spanish, English, and Caló seeks to present the rise and evolution of contemporary Mexican American literature from 1965 to 1995—three decades—around its major themes: the search for identity, feminism, conservatism, revisionism, homoeroticism, and internationalism. Grounded in the Chicana/o subject's desire to create, they are the symbolizing units that provide through language a specific ideological vision (Hernández-Gutiérrez 51-53). These six main thematic clusters have helped Chicano literary production from the past thirty-one years to earn national and international literary prizes, among them the Annual Premio Quinto Sol, the Premio Casa de las Américas, the Before Columbus Foundation American Book Award, the Walt Whitman Award, the Western States Book Award, Premio Nacional de Literatura José Fuentes, and the Western Arts Foundation Award. In addition, the texts presented in this anthology take into account late-nineteenth and early twentieth oppositional texts, as well as works featuring a dominant rural or urban space. Selected authors include three of the five—Gloria Anzaldúa, Lorna Dee Cervantes, and Luis Valdez—whose work has been included by the College Board in the Recommended Reading List for the Advanced Placement Exam of the Educational Testing Service. Using eight essays, sixteen short stories, thirty poems, three plays, and two complete novels, the collection intends to reach not only a new generation of Chicana/o students but also the general Anglo-American, Afro-American, Latin American, and Peninsular reader. Language expression is diverse across all selected texts: English, Spanish, and Spanglish.

Like the publication of numerous anthologies of Mexican American letters—under the term *Chicano literature*—in the late 1960s and early 1970s,[1] the present decade has brought the reader a similar phenomenon that signals a greater interest on Mexican American writing among Americans; however, this time it includes an interest in work by Chicanas, that is, by women. A broad reading of the new anthologies shows a diverse intent that runs from hailing the mainstreaming of Chicana/o letters,[2] to documenting diverse Chicana voices,[3] to the introduction of new writers,[4] to seeing Chicana/o writing as part of U.S. Latino

---

[1]Octavio Romano-V., ed., *Espejo/The Mirror: Selected Mexican American Literature* (Berkeley: Quinto Sol Publications, 1969); Ed Ludwig and James Santibáñez, eds., *The Chicanos: Mexican American Voices* (Baltimore: Penguin Books, 1971); Edward Simmen, ed., *The Chicano: From Caricature to Self-Portrait* (New York: Mentor, 1971); Antonia Castañeda-Shular *et al.*, eds. *Literatura chicana: texto y contexto* (Englewood Cliffs: Prentice Hall, 1972); *Aztlán: An Anthology of Mexican American Literature* (New York: Vintage Books, 1972); Philip D. Ortego, ed., *We Are Chicanos: An Anthology of Mexican-American Literature* (New York: Pocket Books, 1973); and Dorothy E. Harth and Lewis M. Baldwin, eds., *Voices of Aztlan: Chicano Literature of Today* (New York: Mentor Books, 1974).

[2]Charles Tatum, "Introduction," xi-xiv, *New Chicana/Chicano Writing 1*, Charles Tatum, ed. (Tucson: The University of Arizona Press, 1992); Denis Lyn and Daily Heck, eds. *Barrios and Borderlands: Cultures of Latinos and Latinas in the United States* (New York: Routledge, 1994); and Ray González, "Preface," xiii-xiv, *Currents from the Dancing River: Contemporary Latino Fiction, Nonfiction, and Poetry* (1994), edited by Ray González (San Diego: Harcourt Brace Company, 1994).

[3]Tey Diana Rebolledo and Eliana S. Rivero, eds., *Infinite Divisions: An Anthology of Chicana Literature* (Tucson: The University of Arizona Press, 1993); and Roberta Fernández, ed., *In Other Words: Literature by Latinas of the United States* (Houston: Arte Público Press, 1994).

[4]Charles Tatum, ed., *New Chicana/Chicano Writing 2* (Tucson: University of Arizona Press, 1992); and Charles Tatum, ed., *New Chicana/Chicano Writing 3* (Tucson: The University of Arizona Press, 1993).

writing,[5] and to reaching the Mexican and Peninsular reader.[6] In the 1990s, mainstreaming is perhaps the strongest word on the lips of the anthologizers (González, Tatum, Augenbraum and Stavans, Lyn and Heck). In fact, the assiduous reader of Chicana/o writing during the past thirty-one years now finds female and male writers from as long ago as the 1500s to the current decade in two recent mainstream anthologies: *The Heath Anthology of American Culture I* (1994), edited by Paul Lauter, and *The Norton Anthology of Modern Poetry*, 2nd edition, (1988), edited by Richard Ellmann and Robert O'Clair.

However, neither the numerous anthologies of the 1990s edited by Mexican American authors nor the inclusion of a few works in mainstream anthologies by Anglo-American authors offer a broad representation and a historical evolution of Chicana/o literature published during the past thirty-one years.[7] In recognition that 1995 represented the thirtieth anniversary of the founding of Contemporary Chicano letters (Lomelí 111; Fernández xxvii), *Literatura chicana, 1965-1995: An Anthology in Spanish, English, and Caló* was organized under the goal of fulfilling such a necessary task. The selections represent an internal dialogue among Mexican American writers and a discovery to other Americans—white or of color—that promises to enrich the multicultural project

---

[5]Delia Poey and Virgil Suárez, eds., *Iguana Dreams: New Latino Fiction* (New York: HarperCollins, 1992); Denis Lyn and Daily Heck, eds., *Barrios and the Borderlands: Cultures of Latinos and Latinas in the United States* (New York: Routledge, 1994); Ray González, ed., *Currents from the Dancing River: Contemporary Latino Fiction, Nonfiction, and Poetry* (San Diego: Harcourt Brace Company, 1994); and Roberta Fernández, ed., *In Other Words: Literature by Latinas of the United States* (Houston: Arte Público Press, 1994).

[6]María Eugenia Gaona, ed., *Antología de la literatura chicana* (México: Centro de Enseñanza para Extranjeros, 1986); and Manuel M. Martín-Rodríguez, ed., *La voz urgente: antología de literatura chicana en español* (Madrid: Editorial Fundamentos, 1995).

[7]The short-story anthology *North of the Rio Grande: The Mexican-American Experience in Short Fiction* (1992), edited by Edward Simmen, represents an effort toward achieving such a broad representation; however, the use of only one genre and the ahistorical presentation limit its impact. See Edward Simmen, ed. *North of the Rio Grande: The Mexican-American Experience in Short Fiction* (New York: Mentor, 1992).

and American literature in general. The broad representation and historical evolution of Chicana/o writing unfolds from the presence of the above-mentioned
themes. Whereas understanding the search for identity, feminism, and conservatism should be no problem, revisionism means an interest in the Southwest of the
nineteenth-century from the perspective of the contemporary writer; homoeroticism includes both lesbian and gay writings; and internationalism pertains to texts
whose primary events occur outside the United States and interest the Chicana/o
subject. Historically evolved, the discourse present in *Literatura chicana, 1965-
1995: An Anthology in Spanish, English, and Caló* is not to be seen as a set and
frozen system, but as an organic and dialectical one in relation to the Mexican
American experience of the past thirty-one years.

From its earliest discussion and planning, this anthology was developed
with the goal of reaching college and university students housed in various departments and programs in humanities and the social sciences. We had in mind
bilinguals and students in Spanish programs who have at least three years of
university Spanish and, preferably, an introductory course in literary criticism
with the concepts of period, genre, and literary movement. We thought of upper-
division students in departments of English, in ethnic and women studies programs, and in social science departments. For them and all readers of *Literatura
chicana, 1965-1995: An Anthology in Spanish, English, and Caló*, we recom-
mend as reference texts the following works: for biography, *Chicano Authors:
Inquiry by Interview* (1980) by Juan Bruce Novoa and volumes 82 and 122 in the
Dictionary of Literary Biography, respectively entitled *Chicano Writers: First
Series* (1989) and *Chicano Writers: Second Series* (1992), both edited by Francisco A. Lomelí and Carl R. Shirley; in the novel, *Contemporary Fiction: A Critical
Survey* (1986) by Vernon E. Lattin, *Chicano Narrative: The Dialectics of Dif-
ference* (1990) by Ramón Saldívar, and *El colonialismo interno en la narrativa
chicana: el barrio, el anti-barrio y el exterior (1994)* by Manuel de Jesús Hernández-Gutiérrez; in drama, *Chicano Theater: Themes and Forms* (1982) by
Jorge A. Huerta and *El Teatro Campesino: Theater in the Chicano Movement*
(1994) by Yolanda Broyles-González; in poetry, *Chicano Poetry: A Critical
Introduction* (1986) by Cordelia Candelaria and *Movements in Chicano Poetry:
Against Myths, Against Margins* (1995) by Rafael Pérez-Torres; in Chicana
writing, *Beyond Stereotypes: The Critical Analysis of Chicana Literature* (1985)
by María Herrera-Sobek and *Women Singing in the Snow: A Cultural Analysis
of Chicana Literature* (1995) by Tey Diana Rebolledo; in the short story, "Cuentos y cuentistas chicanos: perspectiva temática y producción histórica del género,

1947-1992" (1993) by Rosamel Benavides; in the essay, *Pain and Promise: The Chicano Today* (1972), edited by Edward Simmen and *Chicano Studies: A Multi-disciplinary Approach* (1984), edited by Eugene E. García *et al.*; and in history, *Occupied America: A History of Chicanos*, 3rd edition (1988) by Rodolfo Acuña and *Roots of Chicano Politics, 1600-1940* (1994) by Juan Gómez-Quiñones. In the case of barrio Spanish vocabulary, the reader can consult *El Lenguaje de los Chicanos: Regional and Social Characteristics of Language Used by Mexican Americans* (1975) by Eduardo Hernández-Chávez *et al.*, *El libro de caló/Pachuco Slang Dictionary* (1983) by Harry Polkinhorn *et al.*, and *El diccionario del español chicano/The Dictionary of Chicano Spanish* (1986) by Roberto Galván and Richard V. Teschner.

In addition to following the historical axis in the production of con-temporary Chicana/o literature and in selecting texts as manifestations of do-minant themes, this anthology is organized around the five traditional literary genres: essay, short story, poetry, theater, and novel.

The essay section features historicism, conservatism, feminism, post-modernism, and popular culture. In seeking to indicate an evolution in Chicana/o thought over the past thirty-one years, the section begins with the essay "Chica-nology: A Postmodern Analysis of Meshicano Discourse" (1992) by Francisco H. Vázquez which represents, in its embracing of post-modernism, a vanguard direction in Chicana/o thought, particularly in its criticism of programs in Chica-na and Chicano Studies. We then return to earlier texts in their chronological order of publication. "The Evolution of the Mind" (1969) by Ysidro Ramón Macías, a text from the Chicano Renaissance (Ortego 294-96), shows ideological diversity among Mexican Americans from the very start of contemporary Chica-na/o literature. Originally published as a student publication, Macías's article may exhibit some stylistic weaknesses, however, its intellectual resonance remains high twenty-seven years later. "The Historical and Intellectual Presence of Mexi-can Americans" (1969) by Octavio Ignacio Romano-V. features indigenism and cultural nationalism as the key to the early militant Chicano thought. "Prologue: Middle-Class Pastoral" (1981) by Richard Rodriguez defends a conservative Chicano subject who wishes to partake of ruling America—a line embraced by other Mexican American conservatives like Linda Chávez and Rubén Navarrete, Jr. "La Güera" (1981) by Cherríe Moraga, "La conciencia de la mestiza: Towards a New Consciousness" (1987) by Gloria Anzaldúa and "Letting La Llorona Go, or, Re/reading History's 'Tender Mercies'" (1993) by Cordelia Candelaria are an expression of feminism. Lastly, "Pendejismo" (1993) by José Antonio Burciaga exposes the reader to Chicana/o popular culture and humor.

From 1965 to 1996, the Chicano short story has a rich production among whose practitioners we find an immense number of male and female writers. We have selected the most representative works, some of which have received national and international prizes. The selections begin with "Do You Speak Pocho...?" (1924) by Jorge Ulica, who published in Spanish from the late 1910s to the early 1920s in San Francisco. This text and many others exhibit an artful and whimsical use of Chicano Spanish in Northern California. In terms of the search for identity, we have "El Hoyo" (1947) by Mario Suárez. Among others, "The Paris Gown" (1975; 1993) by Estela Portillo Trambley and "The Moths" (1985) by Helena María Viramontes represent feminist concerns, while "Then They'd Watch Comedies" (1984) by Alberto Álvaro Ríos exhibits the feminization of the male narrator. Rural space is represented in Tomás Rivera's "Las salamandras" (1972), while Gary Soto's "Looking for Work" (1985) represents urban space. This last short story comes from the award-winning collection *Living Up the Street*, winner of the 1985 American Book Award. With a particular focus on AIDS, "Fugitive" (1987) by Gloria Velásquez represents homoeroticism. In other selections, "La junta" (1980) by Jim Sagel and "A Long Walk" (1980; 1996) by Alejandro Murguía represent militancy, while "El conejo pionero" (1988) by Sabine Ulibarrí, in the form of a fable, dwells on middle-class conservatism. "Feliz cumpleaños E.U.A." (1979) by Rolando R. Hinojosa-Smith, "Huachusey" (1986) by Miguel Méndez-M., and "Cumplir mi justa condena..." (1987) by Ricardo Aguilar Melantzón exhibit the spatial expansion of the Chicano subject across the continental United States. Lastly, "Coyote emplumado" (1988) by Sergio Elizondo is a magic-realist text.

With its twenty-nine writers, both male and female, the poetry section is the richest and most diverse in viewpoint. It is here where we include the three oppositional texts from the late nineteenth-century: the anonymously written "Corrido de Joaquín Murrieta" (1850?) and "Corrido de Gregorio Cortez" (1901?), plus "El idioma español" (1889) by the New Mexican Jesús María H. Alarid. The search for identity is represented in the poetry section by *I Am Joaquín* (1967) by Rodolfo "Corky" Gonzales and "Crisis de identidad, o, Ya no chingues" (1970) by Margarita Cota-Cárdenas. Feminism manifests itself in "Notes from a Chicana 'Coed'" (1977) by Bernice Zamora, "Aborto" (1975) by Yolanda Luera, and "Beneath the Shadow of the Freeway" (1977) by Lorna Dee Cervantes. "Are You Doing That New Amerikan Thing?" (1983) by Juan Felipe

Herrera stands as a criticism of conservatism. Homoeroticism finds expression in "Me gusta caminar junto a tu lado" (1991) by Francisco Alarcón. "Barrios of the World" (1971) by Ricardo Sánchez, "Death in Vietnam" (1972) by Luis Omar Salinas, "Nativity: For Two Salvadoran Women, 1986-1987" (1989) by Demetria Martínez, "Kilotons and Then Some" (1985) by Carlos Cumpián, and "Trust" (1992) by Alma Luz Villanueva best represent internationalism. Rural space is represented by "Daybreak" (1977) by Gary Soto and "Pinos Wells" (1984) by Jimmy Santiago Baca. "Tarde sobria" (1971) by Alurista, "El Louie" (1969) by José Montoya, "Barrios of the World" (1971) by Ricardo Sánchez, "Mexicans Begin Jogging" (1981) by Gary Soto, "Padre Nuestro Que Estás en el Banco" (1986) by Reyes Cárdenas and "The Blast Furnace" (1991) by Luis Rodríguez represent urban space. A masterful display of linguistic artistry is "Poema en tres idiomas y caló" (1977) by José Antonio Burciaga, one of the original founders of the comedy group Culture Clash. Finally, love poetry has a place in this anthology with "Cómo desnudar a una mujer con un saxofón" (1986) by Rubén Medina, from the book, *Amor de lejos . . . Fools' Love*, which won in 1986 an honorable mention in poetry from the Cuban Premio Casa de las Américas, "Comiendo lumbre" (1986) by Gina Valdés, and "Me gusta caminar junto a tu lado" (1991) by Francisco Alarcón. This last poem comes from *De amor oscuro/Of Dark Love*, the only profound book of love poetry written in the last thirty-one years by a heterosexual or homoerotic poet. Other historically significant poems appear such as "Los caudillos" (1970) by raúlrsalinas, "Stupid America" (1969) by Abelardo, "Mi abuelo" (1982) by Alberto Álvaro Ríos, "Unción de palabras" (1987) by Tino Villanueva, and "Recipe: Chorizo con Huevo Made in the Microwave" (1989) by Bárbara Brinson Curiel.

From Chicana/o theater, we have selected two short works by Luis Valdez, *Las Dos Caras del Patroncito* (1965) and *Los Vendidos* (1967), as well as *Giving Up the Ghost* (1986; 1994) by Cherríe Moraga. Added to the fact that *Las Dos Caras del Patroncito* marks the beginning of contemporary Chicano literature, both Valdez plays symbolize rural and urban space respectively, fore-grounding thereby the transition of Mexican Americans from a pastoral to a primarily modern urban culture. With its diverse characters, *Los Vendidos* also represents the search for identity. As for *Giving Up the Ghost*, this play is a marked example of homoeroticism in its lesbian face. The play dramatizes the personal initiation into and the complex manifestation of an alternative lifestyle strongly conscious of its subjective participation in Chicana/o culture. In between these texts, and after the last one, there is a phenomenal catalogue of plays that the reader can research and read.

From the numerous novels written in the past thirty years, we have selected *El diablo en Texas* (1976) by Arizonan Aristeo Brito and *There Are No Madmen Here* (1981; 1996) by Californian Gina Valdés. An early novel from the Renaissance of Chicano letters, *El diablo en Texas* not only presents the search for identity but also announces an interest in revisionism. That is, like in the novel *Not by the Sword* (1982) by Nash Candelaria—winner of the Before Columbus Foundation American Book Award—*El diablo en Texas* takes place primarily in the nineteenth century. One of the very first openly feminist novels, *There Are No Madmen Here*, as its title implies, dramatically opens a space in Chicano literature profoundly feminized where male characters are strictly secondary. In this particular novel, as symbolized by a violent and reclusive father, an eccentric and irresponsible husband, and a confused generation of young men, patriarchy has failed to hold the family together, leaving such a central and important task to the protagonist, María Portillo Vega. The same message repeats itself in Chicana novel after novel like in *Trini* (1986) by Estela Portillo Trambley and *So Far from God* (1993) by Ana Castillo.

We wish to thank the presses and authors who have granted us the right to reprint the texts making up this anthology as well as several graduate students who have participated in the process: Fabio Correa Uribe, Elizabeth Flores, José María García Sánchez, Loida Gutiérrez, Arthur Hughes, and Francisco Manzo-Robledo.

Headed by Dr. Felipe G. Castro, the Hispanic Research Center at Arizona State University contributed by awarding the editors a substantial grant for preparing the manuscript.

Manuel de Jesús Hernández-Gutiérrez

Works Cited

Fernández, Roberta. "Introduction: A Mosaic of Latino Literature of the United States." *In Other Words: Literature by Latinas of the United States*. Ed. Roberta Fernández. Houston: Arte Público Press, 1994. xxv-xxxvii.
Hernández-Gutiérrez, Manuel de Jesús. "El proyecto ideológico: la autorrepresentación chicana en la narrativa." *El colonialismo interno en la narrativa*

chicana: el barrio, el anti-barrio y el exterior. Tempe: Bilingual Press/Editorial Bilingüe, 1994. 28-56.

Lomelí, Francisco. "An Overview of Chicano Letters: From Origins to Resurgence." *Chicano Studies: A Multidisciplinary Approach.* Eds. Eugene E. García, Francisco Lomelí, and Isidro D. Ortiz. New York: Teachers College Press, 1984. 103-19.

Ortego, Philip D. "The Chicano Renaissance." *Social Casework* 52.5 (May 1971): 294-307.

PRESENTACIÓN

Chicana/o Literature: A Generational Tapestry of Colors

At the dawn of a new century, a multitude of works identified as Chicana/o literature have appeared, works that have come to define our collective identity. Illuminated by the morning light, our culture emerges from the darkness as dynamic, evolving tapestry, a quilt that captures the Chicana/o experience. We all inherit a culture. Yet, as writers, artists, investigators, we also create culture by way of the images and ideas presented in our creative expressions. The present anthology has captured the essence of the Chicana/o experience from the collected works of the leading Chicana/o writers of the past thirty years. These works offer rich new colors and bold patterns that have been added to the previously existing strands that have defined our culture. The rich diversity that makes up our culture is well represented in this anthology. At times, this diversity foments tensions that reflect the clash of discordant colors that converge from opposing directions. Yet despite these variations in colors, our Chicana/o cultural tapestry remains intact. Paradoxically, the diverse cultural fibers that make our tapestry a unified whole are made ever stronger because of this diversity of views and lifestyles.

For young Chicanas and Chicanos and other readers who awaken to see this rich tapestry lying before them in the early morning sunlight, feast your eyes! You will witness the handiwork of the elders, and of those not so old; artists who have added their unique threads and patterns to Chicana/o literature so that young minds may know what they have known, and see what they have seen. The dream is that their handiwork will inspire you to add to its tapestry, our tapestry, *nuestra cultura querida*. The present anthology captures a place in history. But more than this, the present anthology serves also as an invitation for you to see the world of our Chicana/o culture, and to understand it more fully. Then, if these images strike a chord in your heart, perhaps you will seek to join these master weavers by adding your own colors and patterns to this growing tapestry. This is an invitation, but also a challenge. If through this anthology you take the challenge of seeing the world through these artists' eyes, to see what they have seen, and feel what they have felt, then perhaps you will find the inspiration to do as they have done. And in this, perhaps you too may pass this handiwork on to your own children. Indeed, is not this what culture is about?

Felipe G. Castro, M.S.W., Ph.D., Associate Professor and Executive
Director, Hispanic Research Center, Arizona State University
Edward Escobar, Ph.D., Associate Professor and Director, Chicana
and Chicano Studies, Arizona State University

ACKNOWLEDGMENTS

Barrio Publications, for Abelardo B. Delgado's "Stupid America."

Curbstone Press, for Luis Rodríguez's "The Blast Furnace."

Rolando R. Hinojosa-Smith, for his "Feliz cumpleaños, E.U.A."

Latin American Literary Review Press, for Lorna Dee Cervantes's "Beneath the Shadow of the Freeway."

MARCH/Abrazo Press, for Carlos Cumpián's "Kilotons and Then Some."

Mexican American Studies and Research Center, University of Arizona, for Miguel Méndez-M., "Huachusey"; and Francisco H. Vázquez, "Chicanology: A Postmodern Analysis of Meshicano Discourse."

West End Press, for Cherríe Moraga, *Giving Up the Ghost.*

Moving Parts Press, for Francisco X. Alarcón's "Me gusta caminar junto a tu lado."

Alberto Álvaro Ríos, for his "Mi abuelo" and his "Then They'd Watch Comedies."

Juan Rodríguez, for Jorge Ulica's "Do You Speak Pocho...?"

Aunt Lute Books, for Gloria Anzaldúa's "La conciencia de la mestiza: Towards a New Consciousness."

Alma Luz Villanueva, for her "Trust."

Gloria Velásquez, for her "Fugitive."

Arte Público Press, for *Las Dos Caras del Patroncito* and *Los Vendidos* by Luis Valdez; Tomás Rivera's "Las salamandras"; Helena María Viramontes's "The Moths"; Ricardo Sánchez's "Barrios of the World"; and Rubén Medina's "Cómo desnudar a una mujer con un saxofón."

José Armas, for Jesús María H. Alarid, "El idioma español."

Gina Valdés, for her "Comiendo lumbre" and her *There Are No Madmen Here.*

Bernice Zamora, for her "Notes from a Chicana 'Coed'."

Cordelia Candelaria, for her "Letting La Llorona Go, or, Re/reading History's 'Tender Mercies.'"

David R. Godine, Publisher, Incorporated, for "Prologue: Middle-Class Pastoral," from Richard Rodriguez, *Hunger of Memory.*

Margarita Cota-Cárdenas, for her "Crisis de identidad, o, Ya no chingues."

Ricardo Aguilar Melantzón, for his "Cumplir mi justa condena..."

Alurista, for his "Tarde sobria."

Ysidro Ramón Macías, for his "The Evolution of the Mind."

Juan Felipe Herrera, for his "Are You Doing That New Amerikan Thing?"

José Montoya, for his "El Louie."

Bilingual Press/Editorial Bilingüe, for Aristeo Brito, *El diablo en Texas*; Estela Portillo Trambley, "The Paris Gown"; Jim Sagel, "La junta"; Beverly Silva, "The Cat"; Sabine Ulibarrí, "El conejo pionero"; Demetria Martínez, "Nativity: For Two Salvadoran Women, 1986-1987."

José Antonio Burciaga, for his "Pendejismo" and for his "Poema en tres idiomas y caló."

Chronicle Books, for Gary Soto, "Mexicans Begin Jogging."

Yolanda Luera, for her "Aborto."

Reyes Cárdenas, for his "Padre Nuestro Que Estás en el Banco."

Tino Villanueva, for his "Unción de palabras."

Persephone Press and Cherríe Moraga, for her "La Güera."

Bárbara Brinson Curiel, for her "Recipe: Chorizo con Huevo Made in the Microwave."

Alejandro Murguía, for his "A Long Walk."

Luis Omar Salinas, for his "Death in Vietnam."

Mario Suárez, for his "El Hoyo."

Octavio Ignacio Romano-V., for his "The Historical and Intellectual Presence of Mexican Americans."

raúlrsalinas/Resistencia Bookstore, for raúlrsalinas's "Los caudillos."

Sergio Elizondo, for his "Coyote emplumado."

Gary Soto, for his "Daybreak" and "Looking for Work."

New Directions Publishing Corporation, for Jimmy Santiago Baca's "Pinos Wells."

Chris Strachwitz, Arhoolie Records, for the two anonymous ballads "Corrido de Gregorio Cortez" and "Corrido de Joaquín Murrieta."

Rodolfo "Corky" Gonzales, for *I Am Joaquín*.

ENSAYO / ESSAY

FRANCISCO H. VÁZQUEZ (1949-)

"Chicanology: A Postmodern Analysis of Meshicano Discourse" (1992)

WORLD,

July 10, 1969
VERDANT VIRGINNY

en el ceno
del cocodrilo
una lágrima
rompe el silencio

i assail you
and
question seriously
all that you espouse
in
the way
of civil rights
and
other power projections

for
i know that the people
will never know
what it is
that they must know
in order
to not only survive you
but to live. . .

world,
you come into the barrio
(ghetto)
and promulgate
means of better
capitulation
from those you oppress. . .

and i know
that you shall ever
            fear
to extend the knowledge
that shall free us. . .

Ricardo Sánchez[1]

Why, indeed, will the people never know what they must know in order to live, to survive? Why the fear to extend the knowledge that shall free us? Poets like Sánchez were probably banished from Plato's republic for asking this kind of question. Today, however, the status of knowledge (what is truth? how do we know?) is considered a crucial issue in academic circles. For example, Mario Barrera states:

. . .the politics of the Chicano can be expected to revolve around both class and colonial divisions in a complex manner whose outlines we can only *dimly perceive* in the current period of confusion and redefinition.[2] (my emphasis)

More recently, in a review of the model used to study Mexican political behavior, Juan Gómez-Quiñones decries the dominant liberal conservative pluralistic myths which "often are not only ahistorical but factually erroneous." He is also critical of the reaction against this analysis by some social scientists who

(in) their haste to replace the dominant liberal interpretation with a more profound one, . . . proved to be too facile in suggesting an "internal colony

---

[1]Ricardo Sánchez, *Hechizospells* (Los Angeles: Chicano Studies Center Publications, 1976), p. 91. Incidentally, I believe Ricardo Sánchez meant "seno" and not "ceno." *Author's note.*

[2]Mario Barrera,

model," a discrimination related to economic structures and later suggesting consciousness and language as explanatory factors.[3]

But this quest for "Knowledge that shall free us," for adequate analytical models, is not characteristic only of Chicano Studies or Chicano reality, In effect,

> (it) seems increasingly probable that Western culture is in the middle of a fundamental transformation: a "shape of life" is growing old. In retrospect, this transformation may be as radical (but as gradual) as the shift from a medieval to a modern society. Accordingly, this moment in the history of the West is pervaded by profound yet little-comprehended change, and uncertainty, and ambivalence.[4]

---

[3] Juan Gómez-Quiñones, *Chicano Politics: Reality and Promise, 1940-1990* (Albuquerque: University of New Mexico Press, 1990), p. 19. It should be noted that, besides misspelling my last name [Vázquez], this author erroneously refers to my work as belonging to the language critical-theory of the Frankfurt School, which he considers "socially abstract or potentially one more manipulation to further veiled interests, or at worse an argument for no politics" (pp. 221-222). Clearly, though, he is against any analysis of discourse. The correct analysis, he claims, involves "(real) politics (involving) conscious individuals acting rationally. . . ." p. 30. This is, however, not the proper place for a critique of his assumption that the self is a coherent, stable individual engaged in an "objective" world through a transparent representational language. *Author's note*

[4] Jane Flax, "Postmodernism and Gender Relations in Feminist Theory." *Signs* 12, 4 (1987): 621. Quoted in Mustafa U. Kiziltan, William J. Bain and Anita Canizares M. "Postmodern Conditions: Rethinking Public Education," *Educational Theory* (Summer 1990, Vol. 40. No. 3), p. 352. For a thorough, concrete analysis of postmodern transformations, look at the working papers produced by *The Post-Industrial Future Project: A Canadian Exploration of the Implications of Profound Societal Change*, Ruben Nelson, Director (Canmore, A. B. Canada: Square One Management, 1989). For a brief discussion of the various definitions of postmodernism, see Stanley Aranowitz and Henry Giroux, *Postmodern Education*, Minneapolis: University of Minnesota Press, 1991, pp. 60-67. *Author's note*.

It is precisely this shift from an industrial to a post-industrial society, this radical transformation of the global economy, of the way we produce Knowledge, and thus culture itself, which is termed "postmodernism."

Clearly, postmodernism includes a variety of transformations that involve everyday practices, economic organization, the grounding of science, aesthetics, ethics and philosophy. But even in the face of a multitude of positions regarding postmodernism, it is generally agreed that its most characteristic thesis addresses the relationship between power and knowledge.[5]

In this vein, I contend that the difficulties we—Meshicano[6] poets, scholars, working men and women—encounter are based precisely on the intertwinement and symbiotic power/knowledge relations specific to the Meshicano. First, Michel Foucault's discussion of two predominant theories of power will be re-produced,

---

[5]Ibid., p. 353. *Author's note.*

[6]The Term "Meshicano" is here used to address three concerns. One is to emphasize the symbiotic relationship between power and language (i.e. discourse). Nearly five centuries ago Cristóbal Colón appropriated the power to define, and thus dominate, what he had encountered: the native peoples became Indians, and later Americans. Another exercise of the power to define took place at the beginning of the Chicano movement when the term 'Chicano' was used as an abbreviated form for "Mexicans north of the Río Bravo, and 'Chicanismo' meant a politically charged Mexicanidad (*sic*)." But, as Juan Gómez-Quiñones astutely observes "with hindsight, one can ask whether 'Chicanismo' . . . was one more effort to subsume Mexican identity with all its implications" (cf. infra, *Chicano Politics*, p. 104). There is also the question of etymology. The letter "x" in México originally had a "sh" sound and it was changed by the Spaniards into a "j" sound ("h" in English). If we want to come close to the original Náhualt word, we would say that some Meshicanos live in Meshico and others live in the United States. Then, in the 1960s some of the latter dropped the "Me-" prefix and simply called themselves "Chicanos." None of these concerns, however, are intended as an argument for what is the "correct" name. Such decisions are made within the context of a political economy of discourse, not by individuals. Thus, Gutiérrez Tibón has found seventy versions of the word "México," yet he considers chicano a "*corrupción pachuca de mexicano*" in *Historia del nombre y de la fundación de México*, Segunda edición (México: Fondo de Cultura Económica, 1983), p. 420. At any rate, it is revealing of the unfortunate state of affairs, that the term with more currency today is "Hispanic." *Author's note.*

along with his tentative hypotheses, suggestions and methodological guidelines for a different, perhaps more adequate, analysis of power.[7] On this basis, the power/knowledge relations manifested by and within Meshicano discourse in general and Chicano Studies in particular will be discussed. Finally after mapping the geography of this discourse, the techniques and mechanisms through which it is robbed of its power will be described. May the following words serve, if for nothing else, as "*una lágrima que rompa el silencio en el ceno del cocodrilo.*"

There are two prominent systems for approaching the analyses of power. Both share a common point of what may be called an economism in the theory of power.[8] In the juridical-liberal conception, power is taken to be a right that one is able to possess like a commodity. It can be transferred or alienated, either wholly or partly, through a legal act or some act that establishes a right, such as contract. Power is what every individual holds, and whose partial or total cession enables political power or sovereignty to be established. This theoretical construction is based on the idea that the constitution of political power obeys a

---

[7] I use the word *re-produced* because at various points in this article I use Foucault's own words which I have "poached" from different texts. This was done for various reasons. One is the difficulty in paraphrasing him. Another is to avoid a cumbersome fragmentation of the text by frequent quoting and interpolation of my own remarks. Most importantly, as Michael de Certau points out in *The Practice of Everyday Life*, reading is "poaching": "The reader takes neither the position of the author nor an author's position. He invents in texts something different from what they 'intended.' He detaches them from their (lost or accessory origin). He combines their fragments and creates something un-known in the space organized by their capacity for allowing an indefinite plurality of meanings" (tr. Steven F. Rendall, Berkeley: University of California Press, 1984), p. 169. I have, however, taken care to note the sources of the various fragments when these deviate from the main discussion which can be found in Michel Foucault's "Two Lectures," in *Power/Knowledge: Selected Interviews and Other Writings, 1972-1977*, Colin Gordon, editor (New York: Pantheon Books, 1980), pp. 78-108. For an intimate discussion of Foucault's writings, see Gilles Deleuze, *Foucault* (Minneapolis: University of Minnesota Press, 1988). For an informative discussion of his work, a complete bibliography and his last interview (five months before he died), see James Bernauer and David Rasmussen's, *The Final Foucault* (Cambridge: The MIT Press, 1988). *Author's note.*

[8] Foucault, "Two Lectures," *Power/Knowledge*, p. 88. *Author's note.*

model of a legal transaction involving a contractual type of exchange. The other view, the general Marxist conception, sees power in terms of the role it plays in the simultaneous maintenance of the relation of production and class domination, which the development and specific forms of production have rendered possible. In this view, the historical justification of political power is to be found in the economy. Several questions need to be asked regarding these analyses of power. Concerning the juridical-liberal: Is power modeled upon the commodity? Is it possessed, acquired, ceded through a force or contract that one alienates or recovers, that circulates or voids on this or that level. With respect to the Marxist conception: Is power always in a subordinate position? Is its end purpose to serve the economy? Is it destined to realize, consolidate, maintain and reproduce the relations appropriate to the economy and essential to its functioning?

Even if we allow that it is the case that the relations of power remain profoundly enmeshed in economic relations, what means are available to us today if we want a non-economic analysis of power? We can begin with the assertion that power is neither given, nor exchanged, nor recovered, but exercised, and only exists in action. Second, power is not primarily the maintenance and reproduction of economic relations. Above all it is a relation of force. The questions to be posed then would be these: If power is exercised, what sort of exercise does it involve? What is its mechanism? The immediate answer of many contemporary analysts is that power is repressive. It represses nature, the instinct, the social class, the individual. So, should not the analyses of power be the analysis of the mechanisms of repression? Another answer may be that if power is the way in which relations of force are put into effect and given concrete expression, it should be analyzed in terms of struggle, conflict and war.

In these terms let us compare these major analyses of power. In the first place there is the old system found in the philosophies of the eighteenth century. This (juridical-liberal) approach is based on the idea of power as an original right that is given up in the establishment of sovereignty, and the social contract as broker of political power. A power so constituted risks becoming oppression whenever it goes beyond the contract. Thus, we have contract-power, with oppression as its limit, or the transgression of this limit. On the Marxist side, we have an approach that analyzes political power in accordance with war-repression. In this view, repression no longer occupies the place of oppression in relation to the contract. It is not a violation of the contract but the mere effect and continuation of a relation of domination. Repression is none other than the play of a continuous relationship of force—warfare under the illusion of peace.

This notion of repression, however, seems inadequate for capturing precisely the productive aspects of power. In defining the effects of power with a law that says "no," power is taken above all as carrying the force of prohibition. If power were never anything but repressive, if it never did anything but say no, would anyone be brought to obey it? What makes power accepted is simply that it does not only weigh on us as a force that says "no," but it traverses and produces things. Power induces pleasure, forms of knowledge, produces discourse.[9] There is, however, a historical reason for the acceptance of the analysis of power in terms of repression—as the mere limitation of liberty.

The monarchies that appeared during the Middle Ages brought a measure of order and peace to the mass of warring forces that preceded them by a system of delimited territory and hierarchical authority. That authority was embodied in the sovereign and his/her law. From the Middle Ages on, the exercise of power has always been formulated in terms of law. Of course, there are times such as in seventeenth-century France when monarchical authority was identified with arbitrary rule. Despite attempts to free law from monarchical rule and politics from juridical concerns, the representation of power is still caught up this system. Whatever criticism the eighteenth-century jurists made of monarchy in the name of the law, they never questioned the principle that power must be formulated in terms of law and exercised within the law—a principle that was established with the monarchy. The nineteenth century saw a more radical critique of political institutions. In this view real power operated outside the role of law. The legal system itself was a form of violence, a weapon to be used to reinforce political and economic inequalities. However, even this critique was based on the postulate that power should be exercised according to a fundamental right. Despite the differences of intent from one period to another, the representation of power has remained affected by the model of monarchy. In political thought and analysis the King has not yet been decapitated. Hence the importance still given, in the theory of power, to the problems of right and violence, law and illegality,

---

[9]Michel Foucault, "Truth and Power," *Power/Knowledge: Selected Interviews and Other Writings, 1972-1977*, Colin Gordon, editor (New York: Pantheon Books, 1980), p. 119. *Author's note.*

will and liberty and, above all, the state and sovereignty (even if sovereignty is no longer embodied in the person of the sovereign, but in a collective being).[10]

What of the role of the state? To pose the problem presented by the analysis of power in terms of the state requires posing it in terms of a sovereign and sovereignty. That is, in terms of the law. If one describes all phenomena of power as dependent on the state machinery, this means grasping them as repressive (i.e., the Army as a power of death, law enforcement and justice systems as punitive instruments). This is, of course, not to say that the state is not important. Rather, that relations of power (and the analysis that must be made of them) necessarily extend beyond the limits of the state. This is so for two reasons: first, the State, for all the might of its apparatuses, is far from being able to occupy the whole field of actual power relations, and second, it can only operate based on other already existing relations.[11] For example, after reviewing several theories on the State and the terms of their applicability to the Meshicano experience, Barrera states:

> The Marxist structuralist perspective appears superior in that it better accounts for the imperfect control of the state by the dominant class. This is because this control is primarily exercised indirectly through the structure of the state rather than through direct control.[12]

He expresses his frustration (perhaps unwittingly) at the inadequacy of the existing analysis:

> . . .the most satisfactory formulation *may be* one that sees the most particular interests of capitalists satisfied through the interest group process and through placement of their own members in state positions, while the general interests of the capitalists as a class are attended to through the mechanisms stressed by structuralists.[13] (my emphasis)

---

[10]Michel Foucault, *The History of Sexuality*, Volume I, tr. Robert Hurley (New York: Pantheon Books, 1978), p. 89. *Author's note.*

[11]Foucault, "Truth and Power," *Power/Knowledge*, p. 112. *Author's note.*

[12]Barrera, *Race and Class in the Southwest*, p. 172. *Author's note.*

[13]Ibid. *Author's note.*

Difficulties in the analysis of power arise precisely because, from medieval times onward, the essential role of Right has been to fix the legitimacy of power. In essence, the function of the discourses and techniques of Right has been to erase the domination intrinsic to power and to present power under two different aspects: as the legitimate right of the sovereign, and as the legal obligation to obey it.[14] Thus, power becomes codified in terms of the Law.

Under these circumstances, one must escape from the limited field of juridical sovereignty and base the analysis of power on the study of the techniques and tactics of domination. Domination is not meant here as the way in which power is exercised by one individual or group over another, but as the manifold forms of domination exercised within society.

It is necessary to show how Right is the instrument of domination. More importantly, there is a need to show the extent to which, and the forms in which, Right defines relations that are not relations of sovereignty but of domination. How was power transformed during the last three hundred years? How did it become less visible and codified in terms of the Law.[15] A map to guide us through this transformation is provided in Chart 1.

The top of Chart 1 illustrates that power under feudalism was dependent upon the earth and its products. It extracted wealth and commodities from human bodies, was distributed with absolute power and absolute expenditure, was exercised through periodic levies and legal obligations, and was centered on the sovereign. Power under capitalism, however, is dependent on human bodies and what they do (bio-power).[16] It extracts from them time and labor. Its distribution is

---

[14]Foucault, "Two Lectures," *Power/Knowledge*, p. 122. *Author's note.*

[15]Ibid. pp. 92-93. This transformation was the object of Foucault's *oeuvre*. Some examples are *Madness and Civilization*, tr. Richard Howard (New York: Pantheon Books, 1965); *The Order of Things*, tr. Alan Sheridan (New York: Pantheon Books, 1970); *The Birth of the Clinic*, tr. Alan Sheridan (New York: Pantheon Books, 1973); *Discipline and Punish*, tr. Alan Sheridan (New York: Vintage Books, 1979); *The History of Sexuality*, Vol. I, tr. Robert Hurley (New York: Pantheon Books, 1978). For a complete bibliography see James Bernauer and Thomas Keenan, "The Works of Michel Foucault, 1954-1984" in James Bernauer and David Rasmussen's, *The Final Foucault* (Cambridge: The MIT Press, 1988), pp. 119-159. *Author's note.*

[16]Foucault, *The History of Sexuality*, pp. 140-41. *Author's note*

according to a new economy of power: minimum expenditure, maximum return. It is exercised through continuous surveillance and is centered on Collective Sovereignty or Public Law. This new type of power, which can no longer be formulated in terms of sovereignty, is one of the great inventions of bourgeois society. It has been a fundamental instrument in the constitution of industrial capitalism. This non-sovereign power is disciplinary power. Yet, the theory of sovereignty has continued to exist as an ideology of Right. It has also provided the organizing principle of the legal codes that Europe acquired with the nineteenth century Napoleonic Code.[17]

---

[17]Foucault, "Two Lectures," *Power/Knowledge*, p. 105. *Author's note.*

CHART 1

Nature of Power in	Feudalism	Capitalism
Dependent upon	Earth and its products	Human bodies and what they do
Extract from human bodies	Wealth and commodities	Time and labor
Distribution of power	Absolute power Absolute expenditure	New economy of power: Minimum expenditure, Maximum return
Exercised through	Periodic levies and legal obligation	Continuous surveillance
Centered on	The sovereign	Collective sovereignty

Rules of law • • • • • • • • • • • • • • • Public Right

Human Sciences: Power linked to Scientific Knowledge

Rules of Norm • • • • • • • • • • • • • • • •

Disciplinary mechanisms

Despite differences between Feudalism and Capitalism, power is conceived in terms of sovereignty. This serves to conceal the increasing invasion of procedures of normalization into the domain of Law.

The lower part of Chart 1 addresses the question of why the theory of sovereignty has persisted as an organizing principle of all major legal codes. There are two discernable reasons. As noted before, it has been a permanent instrument of criticism of the monarchy. At the same time, however, the theory of sovereignty and the organization of a legal code have allowed a system of Law to be superimposed upon the mechanisms of discipline in such a way as to conceal them. It hides the elements of domination inherent in its techniques. Paradoxically, it guarantees to everyone, by virtue of the sovereignty of the State, the exercise of individual rights. Modern society, then, has been characterized, from the nineteenth century to our own day, by (1) the social body and the delegative status of each citizen that articulate an organization (discourse legislation) based on public right, and (2) a closely linked grid of disciplinary coercions whose purpose is to assure the cohesion of this same social body. These two limits define the area in which power is exercised. Now, in reference to the disciplines, such as the human sciences, it is clear they are concerned with scientific discourse. As such they do not have anything in common with the discourse of law, rule or sovereign will. When disciplines speak of a rule, they do not intend this as a juridical rule derived from sovereignty but as a natural law, a norm. Thus, the code they come to define is not that of Law, but of normalization.

The human sciences are disciplines, which produce knowledge regarding human behavior. Ostensibly, this is done from a scientific non-ideological perspective. While it is more or less accepted that the social or human sciences have advanced from increasingly scientific techniques, it is more likely that it is the juxtaposition of the right of sovereignty and a polymorphous disciplinary mechanism that makes them possible. Thus, it can be said that the procedures of normalization increasingly engage in the colonization of those of Law.[18] Disciplines as bodies of knowledge, truth and power, tend to increase the productivity of the human body (in economic terms of utility) and diminish these same forces (in political terms of obedience). They dissociate power from the human body. On one side discipline forms it into an "aptitude," a "capacity," which it seeks to increase. On the other side, it reverses the course of the energy, the power that might result from it, and turns it into a relation of strict subjection.[19] This is precisely what Paulo Freire calls education for domination.[20] If economic ex-

---

[18]Ibid., pp. 106-7. *Author's note.*

[19]Foucault, *History of Sexuality*, p. 141. *Author's note.*

[20]Ira Shor and Paulo Freire, *A Pedagogy for Liberation: Dialogues on Transforming Education* (New York: Bergin & Garvey, 1987), pp. 12-13. See also Henry A. Giroux, *Teachers as Intellectuals: Toward a Critical Pedagogy of Learning* (Massachusetts: Bergin & Garvey, 1988), pp. 114-16. *Author's note.*

ploitation separates the force and the product of labor, disciplinary coercion establishes in the individual the constricting link between an increased aptitude and an increased domination. To be sure, legal and normative standards have intersected in a variety of ways, some positive, others negative. The problem, of course, is not the human sciences or other disciplines per se, but the insidious ways in which power establishes particular relationships with knowledge.[21]

Disciplinary normalization, then, seems to be coming into increasing conflict with the juridical systems of sovereignty. The critical problem is that against the transgression of disciplinary mechanisms, against the ascent of a power tied to scientific knowledge, we find that there is no solid recourse available to us today, except that which lies in the return to a theory of Right organized around sovereignty. This is the predicament in which we find ourselves.

In short, modern society is characterized by manifold relations of power that permeate and constitute it. These relations cannot themselves be established, consolidated or implemented without the production, accumulation, circulation and sanctioning of discourses. Power never ceases its interrogation, inquisition or registration of truth. It institutionalizes, professionalizes and rewards its pursuit. As a material entity, discourse is subjected to a political economy of truth, so that finally we must produce truth as we must produce wealth. Indeed, we must produce truth to produce wealth in the first place. We are also subjected to truth in the sense that it is truth that makes the laws, that produces the true discourse which, at least partially, decides the effects of power. In the end, we are judged, condemned, classified and destined to a certain mode of living or

---

[21]There are many observations of the relationship between social science and disciplinary mechanisms. One very specific example is Alexander Liazos, "The Poverty of the Sociology of Deviance: Nuts, Sluts, and 'Perverts,'" in Stuart I. Traub and Craig B. Little, *Theories of Deviance*, Third Edition (Itasca: F.E. Peacock Publisher, Inc., 1985). More extensive and recent examples are: James Clifford, *The Predicament of Culture: Twentieth-Century Ethnography, Literature, and Art* (Cambridge: Harvard University Press, 1989), and Renato Rosaldo, *Truth and Culture: The Remaking of Social Analysis* (Boston: Beacon Press, 1989). The most specific discussion of this topic, however, is Michel Foucault's *Discipline and Punish: The Birth of the Prison*, New York: Vintage Books, 1979. *Author's note.*

dying, as a function of the true discourses that are the bearers of the specific effects of power.[22]

This particular idea of the relationship between power and knowledge leads to the following methodological guidelines:

1) Where there is power there is resistance. Thus, the focus is not on the regulated and legitimate forms of power in their central location or on the general mechanisms through which they operate. The focus is on power at its extremities, in its more regional and local forms and institutions. Of main concern is the point where power surmounts the rules of Right that delimit it, invests itself in institutions, becomes embodied in techniques and equips itself with instruments and eventually even violent means of material intervention. One should try to locate power at the extreme points of its exercise, where it is less legal in character.

2) The analysis of power should not concern itself with power at the level of conscious intention or decision. It should avoid questions such as "who has power and what has she or he in mind?" or "what is the aim of some-one that has power?" It is instead a matter of studying power at the point where its intention, if it has one, is completely invested in real and effective practices. The analysis is on the everyday life, on how things work at the level of on-going subjugation, those continuous processes that target the labor of our human bodies, dictate our behaviors, and even attempt to gov-ern our gestures.

3) Power is not to be taken as a phenomenon of one individual's domina-tion over others or that of one group or class over others. What should always be kept in mind is that power is not that which makes the difference between those who exclusively have it and retain it and those who do not have it and submit to it. It is not something that is acquired, seized or shared. Power must be analyzed as something that circulates, as a process, as a continuous chain, a *rhizome*. It is never localized here and there, never in anybody's hands, never appropriated as a commodity or piece of wealth.

---

[22]Foucault: "Two Lectures," *Power/Knowledge*, pp. 93-94. *Author's note.*

Power is exercised from innumerable points, in the interplay of nonegalitarian and mobile relations.

4) Power comes from below. The important point is not to attempt some kind of deduction of power starting at the top and aimed at the discovery of the extent to which it moves down to and permeates the base. Instead, one must conduct an ascending analysis of power, starting from its micromechanisms and then noting how these have colonized, invested, transformed and extended. Anything can be deduced from the general phenomenon of the domination of the bourgeois class. What needs to be examined is quite different. One must suppose that the manifold relationships of force that take shape and come into play in the machinery of production, in families, groups, and institutions, are the basis for wide-ranging effects of cleavage that run through the social body as a whole. These then form a general line of force that transverses the local appositions and links them together. Major dominations are the hegemonic effects that are sustained by all these confrontations.

5) Relations of power are not in some kind of superstructural relationship with other types of relationships, such as economic processes, knowledge relationships, sexual relations, etc. Power relations are the immediate effects of the divisions, inequalities and disequilibriums that occur in said relations and conversely they are the internal conditions of these differentiations. They are not ideological constructs with a role of prohibition or accompaniment; they have a directly productive role whenever they come into play.[23]

We have come full circle in the examination of the juridical-liberal and the Marxist theories of power and their limitations. We discussed the historical reasons for their common grounding in the analysis of power in terms of repression/sovereignty and presented analysis that reverses the trajectory followed by these two theories. The methodological guidelines lead us to the discovery of an

---

[23]These methodological guidelines have been compiled from two sources: "Two Lectures," *Power/Knowledge*, pp. 96-102 and *The History of Sexuality*, pp. 94-95. *Author's note.*

exercise of power that simultaneously increases the forces of domination, and improves the force and efficacy of its techniques of domination. This is made possible by the appearance of mechanisms of discipline concealed under a theory of Right. These mechanisms of power refer to disciplinary discourses, such as the human sciences truth, which behind a constant pursuit of scientific truth, mask their inherent domination and begin to invade the domain of the Law. In the final analysis, knowledge is not so much true or false as legitimate or illegitimate for a particular set of power relations. And now to explore the relevance of this analysis of power to Meshicano discourse.

Meshicano Discourse and the Analysis of Power

In the previous section we referred to power in terms of a political economy of truth. This economy can be characterized by five important traits: Truth is centered on scientific discourse and the institutions that produce it; it is subject to constant economic and political manipulation (for economic production and political power); it is the object of immense diffusion and consumption (circulating through systems of education and information); it is produced and transmitted under the control, dominant if not exclusive, of a few great political and economic systems (university, media, military, literary). Lastly, it is the issue of political debate and social confrontation (ideological struggle).[24] Now we need to ask the following questions: In specific discourses, such as Meshicano discourse, what are the most immediate, the most local power relations at work? How did they make possible this type of discourse? Conversely, how is this discourse used to support power relations? How is the action of these power relations modified by their very exercise? Finally, how are such power relations linked to one another according to the logic of a great strategy?

A clue to the direction that must be followed is provided by two studies based on the analysis of discourse. In *The Invention of Africa*, V.Y. Mudimbe is "directly concerned with the processes of transformation of types of knowledge."

---

[24]Foucault, "Truth and Power," *Power/Knowledge*, p. 131. *Author's note.*

The fact of the matter is that, until now, Western interpreters and African analysts have been using categories and conceptual systems that depend on a Western epistemological order. Even in the most explicit "Afrocentric" descriptions, models of analysis explicitly or implicitly, knowingly or unknowingly, refer to the same order. . . . What does this mean for the field of African studies? To what extent can their perspective modify the fact of a silent dependence on a Western *episteme*?[25]

Edward W. Said is more explicit in his analysis of scholarly studies that dealt with the Orient:

Orientalism can be discussed and analyzed as the corporate institution for dealing with the Orient—dealing with it by making statements about it, authorizing views of it, describing it, by teaching it, settling it, ruling over it; in short, Orientalism as a Western style for dominating, restructuring and having authority over the Orient. . . . My contention is that without examining Orientalism as a discourse one cannot possibly understand the enormously systematic discipline by which European culture was able to manage—and even produce—the Orient politically, sociologically, militarily, ideologically, scientifically, and imaginatively during the post Enlightenment period. Moreover, so authoritative a position did Orientalism have that I believe no one writing, thinking or acting on the Orient could do so without taking into account the limitations on thought and action imposed by Orientalism. In brief, because of Orientalism the Orient was not (and is not) a free subject of thought or action. This is not to say that Orientalism unilaterally determines what can be said about the Orient, but that it is the whole network of interest inevitably brought to bear on (and therefore always involved in) any occasion when that peculiar entity "the Orient" is in question.[26]

---

[25]V.Y. Mudimbe, *The Invention of Africa: Gnosis, Philosophy, and the Order of Knowledge* (Bloomington: Indiana University Press, 1988), p. x. *Author's note.*

[26]Edward W. Said, *Orientalism* (New York: Pantheon Books, 1978), p. 3. *Author's note.*

What Mudimbe and Said are stating here are counter-hegemonic positions against a dominant body of knowledge; the discourse of the West. We might say there is a Chicano Studies discourse that plays a similar role with respect to the power relations between Anglos and Chicanos. What is that Anglo body of knowledge that "invents" Chicanos, the counterpart to Orientalism?

To be sure, there are stereotyped images of the Meshicano present almost everywhere. Carlos E. Cortés, for example, has conceptualized the Societal Curriculum "that massive, ongoing informal curriculum of family, peer groups, neighborhoods, mass media, and other socializing factors which 'educate' us throughout our entire lives."[27] Much longer than one lifetime, however, there is also a "historical curriculum" known as the "Black Legend," a collection of anti-Spanish, anti-Catholic statements, that can be traced to the sixteenth century![28] More recently in the early twentieth century, we find an academic discipline, sociology, which played a similar role. It, too, defined Chicanos in terms of a traditional culture, a people who were not free subjects of thought or action.[29] Similarly, Américo Paredes in his search for the folklore of the Anglo Texan finds what he calls "the Texas Legend," which he attempts to categorize as either folklore, fact or "something else."[30] Echoing the "Black Legend" discourse that

---

[27]Carlos E. Cortés, "The Societal Curriculum and the School Curriculum," *Educational Leadership*, XXXVI, 7 (April, 1979), pp. 475-479. More recently he has extended this conception in "The Education of Language Minority Students: A Contextual Interaction Model," in *Beyond Language: Social and Cultural Factors in Schooling Language Minority Students* (Los Angeles: Evaluation, Dissemination and Assessment Center, California State University, Los Angeles, 1986), pp. 3-33. *Author's note.*

[28]Raymund Paredes, "The Origins of Anti-Mexican Sentiment in the United States," *New Directions in Chicano Scholarship*, Ricardo Romo and Raymund Paredes, editors (San Diego: University of California, 1978), pp. 139-165. *Author's note.*

[29]Octavio Romano-V. developed a critique of this view through his journal *El Grito*. See for example "The Anthropology and Sociology of the Mexican American: The Distortion of Mexican American History," *El Grito* Vol. 1, No. 2 (Fall 1968). *Author's note.*

[30]Américo Paredes, *With His Pistol in His Hand* (Austin: University of Texas Press, 1978), p. 18. *Author's note.*

has functioned since the sixteenth century, the Texas Legend basically states that "the Mexican is cruel by nature . . . cowardly and treacherous . . . as degenerate a specimen of humanity as found anywhere . . . he descends from the Spaniards, a second-rate type of European, and from the equally substandard Indian of México . . . and the Mexican has always recognized the Texan as his superior."[31] Paredes is puzzled that this legend is not found in the cowboy ballads, the play-party songs, or the folktales of the people of Texas. Paredes concludes this legend is pseudo-folklore which, disguised as fact, still plays a major role in Texas (we might say Meshicano) history. Implicit in this conclusion is the relation of the legend to two sources of power where it appears; that is "the written works of the literary" (where the power of knowledge is exercised) and "among a class of rootless adventurers who have used the legend for their own purposes (where raw, physical power is exercised)." This illustrates the contention that power is tolerable only on the condition that it masks a substantial part of itself. Its success is proportional to its ability to conceal itself. Stereotypes, academic disciplines, and legends or pseudo-folklore disguised as fact, however, do not quite fit the role of a "corporate institution that manages or produces Chicanos politically, sociologically and imaginatively" that Said finds in Orientalism. Yet, we know such discourse exists as a hegemonic power because we live with it, struggle against it, analyze it, and write about it. How can a discourse like that have so much influence on our everyday life and remain unnamed? This is no mystery; it illustrates the power relations between Chicanos and Anglos. For example, the subject of this discourse, the Meshicano, is identified as "a forgotten people," "a minority nobody knows," and "the invisible minority." Or, once "discovered" or "awakened" Chicanos are defined as Hispanics, Latinos, Mexican Americans, Spanish Americans, and so many other names that no single definition is possible. This highly diffused discourse that appears as stereotypes, social science, legends, or pseudo-folklores disguised as fact is, in effect, a politicized science of Chicanos. This *logos* gives statements about Chicanos the status of truth, thus it is a *Chicanology* that serves as a fundamental tool of domination. Paraphrasing Said, we can say that Chicanology is the whole network of interests inevitably brought to bear on any occasion when that peculiar entity "the Meshicano," is in question. No one writing, thinking or acting on the Meshicano can

---

[31]Ibid., p. 16. *Author's note.*

do so without taking into account the limitations on thought and action imposed by Chicanology.

It is precisely the expression of power intrinsic to Chicanology that engenders a Meshicano discourse, understood poetically as "that which we must know in order to survive." More specifically a knowledge that in the politics of truth of Anglo America is never allowed the status of truth. Without the status of truth, Meshicano discourse cannot invest its statements on institutions and their practices. It is a subjugated, oppositional knowledge. Such knowledge is defined as the historical contents that have been buried and disguised in a functionalist coherence or formal system. It is the whole body of knowledge that has been disqualified as inadequate or insufficiently elaborated. It is popular knowledge, though not common sense. It is a particular, local, regional knowledge, a heterogeneous knowledge incapable of unanimity that owes its force only to the harshness with which it is opposed by everything surrounding it.[32] Consequently, subjugated and oppositional knowledges are concerned with a historical knowledge of struggles. Whether it is in specialized areas of erudition (such as doctoral dissertations) or in the disqualified popular knowledge (such as *corridos*, rap songs, and jokes) we find the memory of hostile encounters. Films like *Según, The Ballad of Gregorio Cortez*, and *Zoot Suit* are examples of these memories. In the context of availability to the dominant culture, these are, even up to this day, confined to the margins of knowledge. (And they were intended for the general public!)

Within the power relations between Chicanology as a discourse of dominance and Meshicano discourse as a subjugated (and thus oppositional) knowledge we can see the conditions for the appearance of Chicano Studies as we commonly understand the term. Chicano Studies is a specific form of struggle, a particular practice within Meshicano discourse that stands in a counterhegemonic position to Chicanology. In effect, the claim that Chicano Studies is an academic discipline (that it is based on a logical, empirical structure and that therefore its propositions are the outcomes of verifiable procedures) is the attempt to invest it with the effects of power that have been attributed to science since medieval times.[33] The important point is that this is not a battle "on be-

---

[32]Foucault, "Two Lectures," *Power/Knowledge*, p. 81. *Author's note.*

[33]Ibid., p. 85. *Author's note.*

half" of truth but a struggle "about the status of truth" and the economic and political role it plays. Until this is clearly understood, there is the possibility that Chicano Studies may be appropriated by Chicanology.

We have defined Chicanology as an elusive yet systematic hegemonic discourse that expresses and actualizes Anglo domination over Chicanos, and Meshicano discourse as a diffuse, subjugated, oppositional knowledge resulting from the struggle against Anglo power. Chicano Studies has been defined as a specific discursive practice within Meshicano discourse that attempts to acquire power by claiming academic and scientific validity. Several questions remain, however, regarding the scope and configuration of Meshicano discourse and the procedures by which it is controlled.

The Geography of Meshicano Discourse

A map of the power/knowledge relations that define the Meshicano people since the United States invaded northern México (or since Columbus tripped over this continent) needs to be drawn. Because of space limitations, however, here it is only possible to trace the key statements of this discourse. Now, according to the guidelines that have been established above, power must be analyzed as something that circulates, as a process, as a continuous chain, and Meshicano discourse as an oppositional knowledge, which owes its power precisely to the harshness with which it is opposed by everything that surrounds it. To adhere to these points, then, it is necessary to refer to rhizomes:[34]

> (Any) point of a rhizome can be connected to any other, and must be. . . Semiotic chains of every nature are connected to very diverse modes of coding (biological, political, economic, etc.).
>
> ....
>
> It is not a question of this or that place on earth, or of a given moment in history, still less of this or that category of thought. It is a question of a

---

[34]Gilles Deleuze and Felix Guattari in "Introduction: Rhizome," *A Thousand Plateaus: Capitalism and Schizophrenia* (Minneapolis: University of Minnesota Press, 1987), pp. 7-21 passim. *Author's note.*

model that is perpetually in construction or collapsing, and of a process that is perpetually prolonging itself, breaking off and starting up again.

....

(The) rhizome pertains to a map that must be produced, constructed, a map that is always detachable, connectable, reversible, modifiable, and has multiple entryways and exits and its own lines of flight.

On this basis, a specific event is here presented as an entryway into the geography of Meshicano discourse. It is one that exhibits a very particular kind of semiotic chain. On April 13, 1972, Ricardo Chávez Ortiz, a Mexican national, hijacked a Frontier Airlines 737 Jet from Albuquerque, New Mexico, with an unloaded gun. The hijacker ordered the plane flown to Los Angeles, California. According to the *Los Angeles Times*, his request was not for money or to be flown somewhere, or to release prisoners. He requested "live broadcast time in which to voice the frustrations of a man who feared the world would not listen to his problems, and those of his people, under any other circumstances."[35]

Thus, in terms of the analysis here discussed, this event shows power at its extremes. It involves an illegal act, the threat of violence and, potentially, an international incident. It also involves issues that were being discussed at the academic level. Ironically, while Chicano faculty and students were trying to prove the truth of their statements, Chávez and students were trying *to prove the truth* of their statements, Chávez Ortiz appropriated the means to *give the status* of truth to his statements.

Addressing himself to Anglo Americans, Chávez Ortiz made the following statements:

I have felt an obligation to do this bad deed but not only for the situation of my family but . . . it is much more delicate and dangerous for the new generation than you can imagine. . . . I (told) myself: ask for what you need and make them realize that we are also the children of god. . . . I wanted to attract the attention of everyone in this nation and to say to everyone once and for all, what type of human beings we are. . . . What I

---

[35]This is a paraphrase of the event as described in the *Los Angeles Times*, July 6, 1972. *Author's note.*

need to say to you and that you need to pay very close attention to (is that) on the path we are following, there are going to come very disastrous and terrible days. . . . All you do is let the days go by and maybe tomorrow, maybe the next day, there will be a chance, there will be a new governor or a new president, yakkity, yakkity. . . .

Don't always think about your good clothes and having enough to eat and your good friends. . . . The Americans (Anglos) go and send rockets to the moon. Yes, go ahead and do whatever you want to do while we become rebellious. . . .

All I want is for Mexicans to know that this is Mexican land and always will be. . . . This land that we are working on was a divine gift. . . . I would not admit to any son of a bitch that my nation is for sale or in servitude. . . .

I was held in captivity for two years and all I had was the right to search through garbage cans for something to eat. I also worked for two years without being paid one single cent. . . . Where was justice at this time? Where were the authorities? I have a great fear of going out into the street because I am afraid that at any moment a policeman will take his pistol and shoot me.[36]

Thus, in thirty-five minutes of air time, bought with the violation of a federal law, Chávez Ortiz revealed to the world the harshness that surrounds Meshicano discourse. His statements include the following key points: (1) an assertion of the basic humanity of the Meshicano with reference to god, (2) Anglo indifference to social justice and emphasis on materialistic values, (3) empty political promises, (4) the land grab, (5) Meshicano nationalism, (6) the imposition of a colonial labor system, and (7) police brutality. This collection of observations and accusations, however, is not only the "frustrations of a man" or an example of individual alienation. It is that and much more. Leaving aside the

---

[36]David F. Gómez, *Somos Chicanos: Strangers in Our Own Land* (Boston: Beacon Press, 1973), pp. 177-187, passim. *Author's note.*

question of how "aware" he was of the significance of his act, what he said is equivalent to a microcosm of Meshicano discourse. It is a holographic fragment of the Meshicano experience, a rhizome.

The critical relationship to the geography of Meshicano discourse is that these statements represent a specific articulation, of the "governing" statements that emerge, to some extent, in every event in Meshicano history. These are: (1) racial theories, (2) the land grab, (3) the establishment of a colonial labor system, (4) the system of justice, (5) nationalism, (6) education, (7) internal divisions, and (8) the right of self-preservation. In other words, specific arrangements of assemblages of these statements give Meshicano discourse a sort of regularity that has been in operation since the United States invaded Northern México now known as the Southwest. A regularity that can also be seen in rhizome terms, as "a model that is perpetually in construction or collapsing, and of a process that is perpetually prolonging itself, breaking off and starting up again."

At any rate, this discursive regularity appears at different times, and in different circumstances. Thus, one could take a journey tracing these metamorphoses from, say, the guerrilla tactics of Juan N. Cortina or *Las Gorras Blancas*, the social banditry of Tiburcio Vásquez or Joaquín Murrieta, the increasing sophistication in organizing from the *mutualistas*, the *Magonistas*, and other union efforts to the G.I. Forum, L.U.L.A.C. (League of United Latin American Citizens), the Viva Kennedy Clubs and *La Raza Unida* Party. The journey would take us to different levels of the Power/Knowledge relationship, with the emergence of particular discourses: the Chicano Student Movement, the Chicano Artistic Renaissance, and the Chicano Studies programs/curriculums. Today we witness the appearance of a new object of political, economic and epistemological attention: the Hispanic. Despite the variation, that is, no matter the level of specificity of the statements, they constitute a Meshicano discursive regularity because of the implicit or explicit threat, or actual practice of violence.

Procedures for the Control of Chicano Discourse

There is, however, another aspect to the statements made by Chávez Ortiz that go beyond the geography of Meshicano discourse and point to the specific procedures by which it is dominated:

I could very easily force this plane to go to Mexico and I could have demanded three or four million dollars . . . and I assure you that I would have
been able to avoid capture there. . . . I am a pretty smart person. And I
know how to use my intelligence so I can get along well with my family.

You are the ones that make the laws and elect the governments. Well what
are you doing, what kind of governments are you electing? What kind of
society are you making? I want . . . a clean society, not a filthy traitorous
society like the one we are presently living in. . . . If that is what the laws
are like, then the laws are for the protection of the capitalists, or, in other
words, to protect the government.

There is a Mrs. Bañuelos (U.S. Treasurer 1971 to 1974). . . . She has tram-
pled on a lot of people and because of this she is a son of a bitch[37] . . .
only very capable people and good hearted with good intentions . . . have
the right to obtain positions like these. . . .

The children that I have . . . attended school for many years and they know
absolutely nothing.[38]

These statements refer to points of struggle between Chicanology and Meshicano discourse: (1) the question of intelligence, (2) the ambiguous nature of
the law as applied to Chicanos, (3) the status given to speakers of Meshicano
discourse and (4) educational institutions and processes. These points will be
used to illustrate some of the techniques, mechanisms and procedures for the
control of discourse. Through these, Chicanology selects, organizes, and redistrib-
utes Meshicano discourse in order to deflect its power, to neutralize its impact

---

[37]"(Nominated) by President Richard Nixon and subsequently confirmed by
the Senate as Treasurer of the United States. During the Senate investigation into
her qualifications, it was discovered she was hiring 'illegal aliens' from Mexico. . . . In the barrio it is common knowledge that she has made her fortune in
the Mexican food business exploiting cheap labor from Mexico." *Ibid.*, p. 183.
Author's note.

[38]Ibid., pp. 177-187 passim. *Author's note.*

on public policy.[39] However, let us first finish the story of the hijacking. The event ended with the conviction of Chávez Ortiz on charges of air piracy. He was given a life sentence and released in 1978. To the chagrin of his supporters, his only logical defense was based on "diminished capacity," not being "mentally competent and criminally responsible."[40] This may seem ironic. However, from a Chicanological perspective, this is a technique to invalidate this tactical (as opposed to strategic)[41] articulation of Meshicano issues.

The procedures for the control of Meshicano discourse are illustrated by the following examples that include the points raised by Chávez Ortiz and others taken from Meshicano history.

Prohibition

This is perhaps the most obvious procedure and many examples of it are found in Meshicano history. There was the prohibition to speak Spanish under penalty of bodily punishment or suspension from school (some people swear it still happens). In the late nineteenth century the singing of *corridos* about Meshicano *bandidos* was illegal, and early in this century the practice of red-baiting inhibited Mexicanos and Chicanos from speaking up for better wages and working conditions. This led to the demise of unions such as the Cannery and Agricultural Workers Industrial Union (CAWIU) and organizations like the *Congreso de Habla Española* during the 1930s. Certainly Ricardo Flores Magón experienced the effects of prohibitions around the turn of the century. He was incarcerated nine times for speaking or writing radical political doctrines.

---

[39]Michel Foucault, "The Discourse on Language," *The Archaeology of Knowledge*, tr. Alan Sheridan (New York: Pantheon Books, 1972), pp. 215-237. This appendix contains a discussion of the various forms of exclusion of discourse. *Author's note.*

[40]Gómez, *Somos Chicanos*, p. 186. *Author's note.*

[41]For the meaning of "tactic" as an act of resistance against a "strategic" force, see Michel de Certeau, *The Practice of Everyday Life* (Berkeley: University of California Press, 1984), pp. xvii-xx. *Author's note.*

Reason vs. Insanity

There is more subtle technique of intervention in the control of discourse that is based on the contrast between Reason (usually on the side of the dominant power) and Insanity (usually on the side of those who are subjugated). Thus, Ricardo Chávez Ortiz had to plead insanity for hijacking a plane in order to protest the oppression of the Mexicano in the United States. Furthermore, Meshicanos have not only been overrepresented in mentally retarded classes, but their cultural characteristics have been categorized as deviant. A revealing example of this practice is the statement made by the Texas historian Walter Prescott Webb about the *Plan de San Diego* of 1815. He does not believe that Mexicans wrote the plan because "the disturbances had behind them a purpose, an intelligence greater than that of the bandit leader or of his ignorant followers." Instead, he attributes it to an ambitious Texan or German. While it is not clear who the author of this plan was, it is known that Aniceto Pizaña and Luis de la Rosa, Mexicans native to Texas, led military actions at that time.[42] Similarly Commodore John D. Sloat, who took over Monterey Port in 1846, could not understand why Chicanos were planning to rise against him:

> Truly this procedure is more that of insane people than of persons in their right minds, because if they had common sense they would understand that I am too strong to allow myself to be forced to give up what I have acquired.[43]

At a different level, in American fiction, there are many Mexican characters who suddenly and inexplicably, go temporarily crazy. One thinks for example of Spanish Johnny in Willa Cather's *The Song of the Lark*, and Danny in John Steinbeck's *Tortilla Flat*.[44] It is in this context that we can appreciate the force behind Chávez Ortiz's insistence on his intelligence.

---

[42]Juan Gómez-Quiñones, "Plan de San Diego Revisited," *Aztlan* (Spring, 1970), pp. 124-132. *Author's note.*

[43]David J. Weber, *Foreigners in Their Native Land* (Albuquerque: University of New Mexico Press, 1973), pp. 129-130. *Author's note.*

[44]Paredes, "The Origins of Anti-Mexican Sentiment," p. 165. *Author's note.*

Validity

An even more insidious technique to deny the validity of what is said is the assignment of the status of truth to certain events or statements. In other words, the regime of truth appropriates the right to decide the distinction between true and false statements, the correct method to acquire knowledge and who is qualified to speak the truth.[45] This is, as noted before, not a matter of what is true, but of what can be made to appear as true. To find examples of this technique, one need only open any Chicano history book: the violation of the Treaty of Guadalupe Hidalgo, the blurring of what is justice and injustice in the second half of the nineteenth century, the exclusion of Chicanos from labor unions and schools, the manipulation of immigration laws, deportations, the zoot-suit riots, and charges of "reverse discrimination." From the perspective of Meshicano discourse and Chicano Studies, every one of these instances represents a struggle to establish what actually happened as opposed to what has been given the status of truth.

Academic Control of Discourse

Even in academic disciplines we find procedures of control in the production of truth.[46] Disciplines allow us to build a discourse, but only within a narrow framework. They are defined by groups of objects of study, methods, a body of propositions considered to be true (the literature), and the interplay of rules, definitions, techniques and tools. In order to speak the truth within a discipline, one must obey the rules of some discursive policy that takes the form of a permanent reactivation of a set of rules. It is precisely the resistance to these rules and regulations that gives rise to a Chicano Studies discipline. The first generation of Chicanos who entered academia found that history, political science, sociology and other academic disciplines were somehow detrimental to their search for knowledge about their own culture. Through the establishment of Chicano Studies, these scholars hoped to validate their discourse. But this valida-

---

[45]Foucault, *Archaeology*, pp. 217-220. *Author's note.*

[46]Ibid., pp. 222-224. *Author's note.*

tion was thwarted by restrictions in terms of material support. Meshicano professors were denied tenure; Chicano Studies courses were not required for graduation; programs were funded with "soft" monies; editors and publishers would not publish articles or books by Chicanos, and many that were published soon were out of print. There are, of course, exceptions. The rule is, however, that the knowledge provided by hundreds of dissertations, studies and research projects did not have the effect on institutional practices that they might have if the authors had been speaking from positions within the dominant culture.

Status of Chicano Intellectuals

There are various methods to limit the number of people who are given the charge of speaking the truth. One of these methods is the establishment of the status of the speaking individual through (1) the criteria of competence; (2) systems of differentiation and relation with other individuals or groups with the same status; (3) the functions of this status in relation to society in general and the Meshicano community in particular; (4) the institutional sites that lend legitimacy to their statements; and (5) the various positions occupied by the speaking individual in information networks. This allocation of individuals is determined by a "politics of truth"—a Chicanology. Thus we find ourselves in a very uncomfortable position when we realize that our demand for more Meshicanos in positions of authority has not been realized in terms of the acquisition of power. Rodolfo Acuña refers to this development as the rise of the Meshicano bureaucrats, power brokers who function as agents of social control.[47] This is precisely what Chávez Ortiz denounced in very harsh terms in his reference to Mrs. Bañuelos. To be sure, this is not a matter of labeling successful individuals as "*vendidos*" (sellouts), but a description of the workings of power that go beyond intentionality (or why we never know what we need to know). In effect, this situation may be getting worse:

---

[47]Rodolfo Acuña, *Occupied America: A History of Chicanos*, Third edition (New York: Harper and Row, 1988), pp. 377-386. *Author's note.*

Relative gains are visible in the modest improvements for the middle class—for the most part, college educated professionals and small business persons—and the increment in wealth for the wealthy entrepreneurs. . . . However, because of political self-protection, the advantaged move in step with the reigning conservatism and the distance that separates them from the working poor of their own community potentially could increase.[48]

Fellowships of Discourse

More restricted than academic disciplines is the control of discourse by what may be called fellowships of discourse. Their function is to preserve, reproduce or circulate discourse according to strict regulations and within a closed community. For example, the Anglo Texans in 1832 and 1835, borrowing a technique from their revolutionary forefathers, formed municipal committees for safety and correspondence. These committees, which brought citizens together outside of legal channels, became an important vehicle for bringing on the declaration of independence of Texas.[49] Meshicano organizations such as *mutualistas* and groups such as the *Penitentes*[50] also fall into this category. Meshicano youth in the barrios have their own fellowship of discourse which is restricted by the discourse of *caló*. More commonplace are technical, scientific, medical, economic, teaching discourses and others that follow different schemes of exclusivity and disclosure.

Doctrine

At first sight, doctrine (religious, political, philosophical) would seem to be the reverse of a fellowship of discourse, for among the latter, the number of

---

[48]Juan Gómez-Quiñones, *Chicano Politics: Reality and Promise, 1940-1990* (Albuquerque: University of New Mexico Press, 1990), p. 195. *Author's note.*

[49]Weber, *Foreigners in Their Native Land*, p. 105. *Author's note.*

[50]Robert J. Rosenbaum, *Mexicano Resistance in the Southwest* (Austin: University of Texas Press, 1981), pp. 145-46. *Author's note.*

Francisco H. Vázquez

33

speakers is, if not fixed, at least limited. It is among this number that discourse is allowed to circulate and be transmitted. Doctrine, on the other hand, tends towards diffusion. It is the holding in common of a discourse on which individuals, as many as possible, can define their reciprocal allegiance. In appearance, the only requisite is the recognition of the same truths and the acceptance of a rule of conformity with these truths. If it were a question of just that, doctrines would be barely different from scientific or academic disciplines. The control of discourse would bear only on the form or content of what was said. Doctrines, however, involve both the speaker and the spoken. Doctrines involve the statements of speakers in the sense that they are, permanently, the instruments and the manifestations of an adherence to a class, a social or racial status, a nationality, a struggle, a revolt. In short, doctrine links people to a certain type of statement while barring them from all others. It brings about a dual subjection, that of speaking individuals to discourse and that of discourse to the group of individual speakers. The restriction imposed by doctrine is illustrated by José Antonio Villareal R., author of *Pocho*. Referring to the effects of the "doctrine" of the Chicano Movement on Chicano literature, he states:

> What resulted then is that an unwritten set of standards began to take form. Codes for Chicano literature were explicit. First and foremost was the fact that we could never criticize ourselves as long as we followed this developing pattern.[51]

Education

On a much broader scale there is education as the social appropriation of discourse. Education is the instrument whereby every individual can gain access to any kind of discourse. We well know that in its distribution, in what it permits and in what it prevents, it follows the well-trodden battle lines of social conflict.

---

[51]José Antonio Villareal R. "Chicano Literature: Art and Politics from the Perspective of the Artist," in *The Identification and Analysis of Chicano Literature*, Francisco Jiménez, editor (New York: Bilingual Press, 1979), p. 163. *Author's note.*

Every educational system is a political means of maintaining, or of modifying the appropriation of discourse, with the knowledge and powers that it carries with it. Of course, these forms of control of discourse—the status given to individual speakers, fellowships of discourse, doctrinal groups and social appropriations—are linked together, constituting a corporation that distributes speakers among the different types of discourse. What is an educational system after all, but the allocation of discourse to specific individual speakers, the constitution of a diffused doctrinal group, a distribution and appropriation of discourse with all its pedagogical powers? Thus, the control of Meshicano discourse, the reason that "the people do not know what it is that they must know in order to survive" is to be found in the educational process. This is why Chávez Ortiz's children and the vast majority of Meshicano children "have attended school for many years and they know absolutely nothing."

Education as a mechanism for the control of Meshicano discourse combines all the procedures discussed above. It manifests itself in the curricula of all grades, and is, in effect, an extension of the Societal Curriculum discussed by Carlos E. Cortés. This is because "there is no power relation without the correlative constitution of a field of knowledge, nor any knowledge that does not presuppose and constitute at the same time power relations."[52] If power is to be studied at the extreme points of its exercise, where it is less legal in character, one must look at the very battle line where hegemonic and counter hegemonic practices meet face to face with very tragic results: school failure among Meshicano children, for instance. Such failure leads to other battle fronts such as youth gangs in the barrios and high arrest and incarceration rates for these youths. With reference to bio-power,[53] what we have here is, in effect, a body count of the struggle between Chicanology and Meshicano discourse. Here, too, power is effective to the extent that it is invisible. Thus the difficulty in finding solutions

---

[52]Foucault, *Discipline and Punish: The Birth of the Prison*, tr. Alan Sheridan (New York: Vintage Books, 1979), p. 27. *Author's note.*

[53]Foucault, *The History of Sexuality*, p. 140. *Author's note.*

to the problem of school failure: is it culture, language, a caste-like status, or "dramaturgical communicative competence?"[54]

If we define the property of discourse as the ability to invest discourse into institutional practices (public policy), then what we have just considered are the techniques, procedures and mechanisms by which that corporation of truth called Chicanology appropriates, organizes, rearranges and distributes Meshicano discourse to deflect its impact on these institutional practices. We can now answer Ricardo Sánchez's question. The people do not know what it is they must know because their discourse and its inherent power is either forbidden outright, considered insane or irrational, declared a falsehood, or restricted by academic disciplines, and the educational process, in general.

To reiterate the thrust of these discussions, what is being proposed here is an analysis of discourse that includes both erudite knowledge and local memories. This will establish a historical knowledge of struggles and make use of this knowledge tactically today. Discursive analysis is not a return to a more careful or exact form of science; though it does not call for a lyrical knowledge or the right of ignorance. Such analysis seriously considers the claims of local, discontinuous, disqualified, illegitimate knowledge against the claims of a unitary body of theory that filters and orders them in the name of true knowledge and a politicized idea of science. The focus of analysis, then, is on the insurrection of knowledges that are opposed primarily to the effects of centralizing powers linked to scientific discourse.[55] Further study along these lines would address, *for a specific historical event*: (1) the goals and objectives of Meshicano discourse; (2) the status given to the speakers of such discourse; (3) the operational conceptual scheme; (4) the institutionalization of these three aspects; and (5) the

---

[54]See John Ogbu and Maria Eugenia Matute-Bianchi, "Understanding Sociocultural Factors: Knowledge, Identity, and School Adjustment," in *Beyond Language: Social and Cultural Factors in Schooling Language Minority Students* (Los Angeles Evaluation, Dissemination and Assessment Center, California State University, Los Angeles 1986). A critique and attempt to improve this assessment is provided by Douglas E. Foley, "Reconsidering Anthropological Explanations of Ethnic School Failure," *Anthropology and Education Quarterly*, Volume 22, 1991. The latter publication includes a critical commentary of both perspectives by Henry T. Trueba. *Author's note.*

[55]Foucault, "Two Lectures," *Power/Knowledge*, p. 133. *Author's note.*

ultimate effects of this particular discourse on the actual physical body of the people (biopower).

It is critical to make one very important clarification. The struggle between Chicanology and Meshicano discourse has been presented in term of a dialectical relationship for the sake of simplicity. It is not, however, as if all Meshicanos speak from within Meshicano discourse, and all Anglos speak from within Chicanology. As already noted, power functions in terms of manifold relationships that are determined by specific conditions. Thus, depending on the particular struggle under investigation, we may find Chicanos making statements dictated by Chicanology and, conversely, Anglos obeying the rules of Meshicano discourse. Any ethnic group founded in the United States can speak either discourse (from within their own power/knowledge relations). It is precisely the purpose of discursive analysis to reveal the specific, ever-shifting micro-physics of power and its micro-mechanisms. In passing, it should be noted that this is particularly important when culture is conceptualized as a platonic entity: "It's a (brown, black, red, yellow) thing. You wouldn't understand." Often multicultural relations are perceived as being above not only race and class but most critically, above relations of power.

In conclusion, the essential political problem for the intellectual is not to criticize the ideological contents supposedly linked to science or to ensure that his own scientific practice is accompanied by a correct ideology. Rather, it is a matter of ascertaining the possibility of constituting a new politics of truth. The problem is not changing people's consciousness—or what's in their heads—but the political economic institutional regime of the production of truth. It is not a matter of emancipating the truth from every system of power (which would be a chimera, for truth is already power) but of detaching the power of truth from the forms of hegemony within which it operates at the present time. The political question is not error, illusion, alienated consciousness or ideology. It is truth itself.[56]

This version appeared in *Perspectives in Mexican American Studies* 3 (1992): 117-47. This essay is part of a study which was originally developed in 1981-

---

[56]Foucault, "Truth and Power," *Power/Knowledge*, p. 133. *Author's note.*

1982 with the support of a Faculty Fellowships for Minorities grant awarded by The Southern Fellowships Fund.

YSIDRO RAMÓN MACÍAS (1944-)

"The Evolution of the Mind" (1969)

One of the most pressing problems for a person of a Mexican descent in the United States is that of identity, commonly called the identity crisis. For here is a person who is officially classified as white (Spanish surname) by the Census Bureau of this country, yet because the shade of his skin generally is darker than the Anglos', he is effectively designated as a minority. Furthermore, he is also discriminated against because of his desire to retain the Spanish language and some of the customs and traditions of Mexico. Even though the Indian strain in Mexicans is predominant amongst the population, like in all the countries of America (Latina) there are a significant portion who have very definite European features. These light-skinned Mexicans could, if they did not speak with an accent, easily be mistaken for Anglos or some European stock. This multiplicity of shades amongst Mexicans has to some extent historically played a significant role in the level of economic and social achievement for Mexicans living in the barrios of the United States. Those Mexicans who were lighter generally received better treatment in the schools, usually obtained greater opportunities in vocations, and were accepted much easier into the mainstream of American society. All of the above factors plus the realism of obsession with skin color (or racism) in this country served to place many of these light-skinned Mexicans in roles as leaders of the Mexican communities. Since childhood, especially in the school system, the little dark-skinned Mexican was taught that he was inferior in most capacities to the Anglo, and even to his light-skinned Mexican brother. Therefore, what evolved in the barrios to some extent was a hierarchy of types based upon the color of an individual's skin.

The identity problems of the Mexican did not, however, end with the color of his skin. Of even greater importance was the constant attempt by the dominant Anglo society to pressure and humiliate the Mexican into giving up the Spanish language and customs and traditions retained from Mexico. The now recognized lack of Mexican history in U.S. history textbooks; the forcible suppression of the Spanish language in the classrooms and playgrounds; the sick humor directed against the young Mexican's customs, clothes, and even lunch; the inability of teachers and counselors to motivate the youth and encourage higher education goals; these and many other examples served to create a sharp lessening of self-respect and bewilderment in the minds of young Mexican children. Socially he was constantly made aware that he was not acceptable unless he would shed many of his native habits and language. Even when he would conform to the wishes of his Anglo associates he would often find that they considered him nothing more than a "good Mexican" and talk and jokes behind his back continued. At restaurants and theaters he was often led to areas specifically set aside for Mexicans. One of the most insulting displays of bias occurred in the Church where the Mexican took his family on Sunday and proceeded to be ushered to pews on one side of the church or to specific pews where other Mexicans sat.

The above paragraphs attempt to create some understanding as to the identity crisis that has developed amongst many Mexican youth in the United States. For here is a person who is taught since childhood that almost everything he represents is not only inferior to Anglo standards but also anti-American. Even in some homes the young Mexican's parents did not offer an understanding of his cultural background or refused to speak Spanish for fear their children would be discriminated against by the Anglo society. The result has often been, for that Mexican seeking to raise his standard of living, a denial of his native customs and language and a quite-never attained drive for full acculturation and assimilation within the American societal mainstream. For those Mexicans not willing to part with their native ways, it has often meant relegation to a bad education, low-paying job, and social ostracism. Therefore, many Mexicans previously refused to admit their ancestry, instead proclaiming themselves Greeks, Italians, Spanish, etc. Recently, however, beginning in 1966, there has revived a phenomenon predominantly amongst Mexican youth to deny the term Mexican-American and instead to adopt another term (Chicano). The following article will deal with the differences, both semantic and real, among the mentalities of a Mexican-American, a Chicano, a Third World mentality, and the ultimate mentality in the opinion of this author, the humanist.

The Mexican-American

In the contemporary Chicano movement and thought, the term Mexican-American has acquired certain distinguishing aspects which differentiate it substantially from the term Chicano. Aside from differences emanating from emotional or philosophical causes, the term Mexican-American is repugnant to Chicanos because of at least two reasons. The first reason is that the term is semantically wrong. The arrogance of citizens of this country in calling themselves

Americans as if the term is exclusively theirs rankles most Latin Americans. If one travels to Latin America, he is constantly made aware that he is regarded as a Norteamericano. Mexicans have historically stressed the above point and therefore Chicanos have noted that by virtue of being Mexican one is automatically American also. Therefore, it is semantically correct to say Italian-Americans, Irish-Americans, Chinese-Americans, etc., because these U.S. citizens are descended from those areas in the world not in the Americas. But the attempt by Anglos to further define Mexicans by adding the hyphen and American is wrong and arrogant. The second reason the term Mexican-American is unacceptable to Chicanos is because it is a term which has been attached to us by the Anglo society. One of the major points of contention between ethnic minorities and the dominant Anglo culture in this country is the concept of self-determination. The concept of self-determination is of paramount importance to Chicanos, and one manifestation of this concept is to be able to define what certain words and terms mean to us and what we wish to call ourselves. Mexican-American is a term which persons of Mexican descent in this country never called themselves, instead proclaiming themselves Mexicanos, Hispanos, Chicanos, etc. Therefore, after years of passively accepting the Anglo designation for us, Chicanos have begun to understand that one of the prime motivating factors for a movement is positive self-identity, and acceptance of a term that the system and culture we are directly in conflict with has applied to us is unacceptable. For it is understood that we could have easily been accepted as Americans, yet the tokenism involved in naming us Mexican-Americans is nothing more than an attempt to isolate us and maintain a master-servant relationship.

The view of the term Mexican-American in contemporary Chicano thought, then, is that of a Mexican who seeks acculturation with the dominant Anglo culture and society. This desire for assimilation features certain aspects which are negative for positive self-identity and self-respect. One aspect is that the Mexican-American either rejects his Mexican heritage or else places it in a role of secondary importance to the Anglo culture. In effect what the Mexican-American is doing when he devalues his heritage is admitting that his parents, symbolizing the Mexican heritage, are inferior. Since he is but a product of his parents, the Mexican-American is also admitting that he is inferior and the result is a conscious or subconscious lack of self-respect. In terms of what this acculturationist drive means to the Chicano movement, the Mexican-American is politically ineffective because he either fails to see or rejects the notion that as a Mexican he has a responsibility to his community. Previously too many Mexicans who "made it" left the Mexican communities never to return and instead attempted to assimilate with the Anglo society. Instead the Mexican-American has become indoctrinated with the Protestant or Puritanistic ethic of self-achievement and material gains, because of his search for acculturation which now causes his commitment to the Chicano cause to be a contradiction to his now distorted values. This Puritan ethic, stressing the concept of "lifting yourself up by your bootstraps" is unapplicable to Mexicans in this country because of discrimination and racism by Anglos and the capitalist system. Thus when a Mexican-American accepts this ethic he is in effect denying the existence of the many injustices perpetrated against Mexicans in this country (vendiéndose).

The Chicano

Every Mexican-American is a potential Chicano. Before we can explore what a Chicano is the reader should have a background as to where the term originated and its use in the United States. Although no one has categorically determined how the term was born, it is generally accepted that it came from northern Mexico. It is from northern Mexico that burritos originate, and where menudo, mole, pozole and many other foods prepared by Chicanos also are made in the same manner distinct from the greater southern Mexico. It is also in north-ern Mexico, because of its close contact with the United States, that the language academically called Calo and locally named Pocho also originated. One theory that this author presents as to the origin of the term Chicano is that the Citizens of Chihuahua, a city and state of northern Mexico, took the "Chi" from that name and added the "cano" from Mexicano, arriving at Chicano. Chronologically speaking, the term Chicano has perhaps been common in the United States since the 1930s. It is a term that was used by Mexicans long before Mexican-Ameri-can, and was used as an intimate name to note recognition of our particular status as not full Mexicans nor full Americans (U.S. type). Therefore, the term Chicano is not a new phenomenon, as is popularly supposed. The name perhaps last had significant national attention during the so-called "zoot-suit riots" in Los Angeles during the early 1940s. Recently the name was revived about 1965 at the begin-ning of the Delano Strike and is continuing to grow in popular usage and in building of a definite civil-rights movement and philosophy. It should be noted that a civil-rights movement does not embrace fully the term Chicano, because many Chicanos want either a complete revision of the U.S. political and econom-ic system or separation from it.

Salient aspects of the Chicano include a self-awareness or self-respect and a personal commitment to the Chicano communities. The high degree of self-respect amongst Chicanos exists because this individual accepts his Mexican culture and language as at least equal to if not superior to the Anglos. He rejects the notion that he must subjugate his heritage in order to rise within the American society and instead presents the Anglo with the alternative to accept him as an equal human being. If the Anglo refuses to allow him his self-respect, as is often the case, the Chicano is now seeking to establish political and economic hegemony over his communities in order to control them and perpetrate his existence as a distinct entity. Increasingly the Chicano is becoming more isolated in many respects from the Anglo society than ever before because of the Anglos' refusal to accept him. For the Chicano asks himself: "Why should I try to prove myself to the Anglo? I am going to be my own man, respecting my heritage, and if accepted as such, it's well, if not, that is also all right." A Chicano is also very much aware of the history of Mexican peoples in this country. He recognizes that Mexican citizens defending the Mexican flag fought against Santa Ana at the Alamo; that 20 percent of the G.I.s on the front lines in Vietnam are Chicanos when we comprise but 3 percent of the total population of this country; that educationally, politically, economically, and socially gross injustices have been perpetrated against our communities by the dominant Anglo society, etc. Linguistically, the Chicano recognizes that he possesses a different mentality or outlook towards life than the Anglo due to some extent to the differences between the Spanish and English languages. As an example, the Anglo will say, "I missed the bus," while the Chicano will say "me dejó el camión" (The bus left me). Or notice the difference between "I broke the glass" and "se quebró el vaso" (The glass broke itself). The above examples are but two illustrations of how, because of the language, Spanish-speaking peoples develop a somewhat different outlook on life from that of English-speaking U.S. citizens. This denial to accept the blame for some incidents that occur to us, coupled with many other peculiar aspects of the Spanish language and Mexican culture, distinguish us from the great majority of only English-speaking citizens of this country. It is not to say that we have an inferior mentality; conversely, our way of thinking is something innate, and Chicanos who recognize this view this difference positively, for it represents a more communal philosophy and a greater responsibility to our fellow Chicanos. It is to say that the spirit of compadrazgo, or close ties to certain individuals, is part of the Mexican heritage and is connected with the Spanish language. This sense of responsibility or personal commitment to our communities is the second point that distinguishes the Chicano from the Mexican-American. Rejecting the Puritan ethic of self-improvement above all else, the Chicano recognizes that just because he "makes it" does not make the system in this country valid or responsible to all Chicanos. He recognizes that he is part of a brotherhood and that he has a responsibility to work for the betterment of his people in whatever way that he can. Therefore, he automatically devotes a portion of his lifetime energies to exclusively work for the Chicano communities and for his carnales and carnalas who live in these communities.

The third item that distinguishes Chicanos is the concept of Chicanismo. This concept, or philosophy, has currently not been entirely defined or outlined yet one can say that it includes the previous two points noted above plus the continued maintenance and enrichment of our peculiar Chicano, or Mexican, heritage. Chicanos note that we are heirs to a great mixture of cultures, the Indian and Spanish; and added to this Mexican culture is the experience of living in an English-speaking country with its continuous attempt to erase our Mexican heritage. Out of this historical conflict has arisen our own unique mentality and language, different from both the Mexican and the American. Chicanos now accept these characteristics as positive and beautiful points instead of the previous relegation of them as inferior and vulgar forms of behavior and expression. Chicanos perceive that their culture must not be allowed to remain stagnant, and therefore throughout the greater Aztlan (U.S. Southwest) he is daily expressing himself in his native tongue, Pocho, and seeking new and more effective ways of reviving, maintaining, and enriching his Chicano culture. Finally, no longer does the color of a Chicano's skin determine his status within his community. The lighter-skinned Mexican is not the favored son; quite the contrary, the darker Indian type is now exemplified along with other characteristics and customs derived from our Indian heritage.

Third World

A Third World mentality can be expressed as an extension of Chicanismo expanded to embrace those ethnic minorities who are also suppressed and are victims of Anglo exploitation and discrimination. In order to understand further the concept of the Third World, one must first be aware of the origins of the term. The First World includes the white capitalist countries of the Earth (U.S., Australia, W. Europe, etc.). The Second World features the White communist countries (U.S.S.R., E. Europe). The Third World necessarily embraces all those countries not in either of the first two worlds. There is no standard economic or political ideology common to those countries of the Third World, as illustrated by China, Chile, Egypt, Cuba, India, etc. It also includes those countries which are geographically in the Third World despite the fact that they are dominated by a racist white minority (South Africa, Rhodesia, etc.). In these white minority-dominated nations, the Third World embraces the native inhabitants who are suppressed and optimistically views their liberation from the white exploiters. Despite the fact that there exists no uniform political and economic doctrine amongst Third World countries, they all have something in common (it should be mentioned than an exception is Japan, a capitalist country which more naturally is ideologically and economically allied with the First World, and Albania, which is closer to the Third World than the Second World). The uniqueness of the Third World is that it is economically and politically subjugated or exploited by either or both of the first two worlds. Whatever the Third World country, it is a fact that today they are suffering from mass starvation, economic exploitation, and political interference of their internal affairs at the hands of the white capitalists or communists.

Within the United States, the Third World is comprised of those individuals or ethnic groups which are descended from the geographical areas of the Third World. These would include the Chicanos, Blacks, Puerto Ricans, Chinese, Japanese, etc. Also included in the Third World are the Native Americans, more commonly known as the American Indians. Furthermore, in keeping with an international philosophy, there are substantial numbers of white people in this country who can also be classified as Third World because of their low economic status. For there exist many so-called "Third World" people in the United States who realistically have more in common with the dominant capitalist majority and are oppressing their brothers as much the white capitalists. It is to say that the Third World as a philosophy is beginning to adopt a development of a class consciousness, with less emphasis on the ethnic background of an individual. Similar to the situation of the Third World countries, the Third World peoples of the United States also do not have common political views nor common economic levels of affluence. Yet these peoples unfortunately have many things in common, precisely that they are politically, economically, educationally, and socially impotent to a large extent under the dominant Anglo society. It is this lack of basic human rights and participation denied to them by the racist and exploitative Anglo majority of this country that is now serving to develop a still embryonic Third World movement in the United States. For just as Chicanos are striving to further develop the concept of Chicanismo, other Third World peoples of this country are also beginning to take renewed pride in their own political heritages. No longer are many Third World peoples willing to deny or subjugate their cultures in order to be accepted into the American societal mainstream. In addition, many of them understand that in past times the anglo majority has attempted to create animosities and divisions amongst the various Third World groups in order to divert attention from the problems created by white racism and capitalist exploitation.

Thus, what is evolving today, while at present still only to a small degree, is a philosophy or mentality of a Third World which features self-determination, or that concept that all human beings have the right to determine their own destinies. Many sophisticated Third World peoples in this country recognize that while vast cultural differences exist amongst them, they are all generally existing as second-class citizens and suffering much the same lack of opportunity or oppression in this country. Increasingly, coalitions of various Third World peoples are being formed, seeing in unity a more effective means of achievement of a common or peculiar goal. One can thus state that a Third World mentality exists when particular Third World groups recognize their common ties of misfortune and, tossing aside reluctance to work together because of past friction, make a commitment to work for the betterment and improvement of all Third World communities in this country. It should be noted that when Third World groups coalesce, they do not cease to continue striving for the maintenance or enrichment of their particular heritages. It does, however, mean that those groups do not allow cultural nationalism (ethnic identity and self-pride) to interfere with inter-group relations. In effect, what the above means is a new concept of brotherhood, created and maintained because of the common oppression suffered. At present, unfortunately, the idea or philosophy as stated above is but beginning to grow, yet as dedicated people continue to seek better means of effecting basic human rights, the Third World philosophy will continue to mature and afford new participation and rewards for its advocates.

The Humanist

The ultimate mentality that can be possessed by an individual, in the opinion of this author, is that of a humanist. Forgetting momentarily the popular definition that can be found in a dictionary, a brief viewpoint of the humanist mentality shall be represented here. This author wishes to stress that he will present the humanist mentality in context with interaction amongst various ethnic types. Basically, the humanist philosophy can be said to be an extension of the idea of brotherhood for Third World peoples to now embrace all people as human beings, having basic rights. Thus a Chicano, for example, will judge a white or Black person not because of his color or culture, but on his merits as an individual. This is the old, but unfortunately too little practiced, concept of not prejudging a person because of race, creed, or color. For most persons with any degree of native intelligence understand that there are people good and bad amongst all races or ethnic types, and to categorically assign or stereotype an individual because of his color or culture is not an intelligent strategy. Unfortunately, in considering the current situations in the United States, one would probably be correct if he stated that 75 percent of all whites are racists, either consciously or subconsciously. However, just as Malcolm X discovered that not all whites are devils, Third World peoples must guard against becoming so obsessed with a Third World cultural nationalism that they reverse the racism of whites and stereotype all whites as racists. It has too often been the case that when an ethnic minority militantly voices its intention to retain its culture or assert itself, some of the overobsessed cultural nationalist leaders have categorically debased whites and all other minorities as well.

This author recognizes that general statements are at times convenient, yet Third World peoples and whites as well must guard against oversimplification when referring to other ethnic types. The humanist, therefore, views and respects the peculiar ethnic heritages of his fellow human beings, neither exalting nor degrading them. The Chicano will continue to maintain and enrich his Chicanismo, the Black his Black pride, the white man his, etc. Of all the mentalities discussed above, the humanist mentality is unfortunately the most difficult to achieve. Perhaps this is because it is the most demanding and calls for an outstanding effort from its advocates. Nevertheless, all persons should strive to achieve this mentality because, needless to say, a great measure of peace and brotherhood amongst men could be attained if all persons shared this philosophy towards their fellow men.

NOTE: it is the author's contention that the mentalities or philosophies discussed above are achieved through a progression, starting at the Mexican-American level, then Chicano, Third World, and finally humanist. However, it is quite possible for a Chicano, for example, to bypass the Third World mentality and become a humanist. This author strongly contends that it is impossible for a Mexican-American to adopt either a Third World or humanist mentality because in order for a Mexican-American to interact with other ethnic groups equally he must first accept and recognize his particular ethnic identity and heritage.

Reprinted from *El Pocho Che* (Oakland, 1969).

OCTAVIO IGNACIO ROMANO-V. (1923-)

"The Historical and Intellectual Presence of Mexican Americans" (1969)

Muchos murieron, otros se fueron

During and following the Mexican Revolution of 1910, it is estimated that one of every ten people left the country. Some went to Spain, some to France, some went to Cuba, to Guatemala, but most went north to the United States. Among those who went to the north were printers, poets, civil servants, merchants, farmers, school teachers, campesinos, musicians, bartenders, blacksmiths, jewelers, carpenters, cowboys, mestizos, village Indians, religious people, atheists, infants, mothers, Masons, counter-revolutionaries, philosophers.

Among those who went north was José Vasconcelos, who later became Secretary of Education in Mexico. So did Martín Luis Guzmán, author of the classic novel of the Revolution, *El Aguila y la Serpiente*. Adolfo de la Huerta started the rebellion in northwest Mexico, was Provisional President (1920), and persuaded Pancho Villa to settle on the Canutillo Ranch. Huerta finally fled to Los Angeles, California, worked there as a singing instructor, and later returned to Mexico. Another northern migrant was José María Maytorena, governor of Sonora, supporter of Madero, follower of Villa who finally ended up in California. Ramón Puente was a doctor, teacher, journalist and writer in the Villa army. Following Villa's defeat, Puente left for the United States. Along with the others, these men were among the great number of people who became the "immigrants" and "refugees" from the Mexican Revolution. In the words of Ernesto Galarza:

> As civil war spread over the republic after 1911 a major exodus from the country began. Landowners fled to the large cities, principally the capital, followed by hundreds of thousands of refugees who could find no work. This was one of the two great shifts that were to change radically the population patterns, until then overwhelmingly rural. The other current was in the direction of the United States, now accessible by rail. It moved in the dilapidated coaches with which the Mexican lines had been equipped by

their foreign builders, in cabooses fitted with scant privacy, on engine tenders and on flat cars for the steerage trade. "A la capital o al norte" (to Mexico City or to the border) became the alternatives for the refugees from the cross-fires of revolution.[1]

In the north they worked on the railroad, in the clearing of mesquite, in fish canneries, tomato fields, irrigation, and all other such work that became so drearily familiar to the people living in the colonias. At the same time, for many, the Revolution continued to be fought in the barrios in the United States, as described by José Antonio Villareal in his novel, *Pocho*:

The man who died under the bridge that night had no name. Who he was, where he came from, how he lived—these things did not matter, for there were thousands like him at this time. This particular man had fought in the army of General Carrillo, who, in turn, was one of the many generals in the Revolution. And, like thousands of unknown soldiers before and after him, this man did not reason, did not know, had but a vague idea of his battle. Eventually there was peace, or a lull in the fighting, and he escaped with his wife and children and crossed the border to the north.[2]

Not only did an attenuated version of the Revolution continue in the north, with plot and counterplot, avoidance and memories of hate, but there also continued the ideas, the intellectualizations, and the philosophies of the day. In the northern colonias, as was happening in Mexico, people still discussed and argued over the relative merits of Indianist philosophies, of Historical Experience and Confrontations, and about the philosophical and historical significance of the Mestizo. These relevant philosophies became a part of the common poetry readings of those days in the barrios. They also appeared in the colonia newspaper of the day, in stage and other dramatic presentations, in the music of the trumpet and guitars, in schools of Mexican culture, in the rationales and goals of the autonomous labor unions as well as in the constitutions and by-laws of the sociedades mutualistas. In some cases, the ideas had been transplanted from Mexico.

---

[1] Galarza, Ernesto. 1964. *Merchants of Labor*, McNally & Loftin, Charlotte, Santa Barbara, page 28. *Author's note.* Note that the bibliographic format of these references conform to the style chosen by the author.

[2] Villareal, José Antonio. 1959. *Pocho*, Doubleday & Co., Garden City, New York, page 29. *Author's note.*

In others, they were merged with pre-existent philosophies among the Mexican descended people already in the United States. And through it all, there continued the human quest and the conflict between Nationalistic Man and Universal Man, between Activist Man and Existential Man, Cleric and Anti-cleric, Mutualist, Classical Anarchist,[3] Nihilist man, Agrarian and Urban Man, Indian Man and Mestizo.

These are the principal historical *currents of thought* that have gone into the making of the mind of el Mexicano, the "refugee," el cholo, the Pocho, the Chicano, Pachuco, the Mexican-American. They have their roots in history and currently appear in three mainstreams of thought—Indianist philosophy, Historical Confrontation, and the philosophically transcendent idea of the Mestizo in the form of Cultural Nationalism. These are philosophies, styles of thought, ideas as they persist over time. At times they coincide with actual historical occurrences. Other times they lie relatively dormant, or appear in a poetic metaphor, a song, a short story told to children, or in a marriage pattern. These philosophies were articulated in the post-Diaz days in Mexico and in the days of the Revolution.

En aquellos días

The ideologies and philosophies that gave air to the smoldering fires of the Mexican Revolution of 1910 were pluralistic, reflecting the compositions of Mexico at that time. Many world views, numerous projected plans, desires for power, and historical precedents all contributed to this fiery outburst that led to untold human agonies, an attempted reconstruction, and a massive exodus. In the *Labyrinth of Solitude*, the philosopher-poet Octavio Paz attempted bravely to deal with these criss-cross currents in their historical relation to the present. His published effort resulted in a somewhat Quixotic quest for *THE* Mexican—El puro Mexicano—a quest that fluttered between the two extremes of National Man and Universal Man. What emerged from his search were NOT many masks, as Octavio Paz insisted in the Freudianesque overtones of his work. Instead, what emerged from his search were but different lifestyles which represented different historical trends, a variety of individual experiences, and multiple intellectual

---

[3]Classical anarchism as used here refers to the original anarchist movement promoting the decentralization of power, the opposition of dictatorships in any form, co-operative movements, and not the "mad bomb plot and madman" stereotype of later years. *Author's note.*

currents—in short, Many Mexicans, just as today there are Many Mexican-Amer-icans. Quite often, this seemingly endless multiplicity represents many men. Equally often, it represents every man.

Cada loco con su tema (dicho)

In 1926, José Vasconcelos, former Secretary of education in Mexico, wrote, "The Struggle of the Latin-Americans revolutionist is the struggle of democratic European ideas to impose themselves upon the Oriental indigenous type of des-potism."[4] Vasconcelos condensed his notions into the "philosophy of the Ibero-american race," having its origins in an ethnically pluralistic Spain, transplanted to an equally pluralistic Mexico, reinforced by the universalistic components of the Catholic faith, and ultimately manifested in the Mestizo—genetic assimila-tion with European ideology integrated into the contemporary Mexico of his day.[5] The heart of his argument, of course, was that ideas invariably supercede the biological imperatives of miscegenation. Therefore, if miscegenation was the best vehicle for advancing pre-existent ideas, then such a course was desirable for Mexico. In all this process he envisioned ". . .the hope that the mestizo will produce a civilization more universal in its tendency than any other race of the past."[6]

This was not only the view that depicted the thought currents of the time. For example, Octavio Paz has written, "The Revolution had antecedents, causes and motives, but in a profound sense it lacked precursors. . . . The Revolution began as a demand for truth and honesty in the government, as can be seen from the Plan of San Luis (Oct. 5, 1910). Gradually the movement found and defined itself, in the midst of battle and later when in power. Its lack of a set program gave it popular authenticity and originality. This fact accounts for both its great-ness and its weaknesses."[7] Then, "the revolution, without any doctrines (whether imported or its own) to guide it, was an explosion of reality and a groping search for the universal doctrine that would justify it and give it a place in the history

---

[4]Vasconcelos, José, and Manuel Gamio. 1926. *Aspects of Mexican Civiliza-tion*, University of Chicago Press, pages 51-52. *Author's note.*

[5]Vasconcelos, José. 1926. See above, pages 90-102. *Author's note.*

[6]Vasconcelos, José. 1926. See above, page 92. *Author's note.*

[7]Paz, Octavio. 1961. *The Labyrinth of Solitude*, Grove Press, Inc., New York, page 136. *Author's note.*

of America and the world."[8] Finally, "our movement was distinguished by a lack of any previous ideological system and by a hunger for land."[9]

The views of José Vasconcelos and those of Octavio Paz reflect two major trends of thought at the time of the Revolution. First, there was the articulation of the desire to emulate pre-existent ideologies, i.e., el Mestizaje. Second, there was the desire to do autonomously, to confront, and then to articulate. Both ultimately envisioned something uniquely Mexican in its final outcome, a new synthesis. There was a third trend, the Zapata movement. This movement was a form of Indianism as intellectualized largely by the school teacher Montaño, a pure Indian. According to Vasconcelos, "there was a time when the European dress was not allowed in the Zapata territory; and those Mexicans of white Spanish skin that happened to join the Zapata armies had to adopt the dress and the manner of the Indian, in a certain way had to become indianized before they could be accepted."[10] As Paz describes it, "The Zapatistas did not conceive of Mexico as a future to be realized but as a return to origins."[11] It seemed almost as if a star had exploded long before, and only now could they see its light.

The Zapatista-Indianist philosophy, the Historical Confrontation, and the philosophy of the Mestizo were the three dominant philosophies of Revolutionary Mexico. Sometimes elements of one trend of thought would blend with another, as did the Indianist with Historical Confrontation. But when this took place it was in a complementary fashion, and not at the expense of the ideological premises that were guiding each chain of thought. In the same manner, any given individual could ally himself with any of three philosophies in the course of his life, or shift from one to the other depending on surrounding circumstances, just as was the case with the "white" who joined the Zapatista Indian forces, In short, the three ideological currents actually gave individuals alternatives from which to choose. These alternatives, in turn, represented relatively new historical manifestations at the turn of the century—cumulative changes that had been taking place in Mexico. They represented, therefore, the historical development of thought and not the rigid, unbending and unchanging Traditional Culture so commonly and uncritically accepted in current sociological treatises that deal with people of Mexican descent. At the same time, *these three alternatives also*

---

[8]Paz, Octavio. 1961. See above, page 140. *Author's note.*

[9]Paz, Octavio. 1961. See above, page 141. *Author's note.*

[10]Vasconcelos, José. 1926. See above, page 90. *Author's note.*

[11]Paz, Octavio. 1961. See above, page 144. *Author's note.*

*made it possible for individual people, even families, to be living three histories
at once,* a fact that escaped Octavio Paz when he accepted the notion of the
Freudianesque masks.

In any event, when the time came for people to change locale and move to
the United States, this was but another in a long series of changes that had been
taking place.

Cada cabeza un mundo (dicho)

It is this complexity of thought and its many individual manifestations that
made so popular the saying, "Each head a world in itself." For multiple histories
could hardly have done other than breed complex and equally complex families.
It is this complexity, actually pluralism, that was transferred with the "refugees"
and the "immigrants" to the north and which appeared in the colonias and barrios. This complexity was condensed in the recent poem by Rodolfo Gonzales
of Denver, Colorado, titled "I am Joaquin."[12] Just who is this Joaquin? Joaquin
is Cuauhtémoc, Cortez, Nezahualcoyotl of the Chichimecas. Joaquin is Spaniard,
Indian, Mestizo, the village priest Hidalgo, Morelos, Guerrero, Don Benito Juarez, Zapata, Yaqui, Chamula, Tarahumara, Díaz, Huerta, Francisco Madero, Juan
Diego, Alfego Baca, the Espinoza brothers, Murietta; Joaquin is slave.[13] Joaquin
is master. Joaquin is exploiter, and he is the exploited. Joaquin is corridos, Latino, Hispano, Chicano. Joaquin is in the fields, suburbs, mines, and prisons.
Joaquin's body lies under the ground in Mexico. His body lies under the ground
in the United States, and in the "hills of the Alaskan Isles, on the corpse-strewn
beach of Normandy, the foreign land of Korea, and now, Vietnam."[14] Joaquin
is many men. Joaquin is every man.

The ideas that were, and are, present wherever people of Mexican descent
live involve the Indianist philosophy, Historical Confrontation, and Cultural

---

[12]Gonzales, Rodolfo. 1967. *I Am Joaquin*, Denver, Colorado. *Author's note.*
See the text of the poem reproduced in this anthology.

[13]Romano shows variation in the use of the written accent on words from the
Spanish, as for example in the case of Joaquin/Joaquín and Garcia/García. Roma-
no also uses "Murietta" rather than the more common form, "Murrieta," which
in turn also appears as "Murieta."

[14]Gonzales, Rodolfo. 1967. See above, page 15. *Author's note.*

Nationalism. Now, to the three currents of thought manifested historically there was added a fourth, the Immigrant Experience.

Indianism

Indianism has never been a focus or a rallying cry for action among Mexican-Americans as was Indigenismo during the War for Independence and the Revolution in Mexico. Yet, symbolically, the Indian penetrates throughout, and permeates, major aspects of Mexican-American life, and hardly a barrio exists that does not have someone who is nicknamed "El Indio" or "Los Indios." For decades, Mexican-American youth have felt a particularly keen resentment at the depiction of Indians in American movies, while Indian themes consistently have been common subject matter for the neighborhood's amateur artists, a fact that may be called an anachronism by some or the dislodging of history by others. On occasion, los Matachines[15] still make their Indian appearance in churches, and Aztec legends still pictorially tell and retell their stories in barrio living rooms, in kitchens, in bars, restaurants, tortillerias, and Chicano newspapers. The stern face of Don Benito Juarez still peers out of books, still surveys living rooms, and still takes a place of prominence in many sociedad mutualista halls and in the minds of men throughout the Southwest. Small wonder, then, that several hundred years after the totally indigenous existence of Mexico, reference is still made to these roots and origins in the Mexican-American community. Small wonder, also, that thousands of miles away from the Valley of Mexico, in contemporary Denver, Colorado, Señor Rodolfo Gonzales utilizes recurrent Indian themes in his poetic work. At the same time, such [themes are] found in the wall paintings at the Teatro Campesino center in Del Rey, California, and Indian art and life are common subject matter in such newspapers as *Bronze, La Raza, El Gallo,* as well as others. One should not be surprised, therefore, that the poet Alurista wrote in 1968:

> Unexpectedly
>   my night gloom came
> injusta capa fúnebre
> ....
> y corrí hacia el sol

---

[15]Traceable to the Spanish colonial period, the Matachines are an Indian group that performs at Catholic celebrations in the New Mexican barrio.

el de mis padres
the one that printed
on my sarape

fantastic colors
through the prism
—la pirámide del sol
at the sacrificial Teocatl
my fathers wore their plumage
to listen
and soplaron vida con sus solares rayos
en mi raza[16]

Chichimeca, Azteca, Indio, Don Benito Juarez, Emiliano Zapata y Montaño; in art, prose, poetry, religion, and in Mexican-American study programs initiated by Mexican-Americans themselves in colleges, universities, and high schools, the presence of the Indian is manifested. It hardly need be added that the Indian is also manifested in the faces of so many Mexican-Americans. The Indian is root and origin, past and present, virtually timeless in his barrio manifestations—a timeless symbol of opposition to cultural imperialism.

Historical Confrontation

The philosophy of confrontation has had thousands of manifestations, from the retelling in an isolated corrido to protest demonstration by thousands of people of Mexican descent in the United States. It, too, has an old history which in the north began with personages, such as Joaquin Murietta, Alfego Baca, the Espinoza brothers, and Pancho Villa. Memories of these manifestations spread widely, as attested to by Enrique Hank Lopez when he wrote about his childhood in the United States:

. . .Pancho Villa's exploits were a constant topic of conversation in our household. My entire childhood seems to be shadowed by his presence. At our dinner table, almost every night, we would listen to endlessly repeated

---

[16]Alurista. 1968. "The Poetry of Alurista," *El Grito*, Quinto Sol Publications, Berkeley, California, page 11. *Author's note.*

accounts of this battle, that strategem, or some great act of Robin Hood kindness by *el centenauro del norte*.[17] I remember how angry my parents were when they saw Wallace Beery in *Viva Villa!* "Garbage by stupid Gringos," they called it. They were particularly offended by the sweaty, unshaven sloppiness of Beery's portrayal.[18]

Confrontationist philosophy continued with the labor protest movement among people of Mexican descent in the United States, which at one time became manifest in eight different states and which now has lasted for over eighty-five years. It also has taken other forms, such as the Pachuco who extended the notion of confrontation to a perpetual and daily activity with his own uniform and his own language. *The Pachuco movement was one of the few truly separatist movements in American History.* Even then, it was singularly unique among separatist movements in that it did not seek or even attempt a return to roots and origins. The Pachuco indulged in a *self-separation from history*, created his own reality as he went along, even to the extent of creating his own language. This is the main reason why Octavio Paz, digging as he did into history in search for the "true Mexican," felt it necessary to "put down" the Pachuco. By digging into history for answers, Octavio Paz was forced to exclude people who had separated themselves from history, especially Mexican history. Thus, in denying the Mexicanness of the Pachuco, Octavio Paz denied the Mexican aspect of the processes that went into his creation. That is why Paz ended up by making the Pachuco into a caricature akin to a societal clown, for it was only by doing so that he could enhance the notion of el puro Mexicano in his own mind.

It is unfortunate that Octavio Paz chose to ignore the trend of thought represented by the famous, disillusioned, existential poet of Mexico, Antonio Plaza, who wrote in typical fashion, "Es la vida un enjambre de ilusiones / a cuyo extremos están los desengaños."[19] Had Paz chosen to acknowledge Antonio Plaza, and the philosophical trend he represented in his Mexican, existential, self-separation from history, then perhaps he would have understood a little about

---

[17]*centenauro = centauro.*

[18]Lopez, Enrique Hank. 1967. "Back to Bachimba," *Horizon*, Winter, Vol. IX, No. 1, page 81. *Author's note.*

[19]Plaza, Antonio (Book of Poetry, published in Mexico, handed down for decades and publisher page one. Courtesy of Mr. Rudy Espinosa, San Francisco, California, whose grandfather used to read from this book after dinner each evening.) *Author's note.*

the Pachuco, too, separated himself from history, and in doing so became transformed into Existential Man. And, like existential man everywhere, he too was brutally beaten down.

The language of confrontationist philosophy has been Spanish, English, Pocho, or Pachuco. Almost always, it has addressed itself to an immediate situation spanning the social environment from rural to urban. Normally, it has been regional or local in its manifestations. On different occasions, the confrontationist philosophy has been self-deterministic, protectionist, nationalistic, reacting to surrounding circumstances, and existentialist. The present Chicano movement has incorporated all of these alternatives in its various contemporary manifestations, making it one of the most complex movements in the history of Mexican-Americans.

Having been a recurrent theme in Mexican-American history, like that of Indianism, the confrontationist philosophy also makes up a part of study programs initiated by Mexican-Americans in colleges, universities, and high schools. Like Indianism, it is a history that has yet to be written in its entirety.

Cultural Nationalism

> Vine a Comala porque me dijeron que acá vivía mi padre, un tal Pedro Páramo.[20]

In Texas, New Mexico, Arizona, Colorado, California, Oregon, Washington, Idaho, Nevada, Utah, Oklahoma, Kansas, Arkansas, Ohio, Missouri, Illinois, Michigan, New York, and other states, symbols of Mexican and Mexican-American culture can be seen. Invariably, in one way or another, these symbols are associated with the Mestizos—present descendants of untold Mexican antecedents and reduplicated in an ever-expanding northern arc. Different people have known them as Mexicanos, Cholos, Pochos, México-Norteamericanos, Chicanos, Mexican-Americans. Viewed as a group, they comprise a pluralistic minority within a pluralistic divided nation. They speak Spanish, or English, or both in a great variety of combinations.

The Mestizo-based notion of Cultural Nationalism is prominent among them. But this cultural nationalism is of a very particular kind, unamerican in a

---

[20]Rulfo, Juan. 1968. *Pedro Páramo*, Fondo de Cultura Económica, México, D.F. (novena edición), página 7. *Author's note.*

sense, and considerably unlike the rampant ethnocentrism with its traditional xenophobia (commonly called self-interest) that has been so characteristic of ethnic groups in the United States.

The fiestas patrias, the characteristic foods, the music, the sociedades mutualistas, and all of the other by-products of culture that people write about, are simply appurtenances to more profound conceptualizations regarding the nature and the existence of man. Generally, as a group, Mexican-Americans have been virtually the only ethnic group in the United States that still systematically proclaims its Mestizaje—multiple genetic and cultural origins exhibiting multiplicity rather than seeking purity. Philosophically and historically this has manifested itself in a trend toward Humanistic Universalism, Behavioral Relativism, and a recurrent form of Existentialism, this last of which is often naïvely and erroneously interpreted as fatalism.

The Indianist views, the Confrontationist Philosophy, and Cultural Nationalism with its Mestizaje-based Humanist-Universalism, Behavioral Relativism, and Existentialism, when related to the types of people who have immigrated from Mexico, those born in the United States, as well as people of Mexican descent who were residents in conquered western lands, all give some glimmer of the complexity of this population, especially when one views it internally from the perspectives of multiple philosophies regarding the existence and nature of Mexican-American man. For, in truth, just as "el puro Mexicano" does not exist, neither does "the pure Mexican-American," despite the massive efforts by social scientists to fabricate such a mythical being under the monolithic label of the "Traditional Culture," rather than the more realistic concept of multiple histories and philosophies.

This multiplicity of historical philosophies, to a considerable degree, represents a continuation of the pluralism that existed in Mexico during the Revolution, undergoing modifications and shifts in emphasis. At the same time, it can be said that the philosophies of Indianism, Historical Confrontation, and Cultural Nationalism to this day represent the most salient views of human existence within the Mexican-American population. To these there has been added the immigrant dimension.

The Immigrant Experience

> I'm sitting in my history class,
> the instructor commences rapping,
> I'm in my U.S. History class,

And I'm on the verge of napping.

The Mayflower landed on Plymouth Rock.
Tell me more! Tell me more!
Thirteen colonies were settled.
I've heard it all before.

What did he say?
Dare I ask him to reiterate?
Oh why bother
It sounded like he said,
George Washington's my father.

I'm reluctant to believe it,
I suddenly raise my mano.
If George Washington's my father,
Why wasn't he Chicano?
                    Richard Olivas[21]

Just as could be expected from a pluralistic population exhibiting multiple histories, people of Mexican descent have adjusted to life in the United States in many different ways, including the Pachuco's self-separation from history, the organizers of labor unions, the publishing of bi-lingual newspapers, and the increasingly militant student population. By and large, these adjustments mostly fall into four broad categories: Anglo-Saxon Conformity, Stabilized Differences, Realigned Pluralism, and Bi-Culturalism.

Anglo-Saxon Conformity. A number of people of Mexican descent have eschewed virtually all identity with their cultural past, no longer speak Spanish, and possibly they have changed their name and anglicized it. Most, if not all, of these people can be said to have been acculturated, which, generally, is the process by which people exchange one set of problems for another.

Stabilized Differences. Since 1921 there have been well over 1,000,000 immigrants from Mexico. In various communities they have found pockets of people who have sustained the basic Mexican way of life, along with its multiple histories and philosophies. These pockets vary somewhat as one travels from

---

[21]Olivas, Richard. 1968. *Bronze*, Chicano Newspaper, page 8. (Señor Olivas is a student at San Jose State College.) *Author's note.*

Brownsville, Texas, to El Paso, to Albuquerque, New Mexico, to Tucson, Arizona and through California and over to Colorado. Throughout this area one still hears the respect titles of Don and Doña, the formal Usted, as well as a variety of dialects of the Spanish language. This population comprises the heart of the sociedades mutualistas, the fiestas patrias, the music, food, and the other by-products of culture mentioned elsewhere in this paper.

Realigned Pluralism. It has been the experience of many immigrant groups to take on the general ways of the surrounding society, only to discover that despite their efforts they are still excluded from the main currents for one reason or another. Such has also happened to Mexican-Americans. As a result, those who have participated in such behavior often tend to establish ethnically oriented and parallel activities and institutions, principally organizational, such as ball clubs, gangs, etc. In addition, other organizational activities include scholarship oriented organizations, those that are charity oriented, community service oriented, as well as political organizations. Within this sphere one also finds the common phenomenon of the "third generation return." That is, quite often members of the third generation return to identify themselves with their own ethnic group after having undergone the process of "assimilation."

Bi-Culturalism. Despite the merciless educational pressures to stamp out bi-culturalism and bi-lingualism among Mexican-Americans in schools and colleges, it still persists in many varied and developing forms. It exists, for example, all along the border areas among those entrepreneurs who operate equally well on both sides of the international border. It also exists among the untold number of Mexican-Americans who are interpreters, either on a professional or voluntary basis. There are many others who can deal with a bicultural universe, such as owners of Mexican restaurants, bookstores, gift shops, musicians and the like.

More recently a new phenomenon has begun to appear in increasing numbers. Specifically, more and more Mexican-American students are going to college. Many of them come from impoverished homes where reading resources were unnecessarily limited. Some of these students, attending college, gravitate toward Spanish or Latin-American majors. As a consequence, they begin to read Juan Rulfo, Martin Luis Guzmán, Gabriela Mistral, Pablo Neruda, Gabriel García Márquez, and they hear the classical music of Chavez, Villalobos, Revueltas; or they see the art of Tamayo, Cuevas, Esteban Villa, Salvador Roberto Torres, Rene Yañez. As a consequence, such students do not eschew their cultural past but rather reintegrate into it at the professional and intellectual level and they are well on their way toward bi-culturalism in another dimension.

The recent Mexican-American study programs in colleges and universities are certain to enhance and accelerate this process, especially if they adhere to the bi-lingual base. Therefore, in the near future it will become more and more possible for Mexican-American students to avoid the assimilative fallacies and pitfalls of the past and join in the truly exciting and challenging universe of bi-culturalism. In this way, not only will they participate in significant innovations in higher education, but they will also take a big step toward realizing one of the promises contained in the Treaty of Guadalupe Hidalgo.[22]

Many Mexican-Americans

> Yo, señor, no soy malo, aunque no me faltarían motivos para serlo. Los mismos cueros tenemos todos los mortales al nacer y sin embargo, cuando vamos creciendo, el destino se complace en variarnos como si fuésemos de cera y destinarnos por sendas diferentes al mismo fin: la muerte. Hay hombres a quienes se les ordena marchar por el camino de las flores, y hombres a quienes se les manda tirar por el camino de los cardos y de las chumberas. Aquellos gozan de un mirar sereno y al aroma de su felicidad sonríen con la cara inocente; estos otros sufren del sol violento de la llanura y arrugan el ceño como las alimañas por defenderse. Hay mucha diferencia entre adornarse las carnes con arrebol y colonia, y hacerlo con tatuajes que después nadie ha de borrar ya...[23]

Indianist philosophy, Confrontationist, Cultural nationalism based on Mesti-zaje with trends toward Humanistic Universalism, Behavioral Relativism, and Existentialism. Assimilation, Mexicanism, Realigned Pluralism, and Bi-Cultur-alism. Cholos, Pochos, Pachucos, Chicanos, Mexicanos, Hispanos, Spanish-sur-named people, Mexican-Americans. Many labels. Because this is such a complex population, it is difficult to give one label to them all. And probably the first to resist such an effort would be these people themselves, for such a monolithic treatment would violate the very pluralistic foundations upon which their histori-cal philosophies have been based.

There is another dimension to this complexity, one involving the family. Traditionally, in the United States, the Mexican family has been dealt with as if

---

[22]The promise refers to the right to an education reinforcing and maintaining Mexican-American culture.

[23]Cela, Camilo José. 1961. *La familia de Pascual Duarte*, Appleton Century-Crofts, Inc., page 11. *Author's note.*

it were monolithic, authoritarian, and uni-dimensional. This is a gross oversimplification based on sheer ignorance. The truth of the matter is that virtually every Mexican-American family takes several forms and includes many types of people, from assimilationist to Chicano, to cultural nationalist, and through all varieties including "un Español" thrown in every now and then for good measure. Mexican-American families have individuals who no longer speak Spanish, who speak only Spanish, or who speak a combination of both. In short, the same complexity that is found in the general Mexican-American population is also found in the family of virtually every Mexican-American.

If the day should ever come when all of these people are willingly subsumed under one label or banner, when they align themselves only under one philosophy, on that day, finally, they will have become totally and irrevocably Americanized. On that day, their historical alternatives and freedoms in personal choice of lifestyles, and their diversity, will have been permanently entombed in the histories of the past.

Berkeley, Califa[24]

Reprinted from *Voices: Readings from El Grito, 1967-1973*. Octavio Ignacio Romano-V., ed. 2nd ed. (Berkeley: Quinto Sol Publications, 1973): 164-78.

---

[24]In Chicano Spanish, Califa = California.

RICHARD RODRIGUEZ (1944-)

"Prologue: Middle-Class Pastoral" (1981)

I have taken Caliban's advice.[1] I have stolen their books. I will have some run of this isle.

Once upon a time, I was a "socially disadvantaged" child. An enchantedly happy child. Mine was a childhood of intense family closeness. And extreme public alienation.

Thirty years later I write this book as a middle-class American man. Assimilated.

Dark-skinned. To be seen at a Belgravia dinner party. Or in New York. Exotic in a tuxedo. My face is drawn to severe Indian features which would pass notice on the page of a *National Geographic*, but at a cocktail party in Bel Air somebody wonders: "Have you ever thought of doing any high-fashion modeling? Take this card." (In Beverly Hills will this monster make a man.)

A lady in a green dress asks, "Didn't we meet at the Thompsons' party last month in Malibu?"

I write: I am a writer.

A part-time writer. When I began this book, five years ago, a fellowship brought me a year of continuous silence in my San Francisco apartment. But the words wouldn't come. The money ran out. So I was forced to take temporary jobs. (I have friends who, with a phone call, can find me well-paying work.) In past months I have found myself in New York. In Los Angeles. Working. With money. Among people with money. And at leisure—a weekend guest in Connecticut; at a cocktail party in Bel Air.

Perhaps because I have always, accidentally, been a classmate to children of rich parents, I long ago came to assume my association with their world; came to assume that I could have money, if it was money I wanted. But money, big

---

[1] In William Shakespeare's *The Tempest* (1623), the protagonist Prospero has a servant named Caliban, who represents the newly colonized man from the Americas. As a rhetorical strategy, Rodriguez puts on Caliban's mask, symbolizing an educated slave who will help govern American society.

money, has never been the goal of my life. My story is not a version of Sammy Glick's.[2] I work to support my habit of writing. The great luxury of my life is the freedom to sit at this desk.

"Mr.? . . ."

Rodriguez. The name on the door. The name on my passport. The name I carry from my parents, in a cultural sense. This is how I pronounce it: *Rich-heard Road-ree-guess*. This is how I hear it most often.

The voice through a microphone says, "Ladies and gentlemen, it is with pleasure that I introduce Mr. Richard Rodriguez."

I am invited very often these days to speak about modern education in college auditoriums and in Holiday Inn ballrooms. I go, still feel a calling to act the teacher, though not licensed by the degree. One time my audience is a convention of university administrators; another time high school teachers of English; another time a women's alumnae group.

"Mr. Rodriguez has written extensively about contemporary education."

Several essays. I have argued particularly against two government programs—affirmative action and bilingual education.

"He is a provocative speaker."

I have become notorious among certain leaders of America's Ethnic Left. I am considered a dupe, an ass, the fool—Tom Brown, the brown Uncle Tom, interpreting the writing on the wall to a bunch of cigar-smoking pharaohs.

A dainty white lady at the women's club luncheon approaches the podium after my speech to say, after all, wasn't it a shame that I wasn't able to "use" my Spanish in school. What a shame. But how dare her lady-fingered pieties extend to my life!

There are those in White America who would anoint me to play out for them some drama of ancestral reconciliation. Perhaps because I am marked by indelible color they easily suppose that I am unchanged by social mobility, that I can claim unbroken ties with my past. The possibility! At a time when many middle-class children and parents grow distant, apart, no longer speak, romantic solutions appeal.

But I reject the role. (Caliban won't ferry a TV crew back to his island, there to recover his roots.)

Aztec ruins hold no special interest for me. I do not search Mexican graveyards for ties to unnamable ancestors. I assume I retain certain features of gesture and mood derived from buried lives. I also speak Spanish today. And read García

---

[2]symbol of brash, social-climbing, hustling son of immigrants.

Lorca and García Márquez at my leisure. But what consolation can that fact bring against the knowledge that my mother and father have never heard of García Lorca and García Márquez? What preoccupies me is immediate: the separation I endure with my parents is loss. This is what matters to me: the story of the scholarship boy who returns home one summer from college to discover bewildering silence, facing his parents. This is my story. An American story.

Consider me, if you choose, a comic victim of two cultures. This is my situation: writing these pages, surrounded in the room I am in by volumes of Montaigne and Shakespeare and Lawrence. They are mine now.

A Mexican woman passes in a black dress. She wears a white apron; she carries a tray of hors d'oeuvres. She must only be asking if there are any I want as she proffers the tray like a wheel of good fortune. I shake my head. No. Does she wonder how I am here? In Bel Air.

It is education that has altered my life. Carried me far. I write this auto-biography as the history of my schooling. To admit the change in my life I must speak of years as a student, of losses, of gains.

I consider my book a kind of a pastoral. I write in that tradition of that high, courtly genre. But I am no upper-class pastoral singer. Upper-class pastoral can admit envy for the intimate pleasures of rustic life as an arrogant way of reminding its listeners of their difference—their own public power and civic position. ("Let's be shepherds . . .Ah, if only we could.") Unlike the upper class, the middle class lives in a public world, lacking great individual power and standing. Middle-class pastoral is, therefore, a more difficult hymn. There is no grand compensation to the admission of envy of the poor. The middle class rather is tempted by the pastoral impulse to deny its difference from the lower class—even to attempt cheap imitations of lower-class life. ("But I still *am* a shepherd!")

I must resist being tempted by this decadent solution to mass public life. It seems to be dangerous, because in trying to imitate the lower class, the middle class blurs the distinction so crucial to social reform. One can no longer easily say what exactly distinguishes the alien poor.

I do not write as a modern day Wordsworth seeking to imitate the intimate speech of the poor. I sing Ariel's song[3] to celebrate the intimate speech my family once freely exchanged. In singing the praise of my lower-class past, I remind myself of my separation from the past, bring memory to silence. I turn

---

[3]Also from Shakespeare's *The Tempest*, Ariel represents an angelic, all-knowing spirit. Rodriguez also uses Ariel as a mask.

to consider the boy I once was in order, finally, to describe the man I am now. I remember what I was so grievously lost to define what was necessarily gained.

But the New York editor is on the phone and he can't understand: "Why do you spend so much time on abstract issues? Nobody's going to remember affirmative action in another twenty-five years. The strength of this manuscript is in the narrative. You should write your book in stories—not as a series of essays. Let's have more Grandma."

But no. Here is my most real life. My book is necessarily political, in the conventional sense, for public issues—editorials and ballot stubs, petitions and placards, faceless formulations of greater and lesser good by greater and lesser minds—have bisected my life and changed its course. And, in some broad sense, my writing is political because it concerns my movement away from the company of my family and into the city. This was my coming of age: I became a man by becoming a public man.

This autobiography, moreover, is a book about language. I write about poetry; the new Roman Catholic liturgy; learning to read; writing; political terminology. Language has been the great subject of my life. In college and graduate school, I was registered as an "English major." But well before then, from my first day in school, I was a student of language. Obsessed by the way it determined my public identity. The way it permits me here to describe myself, writing. . . .

Writing this manuscript. Essays impersonating an autobiography; six chapters of sad, fuguelike repetition.

Now it exists—a weight in my hand. Let the bookstore clerk puzzle over where it should be placed. (Rodriguez? Rodriguez?) Probably he will shelf it alongside specimens of that exotic new genre "ethnic literature." Mistaken, the gullible reader will—in sympathy or in anger—take it that I intend to model my life as the typical Hispanic-American life.

But I write of one life only. My own. If my story is true, I trust it will resonate with significance with other lives. Finally, my history deserves public notice as no more than this: a parable for the life of its reader. Here is the life of a middle-class man.

Reprinted from *Hunger of Memory: The Education of Richard Rodriguez* (Boston: David R. Godine, 1981): 3-7.

CHERRÍE MORAGA (1952-)

"La Güera" (1981)[1]

It requires something more than personal experience to gain a philosophy or point of view from any specific event. It is the quality of our response to the event and our capacity to enter into the lives of others that help us to make their lives and experiences our own. Emma Goldman[2]

I am the very well-educated daughter of a woman who, by the standards in this country, would be considered largely illiterate. My mother was born in Santa Paula, Southern California, at a time when much of the central Valley there was still farm land. Nearly thirty-five years later, in 1948, she was the only daughter of six to marry an anglo, my father.

I remember all of my mother's stories, probably much better than she realizes. She is a fine story-teller, recalling every event of her life with the vividness of the present, noting each detail right down to the cut and color of her dress. I remember stories of her being pulled out of school at the ages of five, seven, nine, and eleven to work in the fields, along with her brothers and sisters; stories of her father drinking away whatever small profit she was able to make for the family; of her going the long way home to avoid meeting him on the street, staggering toward the same destination. I remember stories of my mother lying about her age in order to get a job as a hat-check girl at Agua Caliente Racetrack in Tijuana. At fourteen, she was the main support of her family. I can still see her walking home alone at 3 a.m., only to turn all of her salary and tips over to her mother, who was pregnant again.

The stories continue through the war years and on: walnut-cracking factories, the Voit Rubber factory, and the computer boom. I remember my mother doing piecework for the electronics plant in our neighborhood. In the late eve-

---

[1]In Chicano Spanish, *güero* (feminine, *güera*) is used to describe a light-skinned, European-looking person.

[2]Alix Kates Shulman, "Was My Life Worth Living?" *Red Emma Speaks*. (New York: Random House, 1972), p. 288. *Author's note.*

ning, she would sit in front of the T.V. set, wrapping copper wires into the backs of circuit boards, talking about "keeping up with the younger girls." By that time, she was already in her mid-fifties.

Meanwhile, I was college-prep in school. After classes, I would go with my mother to fill out job applications for her, or write checks for her at the supermarket. We would have the scenario all worked out ahead of time. My mother would sign the check before we'd get to the store. Then, as we'd approach the checkstand, she would say—within earshot of the cashier—"oh honey, you go 'head and make out the check," as if she couldn't be bothered with such an insignificant detail. No one asked any questions.

I was educated, and wore it with a keen sense of pride and satisfaction, my head propped up with the knowledge, from my mother, that my life would be easier than hers. I was educated; but more than this, I was "la güera": fair-skinned. Born with the features of my Chicana mother, but the skin of my Anglo father, I had it made.

No one ever quite told me this (that light was right), but I knew that being light was something valued in my family (who were all Chicano, with the exception of my father). In fact, everything about my upbringing (at least what occurred on a conscious level) attempted to bleach me of what color I did have. Although my mother was fluent in it, I was never taught much Spanish at home. I picked up what I did learn from school and from overheard snatches of conversation among my relatives and mother. She often called other lower-income Mexicans "braceros," or "wet-backs," referring to herself and her family as "a different class of people." And yet, the real story was that my family, too, had been poor (some still are) and farmworkers. My mother can remember this in her blood as if it were yesterday. But this is something she would like to forget (and rightfully), for to her, on a basic economic level, being Chicana meant being "less." It was through my mother's desire to protect her children from poverty and illiteracy that we became "anglocized"; the more effectively we could pass in the white world, the better guaranteed our future.

From all of this, I experience, daily, a huge disparity between what I was born into and what I was to grow up to become. Because, (as Goldman suggests) these stories my mother told me crept under my "güera" skin. I had no choice but to enter into the life of my mother. *I had no choice.* I took her life into my heart, but managed to keep a lid on it as long as I feigned being the happy, upwardly mobile heterosexual.

When I finally lifted the lid to my lesbianism, a profound connection with my mother reawakened in me. It wasn't until I acknowledged and confronted my own lesbianism in the flesh, that my heartfelt identification with and empathy for my mother's oppression—due to being poor, uneducated, and Chicana—was realized. My lesbianism is the avenue through which I have learned the most about silence and oppression, and it continues to be the most tactile reminder to me that we are not free human beings.

You see, one follows the other. I had known for years that I was a lesbian, had left it in my bones, had ached with the knowledge, gone crazed with the knowledge, wallowed in the silence of it. Silence *is* like starvation. Don't be fooled. It's nothing short of that, and felt most sharply when one has had a full belly most of her life. When we are not physically starving, we have the luxury to realize psychic and emotional starvation. It is from this starvation than other starvations can be recognized—if one is willing to take the risk of making the connection—if one is willing to be responsible to the result of the connection. For me, the connection is an inevitable one.

What I am saying is that the joys of looking like a white girl ain't so great since I realized I could be beaten on the street for being a dyke. If my sister's being beaten because she's black, it's pretty much the same principle. We're both getting beaten any way you look at it. The connection is blatant; and in the case of my own family, the difference in the privileges attached to looking white instead of brown is merely a generation apart.

In this country, lesbianism is a poverty—as is being brown, as is being a woman, as is being just plain poor. The danger lies in ranking the oppressions. *The danger lies in failing to acknowledge the specificity of the oppression.* The danger lies in attempting to deal with oppression purely from a theoretical base. Without an emotional, heartfelt grappling with the source of our own oppression, without naming the enemy within ourselves and outside of us, no authentic, non-hierarchical connection among oppressed groups can take place.

When the going gets rough, will we abandon our so-called comrades in a flurry of racist/heterosexist/what-have-you panic? To whose camp, then, should the lesbian of color retreat? Her very presence violates the ranking and abstraction of oppression. Do we merely live hand to mouth? Do we merely struggle with the "ism" that's sitting on top of our own heads?

The answer is: yes, I think first we do; and we must do so thoroughly and deeply. But to fail to move out from there will only isolate us in our own oppression—will only insulate, rather than radicalize us.

To illustrate: a gay male friend of mine once confided to me that he continued to feel that, on some level, I didn't trust him because he was male; that he felt, really, if it ever came down to a "battle of sexes," I might kill him. I admitted that I might very well. He wanted to understand the source of my distrust. I responded, "You're not a woman. Be a woman for a day. Imagine being a woman." He confessed that the thought terrified him because, to him, being a woman meant being raped by men. He *had* felt raped by men; he had wanted to forget what that meant. What grew from that discussion was the realization that in order for him to create an authentic alliance with me, he must deal with the primary source of his own sense of oppression. He must first, emotionally come to terms with what it feels like to be a victim. If he—or anyone—were to truly do this, it would be impossible to discount the oppression of others except, by again forgetting how we have been hurt.

And yet, oppressed groups are forgetting all the time. There are instances of this in the rising Black middle class, and certainly an obvious trend of such "unconsciousness" among white gay men. Because to remember may mean giving up whatever privileges we have managed to squeeze out of this society by virtue of our gender, race, class, or sexuality.

Within the women's movement, the connections among women of different backgrounds and sexual orientations have been fragile, at best. I think this phenomenon is indicative of our failure to seriously address ourselves to some very frightening questions: How have I internalized my own oppression? how have I oppressed? Instead, we have let rhetoric do the job of poetry. Even the word "oppression" has lost its power. We need a new language, better words that can more closely describe women's fear of and resistance to one another; words that will not always come out sounding like dogma.

What prompted me in the first place to work on an anthology by radical women of color was a deep sense that I had a valuable insight to contribute, by virtue of my birthright and background. And yet, I don't really understand firsthand what it feels like being shitted on for being brown. I understand much more about the joys of it—being Chicana and having family are synonymous for me. What I know about loving, singing, crying, telling stories, speaking with my heart and hands, even having a sense of my own soul comes from the love of my mother, aunts, cousins. . . .

But at the age of twenty-seven, it is frightening to acknowledge that I have internalized a racism and classism, where the object of oppression is not only someone outside of my skin, but the someone inside my skin. In fact, to a large degree, the real battle with such oppression, for all of us, begins under the skin. I have had to confront the fact that much of what I value about being Chicana, about my family, has been subverted by anglo culture and my own cooperation with it. This realization did not occur to me overnight. For example, it wasn't until long after my graduation from the private college I'd attended in Los Angeles, that I realized the major reason for my total alienation from and fear of my classmates was rooted in class and culture. CLICK.

Three years after graduation, in an apple-orchard in Sonoma, a friend of mine (who comes from an Italian Irish working-class family) says to me, "Cherríe, no wonder you felt like such a nut in school. Most of the people there were white and rich." It was true. All along I had felt the difference, but not until I had put the words "class" and "color" to the experience, did my feelings make any sense. For years, I had berated myself for not being as "free" as my classmates. I completely bought that they simply had more guts than I did—to rebel against their parents and run around the country hitch-hiking, reading books and studying "art." They had enough privilege to be atheists, for chrissake. There was no one around filling in the disparity for me between their parents, who were Hollywood filmmakers, and my parents who wouldn't know the name of a filmmaker if their lives depended on it (and precisely because their lives didn't depend on it, they couldn't be bothered). But I knew nothing about "privilege" then. White was right. Period. I could pass. If I got educated enough, there would never be any telling.

Three years after that, another CLICK. In a letter to Barbara Smith, I wrote:

I went to a concert where Ntosake Shange[3] was reading. There, everything exploded for me. She was speaking a language that I knew—in the deepest parts of me—existed, and that I had ignored in my own feminist studies and even in my own writing. What Ntosake caught in me is the realization that in my development as a poet, I have, in many ways, denied the voice of my brown mother—the brown in me. I have acclimated to the sound of a white language which, as my father represents it, does not speak to the emotions in my poems—emotions which stem from the love of my mother.

That reading was agitating. Made me uncomfortable. Threw me into a week-long terror of how deeply I was affected. I felt that I had to start all over again. That I turned only to the perceptions of white middle-class women to speak for me and all women. I am shocked by my own ignorance.

Sitting in that auditorium chair was the first time I had realized to the core of me that for years I had disowned the language I knew best—ignored the words and rhythms that were the closest to me. The sounds of my mother and

---

[3]Ntosake—also known, preferably, as Ntozake—Shange, an Afro-American writer.

aunts gossiping—half in English, half in Spanish—while drinking cerveza in the kitchen. And the hands—I had cut off the hands in my poems. But not in conversation; still the hands could not be kept down. Still they insisted on moving.

The reading had forced me to remember that I knew things from my roots. But to remember puts me up against what I don't know. Shange's reading agitated me because she spoke with power about a world that is both alien and common to me: "the capacity to enter into the lives of others." But you just can't take your goods and run. I knew that then, sitting in the Oakland auditorium (as I know in my poetry), that the only thing worth writing about is what seems to be unknown and, therefore, fearful.

The "unknown" is often depicted in racist literature as the "darkness" within a person. Similarly, sexist writers will refer to fears in the form of the vagina, calling it "the orifice of death." In contrast, it is a pleasure to read works such as Maxine Hong Kingston's *Woman Warrior*,[4] where fear and alienation are described as "the white ghosts." And yet, the bulk of literature in this country reinforces the myth that what is dark and female is evil. Consequently, each of us—whether dark, female, or both—has in some way *internalized* this oppressive imagery. What the oppressor often succeeds in doing is simply *externalizing* his fears, projecting them into the bodies of women, Asians, gays, disabled folks, whoever seems most "other."

> Call me
> roach and presumptious
> nightmare on your white pillow
> your itch to destroy
> the indestructible
> part of yourself
>
>   Audre Lorde[5]

But it is not really difference the oppressor fears so much as similarity. He fears he will discover in himself the same aches, the same longings as those of the people he has shitted on. He fears immobilization threatened by his own incipient guilt. He fears he will have to change his life once he has seen himself

---

[4]Maxine Hong Kingston is a contemporary Asian Pacific writer.

[5]From "The Brown Menace or Poem to the Survival of Roaches," *The New York Head Shop and Museum* (Detroit: Broadside, 1974), p. 48. *Author's note.*

in the bodies of the people he has called different. He fears the hatred, anger, and vengeance of those he has hurt.

This is the oppressor's nightmare, but is not exclusive to him. We women have a similar nightmare, for each of us in some way has been both oppressed and the oppressor. We are afraid to look at how we have failed each other. We are afraid to see how we have taken the values of our oppressor into our hearts and turned them against ourselves and one another. We are afraid to admit how deeply "the man's" words have been ingrained in us.

To assess the damage is a dangerous act. I think of how, even as a feminist lesbian, I have so wanted to ignore my own homophobia, my own hatred of myself for being queer. I have not wanted to admit that my deepest personal sense of myself has not quite "caught up" with my "woman-identified" politics. I have been afraid to criticize lesbian writers who choose to "skip over" these issues in the name of feminism. In 1979, we talk of "old gay" and "butch and femme" roles as if they were ancient history. We toss them aside as merely patriarchal notions. And yet, the truth of the matter is that I have sometimes taken society's fear and hatred of lesbians to bed with me. I have sometimes hated my lover for loving me. I have sometimes felt "not woman enough" for her. I have sometimes felt "not man enough." For a lesbian trying to survive in a heterosexist society, there is no easy way around these emotions. Similarly, in a white-dominated world, there is little getting around racism and our own internalization of it. It's always there, embodied in someone we least expect to rub up against.

When we do rub up against this person, *there* then is the challenge. *There* then is the opportunity to look at the nightmare within us. But we usually shrink from such a challenge.

Time and time again, I have observed that the usual response among white women's groups when the "racism issue" comes up is to deny the difference. I have heard comments like, "Well, we're open to *all* women; why don't they (women of color) come? You can only do so much. . . ." But there is seldom any analysis of how the very nature and structure of the group itself may be founded on racist or classist assumptions. More importantly, so often the women seem to feel no loss, no lack, no absence when women of color are not involved; therefore, there is little desire to change the situation. This has hurt me deeply. I have come to believe that the only reason women of a privileged class will dare to look at *how* it is that *they* oppress, is when they've come to know the meaning of their own oppression. And understand that the oppression of others hurts them personally.

The other side of the story is that women of color and working-class women often shrink from challenging white middle-class women. It is much easier to rank oppressions and set up a hierarchy, rather than take responsibility for changing our own lives. We have failed to demand that white women, particularly those who claim to be speaking for all women, be accountable for their racism.

The dialogue has simply not gone deep enough.

I have many times questioned my right to even work on an anthology which is to be written "exclusively by Third World women." I have had to look critically at my claim to color, at a time when, among white feminist ranks, it is a "politically correct" (and sometimes peripherally advantageous) assertion to make. I must acknowledge the fact that, physically, I have had a *choice* about making that claim, in contrast to women who have not had such a choice, and have been abused for their color. I must reckon with the fact that for most of my life, by virtue of the very fact that I am white-looking, I identified with and aspired toward white values, and that I rode the wave of that Southern California privilege as far as conscience would let me.

Well, now I feel both bleached and beached. I feel angry about this—the years when I refused to recognize privilege, both when it worked against me, and when I worked it, ignorantly at the expense of others. These are not settled issues. That is why this work feels so risky to me. It continues to be discovery. It has brought me into contact with women who invariably know a hell of a lot more than I do about racism, as experienced in the flesh, as revealed in the flesh of their writing.

I think: what is my responsibility to my roots—both white and brown, Spanish-speaking and English? I am a woman with a foot in both worlds; and I refuse the split. I feel the necessity for dialogue. Sometimes I feel it urgently.

But one voice is not enough, nor two, although this is where dialogue begins. It is essential that radical feminists confront their fear of and resistance to each other, because without this, there *will* be no bread on the table. Simply, we will not survive. If we could make this connection in our heart of hearts, that if we are serious about a revolution—better—if we seriously believe there should be joy in our lives (real joy, not just "good times"), then we need one another. We women need each other. Because my/your solitary, self-asserting "go-for-the-throat-of fear" power is not enough. The real power, as you and I well know, is collective. I can't afford to be afraid of you, nor you of me. If it takes head-on collisions, let's do it: this polite timidity is killing us.

As Lorde suggests in the passage I cited earlier, it is in looking to the nightmare that the dream is found. There, the survivor emerges to insist on a future, a vision, yes, born out of what is dark and female. The feminist movement of such survivors, a movement with a future.

September 1979.

Reprinted from *This Bridge Called My Back: Writings by Radical Women of Color*. Cherríe Moraga and Gloria Anzaldúa, eds. (Watertown, Mass.: Persephone Press, 1981): 27-34.

GLORIA ANZALDÚA (1942-)

"La conciencia de la mestiza: Towards a New Consciousness" (1987)

Por la mujer de mi raza
hablará el espíritu.[1]

José Vasconcelos, Mexican philosopher, envisaged una *raza mestiza, una mezcla de razas afines, una raza de color—la primera raza síntesis del globo.* He called it a cosmic race, *la raza cósmica,* a fifth race embracing the four major races of the world.[2] Opposite to the theory of the pure Aryan,[3] and to the policy of racial purity that white America practices, his theory is one of inclusivity. At the confluence of two or more genetic streams, with chromosomes constantly "crossing over," this mixture of races, rather than resulting in an inferior being, provides hybrid races, a mutable, more malleable species with a rich gene pool. From this racial, ideological, cultural and biological crosspollinization an "alien" consciousness is presently in the making—a new *mestiza* consciousness, *una conciencia de mujer.* It is a consciousness of the Borderlands.

Una lucha de fronteras / **A Struggle of Borders**

Because I, a *mestiza,*
continually walk out of one culture
and into another,

---

[1]This is my own "take off" on José Vasconcelos's idea. José Vasconcelos, *La Raza Cósmica: Misión de la Raza Ibero-Americana* (México: Aguilar S.A. de Ediciones, 1961). *Author's note.* Vasconcelos's text was originally published in 1925.

[2]Vasconcelos. *Author's note.*

[3]Under this racial theory, whites are seen as superior to people of color: Blacks, Asians, Native Americans, and Mestizos or those who are racially mixed.

because I am in all cultures at the same time,
alma entre dos mundos, tres, cuatro,
me zumba la cabeza con lo contradictorio.
Estoy norteada por todas las voces que me hablan
simultáneamente.

The ambivalence from the clash of voices results in mental and emotional states of perplexity. Internal strife results in insecurity and indecisiveness. The mestiza's dual or multiple personality is plagued by psychic restlessness.

In a constant state of mental nepantilism, an Aztec word meaning torn between ways, *la mestiza* is a product of the transfer of the cultural and spiritual values of one group to another. Being tricultural, monolingual, bilingual, or multilingual, speaking a patois, and in a state of perpetual transition, the *mestiza* faces the dilemma of the mixed breed: which collectivity does the daughter of a darkskinned mother listen to?

El choque de un alma atrapada entre el mundo del espíritu y el mundo de la técnica a veces la deja entullada. Cradled in one culture, sandwiched between two cultures, straddling all three cultures and their value systems, *la mestiza* undergoes a struggle of flesh, a struggle of borders, an inner war. Like all people, we perceive the version of reality that our culture communicates. Like others having or living in more than one culture, we get multiple, often opposing messages. The coming together of two self-consistent but habitually incompatible frames of reference[4] causes *un choque*, a cultural collision.

Within us and within *la cultura chicana*, commonly held beliefs of the white culture attack commonly held beliefs of the Mexican culture, and both attack commonly held beliefs of the indigenous culture. Subconsciously, we see an attack on ourselves and our beliefs as a threat and we attempt to block with a counterstance.

But it is not enough to stand on the opposite river bank, shouting questions, challenging patriarchal, white conventions. A counterstance locks one into a duel of oppressor and oppressed; locked in mortal combat, like the cop and the criminal, both are reduced to a common denominator of violence. The counterstance refutes the dominant culture's views and beliefs, and, for this, it is proudly defiant. All reaction is limited by, and dependent on, what it is reacting against.

---

[4]Arthur Koestler termed this "bisociation." Albert Rothenberg, *The Creative Process in Art, Science, and Other Fields* (Chicago, IL: University of Chicago Press, 1979), 12. *Author's note.*

Because the counterstance stems from a problem with authority—outer as well as inner—it's a step towards liberation from cultural domination. But it is not a way of life. At some point, on our way to a new consciousness, we will have to leave the opposite bank, the split between the two mortal combatants somehow healed so that we are on both shores at once and, at once, see through serpent and eagle eyes. Or perhaps we will decide to disengage from the dominant culture, write it off altogether as a lost cause, and cross the border into a wholly new and separate territory. Or we might go another route. The possibilities are numerous once we decide to act and not react.

A Tolerance for Ambiguity

These numerous possibilities leave *la mestiza* floundering in uncharted seas. In perceiving conflicting information and points of view, she is subjected to a swamping of her psychological borders. She has discovered that she can't hold concepts or ideas in rigid boundaries. The borders and walls that are supposed to keep the undesirable ideas out are entrenched habits and patterns of behavior; these habits and patterns are the enemy within. Rigidity means death. Only by remaining flexible is she able to stretch the psyche horizontally and vertically. *La mestiza* constantly has to shift out of habitual formations; from convergent thinking, analytical reasoning that tends to use rationality to move toward a single goal (a Western mode), to divergent thinking,[5] characterized by movement away from set patterns and goals and toward a more whole perspective, one that includes rather than excludes.

The new *mestiza* copes by developing a tolerance for contradictions, a tolerance for ambiguity. She learns to be an Indian in Mexican culture, to be a Mexican from an Anglo point of view. She learns to juggle cultures. She has a plural personality, she operates in a pluralistic mode—nothing is thrust out, the good the bad and the ugly, nothing rejected, nothing abandoned. Not only does she sustain contradictions, she turns the ambivalence into something else.

She can be jarred out of ambivalence by an intense, and often painful, emotional event which inverts or resolves the ambivalence. I'm not sure exactly how. The work takes place underground—subconsciously. It is work that the soul performs. That focal point of fulcrum, that juncture where the mestiza stands, is

---

[5]In part, I derive my definitions for "convergent" and "divergent" thinking from Rothenberg, 12-13. *Author's note.*

where phenomena tend to collide. It is where the possibility of uniting all that is separate occurs. This assembly is not one where severed or separated pieces merely come together. Nor is it a balancing of opposing powers. In attempting to work out a synthesis, the self has added a third element which is greater than the sum of its severed parts. That third element is a new consciousness—a mestiza consciousness—and though it is a source of intense pain, its energy comes from continual creative motion that keeps breaking down the unitary aspect of each new paradigm.

En unas pocas centurias, the future will belong to the mestiza. Because the future depends on the breaking down of paradigms, it depends on the straddling of two or more cultures. By creating a new mythos—that is, a change in the way we perceive reality, the way we see ourselves, and the ways we behave—*la mestiza* creates a new consciousness.

The work of *mestiza* consciousness is to break down the subject-object duality that keeps her a prisoner and to show in the flesh and through the images in her work how duality is transcended. The answer to the problem between the white race and the colored, between males and females, lies in healing the split that originates in the very foundation of our lives, our culture, our languages, our thoughts. A massive uprooting of dualistic thinking in the individual and collective consciousness is the beginning of a long struggle, but one that could, in our best hopes, bring us to the end of rape, of violence, of war.

La encrucijada / The Crossroads

> A chicken is being sacrificed
> at a crossroads, a simple mount of earth
> a mud shrine for *Eshu*,
> *Yoruba* god of indeterminacy,
> who blesses her choice of path.
> She begins her journey.

Su cuerpo es una bocacalle. La mestiza has gone from being the sacrificial goat to becoming the officiating priestess at the crossroads.

As a *mestiza* I have no country, my homeland cast me out; yet all countries are mine because I am every woman's sister or potential lover. (As a lesbian I have no race, my own people disclaim me; but I am all races because there is the queer of me in all races.) I am cultureless because, as a feminist, I challenge the collective cultural/religious male-derived beliefs of Indo-Hispanics and Anglos;

yet I am cultured because I am participating in the creation of yet another culture, a new story to explain the world and our participation in it, a new value system with images and symbols that connect us to each other and to the planet. *Soy un amasamiento*, I am an act of kneading, of uniting and joining that not only has produced both a creature of darkness and a creature of light, but also a creature that questions the definitions of light and dark and gives them new meanings.

We are the people who leap in the dark, we are the people on the knees of the gods. In our very flesh, (r)evolution works out the clash of cultures. It makes us crazy constantly, but if the center holds, we've made some kind of evolutionary step forward. *Nuestra alma el trabajo*, the opus, the great alchemical work; spiritual *mestizaje*, a "morphogenesis,"[6] an inevitable unfolding. We have become the quickening serpent movement.

Indigenous like corn, like corn, the *mestiza* is a product of crossbreeding, designed for preservation under a variety of conditions. Like an ear of corn—a female seed-bearing organ—the *mestiza* is tenacious, tightly wrapped in the husks of her culture. Like kernels she clings to the cob; with stalks and strong brace roots, she holds tight to the earth—she will survive the crossroads.

Lavando y remojando el maíz en agua de cal, despojando el pellejo. Moliendo, mixteando, amasando, haciendo tortillas de masa[7]. She steeps the corn in lime, it swells, softens. With stone roller on *metate*, she grinds the corn, then grinds again. She kneads and molds the dough, pats the round balls into *tortillas*.

> We are the porous rock in the stone *metate*
> squatting on the ground.
> We are the rolling pin, *el maíz y el agua*,

[6]To borrow chemist Ilya Prigogine's theory of "dissipative structures." Prigogine discovered that substances interact not in predictable ways as it was taught in science, but in different and fluctuating ways to produce new and more complex structures, a kind of birth called "morphogenesis," which created unpredictable innovations. Harold Gilliam, "Searching for a New World View," *This World* (January, 1981), 23. *Author's note.*

[7]*Tortillas de masa harina*: corn tortillas are of two types, the smooth uniform ones made in a tortilla press and usually bought at a tortilla factory or supermarket, and *gorditas*, made by mixing *masa* with lard or shortening or butter (my mother sometimes puts in bits of bacon or *chicharrones*). *Author's note.*

la masa harina. Somos el amasijo
Somos lo molido en el metate.
We are the *comal* sizzling hot,
the hot *tortilla*, the hungry mouth.
We are the coarse rock.
We are the grinding motion,
the mixed potion, *somos el molcajete.*
We are the pestle, the *comino, ajo, pimienta,*
We are the *chile colorado,*
the green shoot that cracks the rock.
We will abide.

El camino de la mestiza / The Mestiza Way

Caught between the sudden contradiction, the breath sucked in and the endless space, the brown woman stands still, looks at the sky. She decides to go down digging her way along the roots of trees. Sifting through the bones, she shakes them to see if there is any marrow in them. Then, touching the dirt to her forehead, to her tongue, she takes a few bones, leaves the rest in their burial place.

She goes through her backpack, keeps her journal and address book, throws away the muni-bart metromaps. The coins are heavy and they go next, then the greenbacks flutter through the air. She keeps the knife, can opener and eyebrow pencil. She puts bones, pieces of bark, *hierbas*, eagle father, snakeskin, tape recorder, the rattle and drum in her pack and she sets out to become the complete *tolteca.*[8]

Her first step is to take the inventory. *Despojando, desgranando, quitando paja.* Just what did she inherit from her ancestors? This weight on her back—which is the baggage from the Indian mother, which the baggage from the Spanish father, which the baggage from the Anglo?

Pero es difícil differentiating between *lo heredado, lo adquirido, lo impuesto.* She puts history through a sieve, winnows out the lies, looks at the forces that

---

[8]Gina Valdés, *Puentes y fronteras: coplas chicanas* (Los Angeles, CA: Castle Lithograph, 1982), 2. *Author's note.*

we as a race, as women, have been a part of. *Luego bota lo que no vale, los desmientos, los desencuentos, el embrutecimiento. Aguarda el juicio, hondo y enraizado, de la gente antigua.* This step is a conscious rupture with all oppressive traditions of all cultures and religions. She communicates that rupture, documents the struggle. She reinterprets history and, using new symbols, she shapes new myths. She adopts new perspectives toward the darkskinned, women and queers. She strengthens her tolerance (and intolerance) for ambiguity. She is willing to share, to make herself vulnerable to foreign ways of seeing and thinking. She surrenders all notions of safety, of the familiar. Deconstruct, construct. She becomes a *nahual*, able to transform herself into a tree, a coyote, into another person. She learns to transform the small "I" into the total Self. *Se hace moldeadora de su alma. Según la concepción que tiene de sí misma, así será.*

Que no se nos olviden los hombres

> "*Tú no sirves pa' nada—*
> you're good for nothing.
> *Eres pura vieja.*"

"You're nothing but a woman" means you are defective. Its opposite is to be *un macho*. The modern meaning of the word "machismo," as well as the concept, is actually an Anglo invention. For men like my father, being "macho" meant being strong enough to protect and support my mother and us, yet being able to show love. Today's macho has doubts about his ability to feed and protect his family. His "machismo" is an adaptation to oppression and poverty and low self-esteem. It is the result of hierarchical male dominance. The Anglo, feeling inadequate and inferior and powerless, displaces or transfers these feelings to the Chicano by shaming him. In the Gringo world, the Chicano suffers from excessive humility and self-effacement, shame of self and self-deprecation. Around Latinos he suffers from a sense of language inadequacy and its accompanying discomfort; with Native Americans he suffers from a racial amnesia which ignores our common blood, and from guilt because the Spanish part of him took their land and oppressed them. He has an excessive compensatory hubris when around Mexicans from the other side. It overlays a deep sense of racial shame.

The loss of a sense of dignity and respect in the macho breeds a false machismo which leads him to put down women and even to brutalize them. Coexisting with his sexist behavior is a love for the mother which takes precedence over that of all others. Devoted son, macho pig. To wash down the shame of his acts, of his very being, and to handle the brute in the mirror, he takes to the bottle, the snort, the needle, and the fist.

Though we "understand" the root causes of male hatred and fear, and the subsequent wounding of women, we do not excuse, we do not condone, and we will no longer put up with it. From the men of our race, we demand the admission/acknowledgement/disclosure/testimony that they wound us, violate us, are afraid of us and of our power. We need to say they will begin to eliminate their hurtful put-down ways. But more than the words, we demand acts. We say to them: We will develop equal power with you and those who have shamed us.

It is imperative that mestizas support each other in changing the sexist elements in the Mexican-Indian culture. As long as woman is put down, the Indian and the Black in all of us is put down. The struggle of the mestiza is above all a feminist one. As long as *los hombres* think they have to *chingar mujeres* and each other to be men, as long as men are taught that they are superior and therefore culturally favored over *la mujer*, as long as to be a *vieja* is a thing of derision, there can be no real healing of our psyches. We're halfway there—we have such love of the Mother, the good mother. The first step is to unlearn the *puta/virgen* dichotomy and to see *Coatlapopeuh-Coatlicue* in the Mother, *Guadalupe.*[9]

Tenderness, a sign of vulnerability, is so feared that it is showered on women with verbal abuse and blows. Men, even more than women, are fettered to gender roles. Women at least have had the guts to break out of bondage. Only gay men have had the courage to expose themselves to the woman inside them and to challenge the current masculinity. I've encountered a few scattered and isolated gentle straight men, the beginnings of a new breed, but they are confused, and entangled with sexist behaviors that they have not been able to eradicate. We need a new masculinity and the new man needs a movement.

Lumping the males who deviate from the general norm with man, the oppressor, is a gross injustice. *Asombra pensar que nos hemos quedado en ese pozo oscuro donde el mundo encierra a las lesbianas. Asombra pensar que hemos, como feministas y lesbianas, cerrado nuestros corazones a los hombres, a nuestros hermanos los jotos, desheredados y marginales como nosotros.* Being the supreme crossers of cultures, homosexuals have strong bonds with the queer white, Black, Asian, Native American, Latino, and with the queer in Italy, Aus-

---

[9]The reference is to the Virgen de Guadalupe, whose traditional, religious cult is central to Mexican Catholicism. She is frequently viewed primarily as good and compassionate, as uncombative.

tralia and the rest of the planet. We come from all colors, all classes, all races, all time periods. Our role is to link people with each other—the Blacks with Jews with Indians with Asians with whites with extraterrestrials. It is to transfer ideas and information from one culture to another. Colored homosexuals have more knowledge of other cultures; have always been at the forefront (although sometimes in the closet) of all liberation struggles in this country; have suffered more injustices and have survived them despite all odds. Chicanos need to acknowledge the political and artistic contributions of their queer. People, listen to what your *jotería* is saying.

The mestizo and the queer exist at this time and point on the evolutionary continuum for a purpose. We are a blending that proves that all blood is intricately woven together, and that we are spawned out of similar souls.

Somos una gente

> *Hay tantísimas fronteras*
> *que dividen a la gente,*
> *pero por cada frontera*
> *existe también un puente.*
> —Gina Valdés[10]

Divided Loyalties. Many women and men of color do not want to have any dealings with white people. It takes too much time and energy to explain to the downwardly mobile, white middle-class women that it's okay for us to want to own "possessions," never having had any nice furniture on our dirt floors or "luxuries" like washing machines. Many feel that whites should help their own people rid themselves of race hatred and fear first. I, for one, choose to use some of my energy to serve as mediator. I think we need to allow whites to be our allies. Through our literature, art, *corridos*, and folktales we must share our history with them so when they set up committees to help Big Mountain Navajos or the Chicano farmworkers or *los Nicaragüenses*, they won't turn people away because of their racial fears and ignorance. They will come to see that they are not helping us but following our lead.

---

[10]Gina Valdés, *Puentes y fronteras: coplas chicanas* (Los Angeles, CA: Castle Lithograph, 1982), 2. *Author's note.*

Individually, but also as a racial entity, we need to voice our needs. We need to say to white society: We need you to accept the fact that Chicanos are different, to acknowledge your rejection and negation of us. We need you to own the fact that you looked upon us as less than human, that you stole our lands, our personhood, our self-respect. We need you to make public restitution: to say that, to compensate for your own sense of defectiveness, you strive for power over us, you erase our history and our experience because it makes you feel guilty—you'd rather forget your brutish acts. To say you've split yourself from minority groups, that you disown us, that your dual consciousness splits off parts of yourself, transferring the "negative" parts onto us. (Where there is persecution of minorities, there is shadow projection. Where there is violence and war, there is repression of shadow.) To say that you are afraid of us, that to put distance between us, you wear the mask of contempt. Admit that Mexico is your double, that she exists in the shadow of this country, that we are irrevocably tied to her. Gringo, accept the doppelganger in your psyche. By taking back your collective shadow the intracultural split will heal. And finally, tell us what you need from us.

By Your True Faces We Will Know You

I am visible—see this Indian face—yet I am invisible. I both blind them with my beak nose and am their blind spot. But I exist, we exist. They'd like to think I have melted in the pot. But I haven't, we haven't.

The dominant white culture is killing us slowly with its ignorance. By taking away our self-determination, it has made us weak and empty. As a people we have resisted and we have taken expedient positions, but we have never been allowed to develop unencumbered—we have never been allowed to be fully ourselves. The whites in power want us people of color to barricade ourselves behind our separate tribal walls so they can pick us off one at a time with their hidden weapons; so they can whitewash and distort history. Ignorance splits people, creates prejudices. A misinformed people is a subjugated people.

Before the Chicano and the undocumented worker and the Mexican from the other side can come together, before the Chicano can have unity with Native Americans and other groups, we need to know the history of their struggle and they need to know ours. Our mothers, our sisters and brothers, the guys who hung out on street corners, the children in the playgrounds, each of us must know our Indian lineage, our *afro-mestizaje*, our history of resistance.

To the immigrant *mexicano* and the recent arrivals we must teach our history. The 80 million *mexicanos* and the Latinos from Central and South America must know of our struggles. Each one of us must know basic facts about Nicaragua, Chile and the rest of Latin America. The Latinoist movement (Chicanos, Puerto Ricans, Cubans and other Spanish-speaking people working together to combat racial discrimination in the market place) is good but it is not enough. Other than a common culture we will have nothing to hold us together. We need to meet on a broader communal ground.

The struggle is inner: Chicano, *indio*, American Indian, *mojado, mexicano*, immigrant Latino, Anglo in power, working class Anglo, Black, Asian—our psyches resemble the bordertowns and are populated by the same people. The struggle has always been inner, and is played out in the outer terrains. Awareness of our situation must come before inner changes, which in turn come before changes in society. Nothing happens in the "real" world unless it first happens in the images in our heads.

El día de la Chicana

> I will not be shamed again
> Nor will I shame myself.

I am possessed by a vision: that we Chicanas and Chicanos have taken back or uncovered our true faces, our dignity and self-respect. It's a validation vision.

Seeing the Chicana anew in light of her history. I seek an exoneration, a seeing of ourselves in our true guises and not as the false racial personality that has been given to us and that we have given to ourselves. I seek our woman's face, our true features, the positive and the negative seen clearly, free of the trained biases of male dominance. I seek new images of identity, new beliefs about ourselves, our humanity and worth no longer in question.

Estamos viviendo en la noche de la Raza, un tiempo cuando se hace a lo quieto, en el oscuro. El día cuando aceptemos tal y como somos y para donde vamos y por qué—ese día será el día de la Raza. Yo tengo el compromiso de expresar mi visión, mi sensibilidad, mi percepción de la revalidación de la gente mexicana, su mérito, estimación, honra, aprecio, y validez.

On December 2nd when my sun goes into my first house, I celebrate *el día de la Chicana y el Chicano*. On that day I clean my altars, light my *Coatlapeuh* candle, burn stage and copal, take *el baño para espantar basura*, sweep my house. On that day I bare my soul, make myself vulnerable to friends and family by expressing my feelings. On that day I affirm who we are.

On that day I look inside our conflicts and our basic introverted racial temperament. I identify our needs, voice them. I acknowledge that the self and the race have been wounded. I recognize the need to take care of our person-hood, of our racial self. On that day I gather the splintered and disowned parts of *la gente mexicana* and hold them in my arms. *Todas las partes de nosotros valen.*

On that day I say, "Yes, all you people wound us when you reject us. Rejection strips us of self-worth, our vulnerability exposes us to shame. It is our innate identity you find wanting. We are ashamed that we need your good opin-ion, that we need your acceptance. We can no longer camouflage our needs, can no longer let defenses and fences sprout around us. We can no longer withdraw. To rage and look upon you with contempt is to rage and be contemptuous of ourselves. We can no longer blame you, nor disown the white parts, the male parts, the pathological parts, the queer parts, the vulnerable parts. Here we are weaponless with open arms, with only our magic. Let's try it our way, the mesti-za way, the Chicana way, the woman way."

On that day, I search for our essential dignity as a people, a people with a sense of purpose—to belong and contribute to something greater than our *pueblo.* On that day I seek to recover and reshape my spiritual identity. *¡Anímate! Raza, a celebrar el día de la Chicana.*

El retorno

> All movements are accomplished in six stages,
> and the seventh brings return.
>   —I Ching[11]

> *Tanto tiempo sin verte casa mía,*
> *mi cuna, mi hondo nido, nido de la huerta.*
>   —"Soledad"[12]

---

[11]Richard Wilhelm, *The I Ching or Book of Changes,* trans. Cary F. Baynes (Princeton, NJ: Princeton University Press, 1950), 98. *Author's note.*

[12]"Soledad" is sung by the group, Haciendo Punto en Otro Son. *Author's note.*

I stand at the river, watch the curving, twisting serpent, a serpent nailed to the fence where the mouth of the Rio Grande empties into the Gulf. I have come back. *Tanto dolor me costó el alejamiento.* I shade my eyes and look up. The bone beak of a hawk slowly circling over me, checking me out as potential carrion. In its wake a little bird flickering its wings, swimming sporadically like a fish. In the distance the expressway and the slough of traffic like an irritated sow. The sudden pull in my gut, *la tierra, los aguaceros.* My land, *el viento soplando la arena, el lagartijo debajo de un nopalito. Me acuerdo como era antes. Una región desértica de vastas llanuras, costeras de baja altura, de escasa lluvia, de chaparrales formados por mesquites y huizaches.* If I look real hard I can almost see the Spanish fathers who were called "the cavalry of Christ" enter this valley riding their burros, see the clash of cultures commence.

Tierra natal. This is home, the small towns in the Valley, *los pueblitos* with chicken pens and goats picketed to mesquite shrubs. *En las colonias* on the other side of the tracks, junk cars line the front yards of hot pink and lavender-trimmed house—Chicano architecture we call it, self-consciously. I have missed the TV shows where hosts speak in half and half, and where awards are given in the category of Tex-Mex music. I have missed the Mexican cemeteries blooming with artificial flowers, the fields of aloe vera and red pepper, rows of sugar cane, of corn hanging on the stalks, the cloud of *polvareda* in the dirt roads behind a speeding pickup truck, *el sabor de tamales de res y venado.* I have missed *la yegua colorada* gnawing the wooden gate of her stall, the smell of horse flesh from Carito's corrals. *He echado menos las noches calientes sin aire, noches de linternas y lechuzas* making holes in the night.

I still feel the old despair when I look at the unpainted, dilapidated, scrap lumber houses consisting mostly of corrugated aluminum. Some of the poorest people in the U.S. live in the Lower Rio Grande Valley, an arid and semi-arid land of irrigated farming, intense sunlight and heat, citrus groves next to chaparral and cactus. I walk through the elementary school attended so long ago, that remained segregated until recently. I remember how the white teachers used to punish us for being Mexican.

How I love this tragic valley of South Texas, as Ricardo Sánchez calls it; this borderland between the Nueces and the Rio Grande. This land has survived possession and ill-use by five countries: Spain, Mexico, the Republic of Texas, the U.S., the Confederacy, and the U.S. again. It has survived Anglo-Mexican blood feuds, lynchings, burnings, rapes, pillage.

Today I see the Valley still struggling to survive. Whether it does or not, it will never be as I remember it. The borderlands depression that was set off by the 1982 peso devaluation in Mexico resulted in the closure of hundreds of

Valley businesses. Many people lost their homes, cars, land. Prior to 1982, U.S. store owners thrived on retail sales to Mexicans who came across the border for groceries and clothes and appliances. While goods on the U.S. side have become 10, 100, 1000 times more expensive for Mexican buyers, goods on the Mexican side have become 10, 100, 1000 times cheaper for Americans. Because the Valley is heavily dependent on agriculture and Mexican retail trade, it has the highest unemployment rates along the entire border region; it is the Valley that has been hardest hit.[13]

"It's been a hard year for corn," my brother, Nune, says. As he talks, I remember my father scanning the sky for a rain that would end the drought, looking up into the sky, day after day, while the corn withered on its stalk. My father has been dead for 29 years, having worked himself to death. The life span of a Mexican farm laborer is 56—he lived to be 38. It shocks me that I am older than he. I too, search the sky for rain. Like the ancients, I worship the rain god and the maize goddess, but unlike my father I have recovered their names. Now for rain (irrigation) one offers not a sacrifice of blood, but of money.

"Farming is in a bad way," my brother says. "Two to three thousand small and big farmers went bankrupt in this country last year. Six years ago the price of corn was $8.00 per hundred pounds," he goes on. "This year it is $3.90 per hundred pounds." And, I think to myself, after taking inflation into account, not planting anything puts you ahead.

I walk out to the back yard, stare at *los rosales de mamá*. She wants me to help her prune the rose bushes, dig out the carpet grass that is choking them. *Mama grande Ramona también tenía rosales.* Here every Mexican grows flowers. If they don't have a piece of dirt, they use car tires, jars, cans, shoe boxes. Roses are the Mexican's favorite flower. I think, how symbolic—thorns and all.

Yes, the Chicano and Chicana have always taken care of growing things and the land. Again I see the four of us kids getting off the school bus, changing into our work clothes, walking into the field with Papí and Mamí, all six of us bending to the ground. Below our feet, under the earth lie the watermelon seeds.

---

[13]Out of the twenty-two border counties in the four border states, Hidalgo County (named for Father Hidalgo who was shot in 1810 after instigating Mexico's revolt against Spanish rule under the banner of *La Virgen de Guadalupe*) is the most poverty-stricken county in the nation, as well as the largest home base (along with Imperial in California) for migrant farmworkers. It was here that I was born and raised. I am amazed that both it and I have survived. *Author's note.*

We cover them with paper plates, putting *terremotes* on top of the plates to keep them from being blown away by the wind. The paper plates keep the freeze away. Next day or the next, we remove the plates, bare the tiny green shoots to the elements. They survive and grow, give fruit hundreds of times the size of the seed. We water them and hoe them. We harvest them. The vines dry, rot, are plowed under. Growth, death, decay, birth. The soil prepared again and again, impregnated, works on. A constant changing of forms, *renacimientos de la tierra madre*.

> This land was Mexican once
> was Indian always
> and is.
> And will be again.

Reprinted from *Borderlands/La Frontera: The New Mestiza* (San Francisco: Spinsters/Aunt Lute, 1987): 77-91.

JOSÉ ANTONIO BURCIAGA (1940-)

"Pendejismo" (1993)

Most popular Mexican cuss words begin with a "p." Why words such as *pinchi, puto, político* and *pendejo*, carry such a harsh negative sound, I don't know. I'm not a linguist.

Pinchi, or *pinche*, is used to describe someone who is mean-spirited. The degree of insult depends on the intensity, the context, and who is delivering it. I don't know why the word is considered vulgar. In Spain, a pinche is a kitchen helper, and a few restaurants are named El Pinche, which many Mexican and Chicano tourists find hilarious.

Once when I was a kid, my big sister was angry and wanted to pinch me, so I said, "¡No pinching!" She ran to Mom and said, "¡Mamá! ¡Antonio called me a pinchi!" Well Mother, proper and educated woman that she was, gave me a tongue-lashing that I never forgot, and I could never convince her or my sister that what I had said was "No pinching!" To this day, my sister will only laugh and say she doesn't remember anything, but my ears still sting.

A *puta* is a whore in vulgar Spanish, as opposed to *prostituta* for prostitute. A *puto* is a homosexual.

Pendejo is probably the least offensive of these P words. In Guadalajara and some other parts of Mexico, it is a common everyday word. For the non-Spanish speaking, the word is pronounced pen-deh-ho (not pen-day-hoe); feminine, pen-deh-ha; plural pendejas or pendejos. The noun, or committed act of a pendejo(a), is a *pendejada*. The verb is to *pendejear*. The term pendejo is commonly used outside of polite conversation and basically describes someone who is stupid or does something stupid. It's much stronger to call someone a pendejo than the standard Spanish *estúpido*. But be careful when calling someone a pendejo. Among friends it can be taken lightly, but for others it is better to be angry enough to back it up. Ironically, the Yiddish word for pendejo is a *putz* which means the same thing.

In high school I had a friend whose name I consistently forgot. I must have asked him for the umpteenth time when he finally yelled, "¡Olivas! ¡Pendejo!" So I called him Olivas Pendejo. At that same high school, we had a principal,

Brother Alphonsus, whose favorite proverb was a reminder to students: *¡Naces pendejo, mueres pendejo!*—"you were born a pendejo, you will die a pendejo."

Proverbs on pendejos abound in Mexican culture: Children say what they are doing; old people recall what they did; and pendejos say what they're going to do. Dogs open their eyes in fifteen days, pendejos never do. Of lovers that live far away from each other it is said, *Amor de lejos, amor de pendejos*—"Love from afar, love for pendejos."* The word can also be used to relieve pain: *No hay pena que dure veinte años ni pendejo que la aguante*—"there is no pain that lasts twenty years nor a pendejo that will endure it."

El Diccionario de la Real Academia de la Lengua Española (The Dictionary of the Royal Academy of the Spanish Language) defines pendejo as a "pubic hair." The secondary definition of a pendejo is a coward. Then there are tertiary definitions according to country: In Argentina, a pendejo is a boy who tries to act like an adult. In Colombia, El Salvador and Chile, a pendejo is a fool or a cocaine dealer. There are a lot of those in this country. Here [in the Southwest] and in Mexico a pendejo is more likely to be a fool or an idiot.

Señor Armando Jiménez, author of *Picardía Mexicana*, a collection of Mexican picaresque wit and wisdom, is also Mexico's foremost *pendejólogo* (pendejologist). According to Don Armando, the number of pendejos, even as you read this, is innumerable. It has been estimated that if pendejos could fly, the skies would be darkened and we would enter a new ice age. The pendejos would get a severe sunburn. Some pendejos go so far as to believe that if all pendejos were to be corralled, there would be no one left to close the corral gates. That theory has been discounted by the fact that herding pendejos would be like herding cats. Pendejos have a mind of their own.

The great majority of people regardless of class, color, or creed, are pendejos, according to Señor Jiménez. His research studies claim that up to 90 percent of the world population are pendejos. Of the remaining 10 percent, .5 percent are mentally unstable, 5 percent are geniuses, and 4 percent are unemployed—the exact amount needed for a sound economy. The remaining .5 percent are lost.

According to Jiménez, there are countless categories and types of pendejos. The following are but a few:

• The *políticos*, who think they will change the world with money, charisma or speeches.

• The hopeless pendejos, who blame all their problems on bad luck instead of the fact that they are pendejos.

• The happy ones, who believe in their superiority over other pendejos who look up to them.

• The dramatic pendejos, who can be identified at a distance of one city block, by their stance and by the way they walk, sometimes carrying a book or two.

• The pseudo-intellectuals, who act as if they are deep in thought on some theory when in reality they are wondering where they parked their cars.

• The optimistic pendejos, who are naive, happy, and talkative. They look for hidden treasures, mines, underground water. They also buy lottery tickets, bet on everything and believe in television wrestling.

• The pessimistic or doubting pendejos, who don't believe anything you tell them. If you don't believe this, you fall into this category. And if you do believe this, then you might fall into the category of those pendejos who believe everything.

• Entrepreneurial pendejos, who have grandiose projects, are eloquent, and make great salesmen. If this type convinces you, you are an even bigger pendejo.

This list may be used for self-evaluation, and to classify relatives, friends and lovers. If you did not find yourself in any of these pendejo groups, congratulations! This means you're either a genius, unemployed or mentally unstable. For those on the list, there is still no known cure, but you are not to blame. *¡Naces pendejo, mueres pendejo!*

Reprinted from *Drink Cultura: Chicanismo* (Santa Barbara: Joshua Odell Editions, 1993): 9-13.

CORDELIA CANDELARIA (1943-)

"Letting La Llorona Go, or, Re/reading History's 'Tender Mercies'" (1993)

Killing babies and children isn't nice. Killing your kind seems a particularly depraved violation of parental love and responsibility. In what are still the rare cases of mothers killing their own children, insanity is automatically assumed and usually proven to explain the horror. How paradoxical, then, that one of the most vigorous folk legends among Mexicans and Mexican Americans—we, whose culture places high premium on *mi madre, la familia y el hogar*—is the story of *La Llorona*, the Weeping Woman who kills (or, in some versions, abandons) her children and forever after wanders the world in punishing anguish for her sins. Stories about her have been told and retold over the centuries.

LA LLORONA, the Weeping Woman of Mexican legend, is considered by many historians and folklorists as the mythic form of the historical woman, La Malinche (also known as Doña Marina, Malinalli, and Malintzin), who was given by her village chief to assist Hernán Cortés in what resulted in the conquest of Mexico in 1519-1521. The hundreds of variants of the Llorona tale share a kernel plot: as punishment for her conduct a young, usually beautiful woman is condemned to wander (often by rivers and other bodies of water) forever crying, unloved, and homeless, in grief-stricken search for her lost children. Variants differ as to the nature of her offenses, but they usually include adultery, infanticide, or child neglect, and sometimes homicidal revenge, excessive hedonism, and self-indulgence as well. Often told as *bruja* (witch) or ghost tale to coerce obedience from misbehaving children (e.g., she will steal them to replace the babies she drowned) and overly independent adolescent girls (e.g., her agony will be theirs if they do not repress their sexual longings), the tale has been recorded for centuries, and it is reported throughout Mexico and AmericAztlán (that is, in the United States wherever Mexican Americans, reside; originally Aztlán was the name of the mythological homeland of Mesoamerican ancestors, analogous to the garden of Eden, a myth borrowed in the 1960s by Chicana/Chicano activists eager to recover indigenous roots). La Llorona and her historical prototype, La Malinche, have been interpreted as emblematic of the vanquished condition and reputed fatalism of Mexico and its people.

No longer frightening to me or anyone I know personally, young or old, La Llorona nonetheless still evokes intense passion in me (as this and other personal writings on the subject attest). The phallic propaganda of this tale's face value are as obvious—and in some versions, as banal—as tabloid headlines. In certain moods, she makes me laugh when I'm not crying, makes me screaming angry when I'm not mute in anguish at the remarkable efficacy of patriarchal power to define the terms of its perpetuation. On its face the tale teaches that girls get punished for conduct for which men are rewarded; that pleasure, especially sexual gratification, is sinful for women; that female independence and personal agency create monsters capable of destroying even their offspring; that children are handy pawns in the revenge chess of jealousy, and other lessons of similar scapegoating orthodoxy. Like Greek mythology's Medea, who also bears the stain of evil for maternal infanticide resulting from her love for a man who leaves her, La Llorona and her historical prototype, La Malinche, have served as convenient crucibles for their cultures' coming to terms with conquest, sexual desire, incest, and the multiple-sided nature of love/hate.

As a scapegoat and a crucible, the Llorona legend begs for reconsideration and possible recuperation from what, in another context, historian Emma Peres calls inside *"el sitio y la lengua"* (space and language) of the female subject, rather than from a dominant/dominating patriarchal perspective. But can even such an enlightened viewpoint save the Weeping Woman? Does she even deserve a new image? Yes, suggest several Chicana artists, it's past time for her to cut her hair, put on her Nikes and tie-dyed-shirt, and get the life she's earned. So transformed, she'll learn a new walk to replace the head down, bent over crouch I imagine she's been walking for 400 years and, in the breezy in-charge manner of, for example, artist Yolanda Lopez's twenty-first-century Chicanas, she'll lead the radicals in organizing the quincentennial protests marking La Conquista de Méjico in 2021.

But before that happens, the image of this tragic figure must expand. The mythic Weeping Woman of Mexican-Chicana/o[1] culture, La Llorona is, along with the Virgin of Guadalupe, arguably the most persistent and well-known mestizo folk legend to have emerged from the era of the Spanish Conquest of Tenochtítlán (now Mexico City) in 1521. Four hundred years after the Conquest,

---

[1]For gender inclusiveness, the term, "Chicanas/Chicanos," is used here interchangeably with "Mexican Americans" even though it usually suggests a more politically progressive social consciousness than the latter. For brevity, "Chicana/o" (plural form: Chicanas/os) is used. *Author's note.*

I grew up hearing stories of La Llorona in New Mexico in the 1940s and '50s, and, they are still told today, their persistence undiminished even in the era of "boy toy" Madonnas, Murphy Browns, and a few Gloria Molinas. Admittedly the tale's emotional power may be weakened by the commonplace fact of mass murders and child abuse in society in the late twentieth century.

What explains the paradox and persistence of this tale even in the late twentieth century? Is it that the bone chilling impact of her story on impressionable young minds makes it incredible? What I heard about her as a child is unforgettable, even though I realize that my unrestrained imagination was as much responsible for her image in my mind as anything I heard. Fear and innocence offer the perfect chemistry for mythmaking.

I recall my mother, struggling to raise eight children almost single-handedly since my father nearly always worked out-of-town, using La Llorona as a very effective "rod" of discipline. She would warn us, usually in Spanish, to "settle down and behave or La Llorona will come and get you. Listen, I think I hear her outside. . . . "Her voice would drift off softly, eerily, and we would immediately cease our rambunctious behavior, look toward the windows and doors, and strain to hear what I clearly remember as the awful *bruja's* plaintive moaning. She must be missing her children and crying again, I would think, and she needs someone *just like us* to take with her. And, just remember, she's not going to put up with all the nonsense Mamá does; no, she'll drown us too, just like that [snap!]—like she drowned her own babies.

Invariably effective, the ominous threat of the unseen Llorona lurking dangerously outside quieted our fuss because we didn't want the *brujamala* to hear us and realize that, just behind a flimsy door, sat three desirable children for the taking. Later on, it occurred to me that she wouldn't have been interested in brats like us anyway. In our grade school innocence, though, we could only think of ourselves as very easy prey, for surely in her annoyance with our behavior, Mamá wouldn't even have bothered to save us.

Other versions of the always evolving legend were at hand as we grew up and struggled for independence and self-identity. Of course, as adolescents we no longer believed Mamá's "superstitious crap" as we became aware of what I now call, *con cariño*, my mother's strategic, if Machiavellian, method of kid-control and self-preservation. Yet, those "grown-up" versions of La Llorona stay with me today as vividly as the others. One tawdry version foretells of a teenage girl who, disobeying her parents, sneaks away at night, is seduced by a handsome stranger, and becomes pregnant. Aghast at her condition, she conceals it until the child is born, then in fright and shame she drowns her baby, runs away, and is doomed to the eternal tearful "Llorona" search. Another variant of this plot has as its anti-hero a young, pretty, and very lonely mother whose husband is away in Korea. Succumbing to "temptation," she leaves her children untended to indulge herself with a night on the town. When she returns the children have disappeared. Ashamed to face her family and husband, she spends the rest of her life crying and searching for her kidnapped (and/or murdered) babies.

As an adult I have often exchanged Llorona tales with other Chicanas/os in usually good-humored (though hardly "mock") amazement at our parents' child-rearing tactics. One familiar rendering, whose sexist subtext is particularly blatant, involves a poor *mestiza* (half Indian, half Spanish woman) who falls in love with an aristocratic *criollo* (Mexican-born Spaniard) who, going against social conventions, also falls in love with her. Although social morés prevent their marrying, he keeps her and their children in a comfortable house away from his people until the time comes when he must adhere to tradition and marry an acceptable *criolla*. Understandably broken-hearted, angry, and overcome with passion, the *mestiza* drowns her children in a well and then commits suicide. When her soul appears in heaven to join her children, now angels, she is expelled and condemned to earth to roam, childless and crying in eternal torture for her unpardonable sins. The tale ends there, as of course it must to serve its function as grassroots propaganda intended to reinforce the patriarchy. Presumably the highborn macho lives happily ever after with his proper family, but even if he doesn't, the key point is that *he* is the one who lives—not she or the children—without permanent social stigma for *his* conduct which is identical to hers and which he initiated.

The first thing to stress in recuperating La Llorona for the next century is that she and La Malinche got a bum rap. As Adelaida R. Del Castillo's 1974 article (in *Encuentro Femenil*) and my own 1973 study (first published in *Frontiers: A Journal of Women Studies*, 1980) on La Malinche have established, there is no valid historical basis for "*malinchismo*," the Mexican concept of betrayal that emerged in the nineteenth century. Women didn't have the political or military power to win or lose Mesoamerica to the Spaniards. Thus, the Malinche as traitor and whore image which gave rise to the Llorona folk legend and which was memorialized by, among others, muralist José Clemente Orozco and Nobel poet Octavio Paz in *Labyrinth of Solitude* (1950), lacks legitimacy *except* as reflections of masculinist versions of power.

So why try to save the baby-killer of legend?

One reason which explains part of the persistence of the tale over the centuries is that La Llorona's act of infanticide can be interpreted as a mythic "tender mercy," a concept of irony from biblical folklore which suggests that, within a thoroughly corrupt system, even an act of compassion may be brutal because it, too, partakes of the surrounding corruption. The tale can thus be "read" as political euthanasia, a woman's conscious attempt to save her beloved and cherished children from their parents' awful fate.

Like Toni Morrison's novel *Beloved* in which infanticide is presented as a slave woman's desperate act of maternal protection to save her daughter from slavery, La Llorona persists in folklore because the legend's meanings are multiple, not one-dimensional. Understanding those rich meanings exposes the very injustices which a superficial reading of the tale seems to prefer. In this vein, folklore scholar José Limón argues that "La Llorona [is] a symbol that speaks to the course of Greater Mexican [and Chicana/o] history and does so for women in particular, but through the idiom of women [it] also symbolizes the utopian longing [for equality and justice] of the Greater Mexican folk masses" (in *Between Borders: Essays on Mexicana/Chicana History*, 1990, p. 413).

Whether or not the iconography of folklore's Weeping Woman can be rehabilitated by radical poets, artists, and intellectuals, she can be re/visioned as a resisting woman like Antigone, Sor Juana, Anne Hutchinson, and Morrison's Sethe. My own lifetime fascination with the legend clearly has evolved from the childhood spectre of previous decades into what is now a recognition of its symbolic complexity and a genuine appreciation of its cultural significance. *Today* it tells me that the La Llorona legend survives as potent folk nourishment because it re/presents a hero who bravely exercises her active agency in order to will her own destiny by electing a tragic fate rather than passively allowing herself and her children to live under inescapable tyranny. Usually when men do that they're called heroes, especially if—like kings, presidents, and generals—they kill thousands of *other* people's children on battlefields. It is finally time to let go of a single, narrow, masculinized understanding of the tale and to see La Llorona instead as an always evolving, freshly created emblem of gender, sexuality, and power. And also as another female victim of *his*tory's tender mercies.

Adapted from Cordelia Candelaria's article and poems on "La Llorona" prepared for *The Oxford Companion to Women's Writing in the United States* (1994); published in *Heresies: A Feminist Publication on Art and Politics* (1993) and adapted from the Oxford entry. Reprinted from *Arroyos to the Heart* (Santa Monica: Santa Monica College Press, 1993): 152-31.

CUENTO / SHORT STORY

JORGE ULICA (1870-1926)

"Do You Speak Pocho. . . ?" (1924)

El pocho se está extendiendo de una manera alarmante. Me refiero al dialecto que hablan muchos de los "spanish" que vienen a California y que es un revoltijo, cada día más enredado, de palabras españolas, vocablos ingleses, expresiones populares y terrible "slang".

De seguir las cosas así, va a ser necesario fundar una Academia y publicar un diccionario español-pocho, a fin de entendernos con los nuestros. Hasta las fieles y dulces esposas, si están malas, dicen a sus maridos, hechas un veneno, cuando quieren arrojarlos noramala:

—Vete inmediatamente, "geraut".

Y luego, muy satisfechas, cuentan a sus amigas:

—Le di "leirof" a Justiniano porque no quiere salir de los "dances". Se ha hecho muy "exclusivo" y voy a darle también su divorcio. El Juez es muy amigo mío y lo obligará a que me pague un buen "alimioni". Para que se le quite lo "rug".

Eso, que entre pochos lo entiende cualquiera, necesita intérprete tratándose de otro género de ciudadanos.

* * *

Entre las personas que me honran con su amistad hay una, doña Eulalia, viuda de Pellejón, que en unos cuantos meses de haberse venido de México habla perfectamente el pocho y se ha asimilado más palabras del habla californiana que las que conocía del dulce, hermoso y melífluo parlar de Cervantes.

He recibido una carta suya, cuyo texto copio para regocijo y satisfacción de los lingüistas afectos a estudiar los idiomas raros:

Sr. D. Jorge Ulica, "City". Caballero:

Fui hoy al "posofis" a comprar unas "estampas" y tuve "chanza" de recibir una carta de una hija mía casada que tengo en Piscapochán, de donde soy "nativa". Me he dado mucha "irritación" saber que el "tícher" de inglés de mis nietos es enteramente "crezi", pues no entiende ni una palabra de lo que yo escribo en "english". Figúrese que envié a mi hija "lob y quises," así muy clarito, y el condenado "tícher" dijo que no sabía que era eso, cuando le enseñaron la carta. Ya les "reporté" que estaban pagando el "money por nada" y hasta quise ponerles un "guiarelés" para evitar que les estén quitando peso y medio por "hafanáur" de clase; pero no traían ni "un cinco" en la bolsa. ¡No saber que "lob" y "quises" es amor y besos!

Eso no importa. Lo que yo quiero es que Ud. me diga qué puedo hacer con la "landed" del "bordo" donde vivo, que después de rentarme un "jausquipinrrun", no quiere no que caliente "guor" porque dice que le "esmoqueo" la "parlor". Ayer, a la hora de "bricfast", iba a guisar "jamanegs", y se levantó de cama furiosa, en "blummers" y "bibidí", amenazándome con llamar por el "telefón" al "patrol" para que me llevaran a la "yeil". No quise decirle nada a mi compadre Goyo cuando volvió de la "canería", en donde es "boss", para no "levantar el infierno"; pero si estas cosas no "vienen a un stop", va a haber "jel". No puedo seguir comiendo únicamente "jatdogs", "cofi an donas" y "aiscrim", a riesgo de coger una maladía. A veces tengo que ir, casi en ayunas, "al otro lado de la bahía", y si no fuera porque "en donde don Taun" tomo unos sandwiches de "bicon" y otros de "chis", me moría.

Quiero por eso, que venga a verme. Arreglaremos ese "bisnes" y el de la "aplicación" que tengo que hacer para que "agarren" a mi compadre "los hombres colorados" que les dicen "redmen", porque "dan muchos beneficios" y ahora tienen "abierto los libros" por un mes. Allí no hay "vaporinos" ni "rugness". Si quiere le mandaré mi "aromovil". No será un coche "jaitono"; pero sí una "machina" fuerte para cualquier "raid". Si viene, le prometo llevarlo después a las "muvis", no a los "niquelorios" ni a los de a "daim" sino a los de "don Taun," a alguna "pícchur" de las que hablan mucho en los "papeles". Le enseñaré después mi "redio" para que oiga tocar ese "fox" tan bonito que se llama de "la reina Mora", a los "los musicianos" de la "Lyasband" que toca en el "lobi" del "palas". Es muy "quint". Al fin de la pieza, todos ellos cantan "reina mora, reina mora". "Lob and quises for yu olso".

Eulalia vda. de Pellejón.

* * *

La Sra. Pellejón me ha enviado esta otra misiva:

"Le mando ésta por 'especial de liver'. Quiero 'reportarle' que voy a cambiar mi 'second neim' que no suena 'veri güel' por su 'translécion' en 'inglés'. En vez de Pellejón voy a 'nominarme' Skinejón, que es casi 'di seim'. Así, mi difunto, a quien Dios tenga en el 'jiven', no cogerá 'truble' ni se pondrá 'yelous'.

"Eulalia Skinejon".

Como lo iba diciendo, el pocho avanza a pasos agigantados. Y una de dos: o se escribe un extenso vocabulario de pocherías por connotados académicos de esa lengua o se abre una academia de idioma pocho para los profanos.

Seré uno de los alumnos más aplicados. ¡Y en seguida irá mi "aplicación!"

11 de octubre, 1924

Reprinted from *Crónicas diabólicas (1916-1926) de "Jorge Ulica"/Julio G. Arce.* Juan Rodríguez, comp. (San Diego: Maize Press, 1982): 153-55.

MARIO SUÁREZ (1925-)

"El Hoyo" (1947)

From the center of downtown Tucson the ground slopes gently away to Main Street, drops a few feet, and then rolls to the banks of the Santa Cruz River. Here lies the sprawling section of the city known as El Hoyo. Why it is called El Hoyo is not clear. It is not a hole as its name would imply; it is simply the river's immediate valley. Its inhabitants are *chicanos* who raise hell on Saturday night, listen to Padre Estanislao on Sunday morning, and then raise more hell on Sunday night. While the term *chicano* is the short way of saying *Mexicano*, it is the long way of referring to everybody. Pablo Gutierrez married the Chinese grocer's daughter and acquired a store; his sons are *chicanos*. So are the sons of Killer Jones who threw a fight in Harlem and fled to El Hoyo to marry Cristina Mendez. And so are all of them—the assortment of harlequins, bandits, oppressors, oppressed, gentlemen, and bums who came from Old Mexico to work for the Southern Pacific, pick cotton, clerk, labor, sing, and go on relief. It is doubtful that all of these spiritual sons of Mexico live in El Hoyo because they love each other—many fight and bicker constantly. It is doubtful that the *chicanos* live in El Hoyo because of its scenic beauty—it is everything but beautiful. Its houses are built of unplastered adobe, wood, license plates, and abandoned car parts. Its narrow streets are mostly clearings which have, in time, acquired names. Except for the tall trees which nobody has ever cared to identify, nurse, or destroy, the main things known to grow in the general area are weeds, garbage piles, dogs, and kids. And it is doubtful that the *chicanos* live in El Hoyo because it is safe—many times the Santa Cruz River has risen and inundated the area.

In other respects living in El Hoyo has its advantages. If one is born with the habit of acquiring bills, El Hoyo is where the bill collectors are less likely to find you. If one has acquired the habit of listening to Señor Perea's Mexican Hour in the wee hours of the morning with the radio on full blast, El Hoyo is where you are less likely to be reported to the authorities. Besides, Perea is very popular and to everybody sooner or later is dedicated The Mexican Hat Dance. If one has inherited a bad taste for work but inherited also the habit of eating, where, if not in El Hoyo, are the neighbors more willing to lend you a cup of flour or beans? When Señora García's house burned to the ground with all her belongings and two kids, a benevolent gentleman conceived the gesture that put her on the road to solvency. He took five hundred names and solicited from each a dollar. At the end of the week he turned over to the heartbroken but grateful señora three hundred and fifty dollars in cold cash and pocketed his recompense. When the new manager of the local business decided that no more Mexican girls were to work behind his counters, it was the *chicanos* of El Hoyo who acted as pickets and, on taking their individually small but collectively great buying power elsewhere, drove the manager out and the girls returned to their jobs. When the Mexican Army was enroute to Baja California and the *chicanos* found out that the enlisted men ate only at infrequent intervals they crusaded across town with pots of beans, trays of tortillas, boxes of candy, and bottles of wine to meet the train. When someone gets married celebrating is not restricted to the immediate families and friends of the couple. The public is invited. Anything calls for a celebration and in turn a celebration calls for anything. On Armistice Day there are no fewer than a half dozen fights at the Tira-Chancla Dance Hall. On Mexican Independence Day more than one flag is sworn allegiance to and toasted with gallon after gallon of Tumba Yaqui.

And El Hoyo is something more. It is this something more which brought Felipe Ternero back from the wars after having killed a score of Germans with his body resembling a patch-work quilt. It helped him to marry a fine girl named Julia. It brought Joe Zepeda back without a leg from Luzon and helps him hold more liquor than most men can hold with two. It brought George Casillas, a gunner flying B-24's over Germany, back to compose boleros. Perhaps El Hoyo is the proof that those people exist who, while not being against anything, have as yet failed to observe the more popular modes of human conduct. Perhaps the humble appearance of El Hoyo justifies the discerning shrugs of more than a few people only vaguely aware of its existence. Perhaps El Hoyo's simplicity motivates many a *chicano* to move far away from its intoxicating *frenesi*, its dark narrow streets, and its shrieking children, to deny the bloodwell from which he springs, to claim the blood of a conquistador while his hair is straight and his face beardless. Yet El Hoyo is not the desperate outpost of a few families against the world. It fights for no causes except those which soothe its immediate angers. It laughs and cries with the same amount of passion in times of plenty and of want.

Perhaps El Hoyo, its inhabitants, and its essence can be explained by telling you a little bit about a dish called *capirotada*. Its origin is uncertain. But it is made of old, new, stale, and hard bread. It is sprinkled with water and then it is cooked with raisins, olives, onions, tomatoes, peanuts, cheese, and general leftovers of that which is good and bad. It is seasoned with salt, sugar, pepper, and sometimes chili or tomato sauce. It is fired with tequila or sherry wine. It is served hot, cold, or just "on the weather" as they say in El Hoyo. The Garcias like it one way, the Quevedos another, the Trilos another, and the Ortegas still another. While in general appearance it does not differ much from one home to another it tastes different everywhere. Nevertheless it is still *capirotada*. And so it is with El Hoyo's *chicanos*. While many seem to the undiscerning eye to be alike it is only because collectively they are referred to as *chicanos*. But like *capirotada*, fixed in a thousand ways and served on a thousand tables, which can only be evaluated by individual taste, the *chicanos* must be so distinguished.

Reprinted from *North of the Río Grande: The Mexican American Experience in Short Fiction*. Edward Simmen, ed. (New York: Mentor Books, 1992): 94-96.

TOMÁS RIVERA (1935-1984)

"Las salamandras" (1974)

Lo que más recuerdo de aquella noche es lo oscuro de la noche, el lodo y lo resbaloso de las salamandras. Pero tengo que empezar desde el principio para que puedan comprender todo esto que sentí y también de que, al sentirlo, comprendí algo que traigo todavía conmigo. Yo no lo traigo como recuerdo solamente, sino también como algo que siento aún.

Todo empezó porque había estado lloviendo por tres semanas y no teníamos trabajo. Se levantó el campamento, digo campamento porque eso parecíamos. Con este ranchero de Minesota habíamos estado esperando ya por tres semanas que se parara el agua, y nada. Luego vino y nos dijo que mejor nos fuéramos de sus gallineros porque ya se le había hechado a perder el betabel. Luego comprendimos yo y mi 'apá que lo que tenía era miedo de nosotros, de que le fuéramos a robar algo o de que alguien se le enfermara y entonces tendría él que hacerse el responsable. Le dijimos que no teníamos dinero, ni qué comer, y ni cómo regresarnos a Texas; apenas tendríamos con qué comprar gasolina para llegarle a Oklahoma. Y él nomás nos dijo que lo sentía pero quería que nos fuéramos, y nos fuimos. Ya para salir se le ablandó el corazón y nos dio dos carpas llenas de telarañas que tenía en la bodega y una lámpara y kerosín. También le dijo a 'apá que, si nos íbamos rumbo a Crystal Lake en Iowa, a lo mejor encontrábamos trabajo en la ranchería que estaba por allí, y que a lo mejor no se les había echado a perder el betabel. Y nos fuimos.

En los ojos de 'apá y 'amá se veía algo original y puro que nunca les había notado. Era como cariño triste. Casi ni hablábamos al ir corriendo los caminos de grava. La lluvia que seguía cayendo nos continuaba avisando que seguramente no podíamos hallar trabajo, y así fue. En cada rancho que llegamos, nomás nos movían la cabeza desde adentro de la casa, ni nos abrían la puerta para decirnos que no. Entonces me sentía que no era parte ni de 'apá ni de 'amá, y lo único que sentía que existía era el siguiente rancho.

El primer día que estuvimos en el pueblito de Crystal Lake nos fue mal. En un charco se le mojó el alambrado al carro y papá le gastó la batería al carro. Por fin un garage nos hizo el favor de cargarla. Pedimos trabajo en varias partes del pueblito pero luego nos echó la chota. Papá le explicó que sólo andábamos buscando trabajo pero él nos dijo que no quería húngaros en el pueblo y que nos saliéramos. El dinero ya casi se nos había acabado, y nos fuimos. Nos fuimos al oscurecer y paramos el carro a unas tres millas del pueblo, y allí vimos el anochecer.

La lluvia se venía de vez en cuando. Sentados todos en el carro a la orilla del camino, hablábamos un poco. Estábamos cansados. Estábamos solos. En los ojos de 'apá y 'amá veía algo original. Ese día no habíamos comido casi nada para dejar dinero para el siguiente día. Ya 'apá se veía más triste, agüitado. Creía que no íbamos a encontrar trabajo. Y nos quedamos dormidos sentados en el carro esperando el siguiente día. Casi ni pasaron carros por ese camino de grava durante la noche.

En la madrugada desperté y todos estaban dormidos, y podía verles los cuerpos y las caras a mi 'apá, a mi 'amá y a mis hermanos, y no hacían ruido. Eran caras y cuerpos de cera. Me recordaron a la cara de 'buelito el día que lo sepultamos. Pero no me entró miedo como cuando lo encontré muerto a él en la troca. Yo creo porque sabía que estaban vivos. Y por fin amaneció completamente.

Ese día buscamos trabajo todo el día, y nada. Dormimos en la orilla del camino y volví a despertar en la madrugada y volví a ver a mi gente dormida. Pero esa madrugada me entró un poco de miedo. No porque se veían como que estaban muertos, sino porque ya me empezaba a sentir que no era de ellos.

El día siguiente buscamos trabajo todo el día, y nada. Dormimos en la orilla del camino y volví a despertar en la madrugada y volví a ver a mi gente dormida. Y esa madrugada, la tercera, me dieron ganas de dejarlos a todos porque ya no me sentía que era de ellos.

A mediodía paró de llover y nos entró ánimo. Dos horas más tarde encontramos a un ranchero que tenía betabel y a quien, según creía él, no se le había echado a perder la cosecha. Pero no tenía casas ni nada. Nos enseñó los acres de betabel que tenía y todo estaba por debajo del agua, todo enlagunado. Nos dijo que, si nos esperábamos hasta que se bajara el agua para ver si no estaba echado a perder, y si estaba bien el betabel, nos pagaría bonos por cada acre que le preparáramos. Pero no tenía casas ni nada. Nosotros le dijimos que teníamos unas carpas y que, si nos dejaba, podríamos sentarlas en su yarda. Pero no quiso. Nos tenía miedo. Nosotros lo que queríamos era estar cerca del agua de beber que era lo necesario, y también ya estábamos cansados de dormir sentados, todos entullidos, y claro que queríamos estar debajo de la luz que tenía en la yarda. Pero no quiso, y nos dijo que, si queríamos trabajar allí, que pusiéramos las carpas al pie de la labor de betabel y que esperáramos allí hasta que se bajara el agua. Y pusimos las carpas al pie de la labor de betabel, y nos pusimos a esperar.

Al oscurecer prendimos la lámpara de kerosín en una de las carpas y luego decidimos dormir todos en una sola carpa. Recuerdo que todos nos sentíamos a gusto al poder estirar las piernas, y el dormirnos fue fácil. Luego lo primero que recuerdo de esa noche y lo que me despertó fue el sentir lo que yo creía que era la mano de uno de mis hermanos, y mis propios gritos. Me quité la mano de encima y luego vi que lo que tenía en la mano yo era una salamandra. Estábamos cubiertos de salamandras que habían salido de lo húmedo de las labores, y seguimos gritando y quitándonos las salamandras del cuerpo. Con la ayuda de la luz de kerosín, empezamos a matar las salamandras. De primero nos daba asco porque al aplastarlas les salía como leche del cuerpo, y el piso de la carpa se empezó a ver negro y blanco. Se habían metido en todo, dentro de los zapatos, en las colchas... Al ver fuera de la carpa con la ayuda de la lámpara, se veía todo negro el suelo. Yo realmente sólo las veía como bultitos negros que al aplastarlos les salían leche. Luego parecía que nos estaban invadiendo la carpa, como que querían reclamar el pie de la labor. No sé por qué matamos tantas salamandras esa noche. Lo fácil hubiera sido subirnos al carro. Ahora que recuerdo, creo que sentíamos nosotros también el deseo de recobrar el pie de la labor, no sé. Sí recuerdo que hasta empezamos a buscar más salamandras, para matarlas. Y luego recuerdo me gustaba aluzar con la lámpara y matar despacio a cada una. Sería que les tenía coraje por el susto. Sí, me empecé a sentir como que volvía a ser parte de mi 'apá y de mi 'amá y de mis hermanos.

Lo que más recuerdo de aquella noche fue lo oscuro de la noche, el zoquete, lo resbaloso de las salamandras y lo duro que a veces se ponían de que las aplastara. Lo que traigo conmigo todavía es lo que vi y sentí al matar la última. Y yo creo que por eso recuerdo esa noche de las salamandras. Pesqué a una y la examiné bien con la lámpara, luego le estuve viendo los ojos antes de matarla. Lo que vi y sentí es algo que traigo todavía conmigo, algo puro—la muerte original.

"Las salamandras" by Tomás Rivera edited by Julián Olivares is reprinted with permission from the publisher of *Cuentos hispanos de los Estados Unidos* (Houston: Arte Público Press, University of Houston, 1993): 82-85.

ESTELA PORTILLO TRAMBLEY (1936-)

"The Paris Gown" (1975; revised 1993)

"Cognac with your coffee, Teresa?"

"No, thank you, Gran—Clo." Somehow the word "grandmother" did not suit Clotilde Romero de Traske, sophisticated, chic, and existentially fluent. Teresa had awaited with excitement this after-dinner tête à tête. She knew so little about this woman who had left her home in Mexico so long ago. The young girl curiously searched her grandmother's face for signs of age. There were few. They were indistinguishable in the grace and youthful confidence exuded by this woman. Her gestures, eyes, flexible body, and above all her quick, discerning mind spoke of the joy of living.

Clotilde was an art dealer at the Rue Auber. Back home she was more than that. She was a legend. Tongues wagged incessantly recounting her numerous marriages, her travels, her artistic ventures, her lovers, and the rich and famous that frequented her salon. Then there was the hushed up scandal concerning her departure from Mexico so long ago. No one was willing to tell an innocent girl like Teresa how her grandmother had come to live in Paris. Back home, the wealthy women cushioned in static, affluent, stagnant lives had clacked tongues in furious gossip about the infamous Clotilde. Infamous or not, Clotilde Romero de Traske was to be admired.

"How do you like Paris, child?" There was a daring in her grandmother's eyes.

"Oh, I love it. It's so old-world—so rich in history and culture."

The older woman laughed. "Above all, Paris is a flesh and blood city, the City of Lights. Here the soul blossoms like a flower opening to the sun."

"Yes, I felt it. But I'm not clever enough to put it the way you did."

"You are most clever and lucky. Everybody should see Paris before they are twenty-five. I heard that somewhere. Can't remember where. But, there is no place like it in the world."

You should know, Grandmother, Teresa reminded herself. You've been everywhere but you never returned. It was time to ask.

"You never returned home, Clo. Why?"

"Does anyone really go back home? We change so with time, but home remains the same, and so it's no longer home. Home to me is the pieces of my life that have fitted the puzzle called 'me.' Good or bad—ugly or beautiful. I guess I'm home."

"Were you always so wise?"

The grandmother laughed. "My dear, if you knew the idiotic things I've done. Wisdom is what you learn from the mountain of mistakes you make in life."

It was amazing, the beautiful clear depth of the "legend." Teresa felt a rush of admiration for the emberlike quality of her grandmother's spirit. It filled the room. She knows who she is, thought Teresa. How wonderful to have reached that comprehension of one's place in the universe. Teresa looked about the room and decided that it too was a piece of Clotilde, of what she had become in the life process. The art, the furniture, the flowers were all impressions of a great ferocity of living. Teresa caught herself. Why am I doing this? Analyzing rooms? My Grandmother? Yet the feeling of the room could not be ignored. The colors were wonderful. They seem to awaken feelings she could not really define. Maybe it's all a mystery beyond me.

"So—you are traveling with a university group?" Clotilde's expressive eyes searched her granddaughter's face.

She thinks I'm uncomfortable, thought Teresa. "I escaped."

"Escaped?"

"You know what I mean."

Clotilde laughed. "Assuredly, not in the same way."

"I can't believe the attitudes back home. They all live in the seventeenth century where I must not be exposed to the evils of the world." Teresa realized the petulance of her words.

"You really believe that?" Clo seemed amused.

"They're all stifling, sometimes my mother, my father, my aunts, you name it! Everybody back home is so—so proper."

Clo reflected, "Some moles, some eagles. I don't mean to judge, but you know what they say, 'different strokes'—"

Teresa laughed. "—'for different folks.' Of course. But *you* don't think 'old'!" Teresa saw the fairness in Clo's words.

"What is 'old'? Don't you think it's a knack of seeing what's real?" Clotilde put down her cup and walked to the mantlepiece over the fireplace as if she wanted to observe her granddaughter from a new perspective. Teresa also saw something new. A convex reflection of mood. Clo was the focal point in front of the wild, unkempt order of her art, a form liberated from civilized order. Teresa felt more than she knew it, for she knew little about art.

"I love your paintings, your sculpture. The old mixed in with the new. . . . I know very little about art, but this excites me."

"How discerning! Your feel for art is more important than knowing about it, art without doctrinaire implications."

"What does that mean?"

"You felt something. It left an impression perhaps relating to your experiences. You do not need rules or labels to understand."

Teresa felt inadequate. But it spurred her, so she asked, "Are you an artist yourself, Clo?"

"A very bad one, I'm afraid. When I was your age, I thought I had great talent. I was foolish."

"So you became a dealer in art?"

"It amounted to that after so many years." The collector went up to a massive piece of sculpture and touched its outline reverently. "Have you ever heard of Gaudier-Brzeska?"

"Heavens no." Teresa confessed her ignorance, knowing that she was about to be enlightened.

"Gaudier was a man of great passion, a primitive; he plunged into the world of feeling, and instinct, and energy. Free of barbarism."

This puzzled Teresa. "Primitive—barbarism—don't these go together?"

"Primitives? People of instinct and intuition—free—like children in their thinking, like animals when in fear—brutal. Savages, you might say, but savages do less harm than barbarians. Barbarians are a product of civilization. Artists attempt to preserve our humanity. Civilization destroys it, little by little."

Teresa was intrigued. "Artists are not barbarians?"

Clo checked herself. "*Some* artists cannot be barbarians if they are artists. Remember, barbarians are associated with crudeness of taste, excessive greed, excessive cruelty, and a fondness to be on top. What does that sound like to you?" She did not wait for an answer but continued. "Politicians, big business, warmongers for great gain. All these are creatures of civilization."

"That's not what I learned in history books." Teresa was bewildered.

Clotilde looked apologetic. "I talk too much. I think too much for my own good. Gaudier made out of stone and metal what I have tried to make out of my life—to leave the field of invention open, to step out of apathetic and pathetic comforts."

"You are free. . . ." Why had she said that? She didn't even know why the people back home considered Clotilde so infamous. If the result of infamy led to the kind of woman standing next to her, then it must have redeeming virtues. She touched the figure by Gaudier as if to add a part of herself, to understand what made her grandmother who she was. "I know why you never went back to Mexico, Clo. . . ."

"I may go back one of these days, if the fancy strikes me."

"Why? If I had a choice I would stay in Paris."

"Ah! But you do have a choice."

"No, no, my father would forbid it. You know how fathers are. They're so archaic." But no matter how archaic, I'll always obey him, do what he says, think what he thinks, Teresa realized. She asked Clo, "How old were you when you ran away from home?"

"I didn't exactly run away." Clotilde's eyes were full of memories.

Teresa did not want to press. She got up and walked around the room, looking at paintings, vases, bronze figures. She pondered aloud, "I can't imagine my father being comfortable in this room. It is too primitive and wild and free, without any rules. . . ."

Clotilde concluded, ". . .and fathers love rules. . . ."

"More than they love us?" Teresa looked at her grandmother intently.

"You want to know how I felt about my father's love?"

"Yes. . . ." Teresa's voice anticipated.

"He was proud of me because I was pretty, because I was modest. But he was foremost a businessman and a very rich man. I'm not condemning him. He tried to be fair, but all the rules were his rules. I was a commodity to him, an investment. He could marry me off to a man of property. That was good business."

"That was not love. My father didn't want me to go to the university in Mexico City—but he gave in."

"It's a different time from my time, Teresa. Each generation has its dead ends for women." The grandmother's words were words of experience.

"Did he try to marry you off to a rich man?" Teresa remembered that part of the story from back home.

"Oh yes, he had decided to marry me to Don Ignacio, our neighbor, a widower about my father's age."

"I'm glad I live in this generation." Teresa felt a tinge of relief.

Clo's eyes were back in time. "It was something that rich fathers did. Quite commonplace. Then there were the alternatives: If you refused to marry your father's choice, there was the nunnery. Or—remaining single, an old maid, totally dependent on the charity of others, unwanted and ignored. There were times I considered running away with the stable boy. He was beautiful, so young and strong. But that choice led to poverty, sacrifice, discomforts. That's all there was until the day Tío Gaspar came to visit.

"He had squandered his inheritance living the life of a bohemian. I liked him; he treated my brother and me like people. He didn't talk down to us. Spent hours talking about his gypsy life and the freedom of artists. He painted—badly, but with heart. He bought some easels for my brother and me so we could try our hand at watercolors. When my brother showed his first picture to my father, my father was so proud he fooled himself into thinking that Manolo had great talent. But that was to be expected. He always raved about anything my brother did. The sun rose and set around my brother; after all, he was a boy, a varón, a macho, his future heir. I was only a girl."

"It's like that with many families."

"Oh yes, traditions do not die easy. For thousands of years men have believed themselves superior to women. They do not mean to be cruel. They are just overwhelmed with this self-given image."

Clotilde paused, then asked, "Do you have a young man?"

"I've fallen in love several times. Most men want to possess you. So I run away."

"Are you running away now?"

"In a way. The word 'love' confuses me," Teresa confessed.

"Your instinct is pure. You sense that love can destroy you when it is not love but the illusion of love. I myself have been so careful. I hear the wisdom of the prophet and use it to measure the quality of love. It's a good test."

"What prophet?" Teresa was intrigued.

"Kahlil Gibran. His words—'But let there be spaces in your togetherness. . . .' Real love respects separateness. I have chosen well."

Clotilde made her way to the French windows leading to her garden and opened them. She did not go outside but looked out from the doorway as Teresa came up from behind her. Teresa was amazed. The garden was like the room—lacking neat symmetry, with a cobblestone path leading to nowhere in particular and trailing vines snaking up cypress trees. Here and there flowers grew like surprises. A storybook garden—the secret garden—a garden found in dreams. What was the fragrance? Teresa inhaled it slowly, deliberately. "What is it?"

"Italian jasmine, a gift from a man who knows the pricelessness of our aloneness. This is a must: to find the height of oneself, a solitary journey."

"Where is he now?"

"I don't know. He had a calling to walk the silence among pyramids. But he'll be back. He always surprises me."

"All those alternatives you talked about back home you didn't take any of them, Grandmother." She dared to use the word now. Clotilde's ember eyes accepted.

"My father bought my brother expensive artist's palettes and gave him lessons. But then, Manolo took advantage. He had no talent. His work was awkward and miserable. But he told my father he wanted to study art seriously; would my father finance a stay in Paris? He didn't want to study art, just to have a good time. Tío Gaspar knew I was a much better artist. He bought me books on art and told me I must give it my full dedication if I were ever to go to Paris. An open door! My father could send me to an artists' colony, I could travel. When my father heard these plans, he was enraged. How dare I presume I could have such freedoms! I was only a girl! I should dedicate myself to learning the social graces, to embroidering, practicing meekness, to readying myself for a worthy husband. But I did just the opposite. I spent the days reading all the art books I could get my hands on. Mostly I took Manolo's, for he merely threw them aside and never bothered to read one. I worked and worked on landscapes and painting with charcoal. I was truly convinced I had a talent. I had always competed with Manolo—to dare my father. I needed his approval so badly. My brother and I rode horses, and we loved to ride. I would ride my horse into the hills, without a saddle, my hair wild and unkempt. Again, all this angered my father. Nevertheless, one summer he bought a pair of stallions, beautiful horses, for Manolo and me. Every morning I would race Manolo and beat him every time. My father would watch, and after the race I would run to him, throw back my head, and look him in the eye, hoping for some word of praise. He was oblivious to me, his eyes on my brother, though he chided, 'A man must never allow a woman to outdo him. A varón can ride better than a mere girl. A man must master all things!' Funny, Manolo never mastered anything. I did all things well, but I never heard a word of praise from my father."

They walked into the garden in silence, watching a bird hop along a branch. The cypress looked silver in the slant of shadows and sun. From outside the garden walls came the sounds of moving traffic, whistles, muffled conversations, the splashing of rain puddles left from the night before, a wonderful cacophony touching only the edge of life. Clotilde led her visitor along the cobblestone path that rambled to nowhere in particular. They came to a low stone bench facing an arched terrace lined with colored earthen pots full of flowers. How Mexican! thought Teresa. They sat absorbing sounds until her grandmother picked up the threads of her thoughts and feelings of long ago.

"Well, my brother did not want to go into the banking business, so he talked my father into sending him to Europe with Tío Gaspar to study art! He, of course, had no intentions of doing so; he wanted the good times of the idle rich. He would write letters to me from here, from Montmartre, about the great life, making new friends. He claimed people were alive in Paris. The phrase echoed again and again in my thoughts—where people were alive. . . . I went to my father and asked him if I could go live with Manolo and Tío Gaspar to study art. I reminded him how much more talent I had than my brother. Papá thought I was insane. 'What! You're only a girl! It's time you thought about marriage.' That's when he told me about his plans for marrying me off to Don Ignacio; a great dream of his life—to merge two great estates. I had to pay the price for being *bien gentille!*[1] I argued with him, told him I deserved better than the fates imposed on women in the town. I demanded equality with Manolo; I wanted the same trust and freedom. My mother accused me of wanting to drive my father to his grave. He was close to a nervous breakdown because of my selfish and willful behavior. Why couldn't I behave like a good daughter? Like a good woman?"

Teresa understood. "All choices were dead ends."

Clotilde rose and walked among the earthen pots, feeling the twinges of pain in the memory of a sad experience. Then she stood tall, looked at the blue-hazed sky and smiled down at her granddaughter, continuing her story:

"Dead ends, yes. I had to think of something, something to free myself from a prison that made me a lesser being. I took my horse and ran away into the hills. No, it was not running away, really. When I raced my horse it was the only freedom I knew. I rode and rode, my mind, my body, my spirit melting in the wind, the wild nature of the hills. I stopped racing my horse when I could go no more! My poor little horse was so tired. It was dark and I realized I was lost. I heard the scurrying of some animal in the dark; it terrified me, so I huddled against a clump of bushes and cried myself into a numbness. Then I decided to die with the night's cold.

"I didn't die with the night's cold, but I almost died after three days of thirst, hunger, and exposure to the heat of the days and the cold of the nights. I had given up when my father's search party found me. He had been looking for two days. I remember how he picked me up in his arms. There were tears in his eyes. Poor dear father. In his blind way he loved me. . . . Well, I came down with pneumonia and was delirious for a long time. There were no miracle drugs then. I awoke one afternoon to see my father hovering over me. He was so gentle and concerned. My first thought was to take advantage of that concern. In

---

[1]very genteel, in French.

a weakened voice I begged him not to force me to marry old Don Ignacio, to let me go to Paris. I remember his eyes widening in angry surprise, a look of disbelief on his face. He gave me a long lecture on the consequences of my rebellion, my unloving manner toward my family, my ingratitude, and on and on. . . . He stormed out my room and refused to come visit me during my recovery. In a way, it was a blessing in disguise. I had time to think."

It was time to gather thoughts and feelings and to put them in perspective. Clotilde surveyed her garden as it were some part of a triumphal memory. "Look around. This garden is so different from the garden in my father's house. It was an impressive garden, manicured to perfection. It had a pond with swans and flowers, all in symmetry, according to color and species. I remember hedge after hedge after hedge. I looked out my window during my recovery and saw some of my little cousins playing hide-and-seek just as I had when I was a child, running from one hedge to another. Two children around four years old were happily playing when a toddler ran toward them. They walked him over to the pond to play. When the child saw the water, he took off his clothes and went in. The water came up to his knees. I saw the nurse running to him, picking him up, shaking him in reprimand. She turned him around and spanked his little bottom. A curious episode of innocence. But the whole day the scene kept coming back into my mind. I was trying to find a solution to my life, and this scene kept intruding. Suddenly I had an answer, a real solution to escape my father's tyranny."

Teresa's eyes awaited the wonderful solution, but Clotilde merely motioned for them to return to the house. Teresa followed Clotilde back into the room where light and shadows played in whispered silences. Clotilde walked to the Gaudier sculpture and touched flowing curves that mated. She kept her hand on the figure as if transferring some unknown energy from the figure to herself. Then she went on with her story.

"After that I became the daughter that my parents wanted. I didn't argue or beg. I simply accepted their plans for my marriage. It was all a feigned acceptance, of course. I pretended great interest in an engagement party they were planning to announce my marriage to Don Ignacio. I was to have the best and most exclusive ball any young girl had ever had. Money was no object. My father, overwhelmed by my docility, told me I could have whatever my heart desired. My heart's desire! He had already forgotten what it was. He meant something he could buy for me.

"So I played his game. 'Papa,' I said, 'I would like a beautiful gown from Paris, by the best designer, elegant, expensive. . . .' I remember how his eyes lighted up. To parade me around in finery that would show off his money, he liked that. 'Of course,' he said, the most expensive gown he could buy. Right away my mother and he set about getting hold of the best Paris couturier and ordering a gown to my specifications. In the following weeks I corresponded with a French designer and told him exactly what I had in mind. At the dinner table I would talk of nothing else, like some frivolous fool! My father was so pleased that I had finally fallen into the routine pattern of genteel women.

"Finally the gown arrived. It was a beautiful gown, with masses of tulle and lace and pearl insets, all done by hand. The French designer assured my father there was no other gown like it in the world. Then my life became a whirl of parties with the fawning Don Ignacio by my side. How I hated the man! What makes old, rich, doddering fools think they deserve a young wife? But I went through all the social rituals and pretended gaiety. At night I would lock the door of my room and put on my Paris gown. I would stare at the image in the mirror, at the beautiful gown, at the face wanting courage, wanting enough valor to carry out the plan. I knew that what I intended to do would assure my freedom."

The afternoon sun had lost its full ardor. The pale coolness of early dusk came through the opened doors. On a line of light, pieces of shadows touched the coming night with a gentle sobriety. It was a time suitable for sadness, part of the long ago and part of the present. Clotilde picked up the threads of her design from so long ago. "I spent a lot of time after that planning a grand entrance at the ball. My father decided that at a precise moment he would make a champagne toast and direct the guests' attention to my entrance, down the long staircase. I would come down wearing my Paris gown. Both my father and Don Ignacio were looking forward to the occasion with great pride. How appropriate! My father would show off the precious possession he was turning over to his very rich friend!

"The night of the banquet I stayed in my room, making myself beautiful, but my thoughts were with my racing horse, the wind, and the taste of freedom. I could hear the music from downstairs, people talking and laughing. The gown was laid out on my bed in full glory. It was really a beautiful thing. But then, my plan was a beautiful plan. Close to the appointed time of my descent, I put the finishing touches to my face, my hair; then, I was ready. I had to be brave. When I opened the door, the orchestra had just begun playing the music for my entrance. My father's voice rose above the music for the toast, making some remark about the long friendship of the two families that were to be united, then the voice of Don Ignacio toasting our future happiness. In my mind's eye I could see all the glasses raised.

"I swallowed hard and slipped silently down the hall to the staircase. I could feel my whole body trembling, but I knew I could not falter. I was at the top of the staircase. I remember how cold the banisters were. My throat was tight and my head high. I did not look down. I guided my footing on each step as I counted. That was what was important, counting the steps to my freedom. There would be no marriage, no convent, no old maid existence for me. I remember the next words that came out of my father's mouth: 'May I present. . . .' Then I heard the cries of disbelief and horror, yes, among all present. Still, I held my head high and looked directly into their faces, all frozen by shock. I saw my mother fall into a faint. And poor Don Ignacio, his face was purple, his mouth gaping. He flung his glass to the floor and left the room without ceremony. But no one noticed because all eyes were on me. After all, how often had they seen a girl of my upbringing, betrothed to the richest man in town, come down a staircase—stark naked. . . ."

Clotilde's hands played with the buttons of her blouse, lost in the memory of her triumph. There was a sudden flurry of curtains touched by wind. Teresa went up to her and kissed her cheek. "You were so brave, so brave. . . ."

Clotilde smiled as she talked about the consequences of her act. "My poor darling father! I will really never know the full extent of his distress, his shame. He couldn't abandon an insane daughter rejected by his best friend. But she couldn't remain in his house as a constant reminder of the scandal she had caused. He had the solution. He would send her away forever with enough funds to stay away. Poor darling father!"

"Were you lonely leaving everything behind?"

"Of course I was lonely, but I've never had any regrets."

"It was all worth it then, . . .the solitary journey."

"Oh, yes, it's all that matters, my child."

Both women looked out of the window and caught the last full colors of the day.

Reprinted from *Rain of Scorpions and Other Stories* (Tempe: Bilingual Press/Editorial Bilingüe, Arizona State University, 1993): 36-46.

ROLANDO R. HINOJOSA-SMITH (1929-)

"Feliz cumpleaños, E.U.A." (1979)

Dos cientos años de vida y muerte tiene este país...Y, según ellos, dos cientos años de independencia... ¡Je! Y cómo se la recargan cada rato... sí, in—de—pen—den—cia, pero no para todos, raza, y que no sean tan hipócritas... Y que tampoco me digan que hicieron la independecia ellos solos... Costó sangre, raza, y mucha de esa sangre fue nuestra... miren, aquí donde me ven, tengo ochenta y siete años y el que me vea dirá que no valgo sorbete... 'ta bien, pero yo también anduve en Francia durante la Primera Mundial... así nomás, igualita que el Maistro Castañeda, sí, señor... ¿y qué? ¿que nunca pertenecimos al 'merican Legion? ¿Y eso qué? ¿Apoco por eso no somos veteranos? Lo que pasa es que no somos encimosos, eso es todo...

¿Y los Santoscoy ¿Se acuerdan del difunto Andrés? ¿Aquel viejito que murió de tis? Bueno, ese viejito, don Andrés Santoscoy y su hermano Pablo junto con Práxedis Cervera, viejo, guerrearon en Cuba a fines del otro siglo... Fíjense... ¿qué negocio tenían allá? P's casi nada diría yo, pero fueron y sirvieron... a ver, ¿cuánta bolillada del Valle fue pa llá? Pos Dios sabrá, ¿y quién se lo va a preguntar a El? ¿Verdá? nada, nada... el ejército vino desde San Antonio buscando vaqueros y esos tres muchachos se dieron de alta así, de un día pa otro, sí señor... Eso es tener hombría, no vayan ustedes más allá...

¿Independencia? ¡Jodencia, palomilla!... Si ellos no fueron los únicos, la raza también supo cumplir como cualquiera... Que ahora anden con eso del wélfer pa cá y del wélfer pa llá y que las estampillas y todo lo demás... ¿Qué? ¿Ya no se acuerdan cuando la crisis de los años treinta? Los bolillos eran los primeros que iban a la casa de corte en Klail City para recibir la comida y la ropa de mezclilla. ¿Y la raza? Poca, palomilla, poca porque nos daba pena y porque éramos muy brutos también... si la comida y la ropa eran para todos... pero no, miento, no era pa todos... ni la independencia fue pa todos...

Las familias viejas que sostenían tierra aquí en el Valle y tierra adentro, allá por Flads, por Clayton, y por Tierra Blanca, allí por esos lugares... bueno, esa gente también derramó sangre cuando la guerra de los sediciosos el siglo pasado... ¡Je! pa que ya no hubiera esclavitud... ¿Qué esclavitud? P's sería la nuestra, porque negritos aquí no había... nada, nada, los negritos no vinieron aquí hasta

este siglo cuando se los trajo el ejército... y sí, señor, allí andaba la raza, en el
ejército de la Unión unos, y con los confederados otros... guerreando como si tal
cosa...

En todo andamos; hasta en la Revolución... Allá fue otro montón de raza
de acá, de este lado... que con Madero, que con Villa, y otros que con Obregón
y así... ¡Otra Independencia!...

Ahorita que les hablaba de la crisis del treinta... ¡je! tan fregados esos tiempos y como quiera que sea allí andaba la raza, juntando dinero para mandarlo a
México para que el país pagara las cuentas que se les debía a las compañías
extranjeras por eso de la expropiación petrolera... ¡Qué cosas! no tiene ni qué...
nosotros vivimos dando a los dos lados... pero eso no importa... es dinero y eso
vuela con el tiempo...

Vamos a ver, ayer, como quien dice, en la Segunda Guerra Mundial... ¿fue
la raza? Hell, yes... y hubo mucha que fue y que nunca volvió: allí están Chanito
Ortega en la invasión de Francia, el Amador Mora en Okinawa, y antes de eso:
Clemente Padilla, prisionero de los japoneses, que tampoco volvió... hubo otros
que sí volvieron, como Vale Granjeno y José María Anzaldúa... ¿Y los heridos?
¿Qué me dicen? Los hubo de a montón, como si fueran uvas, raza...

¿Independencia? ¡Je! ¡Mamalones hipócritas! A ver, ¿cuántos jóvenes perdi-
mos en Korea? Muchachos como Chale Villalón, David "el tío", Pepe Vielma y
muchos más como aquel chaparrito Garcés que volvió medio zonzo... ¡Independecia! No la frieguen... El costo de sostenerla también lo ha pagado la raza; con
creces, gentes, con creces... no me ande a mí con eso de la independencia...

¿Se acuerdan de los tiempo de la Segunda Mundial?... sí, h'mbre, ¿cuando
la bolillada no quiso sepultar a Tito Robledo en el cementerio de Ruffing? Bien
pudo morir en Africa, ¿qué no? y bien pudo caber en el ataúd y en el barco en
que lo devolvieron... ¿verdá? p's sí... pero no cabía en el cementerio de Ruffing...
Sí, sí... aquí mismo en Belken County, raza... Que era mexicano, tú... ¿apoco no
lo sabían cuando me lo mandaron pa África? ¡qué bonito, chingao!... Sí, y como
dije, despues vino Korea y de repente, como si tal cosa, vino el Vietná... y allí
va la raza de nuevo... ah, y esta vez muchos de los bolillos rehusaron ir—sí,
raza—que no iban y no iban y no fueron... ¿qué tal si la raza no hubiera ido, eh?
Se pueden imaginar.

Sí, en Vietná nos llevaron a los niños otra vez, como en las cruzadas de
hace mil años; recién salidos del cascarón y a la guerra... ¡Independencia! bonita
palabra... eso de independencia es algo que nosotros tenemos que probar cada
rato igual que cuando teníamos que mostrar papeles para probar que éramos
ciudadanos de acá, de este lado... nosotros, h'mbre, nosotros los que regamos
surcos enteros con sudor teníamos que probar que nacimos aquí... nosotros que

desenraizamos cuánto huizachal y mezquital que había por allí... ¡je! linda la palabra...

No, a nadie le dan ganas de morir, raza, a nadie... y sin embargo este país parece que se propone matar las cosas duraderas, las cosas de valor... ¿Qué falta de tradiciones, raza! ¡Qué falta de respeto! ¿Y ellos? Ah, p's ellos creen que van muy bien... sí señor, que van rieles, como quien dice...¡Independencia! ¡Mecachís en la palabra! ¡Libertad es lo que deben decir! Y si no la entienden, ¡que se lo pregunten a la raza! Libertad, sí, ésa es la palabra... Independencia, no, independencia es una palabra hueca, la libertad es otra cosa... es algo serio... es algo *personal*...

Esteban Echevarría, originario de Flora, Texas, y vecino de Klail City, cuenta con 87 años y es uno de los pocos ancianos que se hayan escapado de una Nursing Home; vive solo, vive en paz, y como dice él, vive en plena libertad.

Reprinted from *Mosaico de la vida: prosa chicana, cubana y puertorriqueña.* Francisco Jiménez, ed. (New York: Harcourt Brace Jovanovich, 1981): 176-79.

ALEJANDRO MURGUÍA (1949-)

"A Long Walk" (1980; written earlier; revised 1996)

Joaquín flung open the conference room door and stepped out, a brown beret at a rakish angle and a brown leather belt tied around the waist of his safari jacket. Tension, thick as clouds of cigarette smoke, swirled out from the meeting he'd just left; behind him, still inside the room, the tense eyes of the Strike Committee members followed him till the heavy door slammed shut again, blocking out the scene and leaving him on the outside. A noisy murmur rose from the students crowded into the hallway of the Administration Building, some with books in their arms, others with strike posters on their shoulders, smoking cigarettes and drinking coffee. A black dude with a blue beret and military coat strode up to Joaquín and gave him a black power handshake. A Chicano said, "Órale carnal, what's coming down?"

Joaquín pressed between the students, acknowledging their remarks but working his way towards the exit. Several formed a circle around him, asking about the plans of the Strike Committee, hanging on to his every word. He stopped and directed them to the flagpole where a rally was about to start. "Everyone needs to hear this at the same time. We're in this together."

Consuelo worked her way through the mob of students, trying to catch his eye. He saw her and waited, giving her time to catch up, her light brown Afro bouncing in a halo around her head as she squeezed herself past the students. She carried school books under one arm and a round strike button pinned on the lapel of her peacoat. But she looked out of place with her clean pretty face and stylish gray, bell-bottom corduroy pants. Her small Puerto Rican voice held all his attention.

"Joaquín, when's this going to stop?"

He held her hand for a second, knowing she was scared, weren't they all? "There's no turning back, baby. Be strong, we'll survive this yet." And he smiled, keeping it quick and short.

She smiled back bravely. "So what's next?"

"I'm taking a long walk to the flagpole. Meet me there." He knew this wasn't the moment to reassure Consuelo that everything was all right because he didn't know if it was all right, if anything would ever be all right again, so he kept going, pushing through the throng of students anxious for news.

Outside the Administration Building, the sky was blue, smogless, belying the chaos that existed below. It was a good day. A good day to die in L.A., he thought. To his right, reporters lolled around the main entrance to City College, where yesterday and the day before students had blocked the gates with a barricade of cafeteria tables and chairs, and the photo came out plastered all over the front of the *Los Angeles Times*,

RADICAL STUDENT MINORITIES ON STRIKE.

The newspaper didn't bother too much with the issues involved in the strike. To them it was just a headline and a photo. Tomorrow a different headline, a different photo. This morning the barricades were cleared by helmeted, club-wielding police. Half a dozen students, including Benjamín, the chairman of the Political Committee, and Kusati, the head of the Black Student Union (BSU), were in the county jail, but still about forty students picketed the front entrance and distributed leaflets. Counter-demonstrators, jocks and Young Republicans, milled around the pickets, hurling insults and sometimes getting into shouting and shoving matches with them.

The wide green lawn in the center of the school was surrounded by beige, three-story, modern, chrome and concrete buildings. Joaquín saw that already a crowd of students was gathering where the silver flagpole stood erect in the sun, minus its flag. As Joaquín hurried along the edge of the lawn, two Black students and a Chicano came running out of the Arts Building and disappeared into the crowd. A fire alarm went off, followed by an instructor bringing out two smoking trash cans that he left outside the building where they continued smoldering, drifting ashes over the grassy lawn and the students.

Near the center of the school where the naked flagpole stood, the students gathered, talking and waving their picket signs. Some hung around the edge of the lawn, not sure whether to join in or stay away. Other students roamed through the lawn with no direction, sometimes gathering in small groups while smoke from the trash fires filtered over them. The chants of students marching through the English and Social Science Building, spilled from the hallways onto the lawn,

"ON STRIKE! SHUT IT DOWN!
ON STRIKE! SHUT IT DOWN!"

Phillip, head of the Vietnam Vets Against the War and in charge of security, ran up in green fatigues and black combat boots. His long blonde hair was pulled back with a red bandana and his eyes were puffy and bloodshot from lack of sleep. "The Tac Squad just pulled into the southside parking lot. I've got security lined up as buffer between them and us. But that's just a diversion. Another unit is assembling on the football field. They're going to launch a heavy duty sweep of the place, man. You should tell the people what's happening."

Joaquín suggested that the Vietnam vet inform the Strike Committee immediately and get word back to him at the flagpole if there was any change in plans. Phillip took off running to the Administration Building, his fatigue pockets flapping with the weight of leaflets. Joaquín made his way to the flagpole, to where Lucha, with a bandana black as her hair, a zarape over her shoulders, and her round face hidden by a megaphone, led the students in a series of slogans.

"POWER TO THE PEOPLE!
¡EL PUEBLO UNIDO, JAMÁS SERÁ VENCIDO!"

The wail of sirens converged on the school from all directions. The high pitched wail rising and falling, then rising again. It had been like this since a Monday, fourteen long days ago when the strike had started. Joaquín woke up early that morning, maybe six or seven, and sirens were already screaming near City College. He'd rustled Consuelo out of her sleep, and told her to get dressed. The strike wasn't supposed to start till noon, but apparently someone had jumped the gun. Consuelo didn't want him to go, she was afraid for him and didn't understand his struggle. But there was no holding him back. When he arrived at the campus a few minutes later, a black Pontiac was burning at the entrance on Vermont Street.

He'd immediately gone to the cafeteria hoping to find the leaders of the Black Student Union, Students for a Democratic Society, the Student Body Government, and his own leadership of the Chicano Student Organization (CSO). The trouble had started the previous Friday on Slauson Avenue when police attacked a group of Chicano and black junior high school students protesting the lack of Chicano and black teachers. Meetings were held that weekend between CSO and BSU members to decide possible actions against police brutality in their communities (seven Chicanos had been found "suicided" in the East L.A. sheriff's substation that year alone), to discuss lack of sensitivity to minority students at the City College campus, and in support of student strikes in San Francisco, Mexico City, Paris, and other parts of the planet.

That Monday morning the groups gathered in the cafeteria—blacks sat with Chicanos, Chicanos with Anglos—formed a strike committee made up of representatives of all their groups, and including the president of the Associated Students, Terry Maguire. They called for a general strike of students and community, with non-negotiable demands—the end to police brutality in their communities, more students from their ethnic background admitted to schools of higher learning, and an end to the Vietnam war that was killing off their generation. Each of these groups took one of the main entrances to picket. The CSO was assigned the southside entrance near the parking lot. Right away Joaquín ordered cafeteria tables stacked around the gates. First blood of the strike was spilled by a right-wing English prof who had his nose punched by Lucha, the fiery Vice-chair of the CSO, for trying to tear down the barricade.

The strike was on and it moved free wheeling, hit-and-run guerrilla style, a disturbance here, a fire there, a rally outside the President's office, barricades spread to the front entrance and large contingents of students marched with picket signs and chanted around the school and through the buildings,

"ON STRIKE! SHUT IT DOWN!
ON STRIKE! SHUT IT DOWN!"

Fourteen consecutive days they struggled, then each night they met over coffee and cigarettes to discuss tactics and the progress of negotiations with the intransigent administration. They lived wired up on benzedrines, burritos and protest songs. Their decisions reflected more spirit than a base for long-range struggle to go with their immediate goals. But they felt that heady rush of youth doing what they know is right, because you had to stand up for what you believed in. If you didn't believe in Vietnam, Nixon, Agnew & Co. and business as usual, you had to take it to the streets. Bring the war home.

But today Joaquín had seen the faces of the Strike Committee members and they were tired. They were haggard and irritable from lack of sleep, bitching and disagreeing with each other, even threatening each other, paranoid about infiltrators and provocateurs—and when the meeting two nights ago in East Los Angeles did not produce the desired community support, it was clear to Joaquín that the strike couldn't last. They'd had to cut their losses. The students were too disorganized and the strike had erupted too quickly. They had jumped in with all energy and corazón they had, and now he knew the CSO, and all the others were burned out and the strike was finished.

The members of the Strike Committee probably knew the same thing. Hatari, with a lion tooth necklace and colorful dashiki, wanted to continue but offered no real tactics. Maguire, president of the Student Council, advocated throwing in the towel, but promised a bail fund from the Associated Students' budget. Joaquín saw that each day dwindled the pickets and their morale. But how to tell three hundred students who supported your every move for fourteen days, who spent hours on the picket lines, going without sleep, missing classes—all this energy wasted—how do you explain about tactics and directions to them, or that non-negotiable demands means the enemy capitulates totally or you lose? They weren't as strong or as wise as they thought, and now it was all over but the burning, a retreating army leaving nothing to the enemy.

Today, Thursday, the fourteenth day of the strike, after the administration refused for the fifth time to accept their demands, the Strike Committee decided to put the word out to trash the school. A decision that the Strike Committee knew was tantamount to taking hemlock. But if Chicano and other Third World students could not participate in the process of education and if the school was not responsive to the communities' needs, then comfortable Anglo students would be denied the campus as well.

As the highest ranking member of the Strike Committee not in jail, the task of announcing the trashing fell on Joaquín.

Sirens whined up and down Vermont Street, each time more of them. Alarms rang inside the buildings and Joaquín could see students looking out the windows at the lawn and the naked flagpole and the crowd gathered around it. Ready to torch the school if need be, he said to himself.

The surge of emotions buffeted him like a toy ship tossed on a stormy sea. He had no choice. He was angry as the rest, knowing the spilled blood would be washed away and forgotten, and that they were not going to win this time, and that the administration was not going to change admission policies, and that the war would go on and tomorrow or the next day another Chicano would be shot down in the streets of East Los or be found hanging in the sheriff's custody and nobody would give a shit. They had tried these last few days, they had tried hard to change the world and they had failed. Now there was nothing left to do but admit defeat bitter as a poison pill.

He stood next to the flagpole and saw their faces, dark and nutmeg colored, with bandanas and berets, waiting, expectant, angry. And the other faces, pale, with beards and long hair glistening in the sun. He didn't see Consuelo though. Lucha handed him the megaphone.

The crowd wanted to trash. They were in the spirit. Their ancestors had withstood centuries of abuse, and poverty, and had been treated no better than dirt on this land. In the name of their ancestors and themselves they were ready to take revenge, these children of the oppressed.

Joaquín explained the situation, briefly and almost senselessly, because it was senseless what the Strike Committee and all of them were up against. The crowd stirred restlessly before his eyes, like waves beating against each other and he was the cliff they smashed against. Someone in the sea of faces shouted, "We want to trash this mother!"

Teach brother, viva and *right on*, the crowd responded. They knew the administration refused to negotiate their demands. They were tired and frustrated and the word was out already about the arrival of the Tac Squad.

He wanted to tell them to go home, to forget the trashing, to study their mistakes and come back another day, better prepared to take up the struggle. But they wanted action and urged him to give them the word from the Strike Committee.

First, Joaquín told them the Tac Squad was assembling in the parking lot and on the football field, and not to be caught between them because they'd do the cause no good in jail. Then he said, "The campus is yours, do whatever the fuck you want with it."

The crowd cheered him, then abruptly calmed down as the realization of what they were about to unleash, sank in. Joaquín returned the megaphone to Lucha, who then led a column of students toward the Administration Building to burn transcripts. But Joaquín not really sure himself where to go, stayed and watched the crowd melt away only to regroup in four and fives, fatigue- or safari-jacket clad students roaming through the buildings trashing empty rooms, disrupting classes, setting off fire alarms. A few students stayed near the flagpole taunting the approaching Tac Squad before scattering.

A phalanx of riot-helmeted police swept through the lawn, then they turned and stopped at the Language Building where many of the students had taken refuge. Joaquín entered the building through a side door to warn the students to get out. On the second floor, inside one of the rooms, two men, a black and a Chicano, and a white woman, were smashing a table to bits with chairs. Joaquín told them to leave. They looked up, recognized him, and then looked at each other for a moment, before running out of the room, shouting slogans and dragging chairs with them.

The tables and chairs were all upended or on their sides and a map of the world lay torn and crumpled on the floor. Joaquín leaned against the blank chalkboard, exhausted, dirty, and almost defeated. He closed his eyes and his mother's face flashed before him, prematurely worn out from laboring in rich houses, her lifelong dream that their children receive an education turned into this pile of ashes. Joaquín had tried to fulfill his mother's dream but this white man's education was just a bitter joke like his mother's life had been.

Joaquín looked over the scattered classroom that couldn't or wouldn't respond to the needs of his people, and in a flash of blinding anger he picked up the nearest chair and smashed it through a window, raining glass on the Tac Squad below.

Reprinted from *Farewell to the Coast* (San Francisco: Heirs Press, 1980): 25-32. Revised in 1996.

JIM SAGEL (1947-)

"La junta" (1980)

Allí andaban todos los vecinos de Corral de Piedra, la Plaza Larga, la Loma, el Guache y, sí, hasta algunos varones del Corucotown. Estaba el White, con su barrigota fabulosa colgando sobre su faja como la panza de una de sus pobres yeguas preñadas. El White pasaba todo su tiempo con sus animales enfermos (nunca estaba en la casa—su mujer decía que ya se olvidaba de cómo se parecía él) pero, quizás por lo jambao, nunca asistía a sus queridas vacas y marranas—nomás un bloquecito de zacate polvoroso una pura vez al día. El chisme por la vecindad era que su vaca de leche estaba tan flaca y triste que la tenía que parar con unos puntales para que no se cayera cuando la ordeñaba.

También andaba el Bennie, casi acostado en su silleta, hablando recio, excitado como siempre. Después de veinte años en el Foodway echando jarros en sacos, al fin se había graduado a su presente posición de manejar la troca de Frito-Lay por todo el condado de Río Arriba. No existía mejor experto en cómo poner los paquetitos de Fritos en los almacenes que el Bennie. Y aunque se le estaba cayendo el cabello, todavía tenía la cara redonda y vacía de un chamaquito de jaiskul.

La Helen, mamá del Bennie, estaba sentada trabajando en su croché. Estaba platicando de sus enfermedades a los que hicieron el equívoco de sentarse cerca de ella. Si sacaría uno nomás una paladita de tierra por cada síntoma de cáncer, cada dolor del corazón e hígado y cada tragedia de su tritísima vida, ya saldría uno por China. La pobre mujer se animaba desanimando a todas las comadres y vecinas con sus reportes oscuros y mórbidos de su frágil mortalidad. Nomás que todavía jalaba todo el día en su huerta a sus setenta y dos años y andaba las cinco millas para la plaza todas las mañanas para ir a misa y había sobrevivido a dos esposos y cuatro hijos. Y nadie por estas partes estaba apostando en el lado de la muerte.

También entró el Peladito, el único anglo en este bonche de plebe, tardecito como siempre. Y hacía años que había puesto su reloj en "Chicanotime" y, no queriendo llegar puntualmente como un gabacho, siempre aparecía exactamente media hora tarde. El Peladito hablaba más español que la raza y hacía adobes cuando los vecinos estaban comprando las casas movibles. Quizás quería probar algo a alguien, pero era buena gente, tercamente barbechando su chile con un caballo espantoso, casi matándose cuando el animal se arrancaba con el ruidazo que hacía el Billy pasando en su tractor.

—Güenas noches—dijo el Billy, agachando la cabeza para entrar por la puerta chaparrita, resbalándose despacio como un somnámbulo a su lugar junto al fogón. Todos sabían que había visitado la cantinita del Godfather antes de venir a la junta. Con sus ojos hinchados y sus manos temblantes se parecía a un ave grandota y fatigada. Le dio crédito al mitote viejo que los pintores siempre salen borrachos porque pintaba casas cuando no la pasaba en las barras. También era comisionado de la acequia y tenía un rancho grande, pero como siempre andaba dormido e insensato, todos se aprovechaban de él.

—Oyes, Bennie, ¿ah...ah...'ónde está el Godfather? —preguntó el Billy, corriendo las manos por su cabello largo y roñoso.

—Pues, yo no sé, hombre. ¿Que no lo vites 'horita?

—¿Yo? No...no me acuerdo.

La Helen dejó su croché un momento para sacudir la cabeza por su pobre primo borracho mientras que el Bennie volvió su atención a su navaja, experimentando con el filo en los cabellitos de su brazo.

El Godfather, hombre chiquito y más barbón que el mero Moisés, era dueño de una tiendita de comidas, de una cantina y la conciencia de la comunidad. Siempre había estado allí, detrás de la registradora, vendiendo dulces, Bull Durham, y copias del periódico "El Hispano"—dándoles crédito a los viejitos que no tenían el conque para comprar los frijoles, y consejo a los borrachitos mientras que les vendía miniaturas de Old Crow y Seagrams. El Godfather estaba allí predicando de la necesidad de recuperar la tierra antes de que Tijerina prendiera su torcha para quemar el Smokey. El estaba recordando a la gente de su cultura cuando el Corky Gonzales estaba todavía estudiando sus libros de historia. Sí, era el Godfather, y tenía el control de un patrón, pero era un mandamiento muy suavecito, entendido, no forzado—y muchos ni sabían la influenica que él tenía en sus vidas.

—Pero, ¿dónde anda ese Godfather?—dijo el Peladito.

—Oyes—le preguntó el Bennie—, ¿qué está pasando con el Waldo Gold?

—Ay, ¿quién sabe? Ahora el cabroncito tiene otro engaño nuevo. Como ya no puede vender los solares en pedazos chiquitos, se ésta vendiendo el terreno a sí mismo, pero en otro nombre. Luego va a subdividir esa tierra en el tamaño que quiere y nos quedamos en lo mismo.

Este Waldo Gold era un desarrollador de tierra, un hombre completamente sin principios y sin vergüenza. Hacía tiempo que él había querido hacer una subdivisión grande de casas movibles. Pero estaba queriendo hacerla en un terre-

no regado, uno de los ranchos más finos y grandes antes que lo vendió el difunto
Pedro por nada. Y los vecinos sabían bien que una ciudad nueva de cienes de
"trailers" iba a acabar con sus jardines y animales, con su agua y soledad, con
su modo de vivir que casi no había cambiado por siglos.

Ahora este Gold quería tirar los álamos ancianos, echar cemento en la
acequia de los Salazares y poner brea en el camino viejo, cambiando su nombre
al "Camino de Oro". El no podía entender a esta gente—hasta había puesto un
nombre español al camino y todavía no se quedaron satisfechos. Pero no le
habían valido todos sus planes grandes de crear una plaza nueva en su imagen
porque los vecinos se habían juntado, cosa que le dio sorpresa, como él había
figurado que eran puros borrachos e ignorantes. Pero el Peladito había estudiado
las leyes sobre el desarrollo de la tierra hasta que sus ojos se quedaron del mismo
color que las manzanas que comía todas las noches. La Helen había interrumpido
su recitación de dolores para telefonear a los miembros del Concilio de la Plaza,
recordándoles que ella había bautizado a sus hermanos y rezado por sus papaces.
Y seguro que el Godfather había platicado con todos, voz que alcanzaba a más
gente que el radio KDCE (¿Qué Dice?) que reverbera de la sierra Jémez hasta
el valle del Río Chama.

Y, al último, este atajo de rancheros, viejitos y, sí, borrachos (porque el
Gold había dicho bien ahí—nomás que como era borrachos de raza, se defen-
dieron) ganaron. Pero, como el ladrón-cabrón que era, de una vez Gold comenzó
a buscar modos de escapar leyes. Y por eso se había juntado la plebe—otra
vez—a decidir qué hacer ahora.

—Pero, ¿cómo vamos a tener una junta sin el Godfather?—dijo el White,
rascándose el estómago.

—Allí viene ahora —reportó el Bennie, mirando por la ventana a una
troquita que se arrimaba.

Pero no era el duende juicioso el que entró, sino los desperados del Mafia.
Estos cincos hombres, amiguitos desde la juventud, vivían cerca del Arroyo Loco
y siempre andaban juntos. Ni uno se había casado todavía aunque el Pollo vivía
a ratos con su pollita, la Corrine, sobrina de la Helen.

Entró el Primo (sobrenombre para Primitivo), que siempre usaba un sombrero aceitoso, uno de esos de cuero y ala grande que usan los bandidos en el
mono. Luego se apareció el José Gordo en la puerta, hombre grosero que todo
el tiempo traiba[1] una risa en la cara y un arma en la bolsa. No era hombre violento, nomás que se sentía más hombre, más macho, con su pistola allí cerca de

---

[1]traía.

sus huevos. Antes, la colgaba en su faja, pero ya el Chief Valdez lo había "bos-teado" tantas veces que la traía escondida en las olas de manteca que llevaba en su cinta.

Luego entraron "los Lovers", el Butch y el Rocky Vigil. Todos les llamaban "los Lovers" aunque naiden supo la razón—quizás era porque eran cuates y tan parecidos que ni su tía Helen los podía distinguir la mitad del tiempo. El último para pasar por la puerta era, naturalmente, el Pollo, un muchacho que no decía más que "ese vato". Y de una vez comenzó a dar la mano a todos (al estilo Chicano), saludándoles con su "ese vato", en veces sustituyendo "ese guy" para la variedad. Después de este ritual, todo el Mafia se sentó en las últimas silletas allí atrás, contra de la pared.

—¿Dónde está el Godfather?—preguntó el Pollo al Billy, pero ya el Billy andaba en el otro mundo.

—Pues, ¿quién sabe?—respondió el White por su compañero pasado.

—Bueno, no está en la cantina—y según la risada que le dio, no había duda que ellos habían andado allá.

—¿Qué vamos a hacer con ese pinche Gold?—anunció el José Gordo, acari-ciando su Colt .45 como si fuera un gatito querido.

—¿Saben que está tirando todos los árboles en la 'cequia?—dijo el Pollo.

—Y no sólo eso, bro—añadió el White—. También puso esos caños en la 'cequia ya.

—El no tenía el permiso de los comisionados pa'hacer eso, ¿no, Billy?

—¿Qu...qué?—respondió el pobre, despertándose un poquito.

La Helen dejó su croché un momento a sacudir la cabeza mientras que el Billy se cayó otra vez en su sueño profundo y el Mafia daba risotadas.

—Yo creo que vamos a tener que conseguir a un abogado—dijo el Peladito, queriendo restablecer un poco de orden.

—¡Qué abogado ni abogado!—exclamó el José Gordo—. ¿Qué chingados queremos con otro ladrón? Yo sí lo puedo correr de aquí.

—¿Cómo?—le preguntó el White.

—Pues, cosa simple, vato. Nomás le damos una espantadita y ahí se va a huir hasta Texas. ¿Que no, Primo?

El Primo, que nunca decía nada porque los bandidos valientes siempre están callados (y también a causa de andar bien engrifado siempre), nomás se zampó el sombrero.

—El Godfather debería de llegar—dijo el Peladito. Ya le estaba dando ansias a él. ¿Qué demontres ha pasado con él?—pensaba entre sí. El Godfather nunca había faltado a una junta—no importara si anduviera casi muerto de cansa-do o enfermo en la cama, él siempre iba a las juntas.

Y había algo en este fregado Mafia que no le gustaba esta noche al Peladito. Estaban bastantes inocentes, nunca haciendo más daño que tirar sus botellas de Michelob en el camino donde se paraban a mearse. Pero el Peladito no tenía nada de confianza en ese José Gordo con sus disimulos, su pistola y su malvado machismo. Y cuando se juntaban reteborrachos como estaban esta noche, pues, un equivoquito y ...

—¡Vámonos, plebe!—gritó el José Gordo—. Vamos a enseñar una lección a ese perrito güero.

—Cuidado—dijo la Helen, con una mirada imperativa en la dirección de su hijo.

—Espérense un ratito, hasta que venga el Godfather—oró el Peladito. El sabía que el Godfather les podía calmar un poco.

—No, no...ya no viene. No se preocupen. No lo vamos a lastimar—nomás espantar un poquito. Vamos. Vamos—Primo, Pollo...

Y se fueron. Con un barullo se salieron—después de que el Pollo dio la mano a todos, diciendo: "Bueno, bro".

Dejaron la casita de adobe en silencio. No se oyó más que el resuello pesado del Billy y la agujas incesantes de doña Helen.

—Dónde está el Godfather?—preguntó el Peladito a la pared. Afuera disparó una pistola.

Reprinted from *Tunomás Honey* (Tempe: Bilingual Press/Editorial Bilingüe, Arizona State University, 1983): 81-91.

ALBERTO ÁLVARO RÍOS (1952-)

"Then They'd Watch Comedies" (1984)

"Leocadio, you've been fighting again."

"Yes, mama."

"What happened? You look terrible."

"They were calling me 'Leo' again."

"No."

"Yes."

"And you fought?"

"Yes."

"Did you win?"

"Yes."

She took a deep breath, too loud to be real breathing. "Get cleaned for dinner. I'll make your favorite."

"I really beat that other guy up."

His mother nodded from side to side, but smiled. "Wait till I tell your father."

"He will be proud, no?"

"Yes."

He *was* proud, and said so, and hit Leocadio on the side of the chin, and even though it hurt, Leocadio smiled. He had done right, now, finally. He had found someone, smaller, who was dumb enough to tease him when he was alone, no guys to back him, so Leocadio beat him up, beat him up good. Finally. Leocadio was as proud as his father, or because of his father, and he was going to look for that guy again tomorrow, maybe. Maybe he would steal his girlfriend, too.

Everyone sat at the table to eat, and Leocadio was smiling.

"Potatoes *con huevo* for that son of mine. You could smell them cooking, no?"

"Yes."

"Of course he could," said his father to his mother, or to himself, "that's a smart head on that son, yes." His father hit him, a little harder, on the chin again, pretending he was a boxer.

"That hurts," said Leocadio this time. His hands stayed on the table and did not try to protect his face.

"Yes, but it feels good, no? Where are the girls tonight?"

"Babysitting. Oh, Leocadio, Julieta wants you to walk her home tonight. She'll call when she's ready. You'll do it?" his mother raised her eyes to ask, as she served the dinner.

"Yes, but I don't see what she's so worried about. She's so ugly nobody will ever try to. . . ."

"Leocadio!" his mother interrupted him.

"No, really, even if it was boot black and they were sure not to get caught . . . ."

"Leocadio!" again. His mother put her hands on her hips.

"And somebody paid them to. . . ."

"Le-o-ca-dio!" this time.

"Where did it happen?"

"What, papa?"

"Where did you hit this guy?"

"In the parking lot. A bunch of my guys. . . ."

"No, I mean, on the face? Did you hit him on the face or did you just push each other around until somebody tripped like a bunch of, you know, *jotitos*?"

"No, I hit him, papa. He was bleeding all over the place. On his shirt."

"Leocadio," said his mother. She was not yelling. Or laughing, now.

"And then I hit him again before I left because he wouldn't promise not to call me Leo."

"So you hit him again?"

"Yes, papa."

"Did you hear that," said his father, looking at his mother this time, "another Reies Madero. That's what we have here, another Madero, but one that doesn't lose."

"It was only one fight, papa. I only ever got beat up before. Every time."

"Eat your dinner, Leocadio, it will get cold. You too," said his mother to his father. She put some tortillas that she had been warming on the table, and took one out for each of them.

"Where are the girls tonight?" asked his father. Leocadio looked at his mother.

"Babysitting. And Leocadio, I want you to leave Maricela alone when she's with her boyfriend this time."

"But mama, they are all by themselves in there when she is babysitting. Do you want something to happen? More babies, maybe?"

"Leocadio!" said his mother.

"Just because she finally gets a boyfriend you're so worried for her. She's only eighteen, what does she know?"

"But Leocadio, you're only fourteen," said his mother.

"I know, and 'what do I know.'"

"What do you know?" said his father. "Ha. Reies Madero sits here and says 'what do I know.' Chh, what a joke." His father laughed, by himself, and hit him on the chin. Never a real laugh, hardly ever, he couldn't even remember when, thought Leocadio.

"Eat," said his mother.

"But my jaws hurt," said Leocadio.

"Ha, hurts. What did you do to that other guy, anyway? What did you say his name was?"

"It was. . . ."

"Besides making him bleed. I mean, why was he bleeding? Teeth? Nose? Both? Ha, lower?"

"Ay, no. Leocadio, you didn't?"

"Like they all did to me, mama, all those times. I just hit him papa. I don't know what I did. I don't know where."

"And he bled, no?"

"Yes."

"What was his name," asked his mother, this time.

"I don't know. I think he's still in Junior High."

"White?" asked his father.

"Yes."

"But not after you left him. Chh."

"Is he okay?" Maybe this was worse than she thought.

"I don't know, but I hope not."

"Leocadio!"

"Madero!" said his father, and tried to hit him again. It was too hard, and Leocadio moved his chin to miss most of it.

"I don't care, mama. They were all calling me Leo, and they wouldn't stop. I kept yelling but they wouldn't."

"So you beat them up, yes?" asked his father.

"No, I just kept yelling first. Then they left except for that one guy who came out and yelled 'Leo Leo Leo Leo, for his breakfast he drinks pee-o!' and I told him to cut it out because. . . ."

"You were alone, no?" asked his father. He was smiling. But it was a father smile, the kind he gave to other men when his wife wasn't looking. Leocadio's stomach got tighter.

"No, there were some other guys, some friends of mine, Johnny and the others. But I told this guy I didn't care what he said like that. . . ."

"What!" No smile now.

"I mean like 'pee-o' and that stuff. Just that he better not call me Leo, just like you said, papa, because that's not my name, not like that, right? I told him he'd better call me Leocadio or else. I told him, a lot of times."

"Leocadio," said his mother. Just like that.

"So you hit him?" asked his father.

"No, not until I asked him what he was going to call me and he said 'Leo' again. Then I hit him. I beat him up."

"Hooo, you showed him. Chh. That will teach him."

"No!" Leocadio shook his head hard, aimed at his father, then got up and left the table.

"Leocadio!" his mother said.

"Where are the girls, anyway?" asked his father, finishing dinner.

Afterward, Leocadio's father washed the dishes, and Leocadio came out of his room to dry. His father would do the dishes, but took no care to clean the grease, the colors from the chips in the plates or the rims of the glasses. Leocadio rubbed them off, the color of potato, of ketchup. The rubbing made a sound like a cat that thinks it's about to get stepped on, but realizes after its first noise, no, still safe.

"The girls should be doing this. Chh," said Leocadio's father, shaking his head from side to side and showing Leocadio the front of his shirt, which was wet.

"They're working." The argument was old, and everyone had been through it. The women should be doing this, the women should be doing that, said his father. But he only worked part-time. They brought in the money, the real money. Leocadio's mother worked at S.H. Kress, and had worked there since high school. The girls were always babysitting, and had been babysitting since before they were women, before almost they could tie their own shoes.

"Still, this is a woman's job, Leocadio. Where is your mother?"

"Washing."

"She should be watching this. Two grown men washing dishes. Washing dishes! Chh."

"I'm only fourteen."

"After today? Ha. Only a man does what you did, beating up those guys like that."

Leocadio shook his head. "One guy. He was smaller than I was, you know. And I think maybe they made him say those things. The other guys he was with before, I mean."

"Made them bleed."

"Because he wouldn't say my name, papa. Like what happened to you when they called *you* 'Leo'—or tried to call you Leo—when you were a kid and came here. Tell me again how you took care of them, all those kids that called you that."

"Beat them up."

Leocadio's mother came into the room with an arm full of clothes. She shook her head as she listened to the last part of the conversation. The clothes she held were mostly women's clothes. "You have nothing more you need washed?"

"Always washing," said Leocadio's father. "You should stop that and wash the dishes, or not use so many dishes. Always grease. You get them so dirty."

"I have to look clean. And you, too. Where are your clothes?"

"There aren't any."

"What do you mean?"

"I didn't dirty any."

They all went quiet. Clean clothes meant no work, and to talk about no work was to talk about the weather—warm, hot, snowing, it didn't matter. It couldn't be changed now. Leocadio motioned to his mother that she was holding his only dirty clothes, so she left the room. She had no time to go through it all now. She had spent half of her life talking about the weather.

"Should be washing dishes," said his father under his breath to Leocadio as his mother left. Leocadio kept drying. "Knocked the shit out of them is what I did," continued his father.

Later, Leocadio's father came out of his room in his underpants to watch TV. He did that whenever the girls weren't home. Everyone watched TV at night, but they always had to watch what Leocadio's father chose. Always a police story. Sometimes a western. Leocadio liked comedies better, and so did his mother, and so did his sisters. The nights his father left and came back drunk or with other men were almost worth the shouting. Sometimes his mother gave his father money. He always got so angry after this that he'd go out again and get more drunk because he said that *he* should be giving *her* money. She couldn't win. She'd say, then, what for? she didn't drink, and he would get even angrier and say that all she was good for was three children, no more, that was no wife, and then he would go out with horse legs, the way a big horse brings all the weight of his body down on each hoof. It was all right, his mother would say. Then they'd watch comedies, Leocadio and his mother and his sisters. It hurt, but sometimes it was better.

Now his father turned the channels. Leocadio watched the bluegreen Virgin de Guadalupe, massive on his forearm, Channel 9, 10, her head turned, 11, her eyes. "There, this one." And hair coming through her, all over, a blanket, high grass. She was always warm. His father went back to the couch which, when he was home, was all his.

"You have a hole in your *calzones*," said Leocadio's mother to his father. She had been watching, too.

His father looked down at his underwear. "So, I told you last week and you still haven't fixed them, and what's happened to the girls, anyway? Are they too good for this kind of work? Hole in everybody's head! Except for Leocadio there." He was talking to no one, no one was in the room except Leocadio, and he wasn't talking to him. "He puts holes in people's heads, other people's heads, where they belong." He reached for an unopened Coors on the shelf next to the couch. He had finished one, but always brought two cans so that he would not have to get up. No one would bring beer for him anymore, no matter how much he shouted. The night was beginning, like others.

"Not other 'people's' heads, papa. One guy. And I doubt it was a hole. And he was smaller than I was, a lot smaller. And they made him do it. And he never would call me Leocadio. And you'll probably get a note from school, or a call or something because they'll say I was picking on him."

"Well maybe it was a hole. You can't say about these things."

"No."

"Humph. But it bled. I mean, you hurt him."

"Yes. A lot."

"Leocadio, stop now." His mother had been in and out of the room, sometimes putting away clothes, sometimes watching TV. She looked tired tonight, thought Leocadio. More than usual.

"But I didn't enjoy it papa, not really. I mean, I really did hurt him. It hurt enough to hit him. I'm sore."

Leocadio's father looked at him and nodded his head up and down, without words. Yes, up, down. Yes, slowly.

"It wasn't worth it, papa."

Leocadio's father looked at him and said, "It was," but turned back to the TV even before he had finished.

Leocadio shook his head from side to side, without words, trying to speak the other language, too.

His mother, father, and Leocadio watched TV for a long time. It was almost time for the news. His father's head was back, chin up so that it almost touched his eyelashes.

"Hey," said his mother to his father, "don't go to sleep. Maricela will be home soon. And it's almost time for you," she looked at Leocadio, "to go get Julieta."

"Okay," said Leocadio.

"Hey," said his mother to his father again, "get dressed or go to bed." His father made a noise from somewhere between languages. Sometimes he got stuck there. "Did you get a check this week?" She had forgotten to ask.

"Yes, I got one. One dollar, that's what I got, one."

"Silly," said his mother. "Where is it? I'm going to the bank tomorrow."

"In my pants. Go get it, will you," his father motioned to Leocadio with his head, the way men do.

Leocadio went into his parents' bedroom to get the check, and came back with it in his hands.

"Papa," said Leocadio.

His father spoke a noise from the space between languages again. He spoke from the lost place a father and a son never share together, but both use. Especially those with the same name.

"Give it to me, Leocadio," said his mother.

"Wait. Papa."

"What do you want," asked his father, but only as a half-question.

"This check says 'Leo' on it."

"Come here, Leocadio, just give it to me," said his mother.

"Mama, stop it. Papa?"

"What?" said his father, trying to close his eyes like before. It didn't look the same.

"This check says 'Leo' on it."

"It's a check. Give it to your mother."

Leocadio dropped the check and looked. "PAPA!" he yelled.

"Leocadio!" His mother tried to turn him from his direction, from his words.

"Papa, it says, 'LEO' on it!"

His father raised himself on his elbow, like the women in old movies.

"LEO!"

"Leocadio," said his mother, without volume. His father waved at her to stop.

"It does, it says that," said his father.

"But you've worked there enough times, a lot of times. They know, they *have* to know."

"I'm not sure." He shrugged his shoulders. His whole body moved, too much for the motion of shrugging.

"Papa!"

"Leocadio, stop!" His father raised his voice. "You stop yelling, what have I taught you, if you *ever* yell at your mother. . . ."

"What have you taught me? What have you *taught* me? And I *wasn't* yelling at my mother. That has nothing to do. . . ."

"Stop it Leocadio. It says 'Leo' on it. What do you think I am, stupid?" He sat up. "You think that I am so stupid that I can't see that the women work in this house and the men stay home?"

"What stupid?"

"Yes, stupid. It says 'Leo' on it, it does, I know it. It could say 'asshole' on it and I'd still take it."

"Ay, no," said his mother. Leocadio wished she wasn't here.

He shook his head, "But. . . ."

"No, you've been doing all the yelling. It's my turn. Twelve-year-old, fourteen, whatever. I've worked all my life, Leocadio, starting when I was younger than you are, with pain." Leocadio clicked his teeth and dropped into a chair. "So, you've heard that, so what. When I was young a man, a black man, I worked with black men, a kind of work that wasn't nice, that's the kind of work I had to do, he told me, 'If you got your head in the lion's mouth you better use the other hand to pet it.' That's what he said and I never forgot it. You know what that means?"

Leocadio turned his face.

"Oh, that's pretty, turn away, sure. I can't. I got a family. You know what that means? It means that I could leave that family all alone, start again, but I never would. It means I could give up everything, but I never would. It means there's a way out, real easy, staring everybody in the face but that doesn't make it like, whatever, the right way. Chh."

"Letting them call you Leo sounds pretty easy. Real easy. Get off it."

"No. No, that's the hardest. You don't know what the hard way is, you've just got to realize. . . ."

"I've got to realize? I almost got killed out there today, and I almost killed. He was bleeding."

"I'm sorry. But you didn't kill him. You don't know what that is. . . ."

"Bleeding because he wouldn't do what you told me he *should* do, *had* to do."

"I'm sorry, well. . . ."

"No you're not, you loved it."

"No, I. . . ."

"You loved it. That's all you could talk about."

"It hurt."

"Hurt? Hurt? You're a liar!"

"Leocadio!" his mother could only say.

"No, no you're right. It felt good. Felt good to make you a man. You could be a man."

"For who? For who, papa? It hurt me, it still hurts, my jaw hurts, from where he hit me, from where *you* hit me even."

"Me. It's true. It felt good. It felt good for me."

"Oh thanks, papa, thank you a lot." Leocadio turned his head fast, as a batter turns to get a call after not swinging.

"Thanks papa is right, that's right. You *should* thank me. You should thank me for *not* fighting, for *not* getting bloody, for *not* getting my jaw hurt."

"Thank you for *what*? I can't believe what you are saying."

"We're alive, we're here. *You* can *fight*!"

"Is that what you've given me, is this a gift? Is that what it is? A Christmas present?"

"But *you can fight*!"

"Fight? Who wants to? And for what? What now? That kid still didn't call me Leocadio, papa. I fought to get the same results you do, only I hurt more. I hurt a lot more. For nothing."

"Hurt? Ha. It feels good, you just don't know." His father showed his teeth, but not really like a smile. It didn't work. Leocadio wanted to shout at it.

"Papa, it doesn't. It doesn't feel good."

"It does." And he was in his underwear.

Leocadio shook his head. His neck felt strong, but because it was tight. "You don't fight, you get along, but that doesn't make it right. *I* fight, I don't get along, but is *that* right? No," his neck felt strong, still, the wrong way, "no, it isn't uh uh. I don't want it."

"It will make you different than I am. More."

"Anything is more. I can take the middle and I am more, too. And it doesn't hurt. I don't bleed. No fighting, no getting along, nothing. Just moving. Just not talking."

"There is no middle." His father shook his head, slowly this time. The other language.

"There is." Leocadio could not hear those other words, but he, too, could speak them. With his whole body, by the roots of his neck, he nodded his head up and down, now, yes and yes.

"No one lives on a bridge, Leocadio."

"Unless he has to, papa, unless that's the only place left, unless that's the only place left that doesn't hurt."

"Then I named you right, Leocadio. Twelve, fourteen, you will see. You're no different from me."

"I'm going to get Julieta."

Reprinted from *The Iguana Killer: Twelve Stories of the Heart* by Alberto Álvaro Ríos, Copyright ©1984 by Alberto Álvaro Ríos. Reprinted by permission of Confluence Press at Lewis-Clark State College, Lewiston, Idaho.

HELENA MARÍA VIRAMONTES (1954-)

"The Moths" (1985)

I was fourteen years old when Abuelita requested my help. And it seemed only fair. Abuelita had pulled me through the rages of scarlet fever by placing, removing and replacing potato slices on the temples of my forehead; she had seen me through several whippings, an arm broken by a dare jump off Tío Enrique's toolshed, puberty, and my first lie. Really, I told Amá, it was only fair.

Not that I was her favorite granddaughter or anything special. I wasn't even pretty or nice like my older sisters and I just couldn't do the girl things they could do. My hands were too big to handle the fineries of crocheting or embroidery and I always pricked my fingers or knotted my colored threads time and time again while my sisters laughed and called me bull hands with their cute waterlike voices. So I began keeping a piece of jagged brick in my sock to bash my sisters or anyone who called me bull hands. Once, while we all sat in the bedroom, I hit Teresa on the forehead, right above her eyebrow and she ran to Amá with her mouth open, her hand over her eye while blood seeped between her fingers. I was used to the whippings by then.

I wasn't respectful either. I even went so far as to doubt the power of Abuelita's slices, the slices she said absorbed my fever. "You're still alive, aren't you?" Abuelita snapped back, her pasty gray eye beaming at me and burning holes in my suspicions. Regretful that I had let secret questions drop out of my mouth, I couldn't look into her eyes. My hands began to fan out, grow like a liar's nose until they hung by my side like low weights. Abuelita made a balm out of dried moth wings and Vicks and rubbed my hands, shaped them back to size and it was the strangest feeling. Like bones melting. Like sun shining through the darkness of your eyelids. I didn't mind helping Abuelita after that, so Amá would always send me over to her.

In the early afternoon Amá would push her hair back, hand me my sweater and shoes, and tell me to go to Mama Luna's. This was to avoid another fight and another whipping, I knew. I would deliver one last direct shot on Marisela's arm and jump out of our house, the slam of the screen door burying her cries of anger, and I'd gladly go help Abuelita plant her wild lilies or jasmine or heliotrope or cilantro or hierbabuena in red Hills Brothers coffee cans. Abuelita would wait for me at the top step of her porch holding a hammer and nail and empty coffee cans. And although we hardly spoke, hardly looked at each other as we worked over root transplants, I always felt her gray eye on me. It made me feel, in a strange sort of way, safe and guarded and not alone. Like God was supposed to make you feel.

On Abuelita's porch, I would puncture holes in the bottom of the coffee cans with a nail and a precise hit of a hammer. This completed, my job was to fill them with red clay mud from beneath her rose bushes, packing it softly, then making a perfect hole, four fingers round, to nest a sprouting avocado pit, or the spidery sweet potatoes that Abuelita rooted in mayonnaise jars with toothpicks and daily water, or prickly chayotes that produced vines that twisted and wound all over her porch pillars, crawling to the roof, up and over the roof, and down the other side, making her small brick house look like it was cradled within the vines that grew pear-shaped squashes ready for the pick, ready to be steamed with onions and cheese and butter. The roots would burst out of the rusted coffee cans and search for a place to connect. I would then feed the seedlings with water.

But this was a different kind of help, Amá said, because Abuelita was dying. Looking into her gray eye, then into her brown one, the doctor said it was just a matter of days. And so it seemed only fair that these hands she had melted and formed found use in rubbing her caving body with alcohol and marihuana, rubbing her arms and legs, turning her face to the window so that she could watch the Bird of Paradise blooming or smell the scent of clove in the air. I toweled her face frequently and held her hand for hours. Her gray wiry hair hung over the mattress. Since I could remember, she'd kept her long hair in braids. Her mouth was vacant and when she slept, her eyelids never closed all the way. Up close, you could see her gray eye beaming out the window, staring hard as if to remember everything. I never kissed her. I left the window open when I went to the market.

Across the street from Jay's Market there was a chapel. I never knew its denomination, but I went in just the same to search for candles. I sat down on one of the pews because there were none. After I cleaned my fingernails, I looked up at the high ceiling. I had forgotten the vastness of these places, the coolness of the marble pillars and the frozen statues with blank eyes. I was alone. I knew why I had never returned.

That was one of Apá's biggest complaints. He would pound his hands on the table, rocking the sugar dish or spilling a cup of coffee and scream that if I didn't go to mass every Sunday to save my godamn sinning soul, then I had no reason to go out of the house, period. Punto final. He would grab my arm and dig his nails into me to make sure I understood the importance of catechism. Did he make himself clear? Then he strategically directed his anger at Amá for her lousy ways of bringing up daughters, being disrespectful and unbelieving, and my older sisters would pull me aside and tell me if I didn't get to mass right this minute, they were all going to kick the holy shit out of me. Why am I so selfish? Can't you see what it's doing to Amá, you idiot? So I would wash my feet and stuff them in my black Easter shoes that shone with Vaseline, grab a missal and veil, and wave good-by to Amá.

I would walk slowly down Lorena to First to Evergreen, counting the cracks on the cement. On Evergreen I would turn left and walk to Abuelita's. I liked her porch because it was shielded by the vines of the chayotes and I could get a good look at the people and car traffic on Evergreen without them knowing. I would jump up the porch steps, knock on the screen door as I wiped my feet and call Abuelita? mi Abuelita? As I opened the door and stuck my head in, I would catch the gagging scent of toasting chile on the placa. When I entered the sala, she would greet me from the kitchen, wringing her hands in her apron. I'd sit at the corner of the table to keep from being in her way. The chiles made my eyes water. Am I crying? No, Mama Luna, I'm sure not crying. I don't like going to mass, but my eyes watered anyway, the tears dropping on the tablecloth like candle wax. Abuelita lifted the burnt chiles from the fire and sprinkled water on them until the skins began to separate. Placing them in from of me, she turned to check the menudo. I peeled the skins off and put the flimsy, limp looking green and yellow chiles in the molcajete and began to crush and crush and twist and crush the heart out of the tomato, the clove of garlic, the stupid chiles that made me cry, crushed them until they turned into liquid under my bull hand. With a wooden spoon, I scraped hard to destroy the guilt, and my tears were gone. I put the bowl of chile next to a vase filled with freshly cut roses. Abuelita touched my hand and pointed to the bowl of menudo that steamed in front of me. I spooned some chile into the menudo and rolled a corn tortilla thin with the palms of my hand. As I ate, a fine Sunday breeze entered the kitchen and a rose petal calmly feathered down to the table.

I left the chapel without blessing myself and walked to Jay's. Most of the time Jay didn't have much of anything. The tomatoes were always soft and the cans of Campbell soups had rusted spots on them. There was dust on the tops of cereal boxes. I picked up what I needed: rubbing alcohol, five cans of chicken broth, a big bottle of Pine Sol. At first Jay got mad because I thought I had forgotten the money. But it was there all the time, in my back pocket.

When I returned from the market, I heard Amá crying in Abuelita's kitchen. She looked up at me with puffy eyes. I placed the bags of groceries on the table and began putting the cans of soup away. Amá sobbed quietly. I never kissed her. After a while, I patted her on the back for comfort. Finally: "¿Y mi Amá?" she asked in a whisper, then choked again and cried into her apron.

Abuelita fell off the bed twice yesterday. I said, knowing that I shouldn't have said it and wondering why I wanted to say it because it only made Amá cry harder. I guess I became angry and just so tired of the quarrels and beatings and unanswered prayers and my hands just there hanging helplessly by my side. Amá looked at me again, confused, angry, and her eyes were filled with sorrow. I went outside and sat on the porch swing and watched the people pass. I sat there until she left. I dozed off repeating the words to myself like rosary prayers: when do you stop giving when do you start giving when you do . . . and when my hands fell from my lap, I awoke to catch them. The sun was setting, an orange glow, and I knew Abuelita was hungry.

There comes a time when the sun is defiant. Just about the time when moods change, inevitable seasons of a day, transitions from one color to another, that hour or minute or second when the sun is finally defeated, finally sinks into the realization that it cannot with all its power to heal or burn, exist forever, there comes an illumination where the sun and earth meet, a final burst of burning red orange fury reminding us that although endings are inevitable, they are necessary for rebirths, and when that time came, just when I switched on the light in the kitchen to open Abuelita's can of soup, it was probably then that she died.

The room smelled of Pine Sol and vomit and Abuelita had defecated the remains of her cancerous stomach. She had turned to the window and tried to speak, but her mouth remained open and speechless. I heard you, Abuelita, I said, stroking her cheek, I heard you. I opened the windows of the house and let the soup simmer and overboil on the stove. I turned the stove off and poured the soup down the sink. From the cabinet I got a tin basin, filled it with lukewarm water and carried it carefully to the room. I went to the linen closet and took out some modest bleached white towels. With the sacredness of a priest preparing his vestments, I unfolded the towels one by one on my shoulders. I removed the sheets and blankets from her bed and peeled off her thick flannel nightgown. I toweled her puzzled face, stretching out the wrinkles, removing the coils of her neck, toweled her shoulders and breasts. Then I changed the water, I returned to towel the creases of her stretch-marked stomach, her sporadic vaginal hairs, and her sagging thighs. I removed the lint from between her toes and noticed a mapped birthmark on the fold of her buttock. The scars on her back which were as thin as the life lines on the palms of her hands made me realize how little I really knew of Abuelita. I covered her with a thin blanket and went into the bathroom. I washed my hands, and turned on the tub faucets and watched the water pour into the tub with vitality and steam. When it was full, I turned off the water and undressed. Then, I went to get Abuelita.

She was not as heavy as I thought and when I carried her in my arms, her body fell into a V, and yet my legs were tired, shaky, and I felt as if the distance between the bedroom and bathroom was miles and years away. Amá, where are you?

I stepped into the bathtub one leg one leg first, then the other. I bent my knees slowly to descend into the water slowly so I wouldn't scald her skin. There, there, Abuelita, I said, cradling her, smoothing her as we descended, I heard you. Her hair fell back and spread across the water like eagle's wings. The water in the tub overflowed and poured onto the tile of the floor. Then the moths came. Small, gray ones that came from her soul and out through her mouth fluttering to light, circling the single dull light bulb of the bathroom. Dying is lonely and I wanted to go to where the moths were, stay with her and plant chayotes whose vines would crawl up her fingers and into the clouds; I wanted to rest my head on her chest with her stroking my hair, telling me about the moths that lay within the soul and slowly eat the spirit up; I wanted to return to the waters of the womb with her so that we would never be alone again. I wanted. I wanted my Amá. I removed a few strands of hair from Abuelita's face and held her small light head within the hollow of my neck. The bathroom was filled with moths, and for the first time in a long time I cried, rocking us, crying for her, for me, for Amá, the sobs emerging from the depths of anguish, the misery of feeling half born, sobbing until finally the sobs rippled into circles of sadness and relief. There, there, I said to Abuelita, rocking us gently, there, there.

"The Moths" by Helena María Viramontes is reprinted with permission from the publisher of *The Moths and Other Stories* (Houston: Arte Público Press, University of Houston, 1985): 23-28.

GARY SOTO (1952-)

"Looking for Work" (1985)

One July, while killing ants on the kitchen sink with a rolled newspaper, I had a nine-year-old's vision of wealth that would save us from ourselves. For weeks I had drunk Kool-Aid and watched morning reruns of *Father Knows Best*, whose family was so uncomplicated in its routine that I very much wanted to imitate it. The first step was to get my brother and sister to wear shoes at dinner.

"Come on, Rick—come on, Deb," I whined. But Rick mimicked me and the same day that I asked him to wear shoes he came to the dinner table in only his swim trunks. My mother didn't notice, nor did my sister, as we sat to eat our beans and tortillas in the stifling heat of our kitchen. We all gleamed like cellophane, wiping the sweat from our brows with the backs of our hands as we talked about the day: Frankie our neighbor was beat up by Faustino; the swimming pool at the playground would be closed for a day because the pump was broken.

Such was our life. So that morning, while doing-in the train of ants which arrived each day, I decided to become wealthy, and right away! After downing a bowl of cereal, I took a rake from the garage and started up the block to look for work.

We lived on an ordinary block of mostly working class people: warehousemen, egg candlers, welders, mechanics, and a union plumber. And there were many retired people who kept their lawns green and the gutters uncluttered of the chewing gum wrappers we dropped as we rode by on our bikes. They bent down to gather our litter, muttering at our evilness.

At the corner house I rapped the screen door and a very large woman in a muu-muu answered. She sized me up and then asked what I could do.

"Rake leaves," I answered, smiling.

"It's summer, and there ain't no leaves," she countered. Her face was pinched with lines; fat jiggled under her chin. She pointed to the lawn, then the flower bed, and said: "You see any leaves there—or there?" I followed her pointing arm, stupidly. But she had a job for me and that was to get her a Coke at the liquor store. She gave me twenty cents, and after ditching my rake in a bush, off I ran. I returned with an unbagged Pepsi, for which she thanked me and gave me a nickel from her apron.

I skipped off her porch, fetched my rake, and crossed the street to the next block where Mrs. Moore, mother of Earl the retarded man, let me weed a flower bed. She handed me a trowel and for a good part of the morning my fingers dipped into the moist dirt, ripping up runners of Bermuda grass. Worms surfaced in my search for deep roots, and I cut them in halves, tossing them to Mrs. Moore's cat who pawed them playfully as they dried in the sun. I made out Earl whose face was pressed to the back window of the house, and although he was calling to me I couldn't understand what he was trying to say. Embarrassed, I worked without looking up, but I imagined his contorted mouth and the ring of keys attached to his belt—keys that jingled with each palsied step. He scared me and I worked quickly to finish the flower bed. When I did finish Mrs. Moore gave me a quarter and two peaches from her tree, which I washed there but ate in the alley behind my house.

I was sucking on the second one, a bit of juice staining the front of my T-shirt, when Little John, my best friend, came walking down the alley with a baseball bat over his shoulder, knocking over trash cans as he made his way toward me.

Little John and I went to St. John's Catholic School, where we sat among the "stupids." Miss Marino, our teacher, alternated the rows of good students with the bad, hoping that by sitting side-by-side with the bright students the stupids might become more intelligent, as though intelligence were contagious. But we didn't progress as she had hoped. She grew frustrated when one day, while dismissing class for recess, Little John couldn't get up because his arms were stuck in the slats of the chair's backrest. She scolded us with a shaking finger when we knocked over the globe, denting the already troubled Africa. She muttered curses when Leroy White, a real stupid but a great softball player with the gift to hit to all fields, openly chewed his host when he made his First Communion; his hands swung at his sides as he returned to the pew looking around with a big smile.

Little John asked what I was doing, and I told him that I was taking a break from work, as I sat comfortably among high weeds. He wanted to join me, but I reminded him that the last time he'd gone door-to-door asking for work his mother had whipped him. I was with him when his mother, a New Jersey Italian who could rise up in anger one moment and love the next, told me in a polite but matter-of-fact voice that I had to leave because she was going to beat her son. She gave me a homemade popsicle, ushered me to the door, and said that I could see Little John the next day. But it was sooner than that. I went around to his bedroom window to suck my popsicle and watch Little John dodge his mother's blows, a few hitting their mark but many whirring air.

It was midday when Little John and I converged in the alley, the sun blazing in the high nineties, and he suggested that we go to Roosevelt High School to swim. He needed five cents to make fifteen, the cost of admission, and I lent him a nickel. We ran home for my bike and when my sister found out that we were going swimming, she started to cry because she didn't have the fifteen cents but only an empty Coke bottle. I waved for her to come and three of us mounted the bike—Debra on the cross bar, Little John on the handle bars and holding the Coke bottle which we would cash for a nickel and make up the difference that would allow all of us to get in, and me pumping up the crooked streets, dodging cars and pot holes. We spent the day swimming under the afternoon sun, so that when we got home our mom asked us what was darker, the floor or us? She feigned a stern posture, her hands on her hips and her mouth puckered. We played along. Looking down, Debbie and I said in unison, "Us."

That evening at dinner we all sat down in our bathing suits to eat our beans, laughing and chewing loudly. Our mom was in a good mood, so I took a risk and asked her if sometime we could have turtle soup. A few days before I had watched a television program in which a Polynesian tribe killed a large turtle, gutted it, and then stewed it over an open fire. The turtle, basted in a sugary sauce, looked delicious as I ate an afternoon bowl of cereal, but my sister, who was watching the program with a glass of Kool-Aid between her knees, said "Caca."

My mother looked at me in bewilderment. "Boy, are you a crazy Mexican. Where did you get the idea that people eat turtles?"

"On television," I said, explaining the program. Then I took it a step further. "Mom, do you think we could get dressed up for dinner one of these days? David King does."

"*Ay, Dios,*" my mother laughed. She started collecting the dinner plates, but my brother wouldn't let go of his. He was still drawing a picture in the bean sauce. Giggling, he said it was me, but I didn't want to listen because I wanted an answer from Mom. This was the summer when I spent the mornings in front of the television that showed the comfortable lives of white kids. There were no beatings, no rifts in the family. They wore bright clothes; toys tumbled from their closets. They hopped into bed with kisses and woke to glasses of fresh orange juice, and to a father sitting before his morning coffee while the mother buttered his toast. They hurried through a day making friends and gobs of money, returning home to a warmly lit living room, and then dinner. *Leave It to Beaver* was the program I replayed in my mind:

"May I have the mashed potatoes?" asks Beaver with a smile.

"Sure, Beav," replies Wally as he taps the corners of his mouth with a starched napkin.

The father looks on in his suit. The mother, decked out in earrings and a pearl necklace, cuts into her steak and blushes. Their conversation is politely clipped.

"Swell," says Beaver, his cheeks puffed with food.

Our own talk at dinner was loud with belly laughs and marked by our pointing forks at one another. The subjects were commonplace.

"Gary, let's go to the ditch tomorrow," my brother suggests. He explains that he has made a life preserver out of four empty detergent bottles strung together with twine and that he will make me one if I can find more bottles. "No way are we going to drown."

"Yeah, then we could have a dirt clod fight," I reply, so happy to be alive.

Whereas the Beaver's family enjoyed dessert in dishes at the table, our mom sent us outside, and more often than not I went into the alley to peek over the neighbor's fences and spy out fruit, apricot or peaches.

I had asked my mom and again she laughed that I was a crazy *chavalo* as she stood in front of the sink, her arms rising and falling with suds, face glistening from the heat. She sent me outside where my brother and sister were sitting in the shade that the fence threw out like a blanket. They were talking about me when I plopped down next to them. They looked at one another and then Debbie, my eight-year-old sister, started in.

She had entered her profanity stage. A year later she would give up such words and slip into her Catholic uniform, and into squealing on my brother and me when we "cussed this" and "cussed that."

I tried to convince them that if we improved the way we looked we might get along better in life. White people would like us more. They might invite us to places, like their homes or front yards. They might not hate us so much.

My sister called me a "craphead," and got up to leave with a stalk of grass dangling from her mouth. "They'll never like us."

My brother's mood lightened as he talked about the ditch—the white water, the broken pieces of glass, and the rusted car fenders that awaited our knees. There would be toads, and rocks to smash them.

David King, the only person we know who resembled the middle class, called from over the fence. David was Catholic, of Armenian and French descent, and his closet was filled with toys. A bear-shaped cookie jar, like the ones on television, sat on the kitchen counter. His mother was remarkably kind while she put up with the racket we made on the street. Evenings, she often watered the front yard and it must have upset her to see us—my brother and I and others—jump from trees laughing, the unkillable kids of the very poor, who got up unshaken, brushed off, and climbed into another one to try again.

David called again. Rick got up and slapped grass from his pants. When I asked if I could come along he said no. David said no. They were two years older so their affairs were different from mine. They greeted one another with foul names and took off down the alley to look for trouble.

I went inside the house, turned on the television, and was about to sit down with a glass of Kool-Aid when Mom shooed me outside.

"It's still light," she said. "Later you'll bug me to let you stay out longer. So go on."

I downed my Kool-Aid and went outside to the front yard. No one was around. The day had cooled and a breeze rustled the trees. Mr. Jackson, the plumber, was watering his lawn and when he saw me he turned away to wash off his front steps. There was more than an hour of light left, so I took advantage of it and decided to look for work. I felt suddenly alive as I skipped down the block in search of an overgrown flower bed and the dime that would end the day right.

BEVERLY SILVA (1930-)

"The Cat" (1986)

I divide the world into cat lovers and cat haters. I have discovered that no matter what people say, deep down in their hearts, no one is indifferent to cats. I had a lot of growing up to do to become a cat lover, and now I test people by their reaction to my cats. Now don't jump to the conclusion that I am one of those eccentric old ladies with eight or ten cats. I once had five cats, but now I only have two, and one of these belongs to my young daughter.

A few months ago I made a resolution that one cat was enough for any woman. With tears in my eyes I set out to find suitable homes for my other three cats. This was not an easy job as cat lovers already had cats, and I could never let a cat hater care for one of my pets out of a sense of pity or obligation. But as determination is one of my weaknesses, within a few days all my cats were comfortably settled.

The reasons for my decision to send away those whom I loved came about due to an unexpected and traumatic moment of insight into my personality. I was luxuriously reclining in my pink bath tub full of warm soft bubbles one Saturday evening when my cats started fighting. This annoyed me immensely as I am a softhearted person who wants above all for everyone to love everyone else.

I had a date with Joe that night which I was complacently looking forward to, and I needed time to make myself beautiful for him. While I lay in the tub thinking that if I ignore the noise for awhile perhaps the cats will quiet down, the phone rang. Damn! I keep saying I'll take the phone into the bathroom during moments like this so if it rings I won't have to jump out all drippy and rattled to answer it. Somewhere in the back of my mind, however, is the unanswered fear of whether or not one can be electrocuted by answering a phone while lying in the tub. I keep intending to ask someone about this, but I never remember until I am in the bath tub and the phone rings.

Oh well. I climbed out of my warm retreat all drippy and rattled and answered the phone.

"Yes," I said.

"Hi baby, this is Super Sam."

Pause. Groan. He was drinking again.

Deep male laugh. "You know who this is?"

"Of course. Pete. Your voice is too distinctive to hide."

"Put on something sexy and come over."

Anger. Compassion. "Look Pete, I've told you before you are a charming, brilliant guy, and lots of fun—when you are sober."

"I'm sober, baby."

"Sure, and I'm Marilyn Monroe."

"You sure are."

Pause. Frustration.

"C'mon. Bring me a pot of coffee and I'll promise to behave. We'll listen to Frank Sinatra, and have a quiet evening by the fire."

Temptation. "Pete. . . ."

Crash. One of the cats had just knocked over my favorite Italian vase full of straw flowers. Ring. The doorbell. "Pete—hold on."

I walked across the loving room careful not to step on the broken pieces of vase, and opened the door a crack. It was Laughing Jack. Standing there in a red turtleneck sweater, tight black slacks, boots, beard, flashing brown eyes, and that everlasting grin. Him you couldn't keep out. He came and went like a falling star.

"Hey," he said in that right on voice of his, "you look fantastic in that towel."

I had forgotten my situation, but then it didn't really matter with Jack.

"Hold on Jack, I'm on the phone."

"Pete. . . ."

"What's going on there?" Anger? Pause.

"Hey beautiful, you got a house full of birds or something?"

I stuck my head around the corner towards the kitchenette and saw Jack picking up pieces of bread which the cats had pulled off the table and dragged around the room. Ordinarily I would have laughed. I wondered why I didn't now.

"Are you still there?" It was Pete. More anger? Anxiety?

"Look Pete, a few things have come up."

"You know what, baby. You've got one of the sloppiest minds I've ever seen."

"What!!"

"I said you've got a sloppy mind."

"Well. . .fuck you. . .goodbye." I slammed down the receiver.

Jack was sitting there laughing at me, in my favorite chair, his feet on my glass top coffee table, a glass of my last bottle of imported Spanish wine in his hand. I looked at him closer than usual.

"What do you want?" I asked him. I wanted to be nice, but deep within me the urge to slug someone was asserting itself.

"Get dressed, beautiful. We're going to the jazz concert."

"Did it ever dawn on you I might have other plans?"

"Change them."

Something inside me was beginning to snap. I had wanted to go to that concert all week. I love jazz. I had even considered going alone. On Wednesday, Tom had called to ask what I was doing over the weekend, and I mentioned the concert, but he doesn't dig that kind of thing. Then Friday, Joe had called and invited me to one of those parties he goes to every Saturday night. As my week had not gone well, and I had no other prospects, and my young daughter was spending the weekend with my ex-husband—I refuse to call him her father— what I had once considered a dull evening sounded very pleasant, and I graciously accepted his invitation.

I became aware that I was glaring at Jack while all this churned through my mind. He was looking me up and down as I sat in the wicker rocker I had slumped into after slamming down the phone, with a damp towel wrapped around me and my hair in rollers. He was grinning as usual. Laughing Jack. He reminded me of a character out of Shakespeare, but I couldn't remember which one.

"Look Jack, I really can't go, and I'd like you to leave now."

"O.K., beautiful. You're still the sexiest girl in a towel I ever knew." Out the door he went, laughing as always. I guess he will die laughing.

I shut the door behind him, and locked it. Now why did I do that, I wondered. Oh well, fuck it. The phone rang again. It was Joe. He called to tell me he would be a little late.

Something was coming over me again. "You know what, Joe?"

"What?"

"Just don't bother coming at all."

"Well what the hell gives with you?"

"You. That's what. I find you boring and inconsiderate, and I always have, and I detest those phony parties you go to every week, and I think you're in a rut, and. . . ."

He hung up. Men, I growled. Men and their stupid screwed up male egos. Who needs them?

I picked up one of my cats at random and clung to it. It was a fluffy, gray, once-stray, alley cat. It cried and tried to get away. I held it tighter. I sank down on the sofa, and the cat eventually relaxed in my arms and quit fighting. Tears started rolling down my face, slowly at first, then stronger until my whole body was torn with sobbing. I gave in, not asking why, or caring. Hours later I realized I had fallen asleep, and it was dark. My cat was still in my lap, sleeping peacefully.

It was after that I decided one cat was enough for any woman. Hesitantly, may I add, I also decided that one man was enough for any woman, if one could find the right man. And if a woman can find the right cat, I guess she can find the right man.

Reprinted from *The Cat and Other Stories* (Tempe: Bilingual Press/Editorial Bilingüe, Arizona State University, 1986): 7-10.

MIGUEL MÉNDEZ-M. (1930-)

"Huachusey" (1986)

Timoteo no era tan pobre, después de todo, era dueño de un burro. El esqueleto del burro de Timoteo no era secreto para nadie, aquel animal analfabeto parecía radiografía. Quién iba a pensar que Timoteo saldría de su pueblo mexicano, Las Animas, y que en ese burro flaco se pasearía por todos los Estados Unidos. Así fue, un día amaneció con la ventolera y sin más ni más agarró camino y se fue. Antes le dijo a su burro, "Anda, vamos, tú y yo tenemos mucho que conocer".

Primero llegó a un pueblo de nombre Tucson. Quiso saber de quién era un hotel muy alto muy bonito. Para luego le preguntó a un güero. ¿De quién es este changarro, oiga? "What'd you say?" ¡Ah! de modo que este hotel es de Huachusey. Qué hombre tan rico debe de ser ¡caramba!

En los Angeles entró con todo y burro a Disneyland. Tanto gozó de ver las maravillas que vio, que abrazó a su burro y de paso a una joven platinada que estaba a su lado. ¿A poco también esto es de Huachusey? "What'd you say?" respondió la mujer. Luego lo dijo, con seguridad, que esto es de Huchusey. ¡Qué rico es!

Timoteo entró a San Francisco montado en su burro. Cuando iba sobre el puente Golden Gate, como había mucha neblina creyó que era puente entre la tierra y el cielo. Asombrado preguntó por el dueño. Una muchacha más rubia que el trigo maduro, de ojos grandes y muy azules, lo miró extrañada con una sonrisa amable y a su vez le preguntó, "What'd you say?" Qué hombre tan poderoso es Huachusey, todo es de él.

Así dijo Timoteo, y siguió en su burro rumbo a Nueva York. Cuando llegó a Nueva York preguntó que si de quién era un edificio muy, muy alto, que se llama Empire State. Un viejo sordo, con perfil de gavilán, poniéndose una corneta en la oreja le gritó, "What'd you say?" Diablo de gringo tan reterrico, pos también esto es de él. ¡Qué va! no cabe duda que es muy rico, Huachusey.

En un pueblo que se llama Boston, le dieron ropa y comida a media plaza. Timoteo le preguntó a uno de los que repartían cosas a mucha gente pobre, que si quién era el que daba "What'd you say?" ¡Ah! con que es él, ya era hora que diera algo, tiene tanto, tanto, tanto. Qué bueno que es generoso Huachusey. Dios le dé más. De cada cosa que le llamaba la atención igual, preguntaba Timoteo por el dueño, y todos le contestaban igual: Huachusey.

Las largas caminatas iban haciendo más y más flaco al burro de Timoteo. Si se le hubiera caído el cuero habría quedado en los puros huesos. Un día, Timoteo le dijo a su burro, "Vámonos, mi flacucho, a nuestro pueblo Las Animas, ya tenemos mucho que platicar".

Al cruzar por un pueblo muy grande que se llama Chicago, Timoteo notó un revuelto de mucha gente. Se acercó y vio a mujeres y a hombres llorando muy afligidos. En la calle yacían muertos a balazos, muchachos y muchachas que sangraban. Timoteo le preguntó a un policía que parecía estatua de concreto, que si quién los había matado. "What'd you say?" dijo el guardián. Qué raro pensó Timoteo, rico este hombre y anda de matón. Si no lo viera no lo creería. A unos les da y a otros los mata. Huachusey...

Por tanto trajín y desvelos, Timoteo se tornó preocupado y sombrío. Huachusey se le había convertido en un dilema, que por más y más que meditaba no podía comprender. Qué raro hombre es este Huachusey: rico, generoso y a veces cruel...

Después de muchos días de caminar, pasaba Timoteo por un pueblo llamado San Antonio, rumbo a Las Animas. A su burro ya no le quedaba cuero y se le había acabado la carne. Timoteo volvía montado en un esqueleto. Fue allí en San Antonio donde Timoteo se topó con un funeral donde marchaban en procesión gentes de todos lugares y de todos los tiempos. Oía cánticos y rezos y el llanto apagado que las pisadas le arrancan a la tierra, camino del cementerio. Timoteo vio que iba hacia él una mujer alta y descarnada que pisaba más arriba de la tierra y se cubría con velo de telaraña. Ni siquiera le dio tiempo a preguntar. ¿Sabes quién murió? preguntó la mujer y antes de que hablara Timoteo agregó, es él, Huachusey. Despertó sonriendo y haciendo planes. Le habían llevado un gran desayuno a la cama. Quiso decir algo y se le quedó entre los dientes una palabra congelada. Ya Huachusey, duerme, duerme, tu mañana será ayer.

Timoteo abrió los brazos en cruz y rezó, los ojos llenos de lágrimas. Luego enfiló rumbo a su pueblo, sin darse cuenta que recién se lo habían borrado del mapa.

Han pasado muchos años y todavía se recuerda esta historia a través de los pueblos de Aztlán. Hay quienes la cuentan en versos que oyeron de sus abuelos.

> Cruzando bosques y pueblos
> por allá va un mexicano
> trota que trota en su burro flaco.
> Se ríe de los desiertos

y no le importa el invierno.
¿Y de quién es ese hotel?
Amigo, es de Huachusey.
¿De quién los caminos pavimentados?
Pos, son del mismo pelao,
el mentado Huachusey.
¡Ah, qué rico debe ser!
Es dueño de Disneyland.
Oiga, el puente ese ¿de quién es?
Pos, diga a cuál puente pues.
El que cruza aquel chamaco.
¿Ud. dice el Golden Gate?
Pos, de quién había de ser
sino del mismo gabacho,
al que nombran Huachusey.
¿Y de quién son estos campos
que cruzan estos caminos?
Son del mismo dueño, amigo.
¡Ay qué rico es ese gringo!
Por allá va el mexicano
cruzando por Nueva York.
¡Qué no se me raje el burro!
Quiero ver a ese señor.
Todos los barcos son de él
y también los aeroplanos.
Tienen tiendas y cantinas
y muchos miles de carros.
¡Ah, qué hombre ese Huachusey
tan rico y tan afamado!
Ya me voy para mi tierra;
tengo hambre y estoy cansado;
ya me duelen mis tripitas.
¡Ay, qué rico americano!
Paloma de las alas negras
pos, ¿qué es aquello que veo?
Están enterrando a un hombre
allá en aquel cementerio.
¡Ay, cómo lloran por él!

Si quieres saber su nombre,
se llamaba Huachusey.

Reprinted from *De la vida y del folclore de la frontera* (Tucson: Mexican American Studies & Research Center, University of Arizona, 1986): 73-77.

GLORIA VELÁSQUEZ (1949-)

"Fugitive" (1987)

Había muerto solo, como Antonio, lejos de su casa, abandonado, sin la presencia de aquellas figuras dulces de su infancia, la caja de chocolate a su lado que Bridget y yo le habíamos traído de París, aquellos chocolates finos dulces que tanto placer le habían ofrecido a su cuerpo delgado, convertido ahora en otra estadística, otro miserable número de aquella ciudad cosmopolita a donde había ido hacía veinte años para hacerse la vida. Se me vino a la memoria aquel día en la capital cuando me había dicho que se iba lejos, que ya no aguantaba vivir de mentiras: "Me voy Esperanza. Ya no aguanto todo esto", y en una voz lejana como la de aquellos ríos solitarios de mi niñez que tantas veces me habían suplicado hasta que me sentaba a escucharlos, me presentó a Marcos comentando que los dos se irían juntos a los Estados Unidos. Había sentido celos al conocer al joven de pelo rubio y ojos azules que parecía demostrarle tanto afecto, pero al mismo tiempo sentí un alivio enorme al saber que alguien lo estaba queriendo como Daniel se lo merecía. Le había dado entonces la dirección de Bridget, haciéndolo prometerme que la llamaría en cuanto llegara a los Estados Unidos.

Años después, al andar con Bridget caminando desoladas en la madrugada por las calles, me acordaría de aquel día y de todas las escenas que actuamos los cuatro en el apartamento pequeño de Bridget; la melancolía de Daniel al escuchar un bolero antiguo de Antonio Aguilar y sus incontrolables celos cuando Marcos se nos acercaba para mostrarnos el álbum más reciente que acababa de comprar. Imposible borrarlo todo. Ni por que dudarlo. Ni por que olvidar aquellas tardes cuando juntos caminábamos por las calles de La Misión comentando la última exposición de arte chicano, la cara orgullosa de Daniel al indicarle a Bridget la artesanía mexicana que aparecía en las ventanas humildes de los negocios latinos y las risas que soltaba cuando Bridget trataba de repetir aquellas palabras con su pronunciación gringa. Pero también me acordaba de otros momentos repletos de amargura y de angustias cada vez que se enfrentaba con un niño abrazando fuerte a su papá en el parque como él había hecho tantos domingos pasados en el parque Chapultepec. Huérfano ahora, prófugo, tratando de olvidar aquellas últimas palabras: "Maricón, joto sin vergüenza, hijo de la chingada".

Recibí su llamada esa mañana y me había regresado a la ciudad para despedirlo y ofrecerle mi apoyo a Bridget que había pasado tantas noches infinitas a su lado limpiándole el sudor de la cara, ofreciéndole chocolates a fin de romper el silencio con sus comentarios frívolos—la última actuación de Raúl Julia o la exposición de arte impresionista que acababa de llegar. En el pasillo me había abrazado fuerte, murmurando, "¿Qué haré sin él, Esperanza? Dímelo, ¿qué haré?" Después en el cuarto, pálida, su cuerpo hinchado aun más por el dolor que la tenía atrapada al lado de su viejo amigo con el cual había suplicado que lo hiciera creer que valía mierda el pasado, que le leyera de las últimas páginas que acababa de escribir, que le cantara de aquellos antiguos versos mexicanos hasta verlo quedarse dormidito en sus brazos inflados. Teníamos que espantar a las sombras, a los malditos recuerdos, a los periodistas con sus cámaras siniestras, listos para retratar al difunto y reportar en el *Chronicle* la nueva estadística, la perdida de otro hijo de Sodoma y Gomorra, aquel infierno de maldad.

Llegaron, pues, los dos ángeles a la ciudad a la caída de la tarde; caminaban en silencio con la cabeza agachada, sus rostros escondidos debajo de sus mantas oscuras, deteniéndose para tocar a cada puerta que encontraban para así poder advertirle a la gente de la peste que se había apoderado de cada rincón de la ciudad. Pero sus advertencias eran inútiles, pues todos estaban asustados por la cantidad de muertos que seguía aumentando y que había dejado las calles llenas de cadáveres—viejos, jóvenes, negros, latinos—todos consumidos ya por la apestosa enfermedad.

Desesperados, los dos ángeles le suplicaron a Dios:

"Y si se salvaran unos cincuenta..."
Pero nadie le respondió.
"Y si se salvaran unos treinta..."
Pero todavía nadie les hizo caso.
"Y si se salvaran unos veinte..."
Pero todavía Dios no quiso escuchar.
"Y si se salvara sólo uno..."

Pero aún así, El no tuvo misericordia. Enojado, uno de los dos ángeles murmuró, "Maldito, maldito sea Dios" y el otro, asustado por las blasfemias que escuchaba le replicó, "No digas eso; ¿qué no ves que nos puede estar escuchando?" Pero aquél no le prestó atención y otra vez lo maldijo. Palideció entonces el ángel asustado, exclamando ansiosamente, "Vámonos ya, muy pronto destruirá la ciudad", pero aquél le contestó, "No, vete tú; yo ya no me voy. Aquí me quedaré ayudando a los que pueda".

Se separaron entonces los dos ángeles, el uno desapareciendo en el camino por donde había llegado y el otro entre la sombra de los grandes edificios de la ciudad que poco a poco se hundían por el peso enorme de la muerte.

Ese mismo año Jimmy Lee Swaggert había profesado: "Not only is the homosexual worthy of death, but also those who *approve* of homosexuality."

Falleció durante una de esas madrugadas grises y lluviosos de la ciudad y lo enterramos Bridget y yo un triste domingo, otro dimanche, sin la presencia de aquellas señoras vestidas de luto apretando sus escapularios, listas para hincarse y rezarle los nueve rosarios, solas las dos, sin la presencia de Marcos que ni una sola vez había querido acercársele, obsesionado por aquel mismo miedo que se apoderaba de todos los habitantes de la ciudad. Bridget se había peleado con Marcos hasta gritarle y echarlo del apartamento de Daniel sin siquiera lograr convencerlo de su responsabilidad. Pero yo no había resistido; lo había persegui-do una tarde, sitio tras sitio hasta que por fin lo había encontrado en un rincón oscuro, borracho, murmurando los versos tristes de los Beatles. Le había rogado que me acompañara.

—Te estoy rogando Marcos. Hazme caso, cada rato pregunta por ti. ¿Qué no comprendes que se está muriendo? ¿Qué te van a costar cinco minutos?

Había subido la cabeza dejándome llevar por la inmensa corriente que parecía querer tragárselo como había hecho con Antonio.

—No puedo Esperanza, lo siento pero no puedo. Me puede contagiar más, ¿no ves que muy pronto seré yo el que sigue?

Lo había maldecido entonces—cobarde, puto, desgraciado—escupiéndole y dándole con una botella hasta partirle la cabeza y ver la sangre escurrir por sus manos. Había ido entonces con una furia a las calles, gritando, dando patadas a los basureros, a los perros hambrientos, a las viejitas chinas, maldiciendo al mar, a los turistas que me miraban con piedad, a mi reflejo, al puente monstruoso, espantando a monjas como en aquellos versos de Neruda, rodando las calles de la ciudad como loca, jalándome las greñas, pellizcándome hasta por fin dejarme caer como bola aplastada en el cemento frío en un rincón sucio y oscuro, acom-pañada por los demás seres perdidos, bag ladies, winos, hundidos todos en el olor de orines y vómitos.

Ahora me han traído a este cuarto rectangular infomándome que necesito descansar, recuperarme, recobrar la razón para poder funcionar de nuevo en la

sociedad. Bridget me ha venido a visitar con una caja enorme de chocolates; me
ha platicado de la película más reciente sobre Frida Kahlo, del nuevo restorán
vietnamita pero no le hago caso. Sigo sentada aquí en el mismo lugar, delante
de la misma ventana recordando los versos de aquel poeta de La Misión que
tanto le gustaban.

"I've had
to bear
the days
anonymously
like a shadow
slip
through the city
without raising
suspicions
I've avoided
innumerable
roads
jumped
every fence
fleeing
always
with a haste
that bites
my heels
& barely
lets me breathe

hiding behind
so many
illusions
during
so many years
now
I don't
even recognize
the face of
my soul
nor remember

what brought me
to this fugitive's life

my crime
must have
been
as huge as
the darkness
found in
my punishment
above all

I've sought
the mute
company
of night

I've learned
to fake
almost
everything
but
still
when next to you
I'm given away
by the empty
pounding
of my heart"[1]

Maricones todos aquellos que no han sabido querer.

Reprinted from *Cuentos chicanos II* (El Paso: Dos Pasos Editores, 1987): 119-24.

---

[1]Poema original de Francisco X. Alarcón, aparece en *Ya vas carnal*, San Francisco, Ca.: Humanizarte Press, 1985. *Author's note.*

RICARDO AGUILAR MELANTZÓN (1947-)

"Cumplir mi justa condena..." (1987)

Le sacaba entrarle al camello,[1] en Alburquerque[2] iba a tener que poner la pompa a andar,[3] le caía buti sura[4] aventarse a pespunte largas cuadras en el sol del desierto, las suelas le quemaban las plantas de los pies y la chompeta le ardía bajo el rayo amarillo a través de la poca greña negra que le quedaba, allí el que no tenía carro estaba jodido, el camión se tarda un friego y cuesta más y las distancias más cortas son enormes a patín,[5] los brazos se le cansaban de cargar las bolsas de papel que le asaban en el Safeway, el mandado a cuestas, lo que habría de refinarse esa semana, un cartón de leche, un apio metido en celofán para que no se hiciera todo lacio al día de estar metido en el refri, unos tomates chicolillos que mejor fueran cerezas, un six de Bud y otras cosas de la casa, a patín porque había dejado la moto parada en el patio del chante,[6] juntando polvo, lluvia, lodo y todas las inclemencias que se le pueden ocurrir al pinche meteoro que pasa a madres de este a oeste continuamente sobre Juárez, sin dar tregua, que se mete por todas las rendijas y se aposenta en todos los rincones de todas las casas, por atrás de todos los muebles, en los dobleces de todas las cortinas, de todas las orejas, de todos los párpados, de las coyunturas y los espacios entre los dedos de los pies, en cada cabello, en todos los lomos de todos los libros y hasta en las intimidades osculantes de los novios, por todas las troneras y las ventanas más herméticas, que hace masticar con el cuidado extremo que requiere ingerir lija y que se complace en crear remolinos precisamente en el pequeño patio en que espera la moto, como perro fiel, con ganas de que el amo la eche a andar y la saque a pasear, aunque sea un ratito, aunque sea nomás

---

[1] el trabajo o la labor.

[2] Albuquerque; las variantes ortográficas en este ensayo son del autor.

[3] esforzarse mucho.

[4] muy seguro.

[5] a pie.

[6] hogar o casa.

alrededor de la cuadra, aunque no la saque de primera, aunque el aceite aún esté frío en el momento de apagarla, pero que le demuestre que la quiere, que no la ha olvidado, que aún siente placer en recibir el aire sobre los párpados y sentirlo estramar el cabello con mayor velocidad que el soplador automático, allí, tapada con un todo bien grueso que la Rosi, compadeciéndose, le amarró para protegerla del marciano ventarrón de octubre que se ha sabido capaz de pelarle la pintura al carro mejor pintado, hasta el vivo metal, en cuestion de

horas.

Con cada paso el loco Edumenio quiere recobrar la dicha que sintió el día que la trajo a la casa, al principio pareció que el paquidérmico dueño no habría de poder montarla, que se le quebraría en tres pedazos bajo las jamónicas piernas, el torso inmenso, el amplio vientre que ya lucía su trigésima llanta de bicicleta inglesa, bajo los suspiros continuos que le causaba cargar con el chaleco de grasa, pero no, pues todos se sorprendieron con la asombrosa destreza, el espíritu de Hell's Angel[7] conque comenzó a maniobrar las vueltas, las esquinas, la increíble suavidad conque cambiaba de velocidades y hacía que su mueble lo transportara veloz sobre una nube de polvo, conque rebasaba a los demás escondiendo una pequeña sonrisa que intimaba su alegría, su gozo, de poder hacer algo mejor que todos los flacos de la cuadra, mejor que todos los elegantes que continuamente se mofaban de su falta de gracia, con una lisura casi automática, se sorprendían al verlo irse al jale[8] en las mañanas, como nuevo caballero, adarga y lanza, y de como llegaba por las tardes quemado del viento y frenaba frente a la casa blanca, a la mitad del callejón, bajando la pierna izquierda y sosteniendo el animal sobre la bota de 30 agujeritos, pasaba el pinche puente sin contratiempos, sin esperas, todas las mañanas, inmiscuyéndose entre los carros que hacían las impacientes e interminables líneas frente al que se le acababa de meter uno que quería cambiar de cola, ante el que ya había llegado hasta la caseta de la aduana gabacha,[9] acelerando para escapar de la multitud de iracundas miradas que sentía querían recordarle su árbol genealógico, o cuando menos eso pensaba al sentir un fuerte rechinido en las orejas, pues todos iban tarde, todos se habían quedado sabrosamente prolongando unos minutos más de semisueño en vez de levantarse y llegar cinco minutos antes, sólo cinco, a las siete veinticinco, antes de que en épica estampida llegaran todos a tratar de pasar al mismo tiempo, antes que la cola inexistente de la izquierda se llenara de tensos y nervioso neuróticos

---

[7]Hell's Angels, el club de motociclistas.

[8]el trabajo.

[9]angloamericana.

que exigían a los demás que ya hacían cola desde mucho antes, que les dieran chance, un quebradita, que se compadecieran de ellos pues iban a llegar tarde y si llegaban los correrían del jale pues era la enésima vez que presentaban la misma excusa al despótico gabacho, al que exigía puntualidad antes que producción, al que juzgaba el carácter no por la firmeza de espíritu sino por la hora en que se levantara su empleado, llegaban en diagonal, las muchachas guapas le hacían ojitos al vecino, le exhortaban que les tuviera clemencia, que se lo agradecerían infinitamente, hasta el cansancio, hasta que las invitaran a cenar, hasta que les viera la piernas al levantarse seductoramente el vestido, hasta los límites del desenfreno, otros menos dotados de belleza física pero si con ganas de chingar a quien fuera se metían a la brava, atentos al menor descuido o al miedo que sentía el vecino de chocar, se le metían a la fuerza, haciendo caso omiso de las mentadas de madre,[10] de los insultos proferidos con rítmico sonar de los cláxones tanto del que sufría la imprudencia como de todos los demás que por detrás perdían un minuto más porque el idiota de enfrente no había podido cuidar su lugar, hasta el momento en que estallaba la violencia, en que uno que no iba a dejar a nadie que entrara a la cola se daba cuenta de que se le metían a güevo,[11] aun cuando ya le había dicho que no, o cuando le había dado al carro un acelerón y fuerte metida de frenos para prevenir la embestida, se decidió, le metió velocidad y chocó por detrás al intruso, se bajó encolerizado, abrió la portezuela del ladrón de lugares de la cola, le tomó por el cuello de la camisa y lo abofeteó, le partió la madre,[12] lo dejó tirado sobre el pavimento ante las sonrisas del público extasiado que no aplaudía por miedo a que le ganaran el lugar, ante el impresionante estallido de bocinas que proclamaban el arribo, finalmente de la justicia a mano propia, el público de guiadores ensimismados que se preguntaban por qué ellos no habían hecho lo mismo, todos iban tarde, muy tarde, todos soñando qué se sentiría poder volar y dejarse de tanta pendejada, todos enojados de tener que negarle la limosna a la creciente multitud de mendigos sureños, de coloridas Marías, de apócrifos sufridores del mal de San Vito, de enjambres de chavos que se tendían, sin permiso, a ensuciarles el parabrisas con agua y un trapo sucio, con el pretexto de luego cobrar por el jale, de parvadas de vendedores de chicles, de golosinas, de nieves que llevaban en hieleras gabachas original-

---

[10]insultos a la madre de uno.

[11]a fuerzas.

[12]lo dejó herido.

mente destinadas a cargar botes de cerveza para el pic nic,[13] de chavos que querían venderte desde un vainillo para perfumar el fétido aroma de cigarro impregnador de coches hasta colchas, cobijas, manteles, patitos coronados de sombreros charros como adorno para el automóvil, boletos de lotería, pasaportes falsos, pistolas de barro, retratos de Pancho Villa, Emiliano Zapata y del ángel de la guarda, muselinas de terciopelo negro en que aparecían retratos de mujeres desnudas y Elvis Presley, de otros chavos que pedían rait,[14] que vamos a la escuela, que nos queremos hacer la zorra, que llevamos un perro rabioso para echarles a los gabas[15] en el Centro Cielovista, que llévanos no seas gacho, que si nos llevas pasamos por American y el gaba no se da cuenta que nos queremos pasar de mojados, y el guiador cierra la ventana, le mienta la madre al pinche manito de Doña Ana, Nuevo México, con razón se los chingan tan seguido si son unos pendejos en todo y más para manejar, pinches güeyes, espavoridos ante el desmadre[16] tan sabroso, al grado del pánico, sin saber si darle o frenar, ante el acoso de maquiavélicos, peritos guiadores, atentos al instante del descuido, luego los camiones de pasajeros y los de carga, unos echando nubes de humo negro que suelen asfixiar al más empedernido fumador, atascados de otros que también van tarde, que se paran antes de llegar a la aduana y causan otro desmadre pues los que van en la línea paralela se aprovechan para meterse enfrente y fregar a los que detrás del camión se ven obligados a esperar pues no hay espacio para darle vuelta, los otros, confiados de su enorme volumen se meten a la brava[17] frente al que sea, se dan cómodamente la vuelta y agarran el carril de la derecha, frenan sobre el inclinado 45 grados del puente y al avanzar se dejan ir un metro, a veces dos, hacia atrás sin ver, sin importarles si al fondo hay algún precavido o un jarioso, un carro que guarda su distancia o uno que se le pega hasta más no poder, todos van tarde, sudan por todos los poros, los motores se calientan, los radiadores se desbordan en borbotones de agua, otros se van quemando, huele a aceite, a hule que se escapa desde las miles de balatas forzadas, chillonas, cuando ya no es posible sostener el peso, hacia arriba, hacia abajo, todos van tarde pero en su extremada neurosis prefieren ese sufrimiento a considerar la
loca solución que ofrece Edumenio, irresponsable,

---

[13]una tardeada.
[14]que pedían ser transportados en coche.
[15]gabachos = angloamericanos.
[16]desorden.
[17]sin permiso.

—pos qué se cree éste, que está en Europa o en algún país civilizado dónde se respeta a los vehículos de dos ruedas, dónde la gente obedece las señales de tránsito y camina por su lado de la calle, dónde el orden es la meta no la represión, qué no tiene familia que proteger, cómo es posible que se le ocurran tales barrabasadas y a su edad, qué no le da vergüenza que la gente lo vea montado como incróspido, el casco atascado hasta las orejas y el maletín amarrado al gril posterior, como si

fuera un pinche cobrador de segunda...

—hombre maestro, qué no le da vergüenza, si va a andar en moto mejor cómprese una mil, cómo es posible que todo un doctor ande en esa pinche moto destartalada, se va a desprestigiar, qué no ve, y a mí que me da mucha vergüenza y soy su amigo, tengo que responder hombre, no se haga güey[18] que ya van muchas veces que le digo, usted debe andar en un Mercedes, un Jaguar, qué es eso de que tenga que entamalarse como pinche oso para aguantar el frío y mire esas botas todas raspadas, parece que no tiene ni pa bolearse los zapatos, no hay que ser y si se lo lleva la chingada,[19] digo, un camión de carga en la carretera o allí mero, por el Paisano, por donde a usted le gusta irse al escuelín, lo van a dejar como pizza embarrado en el pavimento, en serio compa,[20] no vale la pena, tiene que proteger su imagen, al rato cuando lo vean sus alumnos le van a empezar a hablar de tú y eso no es posible, si usted es un catedrático de carrera, qué no se da cuenta, hágame caso, lefio, pazguato, suato, será necesario conseguir algún caco para que se la robe y así acabará su mal, mejor, antes de que muera apachurrado como sapo, como vil sabandija, como torta de huevo batido, como hot cake, como tortilla de harina, pan de peta, crepa de mermelada de naranja, o lo que sea con tal de que entienda lo

que le estoy diciendo.

No, nadie se imaginaba que un simpático cetáceo prieto, como los que se ven en Sea World o en el Circo Ringling Brothers, pudiera reventarse una idea tan revolucionaria para este pueblo de mierda, no se podía negar que el aparato, como los aviones de ala doble, los portaviones americanos o las bicicletas de una rueda, de aquellas que usan los payasos en el circo, representaba algo extraordinario, creaba un sentido entre las gentes como el que ocurre cuando alguien se encuentra un billete de a veinte dólares, no, de cien por lo de la inflación o cuando menos uno de medio millón de pesos, o lo que se siente cuando alguien

---

[18]hacerse el tonto.

[19]la gran bruja.

[20]compadre.

le echa a uno un chisguete de agua fría, sin esperarlo, cualquier día de nuestro saháricos veranos. Fue una ocasión para pegar en el álbum de familia cuando llegó a la casa, relucía el cromo de las salpicaderas, de los rayos de las ruedas, desde los manubrios torcidos como cuernos de vaca vieja y desde los escapes saltones hacia atrás como motores de cohete espacial listo para despegar. El color azul metálico enmarcado por líneas doradas del tanque de gasolina y las chaparreras de cada lado destellaban casi con el tañido de campanitas de chocolate, los asientos amonturados suaves, de nalgahide,[21] relucían como cuero bruñido. Completaban el cuadro los lentes oscuros, los guantes negros, la chaqueta azul, las botas altas y el casco con brújula y radio estereofónico. No hubo forma de negar el prodigio, el vato[22] había cambiado de personalidad, se había convertido en un monstruo, pero en un monstruo muy raro, medio jodido, refriadón, como Lon Chaney[23] cuando la hizo de hombre eléctrico en una película de chiste más que de horror, pues se le ocurre lo inaudito, lo nunca o casi nunca imaginado por gente cuerda, decente, aquella que tiene temor de Dios y procura llevar una vida sana, recta y formal, como los próceres, los prolegómenos de la comunidad, o cuando menos ése es el rollo que te tiran, aquel se había aventurado demasiado, había atentado contra las buenas costumbres, contra la bondad generosa del creador, sea anatema, sea anatema, sea anatema, pues una cosa era andar de loco en la moto poniendo la vida suya y de los demás en artero y constante peligro, además de echar a la pipiluya[24] el futuro de sus deudos, pues a quién se le va a ocurrir venderle seguro de vida a tal individuo, y otra era entrarle a lo seguro poniéndose en hombros a la calaca[25] echando a correr por carretera

y peor aún por una que se dirige al norte.

El viernes salió después de convencer a media humanidad de que iría con el máximo cuidado, de que no dejaría pasar ni un minuto sin que se fuera fijando en todos los acontecimientos y en todas las señales, fueran físicas o imaginarias, místicas o mágicas que pudieran aparecer y en todas las curvas, ranuras, rayas divisorias y salidas de descanso (AUSFAHRT) y las gasolineras y los faros y en

---

[21]un material sintético = suave, reluciente; trueque humorístico con la palabra nalga.

[22]chico u hombre.

[23]reconocido actor americano de cine, conocido por sus papeles de monstruos al estilo de Frankenstein.

[24]a la deriva, sin rumbo.

[25]la muerte en forma de esqueleto.

la caída del sol y los marcadores de millaje, tacómetro, velocímetro, odómetro, aguja de presión de aceite, de aire, de vapor de sangre y de calor que marcan los vasos capilares y en los tornillos del vampiro, en los pedales de velocidades, frenos, las agarraderas de los manubrios, embrague y freno delantero, y en las abrasaderas de todos lados para darse cuenta si iba a caer o si aquello se iba a desbaratar o lo que fuera, pensando en que si se mataba nomás sería un poquito pues luego regresaría convertido en motor de Rolls Royce. Estaba que se zurraba del miedo pues nunca se había aventado un viaje tan largo, en dos ruedas, en carretera y a la intemperie, y a piense y piense que si le lloviera, que si le granizara, se le picara una llanta, se le acabara el aceite al motor, se le calentara demasiado y se le desvielara, se pegaran los pistones, o cualquiera de esas u otras ondas, aquello significaría un frene instantáneo, sin tiempo más que de abrir la boca y empezar a VOLARE OH OH, VOLARE OH OH OH OH, NEL BLU DI PINTO DI BLU.[26] Por fin se dejó de babosadas y se lanzó pensando que al llegar lo haría con las nalgas cuadradas, borrrada la rayita, con necesidad que le plancharan el trasero para recobrar su diseño original pues nunca había pasado más de dos horas sobre ese asiento que, aunque cómodo para paseo, no era para tanto y pensar que son, cuando menos, cuatro horas y media de chinga constante a una velocidad más o menos como de cien a ciento veinte kilómetros por hora, en carro, ni cuando tuvieron que pasar el cerro encabronado de cajas de libros que tuvo que llevarse al exilio el famosísimo zoólogo mexicano Francisco Lupus y que se trajo desde la horrenda capirucha,[27] eran cajas y más cajas, infinidad de jaulas de diversos animalitos, muchos de ellos con las orejitas dobladas como cuando uno marca una página para seguir leyendo sin perder el lugar, cientos de peceras y almohaditas, cobijitas y diminutos utensilios, como los que venden en el mercado, hechos de barro, madera o cobre para que las niñas se diviertan jugando a la cocinita, pero fabricados por la misma mano de mi amigo, individuales, para cada una de sus multitudinarias mascotas a quienes además adiestró a comer como la gente siguiendo todas las reglas de Gloria Vanderbilt, ni aún ese día en que al llegar por fin a la aduana gabacha, en sábado que es lo peor, después de sufrir como nunca momentos de horror espeluznante en que los despiadados antropófagos del lado sur le habían amenazado con comerse aquella colonia ambulante, su lonche, los libros, el camión y a ustedes también si no se dejaban cai con la marmaja correspondiente a quienes exportan reliquias del

---

[26]referencia a una canción angloamericano popular en los años 50; "volare nel blu pinto di blu" es italiano por "volar en el azul pintado de azul".

[27]la capital mexicana o Distrito Federal.

patrimonio nacional y necesaria para hacer engordar su vista de jaguar en celo, no ni cuando ya casi del otro lado el aduanero gabacho, cuya semejanza a Rudolph Hess[28] aún hoy te conmueve, ordenó, con aire de nibelungo, que se bajaran todas la cajas y se quedó lanzándoles una mirada que sin traducirla trasparentaba el más amargo y despiadado desdén para quienes, como éstos, se atrevían siquiera a pensar pasar alguna cosa por allí sin antes humillarse, pedir perdón por todas las inconveniencias que le causaban por la revisión a su excelsamente blanca y ojiazul figura, a su evidente y obvia superioridad intelectual y a su gran bravura, subió por fin, después de horas de trabajo, de cargar u acomodar cada una de las cuatrocientas cajas y jaulas para que las revisara, el individuo aquel miró con desprecio lo que ahí había, se dio media vuelta mirándolos fijamente a los ojos, estaban seguros de que sufrirían la misma o peor suerte que Raoul Wallenberg,[29] seguro los iban a mandar al campo de concentración para braceros que está por la calle Montana o a La Tuna misma por haber osado cometer tan horrendo crimen como intentar pasar ese cargamento a los Estados Unidos, esperaron su juicio resignados, como quien espera recibir su sentencia para morir sobre el potro para después ser quemado y descuartizado frente al público que llenara la Plaza Monumental, después de una presentación de Rafael[30] o Michael Jackson, para que absolutamente todos se dieran cuenta del atroz y terrible crimen cometido, insulto a la sociedad, el tipo se dio la vuelta y ordenó que subieran todo de nuevo, se sacudió las mangas del inmaculadamente planchado uniforme azul marino y se fue, ese día el sudor corrió de abajo a arriba pues el susto les había ocasionado la pérdida de orientación gravitacional, pues no, ni ese día pasaron más de dos horas sobre la moto y ahora tendría

que someter el fuselaje a semejante tortura.

Edumenio pasó el puente y desde el primer momento en que la rueda delantera pegó contra la autopista, la supercarretera de cuatro carriles por lado que ya fuera de la ciudad merma a dos y dos, después de pasar por el desierto lleno de picudas yucas, century plants, nopales, cambios de colores de la tierra, de las montañas, que como dijo Evodio cuando lo llevaste por allí, son todas hermosas, pero muy lejanas de la carretera, y que las distancias que atraviesas, los valles inmensos te dan la impresión de que no viajas pegado al suelo sino que observas desde una altura impresionante, con la sensación que a las 70 millas por hora a que te desplazas jamás llegarás al paso entre los cerros que observas allá entre

---

[28]funcionario de confianza de Adolf Hitler.

[29]De origen sueco, Wallenberg rescató de Hitler a muchos judíos húngaros.

[30]cantante español popular.

la arena, por el oeste conduce a Las Cruces, pasando por la hacienda ribereña del Sergio en donde tiene una cria de perros rabiosos para cometer actos de sabotaje contra los gabas y ortodoxos de todos tipos, incluyendo a quienes no aman la música y en colaboración con el famoso terrorista anárquico, amigo suyo, que se desplaza a todas partes del continente en su compañía desde la urbe fronteriza, dejando atrás los manantiales de agua dulce en Deming, la salida para llegar a Columbus en donde Villa[31] les partió la madre a mil gabachos y los dejó tan enojados que a todos les salieron ampollas en la boca, cuyo mal heredaron a todos sus hijos y éstos a sus nietos y bisnietos, por Lordsburg donde das vuelta a la izquierda si quieres llegar a Douglas, pasando por el parque nacional dedicado a la derrota que los soldados gabachos inflingieron sobre la tropa del Indio Gerónimo,[32] no podría ser de otra forma, no podrían haber hecho un monumento en donde los indios heróicamente le quebraron el alma a los troopers pues eso significaría aceptar que una raza diferente a la blanca, una más inteligente y creativa habría podido utilizar armamentos paleolíticos, arcos, flechas y lanzas y aún así partirles la madonna[33] a aquellos bien uniformados y gallardos genocidas que disparaban desde cañones hasta rifles repetidores y aún así perdieron pues no conocían el terreno ni podrían sobrevivir las vicisitudes de la vida del desierto, aún cuando se desplazaban en camellos traídos desde Arabia, y por esa estrecha vía llegando hasta las frescas planicies pobladas de zacatón donde pastan muchos Aberdinangus,[34] y carasblancas, desde donde se divisa la ciudad que nombra el corrido, "La cárcel de Cananea está situada en una mesa...", montando la sierra poblada de encinos y madroños del mismo nombre por una carreterita en que apenas, apenitas, caben dos carros y no muy grandes, llena de curvas de 270 grados y de vueltas forzadas sobre voladeros pasmosos que prometen la muerte segura si tu auto llega a caer al suelo un kilómetro más abajo, por fin bajando entre sahuaros, chollas y pitayas, unas plantas espinosas que parecen arañas boca arriba, al calorón insoportable de Irmuris, Magdalena y Hermosillo, te pico el...,[35] en que los aires acondicionados de los carros apenas si mantienen la temperatura ambiente aún cuando se llevan puestos a todo vapor, en que los

---

[31]Francisco "Pancho" Villa, renombrada figura de la Revolución Mexicana de 1910.

[32]líder indígena del siglo XIX en el suroeste americano.

[33]partirles la madre = insultarlos.

[34]tipo de vaca originaria de Aberdeen, Escocia.

[35]insulto de índole sexual.

radiadores revientan invariablemente creando larguísimas colas de vehículos a los lados de la carretera, todos provistos de banderas o pañuelos, paliacates colorados colgados en lo alto de sus antenas de radio y que no se te vaya a pinchar una goma pues si te bajas a cambiarla con el calorón te deshidratas, ni se les vaya a echar el aire pues, como aquella vez que viajaban con el Charlie Boy, que en ves de tomarse el agua que llevaban se la vaciaron sobre la cabeza empapándose los cabellos, la ropa, sólo para que a los cuantos minutos, no más de cinco en ninguna ocasión, ya estuvieran completamente secos, hielos y todo, calorones que en Hermosillo hasta han modificado el comportamiento de los habitantes haciéndolos tomar cantidades industriales de cerveza sin permitir que se pongan beodos o previniendo que salgan a la calle desde las diez hasta las siete en que se mete el sol, y que cuando, por necesidad extrema, se avientan a salir a esas horas sorprenden al ingenuo turista ya que después de hacer alto o parar en los semáforos se desplazan a velocidades peligrosas para llegar al siguiente semáforo, todo con el objeto de que durante los instantes que esperan el cambio de luces los proteja la sombra de algún árbol:

ganarle al otro la sombrita.

Pero si no te sales en Lordsburg, puedes seguir derecho por la ruta más antigua de la inmigración, por donde una cantidad muy fuerte de mexicanos, indocumentados y otros similares incluyendo al Alcoholy Quinn (como lo bautizó JEP), han viajado esperanzados de conseguir jale en Califas,[36] desde El Paso sale a diario una limousina exclusivamente a Los Angeles y siempre va llena, la raza llega a Califas, se queda y que, según ella, vive mejor que antes, tanta ha sido la raza que ahora Califas se considera el estado de las mayorías chicanas, sin hablar mucho de la megalópolis horrible que así se ha convertido en un país independiente, por Tucsón que desde lejos es igualito a El Paso, pero que no tiene frontera aunque podría tenerla si la historia no define el cerco a unas millas más al sur, hasta llegar a Aztec, Arizona en donde puedes escoger la ruta oeste que te lleva a Needles y luego a San Bernardino y hasta Los Angeles o de la que, aún antes, puedes desviarte para el norte en Bakersfield y así seguir derecho a la frontera con Canadá que está como a 72 horas de Juárez sin parar, pasando por el valle de San Fernando, Delano, en donde una bola de trabajadores migratorios de todas las nacionalidades, chicanos y gente de todas partes, al mando de César Chávez[37] y al compás de la guitarra de Joan Baez[38] y los discursos y abra-

---

[36]California.

[37]líder laboral y símbolo de la lucha chicana.

[38]cantante de la canción de protesta de los 60 y 70.

zos calurosos del Bobby Kennedy, entre golpanazos de los garrotes de la policía
californiense, insultos y vejaciones de los patrones afectados y no afectados, el
aparato gubernamental, la gente conservadora, como los famosos japoneses de
esa área que después le hicieron de cuadritos la vida al inolvidable Tomás Rivera[39] cuando se le nombró presidente de una universidad chingonométrica[40] de
allá, hicieron su huelga y pararon el consumo nacional de vino Gallo, lechuga
Iceberg y uvas de todas clases, en donde la raza verdaderamente se unió para
darle a conocer al gaba lo que es tener que ver con un pueblo que ya está colma-
do hasta la madre y sin cuyo apoyo y trabajo esa nación se desploma pues es
toda la gente que jala en el fil[41] por una miseria y le pone en la mesa al blanco
el vegetal que se refina sin pensar mucho en todos los problemas que a otros
ocasionó llevarlo hasta allí, Sacramento, las regiones montañosas del norte de
Califas, las praderas, bosques, arroyos, playas, ríos, valles sembrados de flores,
fresas, el jope,[42] con que se sazona la cerveza, los pueblos vaqueros divididos
a la mitad por el ferrocarril, de un lado los blancos, del otro la raza cuya mitad
es igual a cualquier pueblito mexicano con sus tortillerías, panaderías, tiendas de
abarrotes, iglesias, de Oregon y Washington, paisajes continuamente adornados
de picudos volcanes cubiertos de nieve, los famosos Shasta, Mount Angel, Renier
y Santa Elena que hace rato opacó la claridad solar con sus incesante vómitos de
ceniza, tierra y magma y ahora le echan
		la culpa al Chichonal de sus estragos.
	La misma carretera que hacia el este, desde El Paso, te lleva a Van Horn,
pasando por hortalizas raras de girasoles que se cultivan para recoger las semi-
llas, salarlas con todo y cáscara y ofrecerlas a los beodos en los bares, para que
las coman mientras toman cerveza, fuman y juegan al billar, para darle más sed,
para que sigan consumiendo alcohol y así prevenir tanto el deshidratamiento
como la sobriedad, hasta llegar a Fort Stockton, San Anto, y luego seguir por
todo el sur, por Texarcana[43] hasta Miami, pasando por los siniestros estados
esclavistas, racistas discriminadores de Luisiana, Alabama, Mississippi, Arkansas
y si quieres luego desviarte de nuevo hacia el norte para llegar hasta Washington,
Nueva York y la otra frontera canadiense, la mismísima ruta que siguiendo

---

[39]conocido escritor chicano; incluido en esta antología.

[40]enorme.

[41]campo cultivado; la palabra inglesa "field".

[42]lúpulo usado para fomentar la cerveza.

[43]la última ciudad del estado de Texas en la carretera a Luisiana.

derecho al norte, desde el chuco,[44] te lleva a Alburque,[45] Denver, y finalmente
hasta Minnesota o hasta Chicago si tu quieres.

Sientes un miedo feo, hondo, por un lado pasa un camión de carga, casi un
minuto de largo, rompe el viento en capas, te aferras a los manubrios y al pasar-
te, en el preciso momento en que ya no lo ves directamente a tu derecha, sientes
el primer golpe, como una bofetada sobre todo el cuerpo, te estremeces, la moto
comienza a bambolearse, piensas que es poca tu fuerza para enderezarla, para
prevenir que en una de esas violentas zarandeadas te vayas de lado a esa velocidad y contra el negro pavimento, piensas en salirte del carril, que mejor caerte
sobre la arena, que al cabo vas bien protegido y sólo te rasparás las piernas, pero
te acuerdas de lo que le sucedió hace poco a un motociclista por una calle de
Juárez cuando por saltar y esquivar el golpe del choque contra un carro cayó de
cabeza, con casco y todo y nomás se oyó como que se rompía una calabaza
o una sandía.

Pasas por Vado y todavía vas sentado bien, en Mezquite el culo aún resiste
el tormento más o menos, de ahí en adelante vas cambiándote de nalga para dejar
que circule la sangre a esa región que por lo general no se te duerme pero aquí
sí. No, mejor te quedas y luchas contra las olas, las cachetadas sucesivas de
viento que deja atrás el carguero, bajas la velocidad y te metes poco a poco al
carril de la derecha, por si te siguen pegando que, cuando menos, sea de frente,
así podrás balancearte mejor y capotearla, en el momento en que ya no te pega
tan fuerte el aire, cuando recuperaste la compostura y ya vas gozando nuevamente del viento aguantable que te pega en todo el cuerpo y que te masaja bien
padre, como si te hiciera cosquillas una máquina vibradora, ya que te secaste las
lágrimas que de los ojos te ha sacado la fuerza del aire sobre la retina, cuando
ya te decidiste a seguir adelante, pasa otro camión, esta vez por tu izquierda, te
aferras nuevamente sin fijarte que pasa algo más peligroso tal vez, sobre este
trecho de carretera se han entresacado unas ranuritas que pegan verticales contra
tu llanta delantera, no horizontales como los topes o guardaganados, las han
puesto allí para que las llantas de los automóviles cobren más tracción, para que
no derrapen o se salgan del carril, pues ésta es zona de lluvias y resbalones, lo
malo está en que la llanta de la moto es mucho más angosta que las de automóvil
y el efecto es contrario, en vez de agarrarse mejor, la llanta se desvalaga, vacila
de un lado a otro con peligro de una volcadura padre, bajas la velocidad a treinta
con eso ya no te bamboleas pero el que viene detrás no se ha dado cuenta y de

[44]El Paso, Texas.
[45]Albuquerque.

repente oyes un rechinido cabrón que te manda la sangre a los talones, poco a poco sientes que que se te van engarruñando los músculos desde el centro de la espalda, pasando por los homóplatos, hombros, cuello, nuca, antebrazos, brazos, hasta llegar a las manos y a los dedos que de por si ya sientes congelados de tanto apretar el freno con la derecha y el embrague con la izquierda, después te darás cuenta de que tanto esfuerzo, tanta tensión, tanto peligrar y salir del quite sólo para enfrentarte a otro, te han adolorido bastante, lo sentirás en la gasolinera de Las Cruces, cuando cansado y sin ganas de seguir adelante quieras estirarte, es una tortícolis generalizada, los tendones y los músculos no aconstumbrados al uso continuo e intenso han soltado demasiado ácido láctico como para que te sientas normal. Sigues adelante después de pagar $2.50 y darte cuenta de que un tanque te dura exactamente 86 millas sin

contar las 15 que te sobran en la reserva.

Sales destapado, desde Las Cruces hasta Socorro vas piense y piense lo que vas a hacer cuando llegues, ya has estado separado de la familia en otras ocasiones, primero cuando eras marinero y te llevaste a la Rosi a vivir a Worcester, Mass. Allí duraron sólo unos meses pues te llegaron órdenes de cambio de barco y tuviste que traerte todo, ella te ayudaba a manejar y platicaba mucho contigo, desde Rhode Island en el Falcon blanquito que compraste por allá, que los condujo por Massachussets, Connecticut, Nueva York, Pennsylvania, Ohio, Indiana, Missouri, Oklahoma, Nuevo México y hasta El Chuco,[46] y que no se descompuso más que una sola vez en San Louis Missouri cuando la bomba de la gasolina estalló con lujo de desmadre y por mero se van al otro mundo pues chorreó vapor de gasolina sobre todo el motor, que además iba supercaliente de tanto dale y dale, a pesar de que era invierno, te fuiste casi un año aquella vez y te sentiste de la patada,[47] no hiciste más que memoria, viviste de los retratos y de las épicas borracheras con los cuates,[48] quienes, como tú también sufrían de extrema nostalgia marina, también cuando te quedaste solo en Alburque, cuando la Rosi, encinta de Gabi, se fue a Juárez y tú te quedaste dándole molestias a tu cuñada Margarita y a Lorenzo casi seis meses mientras terminabas de estudiar, con pocas esperanzas de terminar, con muchas ganas de salir a ganar lana pues todos tus amigos ya estaban colocados, haciéndose ricos, todos en Juárez y tú convencido de que jamás regresarías allá pues te habías tardado ya seis años más que cual-

[46]El Paso, Texas.
[47]frustrado.
[48]amigos.

quiera, ellos sacaban su BA[49] y listo, a trabajar en una maquila[50] o en alguna compañía de por allí, de ingenieros, contadores, licenciados, pero tú doctorándote para ganar menos y exiliarte definitivamente a alguna universidad del norte en donde hubiera oportunidad de trabajo para un maestro en letras, especializado en literatura latinoamericana, y además sabías que en la uni[51] de El Chuco no habría oportunidad pues eras graduado de allí y en las universidades norteamericanas nunca emplean a sus propios productos para prevenir el famoso inbreeding,[52] y por último cuando por fin conseguiste el jale tan deseado, tan necesitado, después de pasar un terrible verano de indigencia, de incomodidades para todos, cuando tuviste que quedarte con tus suegros, de angustias, pues a pesar de que te fuiste a viajar por todos los sitios del oeste de EU en donde te imaginabas que hubiera universidades, no encontraste nada, ni siquiera alguna posibilidad, ni siquiera la esperanza y dejaste burrícula[53] regados por todas partes, no hasta llegar a Seattle, ya casi en Canadá, se te presentó, pero tendrías que cambiar de onda, enseñar lo que nunca habías aprendido, reeducarte mientras terminabas de escribir el mamotreto[54] que todo mundo exigía y vértelas con el alto grado de desmadre que allí imperaba entre chicanos, estudiantes y profesores, sabiendo que nunca te considerarían como uno de ellos pues, además de provenir de muy al sur, todos eran californios o trasplantados allá desde hacía mucho, hablabas demasiado bien el español y eso querría decir que nunca sufriste las penalidades e inclemencias que todos lucían como medallas de guerra, como si no haber vivido aquello te previniera poder trabajar, comprender la injusticia y el racismo, como si tu piel no fuera igual de morena y los insultos dolieran menos, como si la rabia que te daba fuera postiza y como si tu participación activa en el movimiento no representara igual peligro que para los demás, la claustrofobia, la constante lluvia, la falta de sol, de amigos, de gente que se identificara, aunque fuese superficialmente, con tu forma de pensar, con tu forma de ser, con la necesidad de no desprenderte de lo que para los que viven en la frontera es cosa regalada, que no se piensa, que está por todas partes, gratuitamente, como existen los valores culturales y la lengua, allá no, se tiene que luchar para conservarlos,

---

[49]licenciatura, primer título universitario.

[50]tipo de fábrica en la frontera del lado mexicano.

[51]universidad.

[52]nepotismo.

[53]currículum vitae, récord profesional.

[54]disertación.

para que no se olviden o se pierdan en una masa blanca, en una ola azul de un mar anglosajón, para que a tí no te pasara lo que al muchacho del que te platicaba el bigote de Tomás Ybarra,[55] quien sufría pesadillas recurrentes en las que corría a meterse a un closet para escaparse de un oso polar que lo perseguía continuamente y que cuando por fin se escondía, cerraba la puerta y comenzaba a comerse sus chicharrones, el oso tumbaba la puerta para arrebatárselos, Seattle los forzó a todos a regresar para no perder la cordura, en serio que para eso, para no convertirse en uno más del alto número de jóvenes que cada año se avientan del puente más alto de la ciudad y desaparecen bajo las frías y profundas aguas del canal que conecta los lagos, y luego tuviste que quedarte seis meses en cumplimiento al contrato de trabajo, viviendo en un apartamento de un sólo cuarto, una cocinita minúscula, un closet y un baño sin regadera en donde tenías que sumergirte para enjuagarte, sobre la famosa Ave[56] de la universidad, superslick, como decía el Raúl Salinas,[57] poeta pinto y morador de una reservación indígena de por aquellos lares quien además de escribir poemas más locotones que ningunos se dedicaba a pescar salmón en ríos y arroyos, llegaba a la oficina ajuareado muy extraño, con trenzas, paliacate amarrado a la cabeza, botas montañesas y livais[58]

generalmente muy cansados.

Observas desde la velocidad del vado y la loma la grande extensión del lago del Caballo, piensas que las gentes que viven a la orilla en sus trailers, mobil homes según los gabas pues son casas rodantes posibilitadas para emprender el camino a cualquier confín por carretera, son muy felices, tranquilos y aburridos, pero te dan ganas de parar, de bajarte y de rentar una de la numerosas lanchas para descansar, pasear, hacer nada por largo rato antes de que te desintegre la calaca que traes montada en el pescuezo, paras en Truth or Consequences[59] para echar más gasolina y descansar, comes un pollo que sabe más a cartón que la caja que lo contiene, no hay más, todo lo que en ese pueblo existe se parece a su nombre, pocas gentes te creen cuando les cuentas su historia y no te extrañas,

---

[55]uno de los primeros especialistas en publicar una antología de literatura chicana.

[56]avenida.

[57]uno de los poetas fundadores de la literatura chicana; incluido en esta antología como Raúlrsalinas.

[58]pantalón de mezclilla; la palabra inglesa "Levi's".

[59]ciudad de Nuevo México que lleva el nombre de un programa de radio y televisión popular en los años 40 y 50.

pues es el colmo de ridícula, resulta que llamándose algo así como Tinkerville o Waterbury, un día se les ocurrió a los habitantes promocionarse a nivel nacional para así atraer al turismo y le llamaron a Ralph Edwards quien en ese momento producía un programa de televisión muy popular que se llamaba Truth or Consecuences, le prometieron que si llevaba su programa al pequeño poblado del centro desértico de Nuevo México le pondrían el nombre de su programa al pueblo, el promotor accedió y ellos cumplieron, son audaces en realidad los ignorantes, tal vez sea una virtud desconocida, nuevamente te acosan las ráfagas pero éstas diferentes pues te pegan cuando pasas por algún vado profundo o cuando, al salir de entre dos cerros a un valle, la protección que aquéllos te brindaban desaparece y te encuentras jalando el manubrio en dirección contraria al viento que quiere lanzarte hasta el fondo del barranco o la cuneta, convertirte en aviador involuntario, saltabarrancas, te atacan como fuertes cataratas, de un segundo a otro, sin que tú lo esperes, rezas que tu peso y el de la moto, ladeados, sean lo suficientes para contrarrestar su fuerza.

Un anuncio te informa que ya vas llegando a South Socorro y piensas cómo es posible que una mirruña de pueblo tenga la osadía, el egocentrismo, de denominar sur o norte a un lugar que, si parpadeas, ignoras por completo a tu pasada, te acuerdas que una vez paraste allí con Gilberto en uno de aquellos viajes transcontinentales que te atrevías aventurar, que llegaron a una tiendita y compraron piñones deliciosos, los mejores que jamás hayas comido, te acuerdas que hace un rato pasaste por Red Bluff, Bosque del Apache y te quedas pensando en los pinos, en las bellotas y en la infinidad de piñones que han de desprenderse de tanto árbol, sigues preocupándote, que cómo le vas a hacer, que tienes que completar tu libro para agosto, desde leer hasta escribir y traducirlo todo al inglés, pues nada, tendrás que hacerlo con tranquilidad, investigar cada uno de los multitudinarios libros, escoger lo que te guste y desechar lo demás, anotar al margen todo lo que creas importante y las ondas que se te ocurra explayar mientras los lees, luego te haces de una cantidad pavorosa de diccionarios y emprendes de una vez por todas ese paso caótico, aprender a escribir en ese idioma, te preguntas por qué antes no has intentado traducir nada siendo que toda la vida lo has tenido que hacer por angas o por mangas[60] ya que muchos no hablan español o inglés o viceversa, que desde chavalo en la casa se han hablado las dos lenguas y que en la escuela tuviste que enfrentarte a ellas también, ya podrás encontrar cómo, es cosa de no rajar leña, no te des cuerda más que positiva... ay nanita, agárrate que ahí viene un trailer Mack a madre y por detrás trae una colona de carros que

---

[60]a fuerza.

parece tren, y tú a la mitad del camino y esta mugre que no obedece, chin, qué desmadre, ni las tolvaneras juarenses, este pendejo va levantando arena y piedras por kilo y tú nomás con lentes, para qué te sacaste el casco, y es que pesa una tonelada y con este calor se te van a quemar los sesos como al caballero, el cielo azul hermoso, pasa el peligro, no hay una sola nube, se siente chistoso, como si fueras a caballo pero demasiado rápido, la velocidad se siente al mirar para abajo pero a la vez parece como si todo estuviera muy cerca de ti, como si pudieras bajarte a esa velocidad para tocar las cosas, echártelas a la bolsa, echas de menos la conversación, el radio, poder fumarte un cigarro y tomarte una coca, unas cheves[61] mejor, comerte un sandwich, estirar las piernas a tus anchas como cuando viajas en carro, aquí vas engarruñado

como perico emperchado.

Paras en Isleta del norte, el pueblo indio donde se consigue un cocinado en hornos de barro construidos fuera de casa, compras y comes, te estramas el cabello que viene lleno de tierra y otras verduras, parece que te embarraste medio litro de vaselina, lo traes planchado todo para atrás y duro, ni un pelo fuera de lugar, te miras la pelona en el acero inoxidable de la bomba de gasolina y ves que el aire va jalándote lo poco que te queda del copete, como si a estas alturas te sobrara pelo, como si estas aventuras todavía te correspondieran, pero sigues sintiéndote igual que antes todavía aguantas carnal, te levantas con fuerzas y le entras duro al jale, igual que siempre, pero también es cierto que ya no piensas igual que los chavos de tus clases, te cuesta trabajo hablar de las mismas cosas que a ellos les apasionan y ellos sienten dificultad al conversar contigo de sus cosas, se te hace que la experiencia te da mayor claridad para examinarlo todo pero te limita las posibilidades de acción que la ignorancia permite, y es que cuando no sabes lo que puede

sucederte, no sientes miedo pues no esperas que te pase nada.

Los Lunas, las montañas Manzano y en la distancia la Sandía, en su base al río vallado de álamos y el rosado recuerdo de antiguo Albuquerque, desde allá viene cambiando, viene hierba creciéndole al desierto, las montañas son más negras, menos grises y peladas, sientes más el fresco, más humedad, te acuerdas que ya pasa de diez años que tú y el Fernando hicieron el primer viaje a medio invierno, sobre el hielo y ante el aire rebanador, se pararon por aquí a echarse un cafecito que llevaban en un termo y a orinar preocupados porque los aceptaran, o cuando menos, no los fueran a correr a patadas de la uni, inmigrados, llevaban muchas esperanzas de estudiar y de que poder comer de algún trabajo,

---

[61]cervezas.

de algún día salir doctores, tú crees, y quesque[62] después trabajar como maestros, lo que a ambos motivaba y si fuera posible, también buscar el chance[63] de viajar, a donde fuera, con tal de aventuras, desempolvarse, desprovincializarse, designorantizarse, lecturizarse, el invierno llega más temprano y las estaciones se marcan definitivamente cada trimestre, te acercas, cómo es que no te mataste? la moto perdió un tornillo con las vibraciones y no te diste cuenta hasta después, sólo gastaste $6 de gasolina, pero ya te entraron las ansias, Alburque niega tu llegada, las millas que falta se hacen chicle, se te impone un compás de espera antes de llegar al río, lo cruzas por fin, no has pensado, crees que aquí se acaba el viaje pero no, será de regreso en el verano, cuando todo ya sea distinto, tal vez remolques la moto o te lleven en grua o la vendas de una vez o te quedes, o te vayas nuevamente para el

norte, lo único seguro es que será muy diferente.

Reprinted from *Madreselvas en flor* (Xalapa: Universidad Veracruzana, 1987): 73-91.

---

[62]dizque = dicen que.

[63]oportunidad.

SABINE ULIBARRÍ (1919-)

"El conejo pionero" (1988)

Yo vivo en un barrio de clase media. Un barrio de verdes céspedes, frondosos árboles, tupidos arbustos y multitud de flores y plantas exóticas. Es curioso pero las ciudades del desierto son más verdes y sus jardines son más exuberantes que las ciudades en tierras más hospitalarias. Es que tiene mérito enverdecer el pardo y árido desierto. Tiene mérito hacerle la guerra al sol calcinador y hacer fértil a la tierra estéril. Tienes que despotricarte regando, abonando y protegiendo a las enclenques plantitas de la naturaleza hostil. Hay una competencia feroz entre los vecinos a ver quién luce más verdura y mejores verduras.

A lo largo de mi casa esquinera, por el lado lateral, hay un trecho de juníperos que mide unos treinta y cinco por cinco metros. Es un matorral, una verdadera jungla, tan tupida que allí no entra ni pisa nadie. De vez en cuando yo veía algún perro desesperado ladrando como loco a algo, escondido dentro. Yo suponía que sería un gato, y no le daba importancia.

Un día estaba yo regando los arbustos con la manguera. De pronto me doy cuenta que algo se está moviendo allí dentro. Apunto el chorro de agua al movimiento. Veo unos saltos grises que no alcanzo a identificar. Luego sale despavorido un conejo cimarrón que cruza la calle como un relámpago y se pierde en los arbustos de la casa de enfrente. Los conejos corren de una manera muy rara. Las patas de adelante van atrás y las de atrás van adelante. Una especie de equis movible.

Yo supuse que sería un conejo turista, un indocumentado o un viajero que iba de paso a California. Jipi[1] no era. Andaba muy bien vestido y muy limpio para serlo. Le conté el episodio a mi esposa, y como no lo volví a verlo, pronto me olvidé de él.

Pasó el tiempo y no lo veía. Pero los vecinos empezaron a decirme, "¿Sabes que tienes un conejo cimarrón en tus arbustos?" Al parecer, al volver a sus casas por la noche lo sorprendían a descubiertas. Tenía gustos nocturnos y salía a

---

[1] la palabra en inglés *hippie*.

comer bien tarde por la noche. Al asustarse huía y se escondía en mis juníperos. Por fin un día, al año, se dejó ver. Lo sorprendí al extremo del solar. No huyó. Se quedó allí mirándome. Tranquilo y sereno. Las orejas acostadas. Era como si me dijera, "Déjame solo. Yo para doméstico no sirvo". Luego deliberadamente, saltito a saltito, se metió en el zarzal. Como si estuviera en su propia casa, y muy a su gusto. Supe, de inmediato, que teníamos un húesped permanente, que acaso se convertiría en casi miembro de la familia.

Esa tarde hubo una larga discusión en la familia de sobremesa, llena de especulación y preocupación. Los cómos, por qués y quién sabes. Ya el conejo nos había ganado.

Surgió de inmediato una diferencia de criterio respecto al conejo entre mi esposa y yo. Ella se preocupaba sobre qué comía. Yo le respondía, que hay plantas y arbustos y el césped también que se mantienen verdes durante el invierno. Las hierbas secas tambien son justa comida para esos bichos. En el desierto no hay cosa verde ni en el verano ni en el invierno y los conejos viven y sobreviven de todos modos. ¿Dónde bebe agua? Las hierbas que come tienen el agua que él necesita. Pobrecito, tendrá frío. La naturaleza lo ha preparado para eso. En el campo no tienen calefacción tampoco.

En todo caso mi esposa me hizo ponerle un trasto de agua, hojas de col y lechuga, y una zanahoria. Lo que dicen los libros de niños que comen los conejos. No le hizo caso a nada. Entonces me hizo comprarle comida comercial para conejos, unas bolitas verdes de quién sabe qué. Parecía que el independiente conejo no quería y no necesitaba ayuda del gobierno federal. Mi esposa se sentía decepcionada.

Un día para el desayuno sobraron dos piezas de pan tostado. Cuando salí al trabajo las tomé y se las puse al conejo. Cuando volví al mediodía, habían desaparecido. Ya mi esposa sabía. De ahí en adelante era de rigor tostarle dos rebanandas de pan al conejo todos los días. Después media manzana, fritos, nueces. Gusto refinado el del húesped.

Se fue desarrollando una cierta relación entre el conejo y yo. Aunque no lo viera, como sabía que allí estaba, yo le hablaba. Me gustaba creer que me entendía y que me contestaba a su manera. Hasta le puse nombre. Le llamé Manuel, en honor de un amigo político. Cuando salía a regar, le gritaba, "¡Oye Manuel!" y le contaba muchas cosas, algunas veces cosas muy personales de esas que no se cuentan a nadie. El me escuchaba en silencio y me daba su comprensión. Así se fue acostumbrando a mi presencia y a mi voz. Se dejaba ver de vez en vez, cuando le daba gana. Si yo trataba de acercarme se me deslizaba con dignidad y era como si me volviera a decir, "Déjame solo. Yo para doméstico no sirvo".

El que se dejara ver, el que no huyera era testimonio de que ya no me tenía miedo, que me tenía confianza. Era vivir y dejar vivir. Los animales comparten esta filosofía. En el corral los caballos, las vacas y las gallinas, que pertenecen a diferentes especies, se toleran unos a los otros y no se hacen daño. Ojalá la humanidad aprendiera esta noble lección. Manuel me estaba aleccionando en la animalidad. Me toleraba, una especie de amistad, pero sin sentimentalismo ni condiciones. Esperaba lo mismo de mí. Así giran las especies, como los planetas, sin meterse en el terreno de la otra nunca.

Lo que a mí más me preocupaba de Manuel era su soledad. Esto tenía a mi esposa sin cuidado. No comprendo por qué. A mí me dolía pensar que vivía sólo, que no tenía con quien compartir sus gozos y tristezas, sus ilusiones y esperanzas. Francamente, me molestaba que Manuel no tuviera con quien bailar, con quien dormir. La vida monástica, el celibato, no se hicieron para los conejos.

Cuando el conejo Adán y la coneja Eva fueron expulsados del Paraíso su dios les dijo, "¡Salid y multiplicaos!" El primer mandamiento de la ley de su dios. Los conejos, siendo obedientes, y además siendo adeptos, han venido multiplicándose desde entonces. Nadie ha sabido multiplicarse como los conejos, ni con tanto gusto. Las tablas de multiplicación son un lecho de rosas para ellos. La falta de multiplicación para un conejo debe ser un verdadero desastre, una tremenda tragedia.

Cuando le sugerí a mi esposa comprarle una compañera, no le gustó la idea. Le parecía inmoral. "Además", me dijo, "¿cómo sabes que es conejo? Puede ser coneja". Era verdad. A mí no se me había ocurrido. En el afán de la presente generación del unisexo, de vestirse, peinarse y portarse lo mismo, los conejos nos llevan la delantera. Es imposible distinguir cuál es cual. Es necesario un reconocimiento físico para determinar cuál es el macho y cuál es la hembra. No creo que ellos tienen la menor dificultad en conocer la diferencia—desde lejos. Quién sabe cómo. A lo mejor no resultaría. No hay donde comprar conejos cimarrones, y los conejos domésticos pertenecen a otra raza, son ricos y son la mayoría. Son gente de color. Muy bien puede haber discriminación racial o social, quién sabe por qué lado. Los conejos domésticos son grandes, gordos y torpes. Los cimarrones son finos, escuetos y ágiles. Lo más probable era que el doméstico se moriría de hambre, de frío o de miedo. Parecía que el pobre Manuel estaba fregado de veras.

En todas las sociedades de la humanidad y de la animalidad hay los atrevidos que se lanzan a la aventura y hay los tímidos que se quedan en la vida segura. Manuel era de los atrevidos. Quién sabe por qué razones abandonó su casa, a su familia y la seguridad de su comunidad y se lanzó al desconocido. Cuántos terrores, cuántos sacrificios, cuántas hambres no sufriría Manuel antes de llegar a mi casa. Los ruidos y luces de la ciudad, los automóviles, el gentío, los perros tuvieron que ser horripilantes. Pero no se volvió. Se aguantó. Manuel era un auténtico aventurero, un héroe. En mi matorral encontró el refugio que buscaba. Cuando se le calmaron los nervios deshechos y se le apaciguó el espíritu, Manuel se fue acostumbrando a sus nuevas circunstancias. Se dio cuenta de que el matorral era una fortaleza impregnable. Allí estaba a salvo de perros andantes y de gigantes rectos de dos patas. Poco a poco fue descubriendo que había caído en un verdadero paraíso, la tierra prometida. La leche y la miel lo tenían sin cuidado, pero lo demás era un banquete eterno. Legumbres suculentas, plantas exóticas de sabores raros y gratos. Y para postre infinita variedad de flores jugosas y dulces de perfume intoxicador. El menú más variado que se puede imaginar.

No tardó mucho Manuel en acostumbrarse a la buena vida. Salía bien plantado de paseo y a comer por las noches como caballero de bulevar. Dormía de día como un aristrócrata. La vida no podía ser más rica. Pero algo le hacía falta, y con el tiempo esta falta se le hizo ansia, y el ansia angustia. Yo lo sabía. La vida de soltero puede ser en todo sentido grata—cuando hay solteras, viudas, divorciadas y hasta casadas en todas partes. La vida de soltero debe ser un tormento cuando no hay mujeres.

Una noche volvió mi esposa de una reunión de maestras que había asistido. Llegó tan excitada que apenas podía hablar. "¡Un conejito, un nene! ¡Nuestro conejo es papá!", me dijo.

Manuel había resuelto su problema. Quién sabe cómo. Yo sentí tremenda satisfacción. Manuel, el atrevido, el pionero, ahora era feliz, como se lo merecía.

¿Cómo lo consiguió? No era probable que una coneja atrevida cayera por accidente en el mismo matorral. Lo más probable es que Manuel volvió al desierto, con esa valentía que le caracteriza, y se trajo una esposa.

Es posible que, como en tiempos de la frontera, pusiera anuncios en los periódicos conejiles y se consiguió esposa por correo. No hay manera de saber. Todo lo de Manuel es misterio.

Naturalmente, yo salí la siguiente mañana a felicitar a Manuel por su buena fortuna y su nueva familia. Hablamos largo rato. Ya nos entendíamos muy bien.

Han pasado los días y todavía yo no he visto ningún conejito. Mi esposa vio sólo uno, pero tiene que haber más, dado el talento matemático de los conejos. A Manuel sí lo he visto. Se ve tan relamido y satisfecho que parece indecente. Hay algo tan privado en la felicidad amorosa que no debería dejarse ver. Manuel no sabía o no le importaba. Yo le embromaba, y él sólo se sonría.

Me figuro que Manuel había construido una estupenda casa de clase media, de conejo rico, allí en el matorral para su esposa antes de salir a buscarla. Que le calmó sus penas, sustos y dudas con ternura, que le sigue mimando con todo cariño.

Una cosa me preocupa, algo que Manuel mismo acaso no sepa. Sus hijos. Estos nacieron en la ciudad, en condiciones económicas óptimas. Tienen de todo. No les falta nada. Son niños mimados. Nunca han pasado trabajos ni peligros. No tienen ningún recuerdo del desierto, lo difícil y precaria que era la vida allí. Son la primera generación en un mundo nuevo. ¿Qué va ser de ellos? La disciplina, la cautela y la inteligencia son indispensables para sobrevivir. ¿Sabrán ellos acomodarse a esta realidad urbana y cómoda o se harán rebeldes y radicales? ¿Podrá Manuel inculcarles los viejos valores conejiles, las tradiciones, la cultura? Queda por ver. Los hombres en las mismas condiciones han tenido terribles problemas con sus adolescentes que todavía quedan por resolver.

Allá cuando yo quise comprarle una compañera a Manuel, no soló quería compañía para él. Se me había metido una perra idea en la cabeza, verdaderamente diabólica. Se me occurió que sería lindo poblar todo el vecindario de clase media y conservador de miles de conejos. Ver pulular, más, hervir, los arbustos y matorrales de mis vecinos de conejería. Cuando se lo conté a Manuel se sonrió satánicamente.

Ahora esa idea ya está en marcha, Manuel y yo vamos a conejear al mundo, lo vamos a sacudir de la manera más violenta e inesperada. A pocos les llega la oportunidad de producir un impacto en su comunidad de proporciones tan pasmosas como la que Manuel y yo estamos fraguando. Si me ven con una sonrisa misteriosa es que la alegría que siento es verdaderamente luciférica. Si ven a Manuel, fíjense, él tiene la misma sonrisa. Es una sonrisa indecente.

Bueno, Manuel, ya he contado tu historia. Que el dios del conejo Adán y la coneja Eva esté contigo y con los tuyos.

Por supuesto, yo he creído desde el principio que tú eras conejo. Si eres coneja, la historia sería un tanto diferente. Si ése es el caso, te ruego que me disculpes, Manuela.

Reprinted from *El gobernador Glu Glu y otros cuentos/Governor Glu Glu and Other Stories* (Tempe: Bilingual Press/Editorial Bilingüe, Arizona State University, 1988): 49-59.

SERGIO ELIZONDO (1930-)

"Coyote emplumado" (1988)

Los señores me dijeron que me quedara aquí callado y en silencio el día que me depositaron. Eran dos de ellos los que entraron cargándome, yo no decía nada; quedé apacible desde que terminaron de arreglarme todo en el taller. Callaré y no hablaré a nadie, no conviene dejar de escapar la voz de mi forrado cuerpo de piedra.

Tuve una vida como qualquier coyote, sin ninguna distinción que no fuera más de lo cotidiano; entre nosotros los coyotes no tenemos lujos, ni frivolidades. Mi gente vive en la búsqueda de alimiento desde el momento en que empezamos, siguiendo después al nacer, y en el tiempo de nuestra independencia como adultos; y al morir, ya ven, seguimos dándole a la vida hasta de otra forma...ahora estoy aparentemente inmóvil, y todavía no controlo más que lo que pienso.

Si hubiera sido tejón quizás me habría tocado otra suerte. Es que esos cuates no se dejan, con sus grandes uñas luego se encuevan para que no los alcance quien los caza; será por eso que no se les ve en estos lugares, no es como a uno que lo pescan, lo miran despacio, le hacen ceremonias, lo copian, y finalmente lo ponen en un lugar para que venga a verlo la gente. La misma gente que me atrapó diría que no es fácil coger tejones porque éstos caminan muy pegados a la tierra, tienen mal genio, y cuando el cazador pretende agarrarlos del cuero eso es lo que cogen, el cuero, porque lo tienen bastante suelto sobre el lomo; el animal se da vuelta, gruñe, muerde para que se le suelte y con esta defensa el señor tlalcóyotl se les va, así lo llaman los que hablan el náhuatl, así lo llamaban los antiguos mexicas. Los tejones y nosotros somos parientes.

A mí me pescaron por torpe. A quién se le occure entrar a un huacal de varas inclinando sobre la tierra y sostenido por un palito en la parte que queda abierta. Dentro de esa caja de varillas alguien puso de cebo un conejo muerto. Era una trampa tan sencilla y usual que casi pasaba desapercibida. Esta es la manera de atrapar animales vivos y enteros, que no quedan con ninguna parte del cuerpo quebrada, así quedé yo, vivo, entero y avergonzado.

Esa noche del conejo en la caja de varas ya me tocaba la mala suerte. ¿Qué necesidad tenía de husmear el conejo muerto? Será que la gente que quería agarrarme nos conoce bien, no es como hoy que en cuanto nos ven de lejos nos disparan un cilindro de plomo y...¡pácatelas! Y..., ¡ya! ¡Te amolaron! Además que ya había cenado parte de un venado viejo que hacía días había matado un jaguar que le saltó sobre el lomo y le quebró el pescuezo. Y yo, como no queriendo la cosa visitaba el lugar donde lo tenía escondido el pinto, allí había estado yendo a comer ya varios días. Pero es que a un coyote, un coyote de veras, bien hecho y derecho no le falta la curiosidad.

Antes de la llegada de los españoles era el coyote a quien fregaban por su curiosidad, pero hoy hay gatos que nos acompañan; los trajeron los que andan en dos patas y huelan mal, como luego dicen: "la curiosidad mató al gato". A mí no me mataron, nomás me pescaron, y no por listo, ni por hambriento, ni de veras por curioso, sino por pendejo, sólo por eso; ahora ya ven lo que sucedió: querían su coyotito limpiecito y de cuerpo entero.

Tan augusto que vivía antes de todo eso y lo demás. En el tiempo de antes no había nada de trampas de metal, escopetazos, venenos ni palos; a menos que uno se acercara demasiado a la milpa a entrarle a las calabacitas tiernas, entonces te tiraban una pedrada con la onda y...¡cuerda!, en la costillas.

A ese amigo que me pescó lo conocía desde el día en que llegué a su parcela; en los primeros días anduve con bastante cuidado para medir mi territorio, bueno: era más o menos mi espacio porque había otros animales, que aunque no eran coyotes ya estaban establecidos en la región. Me quedé a vivir allí porque después le di varias vueltas al lugar y no encontré a otros coyotes; digo coyotes porque uno primero se preocupa por la presencia de su misma raza, y a mí me tocaba la de los coyotes. A la demás gente se le deja en paz si no del mismo tamaño que uno, y si son más chicos, se les agarra para comer. En el lugar había conejos y ratoncillos, mi alimento favorito, aunque de vez en cuando tenía que atrapar alguna cordoniz, elote tierno o venados menores como el cuate que perdió la vida en las garras del jaguar.

El señor del lugar, aunque nunca supe su nombre, se dedicaba al cultivo del maíz; cuando no estaba en la milpa salía con su guaje a la espalda a recoger el aguamiel de los magueyes para fermentarlo en pulque, bebida popular de la gente de esa nación. Todo estaba en paz, y precisamente ahí está el detalle de por qué yo, confiado, me creí de la figura del macehual[1] y en una noche cometí la tontería capital de mi vida. Jamás le hice daño a su persona, jamás me metí en su milpa a robarle su maíz tierno, ni calabazas, ni nada. Los elotes que en ese tiempo había probado se los quité a un campesino de otro pueblo parecido a éste,

---

[1]campesino, en náhuatl.

por aquí cerca, de Xochimilco;[2] digo que es un pueblo cercano porque aquí donde me ves en este estado y condición, no estoy lejos ni de mi tierra ni de ese lugar de los canales y flores. A ese campesino sí le pegué duro, podría decir ahora que me cebé con su maicito tierno. ¡Voto al alto Tonatiuh!,[3] ¿pues qué otra cosa va a hacer una boca hambrienta después de probar un alimiento tan sabroso como lo es el maíz tierno? Hay que comer cuando se pueda.

Resulta que a este amigo cuyo nombre nunca supe, se llamaría Torre de Obsidiana, Rayo del Cielo, Flor de Nopal, Caprio de Piedra, o Volcán Blanco, ¡qué sé yo!; a este señor del vestido sencillo, a este bendito señor a quien la Gran Tonantzin cuide, a quien creí ser inofensivo le cayó visita de la vecina y hermosa ciudad de Tenochtitlan. Los huéspedes eran unos señores copetones con plumas de color, tres de ellos, con cabelleras largas, tilmas limpias y huaraches de correas atravesadas, hablaban el náhuatl, la lengua de la región.

Llegaron una mañana cuando mi vecino se encontraba en su milpa desyerbando entre las matas que producen su alimiento. No sé qué platicaban; al principio nomás los escuchaba desde mi escondite que tenía entre las rocas donde yo vivía; tanto hablaron esa mañana que no me dejaron dormir. La noche anterior había sido larga en la sierra a unas tres horas a trote donde fui a cenar venado. Pero como quedaba ya poco cuerpo del cornudo de varios días de muerto alcanzaba su peste a penetrar los bosques, a esto llegaron otros coyotes a servirse de lo que disfrutábamos el jaguar y yo, y nos pelábamos por lo poco que quedaba del muertito. Por eso fue noche pesada para mi cuerpo, y ahora estos lujosos señores de la ciudad de los tenochas estaban hable que hable, ¡quién sabe cuanto hablaban! Al fin, me asomé, pudiendo mirarlos sin que ellos se dieran cuenta, y sin acercarme; como ustedes saben, un buen coyote no se acerca a nada, especialmente a alguien más grande de cuerpo; nosotros siempre podemos mirar antes de que los que anden por ahí nos vean. Aunque no levantaban la voz yo podía escuchar su conversación como un viento lejano, pues este oído que tenemos nosotros los coyotes es tan fino y delicado que a veces creo que podemos oír la caída de una semilla de cacoa en el campo del tianguis[4] de Tlacopan. Decidí no hacerles caso y regresé a acostarme. Me eché con el espinazo hacia donde venía el murmullo de voces de la gente, escondí la trompa en la panza haciendo casi

---

[2]un pueblo cerca de Tenochtitlán, la capital de los aztecas. Ahora es un centro turístico de la capital de México.

[3]el sol o dios principal entre los aztecas.

[4]mercado al aire libre.

una rueda con el cuerpo y me cubrí con la cola. Así pude dormitar alguito el resto de la mañana.

A esa hora del día se levanta una leve neblina cuando la oscuridad de la noche ya no es sombra sino un fulgar delicadamente claro y suave; es el largo momento antes de que se sequen las hojas de los vegetales, cuando la gente y los animales están ya despiertos y levantados, no hacen ruido; también antes de que haya subido el sol y haga que se desvanezca toda esa gasa blancuzca y todo lo demás empiece a colorearse. Las rocas alrededor de mi lecho están algo frías, se nota que las palmas de los nopales lucen fresquecitas. Los animales del monte que trabajan de noche ya están más cerca de sus guardias y lechos; los tecolotes han regresado por última vez y ahora se detienen cerca de donde habían dejado a la cría mientras cazaban, al rato se retiran a quedarse quietecitos el resto del día. Las gotas de agua que se hicieron del rocío empiezan a hacerse ampollitas claras en las puntas de las pencas de los magueyes, en un rato ya no aguantan el peso donde están y ruedan hasta las esquinas de abajo junto al tronco.

Seguiré acostado, pues no me molestan los ruidos familiares: la mujer del macehual[5] muele nixtamal[6] de buen maíz blando en su metate; cuando ya se ha formado una barrita de masa al final de la piedra que le sirve de molino se moja las manos, coge un poco de maíz, lo hace bola que pronto parece un panecito redondo y aplastado, lo pone en medio de la mano izquierda, le da una buena palmada con la derecha causando una pequeña explosión y termina así haciendo la tortilla. Mis orejas lo oyen todo aunque esté dormido, son sonidos de paz y no molestan. El cuerpo hecho un semicírculo recibe todo lo que pasa alrededor: los ruidos de la cocina del macehual, el fresco olor de la tortilla que ya se infla en el comal sobre el fuego de la leña que truena al quemarse, los chiles que se tuestan sobre las brasas, el polvo del sabroso chocolate al mezclarse con el agua hirviente, las vibraciones de la tierra casi tibia cuando por ahí camina la gente. Todo llegará al cuerpo que descansa, mi ser no se detiene, mi vida está en constante movimiento...nunca se muere.

Pero hoy llegaron esos viejos de las plumas de color a hablar con el señor de aquí, el vecino los escucha atento. Después, los señores regresaron a la ciudad que está en una isla, de donde llegaron muy temprano.

---

[5]campesino, en náhuatl.

[6]el maíz hervido para la masa de hacer tortillas.

El campesino los mira alejarse, se queda de pie, apoyado sobre su coa de palo que le sirve para escarbar en la milpa.[7] ¿Qué le dirían aquellos? No sé, no recibe muchas visitas.

Han interrumpido la armonía de mi vivir. En un huacal[8] recién hecho me han encerrado y no entiendo por qué nŏ me han matado. ¿Qué querrán de mí? ¿Por qué me han atrapado y ahora me llevan en hombros dos cargadores a la gran ciudad de colores que está en el centro del lago?

Me alimentan bien, han puesto el huacal a la sombra de un árbol con sumo cuidado, como si fuera de arcilla fina, como para que no me quiebre.

Caminaron dos días, pasando por la calzada que llega hasta el centro de la ciudad de los mexicas, así me trajeron. Ahora estoy rodeado de altos muros, escalinatas, patiecitos y pisos labrados y lisos. Todos estos días escucho el ronroneo de voces de gente que no conozco, nunca he visto tantos, no me miran, sólo pasan de un lugar a otro y yo los veo desde el interior de mi jaula de madera.

Llega un señor acompañado de varios que le sirven, les habla mientras a mí me mira con ojos serenos, de paz. Ahora traen una jaula más grande que ésta en la que me trajeron de la milpa de Tlalpan y me hacen pasar del huacal. En este nuevo lugar puedo caminar a gusto.

Me bañan con agua fresca del lago. El señor de los ojos serenos se pasa bastante tiempo observándome, siempre de día, en este lugar de piedras brutas que tienen en el patio de esta casa. Al fin, este señor llega temprano por la mañana; de una bolsa de cuero sacando una por una unas piedras negras y cuidadosamente las coloca alrededor de otra más grande que han traído. El señor de los ojos serenos saca las piedras negras y las arregla en un semicírculo frente a la piedra grande que ha quedado entre él y yo, ahora ambos estamos sentados, él continúa mirándome en silencio. Llega el día en que se acerca más a mí observándome cómo estoy sentado con mis patas traseras recogidas hasta que las rodillas me llegan a la mitad de la panza. El sigue sentado sobre una piedra cúbica y con cuidado empieza a golpear la piedra grande con una de las negras, de obsidiana. A los dos días me doy cuenta de lo que hace, pues su piedra tiene ya más o menos la forma de un animal que sentado, en silencio lo observa a él.

Pasa el tiempo. Aquí estoy en este lugar de gente que trabaja con piedras, y desde hace varios días que este cuate, con sus obsidianas de varios tamaños, labra...la figura de un canino que silenciosamente y curioso lo mira; ya se le notan las orejas triangulares, erectas, el hocico cerrado, las patas delanteras

---

[7]la planta del maíz, en náhuatl; también el campo de maíz sembrado.

[8]un tipo de jaula o choza, en náhuatl.

apoyan el resto del cuerpo para que la cabeza en alto y los cuartos traseros con la cola pegada alrededor hacia delante. Se ve todo bien, es un coyote sentado.

Ahora trabaja con instrumentos pequeños, tan menudos que los ase con la mera punta de los dedos. Ha dejado de trabajar fuerte, a percusión, y en vez de piel como sería natural, este paciente hombre, después de haber dibujado el cuerpo con plumas, las esculpe una a una. Es la estatua de un coyote emplumado. Es el señor de la tinieblas, el animal misterioso y agorero se ha convertido en inerme objeto cubierto de plumas, es un coyote con plumas, es un pájaro de la tierra, es un animal de piel que parece que está cubierto de flores que apuntan todas hacia abajo; animal que habiendo estado suspendido en la libertad del aire acaba ya de regresar de un vuelo nocturno y ahora se sienta a que descansen su sinnúmero de pequeñas alas silenciosas, reposadas, y lo visten. Es un coyote vestido de aire, un hermoso coyote pájaro, un quetzalcóyotl.[9]

El escultor anónimo, como yo, se pasa horas, días, semanas, labrando más y más las plumas; el resto de la figura sentada está bien, ahora lo que más le importa son las plumas; éstas deben quedar todas bien hechas, suaves, bien talladas y abrazadas al cuerpo para encerrar todo el silencio. Parece que las plumas serán más vitales que el animal que queda dentro de ellas, como si de su obra dependiera el vuelo libre y perfecto de la figura, lo miro; él me observa aún. Me habla con su silencio, con cada talladura de cada una de las plumas y no hay respuesta, luego me mira sentado dentro de la jaula, llegan sus palabras sin sonido y tampoco respondo.

Pienso en el campo como el recuerdo de algo que se confunde en el espacio en silencioso movimiento. Allá en el monte ha quedado todo lo de antes, lo de antes era un todo completo, hasta lo verde que se encontraba por doquier; allá nací y me crié, aquí estoy de nuevo en el mundo de un solo color. Allá era el lugar fijo donde el aire es claro, leve, y huele a madera que se quema dentro de las casa de donde sale aroma de algo de comer. Allá dejé un estelar de huellas de mis patas. Por encima de cada pelo pasó el airecillo cuando caminaba, ondulaba mi figura al trote tendido.

Ahora estoy en este recinto cuadrado donde se oyen ruidos artificales, los sonidos del delicado tallar de este señor que pidió que me trajeran del monte.

El señor de las piedras duras y hermosas ahora trabaja más despacio. Casi no hace ruido con los dedos sobre el quetzalcóyotl; ahora acerca la cara, los ojos, el aliento; una pluma de piedra, le sopla con cuidado, las acaricia, las ama. Dejó

---

[9]palabra compuesta, hecha de "quetzal" (pluma) y "cóyotl" (coyote) = coyote emplumado; alusión al dios Quetzalcoatl, la serpiente emplumada.

de venir unos días hasta que una tarde regresó acompañado de los señores de tilma larga bordada y la cabeza coronada de un penacho de plumas de colores. Hablaron en voz baja, se acercaron al quetzalcóyotl, lo observaron detenidamente, lo apuntaban con la mano como si quisieran tocarle las plumas una por una. A mí no me miran; ni el señor de las piedras fuertes se fija en mí aunque sigo bien en mi juala grande.

Paso días en silencio, solo. Se han llevado al quetzalcóyotl; aquí estoy: el latido del corazón y el rítmico jadeo de mi aliento quisieran que recordara la milpa de Tlalpan.

En el mismo huacal en que me trajeron del campo me han puesto; es la caja de madera bruta, las correas de cuero crudo, ha quedado por aquí un olorcillo de mí. Me acompaña el silencio en hombros de los dos macehuales que caminan con cadencia de paso largo. Poco a poco me alejan del norte y de la ciudad de donde la gente habla fuerte. He cambiado de piel en la ida y vuelta, pero el viaje no ha terminado.

Queda mi figura de piedra ahora para siempre en una jaula de cristal donde la gente que llega, pasa, me mira, sonríe; algunos me adoran, y susurran con el rastreo de los pies en el piso del museo y siempre se alejan. Ahora estoy aquí, hecho de piedra pintada, soy coyote emplumado, Quetzalcóyotl.[10]

Reprinted from *Antología retrospectiva del cuento chicano*. Juan Bruce Ncvoa y José Guillermo Saavedra, comps. (México: Consejo Nacional de Población, 1988): 87-94. Permission granted by author.

---

[10]La letra mayúscula significa que se ha deificado a la escultura.

POESÍA / POETRY

ANÓNIMO

"Corrido de Joaquín Murrieta" (¿1850?)

Yo no soy americano
pero comprendo el inglés.
Yo lo aprendí con mi hermano
al derecho y al revés.
A cualquier americano
lo hago temblar a mis pies.

Cuando apenas era un niño
huérfano a mí me dejaron.
Nadie me hizo ni un cariño,
a mi hermano lo mataron,
Y a mi esposa Carmelita,
cobardes la asesinaron.

Yo me vine de Hermosillo
en busca de oro y riqueza.
Al indio pobre y sencillo
lo defendí con fiereza
Y a buen precio los sherifes
pagaban por mi cabeza.

A los ricos avarientos,
yo les quito su dinero.
Con los humildes y pobres
yo me quito mi sombrero.
Ay, que leyes tan injustas
fue llamarme bandolero.

A Murrieta no le gusta
lo que hace no es desmentir.
Vengo a vengar a mi esposa,

y lo vuelvo a repetir,
Carmelita tan hermosa,
como la hicieron sufrir.

Por cantinas me metí,
castigando americanos:
Tú serás el capitán
que mataste a mi hermano.
Lo agarraste indefenso,
orgulloso americano.

Mi carrera comenzó
por una escena terrible.
Cuando llegué a setecientos
ya mi nombre era temible.
Cuando llegué a mil doscientos
ya mi nombre era terrible.

Yo soy aquel que domino
hasta leones africanos.
Por eso salgo al camino
a matar americanos
Ya no es otro mi destino
¡pon cuidado, parroquianos!

Las pistolas y las dagas
son juguetes para mí.
Balazos y puñaladas,
carcajadas para mí.
Ahora con medios cortados
ya se asustan por aquí.

No soy chileno ni extraño
en este suelo que piso.
De México es California,
porque Dios así lo quizo,
Y en mi sarape cosida
traigo mi fe de bautismo.

Que bonito es California
con sus calles alineadas,
donde paseaba Murrieta
con su tropa bien formada,
con su pistola repleta,
y su montura plateada.

Me he paseado en California
por el año del cincuenta,
Con mi montura plateada,
y mi pistola repleta,
Y soy ese mexicano
de nombre Joaquín Murrieta.

As sung and recorded by Los Madrugadores in 1934 and available on *Corridos y tragedias de la frontera*, Arhoolie CD #7019/20 (Arhoolie Records, 10341 San Pablo Avenue, El Cerrito, Calif. 94530).

ANÓNIMO

"Corrido de Gregorio Cortez" (¿1901?)

En el condado del Carmen
miren lo que ha sucedido.
Murió el sherife mayor
quedando Román herido.

Otro día por la mañana
cuando la gente llegó
Unos a los otros dicen:
No saben quien lo mató.

Se anduvieron informando.
Como tres horas después,
supieron que el malhechor
era Gregorio Cortez.

Insortaron a Cortez
por todito el estado.
Vivo o muerto que se aprenda
porque a varios ha matado.

Decía Gregorio Cortez
con su pistola en la mano:
No siento haberlo matado
al que siento es a mi hermano.

Decía Gregorio Cortez
con su alma muy encendida:
No siento haberlo matado
la defensa es permitida.

Venían los americanos

que por el viento volaban,
porque se iban a ganar
tres mil pesos que les daban.

Siguió con rumbo a Gonzales,
varios sherifes lo vieron,
no lo quisieron seguir
porque le tuvieron miedo.

Venían los perros jaundes
venían sobre la huella,
pero alcanzar a Cortez
era alcanzar a una estrella.

Decía Gregorio Cortez:
Pa' qué se valen de planes,
si no pueden agarrarme
ni con esos perros juandes.

Decían los americanos:
Si lo vemos ¿qué le haremos?
Si le entramos por derecho
muy poquitos volveremos.

En el redondel del rancho
lo alcanzaron a rodear,
Poquitos más de trescientos
y allí les brincó el corral.

Allá por el Encinal
a según por lo que dicen

Se agarraron a balazos
y les mató otro sherife.

Decía Gregorio Cortez
con su pistola en la mano:
No corran rinches cobardes
con un solo mexicano.

Giró con rumbo a Laredo
sin ninguna timidez:
¡Síganme rinches cobardes,
yo soy Gregorio Cortez!

Gregorio le dice a Juan
en el rancho del Ciprés:
Platícame que hay de nuevo,
yo soy Gregorio Cortez.

Gregorio le dice a Juan:
Muy pronto lo vas a ver,

anda háblale a los sherifes
que me vengan a aprehender.

Cuando llegan los sherifes
Gregorio se presentó:
Por la buena sí me llevan
porque de otro modo nó.

Ya agarraron a Cortez
ya terminó la cuestión,
la pobre de su familia
la lleva en el corazón.

Ya con esto me despido
con la sombra de un ciprés
Aquí se acaba cantando
la tragedia de Cortez.

As sung and recorded by Pedro Rocha and Lupe Martínez in 1929 and available on *Corridos y tragedias de la frontera*, Arhoolie CD #7019/20 (Arhoolie Records, 10341 San Pablo Avenue, El Cerrito, Calif. 94530).

JESÚS MARÍA H. ALARID (fechas desconocidas)

"El idioma español" (1889)

Hermoso idioma español
¿Qué te quieren proscribir?
Yo creo que no hay razón
Que tú dejes de existir.

El idioma castellano
Fue orijinado en Castilla
Creencia que da al mejicano
Su gramática hoy en día
Pero quieren a porfía
Que quede un idioma muerto
No se declaran de cierto
Pero lo quieren quitar
Siendo un idioma tan lento
Y tan dulce para hablar.

Afirmo yo que el inglés
Como idioma nacional
No es de sumo interés
Que lo aprendamos hablar
Pues se debe de enseñar
Como patriotas amantes
Y no quedar ignorantes
Mas, no por eso dejar
Que el idioma de Cervantes
Se deje de practicar.

¿Cómo es posible señores
Que un nativo mejicano
Aprenda un idioma estraño
En las escuelas mayores

Dicen, "Vendrán profesores
Para enseñar el inglés
El alemán y el francés
Y toditas las idiomas
Se me hace como maromas
Que voltean al revés.

¿Cómo podrá el corazón
Sentir otro idioma vivo?
Un lenguaje sensitivo
Es muy fácil de entender
Para poder comprender
Lo que se estudia y se aprende
Pero si uno no lo entiende
Lo aprende nomás a leer.

Todavía en la ocación
Existe una mayoría
Que habla el idioma español
Y sostiene su hidalguía
Hablaremos a porfía
Nuestro idioma primitivo
Que siempre, siempre, esté vivo
Y exista en el corazón
Repito, que no hay razón
El dejar que quede aislado
¡Brille en la constitución
Del Estado Separado!

Cuando el mejicano entiende
Bien el idioma materno

Muy fácil será que aprenda
El idioma del gobierno
Rogaremos al eterno
Que nos dé sabiduría
Y que se nos llegue el día
De poder hablar inglés
Pues señores justo es
Que lo aprendamos hablar
Y siempre darle lugar
Al idioma nacional
Es justo y es racional
Pero les hago un recuerdo
Para a San Pablo adorar
No desadoren a San Pedro.

Hoy los maestros mejicanos
Estamos muy atrazados
Pocos de nuestros paisanos
Obtienen certificados
Pues hemos sido educados
En el idioma español
Yo creo fuera mejor
Si se trata de igualdad
Que el tiempo de examinar
Fuera en español e inglés
Pues es de grande interés
Que el inglés y el castellano
Ambos reinen a la vez
En el suelo americano.

Reprinted from *Los pobladores nuevo mexicanos y su poesía, 1889-1950*. Anselmo F. Arellano, ed. (Albuquerque: Pajarito Publicacions, 1989): 37-38. Permission granted by José Armas.

RODOLFO "CORKY" GONZALES (1928-)

I Am Joaquín (1967)

I am Joaquín,
Lost in a world of confusion,
Caught up in a whirl of a
                    gringo society,
Confused by the rules,
Scorned by attitudes,
Suppressed by manipulation,
And destroyed by modern society.
My fathers
        have lost the economic battle
and won
        the struggle of cultural survival.
And now!
        I must choose

Between the paradox of
Victory of the spirit,
despite physical hunger
                    Or
        to exist in the grasp
of American social neurosis,
sterilization of the soul
        and a full stomach.

Yes,
I have come a long way to nowhere,
Unwillingly dragged by that
        monstrous, technical
        industrial giant called
                    Progress

and Anglo success. . .
   I look at myself.
    I watch my brothers.
     I shed tears of sorrow.
      I sow seeds of hate.
   I withdraw to the safety within the
Circle of life. . .

MY OWN PEOPLE

I am Cuauhtémoc[1]
Proud and Noble
    Leader of men,
King of an empire,
civilized beyond the dreams
    of the Gachupín[2] Cortez,[3]
Who also is the blood,
    the image of myself.
I am the Maya Prince.
I am Nezahualcoyotl,[4]
Great leader of the Chichimecas.[5]
I am the sword and flame of Cortez
           the despot.
             And
I am the Eagle and the Serpent of
         the Aztec civilization.
I owned the land as far as the eye
could see under the crown of Spain,
and I toiled on my earth
and gave my Indian sweat and blood

---

[1] last emperor of the Aztecs.

[2] stranger; a pejorative used in the nineteenth century against the Spanish colonialists by Mexican freedom fighters.

[3] the Spanish explorer who conquered the Aztecs in 1521.

[4] a famous Aztec poet alive before the arrival of the Spaniards.

[5] The nation led by Nezahualcoyotl.

for the Spanish master,
Who ruled with tyranny over man and
beast and all that he could trample
                              But. . .
        THE GROUND WAS MINE. . .
I was both tyrant and slave.

As Christian church took its place
        in God's good name,
to take and use my Virgin strength and
                        Trusting faith,
The priests
        both good and bad,
                        took
But
        gave a lasting truth that
                        Spaniard,
                            Indian,
                                    Mestizo
Were all God's children
And
        from these words grew men
                who prayed and fought
                                    for
        their own worth as human beings,
                        for
                            that
                GOLDEN MOMENT
                            of
                FREEDOM.

I was part in blood and spirit
        of that
                courageous village priest

Hidalgo[6]
in the year eighteen hundred and ten
who rang the bell of independence
and gave out the last cry:

"El Grito de Dolores,[7] Que mueran
los Gachupines y que viva
la Virgen de Guadalupe". . .
I sentenced him
        who was me.
I excommunicated him my blood.
I drove him from the pulpit to lead
        a bloody revolution for him and me. . .
                I killed him.
His head,
        which is mine and all of those
        who have come this way,
I placed on that fortress wall
        to wait for Independence.
Morelos!
        Matamoros!
                Guerrero![8]
All compañeros in the act,
STOOD AGAINST THAT WALL OF
                                INFAMY
        to feel the hot gouge of lead
                which my hands made.
I died with them. . .
I lived with them
I lived to see our country free.
Free

---

[6]the George Washington of the Mexican Independence struggle against Spain that began in 1810.

[7]the parish town where Hidalgo worked and in which he made the first call for armed struggle against the Spaniards.

[8]three fighters for Mexican Independence who continued the struggle after Hidalgo's execution by the Spaniards.

from Spanish rule in
                eighteen-hundred-twenty-one.
                        Mexico was Free ? ?
The crown was gone
                but
all his parasites remained
                        and ruled
                        and taught
        with gun and flame and mystic power.
I worked
I sweated,
I bled,
I prayed
        and
waited silently for life to again
                        commence.

I fought and died
                for
                Don Benito Juárez[9]
        Guardian of the Constitution.
        I was him
                        on dusty roads
                                on barren land
as he protected his archives
        as Moses did his sacraments.
He held his Mexico
                        in his hand
                                on
                the most desolate
                        and remote ground
                        which was his country,
And this Giant

---

[9]Juárez reaffirmed republican rule in Mexico in the mid-nineteenth century and successfully fought against France's objective of colonizing Mexico.

Little Zapotec[10]
gave
not one palm's breadth
of his country's land to
Kings or Monarchs or Presidents
of foreign powers.

I am Joaquín,
I rode with Pancho Villa,[11]
crude and warm.
A tornado at full strength,
nourished and inspired
by the passion and the fire
of all his earthy people.
I am Emiliano Zapata.[12]
"This Land
This Earth
is
OURS"
The Villages
The Mountains
The Streams
belong to Zapatistas.
Our life
Or yours
is the only trade for soft brown earth
and maize.
All of which is our reward,
A creed that formed a constitution
for all who dare live free!

---

[10]Juárez was a full-blood Zapotec Indian.

[11]a popular rebel and then a general in the insurrection of 1910 against Mexican dictator Porfirio Díaz.

[12]an Indian leader and then a general from Southern Mexico who also fought against Porfirio Díaz in the Revolution of 1910; Zapata defended land rights for the peasants.

"This land is ours. . .
    Father, I give it back to you.
           Mexico must be free. . ."
I ride with Revolutionists
           against myself.
I am Rurale
      Coarse and brutal,
I am the mountain Indian,
    superior over all.
The thundering hoof beats are my horses.
The chattering of machine guns
    are death to all of me:
        Yaqui
          Tarahumara
         Chamula
        Zapotec
         Mestizo
         Español[13]

I have been the Bloody Revolution,
The Victor,
The Vanquished,
I have killed
    and been killed.
          I am despots Díaz[14]
          and Huerta[15]
and the apostle of democracy
          Francisco Madero.
I am
the black shawled
faithful women
who die with me

---

[13]a series of references to the principal minority groups that make up Mexican society.

[14]Porfirio Díaz (1830-1915) who ruled Mexico until the 1910 Revolution.

[15]Victoriano Huerta, a general under Díaz who killed President Francisco Madero in order to take over the government.

or live
depending on the time and place.
I am
   faithful
      humble,
         Juan Diego
         the Virgen de Guadalupe,[16]
         Tonatzin,[17] Aztec Goddess too.

I rode the mountains of San Joaquín.
I rode as far East and North
         as the Rocky Mountains
              and
all men feared the guns of
              Joaquín Murrieta.[18]
I killed those men who dared
   to steal my mine,
      who raped and Killed
                my Love
                my Wife
Then
I Killed to stay alive.
I was Alfego Baca,
   living my nine lives fully.
I was the Espinoza brothers
   of the Valle of San Luis.
All,
were added to the number of heads
that
   in the name of civilization
were placed on the wall of independence.
Heads of brave men

---

[16] the patron saint of Mexico.

[17] the Aztec goddess of fertility.

[18] After the conquest by the United States of the Southwest in 1848, Murrieta led a rebellion against Anglo prejudice and injustice.

who died for cause or principle.
Good or Bad.
              Hidalgo! Zapata!
              Murrieta! Espinozas!
are but few.
They
dared to face
The force of tyranny
         of men
             who rule
                By farce and hypocrisy
I stand here looking back,
and now I see
             the present
and still
      I am the campesino
      I am the fat political coyote
                  I,
of the same name,
               Joaquín.
In a country that has wiped out
all my history,
             stifled all my pride.
In a country that has placed a
different weight of indignity upon
              my
               age
               old
                    burdened back.
         Inferiority
is the new load. . .
    The Indian has endured and still
emerged the winner,
    The Mestizo must yet overcome,
         And the Gachupin will just ignore.
    I look at myself
      and see part of me
who rejects my father and my mother
and dissolves into the melting pot

to disappear in shame.
I sometimes
sell my brother out
and reclaim him
for my own, when society gives me
token leadership
in society's own name.

I am Joaquín,
who bleeds in many ways.
The altars of Moctezuma[19]
I stained a bloody red.
My back of Indian Slavery
was stripped crimson
from the whips of masters
who would lose their blood so pure
when Revolution made them pay
Standing against the walls of
Retribution.
Blood. . .
Has flowed from
me
on every battlefield
between
Campesino, Hacendado
Slave and Master
and
Revolution.

I jumped from the tower of Chapultepec[20]

into the sea of fame;

[19]the Aztec priest and leader who was tricked and conquered by Hernán Cortez.

[20]a military academy whose cadets chose suicide over surrender to invading Anglo-American troops.

My country's flag
    my burial shroud;
With Los Niños,
    whose pride and courage
could not surrender
        with indignity
          their country's flag
To strangers. . .in their land.
Now
    I bleed in some smelly cell
    from club
    or gun
    or tyranny.
I bleed as the vicious gloves of hunger
    cut my face and eyes,
as I fight my way from stinking Barrios
    to the glamour of the Ring
      and lights of fame
      or mutilated sorrow.
My blood runs pure on the iced caked
hills of the Alaskan Isles,
on the corpse strewn beach of Normandy,
the foreign land of Korea
    and now
      Viet Nam.

Here I stand
        before the Court of Justice
          Guilty
for all the glory of my Raza
        to be sentenced to despair.
Here I stand
    Poor in money
    Arrogant with pride
        Bold with Machismo
        Rich in courage
          and
        Wealthy in spirit and faith.
My knees are caked with mud.

My hands calloused from the hoe.
I have made the Anglo rich
                              yet
        Equality is but a word,
          the Treaty of Hidalgo has been broken
          and is but another treacherous promise.
My land is lost
                          and stolen,
My culture has been raped,
                  I lengthen
                  the line at the welfare door
and fill the jails with crime.
                  These then
are the rewards
                  this society has
For sons of Chiefs
                  and Kings
                  and bloody Revolutionists.
Who
gave a foreign people
        all their skills and ingenuity
to pave the way with Brains and Blood
for
those hordes of Gold starved
                              Strangers
Who
changed our language
and plagiarized our deeds
                          as feats of valor
                          of their own.
They frowned upon our way of life
        and took what they could use.
                  Our Art
                  Our literature
                  Our music, they ignored
so they left the real things of value
and grabbed at their own destruction
                  by their Greed and Avarice
They overlooked that cleansing fountain of

                    nature and brotherhood
Which is Joaquín.
     The art of our great señores
                         Diego Rivera
                         Siqueiros
                    Orozco[21] is but
another act of revolution for
                    the Salvation of mankind.
                    Mariachi music, the
                    heart and soul
                    of the people of the earth,
                    the life of child,
                    and the happiness of love.
                    The Corridos tell the tales
                    of life and death,
                         of tradition,
                    Legends old and new,
                    of Joy
                         of passion and sorrow
                    of the people. . .who I am.

I am in the eyes of woman,
                    sheltered beneath
her shawl of black,
                    deep and sorrowful
                    eyes,
That bear the pain of sons long buried
                    or dying,
                    Dead
on the battlefield or on the barbwire
                    of social strife.

Her rosary she prays and fingers
endlessly

---

[21]Diego Rivera, Alfaro Siqueiros, José Clemente Orozco: the founders of the post-Revolutionary muralist movement in Mexico.

like the family
working down a row of beets
                to turn around
                and work
                and work
                There is no end.
Here eyes a mirror of all the warmth
                    and all the love for me,
And I am her
And she is me.
                We face life together in sorrow.
                anger, joy, faith and wishful
                thoughts.

I shed tears of anguish
as I see my children disappear
behind the shroud of mediocrity
never to look back to remember me.
I am Joaquín.
            I must fight
                    and win this struggle
                    for my sons, and they
                    must know from me
                    Who I am.
Part of the blood that runs deep in me
Could not be vanquished by the Moors.
I defeated them after five hundred years,
and I endured.
            The part of blood that is mine
            has labored endlessly five-hundred
            years under the heel of lustful
                    Europeans
                    I am still here!
I have endured in the rugged mountains
        of our country.
I have survived the toils and slavery
        of the fields.
                I have existed

in the barrios of the city,
in the suburbs of bigotry,
in the mines of social snobbery,
in the prisons of dejection,
in the muck of exploitation
and
in the fierce heat of racial hatred.

And now the trumpet sounds,
The music of the people stirs the
                              Revolution,
Like a sleeping giant it slowly
rears its head

to the sound of
                              Tramping feet
                         Clamouring voices
                         Mariachi strains
                     Fiery tequila explosions
              The smell of chile verde and
         Soft brown eyes of expectation for a
                                     better life.
And in all the fertile farm lands,
                              the barren plains,
the mountain villages,
smoke smeared cities
                    We start to MOVE.
         La Raza!
Mejicano!
         Español!
            Latino!
               Hispano!
                  Chicano!
or whatever I call myself,
                         I look the same
                         I feel the same
                         I cry
                              and

Sing the same

I am the masses of my people and
I refuse to be absorbed.
                    I am Joaquín
The odds are great
but my spirit is strong
                    My faith unbreakable
                    My blood is pure
I am Aztec Prince and Christian Christ
          I SHALL ENDURE!
          I WILL ENDURE!

I Am Joaquín (Denver, 1967). Permission granted by the author.

ABELARDO ("LALO" DELGADO; 1931-)

"Stupid America" (1969)

stupid america, see that chicano
with a big knife
on his steady hand
he doesn't want to knife you
he wants to sit on a bench
and carve christfigures
but you won't let him.
stupid america, hear that chicano
shouting curses on the street
he is a poet
without paper and pencil
and since he cannot write
he will explode.
stupid america, remember that chicanito
flunking math and english
he is the picasso
of your western states
but he will die
with one thousand masterpieces
hanging only from his mind.

Reprinted from *Chicano: 25 Pieces of a Chicano Mind* (1969). Permission granted by author.

JOSÉ MONTOYA (1932-)

"El Louie" (1969)

Hoy enterraron al Louie.[1]

And San Pedro o sanpinche
are in for it. And those
times of the forties
and the early fifties
lost un vato de atolle.

Kind of slim and drawn,
there toward the end,
aging fast from too much
booze y la vida dura. But
class to the end.

En Sanjo you'd see him
sporting a dark topcoat
playing in his fantasy
the role of Bogart, Cagney
or Raft.[2]

Era de Fowler el vato,
carnal del Candi y el
Ponchi—Los Rodríguez—
The Westside knew 'em
and Selma, even Gilroy.[3]

---

[1] a barrio resident and veteran of the Korean War.

[2] Humphrey Bogart, James Cagney, George Raft: Hollywood tough guys of
the period.

[3] a town south of San Francisco.

'48 Feetline, two-tone—
buenas garras and always
rucas—como la Mary y
la Helen...siempre con
liras bien afinadas
cantando, La Palma, la
que andaba en el florero.[4]

Louie hit on the idea in
those days for tailor-made
drapes, unique idea—porque
Fowler no era nada como
Los, o'l E.P.T. Fresno's
westside was as close as
we ever got to the big time,

But we had Louie and the
Palomar, el boogie, los
mambos y cuatro suspiros
del alma y nunca faltaba
that familiar, gut-shrinking
love-splitting, ass-hole-up
tight-bad news...

> Trucha, ésos! Va 'ber
> pedo!
> Abusau, ése!
> Get Louie

No llores, Carmen, we can
handle 'em.
> Ese, 'on tal Jimmy?
> Hórale, Louie
> Where's Primo?
> Va 'ber catos!

---

[4]reference to a Mexican ballad.

En el parking lot away from
the jura.

Hórale!
Trais filero?
Simón!
Nel!
Chale, ése![5]
Oooooh, este vato!

And Louie would come through—
melodramatic music, like in the
mono—tan tan trán! —Cruz
Diablo, El Charro Negro! Bogart
smile (his smile as deadly as
his vaisas) He dug roles, man,
and names—like "Blackie," "Little
Louie..."

Ese Louie...
Chale, call me "Diamonds!" man!
Y en Korea fue soldado de
levita con huevos and all the
paradoxes del soldado raso—
heroism and the stockade!

And on leave, jump boots
shainadas and ribbons, cocky
from the war, strutting to
early mass on Sunday morning.

Wow, is that 'ol Louie?

Mire, comadre, ahí va el hijo
de Lola!

---

[5]no, man.

Afterward he and fat Richard
would hock their Bronze Stars
for pisto en el Jardín Canales
y en el Trocadero.

At barber college he came
out with honors. Después
empeñaba su velardo de la
peluca pa' jugar pócar serrada
and lo ball en Sanjo y Alviso.

And "Legs Louie Diamond" hit
on some lean times...

Hoy enterraron al Louie.

Y en Fowler at Nesei's
pool parlor los baby chooks
se acuerdan de Louie, el carnal
del Candi y el Ponchi—la vez
que lo fileriaron en el Casa
Dome y cuando se catió con
La Chiva.

Hoy enterraron al Louie.

His death was an insult
porque no murió en acción—
no lo mataron los vatos,
ni los gooks en Korea.
He died alone in a rented
room—perhaps like a
Bogart movie.

The end was a cruel hoax.
But his life had been
remarkable!

Vato de atolle, el Louie Rodríguez.

Reprinted from *Information: 20 Years of Joda* (San José: Chusma House Publications, 1992): 16-18. Permission granted by the author.

MARGARITA COTA-CÁRDENAS (1941-)

"Crisis de identidad, o, Ya no chingues" (1970)

Soy chicana macana
o gringa marrana,
la tinta pinta
o la pintura tinta,
el puro retrato
o me huele el olfato,
una mera gabacha,
o cuata sin tacha
una pocha biscocha,[1]
o una india mocha,
(me pongo lentes rosas o negros
para tomar perspectiva,
todo depende, la verdad es relativa)
la vista aguda
o ciega nariguda,
parece que sí
pero mira que no,
me entiendes, Mendes,
o no me explico, Federico,
están claras las cosas,
pues no es por las moscas...
Ya, ya cierra la boca
y si te parece poco,
te echo un jarro de mole
en el falso pinche atole.

---

[1]bizcocha.

Reprinted from *Infinite Divisions: An Anthology of Chicana Literature.* Tey Diana Rebolledo and Eliana S. Rivero, eds. (Tucson: University of Arizona Press, 1993): 88-89. Permission granted by the author.

RAÚLRSALINAS (1934-)

"Los caudillos" (1970)

written from aztlán de leavenworth[1]

Stifling
    Crystal City
        heat
rouses Texas sleepers
    the long siesta finally over
at last, at long, long last
    politics wrested from
tyrannical usurpers' clutches
    fires are stoked
flames are fanned . . .

        conflagrating flames
of socio-political awareness.

    In rich Delano vineyards
        Chávez[2] does his pacifist thing
    "lift that crate
        & pick them grapes"
    stoop labor's awright—with God on your side.

Small wonder David Sánchez[3]
    impatient & enraged in East L.A.
dons a beret, its color symbolizing

---

[1]Leavenworth, Texas.

[2]César Chávez was the major Chicano farmworker organizer in the Southwest in the 1960s and 1970s.

[3]leader of the Brown Berets, a youth community service organization.

Urgent Brown.

Voices raised in unison
    in Northern New Mexico hills
    "¡esta tierra es nuestra!"
       cached clutter: invalid grants/unrecognized treaties
    their tongues are forked,
       Tijerina;[4]
    Indo-Hispano
    you're our man.

Denver's Corky[5] boxing lackeys' ears back
    let them live in the bottoms for awhile
see how they like a garbage dump
    for a next-door neighbor.

    José Angel Gutiérrez[6]: MAYO's fiery vocal cat
       the world does not love energetic noisemakers
    or so says papa henry b. (the saviour of San Anto)[7]
       who only saved himself.

In Eastern Spanish Ghettos
    Portorro street gangs do
Humanity.

    Young Lords[8]: (Cha-Cha, Fi & Yoruba)
       burglarize rich folk's antibiotics
    rip off x-ray units/hospital

---

[4]Reis López Tijerina, New Mexican leader of the land grant reclaim movement in the 1960s.

[5]Rodolfo "Corky" Gonzales, civil rights activist during the 1960s and 1970s; author of the poem *I am Joaquín* included in this anthology.

[6]political activist in 1960s and 1970s and founder of La Raza Unida Party.

[7]Henry B. González, an important political leader from San Antonio.

[8]reference to a Neo-Rican youth service organization (Neo-Rican refers to mainland Puerto Ricans).

> —become medics of the poor—
> ghetto children must not die
> of lead poisoning & T.B.

Latin Kings[9]: (Watusi Valez & the rest)
> if you're doing social service
how can you be on
> terrorizing sprees (with priest accompanist)
in near Northside Chicago?

> Ubiquitous? We're everywhere!

Arise! Bronze People,
> the wagon-wheels gather momentum.

Reprinted from *Un Trip Through the Mind Jail y Otras Excursions: Poems by raúlrsalinas* (San Francisco: Editorial Pocho-Che, 1980): 69-70. Permission granted by the author.

---

[9]a Chicago-based youth service organization.

ALURISTA (ALBERTO BALTAZAR URISTA; 1947-)

"Tarde sobria" (1971)

tarde sobria
    caminas en el agua pavimento cruel
bolsillos sin papel
    sin ruido tus pasos
        past ortega's store—no dimes to spend
gotta look for jesse
        go down see cindy—la gabacha
go to joe's
        go down see virginia
mañana el jale
pero "orita" el tiempo es mío
patrol car—he stop me
no time to walk, too young
the man
        he doesn't know my Raza is old
on the streets he frisk me
        on the job he kills al jefe
en la tienda no atiende a mi mamá
the man
        he say he wanna marry mi carnala
hell no!
        ella es mujer, no juguete
the man
        he likes to play
        he get a lot o' toys
and he don't know
        que las tardes que me alumbran
y las nubes que me visten
        pertenecen a mi raza
        a mi barrio

along with ortega's store
in the afternoons
   dust built walled castles
as i swim through the smog
   and the smell of the cannery
basin headed man of black-white stroll
   stick in hand don't know
no papers in my pockets
   mi bigote for i.d.
gonna look for jesse—forget the gabacha
   go get joe
to see virginia

Reprinted from *Floricanto en Aztlán* (Los Angeles: Chicano Cultural Center, UCLA, 1971): 96. Permission granted by the author.

RICARDO SÁNCHEZ (1941-1995)

"Barrios of the World" (1971)

barrios of the world,
where we live and strive,
where rich and poor separate
    their worlds
into different realities;
barrios of the world,
paradoxes
seething with rage/unsanity

a new world cometh,
world of awareness,
plagueless world,
spectral world,
love struck world,
composite of man's humanity,
cauldron of sister/brother-hood.

el chuco, los, alburque,[1] denver,
san anto, el valle, laredo,
the midwest, boricua[2] harlem,
change is coming to you
birdlike, vibrant, vehemently virile.

la voz del Chicano proclaims
hermandad-carnalismo-humanidad,
like bumper stickers cauterizing
gods of all dimensions.

---

[1] Albuquerque.

[2] boricua = puertorriqueño, Puerto Rican.

god is chicano, mexican, hispano,
 cholo,[3] pocho,[4] mexican-american,
 american of spanish surname (ASS!)
 boricua, puertorro[5] and a host
 multihued
 proclamando divinity, dignity,
 humankind moving forth. . .
 for us, there is our reality,
 it is real and virile/fertile,
 simplicity unadorned
 scorched by sun and drenched in love,

 chicano destiny being created
 carnales one and all, we do not fear
 the providence others claim,
 we just seek our own horizons;
 peaceful people that we are,
 we'll defend our right to live.
 somos la raza, hogan/jacal creators,
 pyramid builders, cathedral makers,
 living en el diablo, siete infiernos,
 coronado, la loma y kern place,
 creators of our destinies
 desde bareles a maravilla. . .

"Barrios of the World" by Ricardo Sánchez is reprinted with permission from the publisher of *Selected Poems* (Houston: Arte Público Press, University of Houston, 1985): 51-52.

---

[3]street youth in a barrio, known today as a homeboy.

[4]a person of Mexican descent who seeks to assimilate into Anglo-American culture.

[5]puertorro = puertorriqueño, Puerto Rican.

LUIS OMAR SALINAS (1937-)

"Death in Vietnam" (1972)

the ears of strangers
          listen
fighting men tarnish the ground
      death has whispered
              tales to the young
and now choir boys are ringing
            bells
   another sacrifice for America
      a Mexican

    comes home
his beloved country
    gives homage
and mothers sleep
        in cardboard houses

     let all anguish be futile
tomorrow it will rain
and the hills of Vietnam
resume
     the sacrifice is not over

Reprinted from *Literatura chicana: texto y contexto/Chicano Literature: Text and Context*. Antonia Castañeda Shular et al., eds. (Englewood Cliffs: N.J.: Prentice Hall, 1972): 43. Permission granted by the author.

YOLANDA LUERA (1953-)

"Aborto" (1975)

mis entrañas me
gritan un hijo
y yo me niego
mi vientre pide
abultarse, hincharse
y yo me niego
mis brazos piden arrullos
y yo me niego
mis labios quieren
cantar canciones de
cuna y yo me niego
yo me niego
y yo me...

Reprinted from *Chicanos: antología histórica y literaria* (México: Fondo de Cultura Económica, 1980): 313. Permission granted by the author.

GARY SOTO (1952-)

"Daybreak" (1977)

In this moment when the light starts up
In the east and rubs
The horizon until it catches fire,

We enter the fields to hoe,
Row after row, among the small flags of onion,
Waving off the dragonflies
That ladder the air.

And tears the onions raise
Do not begin in your eyes but in ours,
In the salt blown
From one blister into another;

They begin in knowing
You will never weaken to bear
The hour timed to a heart beat,
The wind pressing us closer to the ground.

When the season ends,
And the onions are unplugged from their sleep,
We won't forget what you failed to see,
And nothing will heal
Under the rain's broken fingers.

"Mexicans Begin Jogging" (1981)

At the factory I worked
In the fleck of rubber, under the press
Of an oven yellow with flame,
Until the border patrol opened
Their vans and my boss waved for us to run.
"Over the fence, Soto," he shouted,
And I shouted that I was American.
"No times for lies," he said, and pressed
A dollar in my palm, hurrying me
Through the back door.

Since I was on his time, I ran
And became the wag to a short tail of Mexicans—
Ran past the amazed crowds that lined
The street and blurred like photographs, in rain.
I ran from that industrial road to the soft
Houses where people paled at the turn of an autumn sky.
What could I do but yell *vivas*
To baseball, milkshakes, and those sociologists
Who would clock me
As I jog into the next century
On the power of a great, silly grin.

Reprinted from *New and Selected Poems* (San Francisco: Chronicle Books, 1995): 51.

JOSÉ ANTONIO BURCIAGA (1940-)

"Poema en tres idiomas y caló" (1977)

Españotli titlán Englishic,
titlán náhuatl, titlán Caló.
¡Qué locotl!
Mi mente spirals al mixtli,
buti suave I feel cuatro lenguas in mi boca.
Coltic sueños temostli
y siento una xóchitl brotar
from four diferentes vidas.

I yotl distinctamentli recuerdotl
cuandotl I yotl was a maya,
cuandotl, I yotl was a gachupinchi,
when Cortés se cogió a mi great tatarabuela,
cuandotl andaba en Pachucatlán.

I yotl recordotl el toniatiuh
en mi boca cochi
cihuatl, náhuatl
teocalli, my mouth
micca por el english
e hiriendo mi español,
ahora cojo ando en caló
pero no hay pedo
porque todo se vale,
con o sin safos.

[traducción]

Español entre inglés
entre náhuatl,[1] entre caló.[2]
¡Qué locura!
Mi mente en espiral asciende a las nubes
bien suave siento cuatro lenguas en mi boca.
Sueños torcidos caen
y siento una xóchitl[3] brotar
de cuatro diferentes vidas.

Yo indudablemente recuerdo
cuando yo era maya,
cuando yo era gachupín,[4]
cuando Cortés[5] se cogió a mi gran tatarabuela,[6]
cuando andaba en Aztlán.

Yo recuerdo el sol
en mi boca duerme
mi mujer náhuatl,
templo mi boca
muerta por el inglés,
e hiriendo mi español,
ahora cojo ando en caló
pero no hay problema
porque todo se vale,
con o sin seguridad.

---

[1]la lengua de los aztecas.

[2]el lenguaje de los jóvenes del barrio.

[3]"flor", en la lengua náhuatl.

[4]el apodo peyorativo dado a los españoles por los independentistas mexicanos de 1810.

[5]Hernán Cortés, el conquistador del imperio azteca.

[6]la madre indígena del mestizo; puede aludir a Malitzin, la esclava-traductora-amante de Cortés.

BERNICE ZAMORA (1938-)

"Notes from a Chicana 'Coed'" (1977)

for P.H.

To cry that the *gabacho*[1]
is our oppressor is to shout
in abstraction, *carnal*.[2]
He no more oppresses us
than you do now as you tell me
"It's the gringo who oppresses you, Babe."
You cry "The gringo is our oppressor!"
to the tune of $20,000 to $30,000
a year, brother, and I wake up
alone each morning and ask,
"Can I feed my children today?"

To make the day easier
I write poems about
pájaros, *mariposas*,
and the fragrance
of perfume I
smell on your collar;
you're quick to point out
that I must write
about social reality,
about "the gringo who
oppresses you, Babe."
And so I write about
how I worked in beet fields

---

[1]"stranger"; i.e., Anglo-Americans.
[2]"brother," among youths.

as a child, about how I
worked as a waitress
eight hours at night to
get through high school,
about working as a
seamstress, typist, and field clerk
to get through college, and
about how, in graduate school
I held two jobs, seven days
a week, still alone, still asking,
"Can I feed my children today?"
To give meaning to my life
you make love to me in alleys,
in back seats of borrowed Vegas,
in six-dollar motel rooms
after which you talk about
your five children and your wife
who writes poems at home
about *pájaros*, *mariposas*,
and the fragrance of perfume
she smells on your collar.
Then you tell me how you
bear the brunt of the
gringo's oppression for me,
and how you would go
to prison for me, because
"The gringo is oppressing you, Babe!"

And when I mention
your G.I. Bill, your
Ford Fellowship, your
working wife, your
three *gabacha guisas*[3]
when you ask me to
write your thesis,
you're quick to shout,

---

[3]"women," in the language of barrio youths.

Bernice Zamora   247

"Don't give me that
Women's Lib trip, *mujer*,
that only divides us,
and we have to work
together for the *movimiento*;
the *gabacho* is oppressing us!

Oye carnal, you may as well
tell me that moon water
cures constipation, that
penguin soup prevents *crudas*,
or that the Arctic Ocean is *menudo*,
because we both learned in the barrios,
man, that pigeon shit slides easier.

Still, because of the *gabacho*,
I must write poems about
pájaros, *mariposas*, and the fragrance
of oppressing perfume I smell somewhere.

Originally published in *Caracol* 3.9 (1977) and subsequently published in *Making Face, Making Soul/Haciendo caras: Creative and Critical Perspectives by Women of Color*. Gloria Anzaldúa, ed. (San Francisco: An Aunt Lute Foundation Book, 1990): 131-32. Permission granted by the author.

LORNA DEE CERVANTES (1954-)

"Beneath the Shadow of the Freeway" (1977)

1

Across the street—the freeway,
blind worm, wrapping the valley up
from Los Altos to Sal Si Puedes.
I watched it from my porch
unwinding. Every day at dusk
as Grandma watered geraniums
the shadow of the freeway lengthened.

2

We were a woman family:
Grandma, our innocent Queen;
Mama, the Swift Knight, Fearless Warrior.
Mama wanted to be Princess instead.
I know that. Even now she dreams of taffeta
and foot-high tiaras.

Myself: I could never decide.
So I turned to books, those staunch, upright men.
I became Scribe: Translator of Foreign Mail,
interpreting letters from the government, notices
of dissolved marriages and Welfare stipulations.
I paid the bills, did light man-work, fixed faucets,
insured everything
against all leaks.

Lorna Dee Cervantes

3

Before rain I notice seagulls.
They walk in flocks,
cautious across lawns: splayed toes,
indecisive beaks. Grandma says
seagulls mean storm.

In California in the summer,
mockingbirds sing all night.
Grandma says they are singing for their nesting wives.
"They don't leave their families
borrachando."

She likes the ways of birds,
respects how they show themselves
for toast and a whistle.

She believes in myths and birds.
She trusts, only what she builds
with her own hands.

4

She built her house,
cocky, disheveled carpentry,
after living twenty-five years
with a man who tried to kill her.

Grandma, from the hills of Santa Barbara,
I would open my eyes to see her stir mush
in the morning, her hair in loose braids,
tucked close around her head
with a yellow scarf.

Mama said, "It's her own fault,
getting screwed by a man for that long.
Sure as shit wasn't hard."

soft she was soft

5

in the night I would hear it
glass bottles shattering the street
words cracked into shrill screams

inside my throat   a cold fear
as it entered the house in hard
unsteady steps stopping at my door
my name   bathrobe   slippers
outside at 3 A.M. mist heavy
as a breath full of whiskey
stop it   go home   come inside
mama if he comes here again
I'll call the police

inside
a gray kitten   a touchstone
purring beneath the quilts
grandma stitched
from his suits
the patchwork singing
of mockingbirds

6

"You're too soft. . .always were.
You'll get nothing but shit.
Baby, don't count on nobody."
—a mother's wisdom.
Soft. I haven't changed,
maybe grown more silent, cynical
on the outside.

"O Mama, with what's inside of me

I could wash that all away. I could."

"But Mama, if you're good to them
they'll be good to you back."

Back. The freeway is across the street.
It's summer now. Every night I sleep with a gentle man
to the hymn of mockingbirds,

and in time, I plant geraniums.
I tie up my hair into loose braids,
and trust only what I have built
with my own hands.

Reprinted from *Emplumada* (Pittsburgh: Latin American Literary Review Press, 1977): 11-14.

ALBERTO ÁLVARO RÍOS (1952-)

"Mi abuelo" (1982)

Where my grandfather is is in the ground
where you can hear the future
like an Indian with his ear at the tracks.
A pipe leads down to him so that sometimes
he whispers what will happen to a man
in town or how he will meet the best
dressed woman tomorrow and how the best
man at her wedding will chew the ground
next to her. Mi abuelo is the man
who speaks through all the mouths in my house.
An echo of me hitting the pipe sometimes
to stop him from saying *my hair is a*
sieve is the only other sound. It is a phrase
that among all others is the best,
he says, and *my hair is a sieve* is sometimes
repeated for hours out of the ground
when I let him, which is not often.
An abuelo should be much more than a man
like you! He stops then, and speaks: *I am a man*
who has served ants with the attitude
of a waiter, who has made each smile as only
an ant who is fat can, and they liked me best,
but there is nothing left. Yet I know he ground
green coffee beans as a child, and sometimes
about when he was deaf and a man
cured him by mail and he heard groundhogs
talking, or about how he walked with a cane
he chewed on when he got hungry.
At best, mi abuelo is a liar.

I see an old picture of him at nani's[1] with an
off-white yellow center mustache and sometimes
that's all I know for sure. He talks best
about these hills, *slowest waves*, and where this man
is going, and I'm convinced his hair is a sieve,
that his fever is cooled now underground.
Mi abuelo is an ordinary man.
I look down the pipe, sometimes, and see a
rippled-topped stream in its best suit, in the ground.

Reprinted from *Whispering to Fool the Wind* (New York: The Sheep Meadow Press, 1982): 22-23. Reprinted by permission of the author.

---

[1]grandmother's.

JUAN FELIPE HERRERA (1948-)

"Are You Doing That New Amerikan Thing?" (1983)

for all movement, ex-movement and anti-movement affiliates and for Brandi Treviño

Are you doing that new Amerikan[1] thing?
Sweet thing, handsome thing, that thing about coming out, all the way out
About telling her, her telling him, telling us, telling them that we
Must kill the revolutionary soul, because it was only a magical thing
A momentary thing, a thing outside of time, a sixties thing, a sacred thing
A brown beret thing, a grassroot thing, a loud thing, a spontaneous thing
A Viet Nam thing, a white radical thing, an Aztlan thing, a Cholo thing
A nationalist thing, a for Pochos only thing, a college thing, an August 29th
    1970[2]
Chicano Moratorium thing, an outdated thing, a primitive thing.

Sweet thing, handsome thing, that thing about coming out, all the way out
On a communist scare thing, a Red thing, a let's go back to war thing
Because we must stop the El Salvador thing because it could lead to another
    Nicaragua
Thing because we need Reagun[3] and Order in the Americas thing.

Are you doing the new Amerikan thing?

The chains, pins and leather thing
The aluminum thing

---

[1]The "k" in Amerika is meant to symbolize right-wing thinking in U.S. society.

[2]Date of an anti-Vietnam march held in East Los Angeles with an attendance of around 30,000 people from the Southwest and other parts of the United States.

[3]Intended mispelling of the name of Ronald Reagan.

The transparent plastik underwear thing
The lonely boulevard thing
The hopeless existentialist thing
The neo-Paris melancholy thing
The nightmare thing
The urban artist thing
The laughing thing
The serious suicide thing
The New Amerikan Chicano thing
The end of the world thing
The victim thing
The enlightened quasi-political thing
The university hussle for the pie thing?
The *We Are the Community* thing

Are you doing that new Amerikan thing?

The *nacimos para morir* thing
The *yo te protejo* thing
The *Dios y Hombre* thing
The *quién sabe* thing
The *así nomás* thing
The *todo se acaba* thing
The *la vida es un misterio* thing
The *quisiera ser* thing
The *vato firme*[4] thing
The *chavala de aquellas*[5] thing
The *no me toques* thing
The *no quiero problemas* thing

Are you doing that Amerikan thing?

Doing the be clean be seen by the right people thing
Doing the be macho again because women like it anyway thing
Doing the look out for number one because you tried the group thing thing

---

[4]in barrio youth culture, a young man who lives by his principles.
[5]in barrio youth culture, a proud and beautiful woman.

Doing the be submissive again because after all a woman needs a man thing
Doing the Army thing because it really pays more than hanging around the
    Barrio thing
Doing the women's draft thing because you can do it better than the men
    thing
Doing the purity thing because no one got to be president by eating greasy
    tacos thing
Doing the spa thing because there you will meet the right tall &
    dark & blond & tender thing
Doing the homophobic thing because you caught yourself lusting at
    an aberration thing

Are you doing that new Amerikan thing?

Sweet thing, handsome thing, that thing about coming out, all the way out
About telling her, her telling him, telling us, telling them that we
Must kill the revolutionary soul?

Reprinted from *Exiles of Desire* (Fresno: Lalo Press Publications, 1983): 54-55.
Permission granted by the author.

JIMMY SANTIAGO BACA (1952-)

"Pinos Wells" (1984)

Pinos Wells—
an abandoned pueblo now.
The presence of those who lived
in these crumbling adobes
lingers in the air
like a picture
removed
leaves its former presence on the wall.

In corral dust
medicinal bottles
preserve rusty sunshine
that parched this pueblo
30 years ago.
Blackened sheds rust
in diablito barbs.
In barn rafters cobwebs
hang intricate as tablecloths
grandma crocheted for parlors
of wealthy Estancia ranchers.
Now she spins silken spider eggs.

My mind circles warm ashes of memories,
the dark edged images of my history.
On *that* field
I hand swept smooth
top crust dirt and duned a fort.
Idling sounds of Villa's horse
I reared my body and neighed at weeds.

From the orphanage my tía Jenny

drove me to Pinos Wells
to visit grandma. All Saturday afternoon
her gnarled fingers
flipped open photo album pages
like stage curtains at curtain call
the strange actors of my mestizo familia
bowed before me wearing vaquero costumes,
mechanic overalls and holding hoes in fields.

At the six o'clock mass
with clasped hands I whispered
to the blood shackled Christ on the cross,
begging company with my past—
given to Christ who would never tell
how under the afternoon sun in Santa Fe
the rooster slept and black ants
formed rosaries over the hard dirt yard,
when. . .

       Sanjo barrio,
          Chucos parked
at Lionel's hamburger stand
to watch Las Baby Dolls
cruise Central avenue
chromed excitement of '57 Chevies
flashing in their eyes.

In the alley behind Jack's Package Liquors
dogs fight for a burrito
dropped from a wino's coat pocket.
The ambulance screams down Edith
into Sanjo where Felipe bleeds red whiskey
through knife wounds.

On Walter street
telephones ring in red-stone apartments
while across Broadway
under Guadalupe bridge
box-car gypsies and Mejicanos swig Tokay.

Corridos—
  chairs splintering on kitchen floors—
   arguing voices in dark porches—
    doors angrily slammed—
     Seagrams bottles shatter on the streets—

I fell
into Sanjo, into my own brown body,
not knowing how to swim
as tongues lashed white spray warning
of storms to come,
                 I prayed.

In Santa Fe as a boy
I watched red tractors crumble dirt,
the black fire of disc blades
upturning burned leaves and cornstalks in their wake,
while I collected green and red commas
of broken glass in my yard,
and romped in mud slop of fallen tomb-trunks
of cottonwoods
that steamed in the dawn by the ditch.
Then,
        the fairytale of my small life
         stopped
when mother and father
abandoned me, and the ancient hillgods of my emotions
in caves of my senses
screamed, and the corn seedling of my heart
withered—like an earth worm out of earth,
I came forth into the dark world of freedom.
I ran from the orphanage at ten,
worked at Roger's Sheet Metal shop.
I'd open the window to let morning breeze
cool my boy body, and shoo
sparrows from their window ledge nest.

At the Conquistador Inn on south Central

I made love to Lolita,
and after her father found out, Lolita
slashed her wrists,
sitting on the toilet, blood scribbling
across the yellow linoleum,
as her brother pushed me aside, lifted her,
and drove her away, I nodded goodbye.

Teenage years
I sought the dark connection
of words become actions, of dreams made real,
like Tijerina's courthouse raid,
or César Chávez and thousands of braceros[1]
enduring the bloody stubs of police batons
that beat them as they marched.

I ransacked downtown stores
for winter coats to give my friends,
and the National Guard gassed me
at the Roosevelt Park when we burned
a cop's car to the ground.
He clubbed a Chicana for talking back.

On the West Mesa,
I took long walks and listened for a song
to come to me, song of a better life,
while an old Navajo woman sat on her crate
and groaned wet lipped at the empty wine bottle,
in front of Louie's Market
and gummy drunks staggered to sun by the wall,
mumbling moans for money.

Vatos in Barelas
leaned into their peacoats
against winter wind, faces tempered
with scars, as they rattled down pebbly alleys

---

[1]farmworkers from Mexico.

to their connection's house.

At the University of New Mexico
learned Chicanos
lugged book-heavy ideas to bed
and leafed through them sleeplessly,
while I slept under cottonwood trees
along the Río Grande
and cruised with Pedro
drinking whiskey through the Sangre De Cristo
mountains, until we hurled off
a sharp snowy curve one December morning
into a canyon, and I carried his dead body to a farm house.

Months after I headed West
on I-40,
in my battered Karmen Ghia.
Desperate for a new start,
sundown in my face,
I spoke with Earth—

I have been lost from you Mother Earth.
No longer
does your language of rain wear away my thoughts,
nor your language of fresh morning air
wear away my face,
nor your language of roots and blossoms
wear away my bones.
But when I return, I will become your child again,
let your green alfalfa hands take me,
let your maíz roots plunge into me
and give myself to you again,
with the crane, the elm tree and the sun.

Reprinted from *Martin and Meditations on the South Valley* (New York: New
Directions Books, 1987): 3-8. Copyright ©by Jimmy Santiago Baca. Reprinted
by permission of New Directions Publishing Corp.

CARLOS CUMPIÁN (1953-)

"Kilotons and Then Some" (1985)

Bombs on hot and crowded Nagasaki
and Hiroshima.
Bombs on hated Hai-phong harbor and Hanoi.
Bombs on the Caribbean jewel Puerto Rico
for almost a century—
bombs on the presidential building
of socialist Chile in '73.

Bombs off Mexico's Veracruz
shot by U.S. Marines in 1914.
Bombs over the once many starfish
of now-radiated Pacific Isles.
Bombs over the Buddha's blood fields
in Cambodia.
Bombs over Christ's homeland of Palestine.

Bombs over the cactus and lizards
of the New Mexican desert.
Bombs over the Nevada oasis scattering
Las Vegas.
Bombs under the Utah Mormon paradise.
Bombs with no markings sold to
those with no future.

Bombs under the Mongolian Gobi desert.
Bombs under the Siberian rock ice.
Bombs on the heads of Afghanistan.
Bombs with Moslem moon and star
of Pakistan.

Bombs with designer shades from France.

Bombs with mantras and incense
reincarnates India.

Bombs from David's six-pointed star
into the oil rigs of Iraq.
Bombs with red stars over
rich rice fields of Asia.

Bombs with question marks
from South Africa's white elite.
Bombs with passages from the Koran
canned in Libya.
Bombs from the 14th century of lonely Iran.
Bombs from the illreputed saint
of North Korea Kim Il Sung.

Bombs with no consideration
from his cousins in South Korea.
Bombs of the underdeveloped nations
just laying around.
Bombs of the SuperPowers leaving them dumb.
Bombs of the captive people getting louder,
Bombs of the captors making them captives.

Bombs with names such as "TRINITY, 666,
LITTLE BOY, BLISTER BUSTER, HEAVY
METAL, BAR-B-QUED."
Bombs blessed by drunk church sinners
with sweaty palms.
Bombs with no chance of ever learning a trade.
Bombs four days old on the discount table.

Bombs the kind you'll never see.
Bombs the ones you only have to listen to
once—
and you'll never hear again.

Reprinted from *Coyote Sun* (Chicago: MARCH/Abrazo Press, 1990): 57-58.

REYES CÁRDENAS (1948-)

"Padre Nuestro Que Estás en el Banco" (1986)

The evangelists
on the radio
and the television
tell you
all about your sins;
then they
ask you for money.
They condemn
the sinful,
the unrighteous,
they condemn
the young;
they shout
that Jesus
is coming.
And then
they ask
for money.
Money to build
big churches,
money so they too
can be rich
like Billy Graham
and Oral Roberts.
Money is no longer
the root
of all evil;
money it seems
has now become
the source
of salvation.
Well, I just got paid today
and I'm looking
for a clergyman.
I just got paid today
and I think it's enough
money with which
to save my soul—
if not
I'll ask my boss
for a raise next week.

Reprinted from *I Was Never a Militant Chicano* (Austin: Relámpago Press, 1986): 23-24. Permission granted by the author.

RUBÉN MEDINA (1955-)

"Cómo desnudar a una mujer con un saxofón" (1986)

No es fácil.
El aire que sale del estómago
debe traer
la sal del mar.
Las yemas de los dedos
deben hablar
de palmeras
de membrana a surco
o de soles que trabajan
de noche.
Los sonidos,
agua y metal,
casi vena,
deben confundir
oído y hombro,
y descender
hasta las rodillas
con la misma suavidad
de quien maneja
un chevrolet 53
a 30 millas por hora,

en un freeway de Los Angeles.
Los ojos deben permanecer
cerrados
hasta que la noche
tenga 24 horas,
la semana más de siete días
y no exista la palabra
desempleo.
Y entonces,
abres los ojos,
y quizá
encuentres la sonrisa
de ella.
Pero esto no significa
más que un categórico
saludo de hola,
quihúbole,
What's going on, ése,
porque también
en la plusvalía
hay
pasión.

"Como desnudar a una mujer con un saxofón" by Rubén Medina is reprinted with permission from the publisher of "Amor de lejos..."/...Fool's Love (Houston: Arte Público Press, University of Houston, 1986): 59-60. Permission also granted by the author.

GINA VALDÉS (1943-)

"Comiendo lumbre" (1986)

Con tu boca suelta
le haces el amor
a mi boca. Sabes
mejor que aquel mango,
el más jugoso que comí
lentamente un día hasta
que no quedó ni una
hebra anaranjada en
el hueso blanco.

No pares,
deja que el sol explote
silencioso en mi boca,
así me gusta vivir,
comiendo lumbre, probando
tu pulso, tus sueños, tu
corazón en mi boca.

No pares,
quiero que tu beso dure un
poema, una mirada de buho.

Allá, a un planeta de tu beso
está mi casa, la alfombra
blanca con los poros empolvados,
las sábanas lilas percudidas,
el mantel manchado, la chequera
sin sumar, el carro con la llanta
gastada, la libreta con dos poemas
empezados, mil por empezar, mi
hija creciendo como helecho.

Y fuera de mi casa, casi adentro,
el mundo rasgándose más con cada
mentira. La gente mala de codicia
apuntando con su hierro a la gente
rabiosa de hambre. Las mentiras
y las balas me hieren día y noche.
Cien mujeres salvadoreñas se desangran
por mí, por mi silencio. Sus gritos
son mis pesadillas.

No sé de dónde oigo un suspiro, no
sé si es mío o tuyo o de que moribunda o recién nacida.

En tu boca no suspiro, sorbo
tu aliento de nubes, me gusta
lo que me dice tu lengua; tu
corazón en mi boca me hace
sentir por lo que escribo, por
lo que lucho, por lo que, cuando
carece, me indigno.

       No pares,
dame eso que sientes al abrir los
ojos en la alborada, lo que te hace
saltar de tu cama hasta el sol.
No quiero que pares, estoy atrapada
en la soltura de tu boca.

Pero suéltame, déjame ir, dame
tu aliento y suéltame, quiero irme
acercando a otros fuegos. Necesito
escribir, necesito escribir del amor,
de las manos de pétalos, de los puentes,
de las puertas. Necesito escribir
de ese amor apasionado: el amor
al pan, al arroz, al maíz
en la mesa de todos.

TINO VILLANUEVA (1941-)

"Unción de palabras" (1987)

¿Qué dirán mañana estas palabras,
qué dirán
entre las manos de los hijos
de este padre que aún no lo es?
¿Verán
que he interrumpido la vida
para contar estas constancias,
estos retazos de lamento,
y que he venido con los míos
de un pueblo perseguido
por la historia irracional?
¿Comprenderán
que este fragor de consonantes
es el asco
en conciencia transformada,
cabal comprobación de que he existido?

Llévate, hija,
llévate, hijo,
de mí esta unción de palabras
con las que me curo diariarmente,
porque el recuerdo es poderoso
y se vuelve contra mí al improviso,
tiene vida como tú,
aunque todavía no existes,
y sin embargo, dulcemente,
ya de ti hago memoria.

Hoy me desamarro
del trágico trasunto de la vida,
y te entrego, pues,

las cosas familiares: cómo
y por qué una mitad de tus abuelos,
más quien esto escribe,
tardamos largamente en despedirnos
de la vecindad donde dolían
nuestros nombres.

Para siempre:
llévate esta fe enmarcada
a fin de que retengas el retrato
y tu linaje
inquietados en el fondo
por las fracturas del pasado
y la entereza que ya soy.

DEMETRIA MARTÍNEZ (1960-)

"Nativity: For Two Salvadoran Women, 1986-1987" (1989)

Your eyes, large as Canada, welcome
this stranger.
We meet in a Juárez train station
where you sat hours,
your offspring blooming in you
like cactus fruit,
dresses stained where breasts leak,
panties in purses tagged
"Hecho en El Salvador,"
your belts, like equators,
mark north from south,
borders I cannot cross,
for I am a North American reporter,
pen and notebook, the tools
of my tribe, distance us
though in any other era I might
press a stethoscope to your wombs,
hear the symphony of the unborn,
finger forth infants to light,
wipe afterbirth, cut cords.

"It is impossible to raise a child
in that country."

Sisters, I am no saint. Just a woman
who happens to be a reporter,
a reporter who happens
to be a woman,
squat in a forest, peeing
on pine needles,
watching you vomit morning sickness,

a sickness infinite as the war in El Salvador,
a sickness my pen and notebook will not ease,
tell me, ¿Por qué están aquí?,
how did you cross over?
In my country we sing of a baby in a manger,
finance death squads,
how to write of this shame,
of the children you chose to save?

"It is impossible to raise a child
in that country."

A North American reporter,
I smile, you tell me you are due
in December, we nod,
knowing what women know,
I shut my notebook,
watch your car rock
through the Gila,[1]
a canoe hangs over the windshield
like the beak of an eagle,
babies turn in your wombs,
summoned to Belén to be born.

Reprinted from *Three Times a Woman: Chicana Poetry* (Tempe: Bilingual Press/Editorial Bilingüe, Arizona State University, 1989): 132-33.

---

[1] a border river.

BÁRBARA BRINSON CURIEL (1956-)

"Recipe: Chorizo con Huevo Made in the Microwave" (1989)

I won't lie,
It's not the same.

When you taste it
memories of abuelita
feeding wood into the stove
will dim.

You won't smell the black crisp
of tortillas
bubbling on cast iron.
Microwaved,
they are pale and limp as avena—
haven't a shadow of smoke.

There's no eggy lace
to scrape from the pan.
No splatters of grease
on the back of the stove.
Everything is clean:
vaporized
dripless.

It's not the same.

If your mother saw you
she'd raise an eyebrow—
the same one she arched
when, at eight,
you turned down sopa de fideo
for peanut butter and jelly at lunch.

You can turn away
from that eyebrow,
but there's no escaping the snarl
grandma will dish out
from her photo in the mantle.

It's the same hard stare
you closed your eyes to
on the day you brought
that microwave home.

Ni modo, pues.

Get out a plastic dish.
Cook the chorizo on high for 4 minutes.
Crack the eggs.
Fold them in.
Microwave 2 minutes
Stir.
Microwave 2 minutes.
Serve.

Eat your chorizo con huevo
with pale tortillas.
Remember grandma eating,
craving chorizo cooked
over an outdoor stove
in a Tucson summer.

As the grease runs into your sleeve,
peer into her mind's eye:
a childhood of dust
swirls around feet;
in her mouth
a futile search
for a relic of grit.

While your mouth is full,
recall that her appetite

ached
for a seasonless sky
suspended, a firmament,
over a horizon of sand.

Reprinted from *Speak to Me from Dreams* (Berkeley: Third Woman Press, 1989):
64-66. Permission granted by the author.

FRANCISCO ALARCÓN (1954-)

"Me gusta caminar junto a tu lado" (1991)

me gusta caminar junto a tu lado,
ir pisando en el malecón tu sombra,
dejar que tus pasos marquen mis pasos,
seguirte como barco remolcado

ajustando mis pies en las huellas
que como puma dejas en la playa,
quiero ser la toalla con que te secas,
donde te extiendes a tomar el sol

qué suerte la del cinturón que abraza
tu cintura, la del cristo que cuelga
de una cadena entre tus pectorales

qué alegría llegar como peine diario
a oler la mañana en tus cabellos
y en vez de peinarte, despeinarte

Reprinted from *De amor oscuro/Of Dark Love* (Santa Cruz: Moving Parts Press, 1991): 22. Permission granted by the author.

LUIS RODRÍGUEZ (1959-)

"The Blast Furnace" (1991)

A Foundry's stench, the rolling mill's clamor,
the jackhammer's concerto leaving traces
between worn ears. Oh sing me a bucket shop blues
under an accordion's spell
with blood notes cutting through the black air
for the working life, for the rotating shifts,
for the day's diminishment and rebirth.
The lead seeps into your skin like rainwater
along stucco walls; it blends into the fabric of cells,
the chemistry of bone, like a poisoned paintbrush
coloring skies of smoke, devouring like a worm
that never dies, a fire that's never quenched.
The blast furnace bellows out a merciless melody
as molten metal runs red down your back,
as assembly lines continue rumbling
into your brain, into forever,
while rolls of pipes crash onto brick floors.
The blast furnace spews a lava of insipid dreams,
a deathly swirl of screams; of late night wars
with a woman, a child's book of fear,
a hunger of touch, a hunger of poetry,
a daughter's hunger for laughter.
It is the sweat of running, of making love,
a penitence pouring into ladles of slag.
It is falling through the eyes of a whore,
a red-core bowel of rot,
a red-eyed train of refugees,
a red-scarred hand of unforgiveness,
a red-smeared face of spit.
It is blasting a bullet through your brain,
the last dying echo of one who enters
the volcano's mouth to melt.

ALMA LUZ VILLANUEVA (1944-)

"Trust" (1992)

I wouldn't be surprised if I opened
the front door and nuclear winds
were blowing, the sky a crazy color,

like a tornado, everything swept away—
my child, myself, and everyone else
(this is only a fantasy, now) (I know

the power of words, I know)—the sun
strolling down the street, tired of her
place, a distant star—she wants to embrace

us, make us disappear—well, okay, what
does this mean?

Who do you trust when love turns its
back on you? When the ozone tatters,

bit by bit? When wars are more popular than
teaching children? When people have no memory

of what a bed was like, clean sheets? When
children, everywhere, go to sleep hungry? When

the children of Baghdad are slaughtered?
When South Africa comes to its senses?

When the rainforests curse the sky?
When all the murdered in Latin America

return to their families, intact and singing?

When the radiation at Chernobyl stops killing

the innocent? When children in our cities
stop dying for lack of hope, stray bullets,

the crack dealer's promises, our leader's
promises, their convenient lies

to the children of the poor, the forgotten?
When our Drug Wars turn into Fierce Peace:

medical coverage, dental coverage, food, clothing,
shelter, real, substantial, *free* education? When

the birds become mute and tired of flying? When
Spring turns her back on us, withholding her

matrix, source; whispering in the wind,

"There was a web, but you destroyed it—

there was a seed, but you crushed it—

there was a way, but you forgot."

Oh, and me standing in the sun, praising her
to the very end.

Reprinted from *Revista Apple* 3.1-2 (1992): 9-10.

TEATRO / THEATER

LUIS VALDEZ (1940-)

Las Dos Caras del Patroncito (1965)

First Performance 1965: the Grape Strike,
Delano, California on the Picketline

CHARACTERS:

Esquirol
Patroncito
Charlie: Armed Guard

In September, 1965 six thousand farmworkers went on strike in the grape fields of Delano. During the first months of the ensuing Huelga, the growers tried to intimidate the struggling workers to return to the vineyards. They mounted shotguns in their pickups, prominently displayed in the rear windows of the cab; they hired armed guards; they roared by in their huge carruchas, etc. It seemed that they were trying to destroy the spirit of the strikers with mere materialistic evidence of their power. Too poor to afford la causa, many of the huelguistas left Delano to work in other areas; most of them stayed behind the picket through the winter; and a few returned to the fields to scab, pruning vines. The growers started trucking in more esquiroles from Texas and Mexico.

In response to this situation, especially the phoney "scary" front of the ranchers, we created "Dos Caras." It grew out of an improvisation in the old pink house behind the huelga office in Delano. It was intended to show the "two faces of the boss."

A **Farmworker** *enters, carrying a pair of pruning shears.*

Farmworker: (*To audience*). ¡Buenos días! This is the ranch of my patroncito, and I come here to prune grape vines. My patrón bring me all the way from México here to California, the land of sun and money! More sun than money. But I better get to jalar now because my patroncito he don't like to see me talking to strangers. (*There is a roar backstage.*) Ay, here he comes in his big car! I better get to work. (*He prunes. The* **Patroncito** *enters, wearing a yellow*

*pig face mask. He is driving an imaginary limousine, making the roaring sound
of the motor.*)

Patroncito: Good morning, boy!

Farmworker: Buenos días, patroncito. (*His hat in his hands.*)

Patroncito: You working hard, boy?

Farmworker: Oh, sí patrón. Muy hard. (*He starts working furiously.*)

Patroncito: Oh, you can work harder than that, boy. (*He works harder.*)
Harder! (*He works harder.*) Harder! (*He works still harder.*) Harder!

Farmworker: Ay, that's too hard, patrón! (*The* **Patroncito** *looks downstage, then upstage along the imaginary row of vines, with the farmworker's head
alongside his, following his movement.*)

Patroncito: How come you cutting all the wires instead of the vines, boy?
(*The* **Farmworker** *shrugs helplessly, frightened and defenseless.*) Look, lemme
show you something. Cut this vine here. (*Points to a vine.*) Now this one.
(**Farmworker** *cuts.*) Now this one. (*The* **Farmworker** *almost cuts the* **Patroncito***'s extended finger.*) Heh!

Farmworker: (*Jumps back,*) Ah!

Patroncito: Ain't you scared of me, boy? (**Farmworker** *nods.*) Huh, boy?
(**Farmworker** *nods and makes a grunt signifying yes.*) What, boy? You don't
have to be scared of me! I love my Mexicans. You're one of the new ones, huh?
Come in from. . .

Farmworker: México, señor.

Patroncito: Did you like the truck ride, boy? (**Farmworker** *shakes head
indicating no.*) What?!

Farmworker: I loved it, señor!

Patroncito: Of course, you did. All my Mexicans love to ride in trucks!
Just the sight of them barreling down the freeway makes my heart feel good;
hands on their sombreros, hair flying in the wind, bouncing along happy as
babies. Yes, sirree, I sure love my Mexicans, boy!

Farmworker: (*Puts his arm around* **Patroncito**.) Oh, patrón.

Patroncito: (*Pushing him away.*) I love 'em about ten feet away from me,
boy. Why, there ain't another grower in this whole damn valley that treats you
like I do. Some growers got Filipinos, others got Arabs, me I prefer Mexicans.
That's why I come down here to visit you, here in the field. I'm an important
man, boy! Bank of America, University of California, Safeway stores, I got a
hand in all of 'em. But look, I don't even have my shoes shined.

Farmworker: Oh, patrón, I'll shine your shoes! (*He gets down to shine*
Patroncito*'s shoes.*)

Patroncito: Never mind, get back to work. Up, boy, up I say! (*The* **Farmworker** *keeps trying to shine his shoes.*) Come on, stop it. Stop it! (**Charlie,** *"la jura" or "rent-a-fuzz," enters like an ape. He immediately lunges for the* **Farmworker.**) Charlie! Charlie, no! It's okay, boy. This is one of my Mexicans! He was only trying to shine my shoes.

Charlie: You sure?

Patroncito: Of course! Now you go back to the road and watch for union organizers.

Charlie: Okay. (**Charlie** *exits like an ape. The* **Farmworker** *is off to one side, trembling with fear.*)

Patroncito: (*To* **Farmworker.**) Scared you, huh boy? Well lemme tell you, you don't have to be afraid of him, as long as you're with me, comprende? I got him around to keep an eye on them huelguistas. You ever heard of them, son? Ever heard of huelga? or Cesar Chavez?

Farmworker: ¡Oh, sí patrón!

Patroncito: What?

Farmworker: ¡Oh, no, señor! ¡Es comunista! Y la huelga es puro pedo. ¡Bola de colorados, arrastrados, huevones! ¡No trabajan porque no quieren!

Patroncito: That's right, son. Sic'em! Sic'em, boy!

Farmworker: (*Really getting into it.*) ¡Comunistas! ¡Desgraciados!

Patroncito: Good boy! (**Farmworker** *falls to his knees, hands in front of his chest like a docile dog; his tongue hangs out.* **Patroncito** *pats him on the head.*) Good boy. (*The* **Patroncito** *steps to one side and leans over.* **Farmworker** *kissed his ass.* **Patroncito** *snaps up triumphantly.*) 'At's a baby! You're okay, Pancho.

Farmworker: (*Smiling*) Pedro.

Patroncito: Of course you are. Hell, you got it good here!

Farmworker: Me?

Patroncito: Damn right! You sure as hell ain't got my problems, I'll tell you that. Taxes, insurance, supporting all them bums on welfare. You don't have to worry about none of that. Like housing, don't I let you live in my labor camp, nice, rent-free cabins, air-conditioned?

Farmworker: Sí, señor, ayer se cayó la puerta.

Patroncito: What was that? English.

Farmworker: Yesterday the door fell off, señor. And there's rats también. Y los excusados, the restrooms, ay, señor, fuchi! (*Holds fingers to his nose.*)

Patroncito: Awright! (**Farmworker** *shuts up.*) So you gotta rough it a little. I do that every time I go hunting in the mountains. Why, it's almost like camping out, boy. A free vacation!

Farmworker: Vacation?

Patroncito: Free!

Farmworker: Qué bueno. Thank you, patrón!

Patroncito: Don't mention it. So what do you pay for housing, boy?

Farmworker: Nothing! (*Pronounced naw-thing*)

Patroncito: Nothing, right! Now what about transportation? Don't I let you ride free in my trucks? To and from the fields?

Farmworker: Sí, señor.

Patroncito: What do you pay for transportation, boy?

Farmworker: Nothing!

Patroncito: (*With* **Farmworker.**) Nothing! What about food? What do you eat, boy?

Farmworker: Tortillas y frijoles con chile.

Patroncito: Beans and tortillas. What's beans and tortillas cost, boy?

Farmworker: (*Together with* **Patrón**) Nothing!

Patroncito: Okay! So what you got to complain about?

Farmworker: Nothing!

Patroncito: Exactly. You got it good! Now look at me, they say I'm greedy, that I'm rich. Well, let me tell you boy, I got problems. No free housing for me, Pancho. I gotta pay for what I got. You see that car? How much you think a Lincoln Continental like that costs? Cash! $12,000! Ever write out a check for $12,000, boy?

Farmworker: No, señor.

Patroncito: Well, lemme tell you, it hurts. It hurts right here! (*Slaps his wallet in his hind pocket.*) And what for? I don't need a car like that. I could throw it away!

Farmworker: (*Quickly.*) I'll take it, patrón.

Patroncito: Get your greasy hands off it! (*Pause.*) Now, let's take a look at my housing. No free air conditioned mountain cabin for me. No sir! You see that LBJ ranch style house up there,[1] boy? How much you think a house like that costs? Together with the hill, which I built? $350,000!

Farmworker: (*Whistles.*) That's a lot of frijoles, patrón?

Patroncito: You're telling me! (*Stops, looks toward house.*) Oh yeah, and look at that, boy! You see her coming out of the house, onto the patio by the pool? The blonde with the mink bikini?

---

[1]The reference is to a kind of ostentatious Texas residence associated with Lyndon Baines Johnson (1908-73), who served as President, 1963-69.

Farmworker: What bikini?
Patroncito: Well, it's small, but it's there. I oughta know, it cost me $5,000! And every weekend she wants to take trips. Trips to L.A, San Francisco, Chicago, New York. That woman hurts. It all costs money! You don't have problems like that, muchacho, that's why you're so lucky. Me, all I got is the woman, the house, the hill, the land. (*Starts to get emotional.*) Those commie bastards say I don't know what hard work is, that I exploit my workers. But look at all them vines, boy! (*Waves an arm toward the audience.*) Who the hell do they think planted all them vines with his own bare hands? Working from sun up to sunset! Shoving vine shoots into the ground! With blood pouring out of his fingernails. Working in the heat, the frost, the fog, the sleet! (**Farmworker** *has been jumping up and down trying to answer him.*)
Farmworker: You, patrón, you!
Patroncito: (*Matter of factly.*) Naw, my grandfather, he worked his ass off out here. But, I inherited it, and it's all mine!
Farmworker: You sure work hard, boss.
Patroncito: Juan. . . ?
Farmworker: Pedro.
Patroncito: I'm going to let you in on a little secret. Sometimes I sit up there in my office and think to myself: I wish I was a Mexican.
Farmworker: You?
Patroncito: Just one of my own boys. Riding in the trucks, hair flying in the wind, feeling all that freedom, coming out here to the fields, working under the green vines, smoking a cigarette, my hands in the cool soft earth, underneath the blue skies, with white clouds drifting by, looking at the mountains, listening to the birdies sing.
Farmworker: (*Entranced.*) I got it good.
Patroncito: What you want a union for, boy?
Farmworker: I don't want no union, patrón?
Patroncito: What do you want more money for?
Farmworker: I don't want. . . I want more money!
Patroncito: Shut up! You want my problems, is that it? After all I explained to you? Listen to me, son, if I had the power, if I had the power. . . wait a minute, I got the power! (*Turns toward* **Farmworker**, *frightening him.*) Boy!
Farmworker: I didn't do it, patrón.
Patroncito: How would you like to be a rancher for a day?
Farmworker: Who me? Oh no, señor. I can't do that.
Patroncito: Shut up. Gimme that. (*Takes his hat, shears, sign.*)
Farmworker: ¡No, patrón, por favor, señor! ¡Patroncito!

Patroncito: (*Takes off his own sign and puts it on farmworker.*) Here!

Farmworker: Patron. . .cito. (*He looks down at the "Patrón" sign.*)

Patroncito: All right, now take the cigar. (**Farmworker** *takes cigar.*) And the whip. (**Farmworker** *takes whip.*) Now look tough, boy. Act like you're the boss.

Farmworker: Sí, señor. (*He cracks the whip and almost hits his foot.*)

Patroncito: Come on, boy! Head up, chin out! Look tough, look mean. (**Farmworker** *looks tough and mean.*) Act like you can walk into the governor's office and tell him off!

Farmworker: (*With unexpected force and power.*) Now, look here, Ronnie![2] (**Farmworker** *scares himself.*)

Patroncito: That's good. But it's still not good enough. Let's see. Here take my coat.

Farmworker: Oh, no patrón, I can't.

Patroncito: Take it!

Farmworker: No, señor.

Patroncito: Come on!

Farmworker: Chale. (**Patroncito** *backs away from* **Farmworker**. *He takes his coat and holds it out like a bullfighter's cape, assuming the bullfighting position.*)

Patroncito: Uh-huh, toro.

Farmworker: ¡Ay! (*He turns toward the coat and snags it with an extended arm like a horn.*)

Patroncito: Ole! Okay, now let's have a look at you. (**Farmworker** *puts on coat.*) Naw, you're still missing something! You need something!

Farmworker: Maybe a new pair of pants?

Patroncito: (*A sudden flash.*) Wait a minute! (*He touches his pig mask.*)

Farmworker: Oh, no! Patrón, not that! (*He hides his face.* **Patroncito** *removes his mask with a big grunt.* **Farmworker** *looks up cautiously, sees the* **Patrón***'s real face and cracks up laughing.*) Patrón, you look like me!

Patroncito: You mean. . . I. . .look like a Mexican?

Farmworker: ¡Sí, señor! (**Farmworker** *turns to put on the mask, and* **Patroncito** *starts picking up farmworker's hat, sign, etc., and putting them on.*)

Patroncito: I'm going to be one of my own boys. (**Farmworker**, *who has his back to the audience, jerks suddenly as he puts on* **Patroncito***'s mask. He*

---

[2]Ronald Reagan, who was governor of California in the 1960s.

Luis Valdez   289

*stands tall and turns slowly, now looking very much like a patrón. Suddenly
fearful, but playing along.)* Oh, that's good! That's. . .great.

Farmworker: (*Booming, brusque, patrón-like.*) Shup up and get to work,
boy!

Patroncito: Heh, now that's more like it!

Farmworker: I said get to work! (*He kicks* **Patroncito.**)

Patroncito: Heh, why did you do that for?

Farmworker: Because I felt like it, boy! You hear me, boy? I like your
name, boy! I think I'll call you boy, boy!

Patroncito: You sure learn fast, boy.

Farmworker: I said shut up!

Patroncito: What an act. (*To audience.*) He's good, isn't he?

Farmworker: Come here boy.

Patroncito: (*His idea of a Mexican*). Sí, señor, I theeenk.

Farmworker: I don't pay you to think, son. I pay you to work. Now look
here, see that car? It's mine.

Patroncito: My Lincoln Conti. . .oh, you're acting. Sure.

Farmworker: And that LBJ ranch style house, with hill? That's mine too.

Patroncito: The house too.

Farmworker: All mine.

Patroncito: (*More and more uneasy.*) What a joker.

Farmworker: Oh, wait a minute. Respect, boy! (*He pulls off* **Patroncito's**
farmworker hat.) Do you see her coming out of my house, onto my patio by my
pool? The blonde in the bikini? Well, she's mine too!

Patroncito: But that's my wife!

Farmworker: Tough luck, son. You see this land, all these vines? They're
mine.

Patroncito: Just a damn minute here. The land, the car, the house, hill, and
the cherry on top too? You're crazy! Where am I going to live?

Farmworker: I got a nice, air conditioned cabin down in the labor camp.
Free housing, free transportation. . .

Patroncito: You're nuts! I can't live in those shacks! They got rats, cockroaches. And those trucks are unsafe. You want me to get killed?

Farmworker: Then buy a car.

Patroncito: With what? How much you paying me here, anyway?

Farmworker: Eighty-five cents an hour.

Patroncito: I was paying you a buck twenty five!

Farmworker: I got problems, boy! Go on welfare!

Patroncito: Oh no, this is too much. You've gone too far, boy. I think you better give me back my things. (*He takes off* **Farmworker**'*s sign and hat, throws down shears and tells the audience.*) You know that damn Cesar Chavez is right? You can't do this work for less than two dollars an hour. No, boy, I think we've played enough. Give me back. . .

Farmworker: Get your hands off me, spic!

Patroncito: Now stop it, boy!

Farmworker: Get away from me, greaseball! (**Patroncito** *tries to grab mask.*) Charlie! Charlie! (**Charlie** *the rent-a-fuzz comes bouncing in.* **Patroncito** *tries to talk to him.*)

Patroncito: Now listen, Charlie, I. . .

Charlie: (*Pushes him aside.*) Out of my way, Mex! (*He goes over to* **Farmworker.**) Yeah, boss?

Patroncito: This union commie bastard is giving me trouble. He's trying to steal my car, my land, my ranch, and he even tried to rape my wife!

Charlie: (*Turns around, an infuriated ape.*) You touched a white woman, boy?

Patroncito: Charlie, you idiot, it's me! Your boss!

Charlie: Shut up!

Patroncito: Charlie! It's me!

Charlie: I'm gonna whup you good, boy! (*He grabs him.*)

Patroncito: (**Charlie** *starts dragging him out.*) Charlie! Stop it! Somebody help me! Where's those damn union organizers? Where's Cesar Chavez? Help! Huelga! Huelgaaaaa! (**Charlie** *drags out the* **Patroncito.** *The* **Farmworker** *takes off the pig mask and turns toward the audience.*)

Farmworker: Bueno, so much for the patrón. I got his house, his land, his car. Only I'm not going to keep 'em. He can have them. But I'm taking the cigar. Ay los watcho. (*Exit.*)

Las Dos Caras del Patroncito by Luis Valdez is reprinted with permission from the publisher of *Luis Valdez—Early Works: Actos, Bernabé and Pensamiento Serpentino* (Houston: Arte Público Press, University of Houston, 1990): 17-27.

Los Vendidos (1967)

First Performance in 1967: Brown Beret junta,
Elysian Park, East Los Angeles

CHARACTERS:

Honest Sancho
Secretary
Farmworker
Pachuco
Revolucionario
Mexican-American

Scene: **Honest Sancho**'s *Used Mexican Lot and Mexican Curio Shop. Three models are on display in* **Honest Sancho**'s *shop. To the right, there is a* **Revolucionario**, *complete with sombrero, carrilleras and carabina 30-30. At center, on the floor, there is the* **Farmworker**, *under a broad straw sombrero. At stage left is the* **Pachuco**, *filero in hand.* **Honest Sancho** *is moving among his models, dusting them off and preparing for another day of business.*

Sancho: Bueno, bueno, mis monos, vamos a ver a quién vendemos ahora, ¿no? (*To audience.*) ¡Quihubo! I'm Honest Sancho and this is my shop. Antes fui contratista, pero ahora logré tener mi negocio. All I need now is a customer. (*A bell rings offstage.*) Ay, a customer!

Secretary: (*Entering.*) Good morning, I'm Miss Jimenez from. . .

Sancho: Ah, una chicana! Welcome, welcome Señorita Jiménez.

Secretary: (*Anglo pronunciation.*) JIM-enez.

Sancho: ¿Qué?

Secretary: My name is Miss JIM-enez. Don't you speak English? What's wrong with you

Sancho: Oh, nothing, señorita JIM-enez. I'm here to help you.

Secretary: That's better. As I was starting to say, I'm a secretary from Governor Reagan's office, and we're looking for a Mexican type for the administration.

Sancho: Well, you come to the right place, lady. This is Honest Sancho's Used Mexican Lot, and we got all types here. Any particular type you want?

Secretary: Yes, we are looking for somebody suave. . .

Sancho: Suave.

Secretary: Debonaire.

Sancho: De buen aire.

Secretary: Dark.

Sancho: Prieto.

Secretary: But of course, not too dark.

Sancho: No muy prieto.

Secretary: Perhaps, beige.

Sancho: Beige, just the tone. Así como cafecito con leche, ¿no?

Secretary: One more thing. He must be hard-working.

Sancho: That could be one model. Step right over here to the center of the shop, lady. (*They cross the* **Farmworker**.) This is our standard farmworker model. As you can see, in the word of our beloved Senator George Murphy,[1] he is "built close to the ground." Also, take special notice of this 4-ply Goodyear huaraches, made from the rain tire. This wide-brimmed sombrero is an extra added feature; keeps off the sun, rain and dust.

Secretary: Yes it does look durable.

Sancho: And our farmworker model is friendly. Muy amable. Watch. (*Snaps his fingers.*)

Farmworker: (*Lifts up head.*) Buenos días, señorita. (*His head drops.*)

Secretary: My, he is friendly.

Sancho: Didn't I tell you? Loves his patrones! But his most attractive feature is that he's hard-working. Let me show you. (*Snaps fingers.* **Farmworker** *stands.*)

Farmworker: ¡El jale! (*He begins to work.*)

Sancho: As you can see he is cutting grapes.

Secretary: Oh, I wouldn't know.

Sancho: He also picks cotton. (*Snaps.* **Farmworker** *begins to pick cotton.*)

Secretary: Versatile, isn't he?

Sancho: He also picks melons. (*Snap.* **Farmworker** *picks melons.*) That's his slow speed for late in the season. Here's his fast speed. (*Snaps.* **Farmworker** *picks faster.*)

Secretary: Chihuahua. . .I mean, goodness, he sure is a hardworker.

Sancho: (*Pulls the* **Farmworker** *to his feet.*) And that isn't the half of it. Do you see these little holes on his arms that appear to be pores? During those hot sluggish days in the field when the vines or the branches get so entangled,

---

[1]A California senator who favored agribusiness.

it's almost impossible to move, these holes emit a certain grease that allows our model to slip and slide right through the crop with no trouble at all.

Secretary: Wonderful. But is he economical?

Sancho: Economical? Señorita, you are looking at the Volkswagen of Mexicans. Pennies a day is all it takes. One plate of beans and tortillas will keep him going all day. That, and chile. Plenty of chile. Chile jalapeños, chile verde, chile colorado. But, of course, if you do give him chile (*Snap.* **Farmworker** *turns left face. Snap.* **Farmworker** *bends over.*) then you have to change his oil filter once a week.

Secretary: What about storage?

Sancho: No problem. You know these new farm labor camps our Honorable Governor Reagan has built out by Parlier or Raisin City? They were designed with our model in mind. Five, six, seven, even ten in one of those shacks will give you no trouble at all. You can also put him in old barns, old cars, riverbanks. You can even leave him out in the field overnight with no worry!

Secretary: Remarkable.

Sancho: And here's an added feature: every year at the end of the season, this model goes back to Mexico and doesn't return, automatically, until next Spring.

Secretary: How about that. But tell me, does he speak English?

Sancho: Another outstanding feature is that last year this model was programmed to go out on Strike! (*Snap.*)

Farmworker: ¡Huelga! ¡Huelga! Hermanos, sálganse de esos files. (*Snap. He stops.*)

Secretary: No! Oh, no, we can't strike in the State Capitol.

Sancho: Well, he also scabs. (*Snap.*)

Farmworker: Me vendo barato, ¿y qué? (*Snap.*)

Secretary: That's much better, but you didn't answer my question. Does he speak English?

Sancho: Bueno. . .no, pero he has other. . .

Secretary: No.

Sancho: Other features.

Secretary: No! He just won't do!

Sancho: Okay, Okay, pues. We have other models.

Secretary: I hope so. What we need is something a little more sophisticated.

Sancho: ¿Sophisti-qué?

Secretary: An urban model.

Sancho: Ah, from the city! Step right back. Over there in this corner of the shop is exactly what you're looking for. Introducing our new 1969 **Johnny Pachuco** model! This is our fast-back model. Streamlined. Built for speed, low-riding, city life. Take a look at some of these features. Mag shoes, dual exhausts, green chartruese paint-job, dark-tint windshield, a little poof on top. Let me just turn him on. (*Snap.* Johnny walks to stage center with a Pachuco bounce.)

Secretary: What was that?

Sancho: That, señorita, was the Chicano shuffle.

Secretary: Okay, what does he do?

Sancho: Anything and everything necessary for city life. For instance, survival: he knife fights. (*Snaps.* Johnny *pulls out a switchblade and swings at* **Secretary.** **Secretary** *screams.*) He dances. (*Snap.*)

Johnny: (*Singing.*) "Angel Baby, my Angel Baby. . ."[2] (*Snap.*)

Sancho: And here's a feature no city model can be without. He gets arrested, but not without resisting, of course. (*Snap.*)

Johnny: En la madre, la placa. I didn't do it! I didn't do it! (**Johnny** *turns and stands up against an imaginary wall, legs spread out, arms behind his back.*)

Secretary: Oh no, we can't have arrests! We must maintain law and order.

Sancho: But he's bilingual.

Secretary: Bilingual?

Sancho: Simón que yes. He speaks English! Johnny, give us some English. (*Snap.*)

Johnny: (*Comes downstage.*) Fuck-you!

Secretary: (*Gasps.*) Oh! I've never been so insulted in my whole life!

Sancho: Well, he learned it in your school.

Secretary: I don't care where he learned it.

Sancho: But he's economical.

Secretary: Economical?

Sancho: Nickels and dimes. You can keep Johnny running on hamburgers, Taco Bell tacos, Lucky Lager beer, Thunderbird wine, yesca. . .

Secretary: Yesca?

Sancho: Mota.

Secretary: Mota?

Sancho: Leños. . .marijuana. (*Snap.* **Johnny** *inhales on an imaginary joint*).

Secretary: That's against the law!

Johnny: (*Big smile, holding his breath.*) Yeah.

---

[2]A popular rock-n-roll ballad from the 1960s.

Sancho: He also sniffs glue. (*Snap.* **Johnny** *inhales glue, big smile.*)

Johnny: Tha's too much man, ése.

Secretary: No, Mr. Sancho. I don't think this. . .

Sancho: Wait a minute, he has other qualities I know you'll love. For example, an inferiority complex. (*Snap.*)

Johnny: (*To* **Sancho.**) You think you're better then me, huh, ése? (*Swings switchblade.*)

Sancho: He can also be beaten and he bruises. Cut him and he bleeds, kick him and he. . . (*He beats, bruises and kicks* **Pachuco.**) Would you like to try it?

Secretary: Oh, I couldn't.

Sancho: Be my guest. He's a great scapegoat.

Secretary: No, . . .really.

Sancho: Please.

Secretary: Well, all right. Just once. (*She kicks* **Pachuco.**) Oh, he's so soft.

Sancho: Wasn't that good? Try again.

Secretary: (*Kicks* **Pachuco.**) Oh, he's so wonderful! (*She kicks him again.*)

Sancho: Okay, that's enough, lady. You'll ruin the merchandise. Yes, our Johnny Pachuco model can give you many hours of pleasure. Why, the LAPD[3] just bought 20 of these to train their rookie cops on. And talk about maintenance. Señorita, you are looking at an entirely self-supporting machine. You're never going to find our Johnny Pachuco model on the relief rolls. No, sir, this model knows how to liberate.

Secretary: Liberate?

Sancho: He steals. (*Snap.* **Johnny** rushes to **Secretary** and steals her purse.)

Johnny: ¡Dame esa bolsa, vieja! (*He grabs the purse and runs. Snap by* **Sancho**, *he stops.* **Secretary** *runs after* **Johnny** *and grabs purse away from him, kicking him as she goes.*)

Secretary: No, no, no! We can't have any more thieves in the State Administration. Put him back.

Sancho: Okay, we still got other models. Come on, Johnny, we'll sell you to some old lady. (**Sancho** *takes* **Johnny** *back to his place.*)

Secretary: Mr. Sancho, I don't think you quite understand what we need. What we need is something that will attract the women voters. Something more traditional, more romantic.

---

[3]Los Angeles Police Department.

Sancho: Ah, a lover. (*He smiles meaningfully.*) Step right over here, señorita. Introducing our standard Revolucionario and/or Early California Bandit type. As you can see, he is well-built, sturdy, durable. This is the International Harvester of Mexicans.

Secretary: What does he do?

Sancho: You name it, he does it. He rides horses, stays in the mountains, crosses deserts, plains, rivers, leads revolutions, follows revolutions, kills, can be killed, serves as a martyr, hero, movie star. Did I say movie star? Did you ever see *Viva Zapata*? *Viva Villa, Villa Rides, Pancho Villa Returns, Pancho Villa Goes Back, Pancho Villa Meets Abbott and Costello*?

Secretary: I've never seen any of those.

Sancho: Well, he was in all of them. Listen to this. (*Snap.*)

Revolucionario: (*Scream.*) ¡Viva Villaaaaa!

Secretary: That's awfully loud.

Sancho: He has a volume control. (*He adjusts volume. Snap.*)

Revolucionario: (*Mousey voice.*) Viva Villa.

Secretary: That's better.

Sancho: And even if you didn't see him in the movies, perhaps you saw him on TV. He makes commercials. (*Snap.*)

Revolucionario: Is there a Frito Bandito in your house?

Secretary: Oh yes, I've seen that one!

Sancho: Another feature about this one is that he is economical. He runs on raw horsemeat and tequila!

Secretary: Isn't that rather savage?

Sancho: Al contrario, it makes him a lover. (*Snap.*)

Revolucionario: (*To* **Secretary**.) Ay, mamasota, cochota, ven pa 'cá!
(*He grabs* **Secretary** *and folds her back, Latin-lover style.*)

Sancho: (*Snap.* **Revolucionario** *goes back upright.*) Now wasn't that nice?

Secretary: Well, it was rather nice.

Sancho: And finally, there is one outstanding feature about this model I know the ladies are going to love: he's a genuine antique! He was made in Mexico in 1910!

Secretary: Made in Mexico?

Sancho: That's right. Once in Tijuana, twice in Guadalajara, three times in Cuernavaca.

Secretary: Mr. Sancho, I thought he was an American product.

Sancho: No, but. . .

Secretary: No, I'm sorry. We can't buy anything but American made products. He just won't do.

Sancho: But he's an antique.

Secretary: I don't care. You still don't understand what we need. It's true we need Mexican models, such as these, but it's more important that he be American.

Sancho: American?

Secretary: That's right, and judging from what you've shown me, I don't think you have what we want. Well, my lunch hour's almost over, I better. . .

Sancho: Wait a minute! Mexican but American?

Secretary: That's correct.

Sancho: Mexican but. . . (*A sudden flash.*) American! Yeah, I think we've got exactly what you want. He just came in today! Give me a minute. (*He exits. Talks from backstage.*) Here he is in the shop. Let me just get some papers off. There. Introducing our new 1970 Mexican-American! Tara-ra-raaaa! (**Sancho** *brings out the* **Mexican-American** *model, a clean-shaven middle class type in a business suit, with glasses.*)

Secretary: (*Impressed.*) Where have you been hiding this one?

Sancho: He just came in this morning. Ain't he a beauty? Feast your eyes on him! Sturdy U.S. Steel frame, stream-lined, modern. As a matter of fact, he is built exactly like our Anglo models, except that he comes in a variety of darker shades: naugahide, leather or leatherette.

Secretary: Naugahide.

Sancho: Well, we'll just write that down. Yes, señorita, this model represents the apex of American engineering! He is bilingual, college educated, ambitious! Say the word "acculturate" and he accelerates. He is intelligent, well-mannered, clean. Did I say clean? (*Snap.* **Mexican-American** *raises his arm.*) Smell.

Secretary: (*Smells.*) Old Sobaco, my favorite.

Sancho: (*Snap.* **Mexican-American** *turns toward* **Sancho.**) Eric? (*To* **Secretary.**) We call him Eric García. (*To* **Eric.**) I want you to meet Miss JIM-enez, Eric.

Mexican-American: Miss JIM-enez, I am delighted to make your acquaintance. (*He kisses her hand.*)

Secretary: Oh, my, how charming!

Sancho: Did you feel the suction? He has seven especially engineered suction cups right behind his lips. He's a charmer all right!

Secretary: How about boards, does he function on boards?

Sancho: You name them, he is on them. Parole boards, draft boards, school boards, taco quality control boards, surf boards, two by fours.

Secretary: Does he function in politics?

Sancho: Señorita: you are looking at a political machine. Have you ever heard of the OEC, EOC, COD,[4] WAR ON POVERTY? That's our model! Not only that, he makes political speeches.

Secretary: May I hear one?

Sancho: With pleasure. (*Snap.*) Eric, give us a speech.

Mexican-American: Mr. Congressman, Mr. Chairman, members of the board, honored guests, ladies and gentlemen. (**Sancho** *and* **Secretary** *applaud.*) Please, please. I come before you as a Mexican-American to tell you about the problems of the Mexican. The problems of the Mexican stem from one thing and one thing only: he's stupid. He's uneducated. He needs to stay in school. He needs to be ambitious, forward-looking, harder-working. He needs to think American, American, American, American! God bless America! God bless America! God bless America! (*He goes out of control.* **Sancho** *snaps frantically and the* **Mexican-American** *finally slumps forward, bending at the waist.*)

Secretary: Oh, my, he's patriotic too!

Sancho: Sí, señorita, he loves his country. Let me just make a little adjustment here. (*Stands* **Mexican-American** *up.*)

Secretary: What about upkeep? Is he economical?

Sancho: Well, no, I won't lie to you. The Mexican-American costs a little bit more, but you get what you pay for. He's worth every extra cent. You can keep him running on dry Martinis, Langendorf bread. . .

Secretary: Apple pie?

Sancho: Only Mom's. Of course, he's also programmed to eat Mexican food at ceremonial functions, but I must warn you, an overdose of beans will plug up his exhaust.

Secretary: Fine! There's just one more question. How much do you want for him?

Sancho: Well, I tell you what I'm gonna do. Today and today only, because you've been so sweet, I'm gonna let you steal this model from me! I'm gonna let you drive him off the lot for the simple price of, let's see, taxes and license included, $15,000.

Secretary: Fifteen thousand dollars? For a Mexican!!!!

Sancho: Mexican? What are you talking about? This is a Mexican-American! We had to melt down two pachucos, a farmworker and three gabachos to

---

[4]A reference to several federal programs from the 1960s established to fight poverty.

make this model! You want quality, but you gotta pay for it! This is no cheap run-about, He's got class!

Secretary: Okay, I'll take him.

Sancho: You will?

Secretary: Here's your money.

Sancho: You mind if I count it?

Secretary: Go right ahead.

Sancho: Well, you'll get your pink slip in the mail. Oh, do you want me to wrap him up for you? We have a box in the back.

Secretary: No, thank you. The Governor is having a luncheon this afternoon, and we need a brown face in the crowd. How do I drive him?

Sancho: Just snap your fingers. He'll do anything you want.

(**Secretary** *snaps.* **Mexican-American** *steps forward.*)

Mexican-American: ¡Raza querida, vamos levantando armas para liberarnos de estos desgraciados gabachos que nos explotan! Vamos. . .

Secretary: What did he say?

Sancho: Something about taking up arms, killing white people, etc.

Secretary: But he's not supposed to say that!

Sancho: Look, lady, don't blame me for bugs from the factory. He's your Mexican-American, you bought him, now drive him off the lot!

Secretary: But he's broken!

Sancho: Try snapping another finger. (**Secretary** *snaps.* **Mexican-American** *comes to life again.*)

Mexican-American: Esta gran humanidad ha dicho basta! ¡Y se ha puesto en marcha! ¡Basta! ¡Basta! ¡Viva la raza! ¡Viva la causa! ¡Viva la huelga! ¡Vivan los brown berets! ¡Vivan los estudiantes! ¡Chicano power! (*The* **Mexican-American** *turns toward the* **Secretary**, *who gasps and backs up. He keeps turning toward the* **Pachuco**, **Farmworker** *and* **Revolucionario**, *snapping his fingers and turning each of them on, one by one.*)

Pachuco: (*Snap. To* **Secretary**.) I'm going to get you, baby! ¡Viva la raza!

Farmworker: (*Snap. To* **Secretary**.) ¡Viva la huelga! ¡Viva la huelga! ¡Viva la huelga!

Revolucionario: (*Snap. To* **Secretary**.) ¡Viva la revolución! (*The three models join together and advance toward the* **Secretary**, *who backs up and runs out of the shop screaming.* **Sancho** *is at the other end of the shop holding his money in his hand. All freeze. After a few seconds of silence, the* **Pachuco** *moves and stretches, shaking his arms and loosening up. The* **Farmworker** *and* **Revolucionario** *do the same.* **Sancho** *stays where he is, frozen to his spot.*)

Johnny: Man, that was a long one, ése. (*Others agree with him.*)

Farmworker: How did we do?

Johnny: Pretty good, look at all that lana, man! (*He goes over to* Sancho *and removes the money from his hand.* Sancho *stays where he is.*)

Revolucionario: En la madre, look at all the money.

Johnny: We keep this up, we're going to be rich.

Farmworker: They think we're machines.

Revolucionario: Burros.

Johnny: Puppets.

Mexican-American: The only thing I don't like is how come I always get to play the goddamn Mexican-American?

Johnny: That's what you get for finishing high school.

Farmworker: How about our wages, ése?

Johnny: Here it comes right now. $3,000 for you, $3,000 for you, $3,000 for you, and $3,000 for me. The rest we put back into the business.

Mexican-American: Too much, man. Heh, where you vatos going tonight?

Farmworker: I'm going over to Concha's. There's a party.

Johnny: Wait a minute, vatos. What about our salesman? I think he needs an oil job.

Revolucionario: Leave him to me. (*The* **Pachuco, Farmworker** *and* **Mexican-American** *exit, talking loudly about their plans for the night. The* **Revolucionario** *goes over to* **Sancho,** *removes his derby hat and cigar, lifts him up and throws him over his shoulder.* **Sancho** *hangs loose, lifeless. To audience.*) He's the best model we got! ¡Ajúa! (*Exit.*)

Los Vendidos by Luis Valdez is reprinted with permission from the publisher of *Luis Valdez—Early Works: Actos, Bernabé and Pensamiento Serpentino* (Houston: Arte Público Press, University of Houston, 1990): 40-52.

CHERRÍE MORAGA (1952-)

Giving Up the Ghost; A Stage Play in Three Portraits (1986; revised 1994)

> *If I had wings like an angel*
> *over these prison walls*
> *I would fly*
> > *(song my mother would sing me)*

CHARACTERS:

Marisa, *Chicana in her late 20s*
Corky, Marisa *as a teenager*
Amalia, *Mexican-born, a generation older than* **Marisa**
The People, *those viewing the performance or reading the play.*

SET

*The stage should be simple, with as few props as possible. A crate is used for street scenes downstage. A raised platform, stage left, serves as the bed in a variety of settings, including a hotel room, a mental hospital, and both **Amalia**'s and **Marisa**'s apartments. A simple wooden table and two chairs, stage right, represent **Amalia**'s kitchen. Windows, doorways, and furniture appear in the imagination when needed. The suggestion of a Mexican desert landscape is illuminated upstage during scenes evoking indigenous México. Scrims can be used for the dreamlike sequences. Aside from the minimal set pieces mentioned above, lighting and music should be the main features in providing setting. Music should be used to re-create the "streetwise ritmo" of the urban life of these Chicanas, spanning a generation of Motown, soul, Tex-Mex, and Latin rock. It should also reflect the profound influence of traditional Mexican folk music—rancheras, corridos, mariachi, etc.—as well as the more ancient indigenous sounds of the flauta, concha, and tambor. Throughout the long monologues (unless otherwise indicated) when the non-speaking actors remain on stage, the lighting and direction should give the impression that the characters both disap-*

pear and remain within hearing range of the speaker. In short, direction should reflect that each character knows, on an intuitive level, the minds of the other characters.

RETRATO I
"La Pachuca"

Prologue

*This is the urban Southwest, a Chicano barrio within the sprawling Los Angeles basin. Street sounds fill the air: traffic, children's schoolyard voices, street repairs, etc. **Marisa** sits on a wooden crate, centerstage. She wears a pair of Levi's, tennis shoes and a bright-colored shirt. Her black hair is pulled back, revealing a face of dark intensity and definite Indian features. She holds a large sketchbook on her lap. **Corky** enters upstage. Their eyes meet. As **Marisa**'s younger self, **Corky** tries to act tough but displays a wide open-heartedness in her face which betrays the toughness. She dresses "Cholo style"—khaki pants with razor-sharp creases, pressed white undershirt. Her hair is cut short and slicked back. She approaches the upstage wall, spray can in hand, feigning the false bravado of her teenage male counterparts. She writes in large, Chicano graffiti-style letters, as **Marisa** writes in her sketchbook.*

Dedicación

Don't know where this woman
and I will find each other again,
but I am grateful to her to something
that feels like a blessing

that I am, in fact, not trapped

which brings me to the question of prisons
politics
sex.

*Corky tosses the spray can to **Marisa**.*
Corky *(with **Marisa**):* I'm only telling you this to stay my hand.

Marisa: But why, cheezus, why me?
Why'd I hafta get into a situation where all my ghosts come to visit?
I always see that man. . .thick-skinned, dark, muscular.
He's a boulder between us.
I can't lift him and her, too. . .carrying him.

He's a ghost, always haunting her. . .
lingering.
Fade out

Scene One

A Chicano "oldie" rises. Crossfade to Corky coming downstage, moving "low and slow" to the tune.

Corky: the smarter I get the older I get the meaner I get
tough a tough cookie my mom calls me
sometimes I even pack a blade
no one knows I never use it or nut'ing
but can feel it there there in my pants pocket
run the pad of my thumb over it to remind me I carry somet'ing
am sharp secretly
always envy those batos who get all cut up at the weddings
getting their rented tuxes all bloody
that red 'n' clean color
against the white starched collars
I love that shit!

the best part is the chicks all climbing into the ball of the fight
"¡Chuy, déjalo! ¡Leave him go, Güero!" tú sabes
you know how the chicks get all excited 'n' upset 'n' stuff
they always pulling on the carnales 'n' getting nowhere
'cept messed up themselves 'n' everybody looks so
like they digging the whole t'ing tú sabes
their dresses ripped here 'n' there. . .like a movie
it's all like a movie

when I was a real little kid I useta love the movies

every Saturday you could find me there
my eyeballs glued to the screen
then later my friend Arturo 'n' me
we'd make up our own movies
one was where we'd be out in the desert
'n' we'd capture these chicks 'n' hold 'em up for ransom
we'd string 'em up 'n' make 'em take their clothes off
"strip" we'd say to the wall all cool-like
funny. . .now when I think about how little I was at the time
and a girl but in my mind I was big 'n' tough 'n' a dude
in my *mind* I had all their freedom
the freedom to see a girl   kina
the way   you see
an animal   you know?

like imagining
they got a difernt set
of blood vessels or somet'ing like so
when you mess with 'em
it don't affect 'em the way it do you
like like they got a difernt gland system or somet'ing that
that makes their pain cells
more dense

hell I dunno

but you see
I never could
quite
pull it off

always knew I was a girl
deep down inside
no matter how I tried to pull the other off

I knew
always knew
I was an animal that kicked back. . .
*(with Marisa). . .*cuz it hurt! *(Corky exits.)*

Marisa (*from the platform, coming downstage*): I never wanted to be a man, only wanted a woman to want me that bad. And they have, you know, plenty of them, but there's always that one you can't pin down, who's undecided. (*Beat.*) My mother was a heterosexual, I couldn't save her. My failures follow thereafter.

Amalia (*entering*): I am a failure.

*Amalia is visibly "soft" in just the ways that **Marisa** appears "hard." She chooses her clothes with an artist's eye for color and placement. They appear to be draped over her, rather than worn; a rebozo wrapped around her shoulders, a blouse falling over the waist of an embroidered skirt. Her hair is long and worn down or loosely braided. As a woman nearing fifty, she gives the impression of someone who was once a rare beauty, now trading that for a fierce dignity in bearing.*

Amalia: I observe the Americans. Their security. Their houses. Their dogs. Their children are happy. They are not *un.* . .happy. Sure, they have their struggles, their problemas, but. . .it's a life. I always say this, it's a life. (*She sits at the table stacked with art books, puts on a pair of wire-rim glasses, leafs through a book.*)

Marisa: My friend Marta bought her mother a house. I admire her. Ever after the family talked bad about her like that for leaving home with a gabacha, she went back cash in hand and bought her mother a casita kina on the outskirts of town. Ten grand was all it took, that's nothing here, but it did save her mother from the poverty her dead father left behind. I envy her. For the first time wished my father'd die so I could do my mother that kind of rescue routine.

I wanna talk about betrayal, about a battle I will never win and never stop fighting. The dick beats me every time. I know I'm not supposed to be sayin' this cuz it's like confession, like still cryin' your sins to a priest you long ago stopped believing was god or god's sit-in, but still confessing what you'd hoped had been forgiven in you. . . (*Looking to **Amalia**.*) That prison. . .that passion to beat men at their own game.

Amalia: I worry about La Pachuca. That's my nickname for her. I have trouble calling her by her Christian name. (*Savoring it*). Marisa. (*"Rain sticks" in the background.*) I worry about La Pachuca. I worry what will happen to the beautiful corn she is growing if it continues to rain so hard and much.

Corky (*entering*): one time Tury 'n' me stripped for real
there was this minister 'n' his family down the street
they was presbyterians or methodists or somet'ing
you know one of those gringo religions

'n' they had a bunch a kids
the oldest was named Lisa or somet'ing lightweight like that
'n' the littlest was about three or so, named Chrissy
I mean you couldn't really complain about Chrissy
cuz she wasn't old enough yet to be a pain in the cola
but you knew that was coming

Lisa'd be hassling me 'n' my sister Patsy all the time
telling us how we wernt really christians
cuz cath-lics worshipped the virgin mary or somet'ing
I didnt let this worry me though cuz we was being tole at school
how being cath-lic was the one true número uno church 'n' all
so I jus' let myself be real cool with her
'n' the rest of her little pagan baby brothers 'n' sisters
that's all they was to me as far as I was concerned
they dint even have no mass
jus' some paddy preaching up there with a dark suit on
very weird
not a damn candle for miles
dint seem to me that there was any god happening in that place at all

so one day Tury comes up with this idea how we should strip
"for real"
I wasn't that hot on the idea but still go along with him
checkin' out the neighborhood looking for prey
then we run into Chrissy 'n' Tury 'n' me eye each other
the trouble is I'm still not completely sold on the idea
pero ni modo cuz I already hear comin' outta my mouth
real syrupy-like
"come heeeeere Chrissy, we got somet'ing to shooooow you"
well, a'course she comes cuz I was a big kid 'n' all
'n' we take her into this shed

I have her hand 'n' Tury tells her. . .
no I tole her this
I tell her we think she's got somet'ing wrong with her
"down there"
I think. . . I think I said she had a cut or somet'ing
'n' Tury 'n' me had to check it out

so I pull her little shorts down 'n' then her chones
'n' then jus' as I catch a glimpse of her little fuchi fachi. . .
it was so tender-looking all pink 'n' real sweet like a bun
then stupid Tury like a menso goes 'n' sticks hir dirty finger on it
like it was burning hot

'n' jus' at that moment. . .I see this little Chrissy-kid
look up at me like. . .like I was her mom or somet'ing
like tú sabes she has this little kid's frown on her face
the chubby skin on her forehead all rumpled up
like. . .like she knew somet'ing was wrong with what we was doing
'n' was looking to me to reassure her
that everyt'ing was cool 'n' regular 'n' all
what a jerk I felt like!
(*She pushes "Tury" away, bends down to "Chrissy."*)

so, I pull up her shorts 'n' whisper to her
"no no you're fine really there's nut'ing wrong with you
but don' tell nobody we looked
we don' want nobody to worry about you"
what else was I supposed to say? ¡Tonta!
'n' Tury 'n' me make a beeline into the alley 'n' outta there!
(*She exits.*)

Scene Two

*Crossfade to **Amalia** rising from the bed. It is morning.*

Amalia: I remember the first time I met her, the day she first began to bring me
her work. It was early morning, too early really, and there was someone at
the door. At first I think it is my son, Che. Like him to appear at my door-
step with the least amount of warning. (*She goes to the "window," looks
down to the front steps. **Marisa** appears carrying a portfolio.*) But it was
Marisa, standing there with a red jacket on, I remember, a beautiful color
of red. Maybe if I had not dreamed the color the night before I might not
even have bothered to open the door so early, such a hermit I am. (*To
Marisa:*) ¿Sí?
Marisa: Hello. I got these. . .paintings. I. . .heard you could help me.

Amalia: ¿Quién eres?

Marisa: Marisa. Marisa Moreno

Amalia: It's a little early ¿qué no?

Marisa: I'm sorry. Frank Delgado—

Amalia: Súbete.

Amalia "buzzes" Marisa in. Amalia puts on a robe, brushes back her hair. Marisa enters.

Marisa: Good morning.

Amalia: It's too early to tell.

Marisa: I'm sorry.

Amalia: That's two "sorrys" already and I don't even got my eyes on yet.

Marisa: Sor. . .

Amalia (*smiling*): Pásale. Pásale.

Marisa (*handing her a small paper sack*): Here, this is for you.

Amalia: Siéntate.

Marisa: It's pandulce.

Amalia (*looking inside*): Conchas. They're my favorites.

> *Amalia puts the pastry on the table. Marisa sits down, holds the portfolio awkwardly in her lap. During the following scene there are brief lapses in the conversation.*

Amalia: ¿Quieres café?

Marisa: Gracias. No.

Amalia: Pues, yo. . .sí. (*Goes to prepare the coffee.*) I can't even talk before I have a cup of coffee in me. Help yourself to the pandulce.

Marisa (*Indicating the books on the table*): Are all these yours?

Amalia: The books? Claro.

Marisa: They're wonderful.

Amalia: Take a look at them if you want.

> *Marisa carefully props up her portfolio onto a chair and begins to leaf through one of the books. Amalia reenters, looking for her glasses.*

Marisa: You got a lotta. . .things.

Amalia: What? Yes. Too much. My son, Che, he calls me a. . .rat pack.

Marisa: A pack rat.

Amalia: Whatever you call it, I can't even find my glasses.

Marisa (*pointing to the painting on the upstage wall*): And this?

Amalia: Well, I couldn't afford a room with a view, so. . .bueno, pues I improvised a little. ¿Te gusta? (*She finds her glasses in her robe pocket, puts them on.*)

Marisa: Yeah. Mucho.

Amalia (*observing her*): You don't seem quite as awesome as Delgado describ-
    ed you.

Marisa: He told you about me?

Amalia: Ay, all los boys at El Centro were talking about you, telling me how
    I should see your work. . .this new "Eastlos[1] import."

Marisa: I didn't think they liked me.

Amalia: Pues, I didn't say they *liked* you.

Marisa: Oh.

Amalia: I think you scared them a little. Una pintora bien chingona, me dijo
    Frank.

Marisa: That's what he said?

Amalia: Más o menos. Bueno. . . (*Indicating the portfolio*) Abrelo. Let's see
    what makes those machos shake in their botas so much.

As Marisa opens the portfolio, the lights crossfade to Corky entering.

Corky: the weird thing was that after that episode with Chrissy
    I was like a maniac all summer
    snotty Lisa kept harassing me about the virgin mary 'n' all
    'n' jus' in general being a pain in the coolie
    things began to break down with her 'n' her minister's family
    when me 'n' Patsy stopped going to their church meetings
    on wednesday nights
    we'd only go cuz they had cookies 'n' treats after all the bible stuff
    'n' sometimes had arts 'n' crafts where you got to paint
    little clay statues of blond jesus in a robe
    'n' the little children coming to him
    the drag was that you also had to do these prayer sessions
    where everybody'd stand in a circle squeezing hands
    'n' each kid'd say a little prayer
    you know like "for the starving people in china"
    Patsy 'n' me always passed when we got squeezed
    jus' shaked our heads no
    cuz it was against our religion to pray with them
    well, one time, this Lisa punk has the nerve to pray that Patsy 'n' me
    would (*mimicking*) "come to the light of the one true Christian faith"
    shi-it can you get to that? 'course we never went again
    Amalia puts on an apron, becomes Corky's "mother."

---

[1]East Los Angeles.

Corky: but I remember coming home 'n' telling my mom . . .
"Mother": It's better mi'jitas, I think, if you don' go no more.
Corky: 'n' it was so nice to hear her voice so warm
    like she loved us a lot
    'n' that night being cath-lic felt like my mom
    real warm 'n' dark 'n' kind

Fade out.

Scene Three

At rise, **Marisa** *straddles the kitchen chair, addresses* **The people**. **Amalia** *is upstage by the bed. During* **Marisa**'s *monologue,* **Amalia** *ties her hair back into a tight bun, applies a grey powder to her face, and draws dark circles under her eyes.*

Marisa: The women I have loved the most have always loved the man more than me, even in their hatred of him. I'm queer I am. Sí, soy jota because I have never been crazy about a man. (*Pause*) My friend Sally the hooker told me the day she decided to stop tricking was when once, by accident, a john made her come. That was strictly forbidden. She'd forgotten to resist, to keep business business. It was very unprofessional. . .and danger-ous. No, I've never been in love with a man and I never understood women who were, although I've certainly been around to pick up the pieces. My sister was in love with my brother.
Corky (*entering*): My mother loved her father.
Marisa: My first woman—
Corky: The man who put her away.
Marisa: The crazy house. Camarillo, Califas. Sixteen years old.
    Blue light. Haunting music. **Amalia** *becomes* **"Norma,"** **Marisa**'s *"first woman." She sits on the bed in a kind of psychotic stupor.* **Corky** *goes over to her.* **Marisa** *narrates.*
Marisa: When I come to get my cousin Norma, she has eyes like saucers, spin-ning black and glass. I can see through them, my face, my name. She says . . .
"Norma": I am Buddha.
Corky: How'd you get that black eye? ¿Quién te pegó?
"Norma": I am Buddha.

Fade out.

Scene Four

Corky *is alone on stage. She takes out a yo-yo, tries a few tricks. She is quite good.*

Corky: since that prayer meeting night
    when Patsy 'n' me wouldn't get squeezed into the minister's jesus
    Lisa's nose was gettin' higher 'n' higher in the air

    one day Patsy 'n' her are playing dolls up
    on the second-story porch of Mrs. Rodríguez' house
    it was nice up there cuz Mrs. R would let you move the tables
    'n' chairs 'n' stuff around to play "pertend"

    my sister had jus' gotten this nice doll for her birthday
    with this great curly hair
    Lisa only had this kinda stupid doll
    with plastic painted-on hair 'n' only one leg
    she'd always put long dresses on it to disguise the missing leg
    but we all knew it was gone

    anyway, one day this brat Lisa throws my sister's new doll
    into this mud puddle right down from Mrs. R's porch *(She lets
    out the yo-yo. It dangles helplessly.)*

    Patsy comes back into our yard crying like crazy
    her doll's all muddy and the hair has turned bone straight
    I mean like an arrow!
    I wanted to kill that punk Lisa!
    so me 'n' Patsy go over to Lisa's house
    where we find the little creep all pleased with herself
    I mean not even feeling bad
    suddenly I see her bike which is really a trike
    but it's huge. . .I mean hu-u-uge!
    to this day, I never seen a trike that big
    it useta bug me to no end that she wasn't even *trying*

to learn to ride a two-wheeler
so all of a sudden. . . (*Winding up with the yo-yo like a pitcher.*)
that trike 'n' Lisa's wimpiness come together in my mind
'n' I got that thing (*Throwing the pitch.*)
'n' I threw the sucker into the street

I dint even wreck it none (*She stuffs the yo-yo in her back pocket.*)
but it was the principle of the thing.

a'course she goes 'n' tells her mom on me
'n' this lady who by my mind don' even seem like a mom
she dint wear no makeup 'n' was real skinny 'n' tall
'n' wore her hair in some kina dumb bun
she has the nerve to call my mom 'n' tell her what I done
*Amalia, as Corky's "mom," appears upstage in an apron. She is stirring a
pot in her arms. She observes Corky.*
Corky: so a'course my mom calls me on the carpet
       wants to know the story
       'n' I tell her 'bout the doll 'n' Patsy 'n' the principle of the thing
       'n' Patsy's telling the same story 'n' I can see in my mom's eyes
       she don' believe I did nut'ing so bad but she tells me. . .
"Mother": We got to keep some peace in the neighborhood, hija.
Corky: cuz we was already getting pedo from the paddy neighbors
       'bout how my mom hollered too much at her kids. . .her own kids!
       I mean if you can't yell at your own kids who *can* you yell at?
       but she don' let on that this is the real reason
       I hafta go over to the minister's house and apologize
       she jus' kina turns back to the stove 'n' keeps on
       with what she was doing
"Mother": Andale, mija, dinner's almost ready. (*Corky hesitates.*)
          Andale. Andale.
Corky (*coming downstage*): so, a'course I go. . .
       I go myself
       with no one to watch me to see if I really do it
       but my mom knows I will cuz she tole me to
       'n' I ring the doorbell 'n' Mrs. Minister answers
       'n' as I begin to talk that little wimp Lisa runs up
       'n' peeks out at me from behind her mother's skirt
       with the ugliest most snottiest shit-eating grin

I'd ever seen in a person.
while all the while *I* say *I'm* sorry
'n' as the door shuts in front of my face
I vow I'll never make that mistake again. . .
(*with Marisa*) I'll never show anybody how mad I can get!
Black out.

Scene Five

Marisa is pacing about Amalia's room. Amalia sits on the floor mixing paints. She wears a paint-splattered apron.

Marisa (*to The People*): I have a very long memory. I try to warn people that when I get hurt, I don't forget it. I use it against them. I blame women for everything. My mistakes. Missed opportunities. My grief. I usually leave just when I wanna lay a woman flat. When I feel that vengeance rise up, I split. I desert.

Amalia: Desert. Desierto. For some reason, I could always picture mi cholita in the desert, amid the mesquite y nopal. Always when I closed my eyes to search for her, it was in the Mexican desert that I found her. I *had* intended to take her. . .to México. She would never have gone alone, sin gente allá.

Marisa: This is México! What are you talking about? It was those gringos that put up those fences between us!

Amalia brings Marisa to the table, takes out a piece of charcoal from her apron, puts it into Marisa's hand. Marisa begins to sketch.

Amalia: She was hardly convincing. Her nostalgia for the land she had never seen was everywhere. In her face, her drawings, her love of the hottest sand by the sea.

Coming around behind her, Amalia wraps her arms around Marisa's neck. Indigenous flutes and drums can be heard in the background.

Amalia: Desierto de Sonora. Tierra de tu memoria. (*Turning Marisa's face to her.*) Same chata face. Yaqui. (*They hesitate, then kiss their first kiss.*)

Amalia: I've just never believed a woman capable of loving a man was capable of loving. . .me. Some part of me remains amazed that I'm not the only lesbian in the world and that I can always manage to find someone to love me. (*Pause.*) But I am never satisfied because there are always those women left alone. . .and unloved.

Lights slowly fade to black. Musical interlude.

RETRATO II

"La Loca"

Scene Six

A sunny morning. Amalia is kneeling on a chair, bent over the table, painting in thick strokes and occasionally sipping at a cup of coffee. Her hair is combed into a braid and tied up. Marisa lies on the bed, hands behind her head.

Amalia: I've only been crazy over one man in my life. Alejandro was nothing special. Era pescador, indio. Once we took a drive out of the small town he lived in, and he was terrified, like a baby. I'm driving through the mountains and he's squirming in his seat, "Amalia, ¿pá dónde vamos? Are you sure you know where we're going?" I was so amused to see this big macho break out into a cold sweat just from going no more than twenty some miles from his home town. Pero ¡ay, Dios! how I loved that man! I still ask myself what I saw in him, really. (*Pause.*) He was one of the cleanest people I had ever met. Took two, three baths a day. You have to, you know. That part of la costa is like steam baths some seasons. I remember how'd he even put powder in his shorts and under his huevos to keep dry. He was that clean. I always loved knowing that when I touched him I would find him like a saint. Pure, somehow. . .that no matter where he had been or who he had been with, he would have washed himself for me. He always smelled. . .so clean. (*She wipes her hands, sits at the foot of the bed.*) When I went back home that first time, after my son was already grown, I had never dreamed of falling in love. Too many damn men under the bridge. I can see them all floating under the river like so many sacks of potatoes. "Making love," they call it, was like having sex with children. They rub your chi-chis a little, then they stick it in you. Nada más. It's all over in a few minutes. ¡Un río de cuerpos muertos!

Marisa: Sometimes I only see the other river on your face. I see it running behind your eyes. Remember the time we woke up together and your eye was a bowl of blood? I thought the river had broken open inside you.

Amalia: I was crazy about Alejandro. But what I loved was not so much him . . .I loved his children. I loved the way he had made México my home again. (*Pause.*) He was not a strong man really. He was soft. An inside softness, I could feel even as his desire swelled into a rock hardness. Once he said that with me he felt as though he were "a heart that knew no sex." No man-woman, he meant, only heat and a heart and that even a man could be entered in this way. (*Indigenous music rises in the background.*) I, on the other hand, was *not* clean, forgot sometimes to wash. Not when I was around others, pero con mí misma, I became like the animals. Uncombed. El olor del suelo.

Marisa: I remember the story you told me about the village children, how they had put una muñeca at the door of your casita. How you had found it there . . .there, in your likeness and you thought—

Amalia: I must be mad.

*Suddenly, the beat of tambores. **Corky** enters, wearing a native bruja mask. She dances across the stage with rattles in her hand. As she exits, **Marisa** goes to **Amalia**, unbraids her hair.*

Marisa: So we take each other in doses. I learn to swallow my desire, work my fear slowly through the strands of your hair.

***Marisa** bends to kiss **Amalia** on the kneck. **Amalia** pulls away, comes downstage.*

Amalia: Of course, soon after, Alejandro ran to every whore he could find, but not without first calling me that: "puta, bruja." He claimed I was trying to work some kind of mala suerte on him, that I was trying to take from him his manhood, make him something less than a man. (*Pause, to Marisa:*) I have always felt like an outsider.

***Marisa** starts toward her, then changes her mind and exits.*

Amalia (*to **The People***): Ni de aquí, ni de allá. Ask me in one word to describe to you the source of all my loneliness and I will tell you, "México." Not that I would have been any happier staying there. How *could* I have stayed there, been some man's wife. . .after so many years in this country, so many years on my own? (*Pause.*) I'll never forget the trip, the day our whole tribe left para el norte.

*Sudden spiritedness. A Mexican mariachi instrumental rises. **Amalia** ties a bandana around her head. She is a young girl.*

Amalia: All of us packed into the old blue Chevy. I was thirteen and la regla had started, the bleeding, and I was ashamed to tell my mother. Tía Fita had been the one to warn me that at my age, any day, I could expect to become sick. "Mala," she said, and that when it happened I should come to her and she would bless me and tell me how to protect myself. It came the morning of our long jornada to California.

Amalia sees the "blood" coming down her leg. She takes the bandana from her head, looks around nervously, then stuffs it under her skirt, flattening it back into place.

Amalia: Tía Fita was not speaking to my mother so angry was she for all of us leaving. We had asked her to come with us. "What business do I have up there with all those pochos y gringos?" My father said she had no sense. It broke her heart to see us go. So, there was no running to Tía Fita that morning. It seemed too selfish to tell her my troubles when *I* was the one leaving *her*.

Southwestern desert and distant highway sound can be heard. Amalia trying to hide from the others, pulls the bandana out from under her skirt. Kneeling by the "river," she secretly begins to wash the blood from it. Sound and lights gradually fade out.

Scene Seven

Marisa sits at the table in soft light sipping at a beer. She is dressed for the evening in a man's suit jacket. She wears a kind of classic androgynous look. Amalia enters in a slip, crosses to the bed where she begins to dress.

Marisa: If I were a man, things would've been a lot simpler between us, except . . . she never would've wanted me. I mean, she would've seen me more and all, fit me more conveniently into her life, but she never would've, tú sabes . . . wanted me.

Amalia: Sometimes I think, with me, that she only wanted to feel herself so much a woman that she would no longer be hungry for one. Pero, siempre tiene hambre. Siempre tiene pena.

Marisa: She'd come to me sometimes, I swear, like heat on wheels. I'd open the door and find her there, wet from the outta nowhere June rains, and, without her even opening her mouth, I knew what she had come for. I never knew when to expect her this way, just like the rains. Never ever when I wanted it, asked for it, begged for it, only when she decided.

Amalia: I always had to have a few traguitos and then things would cloud between us a little and I could feel her as if underwater, my hands swimming towards her in the darkness, discovering breasts, not mine. . .not these empty baldes, pero senos firmes, like small stones of heat. Y como un recién nacido, I drink and drink and drink y no me traga la tierra.

Lights suggest memory. Nighttime freeway sounds, car radio music. Marisa and Amalia hold each other's eyes. Voice over.

Marisa: I'll keep driving if you promise not to stop touching me.

Amalia: You want me to stop touching you?

Marisa: No, if you promise *not* to stop.

Amalia crosses in front of Marisa. She prepares herself a drink. Marisa watches her.

Marisa: It's odd being queer. It's not that you don't want a man, you just don't want a man in a man. You want a man in a woman. The woman part goes without saying. That's what you always learn to want first. Maybe the first time you see your dad touch your mom in that way. . .

Corky *(entering)*: ¡Hiiiijo! I remember the first time I got hip to that! My mom standing at the stove making chile colorado and flippin' tortillas. She asks my dad. . .

Amalia *(as "Mom," to Marisa)*: ¿Quieres otra, viejo?"

Corky: Kina like she's sorta hassled 'n' being poquita fría, tú sabes, but she's really digging my dad to no end. 'N' jus' as she comes over to him, kina tossing the tort onto the plate, he slides his hand, real suave-like, up the inside of her thigh. Cheezus! I coulda died! I musta been only 'bout nine or so, but I got that tingling, tú sabes, that now I know what it means. . .

As Corky exits, she throws her chin out to Marisa, bato-style. Marisa, amused, returns the gesture. The lights shift. Marisa puts on a tape. A Mexican ballad is played—"Adios Paloma" by Chavela Vargas. Amalia hums softly along with it.

Marisa: Hay un hombre en esta mujer. Lo he sentido. La miro, cocinando para nosotras. Pienso...¿cómo puede haber un hombre en una persona, tan femenina? Su pelo, sus movimientos de una serenidad imposible de describir.

Amalia *(softly singing)*:

Ya se va tu paloma, mi vida
lleva en sus alas dolor
lleva en sus ojos tristeza
y es un lamento su voz.

Marisa *(going to her)*: Tu voz que me acaricia con cada palabra. . .tan suave . . .tan rica. *(Takes her by the hand.)* Vente.

The music rises. They dance for a few moments, then Marisa takes Amalia to the bed. The music fades as Marisa slowly removes Amalia's blouse.

Marisa: Con ella, me siento como un joven lleno de deseo. I move on top of her. She wants this. The worn denim and metal buttons are cotton and cool ice on my skin. And she is full of slips and lace and stocking. . .

Amalia: Quítate los pantalones.

Marisa: And yet it is she who's taking me.

*A soft jazz rise. **Marisa** takes off her jacket. They kiss each other, at first tenderly, then passionately. They hold and caress each other. **Marisa** takes **Amalia**'s hand, brings it to her chest. The music softens.*

Marisa: I held the moment. Prayed that if I looked long and hard enough at your hand full inside me, if I could keep this pictured forever in my mind. . .how beneath that moon blasting through the window, . . .how everything was changing at that moment in both of us.

Amalia: How everything was changing. . .in both of us.

The jazz rises again. The lights slowly fade as they hold a deep kiss.

RETRATO III

"La Salvadora"

Scene Eight

Corky writes graffiti-style on upstage wall.
  I have this rock in my hand
  it is my memory
  the weight is solid
  in my palm it cannot fly away

  because I still remember
  that woman
  not my savior but an angel
  with wings
  that did once lift me
  to another
  self.

Marisa and Amalia appear in shadow on opposite ends of the stage.

Amalia: You have the rest of your life to forgive me.

Marisa: Forgive you for what?

Amalia: Por lo que soy.

Black out.

Scene Nine

Marisa enters carrying a small suitcase. She sets it down at the foot of the bed, removes her rebozo and holds it in her lap.

Amalia: All I was concerned about was getting my health back together. It was not so much that I had been sick, only I lacked. . .energy. My body felt like a rag, squeezed dry of any feeling. Possibly it was the "change" coming on. But the women in my family did not go through the change so young. I wasn't even fifty. I thought. . .maybe it was the American influence that causes the blood to be sucked dry from you so early. Nothing was wrong with me, really. My bones ached. I needed rest. Nothing México couldn't cure.

She lies down, covers herself with the rebozo. Marisa enters, barefoot.

Marisa: For the whole summer, I watched the people fly in bright colored sails over the Califas sea waiting for her. Red- and gold- and blue-stripped wings blazing the sky. Lifting off the sandy cliffs, dangling gringo legs. Always imagined myself up there in their place, flying for real. Never ever coming back down to earth, just leaving my body behind. (*Pause.*) One morning I awoke to find a bird dead on the beach. I knew it wasn't a rock because it was light enough to roll with the tide. . .I saw this from a distance. Later that day, they found a woman dead there at the very same spot, I swear. Una viejita. (*A soft grey light washes over Amalia.*) A crowd gathered 'round her as a young man in a blue swimsuit tried to spoon the sand from her throat with his finger. Putting his breath to her was too late. She was so very very grey and wet, como la arena. . .y una mexicana, I could tell by her house dress. How did she drown? Then I remembered what Amalia had told me about bad omens. (*A sudden ominous tambor, Amalia bolts up in bed.*) I stopped going. I stopped waiting.

Marisa exits.

Amalia: When I learned of Alejandro's death, I died too. I just started bleeding and the blood wouldn't stop, not until his ghost had passed through me or was born in me. I don't know which. That Mexican morning I had awakened to find the hotel sheets red with blood. It had come out in torrents and thick clots that looked like a fetus. But I was not pregnant, my tubes had been tied for years. Yet, lying there in the cool dampness of my own blood, I felt my womanhood leave me. And it was Alejandro being born in me. Does this make sense? I can't say exactly how I knew this, except. . .again . . .for the smell, the unmistakable smell of the man, as if we had just made

love. And coming from my mouth was *his* voice. . . "¡Ay mi Marisa! ¡Te
deseo! ¡Te deseo!" (*Her eyes search for* **Marisa**.) Marisa!
Lights rise. Morning in Mexico City. **Amalia** *gets up from the bed.*

Amalia: It is barely dawn and the sun has already entered my hotel window.
Afuera los hombres are already at work tearing up the Mexican earth with
their steel claws. (*Indigenous music.*) Pero La Tierra is not as passive as
they think. "Regresaré," Ella nos recuerda. "Regresaré," nos promete. When
they "discovered" El Templo Mayor beneath the walls of this city, they had
not realized that it was She who discovered them. Nothing remains buried
forever. Not even memory. Especially not memory.
Fade out.

Scene Ten

The indigenous music blends into Chicano urban sounds. **Marisa** *enters. Her
posture is noticeably more guarded than in the previous scene. The music fades.
There is a pause as* **Marisa** *scans the faces of* **The People**.

Marisa: Got raped once. When I was a kid. Taken me a long time to say that
was exactly what happened, but that was exactly what happened. Makes
you more aware than ever that you are one hunerd percent female, just in
case you had any doubts. One hunerd percent female whether you act it
. . . or like it. . .or not. Y'see, I never ever really let myself think about it,
the possibility of rape, even after it happened. Not like other girls, I didn't
walk down the street like there were men lurking everywhere, every corner,
to devour me. Yeah, the street was a war zone, but for different reasons,
. . .for muggers, mexicanos sucking their damn lips at you, gringo stupidity,
drunks like old garbage sacks thrown around the street, and the rape of
other women and the people I loved. They weren't safe and I worried each
time they left the house. . .but never, never me. I guess I never wanted to
believe I was raped. If someone took me that bad, I wouldn't really want
to think I was took, you follow me? But the truth is. . .

Corky (*entering*): I was took.

Marisa crosses to the platform. **Corky** *"stakes out the territory."*

Corky: I was about twelve years old,
    I was still going to cath-lic school then
    'n' we wore those stupid checkered jumpers
    they looked purty shitty on the seventh 'n' eighth grade girls

cuz here we was getting chi-chis 'n' all
'n' still trying to shove 'em into the tops of these play suits.
I wasn't too big, pero the big girls looked terrible!

anyway in the seventh grade I was trying to mend my ways
so would hang after school 'n' try to be helpful 'n' all to the nuns
I guess cuz my older cousin Norma got straight A's
'n' was taking me into her bed by then
so I figured. . .that was the way to go.
she'd get really pissed when I fucked up in school
threatened to "take it away" tú sabes if I dint behave.
Can you get to that? ¡Qué fría! ¿no?

anyway Norma was the only one I ever tole
about the janitor doing it to me
'n' then she took it away for good.
I'd still like to whip her but for that
her 'n' her goddamn hubby 'n' kids now   shi-it
puros gabachos, little blonde-haired blue-eyed things
the oldest is a little joto if you ask me
sure he's barely four years old but you can already tell
the way he goes around primping all over the place
pleases me to no end
what goes around comes around
"Jason" they call him
no, not "Ha-són" pero "Jay-sun"
puro gringo.

anyway so I was walking by Sister Mary Dominic's classroom,
"the Hawk" we called her cuz she had a nose 'n' attitude like one
when this man a mexicano motions me to come on inside.
"Ven p'acá," he says.
I dint recognize him but the parish was always hiring
mexicanos to work around the grounds 'n' stuff
I guess cuz they dint need to know English
'n' the priest dint need to pay 'em much.
they'd do it "por Dios" tú sabes.
So he asks me, "Señorita ¿hablas español?" muy polite y todo
'n' I answer, "Sí, poquito," which I always say to strangers

cuz I dunno how much they're gonna expect outta me
"Ven p'acá," he says otra vez
'n' I do outta respect for my primo Enrique
cuz he looks a lot like him but somet'ing was funny
his Spanish   I couldn't quite make it out cuz he mumbled alot
which made me feel kinda bad about myself tú sabes
that I was Mexican too but couldn't understand him that good

he's tryin' to fix this drawer that's loose in the Hawk's desk.
I knew already about the drawer
cuz she was always bitchin' 'n' moanin'
about it getting stuck cuz the bottom kept falling out
so he tells me he needs someone to hold the bottom of the drawer up
so he can screw the sides in
(She goes to the "desk," demonstrates.)
so standing to the side I lean over
and hold the drawer in place así
then he says all frustrated-like, "No, así, así."
it turns out he wants me to stand in front of the drawer
with my hands holding each side up así
(She stands with her legs apart, her pelvis pressed up
against the edge of the "desk.")
'n' believe it or not, this cabrón sits behind me on the floor
'n' reaches his arm up between my legs
that I'm straining to keep closed
even though he keeps saying all business-like
"Abreté más por favor las piernas. Abrételas un poco más."
'n' like a pendeja I do.

(She grips the edge of the "desk.")
I feel my face getting hotter
'n' I can kina feel him jiggling the drawer
pressed up against me down there
I'm staring straight ahead don' wanna look at what's happening
then worry how someone would see us like this
this guy's arm up between my legs
n' then it begins to kina brush past the inside of my thigh
I can feel the hair   that first
then the heat of his skin

(*Almost tenderly.*) the skin is so soft I hafta admit
young kina like a girl's like Norma's shoulder
I try to think about Norma 'n' her shoulders
to kina pass the time hoping to hurry things along
while he keeps saying, "Casi termino. Casi termino"
'n' I keep saying back, "Señor me tengo que ir, mi mamá me espera."
still all polite como mensa!
until finally I feel the screwdriver by my leg like ice
then suddenly the tip of it it feels like to me
is against the cotton of my chones.

"Don't move," he tells me. In English. His accent gone. 'n' I don'

from then on all I see in my mind's eye. . .
were my eyes shut?
is this screwdriver he's got in his sweaty palm
yellow   glass   handle
shiny   metal
the kind my father useta use to fix things around the house
remembered how I'd help him how he'd take me on his jobs with him
'n' I kept getting him confused in my mind
this man 'n' his arm with my father
kept imagining him was my father returned come back
the arm was so soft but this other thing. . .
hielo   hielo   ice!
I wanted to cry, "¡Papi! ¡Papi!"
'n' then I started crying for real
cuz I knew I musta done somet'ing real wrong
to get myself in this mess

I figure he's gonna shove the damn thing up me
he's trying to get my chones down, "Por favor señor please don'."
but I can hear my voice through my own ears
not from the inside out but the other way around
'n' I know I'm not fighting this one
I know I don' even sound convinced
"¿Dónde 'stás, papi? ¿Dónde 'stás?"
'n' finally I hear the man answering, "Aquí estoy. Soy tú papá."
'n' this gives me permission to go 'head to not hafta fight.

by the time he gets my chones down to my knees
I suddenly feel like I'm floating in the air
my thing kina attached to no body
flapping in the wind like a bird a wounded bird
I'm relieved when I hear the metal drop to the floor
only worry *who will see me doing this?*
(*Gritting her teeth.*) *get-this-over-with-get-this-over-with*
'n' he does gracias a dios bringing me down to earth

linoleum floor cold
the smell of wax
polish.

y ya 'stoy lista for what long ago waited for me
there is no surprise
n' I open my legs wide wide open
for the angry animal that springs outta the opening in his pants
'n' all I wanna do is have it over so I can go back to being myself
'n' a kid again

then he hit me with it
into what was supposed to be a hole
(*Tenderly.*) that I remembered had to be
cuz Norma had found it once wet 'n' forbidden
'n' showed me too how wide 'n' deep like a cueva hers got
when she wanted it to only with me she said
Marisa: Only with you, Corky.
Corky: but with this one there was no hole he had to make it
    'n' I saw myself down there like a face with no opening
a face with no features
no eyes no nose no mouth
only little lines where they shoulda been
so I dint cry
I never cried as he shoved the thing
into what was suppose to be a mouth
with no teeth
with no hate
with no voice
only a hole.

a hole!

He made me a hole!

Marisa approaches, wraps a rebozo around Corky's shoulders, holds her.

Marisa: I don't regret it. I don't regret nuthin'. He only convinced me of my own name. From an early age you learn to live with it, being a woman. I just got a head start over some. And then, years later, after I got to be with some other men, I admired how their things had no opening. . .only a tiny tiny pinhole dot to pee from, to come from. I thought. . .how lucky they were, that they could release all that stuff, all that pent–up shit from the day, through a hole that *nobody* could get into.

Scene Eleven

Marisa and Corky remain on stage. The lighting slowly shifts. Indigenous music, lively tambores. Amalia enters wearing a rebozo. She covers Marisa's shoulders with one as well. All three, now in rebozos, have become indias. They enter a dream. Corky comes downstage, kneels. She begins making tortillas, slapping her hands together. Marisa and Amalia join her on each side, forming a half circle. They, too, clap tortillas to the rhythm of the tambores. They are very happy. The rhythm quickens, accelerates.

Marisa and Amalia slowly bend toward each other, their faces crossing in front of Corky's. They kiss. Suddenly the scene darkens, the drumming becomes sinister, the clapping frantic. Thunder. Lightning. The gods have been angered. The three scatter. The stage is a maze of colliding lights, searching out the women. Corky has disappeared. Amalia cowers beneath her rebozo. Marisa appears upstage in shadow. She is out of breath. She is being hunted, her arms spread her body pressed up against an invisible wall.

Marisa: Amalia, let me in! ¡Abre la puerta! ¡Vienen a agarrarme!

Amalia wrestles in bed with her "pesadilla."

Marisa: ¡No me dejes, Amalia! ¡No me dejes sola! Let me in!

Amalia can't bear to hear her, covers her ears.

Marisa: Amalia!. . .Amalia!. . .Let. . .me. . .in!

The lights fade out and rise again. Corky can be seen in shadow standing where Marisa had been seconds before. She holds a beer bottle in the air above her head. She comes down with it, like a weapon. The sound of glass breaking. Black out.

Amalia (*in the darkness*): ¿Quién es? ¿Quién es? Who is it? ¿Eres tú, Che? *Lights rise. Amalia is sitting up in bed. There is an opened, unpacked suitcase on the floor and a photo of a man with a candle next to it on the table. Marisa appears in the doorway. She is very drunk, almost in a stupor.*

Amalia: Marisa.

Marisa: Where the...where have you been? (*Amalia gets out of bed, puts on a robe.*)

Amalia: What are you doing here?

Marisa (*menacingly*): I'm asking you a question.

Amalia: Don't come near me.

Marisa: I said, where have you been?

Amalia: What do you want?

Marisa: I wanna know... (*She stalks Amalia.*) I wanna know where you been.

Amalia: You're drunk.

Marisa: Good observation, maestra. Now are you gonna answer me?

Amalia: Stay away from me. Don't touch me.

Marisa: I'm not gonna touch you. No, no. These hands? No, no, Doña Amalia ... us jotas learn to keep our hands to ourselves.

Amalia: ¡Adió!

Marisa: Answer me!

Amalia: You know where I was.

Marisa: I waited for you. I waited three goddamn months! Count them! June, July—

Amalia: I can count.

Marisa: Well, jus cuz it ain't all hanging out on the outside don' mean I don' feel nuthin'. What did you expect from me anyway?

Amalia: Well, not this.

Marisa: Well, honey, this is what you got. Ain't I a purty picture?

Amalia: Estás borracha. Estás loca.

Marisa: Bueno, 'stoy loca. Tal vez quieres que te hable en español, eh? A lo mejor you could understand me then. I'm sorry, y'know, us pochas don' speak it as purty as you do.

Amalia: What are you talking about?

Marisa: I'm talking about going to the goddamn mailbox every day, thinking every llamadita would be you. "Ven, Chatita. Meet me in México." You lied to me.

Amalia: I didn't lie.

Marisa: No?

Amalia: No. (*She turns away.*)

Marisa: What then?

There is a pause.

Marisa: Look at you. You don' got nuthin' to say to me. You don' feel a thing.

Amalia: It's three o'clock in the morning, what am I supposed to feel?

Marisa (*after a beat*): Nuthin'. You're supposed to feel nuthin'.

Amalia: I'm going to get you some coffee.

Marisa: I don' want no coffee! You went back to him, didn't you?

Amalia: Ay, Marisa, por favor no empieces.

Marisa (*seeing the photo*): What is this? A little altar we have for the man? (*She picks it up.*)

Amalia: Don't.

Marisa: ¡Vela y todo! What is he, a saint now?

Amalia: ¡Déjalo!

Marisa: You're still in love with him, aren't you?

Amalia: Put it down, te digo.

Marisa (*approaching*): I'm asking you a question.

Amalia: Stay away from me.

Marisa: Answer me! (*Grabs Amalia.*) Are you in love with him or not?

Amalia: ¡Déjame!

Marisa (*shaking her*): Did you sleep with him?

Amalia: No! Stop it!

Marisa: Did You? Tell me the truth!

Amalia: No! ¡Déjame! (*They struggle. The picture falls to the floor. Amalia breaks Marisa's hold.*) I'm not an animal! What gives you the right to come in here like this? Do you think you're the only person in the world who's ever been left waiting?

Marisa: What was I supposed to think. . .that you were dead? That you were dead or you were with him, those were my two choices.

Amalia (*bitterly*): He's the one who's dead.

Marisa (*after a pause*): What?

Amalia: He's dead.

Amalia slowly walks over to the picture, picks it up, replaces it by the candle. She sits down on the bed, her face impassive.

Amalia (*after a pause*): When I got the news, I was in a hotel in Mexico City. I didn't stop to think about it, I took a bus right away to la Costa. Then I hired a boy to give me a lift in a truck. When I got to the river, I knew where to go. The exact spot. The place under the tamarindo where we used to make love. And for hours until dark I sat there by la orilla as I imagined he had that last time.

Marisa: He drowned.

Amalia: He drowned himself.

Marisa (*going to her*): It's not your fault, Amalia.

Amalia (*after a pause*): Whose face do you think he saw in the belly of that river moments before it swallowed him?

Marisa: It's not your fault. (*There is a long silence.* **Marisa** *makes a gesture to touch* **Amalia**, *but is unable to.*) I shouldn't have come. I'm sorry.

Amalia: No, stay. Stay and keep an old woman company.

Marisa: I'll come back tomorrow. . .fix the window. (*She starts to exit.*)

Amalia: Soñé contigo,

Marisa: You did?

Amalia: last night. (*Pause.*) I dreamed we were indias. In our village, some terrible taboo had been broken. There was thunder and lightning. I am crouched down in terror, unable to move when I realize it is *you* who have gone against the code of our people. But I was not afraid of being punished. I did not fear that los dioses would enact their wrath against el pueblo for the breaking of the taboo. It was merely that the taboo *could* be broken. And if this law nearly transcribed in blood could go, then what else? What *was* there to hold to? What immutable truths were left? (*Pause. She turns to* **Marisa**.) I never wanted you the way I wanted a man. With a man, I just would have left him. Punto. (*Pause.*) Like I left Alejandro.

The lights slowly fade to black.

Scene Twelve

Marisa sits on the platform. *Amalia's rebozo has been left there.*

Marisa: I must admit I wanted to save her. That's probably the whole truth of the story. And the problem is. . .sometimes I actually believed I could, and *sometimes* she did, too.

She was like no woman I had ever had. I think it was in the quality of her skin. Some people, you know, their skin is like a covering. They're supposed to be showing you something when the clothes fall into a heap around your four ankles, but nothing is lost, y'know what I mean? They jus' don' give up nuthin'. Pero Amalia. . .¡Híjole!

She picks up **Amalia's** *rebozo, fingers it.*
She was never fully naked in front of me, always had to keep some piece
of clothing on, a shirt or something always wrapped up around her throat,
her arms all outta it and flying. What she did reveal, though, each item of
clothing removed was a gift, I swear, a small offering, a suggestion of all
that could be lost and found in our making love together. It was like she
was saying to me, "I'll lay down my underslip. ¿Y tú? ¿Qué me vas a
dar?" And I'd give her the palm of my hand to warm the spot she had just
exposed. Everything was a risk. Everything took time. Was slow and de-
liberate.

I'll never forget after the first time we made love, I was feeling muy orgu-
llosa y todo, like a good lover, and she says to me—
Amalia (*voice-over, memory*): You make love to me like worship.
Marisa: And I nearly died, it was so powerful what she was saying.
And I wanted to answer. "Sí, la mujer es mi religión." If only sex coulda
saved us.

Y'know sometimes when me and her were in the middle of it, making love,
I'd look up at her face, kinda grey from being indoors so much with all
those books of hers, and I'd see it change, turn this real deep color of
brown and olive, like she was cooking inside. Tan linda. Kind. Very very
very kind to me, to herself, to the pinche planet. . . , and I'd watch it move
from outside the house where that crazy espíritu of hers had been out
makin' tracks. I'd watch it come inside, through the door, watch it travel
all through her own private miseries and settle itself, finally right there in
the room with us. This bed. This fucking dreary season. This cement city.
With us. With me. No part of her begging to have it over. . .forget. And
I could feel all the parts of her move into operation. Waiting. Held. Suspended. Praying for me to put my tongue to her and I knew she knew we
would find her. . .como fuego. And just as I pressed my mouth to her, I'd
think. . . *I could save your life.*

(*Coming downstage*). It's not often you get to see people that way in all
their pus and glory and still love them. It makes you feel so good, like
your hands are weapons of war. And as they move up into el corazón de
esta mujer, you are making her body remember, it didn't have to be that
hurt, ¿Me entiendes? It was not natural or right that she got beat down so

damn hard, and that all those crimes had nothing to do with the girl she once was two, three, four decades ago.

Pause. Music rises in the background.

Marisa: It's like making familia from scratch
each time all over again. . .
with strangers, if I must.
If I must, I will.

I am preparing myself for the worst,
so I cling to her in my heart
my daydream with pencil in my mouth

when I put my fingers
to my own forgotten places.

The lights fade out in silence. Music.

End

Reprinted from *Heroes and Saints & Other Plays*. (Albuquerque: West End Press, 1994).

NOVELA / NOVEL

ARISTEO BRITO (1942-)

El diablo en Texas (1976)

Yo vengo de un pueblito llamado Presidio. Allá en los más remotos confines de la tierra surge seco y baldío. Cuando quiero contarles cómo realmente es, no puedo, porque me lo imagino como un vapor eterno. Quisiera también poderlo fijar en un cuadro por un instante, así como pintura pero se me puebla la mente de sombras alargadas, sombras que me susurran al oído diciéndome que Presidio está muy lejos del cielo. Que nacer allí es nacer medio muerto; que trabajar allí es moverse callado a los quehaceres y que no se debe tomar a mal el miedo del turista cuando llega al pueblito y sale espantado al escuchar el ruido vacío de almas en pena. Quizás sean estas voces las que nunca me dejan retratar a mi pueblo como realmente es, porque cuando me hablan me dejan la cabeza y el alma hechas pedacitos como si hubiera jugado un perro rabioso conmigo dejando despilfarros de cuerpos arrugados, cuerpos agujereados como cedazo por donde se filtra el agua que riega los campos verdes de sudor borracho y risa sofocada por unos miserables uniformes con mapas del país en el brazo derecho buscando a los que se mojan en el río que fertiliza plantas de diablos ojos burladores de la gente y de un Santo Niño que juega a las canicas de rodillas esperando al padre que regrese de prisión, espantapájaros desconocido, niño esperando debajo de un columpio raptor del viento, niño que escucha suspiros en el agua, en el fortín tembloroso de aullidos de perros funerarios a pleno medio día y en la noche el niño muere, la vieja llora, un feto piensa de noche, noche, noche larga como el infinito, noche pesada, monótona como la historia mentirosa así como las damas del zumbido, pero éstas tienen razón, la historia no, porque en los corrales de este lado las vacas flacas de Ojinaga se compran a muy buen precio para engordarlas a expensas de otros y la iglesia mientras tanto que se cae de ojos tristes en los días que no hay domingos así como las casas de queso de chocolate roídas de ratón porque no tienen cemento y los excusados antiguos tronos de los reyes católicos ahora son de lámina y los baños al aire libre en pleno invierno arropados en lona para que no penetren los ojos o en una tina a media sala los sábados para rociar el piso de tierra, tierra con montes de leña prohibida para todos menos el inquilino quien conoce la bondad del Señor que tiene tiendas que fían la comida y gasolina racionada pero en las

boticas no se venden medicinas ya que no hay dotores sólo hojas de laurel,
romero, ruda y yerbabuena para los niños que voltean los ojos legañosos y las
madres tienen cuates cuando comen los chorupes los frijoles con quelites y la
carne del diablo con azadero con trompillo y con empacho la penicilina cura a
todo mal amén cuando las trocas cargadas de humillados escupen el sol blasfe-
mo con el hedor de muerte próxima, olor que penetra, penetra, penetra el espina-
zo derretido, doblado, jorobado, abrazando casi casi el melón que si lo comes
te da torzón si no se te suelta el cuerpo se te escapa y la mente se te vuela con
el aire bochornoso pero cuidado porque te empacan en el vagón refrigerado de
la Santa Fe y te llevan a disneylandia mientras el mapa del gobierno te pregunta
si eres legítimo de la tierra sembrada con hermanos de tus hermanos de tus
hermanos amén y el puente de la frontera se cierra a medianoche pa ponele el
candado al infierno aunque por debajo se escapa todo el río acostumbrado a ser
tecolotl y el sol ya ni lo necesitas porque eres planta, eres tierra infértil, gastada
y el diablo está cansado de reírse en su cama de agua porque el padrecito subió
a la sierra a mediodía en procesión dizque pa desterrarlo y pa que las puertas
se abrieran por todo el río y se cruzara sin temor y la cruz en la cumbre se
bendice al tiempo que el diablo se prepara para ir al baile y los batos locos¹
no se aguantan tampoco en las boticas donde hay vitrolas con Elvis Presley Fats
Domino Little Richard and the blob that creeps and you ain't nothing but a
hound dog finding your thrill on Blueberry Hill bailando solos con zapatos
puntiagudos con taps tapping tap tapping chalupas down the street unpaved no
sound carros con colas arrastrando sus dos pipas with fender-skirts para cubrirse
de vergüenza Dios nos libre, que nos libre, las gallinas dicen en los gallineros
de las casas cuando las cantinas cierran y el pooltable con las buchacas rotas
but still ten cents a game after Tarzan movie over Tarzans wild all over, gritos,
golpes en el pecho de Tarzán el hombre mono que vino a salvar a los pobres in-
dios de una escuela donde enseñaban a fragmentar los idiomas y el chivero que
enseñaba ciencias porque sabía arrearlas a los pastos secos ya que el agua se
la robaron las bombas traca traca trac toda la santa noche hasta que agarraban

---

¹batos locos, jóvenes del barrio.

*aire y se morían pero el "gin" no se paraba, con su whooooooo sorbía las treilas
a la Chancla y a la Mocha y a la Golondrina nombres puestos por la raza para
indicar sello de posesión prestada a medias mientras todos los inquilinos orgu-
llosos de ser jefes de las tierras que antes fueron suyas "yo pago herramientas,
veneno, dinero, tú pones la vida y me das la mitad, ¿qué tal?" pos a toda madre
a toda madre te vas y te vas y te vas y no ganas nada todo el año pero ¿qué tal
al levantar la cosecha de tu vida? en tu vida habrás visto mil dólares juntos que
duran en un marranito mientras no pagas cuentas de mil quinientos y te compras
una troca sin gasolina para llevar a tus trabajadores porque ya eres dueño,
propietario, sembrador simbólico y a los menos afortunados los haces ver el día
más claro cuando les pagas parte de la baba que te tocó a ti de la baba que tu
jefe te pagó a ti esclavo sumido, sin saber que le pisaste la cabeza al otro para
que viniera por otra, Dios perdónalos, porque al cabo allá en el otro cachete la
vida perra, "caray mi amigo, ¿de dónde?" "desde Michoacán" vestido con la
ropa hecha de costales de harina y huaraches de hule marca Goodyear que
nunca conoció Presidio, Presidio bien aventurado, a ti y a vos padre que eres
de Presidio, Amén.*

PRESIDIO 1883

La víbora, estirada como cola de tigre entre las velas que hace mucho tiempo se apagaron, empieza a retorcerse. Se sonríe la juguetona porque es la dueña del mundo, dueña de esta capilla abandonada, dueña de los ríos, de los dos pueblos situados cara a cara, dueña de la gente. Y esto le da gran satisfacción.

Ahora se desliza por encima de los escapularios y las reliquias, numerosos brazos y piernas y cabezas y toda forma de cuerpos humanos metálicos, y se cuela hasta el suelo. Con la lengua de fuera se arrastra lentamente por la puerta descuartizada hacia afuera y de allí comienza a treparse al techo de la capilla, estrangulando la base de la Santa Cruz. Se detiene en esa posición por un instante para luego ceñirse a la parte superior de la cruz. Ahora enroscada cómodamente, se pone a escudriñar los contornos. "Nada ha cambiado", piensa, "desde que vinieron los frailes siguiendo el río hace mucho años". Recuerda que desde un principio quisieron defraudarla, quitarle el dominio, ese valle que nombraron La Junta de los Ríos. "Pero sólo el tiempo es permanente", piensa. "De esa iglesia y de esa misión, ¿qué ha quedado? Nada".

De allí, de arriba se imagina el valle Presidio-Ojinaga como un pedernal verde delineado por los ríos y se jacta de su imaginación. Después enfoca sobre el laborío de Lynch donde de cuando en cuando brotan cabezas y se sonríe placer. Esta vez las cabezas son como gallos enterradas entre un lago lamoso. De repente se le borra la imagen con el pitido del tren que viene cruzando el puente y observa la víbora como al punto de pasar al lado mexicano se hace una parada momentánea. Después continúa despacio como en cámara lenta y vuelve a sonreír la víbora. ¡Qué imaginación! El río y el tren: una cruz chueca y borracha, una cruz serpiente, una cruz derretida. Pero pronto se cansa del juego a las imágenes y se pone a pensar en lo que oyó ayer. Que mañana viene más gente del interior a trabajar los campos de Presidio. ¡Estupendo! Y con el gozo del niño con su nuevo juguete, la víbora se desliza rápido y contenta. Luego empieza el descenso al fondo de la sierra donde se encuentra la cueva.

Chava el idiota no oyó a los cuatro soldados que venían cantando pero el grito que éstos dieron a las mulas lo hizo que brincara y saliera detrás del mezquite. Luego, como si hubiera visto espantos, tiró la cáscara de plátano que estaba comiendo y salió corriendo con las manos en los oídos. No paró de correr hasta que llegó a la esquina de la viuda Nieves. Los soldados mientras tanto celebraban el susto del idiota a risotadas hasta que había desaparecido. Luego que se les había pasado el ataque de risa el arriero de las mulas ordenó a uno de ellos que fuera a avisar la llegada.

—Tell Ben we got the merchandise and that we'll meet him over there at the fortín.

Sam respondió con una mano en la cachucha. Luego picó espuelas hacía el cercano rancho del terrateniente que se encontraba en las afueras del pueblo. Mientras tanto la carreta siguió hacia el fortín.

Chava se estuvo buen rato arrodillado detrás de la casa de Nieves con los ojos tapados. Entre ave maría purísimas[2] y temblorinas, cantaba de un lindo pescadito que no quería salir del agua porque su mamá le había dicho que si salía, pronto moriría.

Cuando la mujer lo oyó salió de la casa y le dijo que ya se descubriera los ojos y el idiota le respondió con que le dolían los muertos de las mulas y que quería a su mamá.

—Ya hombre ya déjate de cosas, ¿no quieres comer?

—...—

—Bueno, si quieres comer, pasa, y ya no te muerdas las uñas que no tienes.

La mujer volvió a entrar y Chava siguió picándose la cara. Trataba de quitarse los pocos pelos de la barba donde la piel estaba para sangrar y así pasó unos instantes de seria concentración mas luego empezó a hablar con sus difun-

---

[2] el rezo "Ave María".

tas, la mamá Pancha, la tía Cuca y la novia Rosario. Entonces decidió proceder por la calle, descalzo y semidesnudo a ciento veinte grados. "Lindo pescadito no quieres venir, a jugar con mi aro, vamos al jardín, mi mamá me ha dicho, que no salga yo". Pero poco a poco fue derritiéndose la canción de Chava en el camino.

—No crea, comadre, si le fue bien a Don Ben este año con su cosecha. Por eso va a hacer fiesta. De otra manera no ...

—Qué va, comadrita. ¿A poco quiere decir que el hombre no tiene corazón?

—No, si no digo que es convenencia, nomás que pos tiene con qué, y nuestros viejos se lo merecen.

—Tiene razón. Ellos sí que echan la lengua.

—Dice Ramón que esta vez se va a lucir en la fiesta que...

Así es. Mandó a Chindo que matara tres becerros grandes pa que hubiera suficiente. Quesque va a tener dos cenas...

—¿De veras? ¿Y dónde va a ser el fandango después comadre?

—Pos quesque viene gente especial de Marfa. Cuentan que hasta ordenó cinco barriles de cerveza de esa de la estrella.

—Oiga pos ¿que no que iban a hacer el baile allí en el fortín también?

—Parece que no...hablando con el trompudo de Jorge, dice que va a tocar en el parque.

—Yo sí que no me la pierdo. Ando reque alborotada y aunque no está mi viejo voy a darme una asomadita. ¿Y usté?

—Ande, si ¿a poco cree que no se me mueve la ala? Si usté va yo la acompaño.

—Ande pues.

Cuando le llegó el mensaje a Ben, de inmediato se puso a ensillar el caballo.

—No, Ben, por favor no lo hagas, por caridad de Dios.

—Y de perro muerto— contestó bruscamente el viejo montándose en el caballo.

La mujer no dijo más y quedó sola con el galope retumbando en los oídos. Cuando el hombre desapareció en la esquina del camino, ella se encerró maldiciendo la ira del esposo. A Rosario le daban ganas de salir a la calle gritándole a la gente que lo colgaran. Mas todavía tenía la esperanza que a Ben se le ablandara el corazón y esto la hizo que se calmara. Después se entretuvo dando órdenes a las criadas que limpiaran las mesas y los manteles de la fiesta. ¡Ah!, y esa cortina maldita que le había ordenado hacer. Sólo Rosario sabía su propósito pues detrás de ella se escondería la maldad del hombre. Que no se le olvidara, le había dicho, pero ella se resistía a sacarla del ropero, como si esta acción fuera a detener la cólera de su viejo. Quizá no viniera por ella, quizá...

—Perhaps we should try to...
—No. You do as I say.
—Sir, our orders...it would be better if...
—No.
—Captain Ramsey said some innocent...
—You tell the captain I'm going ahead as planned. He'll get the damn thing back tomorrow. Now just help me get it into that room.

Los soldados bajaron el cañoncito y lo rodaron hasta el centro del cuarto donde lo quería Ben. Después pidió que lo apuntaran hacia la puerta donde daba el comedor. Los que lo habían traicionado no merecían más que eso, por ladrones. Ya verían cómo pagaban una traición esos cabrones, roba-caballos.

El roba-caballos se llamaba Jacinto y éste nunca pensó en la posibilidad de que lo hubieran delatado así que cuando Lorenzo, el capataz de Ben, cruzó el río para llevarle la invitación, ni siquiera titubeó en aceptarla.

—Pero por qué tanta...
—Se merece trato especial, señor Jacinto. El señor Ben me ha mandado expresamente porque se siente muy agradecido. Nadie como usted y sus compañeros le habían ayudado tanto. Eso no se le olvida. Así que llámelos y allá los espera el fandango. La cena suya es especial, a las ocho.

Lorenzo tenía razón, pensaba Jacinto, aunque al viejo tallado no se le quitaba lo miserable. De otra manera por qué iban a andar robando. Solamente así, robándole, se pagaban ellos mismos las friegas que se llevaban sin nunca recibir sueldo justo. Pero a lo mejor Ben reconocía por fin el valor de sus obreros y con estos pensamientos creyó oportuno invitar a cuanto amigo tenía y para cuando terminó de hacer cuentas ya llevaba veinticinco.

Esa tarde la gente se hartó de lo lindo en el fortín. Se les hizo raro, sin embargo, que nomás el salón que se usaba para servir estaba abierto. Tampoco pudieron entender por qué otros invitados como Jacinto y sus hombres se habían citado a comer para después. Mientras tanto don Benito, con paso garboso y sonrisa de ángel, caminaba legoneando por entre la gente. Y así, poco a poco se fueron olvidando de las puertas bajo llave. Además la comida estaba tan buena como la cerveza y el baile que seguiría después, ¡caramba!

Con la puesta del sol la gente se escurrió para el parque donde los fronteri-
zos se preparaban para comenzar a tocar y para las ocho el fortín quedaba escueto. Sólo los invitados especiales permanecían esperando su recepción. Mientras
tanto Chava, quien no había querido comer, seguía acurrucado detrás de un
chaparro cercano como si lo hubieran enraizado. Allí seguía con su temblorina,
pensativo. Se estuvo allí hasta que el fuerte cañonazo lo hizo salir corriendo
histérico. El el baile, al contrario, la gente ni siquiera oyó los tiros secos de
pistola que terminaban a los que habían quedado vivos. Lo único que corrió por
el baile esa noche, fue el rumor de que un hermoso galán desconocido había
andado bailando con patas de chivo.

"En ese tiempo la gente sembraba trigo, maíz, cosa asina[3] que se levantara
antes de septiembre porque ya nomás llegaba el río y tenían que abandonar los
jacales en las labores y venirse al fortín. El fortín se ocupaba de pura gente pobre
que había perdido su jacal.

"Una vez estaba chica todavía y nosotros sembrábamos allí en la labor,
donde se levantaba más. Teníamos un chilar que se daba muy regular porque lo
lidiábamos muy bien. Cuando no iban unos, iban otros a comprar el chile barato
pero de allí se hacía uno vivir. Lorenzo tenía una vaca muy dañera. La metía en
el corral y sola se salía por debajo. Iba, hacía el daño, y amanecía otra vez dentro
del corral. Cuando pasaba por el chile regado, hacía quebradero de matas y la
vaca se mantenía gorda porque a nosotros nos fregaba. Pues papá le reclamó a
Lorenzo muchas veces pero nunca quería darse que la vaca hacía males y siempre decía ¿con qué le probaba? Claro, la prueba era la huella: papá agarraba la
huella hasta entrar el corral pero Lorenzo no se quería dar. Porque la vaca era
de ésas que dan un balde y más de leche. Mi papá siempre se lo dijo muy claro:
mira, vale más que pongas cuidado porque te la voy a agarrar y me vas a pagar
todo el mal que, anda, mira el destrozo que hace. Mira nomás cómo en el maíz
va arqueando la mazorca. Pues no, siempre ha sido muy diablo Lorenzo. De
todos modos fue mi papá y habló con Fermín que era juez entonces. Fermín fue
y le avisó a Lorenzo pero salió con la misma, ¿con qué me preban? Papá le dijo
a Fermín: nosotros tenemos un perro que la puede agarrar. Yo le echo el perro
y te aseguro que una vez que la agarre, la vaca no vuelve más. Fermín dijo que
estaba bien porque ya le había avisado a Lorenzo que cuidara la vaca o iba a
tener que pagar el daño que había hecho el animal, y había salido con la misma.

---

[3]así.

"Bueno, pues la sentimos. A mi hermano le hacía más caso que qué el perro, así que papá le habló y le dijo que andaba la vaca. Le dijo, échale el perro, y nomás le habló aquél y le echó el perro. No, ¡qué bárbaro! Le hizo garras el hocico y la hizo volar el alambre. Pero no la soltó hasta que le habló porque ya de que agarraba a un animal no lo soltaba.

"Otro día en la mañana se aprontó Lorenzo con un 30-30 a la casa, echándole pestes a papá. Dijo papá: espérame, allí voy. Entonces papá fue y sacó una cuata de dos cañones. Dijo: ándale, a ver quién se va primero. No, se fue para atrás Lorenzo. Y así siguió la cosa".

—En este mundo nadie se va sin pagar las que debe, hija.

—¿Por qué es mi tío Lorenzo, así, mamá?

—Porque tiene el diablo metido.

—Pero él nomás llevó el mensaje, doña Mónica.

—No es lo único que ha hecho, Eduvijes. Entiéndelo bien, Lorenzo va a pagar todo esto muy caro.

"No te equivoques, hija. No siempre estuvimos necesitados. Este terreno que tiene el Ben era de mi mamá Mónica, de mi tía Paz, de Victoria y Zenobio. Eran los dueños del terreno desde aquí casi hasta el río. Entonces mi tía Paz estaba fuera de sí. Apolonio Varela, casado con la tía Victoria, vivía en Marfa y vinieron para llevarla a lidiar una temporada. La tía tenía una petaquilla y allí guardaba los papeles del terreno y nunca se dieron cuenta de que se habían llevado los papeles. En dos o tres días la señora no quiso aguantar pero allá le hicieron que firmara, vendiéndole al viejo Ben. Todo esto vino a causa de su hijo Lorenzo.

"Entonces tu tío Zenobio y todos pusieron abogado, a don Pancho. Pero le dijeron que no tenían con qué pagarle porque la cosa estaba muy mal. Pues no, les dijo que después le pagaban. Y entonces el abogado de Ben entró por otra parte pero Don Pancho ganó; dijo que podía vender la parte de la tía Paz y hacer lo que le diera la gana, pero lo demás no. Pues se pusieron de acuerdo Ben y Lorenzo, el hijo de la tía. Le untó la mano el viejo, le dio dinero, y lo puso a trabajar en el arroyo. Y cuando fue en la mañana papá para las labores, ya había tumbado Lorenzo el alambre. Entonces le preguntaron para qué y él dijo que porque iba a enderezar la línea. Si en esta vez nos ganaron, a la otra no, dijo. Pues el tío Zenobio, papá y todos creyeron que como iba a echarle bordo para que no entrara el arroyo, a ellos les convenía. El mero bueno fue Lorenzo, el que metió la pata. No se tentó el alma para fregar a la viejita, a su propia mamá loca. Dios lo perdone, hija".

No se supo ni cómo le hicieron para llegar hasta Presidio, pero el caso es que cuando llegaron, llegaron echando grito a caballo. Vinieron del sur de Texas con una meta: a enterrar a la gente viva y sumirla todavía más abajo del infierno. Y aunque los invasores habían llegado al abismo más oscuro de la tierra, supieron ser creativos. En Presidio descubrieron que la tierra y el hombre tenían posibilidades lucrativas pero antes había que enterrar a unos. A los pocos meses se fueron directamente al río para sumir al lanchero, hijo de don Pancho, en el agua. Primero porque había golpeado a Ben y segundo porque había intereses más grandes en el transporte de gente. Pero Jesús sólo había pensado en Rosario su hermana. ¿Qué negocios tenía este gringo cabrón con ella? ¡Vamos! ¡A volar paloma y a tronar el pico a otra parte! Así que una noche enterraron a Jesús en agua, llenando la lancha y el cuerpo de tierra para que los dos se quedaran sumergidos. La piedra en el pescuezo aseguraría eso. A don Francisco mientras tanto le sirvió el diploma de abogado para limpiarse la cola, pues el caso se echó fuera de la corte. Y para el colmo, dentro de un año se le fue la hija con el gringo. ¡Chingao! ¡Tras de cornao, apaleao! Pero de ahora en adelante, ¡Cuidado bola e cabrones! Más tarde Santamaría, su hermano continuó el transporte de gente aun cuando avisaban que pronto se construiría un puente internacional y que tan pronto se hiciera, habría que pasar por él. Pero Santamaría con carabina en mano, seguía sin obedecer la ley porque la gente prefería la lancha. ¿Pasar por la garita y presentar papeles? Vayan mucho a la chingada. El puente es cosa del diablo. (El puente es el arco iris del diablo: dos patas de chivo puestas en dos cementerios. El puente es un resbaladizo para cagarse de risa, ¿que no, Jesús?)

"Los Lynchis tienen historia; los viejos pues. Esos mataron gente a lo bárbaro. Estos trabajaban unas pobres gentes allí y cuando querían irse después de un año o más se llevaban su pago. Pos si te voy a pagar, les decían, pero luego los sacaban y los mataban. La gente no protestaba porque no había de comer; estaba muy duro. Nosotros aquí llegamos a pasarla con una taza de atole y lo que tú quieras. Así es que ¿qué te ibas a poner a hacer? Seguro que hombres sí había como papá, que ya le importaba poco matar. Y asina había algunos como él que podían hacer con cualquiera lo que querían, pero es que pensaban en no dejar a la familia abandonada. Porque valor cualquiera lo tenía. Papá de lo que estaba manco de todo eso. Si no nomás mochales el pescuezo y pasarse pa'l otro lado. Porque aquí no creas que nomás los Lynchis había. Aquí todavía me acuerdo cómo ese capitán Gray era muy bueno pa poner la bota. Era de los rinchis en ese tiempo. Era muy diablo."

Don Pancho no pudo entender la noticia a pedazos que le daba Chava el idiota, así que mejor concentró en apaciguarle los nervios. Luego que se los calmó, abrió la bodega de la tienda y le puso un sarape sobre los costales de frijol para que se acostara. Por lo menos no andará rondando despavorido el resto de la noche, pensó Francisco. Entonces le echó candado a la puerta y se volvió a su casa-tienda-imprenta, al cabo que la luz del día traería la verdad a la puerta. Pero la noche se le hizo larga a Pancho. A las pocas horas llegaron a la puerta unos ojos cristalinos de rabia. Reyes manipulaba la carabina como si fuera de papel al tiempo que hacía chorrear el cuento del fortín por la comisura de los labios. Cuando terminó, el viejo lo convidó a que entrara mas Reyes no quiso. Dijo que prefería ir a averiguar la verdad más allá pues a veces era dudosa la palabra de Chindo.

—Está bien pero no vayas a cometer una locura.

—El desgraciado se va a llevar la suya.

—Asegúrate primero, hijo, y paciencia.

—Si nada más a eso voy, porque quiero estar muy segurito.

—Después hablamos. Pero que no se te olvide, Reyes. Mientras vida haya tiempo sobra.

—Está bien, viejo.

Don Pancho se dirigió a su despacho privado y allí, entre libros y alteros de periódicos, se puso a luchar con su cinismo. Meditaba sobre su vida y su carrera—un verdadero desastre. Nada más. Derrota, rotunda derrota y punto. Los periódicos y los libros polvorosos que lo rodeaban eran los últimos vestigios de una lucha en que había sido vencido. ¿Comprobantes de su edad creadora? Hasta la pregunta era necia. Recordaba cómo su abatimiento era el del pueblo; como los dos habían quedado reducidos a un microcosmos insignificante pero repleto de historia. El, por su parte, había sido rechazado por ambos gobiernos a causa de su fuerte sentido de justicia. De los esfuerzos que había hecho en su tiempo por asegurar los derechos básicos del ser humano no había quedado nada y lo único que lo consolaba era desenterrar su verdad, sepultada en polvo. Los núme-ros del *Fronterizo* que él había guardado en su despacho lo decían todo. Ojalá que algún día alguien viniera y los leyera, pero eso ya cuando estuviera muerto.

Recordaba muy bien el primer año de práctica porque fue en ese mismo año cuando se le derrumbó el mundo que había creado en el aire durante sus estudios. La realidad era otra, caramba. La vida se hacía a gritos y a sombrerazos. Pronto se había dado cuenta que la carrera de abogado no era tan ilustre, y menos cuan-do practicaba en un pueblo de míseras condiciones. Entonces cayó en la cuenta que la mejor manera de ayudar y ayudarse a sí mismo sería por medio del perio-dismo, y de inmediato circuló *El Fronterizo*, un periodiquito que leían no tanto los que necesitaban leerlo sino otros editores del suroeste. Su negocio cobró vigor cuando para su sorpresa, empezó a recibir periódicos de California, de Trinidad, Colorado, de Laredo, de Nuevo México, y de partes que ni sospechaba hubiera gente mexicana. Con el tiempo la comunicación se hizo una gran voz y un mismo interés: polémicas, denuncias, y protestas relacionadas a la vida de la raza de estos lados. Pronto se habían ido colando sus palabras por los periódicos de México y no había tardado en reconocer el gobierno mexicano el beneficio que Francisco Uranga aportaría al país. Con gran entusiasmo había recibido la nombración de cónsul. ¿Las palabras exactas? "Servir como representante de nuestros paisanos en el extranjero y actuar debidamente en defensa de sus derechos y principios asignados por los tratados entre México y los Estados Unidos". Tan pronto como había recibido el nombramiento, se había puesto a poner en orden de prioridad las tareas a emprender. Primero, aclarar la cuestión de terrenos ultrajados del valle de Presidio y buscar la manera de hacer válidos los reclamos de tierras que se habían ido arrollando como alfombra poco a poco. (Pero recuerda que para entonces ya había sido tarde porque los archivos legales estaban escritos en otra lengua y con otro sello.) Después, seguiría la complicada cuestión de ciudadanía y para esto habría que ponerse en contacto con los demás cónsules del suroeste. En seguida, buscar una manera más eficaz de conseguir la repatriación de todos esos individuos que querían hacerlo y que pensaban que el gobierno mexicano los había abandonado. Otra de las causas, y aquí subrayaba, era combatir la insolencia, por parte de los que se consideraban la ley, de cruzar las fronteras sin ningún permiso previo. Este punto era el de los más sensibles, pues había él experimentado numerosos casos en que el perseguido se sacaba de México para venirle a hacer justicia en corte y en un idioma extraño. Sí, había que aclarar esa ley de extradición tan vilipendiada por el conquistador, aunque sabía que era tarea bastante difícil. En otras ocasiones ocurría lo contrario: el acusado, ante las autoridades mexicanas, no podía comprobar que era ciudadano de los Estados Unidos, aun cuando el tratado decía que el que no se repatriara después de dos años, se consideraría como tal. ¿Y los papeles? Se encontraban en el aire. ¿De dónde eres? De la tierra señor. De donde puedo hacer la vida.

No tardó Pancho Uranga en darse cuenta que él también se encontraba en la misma vorágine. Entre el papelerío y la confusión sentía la vida un mareo y una flotación. Resultó con las manos atadas de frustración, convirtiéndose en una de esas personas que de tanta sabiduría sobre cómo marcha el mundo, se crea una mueca cínica que comunica: pendejos, ¿qué esperaban? ¿El bien de Dios envuelto en una frezada? Entiéndanlo, la humanidad está pudrida por dentro. Y cada vez que resultaba el diablo venciendo, se le enterraba más la espinita y para cuando se la había querido sacar ya le había envenenado el alma. Entonces había tomado la pluma como espada. Aparecieron sus escritos en su propio *Fronterizo, El tuc-sonense, El hispanoamericano, El Zuriaco, La vox del pueblo,* y cuarenta periódi-cos más que se publicaban por aquí en ese entonces: "denuncio rotundamente la usurpación de las tierras y apoyo los Gorras Blancas[4] por haber blandido las armas"; "firmo la resolución de la prensa unida hispanoamericana en la que se condena al gobernador de Nuevo México por llamarnos 'greasers'[5] a través de la prensa inglesa de Nueva York y que ahora tiene el garbo de amenazarnos", "protesto expediciones filibusteras[6] por yanquis oportunistas"; "condeno la discri-minación en los trabajos, escuelas y establecimientos públicos", "apoyo las defen-sas hechas por la Alianza Mexicana"; "con rabia y amor lamento la desunión de nuestra raza y lloro por su futuro"; "soy partidario del elemento radical de obre-ros en San Antonio, California y Nuevo México no porque sé que lograron algo sino porque se comprueba el hecho de que estamos todavía vivos y que siempre tendremos lucha"; "sospecho la justicia y la condena que imparten los jueces y que se rigen por una opinión de testigos prejuiciados; es más, sé que Manuel Verdugo no era culpable. Lo supe después que lo condenaron a muerte en El Paso"; "condeno la venta de esclavos negros en Fayetteville, Missouri"; "sepa el editor de dicho periodiquito en Guadalajara que mis esfuerzos por repatriar a los de nuestra raza son genuinos. Que lo hago porque conozco los sufrimientos padecidos en un país que se considera el mejor ejemplo de la democracia y también le hago ver claramente, con ejemplos, que nuestra gente aquí no es un montón de tamaleros como usted tan groseramente nos describe. Esta encuesta que aquí publico contiene la cantidad de personas de ascendencia mexicana y sepa usted que de todos los que respondieron, sólo cuatro tienen el oficio de tamalero y no porque sean holgazanes sino por la adversa fortuna que les ha tocado. Numerosas veces he venido apelando al gobierno mexicano que le conce-da el dinero para el transporte a esta gente que quiera repatriarse así como un pedacito de tierra porque de otra manera ¿cuál sería la garantía de que podrían vivir mejor si regresan a México? El problema radica ahora en que la población china está dispuesta a contratarse por menor sueldo"; "quiero que sepa el señor, que habla sin fundamento cuando dice que nosotros los de aquí somos de los más miserables e ineducados. Sí le concedemos razón que la familia obrera vive mal, pero eso significa que somos ineducados. Reconocemos nuestra realidad y hace-mos lo que podemos. Ahora explíqueme, señor editor, ¿por qué cree usted que

[4]un grupo clandestino organizado para proteger las tierras de los miembros.
[5]grasosos, apodo despectivo.
[6]de conquista, caso de individuos, no del gobierno.

esta gente obrera es la que menos ansía por repatriarse? En otra ocasión me gustaría que usted, en vez de escupir sinrazones, se pusiera a pensar un poquito más. Nosotros, colega, no queremos mudarnos de esta tierra siempre nuestra y si yo hago el esfuezo por la repatriación de alguna gente es porque me mueve la esperanza de que el gobierno mexicano nos auxilie"; "le advierto al señor Gobernador de Chihuahua que ha dado muy malos pasos al conceder bastos terrenos a estas compañías colonizadoras pues no hacen más que apoderarse de las riquezas naturales. Con el tiempo esas compañías seguirán la misma ruta de los grandes capataces que ahora explotan al pobre sin misericordia"; "denuncio ante el público los hechos extraviados del cónsul de Paso, Texas por haber cooperado con el sheriff en la extradición de Rufino Gómez. Los cien pesos que se le pagaron por debajo de cuerda no le servirán para aplacar la conciencia después que se la haya juzgado al acusado"; "no creía que uno de los nuestros (de Laredo) fuera a comentar tan desfavorablemente sobre la poesía que incluimos en la sección literaria, y mucho menos porque está escrita en un español 'bastardo'. Lamentamos mucho que estas actitudes prevalezcan tanto. ¿Por qué se ciega nuestro colega de la realidad? Mejor ¿por qué no se queja el señor ante el sistema educativo o ante el gobierno federal, quien prometió respetar nuestro idioma y nuestra cultura? Si hubiera escuelas donde se enseña en nuestra lengua materna quizás usted no tuviera razón de lamentarse. Pero esto ya es un ideal. Mejor póngase, gaste sus energías en asegurar el bienestar de sus hijos que sabe Dios lo necesitan, y no de mostrarnos esa misma actitud de superioridad que venimos saboreando desde hace mucho tiempo".

Así, con la punta de la pluma, picó crestas sensibles y no tardó para que ambos gobiernos lo consideraran enemigo de la armonía. Cuando defendió la causa de Catarino Garza quien, desde Nuevo México, logró el alzamiento de obreros contra los terratenientes y el gobierno de Chihuahua, ya no era cónsul. Había sido un milagro que escapase de la muerte aunque en ese tiempo la hubiese preferido pues ya nada le importaba. El pueblo que él había defendido con amor ahora le daba la espalda y era lo que más dolía. Unos, tan pronto como les pagaba bien la suerte, se le echaban encima. "Viejo revoltoso, déjese de cosas. Hay prosperidad y usted nos perjudica con sus tonterías. Así que se calla o..." *El Fronterizo* moría una muerte sin gloria. La gente tenía razón, la historia no se detiene. (La historia corre como el agua. A veces mansita, otras con el diablo a cuestas, inflada y rabiosa. Después engendra una mano deforme que estira sus dedos hasta el infinito. Luego la mano de agua se recoge y se engarruña, dejando un pequeño hilito por el cauce del Río Grande. Entonces vuelve la gente con su eterna migración a formar una cruz contorsionada, una miserable cruz de carne y de agua.) Y porque la historia de mi raza es de río, pensé, me voy a hacer una lancha para cruzarlos. Esto me ayudará a mantenerme pero les cobraré solamente a los que puedan pagar. También me dará la oportunidad de guiar y desviar a la gente por los mejores caminos. "Vete por aquí y cuídate con tal y tal y si no te da trabajo sigue el río hasta..." Pero antes recogeré mis tiliches, mis libros y me mudaré a Ojinaga. Haré una casita cerca del río por el otro lado para no dejar que se borre nuestra historia escrita en el agua. Muchos años después, cuando perdí a Rosario y me enteré de que iban a construir el puente, ni me causó sorpresa. Tampoco cuando tuve noticias de que me habían ahogado a Jesús. Me volvió a sangrar la llaga cuando lo enterraron casi deshecho y juré que lo vengaría. Pero yo no podía y pensé que tú lo vengarías, Reyes, por ser su hermano. No te quería criar para que fueras asesino, no. Las armas vendrían después, y esas sólo como último recurso. Lo que quería darte primero era educación de libros pero tampoco de ésos que cuentan histories falsas. Para eso te pondría a estudiar con Mariana la maestra mía, no con la escuelucha ésa donde a barrenazos te inculcan la idea de que debes arrancarle las raíces al idioma que te parió. Después te mandaría allí a Presidio pero sólo después que ya supieras la verdad, por qué son las cosas como son, cuando ya tuvieras orgullo de ser hijo del pueblo. Pero como tú bien sabes, me resultaste un fracaso. No supe por qué desde niño fuiste así, Reyes. Cuando te mandé con Mariana a los pocos días vino a decirme que la habías golpeado porque ella había hecho lo mismo contigo. No quiso verte la cara jamás. Nomás no quisiste escuela, aunque te costó muchos cintarazos, ¿recuerdas Reyes? Hasta ahora no comprendo como aprendiste lo que sabes. Quizá de mis libros que leías escondido porque nunca te vi aplicado en nada. Eras un holgazán y eras un vago. "Anda, vete a la leña para que vendas y compres o vete a ayudarle a tu tío Santamaría con la lancha," te decía, pero no, resultabas por la tarde con comida, leña y dinero. "¿Y de dónde sacaste ese dinero?" "Vendí pescados al gringo del puente". "¡Ya te he dicho que no te andes metiendo con ellos! ¡Endemoniado muchacho!"

El tropel de los cinco caballos quedó amortiguado por la arena suelta del río. Los jinetes se aproximaron a la orilla y se fueron sumiendo en el lodo hasta que pudieron alcanzar el agua. El chamaco Reyes quien jugaba distraído, nunca sintió nada por el chapaleo que hacía en el agua. Los hombres se miraban sonriendo, listos para darle un buen susto, pero en ese momento un caballo no aguantó el quisquilleo en el hocico y estornudó. El muchacho saltó como pescado cuando forcejea con el ansuelo mientras que los hombres soltaron la carcajada.

—Miren nomás qué bien dao el cabrón. A ver, acércate. ¿De dónde eres?

—De aquí, aquella casita que está allá.

—¿Quién es tu padre y qué hace?

—Francisco Uranga, es ranchero.

—¿Conoces bien aquí? ¿Conoces el lugar de los gringos?

—Sí, aquí mataron a mi hermano.

—Y ¿por qué lo mataron?

—No estoy seguro, pero dicen que porque es contra la ley no usar el puente.

—Ah, qué jodidos. Todavía andan conque esa tierra es de ellos. Nomás porque está al otro lado de este maldito charco. Y ¿qué cabrones haces aquí güevoneando?

—Andaba pescando.

—Lo que vas a pescar es un catarro, bruto. ¿Quieres irte con nosotros? ¿Qué dicen muchachos? ¿Nos sirve?

—Pos cómo no, mi jefe.

—Andale pues, ponte la ropa y felicidades.

—No señor, yo no quiero irme con ustedes, ni mi papá...

—Píquele, Píquele, ¿qué fregaos va a estar haciéndose pendejo aquí?

—A ver, Ramiro. Pásame la buena. Allí tienes. Ahora sí. Oigan, cómo se me hace que éste va a salir bueno.

—El chamaco parece tecolote con tamaña carabinota y con esos ojotes que pela, jefe.

Todos rieron. Reyes no se daba cuenta que en ese momento resucitaba en él su hermano Jesús y que la indignación de medio siglo comenzaría a cristalizarse desde ese mismo día.

"No trabajé en Shafter pero sí cuando estaba chica, Camila mi hermana se casó con Cipriano Alvarado y dijo: No te quedes, vámonos. Pos me consiguió a mí y a mi hermano Chente pero le di bien a entender: no me voy a estar todo el tiempo contigo. Dijo, está bien. Cuando quieras venirte yo te vengo a traer. En ese tiempo en Shafter había mucha gente, mucho dinero porque trabajaban las minas de plata. Los hombres ganaban tanto que hasta a mi hermanito le entró la fiebre, asina chico como estaba. Pero asina les fue a los pobres. Se murieron. Cuando entraban a la mina ya salían de abajo enfermos, los pobres. Yo creo que de eso se murió mi hermanito Chente".

"¿Por qué tengo que morir, Eduvijes? Hermana, sólo tengo doce años. No llores por eso. Tú has hecho lo que puedes. Sólo quiero saber, cómo es la vida cuando creces. No he tenido tiempo de preguntarle a abuelito cómo es cuando ya es viejo uno. Pero tú eres grande. Dime, ¿es bonita la vida como la de los niños? Así la veo yo, Vicke. El año pasado cuando murió mi perro yo sí me sentí muy mal, si vieras, porque tenía los ojos muy tristes y todavía así, meneaba la cola. ¿Tú sabes que los perros mueven la cola cuando están contentos? ¿Es verdad que estaba contento, Vicke? ¿Cuándo estaba muriendo? Aun cuando le pegaba meneaba la cola. ¿Así es la gente grande como tú? Yo me sentí muy mal antes de que muriera porque le había pegado yo también. Y antes de morir le prometí que no lo volvería a hacer. Porque yo creo que nadie tiene el derecho de pegarte, de golpearte y si lo hacen, tú debes de pegar también. Porque después te mueres y te vas al cielo sin pagártelas. Bueno, así pensaba yo, Vicke, pero ahora no. Porque creo que si el perro tiene tanto amor así, la gente ha de tener más. Digo esto porque yo siento más amor que el perro, Vicke. ¿Es así con ustedes? ¡Híjole! ¡Pero si estás llorando! No llores, Vicke. Dame un farito. Nunca he fumado pero ahora tengo ganas de saber cómo es fumar. A ver, préndemelo. Quisiera que me quitaras esta enfermedad, Vicke. Esta bola que tengo aquí en el pecho. Me duele mucho. Mira, tócame aquí. Yo quisiera que me la quitaras. Quiero llorar, Vicke, pero ¿qué diría don Jesús? Me daría vergüenza. ¿Qué decía? Que los hombres no lloran. ¿Es verdad eso, hermana? Yo no te diría esto si él estuviera aquí, pero fíjate, una vez lo encontré detrás de un árbol llorando. Yo nunca supe por qué, pero si te viera a ti llorando, te llevaría en su lancha. ¿Te acuerdas, antes que hicieran puente, cómo llevaba gente de un lado pa'l otro? Yo me divertía mucho con él. Entonces todos éramos iguales. No es que no séanos, pero ha cambiado desde que pusieron el puente. Qué curioso, Vicke. La gente se siente separada. ¿Que no los puentes son para que haiga menos de eso? Antes podíamos ir a que los agüelitos sin... ¿pa qué son esos papeles, Vicke? ¿Por qué los piden esos hombres todo el tiempo? ¿Quiénes son? ¿Y el diablo lo has visto, Vicke? ¿Es cierto que estamos en el infierno? Hace mucho calor aquí pero no es verdá, ¿verdá, Vicke? Me dijo mi agüelita que el diablo vivía en aquella cueva donde fuimos, ¿te acuerdas? Yo no lo creo, porque arriba de la sierrita, está bendecido. Pero me contaron que había venido a hacernos mal, que andaba por los dos lados del río. Vicke, no me hablas. Me duele mucho el pecho. Tráeme un trapito caliente por favor. El cigarro no me sirvió. Creía que me quitaría este dolor. ¿Por qué estoy enfermo, Vicke? ¿Por qué no me lo quitan por favor? Cuando vuelvas, Vicke, súbeme a la cama. No estoy a gusto aquí en el piso. Yo no sé pa qué me pusieron aquí abajo. ¡Vicke, yo no quiero morir!"

La noche se estira larga hasta el infinito. Como un chicle negro y pegajoso que envuelve el río, los árboles, las labores. Luego llega hasta los barrios y allí enreda a la gente y la pega fuertemente a las camas, a los pisos y en dondequiera que se quedaron dormidos. El silencio también es oscuro y monótono. Luego

viene la luna botando al compás de los violines y entonces el chicle se torna en
azogue y pone lentamente una capa resbalosa sobre el universo. Platino el río,
plata las hojas de los álamos, todo está plateado como una noche de nieve en
otros rumbos.
La plata da dimensión a la noche. La hace larga y la multiplica. La luna no
es muerte. La luna es vida para los seres que pululan por el río. Las sombras con
la luna cobran vida. Allá está la luna, comiendo tuna, tirando las cáscaras pa...
dame luna, dame de lo que comes. Tú eres mi vida y mi adoración. Yo soy tu
luna. Tu sombra. Soy cuerpo de luz que incendia la noche, que estira la noche.
Soy hombre de noche, soy vida de noche. Soy hijo de la llorona y me llamo
Reyes, hijos de la tal por cual. Yo soy hermano de Jesús del río.

En la parte más honda de la cueva situado al fondo de la sierra de la Santa
Cruz cae un chorrito de luz sobre el agua estancada de un pequeño lago. La
serpiente lo usa como espejo, espejo que ahora refleja una cara humana. La
imagen contempla el disfraz, llena de risa; un traje azul oscuro, una cachucha
militar para cubrir la cabeza puntiaguda donde se acostumbra ver los cuernos y
unas botas aceitosas también pardas. Las botas no sientan bien sobre las patas de
gallo pero no importa. Se usarán sólo por unas horas. Como toque final la serpiente "dirige-trenes" descuelga una lamparilla de aceite que ha guardado para
la ocasión. Con esto, queda lista para aparecer en la estación del ferrocarril.
Después cambiará el disfraz a uno de ranchero pero eso ya cuando esté a punto
de recibir las quinientas almas trabajadoras que vienen del interior. Afuera el
diablo tomando forma humana monta su burro y lo dirige hacia la estación.
Ferrocarriles de Ultratumba está casi vacío cuando llega. Caso raro, pues
siempre hay enjambres de gente esperando los trenes. Quizá por fin han caído en
la cuenta de que nunca llegan a tiempo. El taquillero lo confirma. "El tren viene
con unos minutos de retraso", dice. Eso dice, pero el diablo sabe muy bien que
la palabra 'minuto' no significa nada. Para eso están las advertencias pegadas a
las paredes: *en la salida del paraíso los trenes salen a todas horas pero la llega-*
da es cuando Dios quiere. La otra advertencia que pertenece a la línea del infierno también está subrayada: *en esta línea la salida de los trenes es cuando el*
hombre quiere y llega cuando menos lo piensa. Maldita gente pendeja. Parece
que nunca lee lo que es obvio.
Es la primera vez que el diablo humanizado ha estado en una estación
ferroviaria y siente la misma expectativa de pasajero y de espectador. También
ha oído que los trenes vienen retrasados, y como no está acostumbrado a esperar,
comienza a tener dudas de sí mismo. Ahora no está tan seguro si oyó bien la
noticia de que hoy y a esta hora llegarían los obreros. "No, no es posible que me

equivoque. Estoy segurísimo que los viajeros partieron. De eso nunca hay duda. ¿Pero quizá... ?" Pasa el hombre-diablo a leer las advertencias para ver si por casualidad la información que contienen le quitan las dudas. "A ver..." Lee... pero no saca nada en limpio. "Simples tonterías": ...*en la línea del paraíso no se expenden billetes de ida y vuelta; los niños menores de siete años van gratis en los brazos de la madre; no hay rebaja de precios; solamente las buenas obras se deben llevar de equipaje para no ser detenidos; se reciben viajeros de cualquier procedencia con tal que traigan los pasaportes en regla; y el despacho central de billetes está abierto a todas horas.* "¡Tarugadas! ¡Nada más! La línea al paraíso quebró hace tiempo". El diablo entonces se pasa al anuncio del infierno: *se admite sin descuento, niños menores no, pasajeros llevarán cuanto equipaje gusten pero deben dejar todo menos el alma...* "¡Ah! ¡Aquí!" ...*los que viajan por esta línea podrán seguir la del paraíso si refrenan su billete ante un sacerdote antes de empalmar con el tren de la muerte.* "¡Hijo de la...! ¿Será posible? ¿Que si el tren se detuvo por allí, precisamente para eso? ¿Que habría algún aguafiestas desgraciado? ¿Es?"

—El tren llega en carril número cinco.

La poca gente comienza mientras que el disfrazado queda atónito. Ni siquiera ha oído el tosido del tren.

—Por favor, señoras y señores. Usen precaución. Favor de no acercarse hasta que haya hecho un alto completo.

El diablo dirige-trenes, lamparilla en mano, sigue a la bola de gente con tanto entusiasmo que se le ha olvidado hacer el cambio de vestidura. "Ahora para desviar a los huarachudos", piensa.

Los pasajeros empiezan a bajar. Uno, dos, tres... luego dos... luego... uno... Se pueden contar en la mano. El tren viene vacío. No, no puede ser. El dirige-trenes no sabe qué pensar y se queda allí largo rato hasta que ya no baja nadie.

—Pero ¿qué ha pasado con la demás gente?

—Es todo, señor.

—Oiga, espere. Si deben...

—Le digo que no hay más y ¡ya no me moleste!

El dirige-trenes enrojece de cólera y entonces hace un berrinche estrellando la lámpara contra el riel. En seguida se avienta un pedo que jamás había saboreado ser humano y luego desaparece como rayo por los cielos. El burro se queda rebuznando por su amo mientras que en la esquina de la estación el conjunto Los Pepenados cantan: "el diablo se fue a pasear... y le dieron chocolate... tan caliente se lo dieron que hasta se quemó el gaznate... pero ay, ja, ja, ja... ja ja ja ja... pero ay, ja, ja, ja, ja... ja ja ja ja ja..."

Los quinientos acres de algodón estaban para perderse a causa de la falta de pizcadores. Había sido el primer golpe para Ben, y la situación se puso peor cuando la gente de Presidio pidió el aumento de un centavo más por libra pizcada. No se podía explicar quién había tenido tanta influencia para cortarle el chorro. Además, el "incidente" del fortín era tan insignificante en proporción a los negocios que él hacia, que la misma noche lo había olvidado. Antes, un hecho de justicia como éste no había impedido que el agua corriera mansa y lucrativa. ¿Por qué habría de ser diferente en esta ocasión? ¿Qué habría pasado? ¿Por qué se había negado el gobierno a concederle las quinientas almas que le había pedido? No se lo explicaba. No se explicaba como la excursión que el gobernador Jones, su amigo, había hecho por México, hubiera fracasado.

Sólo Francisco Uranga y su hijo Reyes tenían la respuesta y cuando aquél leyó la noticia en el *Century* de Marfa, se le rodaron las lágrimas. Eran lágrimas de triunfo que había esperado tantos años y eran gozo porque su triunfo había sido doble. La administración mexicana bien sabía el maltrato de sus obreros pero siempre había movidas más beneficiosas y era muy fácil taparle el ojo al macho con dinero. ¡Caramba! Por eso no lo podía creer don Pancho. ¡Hacer arrodillar era casi increíble!

¿Cómo lo había hecho? Cuando se había enterado de que Jones sería, casi por seguro, el siguiente gobernador de Texas, Francisco había ido a estrecharle la mano a Marfa. Allí, el día que había venido a cantinflear[7] frente al público, se había enterado de sus intenciones "internacionales". De inmediato había hecho uso de fraternidades periodísticas y empezó a picar fuerte. Primero les había llegado a los editores de aquí: Rodríguez el del *Zuriago*, Sifuentes el del *Laderense*, Armenta, Armendáriz... de allí pa'l real se había convertido la voz en una red que no detuvo fronteras. Fácil había sido. Hacer pública la masacre del fortín y en seguida trazar el plan excursionista de Jones.

Allá esperaron a Jones en cada parada, martillando las mismas preguntas: "¿Es cierto que el mexicano sufre, más que en otro estado, la discriminación en los empleos y establecimientos públicos? ¿Es cierto de la masacre de Presidio? Hago esta pregunta porque tal y tal corrobora que..." Después de tres días, el gobernador había llegado aturdido a la capital. En la convención oficial había caído Martínez-Vega, el cónsul de Matamoros, pidiendo la palabra. Primero dio los pormenores y situaciones en las cuales se había enfrentado con dicho gobernador, y en seguida leyó una lista de acusaciones. Finalmente terminó leyendo

---

[7]hablar mucho sin decir nada claro; es una alusión al cómico mexicano Cantinflas.

una resolución firmada por los principales editores de habla hispana en el suroes-te. La presión y el escándalo llegaron a tal grado que el mordelón Alcalá tuvo que negarle públicamente la exportación de trabajadores al estado de Texas. Chistoso caso, pensaba Francisco, que semanas antes la raza en Arizona atendiera a la llamada del gobernador arizonense. "Necesitamos el apoyo de todo buen ciudadano para que nuestras cosechas no se pierdan". Los primeros en acudir habían sido los de habla hispana formando tropas de gente los domingos para salvar la cosecha. Paradojas o paradojas. ¡Caray!

Benito recibió las noticias degollando un chivo que cruzó su paso. Luego, como Quijote, corrió a caballo tumbando las carpas que había comprado para la ocasión. Ni en casa pudieron soportarlo esos cinco días.

Sin embargo Benito no se iba a dejar vencer. Mandó a Lorenzo anunciar a los trabajadores de aquí que el aumento pedido se les concedía. Mientras tanto él personalmente iría a pregonar al otro lado que se les pagaría a buen precio la pizca de algodón porque estaba muy necesitado. Después que hizo el hombre la buena oferta en las varias congregaciones, Reyes por otra parte reunió a sus compañeros y les mandó que hicieran público otro aviso contrario, escrito en forma de advertencia: "Se prohibe la cruzada a toda persona que tenga intencio-nes de trabajar en los campos de Benito. Cualquier acto que apoye la causa de este criminal será castigado con dura pena. El Coyote". El segundo día no apare-cía nadie en las labores, excepto Lorenzo quien llegaba con el aviso a casa de su patrón.

—¿Y quién es este Coyote?

—No sé, patrón. Es primera vez que lo oigo mentar por ese apodo. Lo que si he sabido es que anda rondando un montón de bandoleros hace tiempo y que no se tientan el alma para obtener lo que quieren.

—Conque así es, ¿eh? Bueno. Tú vas a México y anuncias que pago a cuatro centavos libra pizcada y que concedo completa protección armada.

Después continuó inquiriendo el paradero del Coyote. Ni le importaba quién fuera, nomás quería darle en la madre.

No fue hasta muy tarde ese mismo día que regresó Lorenzo. Este le trajo dos noticias: primero, que había logrado conseguirle veinte pizcadores de noche, pizcadores que estaban un poco inseguros de arrojarse. De todos modos, les había dicho, si se animan vaya uno de ustedes a avisarme que vienen por la noche. La segunda noticia era que él no era otro sino Reyes Uranga su cuñado. ¡Vaya! Reyes el más mansito de todo el atajo de trabajadores. ¿Reyes? Era causa de risa.

Benito no tardó en ponerse en movimiento. Se comunicó de inmediato con el sherife de Marfa para que éste viniera a socorrerlo y para el tercer día ya andaban husmeando las casas y los contornos de Presidio. Luego, cuando no encontraron nada por este lado, los diez rangers cruzaron el río al lado mexicano y se fueron hasta la sierrita donde se suponía que estaba el escondite de Reyes y su banda. Pero tampoco sacaron nada. Así que al día siguiente anunciaban que se iban, preparando la salida a media luz y por la noche regresaron a ver si por casualidad...pero Reyes no había tragado el anzuelo.

El cuarto día tampoco pasó nada pero de noche vino un mojado a la casa de Ben para avisarle que vendrían los veinte que se habían reclutado. Mas no sería esta noche sino la siguiente. Así que Ben preparó los costales y los dejó metidos en el tronco del árbol gordo cerca de la bomba de agua. Benito no le dijo a Lorenzo que había venido el mojado por miedo a que el plan se descubriera. Ni éste ni los pizcadores sabían que ellos servirían de anzuelo. La estrategia sería sencilla. Picarle el corazón a Reyes, maltratando un poco a la gente y si tenía güevos, saldría al campo libre, el cabrón. Lo que no supo Benito era que Reyes mismo había ensayado a los pizcadores un día antes. ¿Querían trabajar? Ahora jalan o se ahorcan, les había dicho. Tendrán que cooperar. ¿Que una bala les toque? Ese será su castigo.

Benito sonríe al pasar por el barrio oscuro. Ni perro que le ladre, ¿o es que no los oye? Sonríe con el triunfo en la boca. Esa sonrisa hecha de mueca que no engaña a nadie, que se trasluce como radiografía. Pasa el jinete por los cuadritos de adobe, antipoéticos. Adobes que se hicieron con paja nueva en un tiempo y ahora brotan como inútiles barbas de olote. El que quiera hacer poesía es un mentiroso. Sólo les falta a las casitas una cruz al frente para que sean cementerios. No obstante una que otra se defiende de la muerte con sus florecitas y una barandita al frente. Luego la calle polvorosa, sin brea. Burla, burlados todos, el diablo verde sonríe. El diablo manipula títeres. El diablo juega con la vida humana. Y esa vida humana nunca se dio cuenta cómo se coló por entre ellos. Fue como un aire que se les metió entre las piernas y les echó la zancadilla. Otros cuentan que había sido como un sueño del cual habían despertado sin pantalones. Cuando despertaron se habían puesto a las manos del señor, el que les había prometido alivio y lo había cumplido. Les había dado trabajo en sus mismas tierras y la gente volvió a sentir la vida en las tripas. Después les adelantó la raya y fueron a dejársela otra vez en sus manos. "Que a toda familia se les dé una caja de comida como regalo de Navidad, y cuando se haga la cosecha haré una barbacoa. Pero no se les olvide, voten por mí, voten democrat".[8] En dos años los vasallos habían coronado a un rey que apodaron "diablo verde".

Noche sofocante, noche que oprime, noche que aprieta los gaznates de la gente. Calaveras pálidas de exprimida savia, calaveras perdidas en la tierra seca de los algodonales. Postizas plantas regadas con sudor. Gusanos repletos. Presidio, prisión, infierno. Diablo que se carcajea en silencio. ¡Shhh!

Benito apareció como espanto a la puerta de la casa. Luego pegó los labios a la mampara para llamar quedito... ¡Pssst! ¡Lorenzo!

El ladrido del perro dentro del porche le respondió mientras que Benito dio un salto hacia atrás.

—¡Shut up, you bastard!

—Epa, ¿quién es?

—Soy yo, Ben.

—Wayda momen.

—'Ta bien, Lorenzo. Don't get up. Yo nomás avisarte de pizcadores. Andan cerca del río. Date un vuelta más tarde, ¿okay?

—Okay, Don Benito.

Se alejó el Diablo Verde como sombra.

Lorenzo no se acostó luego. La aparición de Ben a esta hora lo había dejado inquieto, así que salió afuera para fumarse un cigarro. Viejo lángaro, desgraciado. Si no fuera porque me paga bien ya le hubiera aventado el harpa. Los problemas que me acarrea. Algún día voy a amanecer tendidito en el cabrón río, agujerado por mi propia gente. Y es que la gente tiene razón, que les hago mal, pero es que uno está fregado por todos lados. Si el viejo cabrón le ayudara a la pobre gente en vez de la baba que les paga, no tuviera problemas. Chingao. Algún día cambiará, después que yo ya esté bien muerto.

Ya en pleno campo aparecen diez jinetes y rodean al viejo Ben. Este les comunica lo esencial: los pizcadores andarán en la sección señalada por el álamo gordo pero para estar seguros, esperen a Lorenzo. Este no necesitará pistola para convencerlo de que debe servir de guía. Que no se les vaya a pasar la mano. Después, veremos qué pasa, les dice.

El señor pica espuelas y se pierde en la noche. Ha sido un día muy largo.

El chiflido al otro lado del río hace trizas el silencio. Se va hasta los oídos del lado mexicano. Pronto se echan al río varias figuras y luego se pierden entre

---

[8]alusión a un partido político controlado por los anglosajones.

el algodonal. Como criminales espantados corren hasta el álamo para coger los costales y se vuelven a sumir en los surcos. Se ciñen los costales a la cintura y empiezan a devorar plantas como peste. Mata tras mata va quedando encuerada. Shas. Shas. Shas. Los costales se van llenando. Se echan el costal al lomo como un chorizo gigante y lo ponen a la orilla del surco.

Esta noche los pizcadores cargan unas orejas larguísimas. Se mueven espantados. Lo peor: no saben si es la espera o no están seguros si el Coyote vendrá. Por eso unos han empezado a mitad de los surcos y se han venido pizcando hacia el río.

Los hombres se arrastran a la luz de la luna. Se cuelan, se retuercen por entre las plantas. Las plantas verdes, con sus motitas blancas parecen arbolitos de Navidad. Los pizcadores quieren treparse hasta la cumbre como si fueran enanos. Pero no pueden escapar la larga cola que los ata a la tierra. Ahora la serpiente, ceñida a la cintura, quiere, con su hocico abierto, tragárselo pero no puede. El pizcador se la tapa con algodón, motitas que la pondrán repleta para que deje en paz a la gente. Las manos, rápidas, rápidas se rasguñan. Quieren despojar el árbol, llevarse esas esperanzas en las bolsas. Quizá algún milagro transformará las motitas en moneditas de oro. Pero todo es inútil. El diablo se las quita. El diablo se multiplica. Después viene otra serpiente tan hambrienta como la otra y otra y otra hasta que alguna noche el bien de Dios les pague la miseria que no merecen. Por ahora los pizcadores platinados seguirán reptando entre mar verde y serpientes blancas. Capullos blancos, puf, billetes verdes. Ojos verdes, dientes verdes. Pudridos, pudrida el alma, verde, verde. Verde mar, cuerpos verdes, verde muerte, descomposición.

La muerte fresca entre un ataúd alfombrado es calientita. El cuerpo puede echarse en él, gozar el calor de sábana eléctrica. Pero estos momentos son efímeros porque después se asienta el sereno de la noche y embarga el cuerpo de frío. Es entonces cuando el alma sale con deseos de prolongar la vida. Se desliza por la alfombra como si fuera gato buscando el calor pero todo es inútil; la caja ya no tiene calor ni ternura. Es el alma como una madre que pierde a su hijo en una tormenta y el viento la estira lejos del niño perdido. Así sucede con Vicente. La brisa de la madrugada convierte su alma en humo de cigarro larguísimo y se la lleva soplando hasta el fortín, allí donde tantas otras han sido depositadas.

Afuera, detrás de la choza, los señores se aposentaron en cuclillas alrededor de una botella. De acuerdo iban llegando las parejas a la casa del difunto, hombres y mujeres, se separaban y tomaban rumbo distinto. Las señoras pasaban adentro; los hombres seguían haciendo la rueda más grande. Al calor de la botella y la lengua animada de Levario, los hombres se olvidaban a ratos del propósito.

Adentro el olor a cera pega de ramalazo pero después lo amortigua el polvo que se levanta del piso de tierra. No son caras las que se ven ante la luz moribunda de velas. Son cuerpos envueltos de negros vestidos, shales que semejan redes pescadoras. Las mujeres que lograron sentarse ven hacia la nada. Son como momias cansadas de jugar con el rosario. Parecen querer hacer más redondas las cuentas y a ratos, como si les dieran cuerda, empiezan a rezar en alta voz. El murmullo es cosa de minutos; luego entra un silencio de plomo, silencio interrumpido por un mosco gigante y fastidioso. El mosco rodea el cajoncito del muerto dos veces y se para. Vuelve a reinar el silencio. Las mujeres se levantan para salir a coger el aire mientras que otras entran a tomar el mismo lugar en los bancos. Filas enlutadas que contrastan con unas paredes recién encaladas. Roberto, el novio de Eduvijes va y viene, entra y sale, pidiéndoles a los hombres que le ayuden a traer sillas de sus casas porque seguramente vendrá más gente. Gracias a Chito, a Levario, a don Francisco y a Reyes, quienes vinieron y se fueron temprano—todos le han ayudado. La pobrecita de Vicke ni siquiera tuvo tiempo de hacerse su vestido, de barrer, de hacer los arreglos. Pero todos habían cooperado. El cajoncito, puesto sobre dos baldes, lo había donado Levario a pesar de que era tan repugnante. Tenías que conocerlo para aguantarlo. Era de esas personas que sólo necesitan abrir la boca para caer como patada de burro. El anuncio a la puerta de su "fábrica de ataúdes", lo resumía todo: MUÉRASE A GUSTO...CON ATAÚDES LOMELÍ. Pero era de buen corazón. Recuerda Roberto cuando llegó buscando cajón para el angelito:

—¿Quién fue esta vez?

—Chentito, el hermano de Vicke.

—¡Ah! Pues que descanse en paz porque aquí no la tuvo. Nació enfermizo el huerco. Ya casi se moría cuando tenía seis meses y peor que sólo le daban galletitas dulces con café pa comer. A ver, mira aquí, de los mejores. En este sí que se va al cielo a gusto, ¿no?, je, je. Con esta alfombrita puede volar a.t.m. Llévatelo, no te lo cobro y dile a Vicke que muchos días d'estos, ja, ja. No te creas, dile que allá iré a verla por la noche. (Por eso, por hablador y porque eres como eres, caes mal, cabrón. También quizá porque te burlas de la muerte, porque la festejas. Allá irás, vestido de lo mejorcito, con tu botella de tequila para lengonear toda la noche. Así la pasarás, cabrón, hasta que tu Virginia te pare el chorro y te arree borracho a casa. Porque eres un parásito de la muerte me caes mal.)

—Gracias, Levario. Que Dios te los pague.

La casucha es chica pero la cal le da dimensión a los dos cuartitos. La cortina de percal tapa el boquete donde no hay puerta pero se trasluce como la faz del sacerdote en el confesionario. Vicke, sentada en su cama, observa los movimientos con ojos opacos y luego pasa la mirada a una vela que amenaza apagarse y que esparce el corazón de Jesús por la pared. El Cristo acompaña a Vicke en su dolor, dolor que parpadea al compás de la danzante luz. El Santo Niño, con su lujoso vestidito, también está presente. Ahora Vicke cambia la vista al retrato del angelito muerto y luego a la imagen del Santo Niño. Una, dos, tres veces. Muchas veces, hasta que ambas imágenes se hacen una sola. Estudia, compara. El pelo rizado, la sonrisa, las manitas pegadas. "¡Ay no, no, a la imagen le falta una mano!" Y recuerda que fue el viento de la noche anterior. Recuerda que cuando se volcó la estatua, su hermanito se iba, el pobrecito. Ella lo había levantado del piso, como él había ordenado, y tan pronto como lo había hecho, el niño se había puesto muy platicador. Cuando le trajo el trapo caliente que pedía, le pidió que lo cogiera de la mano y entonces se puso a acordar de cosas. "A ver, Vicke, a que no te acuerdas de esto: allá está la luna... ¡cómo es eso que la luna come tuna si es de queso? Yo creo que si fuera verdad ya se había redetido, ¿no crees, Vicke? Allá está el sol bebiendo sotol[9]...oye, Vicke, ¡que también las cosas del cielo son como nosotros? Yo por eso no le tengo miedo a la noche, ¿y tú? Cuando sales pa fuera yo no...a la víbora de la mar, de la mar, por aquí puedes[10]...oye, Vicke, ¿recuerdas la canción del lindo pescadito?...en un agua clara que brota la fuente...jugar con mi aro...mi mamá me ha dicho que no salga yo, porque si yo salgo pronto moriré..." Y así había pasado la noche Vicke. Escuchándolo, cantándole, respondiéndole, poniéndole la sonrisita en los labios hasta las horas de la madrugada cuando fue cayendo en sueño. Cuando ya no despertó más y la sonrisa había quedado estampada en su carita, le mandó hablar a Roberto. Su amor vino tan pronto como... "Dios mío, dame fuerzas. Sólo quiero saber por qué haces estas cosas con los chiquitos. Tú sabes que son angelitos y que no hacen nada. ¿Por qué te llevas a este muchachito en vez de a mí? Castíganos, mátanos a nosotros los grandes pero no a ellos. ¿Por qué lo haces? ¿Por qué me has dejado sola, sola, sola?"

Los chistes de Levario se hacen más gordos y más borrachos. Se van filtrando por la ventana como si se burlaran de los padres nuestros y de las avemarías. Como cámara de gas, la casucha se sofoca de cuerpos, de cirios, de noche, de náusea. Mareo. Vicke se siente enferma. "La acompaño en su pésame, no. La

---

[9]un tipo de bebida alcohólica.

[10]fragmentos de una canción infantil.

acompaño en su pésame, no. La acompaño en su pésame, ¡NO! La acompaño en su pésame, ¡NO! ¡NO!" El NO se va haciendo grandote así como dos vejigas infladas. NO. Lentamente se van hinchando en la mente de Vicke hasta que las vejigas no caben en los dos cuartos. Después se derraman por la ventana y se hacen todavía más grandes. Por fin la espina del dolor las revienta. "¡Nooooo!" Empieza a llorar Vicke. Largos llantos intercalados con NO. Afuera la plática cesa para recibir la pena de Vicke por los oídos, pero ya los tapó el licor. ¡No es por eso que se traga en estas ocasiones? ¡Ah, viejos cobardes! ¿Por qué no son tan hombres como las mujeres? ¿Por qué no aguantan a chile pelón, como ellas? Sólo el perro de Levario responde como si estuviera consciente de la angustia. El aullido hace duo al de la mujer.

—¡Shhht! ¡Cállate, perro cabrón!— Levario le da una patada. Este, con la cola entre las patas rodea a los ebrios y luego se echa de nuevo al lado del amo. La plática baja a tono menor.

—Pobre mujer, apenas hace dos años que se le murieron sus viejos, uno tras otro.

—¿Cuando la caminata a Marfa?

—Sí, entonces. Recuerdo también que el chamaco se enfermó mucho. Llevaba la cara abotagada de tanto toser.

—Y ¿qué era?

—Pos no se sabe pero dicen que de allí le vino esto. Otros dicen que cogió algo de las minas cuando estuvo allá.

—Pobre huerco, mejor que ni lo hubieran dejado ir.

—Pobre la Vicke, porque ella siempre lo ha criado.

—Dicen que más temprano vinieron don Benito y doña Rosario a verla.

—¡Ah, Chihuahua! ¿El Patrón?

—Sí, cuando quiere, es buena reata el viejo. Fue el que le hizo a Vicke estos cuartitos en la mera propiedad de él.

—No, pos sí. De eso no hay duda. Yo le ayudé a hacerlos, pero esa vez me dijo quesque iba a hacerlos pa guardar pacas de alfalfa, pero como no se dio...

—Ah, pos ai está. Yo oí al revés, que los hizo pa Vicke porque les debía algo a sus difuntos padres.

—¿Sí? ¿Y cómo está eso?

—No se sabe, pero yo creo que sí hay algo porque cuando vinieron los soldados a ella no se la llevaron hasta Paso. Digo, nomás hasta Marfa, pero luego fue el Ben y la trajo a ella y a Chentito.

—Pos quién sabe cómo estará la cosa pero pa que venga a verla, seguro que hay algo...

Así se va llenando la noche de vida mientras que adentro los restos de la muerte aletean contra los pechos. Pican, hieren como alfiler. Vicke dormita de agotamiento y sueña garabatos. Un puntito luminoso que se torna murciélago indeciso. Luego desciende hasta el velorio como cometa ciego. Vicke lo ve diminuto al principio pero después se hace más grande, más y más y más hasta que ¡PLAS! Se estrella en su frente. Los aleteos en los ojos y en los brazos la estremecen. El murciélago se va. Abre los ojos la mujer. Levario entra bambaleándose y se dirige al cadáver de Chente. "Dios mío, que salga ese borracho, que se vaya a dormir. Que respete al angelito, por Dios". El borracho se acerca mientras que los ojos de las señoras quieren detenerlo pero no pueden. Empieza a palpar el cajón. Con gusto sensual pasa los dedos por la pana. No, no es el cuerpo que le movió a acercarse. Es su obra, su cajón. Tan fascinado está que se olvida de que está montado el ataúd sobre dos baldes y se recarga. El cadáver se ladea. El hombre hace el intento de detenerlo pero está borracho. Los dos caen al suelo con un golpe seco.

—¡Aaaaaaay! ¡Por piedad, por favor no me lo golpeen, que le duele! ¡No! ¡Chentito, mi Chentito querido!

Roberto, quien acaba de entrar, acude a ayudarles a las señoras que se acomiden a poner de nuevo el cajón sobre los baldes. Luego coge a Levario del brazo y lo arrastra para afuera.

—Vete ya, Levario. Ya es hora. Y no vuelvas— Es el tono de una voz con rabia refrenada.

—Sssi yyyo nomás quería tocar el cajón...

—Ya te dije. ¡Vete!

La señora Virginia sale avergonzada pidiendo miles de disculpas y se lo lleva a casa. Mientras tanto allí adentro le frotan a Vicke el cuello con alcohol para calmarla. Llora por unos momentos y entonces vuelve a caer en la trampa del sueño.

El peso que trajo Reyes se hizo sentir en el campamento. Llegaba del velorio de Chente. Un 'buenas noches, muchachos' y luego silencio. Rufino, alias el Grillo, se le acerca.

—¿Qué pasa, jefe? Parece que se le cargó el muertito.

—Pues ¿qué quiere, compa? Pero no es por un angelito más sino porque no le hallo ton ni son a esta perra vida.

—Déjese de cosas, jefe. Mire, aquí le va su preferida.

—Anda pues, échatela.

El Grillo Cantor no iba a recibir premio por esta canción tampoco, pero el corrido de Joaquín Murrieta[11] no se oía mal con el acompañamiento de la guitarra bien afinada.

"Señores, soy mexicano pero comprendo el inglés. Yo lo aprendí por mi hermano, al derecho al revés, y a cualquier americano lo hago temblar a mis pies. Yo me vine..." Reyes no escucha ya. La mente de Reyes se desparrama y se le desborda el rencor. El chamaco que acaba de expirar no es más que otro número de muertes ignobles entre las cuales se cuenta su propio hermano Jesús. Por...

"...cantares me he metido, castigando americanos, y al indio noble y sencillo..." (Desgraciada vida que no respeta ni a los inocentes. Pero yo no me iré sin cobrárselo muy caro.) "Cuando todavía era un niño, huérfano a mí me dejaron, ni quien me hiciera un cariño y a mi hermano lo mataron..." (... y mientras haya injusticia, mientras vea caras viejas maltratadas, seguiré, por Dios que seguiré...) "ya no es otro mi destino, pon cuidado parroquiano..."

—Epa compa, que no se le duerma el gallo.

—¿Eh? A chingao, pos, sí que se me estaba pegando.

—Uu, ¿a poco se la quiere perder?

—¿Pos si quién dijo miedo? Nomás que ya los años, mi amigo. Como quien dice yo me lo llevé en zapetas, ¿que ya no recuerda? De allí del merito puente. Cabrón, que rejiego se nos puso. Pero ya ve, mire dónde anda ahora.

—¿Qué quiere, hombre? En ese tiempo no sabía ni dónde ponían las gallinas. Pero ahora que veo la cosa más de cerca uno no se aguanta, ¿sabe? A uno le hierve el alma.

—Si vienen, nomás hay que asustarlos. Pa que sepan que aquí pesan. Pero que no se nos pase la mano como a aquel otro. Le rechinaron muy feo los dientes.

Bueno, creo que ya es hora de irnos acercando. De aquí vamos a pata y cuiden esos caballos. Y esperen hasta que cante "El Grillo".

Los diez rancheros, guiados por Lorenzo desmontan también como a cien yardas del álamo. Luego, bajo mando del jefe Chester, le atacan la boca a Lorenzo con un pañuelo y le amarran las manos a la cabeza de la montura. Entonces atan su caballo, junto con los otros, a una durmiente clavada en la esquina de la

---

[11]un rebelde mexicoamericano que actuó en California en el siglo XIX.

bomba. En seguida se van escondiendo hasta llegar al álamo y ya allí con el primer tiro al aire, los diez se desparraman por entre los surcos tras la gente. El Grillo canta. Empiezan a oírse chapaleos en el agua. Reyes y sus hombres cruzan el río como si fuera muy natural. Así llegan hasta el árbol sin preocupación ni prisa y allí escuchan calmados las patadas secas en el cuerpo del que salió corriendo al revés. Umph. Umph. Los pujidos no alteran a los jinetes. Y luego...

—¡Aaaagua, muchachos!— grita el Grillo, y entonces empieza la balacera. Los hombres no tiran a pegar pero la sorpresa hace que los azotes de Ben corran espantados dejando el trabajo sin terminar. Eso quiere Reyes. Después sus hombres sacan los chicotes y se llevan a Chester y a su pandilla arreando a golpes hasta caer exhaustos.

Lorenzo mientras tanto ha logrado a fuerza de espuelazos que el caballo reviente la rienda pero no quiere salir a galope porque todavía tiene las manos atadas. Hace un gran esfuerzo por hablar y pedirles piedad mas no puede, por el pañuelo. Entonces logra aflojarse el nudo de las manos pero Rufino lo descubre, y apenas logra picar espuelas para cuando éste se le apareja y lo tumba a la tierra. Luego lo rueda barranco abajo y allí lo zambulle sin darse cuenta que el hombre está mudo. Una, dos, tres, zambullidas. El cuerpo queda flojo. Rufino por fin lo deja allí para atender a los golpeados.

—Epa, Manuel, ¿qué llevas ai?

—Al viejo Rentería. Todavía no despierta de la zurundiada.

—Pues a ver si le vas echando agua.

Uno por uno los pizcadores se fueron haciendo bola bajo el álamo gordo, unos no tan golpeados como el viejo, otros solamente con la boca abierta. Reyes se dirige hacía unos gemidos tirados de panza entre la acequia. Encuentra a un chamaco tiritando. Le tiende la mano. El muchacho parece que le cierra el ojo como burla pero está demasiado morado el golpe para que sea chiste.

—A ver, mira nomás que friega le pusieron. Súbase. Y sepa que para otra vez no es nomás irse a la brava. No crea que le van a pagar ni su trabajo ni su paliza. Tenga, pendejo. Échese esta lanita en la bolsa y...búsquele de otro modo.

Pasaron por donde estaba Lorenzo quien seguía todavía como lo habían dejado en la arena, de panza. El mismo Rufino lo pone boca arriba...

—Oiga, jefe, creo que se nos fue la mano. ¡A qué caray!...hijo de la ching ...pero si es Lorenzo, compa.

—Pues, ¿qué se le va a hacer? Que Dios lo lleve a él y que a nosotros nos perdone, compadre.

Allí cerca de Presidio donde llaman la Loma Pelona, se levanta el fortín como un castillo podrido. Es un castillo de adobe sin puertas que usa el viento como pito de barro y no falta quien pase por allí alguna noche con pelos de puercoespín y diga: el castillo esta espantado. Hay espíritus y hay diablos que pasan de cuarto en cuarto botando. Los incrédulos lo niegan diciendo que son mitotes pero lo cierto es que la historia se intuye. Las leyendas de la gente son las paginas de un libro que se arrancaron y se echaron a la hoguera...

A ver muchachos, vamos a darle una porra a don Benito el de las barbas de chivo. Vamos todos...¡don Beniiito, don Beniiito, don Beniito, que cante don Beniiito, que grite don Beniiito, que ría don Beniiito!...

—*¿Y por qué se te ocurrió darle porra?*

—*Porque ayer lo vi pasar con su traje de catrín, con una pata en el suelo y la otra tocando las barbas blancas del pecho.*

—*Tiene géneros.*

—*No, tiene lana y sal el viejito cabroncito de Presidio.*

—*Otra vez, muchachos, don Beniiito, don beniiito, don benito el de la tienda...*

—*¡Don beniiito!*

—*don benito el del grafitti en...*

—*¡Don beniiito!*

—*en los escusados, en paredes de la calle, en los cheques de banqueros, en los lomos del ganado...*

—*¡Don beniiito!*

—*en el cielo y en infierno, en las tierras de los padres de la Vicke que perdieron en la corte del condado ...*

—*¡Don beniiito!*

—*en los papeles de cuero, don benito el hacendado, don benito el soldado...*

—*¡Don Beniiito!*

—*Alabado sea, digamos todos los muertos.*

—*¡Alabado sea!*

—*por sus obras y sus bienes, por librarnos el señor.*

—*...*

—*Ayer recordé verlo pasar con el pecho tan inflado que se me ocurrió darle porra. No, quería darle una aporreada si pudiera pero el viejo no resiste, Dios lo tenga en sus recuerdos cuando muera.*

—*Espérense, vamos todos a alzar las manos, rezar por él antes de que venga con nosotros al fortín.*

—*No, vamos a darle porra otra vez, por su astucia con el pobre, por sus robos y por los asesinados.*

—*¡Alto! Cállense por el amor de Dios. Tanta calumnia no soporto. Era joven, no sabía. Era militar. Hubo guerra, hubo miedo, hubo riña de gobiernos, él era sólo un empleado. Le dijeron allá por '63, vente para acá muchacho, donde serpentea el río bravo.*

—*A la vibora de la mar...*

—*Y le dijo Captain Gray, todos los gatos son pardos, cuida el río de este lado, crúzalo si necesario.*

—*Por aquí pasó la tropa y se fueron hasta Chihuahua. Don Benito regresó con la gloria de soldado.*

—*¡Porra muchachos! Benito fue a la guerra...*

—*Montado en una perra, la perra se ensució y Benito le lambió.*

—*Y luego se coló entre nosotros, conquistó tierra, puso tienda, dio trabajo a todo mundo.*

—*Cállense gritones, nosotros también tenemos la culpa. ¿Cuántas veces les decía que exigieran sus derechos, que se cuidaran de lobos, que guardaran los papeles.*

—*Nosotros ¿qué sabíamos de gobierno americano?*

—*Bien, pero ¿por qué no nos unimos entonces? ¿Por qué?...sigan pendejos a ver si le encuentran fin. Cuando se escribió el tratado, se aseguraron derechos de tierras en papel. Después se hicieron reclamos, muchos reclamos, al comité federal. ¿Qué pasó? De mil y pico se aprobaron setenta. El resto se les pagó a dólar y medio el acre. ¿Justicia? Bola de pendejos...*

—*Y usted don Rubén, ¿qué pasó con lo suyo?*

—*No pos a mí me trajo la larga muy temprano y lo que ya presentía, pasó. Mi pobre vieja, ¿qué iba a hacer? Con tamaña pistolota le hizo la lucha, pero quedó loquita, o mejor dicho, iba quedando. Dios perdone al vendido de Lorenzo que también la encandungó. No sé qué tratos se hicieron pero allá en la casa de corte Lorenzo la convinció que traspasara su firma. Ni modo, la vieja pendeja firmó y al rato que ya no es dueña pero que el gobierno va a pagarle todo lo que quitaba. Pero dejemos la cosa, ella no tuvo la culpa y con seguridá que yo hubiera hecho lo mismo...*

—*Si yo bien qui la recuerdo. Yo, cuando vine pa esta tierra, yo trabajé con ella.*

—*Y tú ¿qué viniste a hacer aquí?*

—*Pos, siñor, a buscar la vida qui no incontraba en l'otro lado.*

—*¿De dónde eres tú?*

—*Soy el tarasco Melchor, siñor. Vengo de muy lejos. Mi dijeron que por acá si vivía mejor.*

—*Pero si eres bastante joven. ¿Cómo...*

—*Pos, siñor, murí quemadito aquí en el fortín. Nunca pensé murir tan temprano. Tanto qui le rogué a la virgencita*[12] *que mi concidiera ver a mi mamita, pero como ve usté, siñor, no se pudo. Quiría probarle qui sabía ya escribir y qui estuviera mera orgullosa de mí.*

—*¿Y qué es ese papel que traes quemado de las puntas, Melchor?*

—*Pos verá usté, siñor, es una poesía pa mi mamá qui no le mandé. Cuando me quemaron me la eché a la boca porque era lo único que valía en mi vida.*

—*Léela Melchor.*

—*Ay siñor, nomás no se vaya usté a rir.*

—*No, hombre, como me voy a reír. Léela, léela, ¿que no, muchachos?*

—*¡Que lea Melchor! ¡que lea Melchor! ¡que lea Melchor!*

—*¿Ya ves hombre? Tienes público.*

—*Ándale. Y por favor alza la cabeza como si te estuviera oyendo tu mamá.*

—*Pos ai va. Si llama Magrecita Santa:*

   "Tú qui en mi desgracia impeñaste todo pa darme consuelo
   y darme la friega qui nicisitaba,
   tú que le prendites dos velas al santo allá en Igualapa
   Cuando jui juyendo muy muy lejos da ti me encontraba,
   tú qui eres y juites muy güena y sufrida.
   Aceita mis gracias, tamién mis querencias,
   pos no puedo darte más que este manojo
   de flores cortadas, unas en las siembras
   y las más fresquitas allá en la Chinampa,
   Acéitalas dulce magrecita güena,
   Acéitalas chula magrecita santa.
   Ora que es tu santo que Dios te bendiga
   ¿O ya no recuerdas toditas las malas aiciones?
   Pos sabes que jue sin pensalo.
   Pue qué de querencia
   Pue qué de confianza
   Porque yo tu nombre lo llevo metido
   Como a tu sagrada almita de lirio
   Magrecita chula, magrecita güena, magrecita santa.

---

[12]la Virgen de Guadalupe, la santa patrona de México.

Has sido güena todita tu vida.
Por todas mis culpas derramaste lágrimas.
Ora que es tu santo sólo puedo darte
este manojito de flores cortadas
unas, en las siembras, y las más fresquitas
allá en la Chinampa
Acéitalas dulce magrecita güena
Acéitalas chula magrecita santa
y abrasame juerte, bendícime muncho
porque ora en tu santo mi espíritu canta..."
—*¡Que viva Melchor!*
—*¡Vivaaa! Ahora que cante el indio Melchor. ¡Que cante! Una porra muchachos...*
—*¡Que cante, que cante, que cante, que cante Melchor, que cante Melchor, que cante Melchor...*

"Tzitzi, curapi, tzan en an tzetzas et tzana por su me cuaria...ca que tzan tzin, por tunque lo ña miri curiñaaa...[13] *flor de canela sospiro y sospiro porque me acuerdo de tiii...sospiro yo, sospiro porque me acuerdo de tiii, a za guera, aza sentí...porque me acuerdo de ti".*
—*¡Otra! ¡Otra! ¡Otra!*

"Ay, ay, ay, ay, tlazita mutzi caraquia, itzle cuicho, itzla cochitl, aim pero ro quimooo...tzama ri cuaria, maqui ni qui ni quia, matzen flor azul, matze pere tzaratzin, male ña quim pa ña quiii... ay, ay, ay, ay..."
—*... ¿qué decía, señor?*
—*Que están cantando.*
—*Ah, sí... (las lenguas se confunden, se mutilan como pedazos el alma) Bonita canción... (te barrenan otras con la punta de un lápiz y luego le dan vuelta para borrarte la tuya tan fácil como si el alma estuviera en el papel. Luego la lengua se alarga como cuerda y se enreda en tu cuerpo haciéndote bola como le sucedió al gato.)*
—*¿Por qué tan serio, joven?*
—*Por nada, nomás estaba pensando... (que la justicia es una lengua hilada de donde se prende la vida y se hace nudos).*
—*¿Por qué cargas esa cachucha en el pecho?*
—*Lo hago por costumbre. Traté de detenerme la sangre que me salía.*
—*¿Que fue pleito?*

---

[13]poema narrado en tarasco, una lengua indígena de Oaxaca.

—*No, fue un balazo que me dieron cuando salí corriendo.*

—*¿Andabas de mojadito?*

—*No señor, fue cuando se nos puso la cosa tirante el año 30. ¿Se acuerda cuando a todos nos andaba llevando la trampa de hambre?*

—*Pos claro que me acuerdo. En esos tiempos anduve yo por Los Angeles. Decían que nosotros estábamos empeorando la cosa y empezaron a echarnos de a montón. Yo recuerdo que en agosto del mismo año, salió en los periódicos que habían echado a 82,000 de allí nomás, pero lo curioso es que se dieron cuenta muy tarde que nosotros éramos los únicos que no pedíamos ayuda ni nada para comer. Estaba muy confundida la cuestión en esos tiempos. La migra se metía en las casas sin permiso y empezaban a barrer con la gente. Recuerdo del pobre viejo Anselmo, cómo lloró porque lo sacaron de su casa que había habitado más de cincuenta años. Pero esa ya es historia muy larga. Tú, muchacho, dime qué pasó con lo tuyo, pero primero quítate esa cachucha del pecho, parece que estás pidiendo perdón...¡ah caray! ¡Qué tamaño boquetón! Con razón lo traes tapado. A ver cuéntame.*

—*Pues sucedió que mis padres se emigraron cuando tenía seis años. Mi papá encontró trabajo en el rancho del joven Ben, que antes era de su papá, y se sintió feliz aunque yo tuviera que ayudarle después de la escuela. Así estuvo la vida hasta el 31 como usted lo cuenta. Se les puso a los del gobierno que éramos estorbos aunque decían que nos echaban porque nos tenían compasión. Lo que no querían entender era que estaba peor allá. Un día se metieron a la casa y revisaron papeles. Mi papá se había emigrado bien pero le dijeron que yo era ilegal y que tendría que irme al país donde había nacido, a México. Y si no, pues toda la familia tendría que regresar. Mi mamá imploró, lloró y mi papá rezongó pero fue inútil. A mí tanto que me gustaba la escuela. Pues de todos modos me fui a quedar con los abuelos pero no pude aguantar. Después de seis semanas, y a pesar de la advertencia de mi abuela, me vine tempranito a cruzar el río (Güelita, me voy para el otro lado. No muchacho, no cruces el río. Seco está el prado a los dos lados, no cruces. ¿Que no ves que bajo el agua las arañas una red te van tejiendo? ¿Que no ves que las sanguijuelas verdes te calarán en los huesos?) Era todavía oscuro pero así con todo el miedo me arrojé solito...(Sombras frondosas, como peces moribundos...chapaleos en el agua... huellas que se ahogan.) Mi güelita no quería dejarme venir y todo el camino parecía que la oía decirme que me devolviera...(Verdes sombras, tus pupilas con el color de los mares...el sauce te está llorando con sus lágrimas amargas...¡regrésateee!) Pero de todos modos crucé como un eco en las montañas. Parecía que todo estaba contra mí porque tan pronto como crucé, empezó a ponerse más oscuro y a relampaguear...(Se me nublaron los ojos, de nubes grises y negro cielo...tembló la tierra bajo los pies, quebrose el cielo en pedazos, machetazos luminosos.) Entonces sí que me asusté porque si llovía no iba a poder seguir y yo creo que fue el miedo el que me hizo continuar, aunque sabía que no podría protegerme si me agarraba el agua a medio camino y me desorientaría. Pues así fue. Me pescó la lluvia cuando apenas iba a media labor...(pedradas en el rostro, fustigazos en la espalda. ¡Corre! ¡Refúgiate! ¡Regrésateee!) y lo peor del caso es que pronto se convirtió en granizo y me puso bien moretoneado. (Lágrimas, lluvia, munición de hielo. ¡Clemencia!) La cachucha para nada me ayudó y como loco empecé a correr llorando. Ni siquiera me acuerdo como di con el árbol (bajo el sauce triste tiritaba mientras que las gotas en las hojas de las plantas aplaudían). Allí me hice pelotita y lloré mucho tiempo hasta que me quedé dormido. Por la mañana me puse otra vez a caminar pero llevaba un peso bruto en el alma, como si todo el mundo se burlara de mí. Y cuando llegué, lloré en los brazos de mi mamá como un niño. (Y tú, mamita, tú le diste forma al tiempo sondeando la transparencia del mar. Te gustaba recoger las aguas de lagunas y de ríos en tus pupilas redondas. Y aunque los ríos no corrían como antes, te recreabas con el vaivén de tu silla. ¡Te acuerdas que te picaba las costillas y que así llenabas los arroyos de tu piel! Risa de agua multiforme rebosando tus enaguas de percal. Vida sin medida. Mares pululantes. Cielo transparente que se arrulla en tu regazo.)*

—*Ya me lo imagino. Pero entonces ¿cómo te balacearon si no fue en esa ocasión?*

—*Ah, pues fue más luego cuando me puse a trabajar, como ya no iba a la escuela. Andaba solo limipiando en la labor cuando aparecieron los chotas. Los mismos. Yo creo que si no hubiera sido por esta cachucha no me hubieran reconocido. El caso es que de inmediato vinieron hacia mí. Nomás les dije que cuando menos me dejaran ir a traer mi ropa y despedirme. Pues dijeron que estaba bien y me echaron al carro. Me llevaron hasta la casa y me esperaron en el carro hasta que arreglara todo y aunque mis padres armaron un lío, de nada sirvió. Al salir noté que uno de los chotas estaba tomando agua de uno de los grifos que estaba un poco retirado. El otro parecía dormitar sentado en el carro. Entonces no sé qué me pasó pero se me ocurrió correr aun sabiendo que no podría escapar. El que tomaba agua me vio y disparó para asustarme pero después se echó a correr y al ver que no me alcanzaba se hincó para no fallar. Yo como tonto di la vuelta como para encararme con él y de repente sentí un friíto cerca del corazón. Pero no sentí dolor sino una sorpresa grande. Recuerdo que actué como un miedoso porque ya cuando los dos vinieron a ponerme las esposas, yo ya les ofrecía las manos juntitas. Después así esposado recogí mi cachucha y me la puse en el corazón. Me ayudaron a levantarme y caminé con ellos al carro pero las piernas me decían que no. Yo creo que con la cachucha quería tapar el boquete por donde se me iba la vida. ¿Pero cómo se puede guardar la vida en una cachucha? Todos los que vamos a morir somos chistosos, ¿no cree usted?*

—*Es cierto. Pero ¿qué haces tú aquí, si no eres de Presidio?*

—*Soy del mundo, señor. Como la muerte. Que importa ser de aquí o de allá. La ignorancia es grande y es igual. También la pobreza. La realidad es el agujero que traigo aquí, señor.*

—*La realidad soy yo, señores.*

—*¿Y quién eres tú?*

—*Soy Jesús del río, soy de agua.*

—*Estás loco, eres de tierra como nosotros.*

—*Ni de cenizas ni de barro. Viví del agua y morí en el agua. Todo soy de agua.*

—*¿Y por qué estás en el fortín si eres de agua?*

—*Porque el fortín es de vidrio, es aquario.*

—*Sí, cómo no, loquito. Un aquario con puertas de adobe gastado. Eres ridículo.*

—*No, las puertas son de voces.*

—*¿Nuestras?*

—*No, del diablo.*

—*No es cierto, son las nuestras. Son llantos, son silbidos de hombres que quieren cruzar el río. Te hablan a ti, Jesús.*

—*No, son las sirenas del mar. Me quieren, por eso me llaman.*

—*Sí, te quieren. Muerto.*

—*No, me quieren para que cuente cuentos de hadas.*

—*Mitotes tuyos, Jesús. ¿Para qué van a querer idioteces?*

—*Porque mis cuentos son la verdad. Yo también soy sirena.*

—*¿Por qué dices eso Jesús?*

—*Porque mi cuerpo está en Presidio, pero mi alma en el río.*

—*¿Que no se fue al cielo?*

—*No, porque se me seca y quiero que siga viviendo.*

—*¿En un infierno como éste?*

—*Sí, para que aplaque las llamas.*

—*¿Pero cómo, dime tú, vas a lograrlo si estás muerto?*

—*Voy a resucitar, me llamaré José.*

—*¿Tu hijo?*

*—No, el de mi hermano Reyes, y ya me voy cantando señores: "Es mi orgu-
llo haber nacido en el barrio más humilde...*[14] *(este hombre es un loco de atar,
ojalá que se calle pronto)...y el día que el pueblo me falle, ese día voy a morir".*

Los pocos turistas que por casualidad se cuelan a Presidio en busca de cosas
viejas, tienen la suerte de hallar una reliquia güera llamada Mack. Este se supone
ser el experto de la historia de Presidio, del fortín y de Ben Lynch. Así que para
cuando salen de Nancy's Cafe ya quedaron enterados del número de colgadas,
de cogidas y de todas esas cosas que es capaz de hacer el hombre. Lo demás es
fácil. Por unos dólares organiza la excursión al fortín. Ya allí, los hace formar
un semicírculo antes de entrar para que...pero mejor que te lo cuente el viejo
cabrón...

"Yes siree, Old Ben came to this part of the country from his dad's in
Alabama. Guess he got tired of driving them dark folks over there and so headed
fer San Antone. Ben was still young then and I guess them wild hairs of his
stood up when he heard 'bout the trouble with Mexicans. The story 'bout the
slaughter at the Alamo made him mad a plenty. Now I ain't sure when he get to
San Antone but I know he arrive too late. Musta been a sight when he ride into
town. You should see a picture of him, here, see? Big, and tall in the saddle,
with all that fair hair a bristling in the wind. Anyway, he got there a day after
all this happened and he sure got burnt up when he hear about Crockett and
Bowie[15] died. Couldn't do nothing about it, though, just get mad over the whole
mess. He wasn't received good either by Mrs. Caulder because she got a patio
full of dead stinking. . .bodies, so she give him a piece of her mind thinking he
had took part in the killing. But he told her different and help her get rid of most
of the carcasses. Young Ben was a hell of a cowpoke. He was a pretty happy-go-
lucky kid them years but I ain't saying he had no sense in him. He was hard-
working and never give his boss reason to talk. He was a tough hombre those
years; sure he could sing and yodel, but people sure wasn't going to mistake him
for no sissy. He could fight damned near anybody and boy, could he ride. He
could ride broncs till they spilt over tired as hell. And them bulls, you would a
think he was born on 'em. But his rough and tough ways don't mean he wasn't
brought up right. Hell no. His folks reared him good. They tell him 'bout the
Lord, and the right living, and all that 'bout being a loyal and proud man. Sure

---

[14]la letra de un corrido mexicano.
[15]héroe anglosajón en la batalla de El Álamo, Texas.

he was ornery—a few fights once in a while but who ain't when you're that age? And specially when you come to a town of...people with different folkways and no care fer law and order. I mean, you know, he come to San Antone fer that there reason. He learned pretty quick how to deal with 'em in the canteenas and he wouldn't let no man beat 'im. And he already know 'bout how conniving these critters can be with knife and all, you know what I mean. Fact I heard the reason there ain't no Indians in this part of the country no more is 'cause these folks beat 'em at their own game. The first time he fight, he fight five of them at once and he licked 'em clean. And when he whipped 'em pretty good, that's when he got his reputation. He didn't need no gun; the bastards would disappear like shitflies. . .pardon the expression. . .and after that they would turn yeller and run. O yea, they knew what he stood fer. Anyway, guess it was about that time that things started getting pretty stinky down the Río Grand and they start organizing the Texas brigade and other lawful organizations to clear the mess. You know, horse stealing, cattle rustling, killing white folks. People nowadays don't pay much attention to the service these constabulary, Texas Rangers they call 'em, give to their country. Remember there wasn't no law to protect the citizenry so they take it in their own hands. Sometimes when there wasn't no courthouse judge around, a noose on a tree was enough fer'em. Hell, with all these desperados running wild, they had to do something, hoosegow or no hoosegow. Sure, they made some mistakes, but hanging innocent people was rare. And although they crossed the border and followed them outlaws clear to hell, there was not enough of them to clear up the mess. Anyway, to make a long story short, the Rangers went recruitin' by way of San Antone and they hear of Ben's reputation soon enough. In fact, they found that the only bad habit he had was seeñoritas and tobacco chewing so they hired him. But first they talk to his boss directly and of course there wasn't no problem. Mixin' with them don't spoil 'im. So he pack his saddlebags with dried beef and off he goes (come a ti yi yippi yippi yea, come a ti yi yippi yippi yea, tis cloudy in the west and looks like rain and my old slickers in the wagon again. . .on a ten-dollar horse and a forty-dollar saddle. . .) I ain't sure what good he done over the Valley by the Rio Grand, but next thing, he show up in Presidio. It was about the time the government start getting pretty worried about border troubles so they start moving soldiers up and down the river. Ha, ha, but I cain't figure why they sent soldiers to Presidio 'cause it was just a poor Mexican settlement and there was no white folks yet. All they find was poor people and a few savages, Jumanos, they call them. They say the name's Mexican which means humans, and I guess that's true, he, 'cause they sure as hell didn't cause no trouble. That's funny. Sometimes you cain't tell the difference between Mexicans and Indians. They mix up pretty good, ha, and they sent the whole company to fight and there was none to fight. Truth is, they only find a forteen built of adobe by Spanish soldiers, long time before, and it look like it never been used; yea, this one here you're seeing. They say it was a custom to build them everywhere they went, just like the Alamo in San Antone, but this one here wasn't no beauty. Sure doesn't look like it can even hold water out. . .fact you probably could blow at it and it'd fall. Anyway, they find themselves this Presidio del Norte with nothing to do so they move up to Marfa sixty miles away where there was white folks already. But Ben stayed 'cause he was smart. He know what he was doing but you know, this is where the story become different. I mean, Ben was different. He changed, no doubt about it, 'cause he married a seeñorita. By this time he was pretty savvy in the language and took to marrying. Of course she was different, too, educated, pretty, clean—you know what I mean. But I ain't saying he was a turncoat though. He still loved law and order. He always done good like he used to. He never quit being a ranger either and he would run anybody out of town that give him reason to. One night when he was a courting Rosary, he got pistolwhipped pretty bad by his brothers but he got even soon enough. But that's what I mean, he become different 'cause he didn't hold no grudge. He learn how to love these people. I guess that's what love does to you, get soft in the guts. Anyway, he was a well-respected feller by the community and of course they couldn't help it 'cause he was kind to them. He gave 'em work and food, everything, and of course they look up to him like a daddy. He learned how to handle 'em and I say this 'cause next thing, he own a hell of a lot of farmland and longhorns. Fact he even take over the forteen and use it as a office once his business went good and the soldiers had move out. He started using a lot of Mexican help and from here he would pay 'em with all them wads of bills. Yup, Ben was a good old critter with a big heart, you have to admire a guy like him. Sh. . . Hell, he even make big barbacoas and invite the whole lot of them to eat. He was fair if they do the job but if they fail or trick him, boy, he would turn meaner than a. . .angry mama bear. It ain't no bu. . .lie either. But people remember more than good deeds. For example, he never forget Paz, the old lady that sell him the land. He done a lot of favors fer her, and even after she died, he took in her daughter Vicke once she lost her husband. Anyway, people remember old Ben Lynch. He was hardworking, kind, lawabiding, etcetera and all them qualities that an hombre should have. And I ain't saying all about him is true though. But damned near all of it. . . Okay folks, let's go in. . ."

"Mi papá trabajaba en Ojinaga en una labor, rentada a medias y levantaba mucho trigo. Ya se nos acabó la necesidad porque trabajaba mamá haciendo tortillas y lavaba ropa pa darnos comida a los que estábamos chicos. Entonces él agarró esa labor y ya se nos acabó el hambre. Levantaba frijol, calabazas, lentejas y todo iba alzando. Cuando nos vinimos hacía muy poco que había levantado el maíz, unas mazorcas grandotas y hizo una trofa[16] grande allí junto de la casa. Hizo una testera grande con palos pa echarle maíz. Pos bastante dejamos cuando vino Pancho Villa. No logramos nada. Nos vinimos porque los caballos de Pancho se lo comieron. Una pérdida bárbara. Dejamos las garras que teníamos, las chanclas que teníamos, porque no teníamos zapatos, camas y todo se quedó. Nos vinimos nomás de con una burra, con una angarilla y una bandeja grande llena de masa que habíamos amasado pa hacer pan. Eso fue lo que sacamos y vinimos a hacer tortillas al campo donde se acampó toda la gente; también sacamos una esquilia y un sartén y unas cucharas nomás.

"Pasando todo la burra se fue adelante con los triques y nosotros atrás. Pa cuando salimos a la orilla de río, ya nos daba l'agua muy arriba porque creció el río. Pos todos los que sabían nadar se retiraron y los que no pos se quedaron allá. Anda, si fue un desgarriate esa tarde. El hermano de Carmen Chávez cuando se soltó el tiroteo fuerte allá en el pueblo entonces se vino él y otro. Hicieron una balsa pos sin saber cómo se hacía. Hicieron la balsa pa tirarse al río y sí lo hicieron pero se 'hogaron. No, si fue un desgarriate bárbaro. Nosotros cruzamos porque la casa de nosotros estaba arriba de la loma. Allí nomás bajaba uno y allí estaba el río. Pasó mucha gente y se acampó en el bosque. Unos ganaron pa una parte y otros para otra. Se desparramó la gente y nosotros nos vinimos pa Puerto Rico a vivir".

"Cuando vino la revolución de 1910, los soldados agarraban a la gente y la metían de soldado así que los que vivían en Ojinaga, casi todos se fueron pa'l otro lao. Y nosotros como no teníamos trabajo pos andábamos de vagos, como luego dicen, sueltos. Estaba poco dura la cosa así que nos manteníamos pescando. Estaba muy bajo el río, el agua muy clara y limpia y donde había hondables nos metíamos con horquillas a hacerle ruido al pescao pa echarlo fuera pa fisgarlo en las horquillas, cuando salía pa afuera de lo hondo. Ese día que nos agarraron allí andábamos.

"Nos vinimos en la mañana yo, Francisco mi hermano, que estaba de este tamaño, Francisco Brito mi primo y Chamalía Heredia un tío mío. Nos metimos al río hechos ala, en forma de ala, y con las horquillas le hacíamos ruido al pescado. Mi tío no se metió sino que se subió al barranco porque de arriba del

---

[16]tejido parado de cañas de maíz.

barranco se veía el pescado si salía o no, tan clara así estaba l'agua, y de allí nos decía si salía el pescado. Y a poco rato en el mero frente de Quivira oímos un tropel de caballos. Era una avanzada que iba de Ojinaga pa donde estaban peleando en el Mulato. Entonces Chamalía nos preguntó si les hablaba pero yo le dije que no porque como andaba la revolución pos no podía uno saber qué podrían hacernos. Bueno, pues éste les habló; les pegó un grito y ellos se dejaron venir. Nomás llegaron y luego luego, con los rifles en la mano, agarraron a Chamalía. Luego nos dijeron a nosotros que saliéramos pero nos encaminamos pa'l otro lao (y a mí me podía mucho, por ejemplo, que no fuera y que me llevaran a mi hermano, tan chico; Francisco estaba chamaco de a tiro) pero nos agarraron a tiros. Tuvimos que salirnos y nomás pasamos y nos amarraron. Nos trataron muy mal. Nos decían que éramos maderistas y que estábamos pasándoles parque a los maderistas. Eduardo Salinas, el jefe de ellos, les ordenó que nos amarraran con las sogas de los caballos. Nos mancornaron y nos echaron descalzos por arriba de los mesquites. Entonces dijo que nos iban a fusilar. Allí en Quivira arriba de la loma estaba un camposanto y les ordenó que nos llevaran a la loma pa matarnos allí. Nos acusaban de algo que ni cuenta nos dábamos. Si sabíamos de la revolución pero no andábamos. Pos nos llevaron hasta allí y todos se fueron rumbo al Mulato menos dos. Ellos se quedaron con nosotros en la loma. Estaba un solón muy fuerte y nosotros descalzos y todo lo que usted quiera. Pos se pusieron de acuerdo y llevaron a Francisco, como era el más chico, a que nos pasara la ropa y después nos vistieron en la loma. Aunque tenían orden de que nos mataran, no lo hicieron, y uno de ellos sí nos hizo una movida muy buena. Porque ora verá que en el otro lao nos juntábamos todos los muchachos en la noche a pelear de mentiritas. Unos de Loma Pelona y otros del Terronal. Poníamos lumbre en las palmillas y todo eso pa pelear con tizones prendidos. Unos eran maderistas y otros eran gobiernistas. A mí los muchachos maderistas me pusieron de capitán esa noche. Entonces de un papel hacíamos cheques pa pagarles a los soldados y como me tocó a mi ser jefe, parece hecho adrede que traía todos esos papeles en la bolsa del pantalón. Allí tenía escrito el valor del dinero cuando nos agarraron.

"Si yo estoy viendo porque Dios es muy grande. Entonces pos yo estaba muy apurado pero ni remedio. El soldado que fue a traer la ropa, me esculcó y me sacó todo lo que traía, en la bolsa. Pero ése no lo presentó ni se lo enseñó a ninguno, si no, no estaba contando. Fíjese nomás, cómo estaría yo. ¡Ay, Chihuahua! Pero no dije nada, nomás me hice como que estaba muy enojao y les echaba. Bueno pues nos remitieron a Ojinaga y nomás nos vieron presos y mujeres y soldados nos dijeron barbaridad y media. Después nos soltaron y nos echaron a la cárcel y esa noche allí dormimos. Nos tuvieron el día siguiente también.

Para esto, mi abuelito Cleto Heredia, que era sherife del condado de Presidio, se dio cuenta de que nos echaron tiros pa'l otro lao y les apretó. Pos a los tres días nos echaron fuera y hasta nos ofrecieron un salvo-conducto pa'l otro lao. Entonces, viendo a aquellos que estaban tan enojados, le dije a mi tío Chamalía: vamos a darnos, vamos a darnos de alta con los maderistas. Y así fue como lo hicimos. Así fue como entré yo a la revolución.

"Cuando fregaron a Madero, me vine con Villa. Anduve en las armas hasta el 15. Del 15 me salí y me trasladé al otro lado pero siempre trabajando por el partido hasta el 20 que ya se arregló todo. Trabajé con la cuestión de Villa en muchas formas: llevaba parque, vestuario, bueno, hacía de todo. Tenía labor pa que no se me notara; estaba yo en medio de la labor, cerca del río y allí sembraba. A Hipólito, hermano de Villa, yo lo pasé a los Estados Unidos. Vivía él en San Antonio pero lo vigilaban hasta no poder estar en casa. Y nomás ponga cuidado hasta donde son los americanos de convenencieros. Por cuestión de dinero y todo lo que usted quiera, ellos mismos lo sacaron hasta tráermelo hasta Marfa donde lo recibí. Yo lo tuve en mi casa a él y a otros generales y de allí los marché en la noche hasta juntarlos con los Villistas. Así seguí trabajando hasta el 20 que se acabó la revolución, con mi gente, de acuerdo con él, y cuando teníamos que ir a verlo pasábamos el río en la noche. Así andábamos pa allá y pa acá.

"En esa tomada de Chihuahua, Villa fue muy diablo. Era muy sagaz. Dimos un ataque primero y no pudimos entrar. Como era la capital del estado, estaban todos los soldados reconcentrados allí. Entonces éste pensó hacer una llamada falsa. Así que agarramos al telegrafista de Villahumada y le exigió él que formara una llamada a Juárez, como que era de Chihuahua, diciendo que pedían auxilio de tropas para Chihuahua. Fue trampa porque entonces llamó a Juárez y mandaron unos trenes de soldados. Cuando ya venían, les pegamos, los fregamos. Entonces éste hizo la llamada que iba a atacar Chihuahua y volteó y le pegó a Juárez y la tomó. Fue muy importante porque ya quedó Chihuahua cercada por dondequiera; la única salida era de Ojinaga porque aquí habíamos cuatro gatos. Cuando ya se dio cuenta el gobernador se vino con millonarios y tropas. Todos vinieron a dar aquí.

"Nosotros que éramos unos cuantos aquí andábamos por las lomas con reses y cuando veníamos pa Ojinaga no sabíamos que estaban los contrarios adentro del pueblo. Nomás que Luis Cortez mi cuñado y otros hombres de Presidio, pasaron por la junta y nos avisaron. Esos fueron los que nos libertaron la vida.

"Pocos días después nos juntamos con la gente que Villa había mandado adelante, como dos mil, y mientras tanto las tropas de Ojinaga eran un hervidero. Los contrarios, como no cabían, se desparramaron pa las labores o pa'l Mulato.

Bueno, pues primero avanzamos sobre los del Mulato y los agarramos en la puerta del cañoncito pero muchos se escaparon pa'l otro lao por El Polvo. Les salimos en el arroyo del Alamo y allí nos topamos a pelear. Otro día en la tarde rodeamos Ojinaga pero era un gentío bárbaro. No pudimos hacer nada. Eramos unos cuatro gatos como luego dicen pa ocho mil hombres. Pues resulta que dimos tres ataques, pero no...fíjese que había unos hoyos muy grandes parejitos de costales de arena donde estaban parados toda la gente. Nos mataron mucha gente. Salíamos pa atrás derrotaos. Y luego a los tres días llegó Villa con su gente. Maclovio Herrera, Rosalio Hernández y otros. Bueno, con toda esa gente todavía no les competimos. Pero Villa era muy diablo y me acuerdo como si fuera ahorita, que llegó muy enojado por haber metido la gente en esa forma. Y es que estaba muy dura la cosa. Fíjese que todos los álamos los tenían tumbaos y luego tenían alambres de pico por si entraba la gente a caballo. Bueno nos dijo claramente: no les dé cuidado, muchachos. Pa mañana, siendo Dios servido, para esta misma hora, tenemos que ir a comer de la cena que van a cenar ellos. Tenemos que agarrarlos antes de la cena. Dicho y hecho, como así fue. Ordenó a todos, que ya venían como ala, los echó a pie. Uno que otro oficial venía tras de la gente a caballo pero eso era pa cuando el ataque, con la orden de que el que diera pie atrás, era macheteao. Así que no había quién corriera. Nomás se perdió la mira y a todos les dijeron la seña y la contraseña. Esta era la seña, del cuerpo destapao, sin sombrero, el sombrero aquí y el brazo arremangao y luego la contraseña. Hubo muchos que agarraron la seña pero la contraseña no y todo ése que no la daba, abajo.

"En todo caso, parece hecho adrede que cuando se metió el sol se vino un viento con mucho polvo que ni la mano se veía. Así que pa cuando supieron los contrarios ya estabámos sobre de ellos. Y me acuerdo como si esto fuera ahora, comimos la cena de ellos. Ahora verá que después en la noche nos pusimos a hacer café pa tomar y corría cerca de allí un arroyito donde cogimos el agua. Y todos los del cuartel bebimos café pero otro día nos dimos cuenta que era sangre con la que hicimos café. Corría, estaba corriendo porque en el hoyo grande cayó mucha gente. Cuando habían salido corriendo, pos muchos cayeron muertos y heridos. Venía corriendo mucha sangre y de allí agarramos.

"Otro día en la mañana amanecimos a ver cuántos muertos había allí y pa voltearlos. Anduvieron guayines, carros de mula, levantando gente del mismo pueblo. Los acarrearon y los echaron donde está el tanque, la herradura que le nombraban. Allí había un hoyo muy hondo y estaba tapado de puros difuntos. Todo el santo día anduvieron acarreando gente en cantidad... No, si no crea, está larga la historia..."

PRESIDIO 1942

El conejo, hecho bola sobre sí mismo, duerme placentero. No sabe por qué esta vez sueña tan bonito. Como una sonrisa de bebé disfruta el paisaje alineado de lechuga. Contento está el conejo pues se sueña comiendo, así hincado y sin preocupación. ¡Caray! lo difícil que está la vida por allá especialmente cuando vienen los humanos alborotados a echarle pajuelazos. Trocas esparciendo su luz en busca de sus orejas y de repente, zas...zas...zas. Pobres hermanos conejos. Unos sirven de festín a los perros, otros a los lobos. Pero esta noche el conejo de la luna se repliega sobre sí mismo como feto contento, y sueña...

La luna se viste de amargura y saña. Malhumorada está porque no ha llovido y porque por todos rumbos el universo está ardiendo. El Río Grande ya sólo es un charco, las plantas se queman, y la gente, partículas secas, empiezan a brotar por el río. La luna los odia cuando no puede detenerlos, cuando no hay agua suficiente para taparles el pico. Por eso también está enojada la luna. Porque la gente no cesa de traficar. Por eso gruñe.

—¡Salte! ¡Vete, desgraciado mantenido!

El aposento del conejo se estremece con el grito de la luna y lo hace que pegue el brinco hasta la tierra. Luego, sobresaltado, sale corriendo como si oyera ladrar los perros detrás de los matorrales. De pronto siente un leve dolor cerca de la cola. Se imagina una bala menudita que lentamente le va dejando un hormigueo de pierna cruzada por todo el cuerpo. No puede levantarse. Hace el intento de menear la cabeza y parece que no la tiene. Ahora, hasta los ojos siente pesados. ¿Estará soñando? Medio recuerda que muy entrada la noche le vino el cansancio y se echó cerca allí de la cueva para recobrar un poco las energías pero no recuerda cuando le venció el sueño. Y ahora la sensación extraña. El parálisis que sintió antes, le ha llegado a la lengua. Trata de ver en derredor pero sólo se topa la vista con su cuerpo, a punto de reventar. La hinchazón es extrema. Ya no sabe qué pensar, no sabe si todavía está soñando o si anduvo en la luna. Tampoco está seguro si fue balazo el que sintió en la cadera o simplemente cayó tan fuerte desde arriba que su cuerpo se lastimó. Ahora entre párpados borrosos sólo discierne la víbora aproximarse con movimientos rituales. La víbora de la sierrita de la Santa Cruz se le acerca con la boca sumamente abierta y él no está seguro si se carcajea la serpiente en silencio o quiere decirle algo al oído. Mientras tanto lo único que repite su mente sonámbula es un cuento de un ratoncito pequeño que sin malicia se sentó al frente de su agujero cuando apareció un gato zalamero ofreciéndole todo tipo de delicias, y luego el ratoncito había salido solamente para ser devora...*zzzzzzzz*.

Hay cosas que se repiten como los sueños y mi padre, como tantos otros
hombres, necesita de ellos para tolerar la vida. Esta mañana se ha despertado
soñando sonrisas. Con el mismo espíritu se levanta del piso y va a sentarse al
lado de un enorme vientre que parece derramar la cama. Contempla a mi mamá
con ternura pero ella ni se mueve, ni siquiera siente un moyote que, prendido a
su mejilla, insiste en extraerle otro bocadito más de sangre. Después que se lo
espanta, mi papá se casca unos zapatos torcidos que remedan el rechinar de la
puerta. Al salir, lo saludan unos golpecitos leves en el pantalón. Es la cola cari-
ñosa de Chango.

El perro no necesitará el "ven, vamos a ver el amanecer" porque lo seguirá
como lo ha hecho siempre, y los dos caminarán juntos hasta los algodonales. Irán
al mismo sitio donde papá José nos ha llevado a soñar tantas veces y allí se
sentará hasta que se ponga borracho de Dios. Entonces empezará su cuerpo-
embudo a sorber los mil colores que nacen en el horizonte. Pero pronto se disuel-
ve el paño mágico y las nubes quedarán completamente desvestidas, preparadas
para recibir al rey.

Mi papá siempre ha creído que las nubes son pobres ninfas burladas. Piensa
así porque cuando el sol se destapa la cara, de inmediato comienza a volverse
loco de risa. Y así, a risa y risa, a vuelta y vuelta el sol le inyecta las energías
necesarias para vivir. Pero también se burla de él y la risa se convierte en saña
de perro que se quiere arrancar la cola. Y sólo cuando papá se entera de que se
está tatemando vivo, baja los pies a la tierra. Entonces, meneando la cabeza sin
poder creerlo, le hablará a su Chango: "yo no sería como él, amigo. Sí amanece-
ría con los huesos jóvenes y agradecería mi fortuna pero no quemaría ni me
burlaría ni me volvería loco de rabia". Luego rumbo a casa, seguirá con el sueño
de que algún día vivirá en un reino igual y que algún día dormirá en la casa del
Pintor...a su manera.

José, después de haber celebrado el amanecer, entró de buen humor y antes
de pasar al lavamanos, dio un beso de pichón a su amada encinta, quien estaba
preparándole el almuerzo. Ella le respondió con una sonrisa poco forzada.

—¿Cómo amaneció mi chorriada?

—Bien...

—¿Otra vez el latoso ése que trae?

Marcela meneó la cabeza.

—Ai verá lo que va a salir. Entonces se le va a olvidar todo esto.

—Ojalá y Dios te oiga José. Sólo quiero que nazca bien.

La mujer tenía razón por preocuparse. Tres años a puro muele y muele y
nada, hasta que por fin había logrado el embarazo. La alegría sin embargo había
durado poco, pues desde un principio había comenzado a sufrir. Y ahora nueve

meses después, conque llega retrasado. La viejita Vicke, su mamá, andaba preocupada también y por eso había dejado de trabajar en la casa de Rocha. Ahora el quehacer de lavar y planchar la ropa lo hacía aquí. Después de desayunar en silencio, ella con el amargo sabor en la boca, él con el buen humor que trae el sábado, José le dio otro beso.

—Cuídate mucho, José. Cuídate del sol.

—Pierda cuidado, mi vieja— y salió.

Esa mañana el sol descubrió las casas de chocolate con una grande llamarada de tal modo que a los humos que despedían los cañones de las cocinas ni siquiera se les permitió perfilarse. Este día quemaría el sol y la gente, ardida ya, estaría lista para dar fin a la semana al puro medio día. Poco a poco los cantos de los pájaros se fueron haciendo un fuerte chillido de coraje: después las chicharras continuarían su canto para terminar en autodestrucción—insectos cuyos cuerpos se encontraban engarrotados a los arbustos.

A lo lejos se veían trocas y carros llenos de trabajadores dirigiéndose hacia las diferentes partes de los laboríos. Teléforo, el compadre de José, hacía lo mismo: se fue pitando de casa en casa, recogiendo a los que andaban bajo su mando.

Teléforo depositó a los limpiadores en la sección de algodón menos sucia y al ver éstos lo limpio de los surcos, se les subió el ánimo. De inmediato se hincaron a la orilla para sacarle filo a los azadones enérgicamente y cuando oyeron a Teléforo darle instrucciones a su hijo que se encargara de la supervisión mientras él fuera a echarle un vistazo a los mojados que traía trabajando cerca del río, apenas pudieron contener el entusiasmo. El Chale era reata[17] y cuando quería les hacía la parada. Pero ahora les hablaba en tono serio.

—Orale ésos, ya oyeron el jefe, ¿qué nel[18]? Así que nada de perra. Aviéntense o si no, los reporto.

—Uuuu, que zura[19] el bato, vamos a empelotarlo pa que no se madereye[20] el güey— brincó el Jusito, mientras que las mujeres se enrojecieron y pronto se escurrieron por los zurcos. ¡Chamaco descarado! ¡No tiene pelos en la lengua!

---

[17]tenía sentido de humor.

[18]no.

[19]creído.

[20]no sea soberbio.

El Chale, al notar el enojo en las caras de los otros, soltó la carcajada.

—Puros mitotes, ésos. ¿A poco me creyeron? Este bato no está lurio ni come lumbre, ésos. Llévensela suave, al cabo no te dan premios.

Lentamente fueron entrando y al poco rato se vieron puras cabecitas gorrudas en medio de los algodonales. Tampoco tardaron en descubrir el engaño; la maldita carrijuela se entretejía por las plantas a modo de ni siquiera dejar cruzar. Una sola mata de esa fastidiosa enredadera servía para hacer bola a todo el mundo. Los azadones venían sobrando; había que gatear por debajo y arrancar la raíz con la mano. Y así se pasaba el día, sepultado en un laberinto como si se fuera un borracho que no encuentra la puerta de la casa. A las cansadas aparecían los cuerpos en las orillas, cuerpos empapados con caras que escupen, que tosen, que tiran los azadones sobre la acequia y se dirigen al árbol cercano. Luego eternos movimientos de cabeza, hacia donde debe aparecer el socorro—la troca amarilla del viejo que trae la raya. Pero no se ve nada y entonces la vista se clava en los pechos húmedos femeninos, como si de allí brotara el ánimo más grande del mundo. Los viejos enclenques, al contrario, piensan en cómo hacerle esta vez pa que alcance el cheque mientras que las mujeres milagrosamente ponen zapatos nuevos en los huercos después de haber calculado los biles atrasados de dos a tres semanas. Cabrones chamacos. Tienen patas de fierro. Más adelantito, la pacota de jóvenes saborean el baño frío y las cervezas.

La escena se repite a la orilla del río. Con una excepción: Leocadio el cacarizo está furioso. La audiencia, que por lo general aplaude su don creativo, ahora se burla de él porque sus cuentos tienen la tendencia de terminar demasiado fantásticos o pendejos. Hoy no han podido tragar la historia verdadera del hombre que era tan fuerte que podía quebrase los piloncillos en la frente. Por eso está enojado.

—No se fije en esta bola de groseros, compadre; sígale.

—No, que vayan al jodido. Se creen que son muy sabios los...

—Le digo que no se fije. Yo sé que usted no anda con esas pendejadas de libros.

—Pos usté sabe bien, compa, que aunque no tenemos escuela estamos más al alba[21] que toda esa plebe, ¿verdá? Nomás dígame qué quiere saber, compa, a ver si no sé.

—Pos sabe, siempre he querido saber cómo empezamos los humanos. Nunca estuve claro en eso. ¿Cómo empieza todo ese mitote, compa?

---

[21]preparados, listos.

—Pos ora verá. Dicen quesque estaba muy oscuro y todo y ai tiene usté que Diosito en ese tiempo se sentía muy solo y añídale que no había nada de luz. Pero yo creo que la pelada verdá es que no tenía nada que hacer y un día nomás por curiosidá se puso a soplar así como cuando le sopla uno a los hormigueros pa que se enojen las hormigas, ¿sabe? Y pos dijo, a jodido, y se reculó pa atrás. Y es que se le prendió el sol en la cara y casi lo dejaba tuerto. Ai tiene usté que le gustó lo que había salido del soplo y le siguió con una luna y a ésta le puso arete pa decoración. Se le puso buena la cosa, ¿sabe cómo, compa? Entonces todo alborotado empezó con la tierra y le echó agua. La prueba ai está, compa, este río que pasa por aquí. Luego...

—Párele ai, compa. ¿Usté dice que se aventó todo esto solo?

—Así como se lo digo, por Dios santito.

—Oiga, pos tendrá tamañas manotas como las de Lencho, ¿no cree usté?

—No, señor, si nomás tenía que pensalo, le soplaba y era todo.

—¡A jodido! ¡Me quiere usté decir que lo hizo con la pura cabeza?

—Sí.

—Ai sí que voló puntos.

—Así es la cosa. Dijo, voy a pensar en el sol y ¡puf!, ai lo tiene, bien redondote y caliente como un jodido. ¡Y las estrellas?, ni más ni menos. Pero fíjese, compadre, que todavía le faltaba lo bueno. ¿Qué cree usté que faltaba?

—Pos los animales.

—No, hombre, nosotros. Los jumanos.

—Párele, párele ai. ¿Y qué cree que somos, compa? Puros cabrones animales. Y si no lo quiere creer, fíjese en la cara del Chango Pérez. Si no es animal, está encartao cuando menos.

—No, hombre, no le mueva a eso. Ése ya es otro cuento...pero usté se me está adelantando, compa. Déjeme seguile.

—Ande pues.

—Resulta que en ese tiempo andaban las víboras paradas.

—¡Ah jijo!

—No se asuste, compa, que no picaban. A Diosito menos porque él las había echado al mundo asina como le digo. Ai tiene usté que en ese mismito tiempo pensó hacer el hombre, pero con éste si tuvo más batalla. Aquí sí tuvo que usar las manos. Agarró un pedazo de zoquete por donde pasaba l'agua pa regar el jardín y le sopló. ¿Y qué cree usté que pasó?

—Pos le salió una mujer.

—No, compa, le salió un machote así, del pelo de Sansón,[22] y...

—Oiga, compadre, cómo se me hace que me está reburujiando las cartas.

—No, si así jue.

—Pos yo creo que está todo confundío.

—No se mande, compa. Es confundido.

—Dispénseme, confundillo. Este...¿que no jue mujer la que hizo primero?

—No, si pa allá voy. Dijo Diosito, hay que hacerle compañera a este macho, y le sacó una costilla con las manos.

—No, compa, esto ya huele mal. Es puro pedo suyo. ¿Cómo cabrones...?

—Si ni pestañeó, yo creo que ni cuenta se dio porque ¿no se acuerda usté que en primer lugar nomás tenía que soplar?

—Pos...está poco chillona, si usté me pregunta.

—Y si usté cree que el machote que se aventó estaba bien hecho, debiera ver la hembra.

—Si pero fue al rev...

—Se aventó un cuerote[23] como los que hace Lencho. Ya usté se imagina y pa peor remedio, imagínese usté los dos empelota.[24]

—Está bien, si usté dice que así jue, está bien. Pero de todos modos que me la ponga, está jodida la cosa. ¿Cómo iban a resistir usté sabe qué?

—Ai voy pa allá, pero no se me adelante. Diosito entonces puso las hermosas criaturas en ese jardín que le llaman el paraíso, y allí mero ni el diablo entraba. Si no digo que no había diablo pero Diosito ya les había pitado. Y ya se los haiga si le hacen caso, les dijo, y ellos obedecían la orden.

—¿Y qué comían allí, compa?

—Ah pa eso, Dios le sopló a un árbol de manzanas.

—¿Y a poco se la pasaban comiendo manzanas?

—No, eso no, porque era pecado pero las hojas eran tan buenas y tan dulces como las mismitas manzanas.

—¿Y a poco se pasaban todo el tiempo comiendo? Yo creo que coj...

—Usted no me deja hablar, compa. Cállese y espérese hasta que termine. Después puede hacerme preguntas.

—Está bien, compadre, no se enoje. La cosa es que me la está haciendo un poco dura pa tragar. Andele, sígale, no se enoje.

---

[22]figura bíblica cuya fuerza física residía en su pelo largo.

[23]una mujer bellísima.

[24]desnudos.

—Resulta que como estaban en el paraíso no tenían deseo de nada, usté sabe de...

—Sí, de coger.

—Un aburrimiento de a chingal. Hasta que vino una de esas víboras y le dijo a la mujer: cómete una manzana y verás qué bonitos se te ponen los cachetes. Y la mujer vanidosa...

—¿Pos no me dijo que estaba criada como con leche de burro?

—Sí, pero le faltaba color. Pero lo importante es que la víbora era el enemigo de Diosito. Era el mero diablo. Y ai tiene usté que la tentó.

—¿Dónde le tentó, compa?

—Chingao, compadre. No puede uno platicar en serio con usté. No se haga pendejo. Quiero decir que se la conchabó a que se comiera una manzana. Entonces Diosito se puso de muy mal pelo y los echó de allí. Desde entonces tuvieron todas las cosas que nosotros tenemos, los problemas, los gustos, los deseos.

—Usté dice que pudieron...

—Sí, entonces sí. Se desataron y empezaron a echar cría.

—Pos me va a perdonar y yo sé que se va a enojar, pero no me la pega. No me trago esa parte de la víbora. Eso de echárselo a la víbora y pior a la mujer pos nomás no. ¿Cómo cabrones cree usté que se iba a aguantar un garañón sin curiosear la cosa, prencipalmente cuando andaban empelotados? Dispénseme pero no se lo creo.

—Pues entonces vaya usté al cabrón, compadre. Ya no me pida que le cuente nada, y si quiere saber algo, vaya a otra parte. Conmigo no cuenta y se acabó. Yo ya me voy.

—Espere, compa, no se vaya tan enchilado. Usté no sabe discutir como la gente educada. Luego luego se enchila.

—Vaya usté a la chingada, compadre...

Tardes calladas. Uniformes rayados. Por las tardes se frotan las quemaduras. Las líneas blancas de sudor que se secó en las camisas huelen mal pero no importa. La gente se las deja puestas para comer la primera comida caliente del día. Las cabezas de fiebre comen calladas, los movimientos lentos como si estuvieran viviendo en una eterna monotonía. Pero luego el sol se va apagando y poco a poco los cuerpos resucitan; los jóvenes, como el Chale y el Jusito salen a los billares, a la botica, al mono, al otro cachete para gastar las cinco lanas que les quedó. Los viejos al contrario se van a hacer las compras de la semana y a pagar lo que quedaron a deber. Luego con su six-pack se regresan a la casa contentos de aire fresco, soltando una lengua que todo el día estuvo gorda y seca. Y por allí cerca, detrás de los mezquites y los guames, por el arroyo, y por el llano, los chamacos corren y gritan, palpando la vida. Juegan a los encantados, a la roña, a la víbora de la mar mientras que por otras partes voces viejas, voces apagadas, voces y más voces siguen negando la muerte. Entra la noche gigante y negra. Con sus pasos sordos y un deseo de estrangular. La gente recula. Los moyotes chillones les dicen al oído que ya es hora de meter las sillas. Una por una las lucecitas cuadradas brotan como magia; las casitas de adobe también se engarruñan, se encogen con la noche. Sólo así podrán resistir su peso.

Dicen que Pedro el Tragaplumas nació con un corazón muy grande y que por eso tenía que respirar con la boca abierta. Que no le cabía, dicen, pero creo que eso era sólo parte de la razón. Pedro había nacido con la boca lista para reírse y la cosa más insignificante, el chiste más malo, lo hacía soltar la carcajada. La única vez que cerró la boca fue cuando se tragó las plumas. Le pegaron fuerte y alto a la pelota destripada y Pedro la logró coger: con la boca. Y aun así, después se rió. Por eso yo creo que no había en él lugar para tragedia.

Tampoco puedo creer que su corazón fuera capaz de reventarse. Y es que su corazón era de risa, una risa líquida que se escurría por los pantalones. Por eso después de la escuela, todos se iban a refrescar a la botica. Lo arrinconaban para que no pudiera levantarse, y entonces empezaban los chistes. Ratos después, se levantaba toda la tropa con Pedro en medio, para que no lo viera la gente. Porque la risa líquida ya se había desahogado. Otras veces por la calle:

—A que no se lo picas.

—A que sí...

Y se acercaba Pedro muy despichadito por detrás del señor. Después salía corriendo. Meado de risa.

Esta noche de sábado la plebe cierra la cantina. Pero esta noche, aunque quedan picados, no sacan cerveza. Muy simple. No hay lana. Ni el Nalgas desparramadas que siempre trae de no se sabe dónde, ni el Chango gorila que lo mantiene no se sabe quién, ni el Güero descarapelao, que siempre saca del calcetín. Y aun así, el pueblo apagado no puede convencerlos de que ya es hora de descontarse.

—Que se traiga el Louie la guitarra y nos vamos a las lomas.

—No, que se traiga a su hermana.

—La tuya, hijo 'e tu...

—Órale pues, ésos. Achirápense.[25]

---

[25]cálmense.

Es el mago quien habla, el Nalgas. Se apaciguan.

—Yo no sé ustedes, pero a mí ya me lleva la trampa de hambre. Necesito refinar.

—Sí, pero todo está cerrado.

—Entonces tenemos un problema, ¿no? ¿Qué les parece? Silencio. Todos esperan las sabias palabras del Nalgas.

—Al pollero, vamos a pegale.

Los ojos de todos se abren un poco más y pronto se traza el plan. Aventar a uno de ellos enfrente del gallinero del gringo, entrar y esperar con la mano extendida hasta que la gallina se suba. Eso es, esperar como momia para que no se alboroten, y listo. Sales, le tuerces el pescuezo, y ya. Fácil. Pero ¿quién va? Silencio. No hay héroes... Después, uno por uno voltea hacia el carro. El Traga- plumas está dormido. Como siempre con la boca abierta.

—¡Pedrooo!— grita el Louie lo más fuerte posible. Después, lo demás es fácil.

—Yo voy— consiente medio dormido.

Se detienen bastante retirado, sin apagar el motor. Por todos lados ladran los perros. Y por todos lados la gente duerme como siempre. Muerta.

Se baja Pedro bambaleándose. Pronto se lo traga la oscuridad. Mientras tanto la espera en el carro es peor que el riesgo del Tragaplumas. Los minutos son horas, escopetazos, degüellos, muerte, hasta que por fin aparece la silueta y un bulto colgando al lado. Le abren la puerta y sube, jadeando. Pronto no queda más que el chirrido de las llantas en la esquina de la calle. Todos aguantan el deseo de hablar hasta que por fin dan vuelta en un callejón.

—¿Cómo te fue?

—Bien, pero nomás pude traer una.

La palpa el Chango.

—Oye ¡qué chingona está!

La pesa el Louie,

—Oye, de veras.

La levanta el Güero de las patas.

—¡Hijo de la madre, te trajiste el gallo!

Y en cinco minutos Pedro vacía toda la cerveza que trae en el cuerpo. Esa misma noche también le atacan la boca de plumas de gallo. Dizque para que se meara más. Pero nadie pudo creer que se le reventara el corazón.

El sorbete de los tubos estremece el cuerpo sentado en cuclillas y hasta ahora no había sentido el peso de la inclinada cabeza posada sobre el pecho. Chonito echa un vistazo medio dormido al agua corriente para cerciorarse de que no está soñando pero ve la acequia seca. Se habrá acabado el agua en el río, piensa, al momento que endereza el cuerpo tullido de cansancio. No se puede imaginar que se haya quedado dormido tanto tiempo, que ni siquiera el sol lo haya despertado. Un leve escalofrío le pasa por el cuerpo haciéndose dirigirse hacia el bulto que hace la camisa y el sombrero. Luego coge la pala para ir a la otra orilla con grandes esperanzas de que se haya terminado de regar la melga. Pero no necesita; José su amo se acerca.

—¿Qué pasó, Chonito, ya estuvo?

—Yo creo que no, don José, se paró la pompa.

—Ya sé. De allá vengo. Cuando venía pa acá no la oí, así que me fui a ver. Ya empezó otra vez. Yo creo que mañana acabamos ¿no?

—Si señor, nomás que no se acabe l'agua.

—Ai te traigo un lonchecito pa que te aguantes hasta el mediodía y...

—Pero ¿que no va a jalar usté en lo del viejo?

—Sí, pero voy a poner al chamaco de Leyva que la cuide. Le arreglo la presilla y los tubos nomás pa que la cuide. Al cabo es poco.

—Pos si usté quiere yo...

—No, hombre, los cabrones chotas andan como hormigas. Vale más que te vayas a mediodía y me esperes en el otro lado. Después que me paguen voy y cambio el cheque y te pago.

—Como ¿a qué hora lo veo, señor?

—Me esperas allí en el álamo como a las tres.

—Está bien, patrón.

—Y cuídate porque...

—No se preocupe, don José, en eso ya estoy bien quemao.

—Bueno, allá te veo más tarde.

En un instante José desaparece en el mar algodonero del río mientras que Chonito vuelve a sentarse en el borde, esta vez para ponerse las botas torcidas llenas de misericordia mientras que las nalgas se refrescan con la tierra húmeda. El chamaco, a pesar de que ésta es la tercer noche de insomnio que ha pasado, no hace por irse a dormir en alguna sombra cercana. Se siente feliz porque esta vez su amo va a fregar pato. No se cansa de contemplar los cuarenta acres de plantas bien cargaditas de fruto. Quisiera que el señor José se hubiera estado aquí a su lado para compartir con él los preciosos capullos que empiezan a reventar, verlos besar el agua. Pero Chonito sabe que es mucho pedir. José el enamorado de una tierra que ya no es de él, José el de las piernas arqueadas tiene que ser más que inquilino. Por eso se ha ido a unir con el grupo de limpiadores que dirige Teléforo.

De Presidio sólo el recuerdo de las nubes y del diablo. Flaco éste, gordotas aquéllas, ambos se resbalan por el cielo burlándose de la gente, de los animales, de las plantas. Nunca llueve en Presidio y el estruendo que sale de la garganta de esas nubes sólo sirve para llenar el hueco de silencio por un instante, pero ni siquiera el eco en la sierrita de la Santa Cruz sirve para asustar al diablo. El sinvergüenza nunca se olvida del pueblo. Con su mano firme aplasta los chaparros y la hierba mal crecida. Con las dos exprime las aguas del Río Grande que antes fue y lo reduce a espejismo, a charco.

Pero el patas de chivo no es todo maldad. Tiene un columpio muy largo en la cumbre de la sierra y de vez en cuando aparece en los bailes como galán. Otras veces aparece en forma de burro y se deja montar hasta que los chamacos descubren, con un palo, que no tiene culo y entonces desaparece, dejando el olfato de cologne francés. Sin embargo, la broma que prefiere más es la del gato y el ratón jugando a las escondidas. El chiste es de cuidar la gota de agua que divide dos tierras, como si no fuera la misma. El gato patrullero, con ceño fruncido, espera en acoso al ratón, cuya defensa carga en el estómago en forma de hambre. Brinca el ratón el charco y empieza la pesquisa ridícula mientras que el diablo se rueda por el suelo a carcajadas.

El sol se lo bebe, lo quema. El sol se ríe porque lo marchita. Las plantas, como él, se sienten inútiles, sin saber qué hacer, mientras que el sol bebe sediento hasta chupar la última gota.

Chonito quiere llorar pero no puede. Le duele la garganta, aun cuando está entre el agua hasta el pescuezo. Sabe que no debe moverse porque se le va el agua y tiembla de miedo. Gime. Mientras tanto el chamaco se está convirtiendo en vapor.

Sigue en su misma posición y revive de nuevo el incidente. Había sido rápido. Después que se había ido don José, se había reclinado sobre la pala y de inmediato lo había vencido el sueño. Los jeeps de la migra lo habían despertado y como bocabierta se había puesto a ver la pesquisa sin fijarse en el boquete de la acequia por donde se estaba colando el agua. Parecía como si nunca hubiera visto esa escena—de oír el "aaaagua" de los mojados y luego un montón de cabezas voladas hacia el río. ¿Cuántas veces había presenciado el espectáculo, pataleadas de viejos y niños o de algún accidente como el del mes pasado? Había volado el avión patrullero muy bajito, hasta nivel de cabeza y zas. El señor a caballo había perdido la cabeza muy finito. Quesque por la noche la anda buscando todavía. O de la semana pasada cuando encontraron al chicuelo regordito, flotando en la acequia. Dicen que el chota quería nomás asustarlo con las zambullidas porque seguía cruce y cruce.

Después que se había pasado todo el fandango, se había fijado en el agua
que se salía, y al principio no se alteró pero luego le entraron ansias y empezó
a palear como loco. El agua se llevaba la tierra y el agujero se hacía más grande.
Paleó hasta que le sangraron las ampollas y luego, sin encontrar salida, se había
quitado los zapatos, se había metido al agua y se había atravesado en el boquete.
Y así había que esperar a don José, quien no tardaría en volver, ya que era cerca
de la una.

La angustia y todo se le calma cuando piensa en lo hombre que es. Todo
puede hacer ya aunque apenas tiene doce años—el azadón, la pala, la pizca, el
empaque, todo. Y porque sabe que lo puede hacer como los grandes, siente
orgullo. Pero luego vuelve a la situación en que se encuentra y siente vergüenza.
¿Qué irá a decir don José? Por bruto. El agua está muy escasa y si el viejo la ve
corriendo por el camino, se va a enojar. Qué bruto, se me durmió el gallo.

Ahora vuelve a sentir sueño por el agua fresca que le corre entre los brazos,
las piernas, el pescuezo. El murmullo del agua lo arrulla pero resiste porque se
siente muy raro, algo así como flotando en el aire, como que no hay fin a la
espera. Como aquella vez cuando por casualidad había empezado a marchar el
tractor. No había sabido qué hacer sino dar vueltas y más vueltas en círculo hasta
que se le acabara la gasolina. Había pasado una eternidad borracha hasta que se
le había ocurrido chocarlo contra una treila.[26] Después había salido corriendo
hasta su casa. Pero esa vez había encontrado salida. No como ahora. Ahora
tendría que esperar y esperar y esperar...

José necesita dar grandes estrujones a Chonito enroscado para poder volver-
lo en sí, y cuando por fin abre los ojos, suelta el llanto. Entonces se desahoga el
muchacho entumecido en el pecho del hombre. Pero después que se le ha pasado
el susto a José, no puede contener una sonrisa y el chamaco, al notarlo, para de
llorar y se desprende bruscamente. Luego sale corriendo hacia el río. Mientras
tanto las carcajadas lo siguen golpeando y no cesa la burla hasta que llega a las
orillas del río.

El diablo se pone juguetón pero por el momento no se le ocurre nada; sólo
contemplar su cuerpo en el espejo. Desnudo así, se ve que no tiene sexo. Ni
pelos. De frente su sexo parece un bizcochito de niña recién nacida. Da la vuelta
y no se encuentra al ano. Quiere ahora pensar en algún símil, en alguna metáfora
para su bello cuerpo pero no puede encontrar una "feliz comparación". Piensa y
piensa y lo único que le viene es una serie de interrogantes. Esta incapacidad le

---

[26]una casa portátil, movible por coche.

molesta tanto que lo pone de mal humor y entonces busca otra manera de deleitarse. De inmediato se mete en un traje de payaso y se contempla en el espejo de nuevo. ¡Bah! El juego es demasiado pueril. No le vale afuera. Debe ponerse más serio con sus bromas; tiene que seguir burlándose de la vida humana.

Ahora se arquea las cejas puntiagudas con un negro pincel y en seguida estira el brazo para rascar azul de cielo. Este se lo talla en las pupilas. Como último toque a la parte superior del cuerpo, se casca una peluca rubia y un sombrero tejano. Luego busca un traje para cubrirse lo demás y encuentra el verde oscuro, su preferido. Cuando ya se lo puso, a pujidos se mete unas botas que le cubren las patas de gallo. ¡Ah! Allí está. De paso se guiña el ojo en el lago que usa como espejo. Ya afuera, se monta en su columpio... pero... ¡momento! ¡Por poco se le olvida! Sin embargo, hay tiempo todavía. De manera que no se preocupa. Se cimbra alto, alto, hasta que alcanza una estrella. De inmediato la arranca y se la prende donde debe palpitar el corazón. ¡Listo! El diablo está listo para seguir su chiste eterno.

Cuando quieres llegar a Presidio te vas por un camino apretado de guames y mezquites. Con el aire pegado a las pestañas y una mente retrasada, el cuerpo se te suelta y se te cae en una noria que nunca terminó de escarbarse. O te resbalas por un embudo. Antes de caer te sientas en la cumbre de la loma para divisar, al fondo, las cagarrutas de chiva: casas que resaltan como huérfanas entre los vastos terrenos agrícolas. Casas de adobe maltratado, casas que piden misericordia a Dios. Casas: zapatos viejos que se abandonaron a un sol que engarruña todo. Tú como borracho te sueltas de la cumbre y luego te dejas resbalar por un camino que parte a Presidio en dos. A paso de rueda, Johnny's Bar, Texaco, Ron's Lumber, Halper's (al que le barrenaron la sien para hacerlo que soltara la lana), Phillip's 66, Juárez General Store. A paso de rueda.

—¿Y el centro? ¿Y la vida?

—Ah, pues éste es Presidio, señor. No pregunte más que no sabría decile. ¿Que qué? Ah, sí. La gente la encuentra en la orilla del río, entre lo verde, por debajo del puente, por encima.

—And what's across the border? Mexico?

—Sí, señor, Ojinaga. (Presidio partido en dos hace tiempo.)

—¿Reyes Uranga?

—La segunda casa con gallinero. Pero de día no vive allí, sólo de noche.

—¿Y el joven?

—¿José? Oh, ése ya es otra cosa. Si no está en casa, pos búsquelo en lo verde del melón, de la lechuga, del algodón, entre un costal, o sobre una pala al mediodía de tacos y kool-aid. Quizás en la empacadora. Oiga y ¿quién es usté?

—George Evans de Marfa. Quiero habla con él, ¿entiende?

—¿Que anda mal?

—No no. Nomás habla.

—Entonces si así es lo encontrará entre vagones congelados del Santa Fe jugando a la pelota en el packing shed de Jones entre manos grietudas, pantalonudas, garzoludas, sudadas.

—¿Dónde?

—¿Que dónde está? Pues mire, sigue el mismo camino hasta afuera y allí donde están los corrales de las vacas, allí mero está la empacadora de Jones.

—Muchas gracias.

—De nada.

(Doce horas por 50 por 70 centavos entre 10,000 por 10 menos transporte, menos los melones que se comen, menos los que no vinieron hoy porque les dio vómito y torzón o se emborracharon, menos el adelanto de Carrasco que no regresó. He's still a hardworking ole boy. See if I can get 'im to train for shipping orders.)

—Joe! Here's someone to see you.

—He's in the toledo, Mr. Jones.

—Done something wrong, Mr. . . .

—Evans. No, I just came to talk to him about some incident last night.

—He'll be out in a minute. Hey! Son of a bitch! I told you. . .más rapido, Manuel. Cajones aquee. The fellow's getting old, you know? I just keep him around to help 'im out, but we get old sometime, you know? Hey, here he comes.

—Joe Uranga? I'm George Evans from. . .

—No sir, I'm Joe Durango. Uranga is not working here.

—Damn it, I thought you said Durango, Mr. Evans. I'm sorry. . .

—Know where I can find him?

—Yes sir. He work with Mr. Lynch at the farm. But he don't go by the name of Joe. They call 'im José.

—What's the dif. . .oh well, thank you, and sorry to bother you, Mr. Jones.

—No bother. . . Hey! Son of a. . .more cajones over there!

La lluvia quiere derretir la casa de Dios pero no puede. Picotea la ventana inútilmente y cuando se cansa, desliza sus lágrimas de rabia por la pared. Luego, para conformarse en su derrota, entra por la puerta que de vez en cuando se abre y rocía a los cuerpos cercanos. Pero a estos hombres atrincherados tampoco les importa que los moje. Están allí por gusto. Están para pasar revista de las piernas y para adivinar la razón por qué ha llegado tarde tal y tal, como ahora lo hacen con Marcela. Todos la miran, todos la piensan—la mujer que espera eternamente... No se sabe si al pasar por el agua bendita se le olvidó hacerse la cruz o no quiso; sólo toma asiento y empieza a limpiarse la cara con un paño. (No debía haber venido. Todos los ojos me ven, saben. Bien me lo dijo mamá, no vayas, pero yo insistí. Ahora lo que voy a pasar aquí son puros nervios.) "Queridos hijos míos, no hay que temer, dejad de preocuparos. Tengamos confianza en Dios, él sabe lo que hace". (Si padre, pero ahora el río no me va a dejar pasar. Yo quiero irme con José. Tengo mucho miedo de que me estén esperando afuera y me lleven a la oficina.) "Sabemos que la creciente puede ser desastrosa para nosotros pero el evangelio..." (Dios mío, ¿qué voy a hacer si no me dejan ir a casa, si me detienen y me preguntan por José? Dios mío, ayúdame...) "Y ahora recemos, roguémosle al Señor que nos saque de peligro, que nos eche la bendición. Oremos..."

Ha sido breve el sermón. El cura siente la misma impaciencia de la congregación. No hay más que decir; todos saben que sus esperanzas quedaron en bancarrota. Ahora se ponen de pie, menos Marcela. Se queda sentada un ratito más porque en estos momentos sus piernas son de hule y porque ya no se puede mover como antes. Ya se cansa mucho. Se le hinchan los pies. Su vientre de río crecido la hace sentirse muy incómoda, ahora más que de costumbre porque "ya hace bastante rato que le estoy dando lata. Eso digo yo porque ni siquiera hace el esfuerzo de pararse. Juzgo que ahora la molesto más porque he oído comentar que cuando me muevo la lastimo, y me imagino que ahora que estoy más desarrollado y más fuerte será un tanto peor. Sin duda que eso estará pasando en este momento; le estaré torciendo el estómago de lo lindo porque así me pasa cuando se me ocurren cosas. Me muevo mucho. Yo no quiero hacerlo pero hace poco decidí afilar la poca memoria que tengo y acumular cosas que han pasado para escribirlo todo cuando nazca. Y el esfuerzo por recordar y ponerlo en orden me hace moverme, como ahora lo estoy haciendo. Mi pobre mamá no sabe de mis facultades; no sabe que tengo una imagen bastante precisa de ella y de lo que ocurre afuera. Piensa que lo que trae en el estómago no siente, ni oye, ni piensa. Pero está equivocada. La sorpresa que se llevará cuando pueda escribir tan pronto como nazca. Es algo fastidioso para mí estar metido aquí, estar flotando siempre como en un chicle líquido y pegajoso. Cuando me estiro siento de inmediato pegar los pies y las manos contra una red. Me imagino que así se sienten las moscas cuando quieren despegarse de la telaraña. También pienso en mi pobre mamá. Lo que le duele. Yo quisiera ya haber nacido pero ella insiste en que no, porque cree que así es mejor para mí y como todos los sentimientos de una madre, no quiere ver sufrir a su hijo. Todo por mi hijo, dice. El caso es que yo me siento mal porque sé de los sufrimientos que ella pasa allá afuera y no puedo hacer nada. Estoy con las manos atadas y a veces no me enojo con ella sino con lo que oigo que está pasando y lo que imagino. Y mi mamá con el mismo tesón. Por eso ha resistido parirme. No quiero que mi hijo sufra, dice, pero yo creo que ya bastó de protección. ¿Se imaginan ustedes lo que será cargar un niño en el vientre tanto tiempo? Yo ya me cansé de...perdón mamá. Voy a acomodarme un poco ah...ay...ya ya oí las campanitas. Ponte, ponte de rodillas así, así... Ahora prometo quedarme quietecito mientras que el padre se toma la sangre de Dios. Si la situación es igual que todos los domingos, la iglesia estará llenita. Y común. Como un retrato cansado que todo representa. El padre al frente con sus ademanes. Vestido igual. Palabras iguales. Todos somos pecadores pero los humildes iremos al cielo. Hay que sufrir para ganar la vida perdurable. Cristo por eso amó y sufrió. El nos puso el ejemplo y hay que imitarlo. Al frente estarán los niños que todavía no aprenden los movimientos en orden ni saben los responsos. Poco les importa. Cerca estarán las beatas vestidas de negro pegadas a las estatuas y a las velas que chorrean, sumidas en oración. Igual. Al otro extremo, mero atrás, estarán los más humildes, como si fuera costumbre de siglos. Igual. El retrato de la iglesia y su congregación sugiere todo. El retrato fastidioso se repite al comulgar. La línea de derecha irá primero, quizá por estar más seguros de la salvación mientras que la otra línea espera. ¡La campanita! ¡Suena otra vez la campanita! Mi mamá y todos agachan la cabeza cuando el padre levanta la representación del cuerpo en pan redondo. Nunca supe por qué lo hace, digo, por qué agachan la cabeza. ¿Será por costumbre o por respeto? ¿Será por el miedo al misterio o por sentir culpa de comerse el cuerpo de Cristo que no creen merecer? Quién sabe. También pienso que es ridículo sentir los golpes que se da mi mamá en el pecho, algo que tampoco entiendo. Parece que quiere castigarse, golpearse el corazón porque le late. ¿Acaso se siente culpable de estar viva o reniega de estarlo? Levántate ya mamá, desentumécete primero. Siquiera esta vez sé tú primera. Andale, gánales. Mira que tú tienes el mismo derecho. La verdad es que ya no te importa. Pero debe. Mira esa niña. Déjame salir para darle una bofetada. ¿Por qué se te adelanta y te hace a un lado? ¿Que tiene también más privilegio que tú aun en la casa de Dios? Pero no debo molestarte con estos berrinches. Te prometo calmarme. Ahora... abre la boca...así, así. Anda, ya regrésate pero no entrelaces las manos por favor porque no quiero que te caigas como la semana pasada. Recuerda que anoche no comiste".

Marcela se regresa al asiento con piernas de mantequilla. Después que el cura le ha dado la hostia, le ha dicho que la espere porque quiere hablarle. Ella, consternada, se ha ido a arrodillar en la última fila detrás de un viejo robusto como si esto fuera a quitarle el miedo. Allí, de rodillas, reza y (¿que si me saliera ahorita, rápido, sin esperar que se acabe la misa? Sin duda el padre ya sabe y quiere preguntarme por José. Dios mío, ya no aguanto más...)

Afuera, el agua menudita sigue picoteando mientras que la congregación se pone de pie. En ese momento nota Marcela a un señor alto, güero que entra sin quitarse el sombrero stetson y se pasa hasta el frente como si ésta fuera su casa. Luego se regresa con unos ojos de águila que se columpian de lado a lado. Ella siente un fuerte estremecimiento pero lo disfraza, componiéndose el velo. Cuando el señor la nota, se detiene momentáneamente frente a ella y le sonríe. Luego le guiña el ojo y sale. Ella queda pasmada sin poderse mover.

"Ya mamá. Ya se acabó la misa. Salte ya. ¿Por qué te late tanto el corazón? Que, ¿qué? ¿Está lloviendo todavía? ¿Cómo le vas a hacer para llegar a casa? No puedes correr... ¡Te sientas a esperar? Pero no...por favor no corras. Mamáaa...

Cuando llegó a casa, Marcela venía agazapándose y echando manoteadas al aire. Gritaba que se lo quitaran.

—Pero, ¿a quién hija?— le preguntaba la viejita mientras que Chonito hacía los ojos más redondos.

—¡El diablo!— aulló la mujer aterrorizada.

Con el ave maría purísima en la boca, Vicke pronto le hizo unas crucecitas en la frente y empezó a rociar el cuarto de agua bendita. Luego que hubo hecho esto le dio una cucharada de azúcar para el susto, y de esta manera fue calmándola lo suficiente para que les dijera lo que había pasado.

—Luego, luego que salí de la iglesia se me pegó una sombra que me repetía que no me iba a dejar pasar. Y se reía y se reía como loca.

—Han de ser los nervios, señora— balbuceaba Chonito.

—Sí, hija. Es el miedo.

—Les digo que lo vi. Tenía diferentes formas. Primero parecía como que se estaba columpiando y me quería tumbar cada vez que se mecía. Fue cuando empecé a correr y entonces él se hizo borrego y a topetes me traía por delante. Cuando me vio caer en el suelo se volvió a reír. Después desapareció en...pol... ¡Aaaay! ¡Quítenmelo! ¡Aaaay viene! ¡Por favor!

Comienza a manotear Marcela, echándose a correr de un cuarto a otro. Se vuelca la mesa y quiebra los trastes. Luego barre con todo lo que se le pone en frente. La viejita y Chonito la atrapan sobre la cama y allí forcejean con ella hasta dominarla. La mujer tiene las manos engarruñadas.

—¡Por favor, ayúdame! ¡Mírame los dedos, Vicke! ¡No puedo estirarlos!

Marcela trata de extendérselos ella misma pero se la traban los dedos unos con otros. Entonces intenta salir corriendo de nuevo pero los dos la sujetan con fuerza mientras que Vicke le habla, le reza, le hace cruces sobre las manos paralizadas y le soba todo el cuerpo. Poco a poco se va calmando la mujer histérica hasta que por fin puede mover los dedos. Pero la vista se llena de lejanía. No contesta a las preguntas. No reacciona a nada aun cuando la viejita trata de darle caldo con su propia mano. Marcela no abre la boca; sólo se queda sentada en la cama como zombie, los ojos paralizados en la pared. Cuando todo ha resultado unútil, tienden el cuerpo sobre la cama. Marcela no resiste. Piensan Vicke y Chonito que quizá con una dormidita se le pase pero no saben que la mujer mantendrá los ojos dilatados el resto del día.

El diablo se retira para morirse de gusto. Luego, cansado se acuesta sobre las piedras húmedas para roncar a sus anchas.

Chonito se levanta del piso donde rendido ha quedado después de pasar el río y va directamente a la cazuela llena de agua. Luego que la vació afuera, vuelve a buscar el gotero a ciegas. Cuando por fin escucha el tin sobre el peltre lo centraliza debajo de la gota. En seguida, saca el paño y lo pone sobre la cazuela porque de otra manera el sonido no lo va a dejar dormir. Hecho esto, se acerca a la cama de Marcela para cerciorarse de que está bien. Los profundos ronquidos lo dejan satisfecho. ¡Vaya! Por fin ha quedado dormida. El ni se acuerda. Tanto que había llorado la mujer. "Ya se me hacía que no la controlábamos. La tembladera que se cargaba. Pobre señora, ni siquiera cuando le aseguré que el señor José estaba bien y que la estaba esperando, se consolaba. Es la primera vez que la veo tan, tan, no sé cómo explicarlo, pero estaba hecha pedazos por dentro. Dicen que las mujeres cuando están esperando se ponen así. Quiera Dios que sea verdad porque si no, esta mujer se nos está volviendo loca. Juraría que ya estaba cuando llegué. Ojalá que no le vaya a seguir ese mal".

"Ah, cómo quisiera platicar contigo Chonito. Darte las gracias por todo lo que has hecho. Hacerte comprender por qué mi mamá está así. Es que trae cien años, fíjate Chonito, cien años de historia indignada en la panza. Su enfermedad es de palabras que no pueden salir de aquí, de sus entrañas. Se quedan pegadas en la boca del estómago hasta hacerla vomitar. Día y noche allí la tienes con ese mal, destinada a nunca acostumbrarse. No, Chonito, mamá no está volviéndose loca. Está enferma de palabras que pronuncia como suspiro en oídos que no retienen nada. Y entonces esas mismas palabras se retachan hacia atrás, entrando de nuevo por la boca y aposentándose aquí. Luego la hacen que devuelva el estómago. Por eso llora mi mamá y quiera Dios que antes de nacer no me vayan a envenenar porque también a mí me hieren. También yo siento la boca como si la tuviera llena de alfileres. Ojalá que salga pronto de aquí porque me fastidia mucho este silencio de hiel. Mientras tanto Chonito, si puedes, no los dejes entrar. No dejes cantar a los poetas esas épicas gloriosas de la vida. Córtales los güevos por mí, mientras yo nazca. Si te hablan de hazañas, pídeles a los muertos que aplaudan y los cubran de besos leprosos; si hay amor en sus versos, cántales corridos; si belleza encuentran en el valle de Presidio, cuéntales del diablo y de su cueva. Muéstrales como se hizo el amor con los indios. Si de virtud se inspiran, Chonito, llévalos arriba, donde la gente de los milagros deja piernas, brazos y unos ojos de metal. Nunca un cuerpo entero. Nunca un cuerpo vivo. Pero descansa, Chonito, al cabo que ni me oyes. Algún día y ya pronto, encenderé la chispa, les quemaré los pies. Algún día no dormirán porque la noche les pesará mucho, como una pelota atada a los pies con una cadena o como pelota de hule muerto. Los cuerpos de los trabajadores cansados se retorcerán en sus lechos, rechinarán sus huesos. Y los muertos les invadirán la mente, los harán llorar, los harán reír, los volverán locos. Sí Chonito, algún día no dormirán, no dormirán, no dormirán..."

Ha cesado de llover. Adentro los goteros se cansaron de cae y cae. Ahora el silencio se hace aplastante, enorme. La noche, como el cuerpo de Marcela, pareció también caer exhausta. Nada se mueve. Ni las estrellas, ni las nubes. Ni la tuna. Nada. Las casas están embadurnadas contra la noche. Engarrotamiento y silencio de plomo. Sólo un vientecito desorientado pasa sus manos frescas por las barbas del álamo afuera de vez en cuando. Entonces el árbol siente el escalofrío y responde con un leve sonido de pandereta.

Marcela entreabre los ojos pero no ve nada por el momento. Sólo adivina los bultos de Chonito y Vicke durmiendo esparcidos en el cuartito. Está acostada de lado porque ya hace mucho que no puede ponerse de espaldas. Ni lucha le hace. El bebé que ha resistido parir es como traer una tonelada de cobre en la panza. Fraguado en forma de cono puntiagudo. Acostumbra un poco más los ojos a la oscuridad mientras piensa en José, José, cómo estará, el río grande, no hay pase, misa, el padre, llovió, lloré, dormí, qué hora, serán las tres.

Detesta levantarse a estas horas y quisiera poder aguantarse hasta que amanezca porque sabe lo que le espera afuera. El zoquetal, el fríto, y luego el asiento de madera mojado. Tiene que salir aunque sea sólo un chorrito insignificante. La presión del niño es mucha. Hace rechinar la cama al incorporarse y busca las chanclas con los mismos pies y cuando los encuentra, se los casca. Luego se cubre hasta la cabeza con la cobija y camina hacia la puerta.

—¿Señora?

—Ahorita vengo, Chonito, voy afuera— le contesta en voz baja.

—Marcela, ¿eres tú?— la viejita se sienta en la cama.

—Sí, voy a hacer aguas.

—¿Quieres que vaya contigo?

—No mamá, si horita vengo— y sale de inmediato sin esperar la insistencia de la viejita.

El excusado de lámina no está lejos pero tiene que pelear con el lodo pegajoso que quiere robarle los zapatos. Pronto se pone a la puerta, anticipando lo mojado que estará adentro. La casita es un verdadero cedazo. Se sube al helado trono, se levanta la capa y luego se sienta, atrapando las manos debajo de cada nalga. Toda esta incomodidad para tan poca cosa. Es que el niño ya anda muy abajo. "A veces parece que traigo la cabecita entre las piernas. Pero no le hace...ya, ai va...se está moviendo otra vez. Muévete, m'ijo, muévete porque sólo así estoy segura de que no te me has muerto. No importa que me duelas. Muévete para que no me preocupes. No sé qué te ha pasado pero ya no te mueves como antes. Debiera sentirte más, con lo avanzada que estoy, Ándale...así...así..."

La mujer regresa y se vuelve a acostar. El feto se sigue moviendo con unos movimientos suaves, serenos. Ella los disfruta. Se siente feliz porque allí en sus entrañas hay vida. "No te preocupes mamá. Sé que no estás sola. No me sientes porque no quiero causarte daño. Nomás cuando me canso de estar así como si estuviera rezando engarruñado, me tengo que estirar. Pero lo hago con cuidado, ahora que he descubierto que si estiro las manos primero y luego las piernas, es menos dolor para ti. Por eso ya no me sientes, porque ya no acostumbro patalearte. Ahora...me estoy acomodando porque sabes, la noche ha sido muy larga y he estado de cabeza dormido. Ya me estaba pesando mucho la sangre. No sé por qué me quedé dormido así. Quizá porque tu corazón latía demasiado fuerte o porque te gruñían las tripas. Sabes, esto te sucede a ti muchas veces, como ayer que no cenaste, ¿recuerdas? ¿Cómo te quedaste dormida? El susto que nos diste a todos. Vino tu comadre a verte y Teléforo casi cruzaba el río para avisar a papá pero entrada la noche te tranquilizaste. Eran puros nervios. Yo los sentí tan apretados como cuerdas aquí dentro. Imagínate como estaba yo, con el tun, tun, de tu corazón a prisa en mi cabeza, y tus nervios y tus tripas revolcándose como creciente. Estos son los momentos cuando sufro yo más, porque tu corazón no es verdad que está en el pecho, sino en el vientre. Aquí lo tengo palpitando entre mis manos y yo hago lo posible por hacer el menor movimiento. Hace días descubrí que me puedo mover como un compás; si te acuestas de lado, me atravieso en tu vientre en posición vertical; si te paras me pongo en posición horizontal; si haces movimientos que no entiendo, me dejo flotar sin resistir. Por eso no me sientes mamá, y ojalá que comprendas. Estoy normal, voy creciendo rápido. No sabes, pero desde que empecé a ejercitar la mente, noté yo mismo el desarrollo. Desde que me puse a pensar en escribir cuando naciera. Y ahora no me importa este desorden. Ya vendrá el tiempo. Ahora lo que importa es dejar todo volar, soltar la lengua hasta que llegue el tiempo. Por primera vez estoy contento de poder ver tan claro desde aquí madre. No hay necesidad de estar fuera ni que sea de día porque tú me lo comunicas. A ti se te trasluce el alma. Cuando estás alegre se te vuelve mariposa blanca y cuando sufres, la mariposita sangra bañándome todo el cuerpo. Esta noche quise hablar con Chonito y explicarle tu locura, pero creo que no me oyó. Esta es una cosa que no entiendo. Parece que unas gentes me oyen cuando pienso y otras no. Yo quisiera saber si de veras tienen sentidos, si de veras oyen. No sé por qué no ha sido hasta ahora que se me haya ocurrido lo lento que ha sido mi vida. Apenas hoy me doy cuenta que yo me extiendo como un hilito muy fino hasta muy atrás, desde tu niñez yo te llevaba en mis venas. Acuérdate también que tú sólo me diste tu vientre para que allí creciera pero que mucho antes, ya venía semilla volando brincando de vientre en vientre. Imagínate cien años de existencia antes de nacer, buscando donde pegar mis raíces. Pero ya descansa, mamá, que la noche ha sido larga".

Después que se descontó l'agua, la nochi se puso buti suave. Muy de aquella se puso, con fregales de estrellas por todas madres. Poco a poco las nubes se vían escurrido como si tenían escame[27] hasta dejar un friego de alfileres aluminados. Simón, el cielo parecía una cuilca[28] calota como ésas que usan los reyes pa taparse el esqueleto.

Downtown toda la raza jue saliendo de los chantes,[29] a ver qué fregaos taba pasando en el pueblo escueto. Todas iban a patín porque los jefitos no vían cooperao con las ranflas.[30] Además se necesita gota pa dar el round y también está escasa de a madre como todo el borlo. La pinchi lluvia no vía dejado camellar[31] toda la semana así que unos batos tenían que contentarse con milal como el chinito la nochi del diciséis. Los otros se vían ponido[32] a tirar crape[33] de a nicle[34] detrás de a que Johnny's Bar, al cabo que con un bola ni siquiera te ponías feeling. Y si la traías parada pos podías hacer roncha y luego te ibas a

---

[27]miedo.

[28]capa.

[29]casas.

[30]coches.

[31]trabajar.

[32]se habían puesto.

[33]jugar a los dados.

[34]una moneda de cinco centavos.

jugar pool por beeria.[35] Pero si no, pos quedabas brujo de a madre y como siempre, así pasaba con los que andaban más jodidos que las mangas de un chaleco. En los cabrones dados el bato más zura[36] siempre salía ganando. Así que aunque les tronaras los dedos de a madre y les soplaras y los trataras como jainas,[37] siempre vinían las jodidas burras. Ni siquiera little Joe, ni Fiva la viva, ni Sixto el ojo de plata te hacían caso. Te tiraban a loco aunque les periquearas. Chingao, parecía que los dados taban loaded.

En otras veces los batos no estaban aquí haciéndose pendejos solos. A esta hora andaban en el Otro tirando chancla, watchando[38] las rucas, cavuleando todo el pedo. En las ramadas y los congales todo bien de aquella. Chavas dando güelta y güelta en la plaza como disco rayado, mascando goma, esperando que te les acercaras y les cantaras. "Esa, vamos a echarnos una cartita allí donde están los trompas de hule[39]; ésa no me corte que estoy chaparro". Después si pegabas, te la llevabas y le apañabas una coca y le tirabas líneas de aquella. Si tenías suerte y le caibas bien a la chava tú le podías cai a la brava: "Esa vamos a lo oscurito pa tirar pichón[40]". Si nel, pos te la llevabas suave nomás tirando chancla.[41] De todos modos vías pegado y el borlote era calmala, llevártela suave. ¿Pero horita? Ni qué pelarle, ta de a madre gacho el pedo. A güevo te la pasas con una pata en la esquina, watchando a los rucos dando el round, todos agüitados, todos escamaos que el jodido río se suelte meando por todos laos. Entonces sí, se joden ellos y tú también. Los cabrones chotas también andan güelta y güelta como si eso iba a detenelo, pero lo suyo es puro pedo porque no tienen ni qué chingaos cuidar. ¿Quién va a pasar pa acá con toda esa agua? Además te cuesta un güevo cruzar en el chalán.[42] Nomás los batos que vienen al borlo de allá del Chuco, Kermit, y el Odesson train lana pa pabuleale cinco grandes al Trompas que se jugó chango y se apañó la lanchita pa estar pase y pase gente pa'l Otro. Pero esta noche jodida, raspa, ni esos pasan. Nomás el cielo está suave. O te quedas en el

---

[35]cerveza.

[36]suertudo, de mucha suerte.

[37]mujeres.

[38]mirando.

[39]músicos.

[40]besarse.

[41]bailando.

[42]canoa o barco.

chante a aplastar oreja[43] o le cais a la jefita con el bola que siempre tiene escondido y te pelas al show. Pero no seas pendejo; no te vayas a jugarlo en los crapes porque ni al mono vas a poder ir.

El Chale que ha estado bonkeado toda la tarde, se levanta y se va al toliro.[44] Recuerda el date que tienen él y Jusito y se pone a alistar. Allí frente al espejo se quita la güeva remojándose la máscara y luego con la lija se hace una barba blanca como Santo Clos. Saca la zura y al recle le quedan los cachetes bien lisos. A su jaina le gustan así. Ahora se embarra la greña con grasa Parrot y se hace un ducktail padre. Al agacharse se da cola que los calcos tan bien cateados y de volada se los pasa por detrás de los Khakis porque no hay tiempo pa'l speedshine. Ya van a ser las eight y aquel bato ya estará esperando con las rucas. Así que pronto se deja cai el zurrón, dejándose la lisa desabrochada de arriba pa esportear su pecho peludo, y listo. "No voy a refinar jefita. Ai la watcho al recle".[45]

Cuando se iba a subir a la carcacha del jefito, se fijó que estaba ponchada y se caldeó tanto que la agarró a patadas hasta que le dolió el dedo gordo. Después que le echó la última madre le puso el bato en el dodge patitas. El agüite[46] no se le calmó de volada porque pensaba todavía en las fiestas que iba a perder aunque sabía bien el peligro de cruzar. Recordó la chinga que le vían ponido al Betabel pero él vía tenido la culpa que lo filerearan[47] porque ¿cómo se pone a tumbale la ruca a aquel bato así a la brava? Simón, él vía tenido la culpa. Ta mejor que no puedas pasar. Mejor calmantes montes aquí hasta que se apacigüe el pedo. ¿Qué le pelas? Aquí tienes pichón con la Mary, ése. No seas jodido con ella, la ruca ta encanicada, te quiere chingos. Si no, ¿cómo te ha aguantado tanto? Pero el bato vía contado con la ranfla pa sacarse de llevala al mono[48] porque andaba bruja. El único bola que le vía quedado se le vía ido en gota[49] y ahora la mugre ponchada. Valía más que el Jusito... a este bato jodido nada le agüita. Toda es pura pinchi risa y yo creo que así lurio va a morir. Nunca sabes qué va a hacer, con qué va a salir, en qué pedo te va a meter. Y esa desgraciada

---

[43]dormir.

[44]baño.

[45]al rato.

[46]enojo o enfado.

[47]apuñalaron.

[48]el cine.

[49]gasolina.

costumbre de andar picando chiclosos cada vez que das la espalda me agüita de a madre. Y las pendejadas que dice, pero eso sí, el bato nunca se te raja en ninguna parte. Vale más que esta noche me aliviane el bato.

Cuando llegó el Chale a la botica brincando charcos, al Jusito le agarró una risota de poco pelo y el Chale nomás lo dejó que se curara a gusto.

—Uuu, qué bato éste. ¿Pos no que la ranfla y que yo y que...

—Nel ése, taba más agujerada que usté, jodido.

—Pos ya la chingamos. Hora vamos a quedar con el...

—¿Y las jainas?

—Ai stán adentro ése. Hace friego que nos calman. Vamos a ponele, carnal...

—Espérate ése. Ando bruja.[50] Ni un...

—Uuu, qué bato. Aquí camarón, wátchele. Cuatro lanotas.

—¿De dónde...?

—Las baterías ése. Cro que los traitores del Johnny no van a estariar[51] mañana.

—Orale, pues. Capea a las rucas.

Pa cuando llegaron a las vistas el Jusito y la Olga ya se vían prendido varios de lengua y la llevaba meándose de risa pero la Mary cortó gacho al Chale por el mal porte del bato. Así que éste le jue cantando que no vía otra chava que lo haciera sentir más de aquélla que ella y que tan pronto como tenía lana le iba a apañar la mancuerna. Dispués le siguió con que su jefito Teléforo se la pasaba cascareando con el viejo porque ya no podía ponele duro al jale y él tenía que alivianalo. Le teoricó el pedo de por qué la vía dejado parada el otro día—la jura lo vía pescado speeding y como andaba bien marrano, vía chisquiado de a madre cuando les quiso pintar el cuatro. Hasta los chonteados le vían quitado en el tabique y dispués cuando salió se vía metido en el pedo del Betabel allá en el Otro. De esta forma alivianó a su chava pa cuando llegaron al mono.

Adentro, garraron chingo de patada con el Tom and Jerry pero nomás eso watcharon porque pa cuando empezó Tarzán a echarse jodazos en el pecho y el cabrón chango haciendo la misma, los batos tenían las manos llenas y un ojo torcido. Pasaron muy buen tiempo pichoneando de aquella hasta que apareció la Jane y jue cuando empezó todo el borlote. Los batos no se daban cola que sus baisas se vían ponido en slow motion hasta que se vían parado a la brava. ¡Hijo de la chingada, la Jane taba buenota de a madre! Las chavas se resintieron cuan-

---

[50]sin fondos, sin dinero.

[51]encender o echar en marcha.

do vieron la curadota⁵² que se estaban dando los batos y las dos protestaron. La Mary le dijo al Chale que no juera tan descarado y boca abierta, pero la Olga sí se jue grande. Empezó a gritarles fregadera y media en voz alta pa que oyeran todos. Entonces no hubo más remedio que salir ajuera pa averiguar y arreglar el pedo. Después entraron otra vez los cuatro pero todos venían de mal humor.

A medio mono las rucas pidieron algo pa tomar nomás de cabronas y vengativas porque sabían que los batos andaban raspas.⁵³ El Chale no supo qué contestar pero el cabrón perico del Jusito, que vía prometido taparse los ojos cuando apareciera Jane, le dijo al Chale que juera con él. Este lo vio rirse y cerrale un ojo. Pos cuando ellos salieron las chavas se quedaron haciéndose ilusiones y cuando los batos duraron mucho pa venir, pensaron que a la brava querían quedar bien con ellas. Que con seguro van a trai cokes y hamborgas y papas y todo el pedo. Que sufran los cabrones pa que no crean que semos cualquieras, ¿que no carnala? Simón, hay que ponerse dura todo el tiempo con estos jodidos.

En eso estaban cuando llegaron los batos y se aplastaron así como que no traiban nada. Pero el Jusito puso un bultote de poca madre en el piso y lo traiba envuelto en su suera.

—¿Ontán las cokes?

—Traimos otra cosa mejor ésas, pero hay que calmala porque es sospresa.⁵⁴

—Tan lurios, trajieron m...

—A la brava, ¿que no, carnal?

—Simón, es...

—Vale más que se la corten. Destapen lo que train o nos vamos.

—Orale pues. ¿Tas listo, carnal?

—...

—Pero tienen que cerrar los ojos primero...

Cuando las chavas siguieron la línea el Jusito levantó el garrafón de Kool-Aid y se lo puso en las piernas a la Olga y pa cuando abrió los ojos la ruca, el Jusito ya estaba casi a la puerta. El Chale también salió hecho madre tras de él y se metieron al toliro pa agarrar chingos de patada. El ruco que cuida el pedo allí los sacó a pushones porque no paraban de rirse. Allá ajuera siguieron cagándose de risa sin pensar en sus jainas, al cabo que esta nochi jodida, raspa,

---

⁵²disfrutando de ver el cuerpo de Jane.

⁵³sin dinero.

⁵⁴sorpresa.

lo único que tiene de bonito es el cabrón cielo. Con fregales de estrellas por todas madres.

El día amaneció como un Grito de Dolores retrasado. ¡Ya voló el puente! ¡El agua ya reventó en la labor de arriba! ¡Ya se metió a las labores del Colorao! La noticia se fue encadenando hasta que llegó a todos los rincones de Presidio. Los dueños empezaron a echar madres, que sacaran los tractores y las herramientas que pudieran salvar. Pronto empezaron a hormiguear trabajadores alborotados, abatidos con la lucha que habían hecho. No se pudo más, presas, palas y costales llenos de arena, pacas de alfalfa, y todo lo que humanamente se había pensado resultaba inútil. El agua fue arrollando los plantíos de algodón y de melón tardío. El agua buscaba espacio para estrechar sus tentáculos entumecidos y cuando encontraba obstáculos más grandes que ellos, les bramaba. Luego los rodeaba lentamente, como si así cobrara fuerzas necesarias para después engullirlos y continuar su despojo. Los señores grandes, los dueños, entonces daban una media vuelta, se montaban en sus vehículos y con un rechinar de llantas se alejaban rabiosos. "Este año te vas a quedar en el hoyo, hermano, porque no aseguraste tu cosecha. Vendrán por tu nueva empacadora de alfalfa, por el Allis Chalmers y su arado, lo mismo que el International que usabas para el disco". "Son of a bitch. When you want the fucking water you don't get it and now. . .goddamn. And all that money I put into repairing the gin. . .all that fucking work for nothing".

Toda la mañana la visita a Sam's Phillips 66 es interminable. La gente del pueblo viene y tankea,[55] alistándose pa salir. Ya no hay más que hacer aquí, sino ponele pa Nuevo México o pa'l Odessón. "El jale en las compañías de petróleo son las que más te pagan". "Sí, pero yo qué jodidos sé de máquinas y tienes que saber bastante totacha[56] pa esos jales". "Nel carnal, yo conozco el bato de esta compañía, es a toda madre. Yo te acomodo". Los más viejos que han dado la vida entera a la labor también vienen pero sólo echan gasolina y se van sin decir palabra. Piensan sólo en la pela que van a llevar, la renta, las malpasadas, el dinero que van a ganar y que se van a comer. Luego regresarán otra vez aquí raspa. Pero cuando menos has vivido, ¿que no?

Al otro lado de la calle, Nancy's Cafe también empieza a animarse. Una por una van llegando las trocas sombrerudas y excitadas. Luego los jeeps de la migra. Sólo falta el carro antenudo del sherife. Entre bocadones de ham and eggs

---

[55]llenar el depósito con gasolina.
[56]inglés.

con café, "Damn, you should a seen how that water topple that tree like a shit-house; the water's pouring all over the fucking place at Johnny's, tried to save his bulldozer but the bank caved in. That stupid Lencho just let'er go and he jump off like a scared rabbit. . . Well, gotta go see if them ole boys done as I told'em to. Guess there's nothing else to do but start buyin' Mexican cattle. I hear this guy down by los Mochis got purty good ones to sell. I'm gonna try and lease some of that Campbell property so I can fatten them carcasses. Six months'll do it. I hear they're payin' pretty good price for beef this year."

Ben Jr. tiene otra idea: "Me voy por tres meses al valle, me llevo las trail-ers, consigo contrato para transportar las cosechas de Vernes, Inc., y me recupero un poco. Después que se baje el río, compongo las tierras y reclamo al gobierno la reducción. El gobierno me paga por no sembrar. 220,000 dólares tax-free por hacerme un favor. ¿Qué más quiero? No puedo pedir más. Así las tierras descan-san".

El pensamiento lo hace generoso con la mesera y le deja cincuenta centa-vos.

—Have a good day, Sir.

—You too, ma'am.

Esa mañana la viejita Vicke y Chonito se levantaron temprano con los pujidos de Marcela y ya para cuando el sol salió, la casa estaba animada. El que estaba para nacer venía tocando con punzadas fuertes y no había manera de detenerlo. —Debe ser el golpe que llevaste ayer, hija. No creas, si todavía te falta tiempo— le decía la señora, en un esfuerzo por conformarla. Luego carre-reaba de la cocina a la sala con tazas de yerbabuena y tortillas frotadas de mante-quilla pero Marcela las rechazaba. —¡Te dije que ya no quiero! Ya me tienes empanzada con tanto mugrero. ¡Llévatelo, no lo quiero!

Chonito las dejó hablando. El salía para la casa de Teléforo. Cuando llegó, encontró a todo mundo en rejuego. —Es que Carlos se va pa California, y tuve que arreglarle la ropa. El viejo también se levantó temprano pa ayudar pero con la humedá de estos días no se ha sentido bien. Ya sabes lo que sufre con las riumas— La comadre Serafina le hablaba al muchacho como si fuera hijo de José... Era de esperarse. El chamaco quería a su amo más que al propio papá y se pasaba más tiempo aquí en Presidio que en Ojinaga. Además, a su papá sólo le importaba el dinero que el muchacho traía a casa, y si no, le alistaba el cajon-cito de shine y "¡a la calle, güevón!" Era difícil transformarse en payaso en esas ocasiones. Hacer reír a los güeros y a los soldaditos mexicanos que rondaban el zumbido. Nomás no podía. Tampoco toleraba a los otros muchachos que, como agentes de seguros, seguían al pobre gringo hasta que se le ponía la cara roja.

Luego que vencían, se lanzaban tres o cuatro al suelo, buscándole más de dos pies, y al ver que el señor era un ser normal, se sentaban en sus cajoncitos pensativos. Hombre güero, enigma de la tierra, plenitud vital, ¿cómo no das a saber tu secreto?

La última semana se le había puesto mal la situación porque desde que José había huido, no había trabajado. Pero estaba decidido a sufrir las consecuencias. Más importante era el bienestar de la familia Uranga. Así que desde un principio le había dicho a Teléforo que no contara con él para llenar sacos de arena y hacer presas en el río. —Cuida a Marcela y a Vicke lo mejor que puedas— le había dicho José. —Que pasen unos días y el sábado cruzas para que me enteres si los cabrones ya se fueron. Estaré en la casa de Bernabé y si hay urgencia cuenta con Teléforo, mi compa.

Había cumplido a la letra. Por las tardes se iba al pueblo. Se metía en las gasolineras, se sentaba afuera del café, paseaba por el hotel y hasta se daba la vuelta al puente, arriesgándose a que lo pescaran. Recuerda muy bien que apenas había cruzado José, cuando habían llegado con "dónde José Uranga" y cuando no lo habían encontrado, se habían regresado. A los pocos días ya estaban en Presidio con orden de arrestarlo por evadir el servicio militar. Mientras tanto Chonito iba y venía con las noticias hasta que por fin había decidido José mudarse al otro lado. El no podía verse matando gentes que nada de culpa tenían en los pleitos de políticos. —Habla con Teléforo y dile que mañana por la noche me haga el favor. El ya sabe lo que debe hacer—le había dicho.

Chonito había matado las primeras horas de la noche anterior debajo de las carpas mojadas que celebraban las fiestas patrias. Entre juegos de dados, remates de ropa y gritería de borrachos, había esperado hasta llegarse las doce. Luego, con el valor necesario, había pasado como gato prendido al costado del puente. A tientas se había ido encontrando las tablas porque el río ya volaba por arriba. Después de un eterno jalar de greñas, la corriente lo había permitido cruzar. A las dos de la mañana Chonito era una sombra mojada que se colaba por el pueblo embadurnado de zoquete. Luego un té caliente, una señora enredándolo con una sábana y una colcha tendida en el piso. Chonito no recordaba más.

—Nomás quería avisarle a usté que esta noche es el encargo de don José.

—Muy bien. Entonces dile a Vicke que allá iré a recogerlas despuesito que se haiga metido el sol. Al rato le aviso a Samuel que se aliste con la lancha. Pero anda, vente a almorzar. ¿Estás seguro que no quieres?

—No, gracias. Si ya comí allá. Mejor me voy a ver en qué puedo ayudar.

—Ese carnalito, ai nos watchamos. Póngala ai.

—Pues que le vaya bien por allá.

—Simón,[57] a ver si nos alivianamos. Pásela suave, ¿eh?

—También usté Carlos.

De noche se encontraron con un río lomudo de chocolate. Parecía más bien una montaña prieta en continuo vaivén. Marcela al contrario se imaginó un gato engrifado que abría el hocico rabioso sin maullar. Lo único que parecía oír era un leve zumbido de abejón en lejanía.

La mujer baja la cabeza como si buscara algo, como si la vista fuera a detenerle la sensación de algo que le chorrea por las piernas. Siente un arroyito caliente que empieza desde los nervios de la cabeza y baja hasta los pies. Pero no dice nada. Sólo mira una escena mecánica, hombres sin diálogo que corren de la troca a la lancha, echando bultos que acumularon Vicke y Chonito durante el día. Parece que la escena toda está encarcelada entre una enorme concha de rumores. Los nervios, hechos cuerda, les tapan los ojos y por eso cuando quedan inundados por la luz de unos faroles ni cuenta se dan. Ni siquiera cuando están para subir a las mujeres. Sólo cuando Teléforo vuelve a la troca es cuando nota el par de luces que se viene haciendo más grande.

—¡Pronto! ¡Súbanse a la lancha que viene alguien!— les grita, a la vez que echa a andar el motor de su troca.

Samuel el lanchero toma a la viejita en los brazos mientras que Chonito coge a Marcela de la mano para estar seguro de que no tropiece. Se mueven los remos con furia esperando la bala de pistola en el estómago. Pero no se oye nada. Las tripas se desanudan.

Mientras, Teléforo espera que lleguen las luces. "Bien me las arreglo. Les digo que vine a darle la vuelta al río y es todo. Saben los cabrones quién soy. Les digo que la lancha lleva a dos amigos de Odessa que tienen a su madre enferma. Que el carro que está allí es el de ellos. ¿Qué más pueden preguntar? Sí, aquí los espero... ¿Qué?... Parece que se están apagando. ¿Quién debe ser?"

El hombre espera un momento más pero nada sucede. Apenas distingue el bulto del auto. Entonces da la vuelta a su troca y se dirige hacia donde habían estado las luces. Pasa despacio y no puede creer que no haya nada allí. Regresa otra vez y se va hasta la orilla del río y tampoco. A fuerza quiere ver algo, las luces, el bulto por lo menos. Cuando se convence de que no hay nada, perplejo sale rumbo a casa. Es entonces que oye el fuerte golpe contra el parabrisas. La lechuza queda pataleando al lado del camino. Pero el hombre no se detiene

---

[57]sí.

porque el rumor del río ahora se convierte en una carcajada de gigante. El diablo regresa a su sierrita querida.

La primera parte de la cruzada se avanzó con suma rapidez pero el forcejeo de los lancheros se fue haciendo más duro al llegar a medio río, y cuando ya no se movía la lancha a despecho de que remaban como locos, dejaban que el agua se los llevara un momento para luego seguir luchando.

La viejita apretaba la mano de su hija cada vez que pegaban los montes de basura contra la lancha y se comía los santos. Marcela al contrario llevaba la mente como pescado muerto en una red. El dolor le venía a intervalos, dolor que le duraba un minuto eterno y luego desaparecía como vibración de campanas. Ella permanecía indiferente. Parecía estar suspendida en el aire, más allá de la emoción humana.

—¿Cómo te sientes, hija?

—Dame agua.

—No hay agua hija.

—Quiero agua.

—Aguántate un poco más hijita.

Marcela cierra los ojos y aprieta juntas las piernas lo más fuerte posible. Parece querer quitarse la obstrucción que trae entre las piernas.

—Quítamelo, Vicke.

—No puedo, hija—. La viejita piensa que Marcela se refiere al dolor.

—Te digo que me lo quites.

—Por el amor de Dios cálmate, hija. Verás que pronto se te quita.

Los hombres reman más duro. Las palabras de las mujeres les sacan fuerzas sobrehumanas que en otra ocasión ya se hubieran acabado, mas no es sólo eso; las acciones de Marcela parecen indicar que la mujer va perdiendo la cabeza porque, ¿quién en ese estado pudiera sentir la indiferencia a tal dolor? No, no puede ser natural, piensan.

Tampoco lo que ahora ven. El cuerpo suelto de la mujer cae sobre la viejita quien grita despavorida, al tiempo que ésta la estruja. Pero Marcela ni se mueve. Los hombres pronto se olvidan de la lancha y buscan la manera de poder volverla en sí pero ya todo es inútil; solamente el agua sucia tiene movimiento. El agua y un recién nacido a medio río. Sobre las copas de los árboles, sobre las cabezas, unas nubes de algodón desmenuzado sueltan el llanto.

PRESIDIO 1970

Ya déjalo así, hijo. Mañana haremos un poco más. Vale más recogernos.

—Está bien, apá— y me enderecé, a la vez echándome el azadón en el lomo.

Nos fuimos los dos caminando hacia la casa taciturnos y silenciosos. No teníamos nada que decir. Parecía que la oscuridad nos apresaba los cerebros fatigados y sudorosos, dejándonos mudos. Sólo se escuchaba el quejido de terrones aplastados por los pies de dos hombres exhaustos.

¿Cuándo terminará esto? pensaba, recordando los días monótonos y eternos. Días cansados. Días sin esperanza. Pobre papá. Es tan viejo y aún no se da cuenta que todos los días son iguales, sin cambio. Que todo se reduce a existencia y muerte. Seguramente ni siquiera se ha fijado bien en el espejo, en las hondas líneas estampadas en su cara, en la joroba encorvada de ayeres, en la fatiga reflejada en sus ojos de hoy.

—Qué sol tan perro hizo hoy, ¿no hijo? Parecía que nos habíamos dado un baño de sudor.

—Pues sí. Por eso me senté buen rato bajo el árbol...al cabo poco se avanza. ¿De qué sirve matarnos?

No me respondió. Volvimos a quedar mudos.

Así ha ocurrido siempre, padre. Siempre se ha quedado esta tierra maldita con tu sangre, con tu sudor. Y me duele que en cada gota de tu cuerpo vaya parte de tu alma, de una vida que muere para vivir mejor. Yo sé que tus pasos apuntan a un vacío día tras día y yo los sigo también. Pero ¿sabes por qué lo hago? Por ti papá. Por no dejarte solo. Pero ya me cansé papá, y no te he dicho que me voy. Me voy porque estoy seguro de que hay otro mundo mejor que Presidio...presidio, tejas. Hasta el nombre me suena enfermo para haber visto la luz primero, bajo tejas de presidio.

—Mañana vamos a seguir limpiando, ¿no papá?

—Sí, hijo. Hay que hacer un poco más. Cuando menos las melgas que se van a regar.

Claro, haríamos más agujeros en los zapatos, zigzaguearíamos como locos por los camellones. Quitaríamos yerba y pisotearíamos y caminaríamos y aparecería otra línea en la frente de mi viejo. Por lo pronto ahora, nos curaríamos las fatigas con descanso de vacío y oscuridad; después nos levantaríamos temprano por la mañana como si fuera algo nuevo en el tiempo. Como si el tiempo tuviera límites. Qué pendejadas. La vida se mide sólo a base de esfuerzo y de acción. Qué brutos los que nos consideran güevones por tener raíces en la "tierra del

*mañana". Pero es que no comprendan que mañana significa esperanza, que hoy
se trabajó quince horas y que hay esperanza de aguantar diecisiete. Es esperanza
de mejorarse, sobrepasando los límites del cuerpo. En Presidio nunca muere. Se
afirma y se hace sustento como pan de cada día, hasta el punto de convertirse
en parásito eterno. Sí, hay que tener esperanza...*
—¿Por qué no fuiste a la guerra, padre?
—Porque no entiendo de riñas entre países. ¿Para qué pelear con otros si
la lucha la traigo aquí dentro, si el hambre es mi propia guerra? Nosotros, hijo,
somos como un par de dados que de tanto rodar hemos tomado forma de canica.
Y no cesaremos de rodar hasta que encontremos un hueco. Es ese hueco con el
cual debemos luchar y no contra nosotros mismos.*
    *Pero los agentes no te escucharon, ¿te acuerdas, padre? Vinieron y te
llevaron sin pestañear a otro presidio, después de que habías perdido a tu mujer.
Y ahora pagabas el crimen de no dar muerte a otros, por no hacerte enemigo de
tu barro. No quisieron entender que para ti la lucha por vivir bastaba y tuviste
que cumplir la sentencia. Con cuatro líneas más en tu frente, con dos alas caí-
das, arrastrando por el suelo, con una marca estampada sobre tu espalda, ¿te
acuerdas, padre? Regresaste con el alma agujereada y con corazón sangriento
para luego volver a caminar por esas tierras. Y después te cansaste y te embo-
rrachaste y te volviste loco de risa endiablada aquí en Presidio. Y luego que vi
tu tragedia me arranqué de las garras y me fui, ¿te acuerdas? Pero ahora he
regresado, después de mucho tiempo, y ¿sabes por qué? Porque te has muerto.
Ayer por fin te enterramos en el polvoroso cementerio de Presidio. Digo que por
fin, pues ya nos estábamos cansando de velarte y yo creo que hasta tú mismo
sentías igual. Ya estarías cansado de estar expuesto a tanta gente, a tantos gemidos. Yo sólo quise verte el primer día. Después me dediqué a hacer los arreglos
necesarios y a soportar condolencias. Hasta entonces no me enteré de los amigos
que tenías, todos ellos caras marchitas de tiempo y pensé que así los mataría la
vida también, como a ti. Después del primer día de palabras rayadas como un
disco, me dediqué a mi abuela Vicke. Cuando llegué no le pude decir nada así
que la dejé que se desahogara en mi pecho diciéndole torpemente que no llorara.
Entonces los dos caminamos para contemplar los últimos vestigios de una cara
cicatrizada, un rostro de cincuenta años arrugados; debajo de la piel un corazón
reventado a golpes —la vida siempre nos tuvo desprecio. Por eso no quise volver
a verte, porque moriste con el mismo gesto de desprecio en la boca. Estoy seguro
que si me hubieras podido hablar en ese momento, me hubieras regañado. —¿A
poco crees que voy a dejar burlarme de la muerte? ¿Que no te dije que me
enterraras con mariachis?— me hubieras dicho. Por eso sientes rencor, papá,
porque naciste en un rencor humeante, en un hoyo de huesos calcinados, en*

*Presidio—siete letras taladradas en semana santa, presidio del tiempo prolonga-
do, presidio suspendido en un vapor a las tres de la tarde, presidio la burla,
presidio mal aventurado, presidio nacido viejo. No, don José, no había que
buscarle amaneceres a Presidio, no había que preguntar por los niños, la gente
nació con arrugas, a las tres de la tarde. Por eso no existían ni existen fiebres
en Presidio. La gente parió quemada, derretida. La sangre de sus cuerpos está
hecha a ciento veinte grados. Y tú por eso amaste y viviste con la sangre hirvien-
do—el odio ya estaba soldado desde mucho antes que tú murieras. Y ese rencor
que viene desde muy atrás ahora se me ha pegado. Se me pegó desde el primer
día que te velamos. Por eso no quise volver a verte. Ahora, tres días después, me
siento mejor aunque me haya despedido de ti para siempre. Pero sabes, he decidido quedarme porque hay que quitar la corona de espinas en Presidio. Sí,
habrá que caminar por los cactos y los mesquites. Habrá que aguantar el camino, quitar la corona y ponérsela a otro. Después, ir hasta el río y lavarse las
llagas, y ya cuando se está limpio habrá que regresar a Presidio y el que quiera
seguir tendrá que regresar fuerte porque necesitará la voluntad más grande que
emana del alma. Porque lo verán y lo creerán loco y le dirán que se vaya a
predicar a las orillas del río. La gente que ha sufrido con él lo comprenderá
pero no lo seguirá porque tendrá miedo, y habrá otros que le escupirán la cara.
Le dirán que todo corre muy bien, que la gente está contenta con sus casas y
trabajos. Pero el milagro obrará y entonces necesitará reunirlos, contarles del
diablo que se desató y que todavía anda suelto. También habrá que decirles de
ese famoso fortín que nació mucho antes de 1683 y de tantas otras cosas. Sí,
habrá que contar, pero no con sufrimiento y con perdón. Habrá que encender la
llama, la que murió con el tiempo.*

The Devil in Texas/El diablo en Texas (Tempe: Bilingual Press/Editorial Bilingüe, Arizona State University, 1990).

GINA VALDÉS (1943-)

There Are No Madmen Here (1981; revised 1996)

Rhythms

    it's your turn,

        hurry up

you make the lines crooked,

        I want to make them

        you can't

    why

        it's my chalk

    the white chalk

took all of Yoli's attention. She winced at the screeching on the board. She looked at her friend, Mirasol, who sat next to her in the last row of the classroom. Can't she hear the screeching? She was 600 years away, designing geometric letters, figures that echoed pyramids, stone temples, hieroglyphics, with mathematical precision, shaman flair, Mirasol, designer of magic domes, architect of the Ninth Wonder. Our last year here. How can I convince her to continue? Twelve years of the crap is enough, is all Mirasol would say. College is different, Yoli tried conveying her sister Lorena's thoughts, her sister already in college. Mirasol's narrowing eyes tell Yoli that she's tired of lies. We don't have to buy everything they say. In college you can do research, unbury facts, unravel mysteries, weave answers, histories, out of data and ideas, Lorena said, arm yourself with hard weapons. Yoli watched Mirasol transforming her American History textbook. Mirasol of the brown velvet skin, black velvet hair, pink velvet lips. They said they looked alike, but her eyes weren't juicy limes like Mirasol's.

Mira Sol, priestess of magic letters. Yoli's eyes half circled from Yoli's pencil to the screeching chalk, the professor's mouth opening by degrees.
Can anyone tell me who wrote the Bill of Rights?
Some rightists.
What did you say Miss Vega? I thought you said something. Nobody knows
. . . knows . . . knows . . .
Mirasol approves the dialogue with a smile. Mira Sol, who carries on a brilliant dialogue with the sun, the sun goddess whispering her secrets which she transposes onto the edges of her textbook, which she now closes. Yoli sees musical notes floating in front of her lime eyes, flute sounds, drum sounds . . . she is moving in time, hears the screeches of the chalk, winces, moves round to Saturday sounds . . . ae timbalero . . . her eyes shine like green sequins . . . ae timbalero . . . breath of life, pulse of the universe . . . the two velvet-eyed beauties enter gracefully into the dance hall filled with young laughter, spiced music, young women and men between sixteen and twenty undulate the floor, the walls, the ceiling, their arms, legs, feet, pulsing

the maracas murmur—shuku shuku
the guitar complains—tran tran
the güiro protests—raka taka
the drum calls—tun tun tun
drum beats

become background music for the professor's voice
Next week we will study about a man who terrorized the southwest, who tried by all means to take advantage of the people. Does anyone know who I'm talking about?
Sam Houston
Miss Vega, raise your hand if you want to say something. Hasn't anyone heard of Villa?
Yoli and Mirasol glance at the circular clock at the same time and see the elongated half hour in each other's eyes. Half an hour listening to history hi story his tory his story . . . Yoli sees Mirasol opening her textbook, picking up a pencil. In half an hour she will design a stone city with labyrinthic gardens where corn grows in animal shapes and cotton grows in rainbow colors, she will erect shrines for the mother of crops, mother of plenty, mother of all, where she will reign as high priestess of fertile arts. In half an hour Yoli will circle the world, lingering in India, China, Japan, places where she flew to as a child riding on favorite fairytales, white silk clinging, she sits on purple cushions in mushroom temples, exchanging haiku with Shintoist priestesses, offering her natural lines to the sun goddess, to the moon goddess, to the earth god, brown-skinned,

long-eyed, earthy, he listens in rapture to the damp syllables and moves close to her, with one hand removing the green sash of his brown kimono, with his other hand, taking hers, inviting her to feel his steam bath smoothness, hard limbs, moss scented, moving closer he whispers golden syllables in numbers she loses count of while they keep rhythm with their merged bodies, landing on the moon, she dances to life and returns with the secret of rhythm. What am I doing here? in this class room? Two more months and it will be summer and she will go stay with her Aunt Emilia in Ensenada, to be kissed by dust and salt air, and Los Angeles will become a waterless cloud. Tía Emilia, who hadn't gone past high school, the storyteller, telling her tales to an audience of her six children, four neighbor children, and to her, her niece Yoli, all the way from Los Angeles to hear her stories. Tía Emilia, sitting in her bedroom at night, after all were asleep, in front of a radio that whispered poems that she whispered back

Desde que nos conocimos,
  moreno, no sé que tengo,
que cuando llega la noche
  me acuesto pero no duermo.

   Quiero ver cuando amanezca
    el sol en tu faz morena
   y cuando caiga la noche
    en tu cuerpo luna llena.

Cuando llueve qué bonito
  suena la lluvia en el techo;
toda la noche escuchando
  el ritmo de nuestro lecho.

   Con tu calor y tu ritmo
    cuanto me has hecho gozar;
   tienes el sol en tus manos,
    en tus caderas el mar.

Tía Emilia, the psychiatrist, classifying her many birds into social types, the homosexual canaries, the paranoid mynah bird, and Zoila, the nihilist parrot. Zoila, pacing, always pacing, searching the four corners of the house for answers to her birdly existence. Tía Emilia, who diagnosed everyone by their farts. Watch out for people like your tío Simón who afterwards shouts at everyone, blaming the one nearest him and leaving the room indignant. The progressive economist, who when feeding her children and their neighbor guests, knew that if she gave everyone a little less they could all eat, not too much, but enough, enough for her children, for her constant guests, for her birds, Federico, Timoteo, Gregorio and Zoila. Zoila with slightly full belly, pacing, pacing, searching the four corners and the heights of the backyard pepper tree for forbidden knowledge

> *so much knowledge*
> *so much forbidden*

Yoli moves close to Mirasol and speaks in whispers. Are you going to the movie with Louie tomorrow? What for? I have to take my little sister, to watch me like a cockroach, to see if Louie places his hands on a good place. You want to go the dance? At least I don't have to take the brat with me
> to the Saturday dance
>   all night
>   dancing
between dances feasting their velvet eyes on one of the few thirty-year-old men who moves his hips to the rhythm of waves, the velvet eyes fixed on the man of medium height, straight black hair, pleasant features. He stands with straight spine, feet barely moving, face expressionless, only his hips sway slowly from side to side in perfect rhythm to the music . . . uno dos cha cha cha . . . slowly . . . uno dos cha cha cha . . . he's doing a very slow cha cha . . . a bolero . . . a danzón . . . Juárez, no debió de morir . . . an inward tango. All. None. An Indian danza . . . tachun tachun tachun ta ra ra . . . a love ritual . . . ah ah ah . . . he's following his own rhythm, that blends with the love sounds of life . . . he's standing waist deep in a warm ocean, frothy slow motion waves breaking around him. The four velvet eyes, transforming to satin, remain fixed on the man's expressive hips, that part of him concentrated with energy. They don't fear that he might become aware of their overt attention, he's oblivious to everything but the music, the music in the room, the music of life, his own inner music
> music
music everywhere, swaying Yoli's hips as she walks, she feels she's a red rumba, needing to dance, on the bus, waiting for a light to change, dance, during mass, dance, when the host is offered, dance, rebirth, new life, dance! dance! and she kneels, bows her head, calms her hips and pounds her chest ¡por mi culpa! ¡por mi culpa! ¡por mi grandísima culpa!
> mercy mercy mercy

they want me safe, married. Everyone has a wonderful man for me, tía Emilia has ten of them. Tía Emilia, matchmaker of the vecindad, could rival the whole team of Lonely Hearts, Incorporated, of West L.A. I have a choice, the seminarist (with the dark eyes) who's not a priest yet, the pimply young man who delivers the bottled water, the stu-stuttering to-to-tortilla maker, the old school gardener with chewed off hair. Well, says tía Emilia, nobody's perfect. No! no! no! tía Emilia, marriage is an odd habit, we're full of odd habits that somehow keep us sane, and bored, tomorrow I'm returning to Los Angeles

L.A.

        Los

Angeles, back to L.A., back to school, back to class, back in class, back of class, watching Mirasol wander from her pyramidical creations into the square of the room. How was the test? Yoli nods, squints, promising her a round answer after class. The aptitude test lasted two days, two days of questioning, hundreds of questions to which they all knew the answers

   What would you like to be?

   How could she tell this man who had never talked to the sun goddess or to a drunk cockroach?

   Have you ever thought of being an actress?

   An actress, a writer, a director, a producer, producer of productive products, of unsilent movies, direct director. An actress plays roles others give her, a writer creates her own roles

   Some people don't like to hear this, but you have mechanical talent

   Down under hard steely oily greasy mechanical talent? or high aptitude for relativistic mechanics?

   unmechanical talent finely tuned motorized

                        electrifying

                  dynamic

world created by Mirasol on the edges of her book, she peeks from it, stares at the white soxs of the history professor, eases back into the book to write herstory in futuristic hieroglyphics that someone might someday decipher. Yoli looks at Mirasol's eyes as distant and ancient as her designs, wise as her mother's brown eyes, her mother, the dress designer, taken out of school by her father because, well, a woman doesn't need so much school, interned in a sewing factory, becoming an expert on threads, bobbins and button holes, nobody could sew a straighter seam, a more perfect dress, that she was paid two dollars to sew, which she later found with a hundred dollar price tag in an exclusive store, pronto, pronto, it doesn't have to be so perfect, we have to get the work out, pronto, pronto, her mother, who sometimes didn't express all the tenderness she felt, to protect her softest parts, I don't want any animals around here, they need too much love, patting, worrying about every dog and cat that she saw, this woman who often didn't express her passion, that showed anyway in her round lips, stretched legs, waterfall laughter, this woman who always repressed anger, an anger that had built up since she was eight, when she had seen her father slapping her mother, anger building toward all those who use their hands for other than work and caresses, compassion for those of weak position, I don't want plants in the house, they're too dependent on my kindness, her eyes, healing as a Yaqui curandera's, reservoirs of hope, saved up to be used by her daughters. Who had saved up for Mirasol? Mirasol with eyes as cynical as her grandfather's, his lids weighed down with dust, smoke, lint, clouded with less hope at end of long work day, hope less, hopelessness, an acid that Yoli saw gnawing at the corner of her grandfather's mattress, its cottony tripes spilling, a bitterness that cracked his walls, pots, dishes, shoes. He said this something sour, acidic, seeped through the cracks of the walls and pulled his feet at night, that sometimes it blew through the window, its cold breath on him, numbing his hands, and so he lights candles and this fire is something the acid can't devour, the flames of his red votive candles that shine like the glue that holds together his crucifix, the beads of his rosary, the ink of the newspaper, the white pages of his library books, the lottery stubs, Yoli gathers the flecks of light from every candle, from every pink geranium, wherever else she can find them, she has been gathering them for years and she knows that someday they will amount to more than a candle flame, closer to a sun

some day sun day she would take every sun note and she would compose a symphony and play it back to her mother, to drown out the hiss of sewing machines, to blow away the million threads sticking to her clothes like cobwebs, music for a fashion show of her own designs, creative creations, to her tía Emilia, as background music for her stories, to make her elves jump, to her grandfather, to pull him out of hell, to Mirasol, to dance with Mira Sol to the beat of their own music, beat of the past beat of the future beat of the present

it's your turn, Yoli, hurry up

forget it, Sammy, you always make the lines crooked

come on, jump, you're holding up the game

I'm tired of this game

Zoila chants

pacing, pacing

fixing her one eye on tía Emilia as she tells her stories

The Elevator

Don Severino entered the old hotel situated in downtown Los Angeles and stood in front of the elevator, that like everything else in the hotel, was decorated with rusted copper. He hit the elevator door with his cane and said, "Tin can!" He walked toward the hotel office and rang the bell until the manager came out.

"Yes, don Severino."

"When the hell are you going to fix that tin can?"

"If you're talking about the elevator, it works fine."

"Can't you hear it squeak like a sick pig? Or are you deaf? You wouldn't get me in that ruin for nothing."

"The other men use the elevator."

"Because they can't climb the stairs. You have no compassion for old people, because you don't know what it's like to be old; but when you get old and your legs cramp—which I hope they do—you won't be able to sleep at night thinking of all the old men you tortured."

"I've already told you, don Severino, that I have nothing to do with this."

"Because you don't want to. Give me the owner's phone and I'll talk to him today."

"I've already told you that I don't have the owner's phone."

"Then who do you give the rent to? Eh? Who?"

"A Mr. Wilson comes by, the owner's secretary, and I give it to him. I've already told you. Why do you keep asking the same questions?"

"Well, give me Wilson's phone. Maybe I can talk to him."

"I don't have his phone."

"I'm not the only one who's got complaints."

"This is a nice hotel, don Severino, it's centrally located, the rent is cheap, the rooms have a good view, and really, I don't know why you complain so much."

"Because this shitty hotel is falling apart, and if I don't go to another one, it's because I can't afford to, and with the rent you charge here, we should have an elevator that works."

"I have already told you that the elevator works fine."

"I've never seen you get in it."

"I like the exercise."

"So would I if I were as young as you."

The manager answered the telephone, and don Severino walked away slowly toward the stairs that would take him to his room on the third floor. He supported himself on his cane with his left hand, and with his right he held on to the rail. Each stair creaked under his heavy foot, and every creak was followed by a "chingado" as if he were saying a litany.

When he entered his room, he took off his hat and coat and walked into the kitchen. He put on the light and cockroaches jumped out of cracks in the floor and out of cabinets. "Damn dirty bugs! Nice welcome you give me." He finished preparing his coffee, warming a piece of French bread and chasing cockroaches. "You're useless animals, you're only good for sickening people." He walked toward a small table at the foot of his bed and sat down to dunk pieces of bread in his coffee. When the bread was gone, he slurred the rest of the coffee while he read "La Opinión." When he finished reading the newspaper, he washed the dishes, made up his bed, and with a rag he dusted all of the statues of saints that stood on an altar that he had built in one of the room's cabinets. "You sure are stubborn, San Martín. Don't be mean, Santa Lucía, don't let my eyesight get worse." He took the statue of San Judas and stood it on its head. "You might work miracles, but you ignore me." He lit all of the candles, sat on a broken rocking chair in front of the altar and began to pray a rosary.

When he had finished his prayers, he sat on a chair in front of a window that faced one of the city's main streets, observing the people that passed by and recalling other times when his relatives visited him.

"Who is it?"

"Young Patricio."

"Come in, Patricio."

An old bent man entered the room, stood near the bed, and with his small eyes stared at the magazine pictures of naked women that covered part of one wall. After going over the pictures several times, he walked toward don Severino and said with a toothless smile, "Don't forget the poker game at my room tonight."

"I thought it was going to be at Gómez's room."

"It's going to be in my room, you're more absentminded than I am."

"If you insult me, I'll never forget it. Sit down a while, sometimes a passable woman goes by." He handed the newspaper to his friend and said, "Look what's happening in Mexicali. The gringos don't want to sell pure water to the Mexicans. They wish we would all die of thirst."

"That's what they would like."

Don Severino spit into an empty coffee can. He stuck his head out of the window and shouted, "Damn cops! Leave that man alone! It's bad enough that he's drunk, they have to give him a blow. Look, Patricio, I'm glad you came because I wanted to talk to you about the elevator. If more of us complain, we'll get quicker results."

"Nobody's deafer than someone who doesn't want to hear."

"Well, I'll continue to complain. And you stop riding on that elevator."

"And how do you want me to get to the third floor? Crawling?"

"And how do you think I get up here?"

"Stubbornness. See you tonight, Severino. Let's not let Crosseyed Gómez beat us."

The following day, when he returned from church, don Severino, as usual stopped at the office and began ringing the bell. "I know you're there, bastard. When you get old even your guts are going to cramp."

Don Patricio saw his friend and walked toward him. "Stop complaining, come to my room, I made chicken soup, I'll offer you a plate."

"If you offer me two, I'll go."

"Come, then, I put cilantro in it, the way you like it."

"I'll be there in a while, I have to finish my novena."

"The older you get, the holier, And you can't even stand the church. You're always saying that it screws people."

"I don't pray to the priests, I pray to God, through the saints."

"Well, I say there's no saints, in this world or any other, if there is another."

"You're an atheist, Patricio."

"And you're a fanatic. Don't forget the soup. If you don't come I'll eat it all and they say that the cemeteries are full of gluttons."

"Don't get into that monster, Patricio, it's broken."

"You won't get me to climb those steep stairs. It's up to you if you want to roll down and break your neck."

"That elevator creaks funny."

"Look, Severino, the elevator's almost here, I'll wait for it."

"Don Severino began to climb the stairs slowly. As he reached the third floor, he heard a loud creak and then a crash. He dropped the cane and held on to the rail with both hands. His legs shaking, he opened the door to his room, dropped on the rocking chair, took the rosary that was hanging on the arm of the chair and began to pray out loud.

Don Severino's shaky voice was swallowed by the siren. He stood, walked toward the window, and with glassy eyes followed the uniformed men who walked into the hotel with three stretchers. He stood there, supporting himself on the window sill, watching the men go in and out of the hotel carrying stretchers with shrouded bodies. He walked toward the altar and took the statues one by one, tightening his hands around their necks and standing them on their heads.

He served himself a glass of purple wine and placed the bottle close to the rocking chair.

There Are No Madmen Here

"When did you get here, Mundo?"

"Three days ago. I came to straighten these people out. And you, María? Why do you risk coming here? Maybe they won't let you leave."

"Don't tell her that," said Chuy.

"Why not? Don't think that because you look alright they can't keep you here. You think there's only crazies here?"

"I know you and Chuy aren't crazy."

"When we arrive here we're not, but they've got it planned so that no one leaves here well. If you knew what they do. . ."

"Don't talk like that to my sister, she's the only one who visits me."

"I'm not trying to scare you, María, I just like to say what I know, the truth. Nobody says the truth. Lies! Lies! Nothing but lies!"

María stares at her brother and his best friend trying to get used to seeing them together in those surroundings. They had both been in hospitals before, but never in the same one, at the same time, Chuy sitting on his bed, resting his head on a pillow and Mundo sitting on a chair at the foot of the bed, alert to everything around him, looking more like an employee than a patient, tall, thin, intense eyes, their physical resemblance always surprised her, as did their opposite personalities. She had seen them together so many times, since they were boys, in her house, talking, drinking beer, passing out, her mother saying, they're at it again. Mundo lost his job yesterday, mamá. They always had a good reason, her mother said, I hate to see them like this, but it's better than out in the street where the cops will pick them up and throw them in jail like stray dogs.

"Chuy can't say I'm not a good friend, even to this place I come to keep him company."

"You came? They brought you, the same as me."

Nobody in the family wanted to see Chuy in the hospital, but when he got the d.t.'s, when they saw him sitting on the bed, holding his knees with his hands, rocking, with a sweaty, distorted face, shouting, There's a man out there! There he is! Everyone became frightened and so they decided to have him committed. She wondered how Mundo had managed to get locked up again.

"Are you surprised to see me here, María?"

She looked up at Mundo. "I'm . . . I'm glad to see you, but not here. You hadn't stopped by the house in a long time."

"I was around, fighting with everyone. They don't let you rest for a minute, out there and in here. Look at that nurse, I've got to keep my eyes on her. The only reason she hasn't killed me is because I haven't let her."

She wondered if he had been committed through the courts like that first time when he had entered the church drunk, stood near the altar, taken his clothes off and shouted, We need to be innocent, like newborn babies! The ushers had thrown coats over him and dragged him out of the church. At the court he had shouted at the judge, Indecent exposure? You are indecent, exposing your indecent lies! He had been taken from the court shouting, Disturbing the peace? How can I disturb what doesn't exist? Chuy never raised his voice, he was always so calm, never complaining about anything. Their mother said of him, This one swallows his troubles.

"Look at everyone here, María," said Mundo, "look at their faces, they keep them drugged so they won't complain, they want us tame and dumb, nice and calm, calm! calm!"

"What's Mundo doing, Chuy?"

"It's his bed."

"I know, but why is he standing on it?"

"They'll come and calm him down soon."

"They're killing you! They're killing you and you're letting them."

"Look, Chuy he's making that man cry."

"That one's always crying."

"Here comes that nurse he can't stand."

"Are you still bothering the other patients?"

"You're the one bothering us, you and all the bastards that work here. Don't put up with it! They want to knot your veins and burn your brains. Don't let them! Don't let them!"

"I'll talk to the nurse, Chuy."

"It's better if you don't bud in, the attendants are coming."

"Kill me! What are you waiting for?"

"Let's do something, Chuy."

"They're not hurting him, they're just giving him a shot of thorazine. He'll calm down soon. The bad thing about Mundo is that he talks too much. If you keep quiet they leave you alone."

Lying in the living room, the more Chuy drank, the quieter he became, and Mundo, with each beer, becoming louder, the words spurting out. What is he so angry about? asked her mother. He wasn't admitted to the university. Chuy wasn't either and he's not shouting about it, but Mundo never stops talking, María, your brother's half gone and Mundo's tongue keeps on wagging.

Mundo's shouts, Chuy's whispers, that patients' cries buzzed in María's head, and visiting time wasn't over yet. If she left now, Chuy would feel hurt, if she stayed, the buzzing would prick her brain.

"Are you going so soon?"

"I promise I'll be here early next week."

During the first months, several relatives visited him, but after a year and a half she was the only one who rode two hours every Sunday from Los Angeles to the dusty town surrounded by soft brown hills that hid the asylum. She could see the white roof now, hoped that, somehow, time would go by faster this Sunday.

"I'm glad you came early, María, Mundo's telling me about the interview he had with the doctor, he sounds just like him, he should be an actor. Start again, so that María can hear it all."

"Evil! evil! I think doctors are evil, and these prisons you call hospitals, and all who run these places. What do you want us to do? open the doors and let everyone out? That would be a good start. Do you know what would happen if these people were let loose. The same thing that's happening with people like you loose. You're the dangerous ones, the ones with the keys. You're the mean ones! mean! mean!"

Mundo was making a fist at the absent doctor, his black hair disheveled; María turned away from him and saw a nurse, the same one as before, walking towards them, two attendants behind her.

"Give him a shot of Thorazine."

"Look how they're holding him, Chuy."

"Don't worry, that's so he won't run away. He'll calm down soon."

"Poison me! Kill me! You'll never kill the truth! The ward filled with Mundo's shouts, Chuy's whispers. . .

". . .he's writing a book . . . can't read or write . . . doesn't let go of that notebook . . . writing a book . . . that . . ."

"What did you say, Chuy?"

". . . filling up paper . . . scribbles . . ."

Echoes . . . buzzing . . . "I better go now, Chuy, it's almost time."

"Wait until the bell rings."

"I'll come early next week."

Next week, last week, this week, her weeks seemed to be getting shorter than her weekends, Sunday was the longest day of all, two hours to reach the hospital, two hours back to the house, and the time at the asylum could no longer be counted in hours, days, a week, weekend, Sunday already, brown hills, white roof, I hope Mundo doesn't talk so much.

"You did come early, María."

"I told you I would. Where's Mundo? I'm surprised he's not here."

"I haven't seen him all week, I've asked for him but they don't answer me, they just . . ."

Whispers, Chuy's soft voice . . . echoes of Mundo's shouts . . . "I'm leaving, Chuy."

"So soon?"

"I'm going to the office to ask about Mundo."

She looked at the two nurses, spoke to the one who smiled at her.

"Mr. Flores? Let me check. He's been transferred to another hospital."

She decided not to return to the ward, it became dark so early, she would go home and call that hospital, she would wait until everyone fell asleep, it was better if they didn't know about this yet.

Such a long ride, it was late and she was tired, the voices on the telephone sounded distant, she was tired of calling so many hospitals, of hearing the same answer, we don't have a patient by that name here. She needed to sleep, in the morning she would go to the hospital, talk to all of the nurses, to the doctors, she wouldn't go alone, she would speak to her brothers, friends, she would call them now, no, nobody could take off work, she'd go alone, she just needed sleep, a good rest for the long ride, she would call in sick to work and leave early in the morning, sleep is all she needed, she had not been sleeping well the last few weeks, and that night wasn't different.

But she called her work the next morning and rode towards the brown hills that hid the asylum that she felt she had just left, it was an odd feeling coming on a Monday, good, there were different nurses at the desk.

"How can I help you?"

"I'm looking for . . . I'd like information about . . . about Mundo Flores."

"Flores?"

"He was a patient here, I just visited him, just saw him last week."

"I don't remember anyone by that name. Let me check."

She doesn't remember . . . she doesn't want to talk . . .

"We did have a Mr. Flores here, but he's been transferred to another hospital."

"That's what they told me yesterday. I've called several hospitals in California and he's not in any of them. Why don't you want to tell me? I'd like to speak to someone who knows. I want to speak to Mundo, where is he?"

"Calm down. I'll take you to the doctor, maybe he can help you."

"Let go of me! Let go of my arm!"

"Calm down."

"Let go of me!"

María Portillo

María Portillo Vega and her three daughters sat in the kitchen of their two room house eating their supper in silence. The wind was strong that day and that always caused tension among them. The first time that they had seen the house one of the girls had said, "It looks like any wind could blow it down." And the others had agreed. The cardboard window blew open and María rushed to fix it. She took a hammer, a bag of nails, and nailed the cardboard to the window frame. It would hold, María knew that it would, just as she knew that the house would not blow down.

That morning, after discovering that she had only one peso and twenty centavos in her purse, María went to church to light a candle. She knelt before the candle stand, rolled the peso like a cigaret, and slipped it into the poor box. After lighting the candle, she placed her hands together and said a prayer to San Martín de Porres. She looked at the candle and wondered if the wind from the nearby door that constantly opened and closed would blow it out or if it would burn all day and melt away her problems. She moved her eyes away from the burning candle and looked at the women scattered throughout the church. They all knelt like her with their heads lowered and covered with black veils as if in mourning. She turned back to the candle and stared at the yellow flame. When she took her eyes away from the candle all she could see were white circles that flashed before her as she walked out of the church. An old woman who sat on the sidewalk in front of the church, surrounded by rosaries, holy medals, novenas, statues of saints and crucifixes, waved a novena and called to her, "These are hard to get—Saint Eduwigis—she helps the poor." María took the novena and gave the woman twenty centavos.

María spent the rest of the day looking for work but the search was futile and in the afternoon she sent her youngest daughter to borrow money from her sister Emilia. Her daughter returned with a dozen tortillas but without the money. "Tía Emilia sent these to you and she said that she was coming to ask you for a loan." Her sister Emilia was her only relative that remained in México, all of her other relatives had moved to the United States. María also had lived in the States and she had become a citizen like the rest of her family, and her three daughters had been born there, but they had returned to México because that was what her husband wanted. In México he could use the knowledge that he had acquired in Mexican schools and through books and experience to work as a professor. In the States he had been unable to obtain a license to teach and ended up working in various factories. María loved México, but felt that life was easier in the States, regardless of the work they were able to find. She had had good and hard times in the two countries, but she knew that when life was hard in México, it reached the point of desperation.

In spite of her 43 years, María's face had the expression of innocence. "You have a face like the Virgin Mary's," her father often told her. But her glances and smiles were flirtatious and subtly tinged with irony as if she knew what everyone was really thinking. Her three teenage daughters all looked like her, but Margarita, the oldest, gave an impression of greater naivete than the others, Lorena's eyes were less flirtatious, and Yoli, the youngest, had a more secretive face. "The two oldest are like me," María would say, "the youngest is a Vega."

María thought of her in-laws. They all lived in México and all were well educated people. Her husband, Efrén, was a literature college professor with a warm smile who often recited stanzas from Amado Nervo and Juan de Dios Peza. People, places and things around him seemed like a dream to him, "a flimsy illusion," he called it. And to keep this dream from becoming a nightmare he periodically jumped into his army jeep and left the city of Ensenada to hide in the Baja California wilderness. He spent days, sometimes weeks communing with animals and mountain spirits, "things he can deal with more easily," said María. He returned to his house, sometimes a month later, reappearing before his family as if he had been gone for only a few moments, perhaps having a beer at a corner bar. When he left, he often forgot to provide for his family, and at those times they had to depend on the generosity of relatives for their survival.

"When is our father returning?"

"Only god and the devil know," said María. She had played hide and seek with him for many years but now he seemed to be in permanent hiding. She had not seen him for several months and the last she had heard of him was that he was diving for lost treasures in Yucatán. As usual, he was doing as he pleased. He had taken her to the States, brought her back to México, and now had taken off to the south, without her. If he had asked her to go with him, she wasn't sure if she would have gone. She had not done what she wanted for so long that she was not sure of what she really wanted, but she knew that it was something other, better than what she had. She felt tired of thinking, of looking for work, of not finding it, of having to get by with so little; she felt tired of trying to figure out her husband's moods and whereabouts, of waiting for him. At night, lying on the edge of the double bed, she often felt alone, more so than when she had been a single woman. They had been together so many times in that bed, and at those times she also often felt alone, not knowing if he would be there when she woke up in the morning, not sure if she would be sleeping with him the following night. The first time he had held her hand it had been such a special feeling, that touch had produced so much pleasure in her and she had wanted him to hold her hand tighter, longer. And that is the way she felt when they made love, a pleasurable feeling that she wanted to heighten and prolong but that always evaporated before she could hold it long enough to fully experience it. They exchanged thoughts during the day, merged their bodies at night, words and limbs mingling, and then he was gone. Yet she could not do the same, come and go as she pleased, have someone always waiting. He had left again, and once more their lives had separated at so many places.

The wind subsided. María stepped out of the house and stood in the back lot filling a large hole in the ground with scraps of wood, twigs and paper. She struck a match, threw it into the pit and looked at the rusted suitcase that lay next to her on the dirt ground. She felt the tiredness. Perhaps the wavering, the indecision, the holding back, added to it. But in routine there was a feeling of safety and comfort. She felt a lack of energy to think and act in different ways, but she wanted to, felt a need to, why couldn't she? She thought of her father, mother, brothers, husband. Who was stopping her? She unlocked the suitcase, took out its content and threw it into the fire, while her daughters stood at the back door of the house following her actions.

"What is she throwing into the fire?"

"I don't know. It looks like cloth, white cloth."

"It's a dress, an evening dress."

"I always wondered what was in that suitcase."

"Let's go see what it is," said Lorena.

Margarita pulled her back. "You stay here."

The orange flames licked the dry air and María stared at them.

"Ay!" cried Margarita, "it looks like her wedding dress!"

"Can't be," said Lorena, as she ran out of the house.

"Mamá! What are you doing?"

María could not hear her daughters' voices, only the crackling of the fire that was devouring the delicate lace. The feeling of relief came to her strong and sudden, and she felt her energy returning, an energy that she had not felt for

many years, a feeling that she could do whatever she decided to. The last traces
of sunlight disappeared and the flames glowed like giant candles. She threw a
box of loose dirt on the dying flames and without saying a word, walked back
into the house.

The following day during breakfast, María announced in a firm voice,
"We're going to go live to[1] the United States."
Margarita embraced her mother. "That's wonderful, mamá,"
"What are we going to do there?" asked Lorena.
"We have many relatives, I'm sure we can manage. I just got a letter from
my Aunt Josefina asking us to stay with them."
"Josefina?"
"Your grandfather's sister. We'll be staying with her and Consuelo until we
can rent our own house."
Margarita turned to Yoli and said, "Isn't it great?" Yoli remained silent.
"When are we leaving?" asked Lorena.
"As soon as we can get a ride to the border."

Several days later María stuffed an old suitcase and several knitted shopping
bags with their clothes and drove with a friend to the border.
"What are you and the girls planning to do on the other side, María?"
"We're staying with my aunts; they have a big house."
"Aren't you staying with any of your brothers?"
"They all have their own families to worry about. I'll call them when I
have a job and a house of my own. We'll just stay with the aunts for a while."
Her friend left them two blocks from the border and María told her daugh-
ters to wait in front of a marriage office. "I'll be back soon, don't get married
while I'm gone."
The girls stood next to a man with a white smile who was sitting on the
sidewalk strumming a guitar. "What would you like me to play for you?"
Yoli answered. "We don't have any money."
"I'm not going to charge you. Just tell me what song you like."
"Whichever one you play," said Margarita.
The man began to sing in a sad tone:
    Ya se va la embarcación;

---

[1]This is an example of the transference of Spanish syntax in English; the
correct preposition should be "in."

ya se va por vías ligeras...

Lorena told Yoli, "That's an old song. Our grandfathers sang it to our grandmothers when they were trying to catch them."

The man overheard. "And they caught them, señoritas." He stopped playing and looked at the three girls, "Why do you girls want to go to the other side? Those gringos don't like Mexicans."

"They're going to have to learn to like us," said Lorena, "because we're planning to stay."

"I'd rather stay here, in God's country. I've been to the other side and I couldn't stand it for long."

He stared at the girls. "Maybe it'll be alright for you girls, but not for me. I could cross the border, I have papers, but I'm planning to stay here for as many years as God will grant me." He bent his head and continued playing.

The border was crowded. All of the gates had long lines of cars waiting their turn to cross. As usual, several men peddled their wares to the passing cars. Some sold velvet paintings, others ceramic animals, hats, leather wallets, anything they could carry. María took off her wedding band and stood next to a car. "Don't pass up this bargain—pure Mexican gold."

"I'll give you two dollars for it."

"Two dollars? You want to steal it from me? This is pure gold, twenty-four karats."

"Okay, I'll give you three dollars for it."

"Tenga!" said María making a fist. "Viejo avaro! You'd probably steal from your grandmother."

A young man who was selling velvet paintings walked up to María. "What are you selling, señora?"

"Nothing."

"No luck?"

"I want to sell my ring so I can buy bus tickets to Los Angeles, but these thieves want it free. How do you people make a living?"

"With great difficulty. May I see your ring, señora?" The young man studied the gold band.

"This is good gold."

"My husband paid thirty dollars for it, and that was a long time ago, it's worth more now. The old man wanted to give me three dollars for it."

The peddler shook his head. "Today has been a bad day for all of us, you should have been here yesterday, yesterday was a good day." He stared at María. "You look like a good person, and you need the money, I'll buy the ring from you."

"Thank you, thank you."

He scratched his head. "I'm sorry, seño, but I can't give you much for it. How much do you need to get across?"

He took a twenty dollar bill from his pocket and gave it to María. "I wish I could give you more, but this is all I have."

"This is fine, it's all I need for today; tomorrow, God will see."

"Good luck, seño."

"Good luck to you. I hope you sell all your paintings."

María returned to her daughters with a smile on her face. "Let's go, we're rich." They walked toward the border crossing, passing by the peddler. "Adiós," said María, "muchas gracias."

"Adiós, seño. You have beautiful daughters. They take after their mother." María saw a man with a cigar pulling at his sleeve, and shouting,

"Hey, amigo, give me a couple of those."

The young man sold two paintings to the man with the cigar, then took out the wedding band from his pocket. "Pure gold . . . best kind . . . twenty-four karat . . . forty dollar. . ."

"Forty dollars? Are you kidding?"

"Mister, this is Mexican gold, best kind."

The man checked the ring. "I'll give you twenty dollars for it."

"Thirty-five dollar. . ."

Near the border María stopped and faced her daughters. "Don't forget what I told you. When the border officer asks you where you were born, just say, 'I was born in Los Angeles, that's all you need to remember.'"

After crossing the border they walked into the bus depot, bought the tickets to Los Angeles and stepped into the empty bus. Each one sat on a separate seat in order to be near a window. They had not been to the States since they were little, and as Margarita said, "I don't want to miss anything."

Soon they were all accompanied. Three young men sat next to the girls and an older man sat next to María. Lorena took a book from her shopping bag and became completely engrossed in it, cutting off the boy's conversation.

"You could have at least given him a few moments, the boy was trying so hard," said Margarita later on the bus they rode from downtown Los Angeles to the aunt's house.

"The book was a lot more interesting."

Yoli had pretended to be a deaf mute. "Why did you do that?" asked Margarita. "He seemed like a nice boy."

"Nice? If I had tried to sit any further from him I would have been out of the window."

Margarita turned toward her mother. "That man that sat next to you looked kind of interesting."

"Ay, Margarita. If someone showed you the head of Pancho Villa, you would say, 'He's kind of short, but he's not bad.'"

"What was he doing with that pipe?" asked Lorena.

"That was his good luck charm. He rubbed it every few minutes and said, 'With a little luck, one can live well anywhere.'"

"It wasn't easy getting rid of them," said Lorena, "especially with Margarita urging them on." They walked out of the bus to their aunts' house.

They stood in front of a white Victorian house and stared at each other. "Are you sure you have the right address, mamá? This place looks like a mansion."

"I heard they had done well," said María, "but I didn't know they had done this well. Come on, let's not just stand here, let's knock on the door."

"María! What are you doing here?" shrieked a large bosomy woman with two white braids pinned on top of her head.

"You wrote to me, inviting me to come."

"I never wrote to you. But come in anyway, come in." said Josefina with a strange high laugh that made her bosom heave. Two tiny Chihuahua dogs stood at her feet barking incessantly.

"Watch out," said Lorena to the others, "They look like they want to take a piece off of us."

Josefina looked the girls over. "María, you should have never brought these young girls to this wicked city, they will soon become loose women."

"But you asked me to come."

"I never did such a thing. Consuelo! Come here! We have company. She's probably primping."

Consuelo walked into the living room wearing a long purple velvet robe with pink ruffles. She embraced María and said in a high voice, "Ay María! We were expecting you. What took you so long?"

"We were expecting her?" shouted Josefina. "So you're the one who invited them. Why didn't you let me in on it?"

"I did tell you; you can't hear, if you could, you'd get rid of those noisy dogs."

"You're the only noisy dog. Make yourself useful and bring these girls a glass of warm milk."

"You do it, you're the cook."

"The only reason I cook is because I'm afraid she'll poison me."

When Josefina was in the kitchen, Consuelo said to María, "Don't pay attention to her, every year she gets worse."

Josefina returned with six glasses of milk. "Not for me," said María. "What I would like right now is a tall glass of Uncle Pepe's wine."

"Is that old drunk still making that awful stuff?" said Josefina. "I thought he had croaked off by now, poisoned by that junk,"

"He's probably thinking the same thing about you and your herbal drinks," said Consuelo. "I would love to have a glass of wine too, maybe I could sleep for a change. I can't sleep with her snoring."

"My snoring? Your guilty conscience."

"I wish I had something to feel guilty about"

"Those nice girls just arrived and you want to pervert them already? Keep your thoughts to yourself." When Consuelo left the room for a moment, Josefina turned towards María and said, "She gets worse every year."

The day after they arrived the three girls enrolled in school and María was left alone with the two aunts. "They're set on making life miserable for each other and for anyone near them," said María. Whenever she left the house they wanted to know where she was going, who she was seeing, what she was doing and when she was returning. "I feel like a criminal."

"This city is very dangerous for a woman alone," said Josefina. "There are a lot of men prowling, ready to pounce on women like you."

When letters arrived addressed to María or her daughters, the aunts steamed them open, or as Margarita said, "One time I caught them with one of my letters, placing it against a lighted lamp."

"I'd put up with anything," said Yoli, "if they got rid of those dogs."

"I'm envious of them," said Lorena.

"Envious?"

"Yes, envious. Whenever I go into the kitchen to look for a snack, they start cooking pieces of filet mignon for the dogs. I glare at the dogs and they growl back at me."

"That's never happened to me," said Yoli.

"To me neither," said Margarita.

"That's because they know that I am the one who likes steak the most."

Every night María returned from job hunting with an aching back and blistered feet.

"You look tired, mamá, stay home tomorrow and rest."

"Rest? With those two women? I must find work so we can save money and move away from here. You'll see. I'll find a job soon, I have to."

The following day María faced her daughters with a smile. "Didn't I tell you I'd find work soon?"

"You did? Where?"

"In a sewing factory, downtown."

"That's kind of far, isn't it?"

"It takes me one hour by bus, but at least I don't have to transfer."

"I thought you said you had gone to all the sewing shops and that they weren't hiring."

"I walked into the only shop I hadn't been to, sat down at an empty sewing machine, and refused to get up."

"What did the owner do?"

"He told me he wasn't hiring, to go home. I told him I really needed the work, that I wasn't leaving. So he brought me a bundle of blouses, asked me to sew one, and when he looked at it and couldn't find anything wrong with it, he told me I was hired, to return tomorrow. I told him I was ready to work today, and continued working on the other blouses. I sewed six blouses today."

"How much do they pay you?"

"A dollar a blouse."

"That's all?"

"It's the same at the other shops. A few of them pay by the hour, but I heard these were harder to get into, and that they don't let you breathe."

As soon as the aunts found out that María was working, Josefina told her, "You have a job now, María, you can afford to pay us a little something." And a little something turned out to be half of her paycheck.

"They have plenty of money," said Yoli, "why do they need our money?"

"To buy filet mignon for their dogs," said Lorena.

"Look," said María, "if we eat less and walk more maybe we can soon afford to move away from here."

"If I eat any less, I'll disappear."

"Maybe you'll disappear to a better place."

"I need a new dress, I feel like Cinderella before she met her godmother."

"Don't flatter yourself, you look more like one of the stepsisters."

"And you act like one"

"¡Ya basta!" shouted María. "You're beginning to sound like the aunts. We better move out of here soon."

That night María began a novena to Saint Ann asking for help in finding a house. When the weeks passed and she still found herself in the aunts' house, she began a novena to Saint Jude, the patron saint of difficult, desperate and impossible cases. She walked to a nearby church, lit a candle and whispered her morning prayers to Saint Jude. She walked out of the church muttering to herself, "God takes his time, but he doesn't forget."

It was a warm Sunday afternoon and María found it intolerable in the house listening to her two aunts. She took the money that she had been saving with great difficulty and decided to treat herself and her daughters to a movie. It was their first night out in the city and they were in good spirits. "The movie wasn't bad," said María, "and it sure felt good getting away from the aunts."

They returned at nine o'clock and found the house dark and locked with a safety lock. "We can't get in" said María, "it's bolted from the inside. Lorena, go see if the back door is open, and you, Margarita, go check all the windows."

Lorena and Margarita soon returned to the front door. "Everything is locked."

"Okay, Yoli, go knock on their bedroom window."

"Let me have the privilege," said Lorena.

"Lorena!" called María, "just knock on the window, don't break it."

"They don't want to answer," said Lorena, "but I know they're in there."

María pounded on the door until a light went on in the house. Josefina stood before them in a long white flannel nightgown with her braids hanging down to her shoulders and her two dogs barking at her feet.

"This is no time for decent young women to be out in the street. Next time I won't let you in."

Lorena whispered to Yoli, "I thought they didn't make those nightgowns anymore."

María called her eldest brother the following day and asked him for a small loan and for help in finding a house. "You should have called me sooner, María, what's a family for?"

"I'm really eager to see you and your family, Ramón, but I didn't want to bother you, I know how busy you are."

"Give me a few days, I'll see what I can do. As soon as I find something I'll call you."

The days passed slowly. As soon as they returned from school and work they locked themselves in the bedroom that they occupied on the upper floor of the two story house. "I feel like a prisoner," said Yoli. They packed their belongings in their suitcase and shopping bags and were ready to leave at a moment's notice. They spent their time listening to the radio and reading. "I've read the same book three times," said Lorena. And they reminisced about their life in México. The window that faced the street became the center of attraction.

Yoli stood by the window and ran her fingers through the fine lace curtains. "How did the aunts get rich, mamá?"

"I'll tell you someday."

"Tell us now."

"It was during the Depression and I was a little girl then, but those times are hard to forget. There were seven of us in the family and your grandfather had lost the two jobs that he held; so he reached a desperate solution. In the garage at the back of the house where we lived, your grandfather filled a barrel with rice, barley, prunes and raisins. One week later, after this mixture fermented, he walked into the garage early in the morning with a starched white coat and the seriousness of a chemist. He boiled the white fermented mixture in a pot, adding burnt sugar to it to give it a golden color. This mixture cooked into a strong liquor, 100 percent proof, and many say, delicious."

"How did grandmother Carlota feel about this?"

"She was strongly opposed to the bootlegging, but not for moral reasons, since it was the Depression and there were five children to feed, and it was not for fear that your grandfather would get caught, since that meant that he would be jailed, and that was the only way that she could hope to keep him at a distance. Her main objection was that he never made any money at it. As soon as he finished, he called a neighbor, an old friend of his, and the tasting began. I watched them from a crack in the garage door, as they tasted with their fingers, and then took sips from a teaspoon, then from a ladle, and then a glass. Then I watched them bottle the liquor, as they continued with the tasting. I already knew more or less when they would pass out, and when they would come to, to continue with the sealed bottles. The garage, or The Portillo Distillery, was off limits to everyone in the family, but I had the privilege of acting as watchdog on brewing days. When the strong mixture was brewing, I stood on the street corner of our house to look out for suspicious looking people, someone from another neighborhood that could turn him in. The smell of the brewing liquor was so strong that it's still a mystery to me that your grandfather never got caught. On brewing days I was a double spy, since your grandmother had me watch the garage so I could let her know when your grandfather and his friend passed out. As soon as I saw them lying on the floor, I ran to tell my mother, and then we would both go into the garage, and with great speed, take out the sealed bottles, as many as we could take out before your grandfather woke up."

"What did grandmother do with the bottles?"

"She passed them to Josefina. Josefina and Consuelo lived next door to us at the time and they were just as quarrelsome then as they are now. Our houses were separated by a tall wood fence, and that's where Josefina waited anxiously, taking the bottles from us for a penny each. Josefina was a curandera, well known in the barrio, and she sold your grandfather's bottles as a cure-all. I always wondered if her patients used the brew as medicine, or if they bought it as medicine but used it as the liquor that it was, but during those times her fame as a curandera soared."

"Josefina was a sharp one."

"She sure was. She also raised chickens. Who knows how many chickens she had in the chicken coop that she built next to the fence that divided our houses, but all of our neighbors complained about the noisy chickens, and some of them even began to say that the chickens were bewitched, since they cackled during those hours when chickens are supposed to sleep. Nobody could figure out why the chickens made such a racket, until I discovered what was happening. When your grandfather finished brewing, while I stood on the street looking out for strangers, he took the sediment of the strong brew and threw it over the fence, and it fell into the chicken coop. The chickens gobbled it up, leaving no trace of the concentrated sediment. Right away the chickens became drunk, cackling wildly. When the Depression was over, we no longer had to put up with drunk chickens; we returned to our usual problems."

"What did our grandfather do then?"

"He got a job in a machine shop."

"So our grandfather was in the liquor business," said Lorena.

"And so was your great-grandfather.

"Was he a bootlegger too?"

"Your great-grandfather was in the legitimate liquor business. He owned and operated one of the best tequila distilleries in México."

Their conversation was interrupted by shouts and loud knocks on the bedroom door. "María! María!" María quickly hid the shopping bags in the closet before opening the door. Josefina stood before her, her bosom heaving. "Someone wants you on the phone. It's a man!" María walked calmly down the stairs while Josefina and her dogs followed noisily behind her.

"Just listen, you don't have to say anything. This is Ramón. I disguised my voice so I wouldn't have to talk to the aunts. Why add to life's miseries? I'll be there tomorrow at six in the afternoon. I'll be waiting for you two blocks north of the aunts' house; watch for a blue camper. See you tomorrow, María."

María looked sideways at Josefina who was standing next to her, and whispered into the telephone. "I'll be counting the minutes."

Josefina looked at her sternly. "You're up to no good, María. I don't like this."

María returned to her bedroom and told her daughters the good news. They embraced her, raised the volume on the radio, and sang, danced, and stomped on the wooden floor. There was soon a loud knock on the door and when Margarita opened it Josefina stormed in and looked around the room as if looking for someone. "Well, where are they? Where are you hiding them?" She looked under the bed. "Where are all those people making that racket? It can't possibly be just the four of you."

"It is," said Lorena.

"Well cut it out."

Consuelo stood at the door in a flowing pink gown. "Where's the party?"

"The party has just ended," said Josefina, as she led her sister down the stairs.

María closed the door and turned to her daughters. "The party has just begun."

The following afternoon they all sat on the edge of their beds glancing at the antique clock on the wall. When the clock marked 5:30, María stood up. They picked up their shopping bags and before opening the door, María told them, "Don't make any noise, go down slowly and quietly, I don't want a scene with the aunts." They tiptoed down the stairs and when María was about to open the door that led to the outside of the house, the dogs began to bark noisily. "Perros desgraciados," said María.

"I think there's someone at the door," shrieked Josefina. María opened the door and was about to step out, when Josefina grabbed her arm and shouted, "Consuelo! Consuelo! Come quickly! They're trying to leave."

Consuelo stood next to Josefina. "María, how can you do this to us, leaving like this, without even saying goodbye."

"We didn't want to bother you, we felt it would be better this way."

Consuelo was crying. "How can you leave us alone?"

Josefina broke in, ". . . to die, to die all alone."

"Neither of you is going to die."

Margarita began to cry with her aunts. "You are going to get lost in the big city," said Josefina, "at least leave the girls with us."

"If we get lost," said María, "we'll get lost together."

Margarita was still crying as they walked away from the aunts. "Maybe they really feel bad about us leaving."

"Of course they do," said María. "They won't have so many people to push around."

They stood at the place that Ramón had indicated, glancing furtively towards the aunts' house. "Hurry up, tío Ramón," said Lorena, "before the aunts catch up with us."

A blue camper parked next to them and a tall, thin man stepped out and embraced them. "Let's go before the aunts come," said María.

"Get in quickly," said Ramón, as he opened the camper's back door and helped them in. He slammed the doors shut and drove away at high speed.

They stopped in front of a small white house. "I saw several houses, but this one is by far the best and the cheapest; and it's furnished. Why don't you and the girls take a look at it, the owners live in the back."

An old woman wearing a black dress and black stockings answered the door.

"We are interested in seeing the house for rent," said María.

A heavy old man with a red face walked up to the door and said, rolling his r's, "I am Mr. Kovacs, the owner, and this is my wife, Maritza. We don't want no drinking, no wild parties. We want to rent to quiet people."

"My daughters and I are quiet."

Mr. Kovacs studied María and the three girls, his eyebrows knitted into a frown. He handed María a key, still frowning. "You may see the house."

The paint on the outside of the house was peeling, the bedroom was painted dark blue and was full of cracks, the kitchen was too small, two windows were broken, one faucet didn't work, "and worst of all," said María, "the owners live in the back." But they all took an immediate liking to the house. "It breathes."

"When would you people like to move in?"

"Today," said María. She returned to the camper. "We're taking the house, Ramón. Thanks for helping us find it. It has its problems but it'll do until we can afford something better."

Ramón gave her five twenty dollar bills. "Here, this should help you a little."

"Thank you, Ramón, it'll help a lot. I'll pay you back as soon as I can." When the blue camper was no longer visible they walked back into their new house.

They walked through the house checking the furniture and opening closets, then they sat down at a sturdy wooden table that took up most of the kitchen. "Well," asked María, "how do you like it?"

"It's better than living with the aunts," said Lorena.

"And better than the last house we rented in México," said Yoli.

"What house?" said Lorena. "You mean that chicken coop? I'll hate chickens for the rest of my life."

"What a life, spending one's time fighting chickens, as if we didn't have anything better to do."

"We didn't."

They recalled the last house they had lived in in México. It was located on a hill, "away from civilization." Their neighbors raised chickens that roamed freely in the neighborhood and that María said had a fondness for her backyard. "That was a small house. Every time I turned I bumped into something."

"It was a doll house."

"A doll house for chickens."

They remembered how early they went to bed in that house since they didn't have electricity. "We slept at the same time as the chickens."

"We did have light on the outside of the house," recalled Lorena. A 100 watt lightbulb on the back porch of their neighbor's house lit a small portion of their backyard, and in the summer the girls sat near that light and read, drew, and talked.

"We can't complain too much about that house," said Lorena, "we had nightly entertainment. Remember Julio El Ruiseñor? Everyone thought he was crazy, but I thought he sang well."

"He wasn't bad, but he never stopped."

"He had talent, he wrote his own words to the songs."

"He couldn't remember the words."

María remembered the boy's songs and the good parties they had in the small house with the borrowed light of the naked lightbulb and the full moon. Their friends brought the food and drinks and the neighbors were invited with the agreement that they keep their chickens and dogs locked up. "Remember the parties?"

"Julio El Ruiseñor always provided the entertainment."

"He really outdid himself on those days."

"Did any of you ever see him?"

"Never. He never came out of that house. He just sat by the dark window and sang."

"I wonder what was wrong with him."

"Maybe he was really ugly."

"His brothers were all good-looking."

"Maybe he was an ugly duckling."

"That house was at least better than the one we lived in before that," said Margarita, and they all agreed with her. María recalled how they had hesitated to look at the house because of its size; it was three storied, had seven bedrooms, two baths and a huge living room. "That living room looked like a dance hall." When they found out the incredibly low rent they took the house immediately, "before somebody else could grab it." But there had been one disturbance after another. "All those strange noises, especially at night."

"If there were ghosts, they were sure noisy ones."

"The ghosts were having more fun than us."

"Remember our neighbor? El Chino Agustín."

"Yeah, the owner of the tortilla shop. They said his store was a front for an opium den . . . high stake gambling and opium orgies."

"No wonder he was so rich."

"He would have gotten rich anyway, with the high price he charged for his tortillas."

"He made good tortillas."

"Maybe we had Chinese ghosts."

"Whatever they were, they got rid of all our guests," said María. "I remember when Chuy and Lucas went to stay with us for one week. One night was all they lasted. They didn't even stay for breakfast. 'This house is haunted, María, you should move out of here, I'm afraid for you and the girls.' It was the same with everyone else who stayed there. They claimed they heard noises all night, whispers, wails, screams, tapping. Nobody lasted more than a night."

"How did we last so long?"

"Necessity. Besides, I always felt it was termites."

"Termites that wailed?"

"They were also afraid of the ghosts."

María stood up. "Enough talk, let's get to work. This house needs to be dusted if we're going to sleep in it tonight." She took her shopping bag, dropped the contents on the table and picked out one of her dresses. "This dress could be sold as an antique, but we'll put it to a good use." She looked at the old evening dress that brought good memories and then quickly tore it into four pieces. "Okay, choose a room and get to work."

Lorena cleaned the large window of the sunroom. "This is a great place to read. I'm going to turn this room into a bedroom and library."

Margarita glided through the living room, dusting the furniture. "We'll have great parties here."

María cleaned the bedroom. "We'll need to paint this room, it looks like a coffin."

Yoli worked quietly, she had chosen the bathroom.

When María finished cleaning the bedroom, she continued with the kitchen, and when she finished, she sat for a moment by the kitchen window and stared at the full yellow moon that reminded her of a corn tortilla.

It was Friday afternoon, one day after María had moved into her new house. Word had spread that she was residing in the United States and her house began to fill with relatives. They came singly, in couples, whole families; there were some that she had not seen for many years and young ones that she had never met. They came with gifts: bags of groceries, food they had prepared themselves, clothes, old furniture and cases of beer. One of them gave María a record player. "It's old, but it works." Ramón walked in with his twenty-two-year-old son, Valentín, looked around the crowded room, shrugged his shoulders, and said to María, "I couldn't keep them away."

María observed them all—the young, the old, the ageless—and felt that it was the same as old times, before she had gone to live to México with her husband. They were all there, gathered in her small house, a mixture of every type of Mexican. There were the Mexican-American, old Pachucos, the Pochos and the Mexicanos; and there were a few who defied description. She heard the fluent Spanish and the fluent English, and the dialects created by the merging of these two languages. She heard the children, arguing as usual, and she noticed that even the arguments were similar.

"Did you hear what she said? She's ten years old and she can't speak English."

"Why should I speak English? I'm Mexican."

"You live in the United States, you should speak English."

"I don't live here. I'm visiting."

"Visiting? You've been visiting for three years."

"At least I speak English better than you speak Spanish. What kind of Mexican are you?"

"I'm not Mexican, I'm American, and so are you, we were born here."

María saw her young niece running to her mother.

"Mamá! Louie says that I'm American because I was born here. Is that true?"

"Tell me, mi hijita, if the kittens are born in the oven, are they kittens or are they biscuits?"

After a few of these assaults by her Mexican-American cousins, the Mexican Portillo would be eager to return to México, where, she felt, people were more civilized. But María knew what would happen in México. Only one Anglicized Spanish word slipping from her tongue and she would be laughed at and labeled Pocha. And the girl would be eager to return to "the other side." María could hear a well meaning aunt advising her young niece.

"Don't forget, Conchita, you are Mexican and you always will be. Spanish is your language and you must speak it all the time so you won't forget it; it would be a great sin if you did."

She saw another relative take Conchita aside and tell her, "Don't listen to your aunt, you'll never get ahead that way. You must stop speaking Spanish or you won't learn English well. You live in the United States, English is your language now."

Conchita shrugged her shoulders. "These gente! Who les entiende, pues."

"Concha! What's that I hear? Speak Spanish or speak English. None of that mixed-up stuff."

María smiled. It was the same as before. It was hard to tell that so many years had passed, except when she saw her grown daughters. She could hear them talking to their cousin Valentín about college. Her daughters didn't need encouragement, only money. "There must be something I can do," thought María. "College is good for these kids." She noticed how Valentín had grown from a small shy boy to a confident, articulate young man. He stood tall, thin, observant, his fast eyes scanning the people around him. Lorena had told María about him, that he was a sociology major in his third year of college, that he talked a lot about changing the world and that Villa was his idol because he didn't let anything get in his way. He felt that the best way to achieve his goal was by acquiring great wealth, and through his wealth, obtain power, that he would use to equalize society. "We must begin by working on our families, they think like peons."

"Isn't that what you want to create?" said Lorena, "A society of peons?"

"Look, it wouldn't be so bad if we were all peons; what's no good is that we've been doing the hard work, while the others have been having all the fun."

María watched Valentín glide across the small room. He stood before a group of men that were discussing the family tequila business, headed by his father, Ramón.

"You should get out of this business, this is no good. You're all going to get caught, and for what? For a few dollars?"

"If we got paid decent wages, we wouldn't have to bother with tequila," said Rufelio, another of María's elder brothers.

"You don't."

"What do you suggest we do?"

"Get rid of the tequila and get into dope."

"Dope!" shouted Ramón. "What do you think we are?"

"That's where the money is . . ."

"Money! Money! That's all you talk about."

"It's not the money I'm interested in, it's the power that money brings. Power! That's what rich people have that poor people don't."

"What do these rich people know about life?" said Ramón. "About friends, music, love, familia . . ."

"And cerveza Tecate," said Rufelio pouring salt and squeezing lemon into his beer, sipping it and smacking his lips.

"You start making money and soon you want more and more, and you don't know when to stop," continued Ramón. "You get so caught up in it that you don't give a damn about nothing else."

"But can't you see," said Valentín, "with the set up you have, you could do great business, and power, man, you could have power."

"Don't listen to my son. ¡Está loco! ¡Loco!"

"Don't worry," said Rufelio, squeezing more lemon into his Tecate beer, "to foolish words, deaf ears."

The relative who had brought the old record player put on a record. From it came a fast beat, then the music stopped for a moment, and a deep voice said "Tequila."

"Hey," said Ramón, "They're playing our song."

"Your song," said Valentín, walking away from the group of men with whom he was talking.

María walked up to Ramón. "Your son has grown up."

"Since he started college he thinks he knows everything."

"But college is good for them. I wish my girls could go, they really want to but . . . you know how it is."

"Yeah, it costs. Want to sell tequila? It'll help pay for the tuition."

María thought of the factory and wondered how many bundles of clothes she would have to bring home to sew to pay for her daughters' school. She looked at Ramón. "When do I start?"

One by one the Portillos left the party, embracing María, and promising, "We'll be here next Friday."

The morning after the Friday night party there was a loud knock on María's door. Mr. Kovacs stood in front of her with his red face redder than usual and the veins of his thick neck bulging. "You must leave at once! You are noisy, loud people! You kept me and my wife awake all night!" María smiled at him and he began to tremble and his voice to shake. "If you don't leave by tomorrow, I will call the police!" he shouted as he walked away.

María's daughters gathered around her. "What are we going to do, mamá? Do we have to move again?"

"We're not moving."

"But he said we had to move."

"Nobody is going to kick us out."

"But mamá, he said he would call the police."

"We're staying."

"What are you planning to do?"

"If all else fails, we'll pray to Saint Jude, but I'm leaving that as a last resort, I'm already too indebted to him."

"But mamá . . ."

María looked at her daughters. "Where's your faith?" The girls did not say anything else; they knew that in matters of faith it was useless to argue with their mother. Or as María would say, "One shouldn't argue with Saint Jude."

The following day Mr. Kovacs stood with his red face at María's door. "Why have you people not left yet? Do I have to call the police?"

"You don't have to do any such thing."

The old man shook his fists in the air. "You are going to be the cause of my heart attack! You loud people!"

"Now, Mr. Kovacs, we can't be all that bad." She took his arm. "Come in, we can talk better sitting down." She guided him into the kitchen and served him a bowl of menudo and a large glass of Uncle Pepe's wine.

Mr. Kovacs sipped the wine. "I know you are not bad people, but I can't stand all that racket."

"Don't worry, Mr. Kovacs, we'll only have parties on weekends."

At these words, the old man choked, and María patted him on the back as she continued talking. "We might be a little noisy, but we're nice people. We'll take good care of your house, you don't have to worry."

After two bowls of menudo and three glasses of Uncle Pepe's wine, Mr. Kovacs was laughing with a laugh that fit his heaviness. "I haven't tasted wine like this since I left the old country." He smacked his lips. "This is good wine, pure, rich, not like that colored water they try to pass for wine in the stores. And this soup, this wonderful, wonderful soup. Ah, María, you are a real cook." He left the house bowing at María. "Thank you, thank you, you are a nice lady. Tomorrow I will bring you Hungarian pastry. My wife makes the best pastry in the world." María could hear him muttering as he walked away, "Fine woman . . . fine woman. . . ."

Every Friday night the Portillos crowded into María's house for the week-end party. Menudo, "the best cure for a hangover," cooked for several hours in a huge pot on the stove. "It revives the dead," asserted María. Several bowls of lemon wedges, oregano and diced onion, and a tall stack of corn tortillas were set on the kitchen table that was covered with an embroidered tablecloth. The long cotton tablecloth was more than a decoration, it covered the cases of tequila that María kept under the table. A plastic icebox filled with beer sat on the floor, the mariachis played on the record player, and the party was about to begin. No one could be sure of what would happen next. But the Portillos were rarely to blame for any disorder. The troublemaker was usually a friend of a friend or most often a bato loco from the neighborhood who was stirred by the smell of menudo and who had caught a glimpse of one of the Portillo girls. He would walk into the party, passing himself off as somebody's cousin, and after a few beers and several unsuccessful advances toward the Portillo girls, he would decide that all Portillos were snobs.

The fights were usually stopped before anyone was seriously hurt. But there were a few Portillos who liked a good fight and when they were around it was usually María who put a stop to it. She stood in front of the intruder with an open bottle of first rate tequila, offered him a drink, and soon had him under the table. "Tequila is responsible for many good deeds."

"How is tequila made?" asked Lorena.

María explained how the sweet juice aguamiel is extracted from the maguey plant, fermented into pulque, a white thick liquid, then distilled into a clear liquid, tequila. "Indians believe the cactus has divine powers, that a god lives in a maguey."

"Maybe it is holy," said Ramón. "Tequila will cure anything."

"They say it's the alcohol in it," said Rufelio, "that it kills all the germs in your body; if you survive, you'll be cured of your illness."

"It's a good body rub," said María, "great for arthritis, and a glass in the bath will stop a cold."

They all kept an open bottle of tequila in their house. They felt it was more reliable than the family doctor. The doctor also had faith in tequila, but María knew that his faith in it was not for backaches but for heartaches. He was not interested in what the strong, fermented drink could do for his body, but in what it could do for his soul.

In any case, Dr. Hernández did not believe in sickness of the body. He strongly believed that the soul suffered and caused the patient a variety of physical discomforts, all illusions of the distorted soul. When anyone in the family called on him, if they were lucky enough to find him, whatever their ailment was, from a mild sore throat to impending death, the doctor would laugh his loud vibrating laugh and assure the suffering Portillo that everything was alright. "Nothing's wrong with you," he said, "nothing at all. You're a healthy man, don't worry." And he laughed his good deep laugh.

At times, when they felt it was a matter of life and death, the Portillos called all of the neighborhood bars until they found Dr. Hernández. He walked into their house with a small black bag and a wide smile. After greeting everyone in the house, he walked up to the sick Portillo, looked him in the eyes and said, "You look fine, just fine. Is this what I was called for? This man is stronger than I am." He then slapped the moribund Portillo on the back, and after firmly refusing payment, he had a quick drink that he was offered and walked out of the house with his unopened black bag.

The sick Portillos always regained their health. Be it faith or luck, nobody had died on Dr. Hernández yet. He had thus gained the reputation of a true healer.

Ramón, who had been cured of typhoid said, "I know it was the slaps on the back that saved me; the doctor has miraculous hands."

"You could be right," said Rufelio, "but I feel that it's his gaze."

"That's right," said another Portillo, "those eyes could frighten away whatever evil spirits are responsible for ill health."

"If you asked me," said María, "I would say that it's his laughter. The doctor's laughter could bring back the dead." Others had different opinions.

The Friday night party was well underway when Dr. Hernández walked in. He went straight to María and embraced her strongly. "Ay María! You're as beautiful as ever." He had brought his guitar and was soon singing songs of lost love and lost hope in his deep voice. He had a wide repertoire and also did a lot of improvising. Everyone joined in the singing. Some had good voices, others couldn't keep a tune, but no one lacked enthusiasm. Besides having a good singing voice, the doctor was also a good orator and he often interrupted his songs to recite poems:

Si porque a tus plantas ruego
Como un ilota[2] rendido
Y una mirada te pido
Con temor, casi con miedo . . .

It had been a long time since María had seen Dr. Hernández and she was happy to see him again. She felt like the night, full of poetry, of music, of laughter, of soul cries.

Valentín stood by the door with watchful eyes. In spite of studies, work, politics, and girls, he always had time for his family. He made time, they were vital to his plan. It was the moment he had been waiting for—everyone had drunk enough to be receptive to him, but nobody had passed out yet. María saw his eyes slanting a little more than usual as he stood in the middle of the room and began his speech. "You're all letting a great opportunity go to waste. With the kind of setup you have you could be making money, real money. Can't you all see it, you're in the wrong business."

"So are you," someone shouted. "The way you like to preach you should become a priest."

"That's right," said another. "Every good family should have a priest. Padre Portillo. It even sounds good."

"Don't give him any ideas," said Ramón. "It's bad enough with a politician; what would we do with a priest?"

"Get rich," said Rufelio. Everyone laughed, and they began to tell priest stories.

As usual, Valentín was left talking to himself. A drunken uncle staggered toward him and lifted his beer bottle. "I'll drink to y-you, y-you sanababichi, you know what you're t-talking about. Ga-gaddamit, I'm ti-tired of being so ga-gaddam poor. E-every night, be-beans and tortillas, to-tortillas and beans, be-beans and to-tortillas . . ." He looked crosseyed at Valentín. "You-you're alright." He staggered toward Ramón. "You have a sha-sharp son."

"I know. Sharp like the corner of a mattress."

Valentín cornered Dr. Hernández who was strumming his guitar. "I try to reason with them, but they won't listen."

---

[2]slave.

Dr. Hernández continued playing his guitar. "You have a nice family, camarada, you should be proud of them."

"I can't figure them out."

Dr. Hernández stopped playing and looked at Valentín. "They're good people, camarada, they know what counts." He saw Valentín's intense face and laughed, slapping the young man on the back. "Cheer up, camarada, you have a fine family."

María stood under the white circle in the sky but she didn't feel warmer. It had been several months since she had left México and she felt that it was time to return. She called Ramón and asked him if she could go with him on his next trip.

"Sure, María, I'll be happy to have someone to complain to."

When their sister Emilia heard the honk of the camper, she ran out of the house shouting, "Ramón. Ya llegó Ramón. María! He brought María." The two sisters embraced while several of Emilia's neighbors stood around them smiling.

"I don't count anymore?" said Ramón.

"I see you every week," said Emilia. "But María, I haven't seen her for . . ."

"For too long," said María, and they embraced each other again.

"That's enough. You're acting as if you hadn't seen each other for twenty years."

"It seems that long," said Emilia, wiping tears from her face. "You look good, María, you must be doing well."

"I'm doing alright, but I miss it here."

"This?" said Emilia, stretching her arms toward the unpaved street and her small, unpainted house.

They walked into Emilia's house and María stopped at the door and exclaimed, "Rufelio! What are you doing here?"

"Same thing you are."

"He's always here," said Emilia. "I can't get rid of him."

"He can't always be here," said María, "he's always at my house. If I didn't know better, I'd swear you had a twin." María knew that Rufelio wasn't the only one who spent a lot of time at Emilia's house. Her sister's house was usually filled with people. Emilia claimed that she didn't have a house but a hotel. Most of the visitors were relatives from the States, some passing by to other parts of México, and those whose final destination was Emilia's house. Crossing the border was a continuous ritual to the Portillos. "In a way the border is invisible," said María. She knew that they never really left México, and that México never left them.

"I know why you come," said Emilia to Rufelio, "you can't stay away from my beans."

"You're right. That's what you get for making the best beans in the world."

Emilia shrugged. "When you cook beans every day, you get pretty good at it."

Emilia stirred a huge pot of beans, poured some into a greased pan, added white cheese to them, and after they had boiled for a few minutes, she served full plates to them and began warming tortillas. While they were eating, she spoke to them rapidly. "Do you know that El Sapo has two women living in his house? La Changa told me all about it. She lives in the apartment next to his and she says that the walls are so thin that one can hear everything that goes on in there. 'It's almost like living with him,' says La Changa. 'Why don't you,' I told her. 'What's one more woman in El Sapo's life?' 'I'm not that desperate,' she said. 'I can still choose, I'm not ready to grab yet.' "I think they would make a good pair," said Emilia. "El Sapo y La Changa, made for each other. I heard from La Tostada who lives on the other side of El Sapo that La Changa had actually tried to move in with him but that he had refused. 'You're too old for me,' he told her. "She's only thirty-two and he's over fifty," said Emilia, "but he likes young girls. La Tostada says that La Changa is spreading a lot of rumors about El Sapo because he wouldn't pay attention to her, but I believe everything she says about him; the way his green eyes bulge and the way he grins, he looks like a pervert."

They all continued eating while Emilia kept on talking. It didn't seem to matter to her that her relatives had not met the people she spoke of, and that they probably never would. She spoke excitedly about all of her neighbors and then continued with her birds. She had many of them, in small cages throughout her house. She pointed to her homosexual canaries, and a mynah bird that was paranoid. But her favorite was Zoila, a small green parrot that paced her house chanting, "Puro pedo. . . puro pedo. . ."

"Haven't you taught her anything else?" asked María.

"The dumb bird doesn't want to learn anything else."

"She's not so dumb," said Rufelio. "In only two words she's summed up the meaning of life."

Ramón finished his beer and turned toward María. "I can't listen to this anymore, María, let's get to work."

"What work? I'm vacationing."

"Hey, Ramón," said Emilia, "all you think about is work, work, work. You're wearing out fast."

"You wear out faster with talk, talk, talk. Come on, María, before she wears out your ear."

"Don't complain, you know you love my stories."

"He does, but he'll never admit it," said Rufelio.

"Come on, María, let's get away from these two. I want to show you how I pack the tequila in the camper, in case you need to make the trip by yourself."

"You'll have to get someone else to do it, Ramón, I don't think I could."

"You'd be the best one for the job, María, you have the most innocent face."

"That makes you the worst one, Rufelio," said Emilia.

Ramón and María walked into Emilia's garage and María watched while Ramón worked in the darkness, filling the custom-made camper. He raised the floor, dropped the walls, and fitted the numerous bottles into the small compartments. The fit was exact to avoid breakage and rattling. Once all of the spaces were filled, he replaced the floor and wall paneling, and once again the camper looked like an average camper.

After saying goodbye to Emilia and Rufelio, María and Ramón drove quietly to the border.

"Bringing anything from México?"

"No. Nothing at all."

"Okay. Have a nice day."

As soon as they passed the border, María said, "Step on the gas, Ramón, let's get far from them."

"Calm down, María, you wouldn't want me to get a speeding ticket."

"If you can't make the trip one day, ask someone else to come; I couldn't cross with the loaded camper. I don't know how you do it."

"I think of Valentín's school. Besides, it gets easier after a while; it becomes a routine, like any other job."

"Leave me out of it, I'll stick to selling it."

It was still afternoon when María arrived at her house. Ramón placed four cases of tequila on her living room floor and left. María still had two cases left from the previous week stacked under the kitchen table where she always kept them, but she knew that she would sell them all soon. She served herself a small glass of Uncle Pepe's wine to relax, sat at the kitchen table and waited for her daughters who would soon be returning from school. She stretched her legs, but she could not feel the cases of tequila. She picked up the long tablecloth and searched under the table.

When her two eldest daughters returned from school, María called to them. "Margarita! Lorena! Did you move the boxes of tequila from under the table?"

"Not me," said Margarita.

"I never touch those boxes," said Lorena.

"Well, where are they then? They're too heavy to move by themselves."

"Let's call Detective Pérez," said Lorena. "The Case of the Missing Tequila, or The Missing Tequila Case."

"Stop joking; help me find the boxes."

They had just begun the search for the tequila, when Yoli walked in. "Yoli! Did you move the tequila from the kitchen?"

"Yes."

"So you're the one. Where did you put it?"

"I sold it."

"You did what?"

"I sold it."

"Who did you sell it to?"

"To Sergio. He came this morning before I left for school and said that he needed it right away, so I sold it to him."

"Listen, all of you. Selling tequila is my business, not yours. I don't want this ever to happen again. Do you hear?" They all nodded. "And I told you many times that I don't want any men coming in the house while I'm not here, especially men like Sergio. How much did you sell it for?"

"Twenty-five dollars a case."

"What? That's five dollars more than I get. How did you get Sergio to agree?"

"I told him that I couldn't sell it to him, that I wasn't allowed to, but he insisted, said he needed it soon, so I told him that if he needed it that badly he would have to pay more for it."

"Maybe you should let her handle the tequila, mamá, we could make more money," said Lorena.

"I give my customers a good price, that's why they keep coming back. Besides, I told you many times that I don't want any of you touching this stuff. And when I'm not around, keep the men out."

María walked out of the room and Yoli whispered to Lorena, "Too bad, I was ready to start my own business."

After her daughters had gone to bed, María sat alone at the kitchen table. She wanted a different life for her daughters, for them to finish high school, to attend college and to have good jobs. She wanted them to have big dreams and to be able to fulfill them. She felt she was doing everything possible to help them achieve their goals . . . or maybe not . . . maybe there was more she could do . . . she was not sure . . . she felt tired. Maybe if she prayed more . . . She would pray to Saint Ann, and to Saint Anthony and to Saint Jude. She would start a novena to San Martín de Porres. She would pray for her daughters and the saints would answer . . . she hoped that they would . . . the saints were good to her . . . they answered her prayers . . . most of the time. She looked at the moon. It was a waning moon . . . or perhaps it was waxing . . .

It was still dark when María woke up. If she hurried, she would have time to go to church before going to work.

She lit a candle and felt the small flame soothing her. She thought of her father. "Lighting candles is no small thing, María. When you light a candle you're asking for light, for understanding, for guidance."

María had not seen her father for several years. No one in the family visited him, except for Valentín, and she knew the reasons. Don Severino was usually in a bad mood from having lost his pension check at poker and for having to drink cheap wine. They all disliked the smell of cheap liquor that was impregnated in the room, and the sight of the shirtless old man with his piercing blue eyes and cynical smile. He had used his fists on his sons, and on occasion, on the women, though the Portillo women were not ones to put up with such treatment. "Do you think we're still in México?" had said his wife after such an incident. "You can't get away with that here; this is a woman's country." The judge who tried his case turned out to be a woman and her father had difficulty getting out of jail. Besides, everyone in the family wanted to keep him there. When that was no longer possible, some of them tried to have him committed to a mental institution. But that plan also failed, which prompted the Portillos to say, "Not even the crazy house wants him." María knew that they all feared him because they knew that he was capable of anything. Some of the Portillos felt that he had mellowed with age, but they weren't taking any chances. She would go see him; he was a relative, her father, familia. She promised Saint Jude that she would pay her father a visit.

On her way to her father's house, María recalled the last time that she had gone to see him. She was told that he was still living in the same place, and though several years had passed since she had gone there, the dilapidated hotel was clear in her mind. When her daughters were small, she had sometimes taken them to visit him, and at those times he would ask them all to wait outside. He would then begin to work on his room as quick as his semi-drunken condition and rheumatic legs would allow. He started by turning over all of the nude pictures that he had cut out of old magazines and that covered the cracked walls of his hotel room. The girls had always been amused by this, it is one of the reasons why they sometimes visited their grandfather; they had seen all of the "dirty" pictures on certain occasions when he had been too drunk to bother with such decencies.

María found her father sitting at the same place where she had last seen him, in front of the makeshift altar. The altar had been set up in a doorless built-in cabinet and was decorated with brightly colored crepe paper, paper flowers and colored votive candles. He sat in front of his place of worship in a broken rocking chair with a glass of purple wine in one hand, glaring at the many statues of saints that rested on their heads. His prayers had not been answered, and this was his revenge. Her father's deities, while capable of outflowing love and divine compassion, were also subject to a variety of human-like frailties. They were jealous, stubborn, morose and open to bribery. They were accordingly treated with impassioned devotion and occasional contempt. María stared at the upside down saints. They would remain in this position until life became progressively worse for the old man and he would begin to suspect that the saints were trying to get even with him. When this fear became strong enough, he would turn the statues to their upright position.

María had brought a pot of soup for her father, as she had always done, and set it on a round table next to his rocking chair. As usual, don Severino greeted her with affection. "You're not only the best cook, but the prettiest in the family."

But María knew that she would not be staying long with her father. She could tell that he had been drinking heavily and if she stayed, she would have to listen to him repeating endlessly whatever topic he had chosen for that particular drunkenness. "Who dares to talk about going to hell?" he shouted as if speaking to a large group. "Nobody goes to hell; we're already in it."

"There's nothing worse than a drunk old man," thought María as she prepared to leave.

"Go ahead, leave your old man alone. I'm used to being alone. Nobody visits me, except Valentín. That boy doesn't forget his old abuelo . . . comes often . . . he's a good boy . . . brings me bottles of tequila every time he comes. Look!" Don Severino opened a cabinet that was near him with his cane and María saw the bottles of tequila lined up. "Don't drink it . . . never did . . . it's medicine. And never drink beer, María, it's poison . . . kill you quicker than anything. Wine!" He held his glass of purple wine in front of him and took a gulp, smacking his lips. He pointed to the bottles of tequila again. "Sell them to my neighbors . . . don't make much . . . but it pays for my wine, my candles, my newspaper. I'm saving these ones for Christmas . . . get twice as much for them." Don Severino closed the cabinet door with his cane. "My boy is coming tomorrow." María could detect a smile.

She recalled that Ramón had said, "The only thing the old man lives for is to meet with Valentín."

"The only reason he's staying alive," had said Rufelio, "is to see if his many curses will come true." María had once seen her aged father and Valentín together.

Don Severino beamed when he met his grandson. "Come here, sinvergüenza. How's my favorite grandson? The smartest one in the family. Getting top grades at school? Driving the girls crazy. Just like your old abuelo." The two of them sat across from each other in front of an open curtainless window that looked out into skid row, and Valentín listened attentively to tales of law and disorder: won and lost battles; easily gained and more easily lost fortunes; conquered love, and the ones that got away. He spoke of the federales who destroyed his booming, legitimate liquor business. "I have never dealt in legitimate business since." He spoke of his escapades with Pancho Villa, his eyes lighting up as he spoke of him. "That cabrón was a real man. There's no one like him around anymore." The old man frequently interrupted his stories to spit into an old coffee can that he kept at his side for such a purpose, or to shout a compliment at a middle-aged woman passing by his window. "Ay, mamacita! ripe but good." Or he would shout obscenities at policemen carrying away drunks. Always at exactly the same time, he stood up and fed the brown and gray pigeons that gathered at his window sill.

Once alone, don Severino sat by his window staring into the street that was beginning to stir with night life. He looked at the young winos, old prostitutes and policemen. "Cops everywhere, with those long nervous sticks." He shook his head at the procession. "They have no hope," he once told María, "yet they keep on living, dragging."

"No, papá, nobody who has lost hope keeps on living; hope is the last to die."

"Maybe, María, maybe you're right." But day after day, night after night he saw them from his window. "This ugly window." His drooping eyes followed bent figures, the crawling humans, the wretched—all those shadows that crept slowly by his window. He caught a downturned mouth, downcast eyes, pallid skin, frowns, "a lack of hope." He felt their aimless steps, their unfixed gaze, their hunches. He felt them scurrying past him, "like vile insects." His eyes felt tired and he stood up and walked toward the altar. He lit all of the candles and sat in front of the glowing saints with his purple wine and his rosary. "Nombre[3] del Padre, del Hijo, del Espíritu Santo . . . Amén." He stood up with great difficulty, repeating in a low pained voice, "Chingado . . . chingado . . . chingado . . ." He walked to the altar, picked up one of the statues and held it tightly around the neck. He spoke to it with clenched teeth, "If you don't answer my prayers, you're going to spend the rest of the week on your head." His nightly ritual performed, he lay on his bed and fell asleep.

As don Severino well knew, the Christmas season was the best time of the year for the selling of tequila. This is when tequila came closest to a full fledged business for the Portillos.

"Everybody wants to buy tequila for the holiday parties," said Ramón.

"The bottles make good Christmas presents," said María.

"It's good to warm up," said Rufelio. "It's more expensive than gas, but cheaper than electricity."

Christmas was celebrated two weeks in advance, beginning on December 12, the day of the Virgin Guadalupe. On that day, the family met at María's house and from there they proceeded to a nearby church. When mass was over, they made a line in front of the candle stand and one by one they knelt, bowed their heads, said a short prayer and lit a candle. María knelt in front of the candle stand and looked at the fully lit rows of candles. She knew that many were thanking the virgin for the full meals that the tequila made possible and asking her for continued protection.

Ramón was not sure if the extra profit that he made with the tequila during Christmas was worth it. At this time, he delivered it not only to his family, but

---

[3]en el nombre.

also to several business establishments: small liquor stores, restaurants, small markets and neighborhood bars. After crossing the border with the tequila, he would drive to his house, unload it, repack it in special boxes, then reload the boxes in his camper and begin the deliveries to the businesses and households.

The Portillos were scattered throughout Los Angeles and its surrounding counties, and it took Ramón until midnight to complete his deliveries. He always arranged his time so he could be at María's house before nine p.m., since María had the habit of sleeping early. If he arrived later than this, one of her daughters would handle the order and there was usually a mix-up: one case less, one case too many, or the wrong amount of gold and white tequila.

It was two weeks before Christmas and Ramón was running unusually late. He arrived at María's house at midnight and Margarita answered the door, half asleep. Ramón was holding a case of tequila and he was out of breath. "Let me put this down quick, it feels like the bottles are made of lead."

"Just leave it in the front room, we'll move them to the kitchen tomorrow."

"Thank you, Margarita," whispered Ramón. "I'm sorry I'm so late, but I'm really behind schedule."

"Do you want me to put the light on?"

"No, no, I don't want to wake anybody else." He brought in several more cases of tequila. "Sorry to wake you up, Margarita, get back to sleep."

A few minutes later María woke up startled. "Something smells strange." She jumped out of bed and called to her daughters. "What's the matter? Don't you have noses? Get up, chicken brains! before the house blows up." The girls jumped out of bed and helped their mother carry the tequila away from the lit heater and out of the house. "Didn't I tell you to turn the heater off before going to sleep?" shouted María. "If it wasn't for my sharp nose we would all be chicharrones."

María and her daughters carried the burnt tequila boxes out of the house carefully and stood shivering in their nightgowns in their backyard, staring at the steaming cases of tequila and hoping that none of their neighbors had sharp noses. After throwing a blanket over the tequila, they returned to their beds.

In the morning, María called Ramón and asked him to pick up the damaged tequila and to replace it since she had customers waiting. "I would let it go, Ramón, but you know how it is during Christmas."

It was one day before Christmas and undoubtedly the happiest time of the year. María was spending the extra money that she made on the tequila on food for her many relatives. She was an excellent cook, the best one in her family, and at Christmas time and Lent her cooking skill was displayed at its best. The

454 LITERATURA CHICANA / CHICANA/O LITERATURE

Christmas season called for special dishes that could only be enjoyed once a year since no amount of coaxing could make María or any other cook prepare Christmas dishes at any other time besides Christmas. Lent was another time that called for special dishes, but Lent was not the happiest time of the year. As María said, "To poor people, the whole year is Lent." But Christmas, thanks to the fast selling tequila, was a bountiful time.

Lorena stepped into the kitchen where María was making the corn tortillas and said, "Mamá! Are you making the tortillas by hand?"

"The eyes don't fool you."

"They make great tortillas at La Esperanza. Why waste time making them yourself?"

"The ones I make taste better."

"But, mamá, nobody makes corn tortillas by hand anymore."

"Everybody's getting lazy."

"You could put your time to better use."

"Like listening to you?"

"But, mamá . . ."

"Are you trying to teach your teacher?"

"Mamá!" called Margarita. "Yoli locked herself in the bathroom again."

"It's the only place in the house that has any privacy," said Yoli.

"She took a book with her," said Margarita.

"Yoli!" shouted María, "come out of there, you're going to shrink."

"Hurry up," said Margarita, "I need to use the toilet."

"Go to the gas station."

"Yoli! Come out of there." Yoli did not answer.

"It's no use," said María, "she's in love with the toilet."

María placed several folding tables together, covered them with a red tablecloth and set the holiday food on it. People began to arrive. There were relatives, friends, friends of relatives, relatives of friends, neighbors, and tequila customers. It wasn't always easy to find the connection of the visitors, but María welcomed them all.

Several bottles of the best tequila stood on the table for the many guests. The Portillos rarely drank tequila. They were all beer drinkers. They drank tequila only on very special occasions, such as Christmas Eve. María began forming the circle, everyone standing close to each other, with a glass of tequila in their hands. There was no lemon, no salt, no tricks and no speeches. Ramón raised his glass and they all gulped the tequila down at the same time. María could see them shuddering and their faces turning red.

Valentín knew this was a good moment. "Everything is changing, every-thing."

"Except your sermons. Wait until midnight so you can join the priest."

Valentín wished that Dr. Hernández was there. He hadn't seen the doctor for several months, and for the first time he realized how much he missed him.

Close to midnight, everyone traded the beer for strong coffee. When most of them had sobered, they began to vacate the house and to fill the various cars that would take them to misa de gallo.

They were all there, sitting together in one section of the church. Ramón looked for Valentín, but he couldn't find him. He stood in the aisle and scanned the church, but his son was nowhere in sight. He left the church and drove back to María's house.

Ramón stood in front of Valentín. "Get up, hereje, you want everyone to say that I raised an atheist son? You want to dishonor me?"

"What has the church done for us, except take what little we have? How have the priests helped our people?"

"You're going to pray to God, not to the priests." Ramón was not stern with his son on matters of religion, but Christmas Eve mass was different; attending together was a strong family tradition. Valentín knew this. He stood up and joined his father.

Everyone in the church turned and looked at Ramón and Valentín as they entered the church, except María. The host that the priest raised in front of the altar filled her vision.

Ramón sat across from María with his back stooped. "Ay, María, my back feels like it's broken."

"What happened, Ramón?"

"I think I picked up one case of tequila too many. It always happens around Christmas, but this year it's worse than ever."

"Have you seen the doctor?"

"Nobody has seen him for over six months. That's the longest he has been away from us."

"I guess you'll have to settle for Josefina."

"I'd rather die than put up with another one of her sermons."

"Try rubbing tequila on it."

"That's what I've been doing, but it doesn't seem to help."

"Sometimes it takes a while."

"I'll keep on rubbing the tequila, María. But anyway, I didn't come just to complain. Tomorrow is the day I pick up the tequila and I don't think I can make it."

"I'll do it for you, Ramón, but only this time. Next time you'll have to get someone else to make the trip."

When Emilia heard the familiar sound of the camper she ran out of her house as usual. "María! What are you doing with the camper?"

"Ramón's having trouble with his back."

Emilia offered her a beer as they walked together into her house.

"No, no beer, I want to be sober when they catch me. She gulped the food that Emilia served her and stood up.

"What's the rush, María? Not even Ramón hurries this much."

María walked toward the garage. "I want to get this over with as soon as possible."

Instead of going straight to Ramón's house as planned, María drove to her own house, took a drink of tequila, showered and took a short nap. When she woke up, she returned the camper to Ramón. "Here's your hot camper. Never again. I thought all the border officers were staring at the camper. I was sure they were going to search me. I was shaking so badly I don't know how I ever made it across. I kept looking in the rear-view mirror and every car behind me looked like a police car."

Ramón laughed. "What's the matter, María, can't get a few bottles across the border?" "A few bottles? I felt like I was carrying enough tequila to get everyone in L.A. drunk."

"That's the way I felt at the beginning, but it gets easier."

"I don't care to find out. Next time, ask someone else."

"I hope that by next week my back is better."

"Have you been rubbing the tequila on it?"

"Yeah. Hey, if rubbing it doesn't help, maybe drinking it will. I think I'll go have a beer at the bar."

"I'll join you."

María immediately recognized the man sitting alone at the counter. No one else could sit as straight on a backless stool. He was drinking tequila in his usual manner, placing the salt on the back of his hand, slapping his hand, and letting the salt jump into his opened mouth, then sucking the lemon, and then finally swallowing the tequila in one quick gulp. "Doctor!"

Dr. Hernández turned, jumped off the stool and embraced them. "María! Ramón! What a surprise, a treat."

"We're surprised," said Ramón. "You gave us a good scare. We thought you had disappeared for good and we would have to settle for Josefina and her sermons."

Dr. Hernández laughed. "She's getting on in years, but she has good hands."

"I know, but her brews and her sermons get more bitter every time. The last time I drank her foul tasting brew I returned home worrying I might turn into a frog."

"That curandera can do better than that. She would at least turn you into a dragon."

"Gonzalo!" shouted Ramón, "bring the good doctor another tequila, bring the whole bottle, serve everyone in the house, this calls for a celebration."

María faced the doctor. "Where have you been hiding?"

"I was down south, in Yucatán. I saw your husband down there."

"You're kidding."

"I saw him alright, stayed with him for a while, he says he'll never leave the place, at least not until his mission is accomplished."

"What mission?" said Ramón. "What is that guy up to now?"

Gonzalo refilled their glasses and Dr. Hernández went through his salt and lemon routine again. "Efrén is convinced that he's a reincarnation of the poet-king Nezahualcóyotl."

"Me lleva la . . . I always thought my brother-in-law was strange, but he sounds like he's really gone now."

"He makes a lot of sense. He says he knows he's crazy, that we are all crazy, that that's the reason we're in this world."

"You mean he thinks the world is an insane asylum?" said Ramón.

"In a way. He thinks we came to this world to recuperate."

"Recuperate?" said María. "This place could drive the sanest person mad."

"Exactly. It's full of lessons."

"But who learns anything?" said Ramón.

"Efrén says that it takes a lot of hard knocks and that too many people go around shielding themselves from everything."

"There's a lot of fools running around with their heads full of bumps," said María.

The doctor laughed. "That's why they keep coming back."

"You mean reincarnation?"

"Recommitment."

"Ramón served himself another tequila. "You believe in all that, doctor?"

"I can see it."

"It sounds like you and Efrén got along fine."

"It was a good experience. Yucatán is beautiful, truly the land of the gods. Efrén built a hut near the sea, that's where he lives. During the day he lectures on Nahua and Maya culture and at night he writes poetry. His poetry is pretty good."

María smiled. "How do the people down there take him?"

"Everyone in the area knows him. The Indians really like him, call him El Gran Efrén. The government doesn't bother him, they take him as a harmless crazy monk."

"Hey, Gonzalo!" called Ramón. "Bring us another bottle and have a drink with us." The bartender served them and himself. María offered a toast. "To the reappearance of our good doctor."

"And to my brother-in-law, El Gran Efrén."

"I'm glad you are back in town, doctor," said Gonzalo, "if you hadn't returned soon, the bar would have had to close down."

"Dr. Hernández laughed and raised his glass.

> *Quetzal, quetzal no calli*
> *zacun no calli tapach*
> *no calli nie cahuaz*
> *au ya, au ya, au quilmach.*

Everyone in the bar clapped and raised their glasses. "To the poet!"

"Efrén taught me this poem. It's a Toltec poem written by Quetzalcóatl Topiltzin when he tasted pulque."

"Me lleva la . . ." said Ramón. "If the kings like this stuff, what can be expected of us pelados?" He called the bartender. "Another bottle, Gonzalo, we'll drink it to Quetzalcóatl."

Dr. Hernández laughed his good deep laugh and slapped Ramón vigorously on the back. María could see her brother's body relaxing. He sat on the backless stool straighter than he had for many months.

With his friend far away in Yucatán, fully committed to ancient gods and well detached from his family, Dr. Hernández felt free to pursue his dream. He walked into María's house with a bouquet of flowers in one hand and a bulging gunny sack in the other. He gave María the flowers, and she busied herself look-

Gina Valdés

459

ing for a vase. When she was through arranging the flowers, he handed her the other present.

"What's this? asked María.

"Open it and see."

María opened the gunny sack and exclaimed, "Just what I always wanted, a dead duck."

"I was hunting near Ensenada this morning and this is what I caught. Can you still roast a duck as well as you used to?"

"Better."

The duck was clean, ready to cook, and María lost no time in preparing it. She recalled when they were living in México, how often Dr. Hernández and Efrén went hunting, always bringing back ducks or rabbits. Efrén liked rabbit meat, but Dr. Hernández liked duck, marinated in wine and herbs. He rarely ate any other meat except for wild game and fish that he caught himself.

As soon as María had seen the flowers she had been aware of the doctor's intentions. She recalled how he had wooed her when she was a single woman. He had taken her flowers regularly and serenades in the middle of the night, songs of unrequited love. He was not a handsome man. He was short and leaned toward the heavy side. "He likes duck too much." He had a drooping black mustache and had worn thick, black rimmed glasses ever since she had known him. But when he spoke, sang or recited poetry, María felt he acquired a strong attractiveness. She might have married him, but when he had left their town to study medicine, she had fallen in love with Efrén.

Shortly after María's and Efrén's wedding, Dr. Hernández had returned to their hometown with a license to practice medicine and a young bride. Two years later his wife had died in an auto accident and since then he had begun to drink.

María stared at the flowers. They had only one meaning. She thought of her daughters. They were all grown. "Which one is he after?" She stood up and walked toward the kitchen cupboard that served as a liquor cabinet. "Place your order, doctor."

"Anything will do, María, anything will taste good as long as you serve it. And don't call me doctor, call me Miguel."

María wondered if those were the words of a hopeful suitor or of a hopeful son-in-law. When she handed him his glass of tequila, he held her hand. "As smooth as ever," he said, staring at her. María was relieved. She didn't like the idea of having a son-in-law older than herself. But she wondered if they could continue where they had left off so many years before. He had become a part of the family, almost like a brother to her. He stared at her and she stared back at him. The old spark was still there.

When María stood up to refill his glass of tequila, Dr. Hernández also stood up, embraced and kissed her. "At last," he said. "All these years waiting to hold you." He kissed her again. "Ay, María, it was worth the wait."

Later that night, María sat by the kitchen window. The full moon looked like a thick tortilla that she could bite into.

María tried to keep her romance with Dr. Hernández as quiet as possible. Sometimes she thought about his marriage proposal. "He's a good man, but he could change; marriage has a way of changing people, often not for the best. Maybe it would be good for two years, if we're lucky. He might want to come and go like Efrén, and once again I'd be the one who's expected to wait. I can see it happening, Miguel deciding he was Moctezuma going off to Yucatán to join Efrén. It could be worse. He could decide he was Moctezuma and not go away."

Dr. Hernández's drinking had dropped since he had begun dating María, but since she refused to marry him, his drinking had become heavy again. Yet María knew that in spite of his heavy drinking, Dr. Hernández could not be considered an alcoholic. This puzzled her. There were her two younger brothers, Chuy and Lucas, whose drinking was an illness, and on the other hand, there was her father, Severino, who had drunk heavily all of his life but had never suffered from alcoholism. "I can take it or leave it," said don Severino, "but I prefer to take it. One needs to be drunk to put up with this world."

María's younger brother, Lucas, who was single and very attractive, appeared at family gatherings only sporadically. But her other younger brother, Chuy, was always the first to arrive. He walked into María's house calling to her, "What's the drink of the day?" That was his greeting; Chuy only drank beer, and by the time that the rest of the family arrived, he was through with his celebration. If he was the first to arrive, he was also the last to leave, for María's house was refuge to him.

It was Friday afternoon and Chuy sat by himself in María's living room drinking beer and strumming a guitar while María was cooking. Valentín walked into the house with his father, and while María and Ramón talked in the kitchen, Valentín approached his uncle. "Hey, good uncle, holding on to the bottle again?"

"That's your Uncle Chuy, always hugging the bottle." He sang in a cracked voice:

> Qué bonito gorgorea
> el tequila en la botella;
> pero más bonito siento
> cuando yo me prendo de ella...

Valentín looked around him. He took a cigaret from his pocket. "Listen, uncle, if you want to feel good, try this."

"Is that what you take to feel good?"

"Yeah, and it works."

"Then why are you always complaining?"

"I know what I'm telling you, uncle, this stuff makes you feel real good. What you're pouring down your throat is going to send you to your grave."

"I'll die happy."

"You'll live happy with this. Come on, don't pass up a good thing."

"It'll just make me crazier."

"Give it a try, I know what I am telling you."

Chuy drank the rest of his beer in gulps and smacked his lips. "Look, Valentín, put that stuff away; it's bad enough that I'm a drunk, stop trying to make a marihuano out of me."

María saw Chuy only when he went to her house, since like the rest of her family, she rarely visited his house. Chuy lived in a broken-down, two-story house in central Los Angeles with his wife, Lupe, his five sons, his mother-in-law, his wife's grandmother and several cats. He was allergic to cats and as soon as he entered his house he would begin to cough and sneeze. His mother-in-law, Eulalia, constantly changed religions and tried to convert everyone near her. The last that María had heard, she was a Jehovah's Witness and spoke continuously of the end of the world.

"Give up that devil's brew that's destroying your soul, Chuy. You have no time to lose, the end of the world is near."

"The world has already ended, this is instant replay." Chuy sometimes recalled, "the good old days when Eulalia was just a fanatical Catholic."

His mother-in-law had moved in with them soon after their marriage. "No one asked her, she came one day to visit and she's been with us ever since." Chuy told María how Eulalia had filled their house with statues and color photographs of saints. "I don't think she left any saints out." She had eventually converted one of their bedrooms into a shrine with candles of all shapes and colors continuously burning, and bouquets of flowers under the major saints. "My house smells like a mortuary."

"I'll get the devil out of this house."

"When are you leaving?" mumbled Chuy. But Eulalia stayed on, and every Sunday they had a confrontation.

"What excuse do you have for not going to mass?"

"When I see the priest drinking wine I feel tempted."

"That is not wine, you fool, that is the blood of Jesus."

Soon after his mother-in-law had moved in with them, Maruca, his wife's ninety-two-year-old grandmother also moved into their house. "She's got it into her head that I'm trying to kill her, María."

"That no good husband of yours is trying to kill me," she told her granddaughter, Lupe.

"Don't be silly, grandmother, my husband could never do a thing like that."

"Don't be so sure," said Eulalia, "that husband of yours is possessed by the devil; he's capable of anything." When no one was looking, Maruca walked past Chuy and hit him with her cane and made obscene signs at him.

"Vieja maldita," muttered Chuy as he walked out of the house.

When life in his house became intolerable, Chuy moved in with his father. "He must be desperate," said the Portillos. Don Severino, who often complained to María about loneliness, complained louder about invasion of privacy.

As soon as Lucas found out that his brother Chuy had moved in with his father, he also moved in with him. "I can't leave Chuy alone with the old man," he told María. "That old man has mean insides."

"I can't even feed myself and I have to feed these two," don Severino told María.

"Don't worry, papá, I'll bring all of you something to eat."

"I don't know how I got by when you weren't around, María. And I don't know what these two boys would do without me."

María knew what their life together was like. The two brothers rarely left the hotel room. Chuy spent most of his time drinking beer, strumming his guitar, remembering his sons and the last job that he had been fired from. "I worked hard, real hard, what more did they want?' Lucas said that he couldn't leave the room because there were too many cops around. "These cops have nothing better to do than to chase Mexicans."

Don Severino sat by the window looking out into the dark street. He stood up and walked to his altar, careful not to step on Lucas who slept on a mattress on the floor. When he lit the candles, cockroaches crept out of crevices, one of them scurrying in front of Chuy who was stroking his guitar.

La Cucaracha, La Cucaracha
ya no puede caminar,

porque no tiene, porque le falta
marihuana que fumar...

Lucas sat up and threw an empty beer can at him. "Do I have to kill both of you to get some sleep?"

"Let him play," said don Severino, "we can use a little music in this miserable place."

"It's miserable because you two are in it," said Lucas.

"You're envious," said don Severino, "because you have no talent."

"You call those screeches talent?"

Una cucaracha pinta
le dijo a la colorada:
"Si yo me fuera contigo,
me llevaba la fregada."

Empty beer cans flew and the arguing continued until it reached a high pitch and then it suddenly ceased, creating a deaf silence. Lucas lay asleep on his mattress and Chuy slept on a sleeping bag near him. Don Severino sat by the window with the light of the street lamp illuminating his ruddy face. A glass of dark wine rested on the window sill and a rosary lay on his hands. He finished saying the rosary and drinking the wine at exactly the same time.

The following day Lucas spoke of leaving. "A man can't breathe here." He stood by the window. "This place is swarming with cops. I'm leaving as soon as it gets dark."

"Why wait that long?" said don Severino.

But perhaps to spite his father, Lucas stayed. "He wants me to leave so he can get after Chuy."

That night, Chuy, who had been drinking heavily, had delirium tremens, otherwise known as d.t.'s. María had once seen him in that condition and his trembling body and sweaty distorted face had frightened her.

"There's a man out there! There he is! He's digging a hole in the wall . . . digging . . . digging . . . he can't come through the wall . . . he's digging a hole . . . he can't come through . . . "

The first thing that don Severino did was to take out from under his bed the statue of Saint Anthony that he had been hiding there all week and place it back on the altar. He then ordered Lucas to call María.

María arrived and helped Lucas carry Chuy to his old Dodge. Together they took him to the nearest hospital where he was admitted immediately. Lucas soon left the hospital and María sat alone in the waiting room praying an invisible rosary, using her fingers as beads. After a long wait, she was informed that Chuy needed to be interned in a mental hospital.

María was at the same time saddened and relieved. She hated to see her brother committed to a mental institution, but she didn't know what else she could do for him.

A few days later, María visited her brother Chuy at the hospital, and she continued to visit him regularly. On one of her visits, María told him, "I'm sorry that you have to stay in a place like this, Chuy."

"It's not a nice place, but there's crazier people out there." He had been in the hospital several weeks and María noticed that he looked comfortable in his surrounding. It was a warm day and the two of them sat on a bench in the hospital's garden. "See that man over there?"

María saw a man with a beach ball, repeatedly throwing it up in the air and catching it. "He's pretty good with the ball, he never drops it."

"He has lots of practice, every day he does the same thing. He thinks the ball is the world and that it's up to him to keep it moving."

"Has he ever dropped it?"

"Once. It was terrible, the poor man was suffering. He fell to the ground and cried uncontrollably, shouting, 'The world has ended! The world has ended!' It took several people to calm him down, and he was shaking for a long time. But here he is, at it again."

"When does he stop?"

"He stands there for hours, until a nurse comes and takes him back to his room. He'll go quietly. That one over there," said Chuy, pointing to a man kneeling on the grass, "is looking for a key. He says it's the key to the kingdom of heaven."

"Has he ever found it?"

"Several times, but as soon as he finds it he loses it. Then he starts to look for it all over again."

María shook her head. "I guess it's true what they say, that every madman has his theme."

Chuy looked at María. "I wish I had a nice cold beer right now." María stared at her brother. She knew that he had not had a drink in a long time. Chuy laughed. "I think these people are driving me crazy." He laughed again. "No joking, they do the same thing every day, same thing. I've been watching them for several weeks, and every day it's the same thing. I get dizzy watching them."

Visiting her brother Chuy at the hospital took all of María's Sundays. After the two-hour bus ride from Camarillo, she sat at the kitchen table trying to relax and to forget about the approaching work week.

"Mamá!" shouted Lorena, "stop rubbing your eyes. You've been rubbing them since you got home. You know what Dr. Harris told you."

Dr. Harris, the oculist, who according to María, "knows everything about eyes," and whom she visited twice a year, told her, "Never rub your eyes, you inflame them more."

"But sometimes they're so itchy that I feel like taking them out and scratching them."

"When you feel like that, come and see me."

"Mamá! Stop rubbing them."

"I can't help it!"

"Are you working on black cloth again?"

María nodded. The lint from colored cloth was bad, but black was worst, and she had been working on black for one week. She knew it was time to see Dr. Harris.

She was glad to have found such a doctor, for she knew that not all doctors were healers. Dr. Hernández was a healer, and so was Dr. Harris. They not only had the degree and the license, but also the special hands. "This is going to sting, but it'll be over soon." And with steady and quick hands, the old oculist turned her eyelids inside out and scraped them with a tiny knife to get the black lint out. He then poured an eye lotion into her eyes and they watered all the way home, and the following day they drained all day. After this treatment her eyes would be bright and clear for a few months, then they would start bothering her again. At these times María considered changing her line of work. "Maybe if I go to night school, learn typing . . ." But after the nine hour work day and the one hour ride in the bus packed with sweaty workers, all she could think of was dinner and sleep, on Friday nights, unwinding with her family, Saturdays, heavy housework, Sundays . . . "It will be different for my daughters." She sometimes heard them discussing education.

"One doesn't need to go to school to be smart," said Yoli. "Look at all those dummies with college degrees, and there are those who haven't made it past the sixth grade, like tío Rufelio, and he's sharper than any college professor."

"Think how smart he'd be if he'd gone to college."

"He would be a smart, boring man. Mamá agrees with me, don't you, Mamá?"

"You're both right. Life is the best teacher. If you live long enough and keep your eyes open, you'll learn plenty, sometimes more than you'd like to know."

"Mamá knows best."

"But especially in this country you need papers to show that you know something. Nobody is going to take your word for it."

María stared at the slice of moon. She would spend more time with her daughters.

The next day, María sat with her three daughters at the kitchen table. Each had a glass of wine in front of her and the large wine bottle stood in the middle of the table. María took a sip of wine and exclaimed, "Ay!" I had forgotten how good Uncle Pepe's wine tasted. I must congratulate him next time I see him. That man knows how to make good wine." She turned toward Margarita. "What is it?"

Lorena spoke first. "It's about her new boyfriend . . ." Margarita gave her a sharp look and Lorena stopped talking.

"Which one?" asked María. Margarita didn't answer. "Well, when do I have the pleasure of meeting him?"

"I invited him to come to the house next Monday."

"Monday's fine. What's his name?"

"Wait till you meet him." Margarita glanced at Lorena and Yoli, and they remained silent.

It was a long wait until Monday. María was disturbed by her eldest daughter's secrecy; she was the most talkative of her daughters.

Monday afternoon, María began to prepare a full course Mexican dinner. It never occurred to her that Margarita's boyfriend might not be Mexican. All of her daughters had consistently shown predilection for Mexican boys.

Margarita's boyfriend arrived at exactly seven o'clock, the time that had been set. "A punctual man," said María. She opened the door and stood quietly before the young man. She hated to hear anyone talk about typical Mexicans, reminding everyone that Mexicans came in all shapes and colors. But she was sure that the young man standing in front of her was not Mexican. He was short, slight, had frizzy blond hair and large languid eyes that were further magnified by thick glasses. He had a studious, melancholic air about him as if he had studied for a final exam all night and failed. María stared at him for a while, and then, realizing her rudeness, she extended her hand to him. "I'm Margarita's mother," she said, forcing a smile.

The young man also forced a smile. "I'm Tim Kirby, may I come in?"

It was soon apparent that Tim Kirby didn't like Mexican food, which didn't help to endear him to María. He looked at the food as if it contained poison and nibbled on it hesitantly which prompted María to say later, "He eats like a rabbit." Not only did Tim scorn the food that María had prepared with so much care but he also disdained Uncle Pepe's wine. "It would have been wasted on him," thought María. "What has happened to Margarita, besides being blinded by love?"

The day after Tim's visit, María sat at the kitchen table with her three daughters and Uncle Pepe's wine that was getting low. "Why hadn't you told me sooner?"

"We just decided on it."

"Are you planning to marry in a Protestant church?"

"Tim is going to become a Catholic."

"What?"

"He's going to start catechism next Saturday."

"Have you set a wedding date?"

"Two years from now, when Tim finishes college."

María sighed. She served herself another glass of wine. "In two years," she thought, "anything can happen. Love can go as easily as it comes. Maybe two years from now she'll be married to a nice Mexican boy." Lorena served herself another glass of wine and spoke to her mother with a smile. "You don't have to worry about me."

"I'm glad to hear that."

"I'm planning never to get married. I'm thinking of going East to study law. I'd like to spend my life helping Mexicans in trouble."

"Law? East? Why can't you study here? We have no relatives in the East."

"Some of my friends are planning to go East, they have great schools there."

"What's wrong with the schools here?"

"I can't study in this house, it's always full of people. I want to go to a quiet place where I can study."

"Go to the library."

"I want to go East, mamá."

María looked at her youngest daughter. "What are you up to?" Yoli didn't answer.

"I should have taken Porfirio's advice and stayed in México. I thought that coming here and sending you girls to college would be a good thing for all of you, but maybe what Porfirio says is true . . ."

Lorena interrupted. "Porfirio is crazy."

"Maybe he is, but children and madmen tell the truth. He always warned me about moving here and sending you girls to college, said you would become crazy. Look at you. Who would think that Porfirio was a prophet?"

Tim visited Margarita once a week, but he rarely took her out anywhere. "If he's stingy now," said María, "what will he be like when they are married?"

On one of his visits, Tim met with the unexpected. It happened that a Portillo had crossed the border on a three day permit and was staying at María's house. The Portillos made a pilgrimage to her house to meet the visiting relative and the party began.

Everyone tried to make Tim feel welcome. They served him food, which he refused, they offered him drinks, which he didn't drink, they flashed their best smiles, which he didn't return; Tim sat through the party as if in a stupor. The Portillos shrugged their shoulders. "Behind that cold exterior lies a warm man," they said. "Why else would Margarita be interested in him?" It was the first and the last Portillo party that Tim attended.

Tim began to visit Margarita twice a week, making sure in advance that there weren't any parties going on. "Once a week was bad enough," thought María. "How would you like to visit your aunt Griselda?"

"Griselda?"

"She has that beautiful house by the sea . . . you could take a little vacation . . . all those palm trees . . . the breezes . . . the warm nights . . . the beautiful dark men in their white outfits . . . soft music . . . dining by the sea . . ." The telephone rang and Margarita ran to answer it. From her lowered voice, María knew that it was Tim.

Margarita told her mother that she was not planning to go anywhere, but María worked hard to convince her, and one week later her eldest daughter was on her way to Mazatlán. María wrote a long letter to Griselda. "I have complete faith in you and I know that when Margarita returns, she will not be able to remember Tim Kirby."

Two weeks later, Tim stood at María's house, speaking to her in a shaky voice. "I can't wait two years until we get married, I want to marry Margarita now. If she doesn't return immediately, I'm going after her."

María was startled; she had never seen so much life in the man. After recovering from the shock, she said, "Nobody shouts at me." And she told Tim to leave her house.

Three days later Margarita was back at her house. Griselda wrote an apologetic letter to María. "I did all I could, but your daughter looked dazed, and when the special delivery arrived, she cried and insisted on leaving."

If María was against her daughter marrying Tim, Tim's father was equally opposed to the wedding. But he didn't try tropical vacations or threats; he quickly disowned his only son. Tim had enough problems. He couldn't hold a job, he suffered from allergies, school was a constant pressure for him, and he lived with his only known relative, his aging, grumbling father who was disowning him. Tim became more morose than ever, but he accomplished his goal.

More than 300 relatives and friends of Margarita Vega Portillo filled the church. Tim was by himself. Even the best man was a Portillo. "The day you marry, you're either cured or killed," said Rufelio, "and Tim looks like he's going to his execution."

After the wedding ceremony, everyone kissed the bride and embraced Tim warmly. He was now a member of the family and was to be treated accordingly. The wedding party moved from the church to a nearby hall where the feasting began. Everyone in the family donated what she or he could to make the wedding a success. One who worked in a winery donated the liquor, a farmer offered a few turkeys and hams, a baker baked the wedding cake, a musician provided the music, and several others helped to decorate, cook and serve. Then they all sat down together to eat, drink and celebrate as best as they knew how. Tim did something he had never done—he became drunk. Not a drinker, it didn't take him long. One toast here, another toast there, and he soon became inebriated.

Margarita stood in the center of the hall dancing with one relative after another. Some couples danced while others sat and clapped to the music. A couple in their eighties stood up and danced with agile movements while everyone cheered them on.

María noticed Valentín pacing the hall, his fast eyes scanning the crowd, looking for attractive girls to dance with. As he continued pacing, he tripped on something. He held on to a chair to keep from falling, and as he looked down he saw Tim lying on the floor. He walked up to Ramón who was drinking a beer with Rufelio. "Do you know where's Dr. Hernández?"

"Probably hiding from you."

"I need him."

"Can't find anyone else to listen to you?"

"Tim passed out?"

"Can't blame him," said Rufelio.

"Tim needs help."

"Let him sleep it off."

Valentín walked to the middle of the hall and tapped the shoulder of the man who was dancing with Margarita. She smiled. "Valentín, I thought you'd never dance with me."

He whispered to her, "Your husband passed out."

"Ay!"

"Don't worry, I'll get a friend to help me; we'll carry him to his car through the side door. If you want, I'll drive you and Tim to México."

Margarita kissed Valentín on the cheek. "Thank you, cousin."

With the help of a friend, Valentín picked Tim up and was about to take him through the hall's side door when a group of relatives began to gather around them making it impossible for them to leave quietly. Valentín spoke to the band while his friend held the bridegroom. When Valentín returned, he held Tim's shoulders, his friend held his legs, and they began the long walk to the main exit of the large hall while the band played the wedding march followed by the funeral march.

"I told you, you marry and you're cured or killed," said Rufelio. "But this guy didn't even last one day."

"He's passed out, not dead," said Ramón.

"Married, dead . . . same thing. Poor Tim, didn't even last one day. . ."

"Poor Tim?" said María. "Poor Margarita."

About once a month, Lorena gave a party for her many friends. Her parties resembled the family parties, except that there was less singing, less drinking, more dancing to slower music and more romancing. If someone wanted to drink hard liquor, smoke a joint, or make out, they had to retire to the privacy of the parked cars. "There's better parties going on in the cars," said Valentín.

Yoli always joined her sister's parties but she never gave one herself. They knew very little about her friends. "That girl keeps everything to herself," said María. Lorena had told her that she had recently seen Yoli holding hands with a Japanese boy that they had both met at a foreign students' meeting, that his name was Makoto Matsuda, but everyone called him Mack, that he was from Osaka and that his father owned an import-export business. María recalled the time when she had caught her youngest daughter kissing a boy in their garage; she was only eleven then but she had thought it was time she should speak openly and clearly about boys. But she hadn't spoken to her older daughters and she never spoke to Yoli, just as her mother had never spoken to her. In her teens all that she knew was that sex was something that all married men enjoyed, that single men also engaged in, but never single women, never anybody's daughter or sister, nor anyone's mother. This was a real mystery. When a young woman became pregnant she was quickly dressed in white and rushed to the altar. When the baby was born, it was either premature or the incident was dismissed as just one more case of immaculate conception. She recalled a friend telling her, "If you do it before you marry, you get warts. She had imagined her body covered with warts; it was not a nice sight, but it was one of the lesser punishments, not as bad as burning in hell. "The human body—a sack of sins," she heard. There were a few women in her town who were different. That's what people said in whispers. For years she wondered about their secrets. She now wished she had spoken to her daughters when they were younger; as they became older, it became more difficult. The first time she had kissed a boy and allowed him to feel her body, together with the feeling of pleasure, she had felt that she had done something wrong, a mortal sin to be quickly confessed unless she might accidentally die and be damned forever. She had been unable to confess at her parish as she did every Saturday and had walked five miles to a chapel in the town's hills, to confess to a priest who would not recognize her voice.

María sat across from her two daughters. She could not read Yoli's face; Lorena was easier to understand; she knew that her middle daughter's main passion was books, but recently, Lorena seemed restless.

"I have to go East, mamá. I have to study and I can't do it here."

"We have no relatives there."

"I can take care of myself. I'm applying to several schools."

María could feel the five-year-old Lorena tugging at her skirt while she was in the kitchen cooking or scrubbing the bathtub, begging her to teach her to read, and pleading with her father and uncles to teach her. But they were all too busy or too tired. When Lorena had run away from kindergarten for the second time, complaining that all they did was play, she was forced to place her daughter in the first grade, where she quickly learned to read and write.

Yoli, who was sitting near Lorena, was more silent than usual. "Who's this Chinese boy at school?"

"He's Japanese," said Lorena. Yoli didn't answer. She stood up and locked herself in the bathroom.

The following day Yoli didn't return from school at the usual time. When it became dark, María called Margarita and Dr. Hernández.

"That girl has always given me trouble," said María glancing at her two daughters, "not that you two haven't."

"Want me to call the police?" asked Lorena. They all agreed that it was the best action to take.

The policeman asked María a few questions, took a photograph of Yoli and assured María that they would do their best to find her missing daughter.

Everyone sat down at the kitchen table and Lorena took out a bottle of Uncle Pepe's wine.

"Not for me," said María.

"Come on, mamá, this will make you feel better."

"Tonight I need something stronger."

Lorena served her mother a small glass of tequila. They were all silent until María spoke. "Lorena, go check Yoli's wooden box, under her bed, see if she took her money with her."

Lorena returned with an envelope addressed to María. "The money is gone, but I found this." María opened it and read it.

> Dear mamá,
> Don't try to look for me, I'm far away.
> I'll write to you soon.
>   Love,
>   Yoli

"Just like her father . . . takes off just like that . . . nothing to it . . . just takes off . . . far away . . . where's far away?"

"Don't worry," said Margarita. "Yoli can take care of herself."

"She'll be back soon," said Dr. Hernández.

"As soon as she pleases," said María.

One week after Yoli's disappearance, a letter arrived from Japan. When Lorena saw the letter, she said, "Mamá is going to faint."

María sat at the kitchen table holding the letter.

"Aren't you going to open it?"

"She's gone, what more do I need to know?"

She threw the letter on the table. "I'll read it later. She's at the other end of the world."

Dr. Hernández took María out often in an attempt to distract her. They usually went to a neighborhood dance hall where they listened to live music and watched the dancers. Dr. Hernández grabbed María's arm. "María! Let's go to The Village."

"The Village? It's been so long since we've been there, you too, Miguel."

"How can I forget?"

"I recall how you and Efrén got old Gurov drunk."

"He was doing alright by himself."

"Old Gurov was dancing like a wild bear. I'll never forget the sight of him. I remember you were dancing with him. You were both great."

"I don't think I could do it now, I'm not so young anymore."

"If old Gurov can do it, so can you."

"Those people are in good shape. Maybe I should try eating rye instead of corn and drinking vodka instead of tequila."

"You're doing fine."

Dr. Hernández held her face. "What would I do without you?" He called the bartender. "Camarada, what time is it?"

"It's the same time that it was yesterday at this same hour."

"So what time was it yesterday at this same hour?"

"Ten o' clock."

"Come on, María, it's still early. Let's go home and call everybody. See if we can leave early tomorrow morning and stay all day."

"You make quick decisions, don't you?"

"It doesn't get me anywhere. When I first met you I decided to marry you, and look at me, more than twenty years later, and I still can't convince you."

María woke up at five o'clock and prepared chorizo con huevos, a large batch of tortillas and a pot of coffee. Dr. Hernández arrived in a large borrowed truck, and soon after Chuy arrived.

"Doctor!"

"Good to see you, camarada. How are the wife and kids?"

"As troublesome as ever."

"Aren't they coming?"

"I left them at home so they could drive each other crazy."

María stood at the door. "So that's what they do when you're not around. You should have brought your mother-in-law at least."

"The worst one?"

"We could have gotten her drunk and left her on a deserted road."

"She would find her way back, like a cat," said Chuy.

"What is she preaching now?"asked Dr. Hernández. "Is she still a Jehovah's Witness?"

"That's over with, She's now into something nobody ever heard of."

María laughed. "I knew that someday she would start making up her own religions."

"I wouldn't mind if she didn't try to convert me."

"How's the ancient one?" asked the doctor.

"Getting deafer and meaner all the time."

"It doesn't look like we'll miss any of them today," said Dr. Hernández.

"The farther from them the better," said Chuy and walked into María's house.

One by one they came. The women, the men, the children, the old folks. Two more trucks arrived, and by eight o'clock, the entire Portillo family was there, ready to leave for The Village.

Soon after crossing the border, the Portillos drove off the main highway and onto a dirt road that would lead them into the hidden Baja California valley. As soon as they were on Mexican soil, lips upturned, eyes widened, faces took color, guitars sprang out of blankets and the air filled with laughter and song.

The valley was green and the summer air was warm and dry. The older Portillos explained to the younger ones how many years before a group of Russian refugees had left their homeland seeking shelter in the Mexican valley. "They must have found the peace they were seeking, for none of them have left the valley. They grow their own food, raise sheep, make their own bread, wine and clothing and worship in the way they want."

The Portillos who lived in México, some of them close to The Valley, went there often. "They always welcome us," they said.

"Mariya! Mariya! cried Gurov. He ran toward her and lifted her up high as if she were a child. "I'm an old man, Mariya, but I can still lift you, see?"

"People like you never get old, Gurov."

"My wife tells me to lay off the wine if I want to live a little longer, but I tell her that that's what keeps me going. Without wine the soul dies." He laughed loudly and his cheeks turned a deeper red.

"Mariya, don't you love us anymore?"

"We all love you, Gurov, you know that."

"But why do you stay away so long? That you call love?"

"I'm sorry, Gurov, I wanted to come, but it's one thing or another."

"When the heart is willing, the body obeys."

"Well, Gurov, here we are."

Gurov looked at the people pouring from the trucks. "Good, you brought them all. Very good." Dr. Hernández and Gurov saw each other and ran to meet. They stood in a strong embrace without speaking. Tears streamed down Gurov's red cheeks and Dr. Hernández blinked under his glasses. "You are here," said Gurov. "You are here, with us, you have not forgotten us."

"I couldn't stay away any longer."

"You look wonderful," said Gurov. "Maybe I should eat corn instead of rye and drink tequila instead of vodka." Dr. Hernández and María looked at each other and laughed. Gurov looked around. "Where's Efrén? I don't see him."

Dr. Hernández spoke. "Efrén is in Yucatán."

"Why so far? Leaving such a beautiful woman alone."

"He has a mission there."

Gurov touched his long white beard. "A mission?" Dr. Hernández nodded. Gurov's eyes narrowed, but they soon brighten again. "He will be with us in spirit."

María saw Gurov's wife, grown children and grandchildren come out of their houses, and soon many of their neighbors were there; it seemed as if the whole Russian village had come out to greet them. They carried loaves of bread, pots of soup, chunks of cheese and jugs of wine, and placed them on long wooden tables that stood under pepper trees.

"Eat as much as you can," said Gurov, "there is more, much more, plenty for everybody."

After sharing a good meal, Gurov and his family and neighbors brought out balalaikas, the Portillos picked up their guitars and they tooks turns playing Russian and Mexican songs. While one of his songs played, Gurov danced for them.

"Gurov can still do it," said Dr. Hernández.

"I knew he could," said María. "And so can you. What are you waiting for?"

Dr. Hernández joined Gurov while everyone clapped and cheered them on. Soon, others joined them.

María noticed the smile on Valentín's face. She couldn't recall seeing such a smile on him before, except when he saw a girl he liked. Others also noticed Valentín's good mood. "It looks like he left his sermons on the other side," said Rufelio.

"We should bring him here more often," said another.

But when Dr. Hernández took a walk by himself into the woods, Valentín followed him. "What do you think, Valentín? Beautiful place, isn't it? Beautiful people."

"Yeah, it's nice here. It's alright to live like this in this kind of place, but you can't do that on the other side. It's a different game there."

"What kind of game, camarada?"

"A power game, a money game. You got the money, you got the power. You try to live like this there and they'll swallow you up."

"So you think that with money you've got it made?"

"Like tía María says, 'With money, the monkey dances.'"

Dr. Hernández laughed. "And without money, if he's a good monkey."

It was late afternoon when the truck began to fill again. It had been an unusual experience for the younger Portillos who had never visited The Village, and it had been a day of magic for the older Portillos who had been there many times. Many of them spoke of returning to The Village soon. "Maybe we could have our yearly picnic here," some of them suggested.

As soon as they returned from The Village, the Portillos began to plan their yearly family picnic. It was always well organized, and the whole family was expected to attend as they were expected to attend every family wedding and funeral. All family matters were discussed at the picnic, existing problems were aired, and hopefully resolved, and the tequila business was reviewed.

Dawn was breaking when the Portillos arrived at the chosen Los Angeles park with pots of menudo, pozol, tortillas, baskets of sweet bread, jugs of chocolate and strong coffee that would be spiked with a touch of tequila to warm up in the cold morning.

Ramón, one of the main organizers of the annual picnic, was the first to arrive. He helped himself to a cup of coffee with a double piquete and waited for the right moment to announce his retirement from the tequila business. He had already told María of his plans and was eager to tell everyone else. "Only three more trips and I'll retire." He finished his spiked coffee and lay under a tree. "Only three more trips," he mumbled as he dozed off.

María looked down and saw Ramón's sleeping face. "It's a good day for him," she thought. She looked up and saw Chuy in the distance. She could see that his whole family was there, even the senile Maruca wrapped in her heavy black shawl and supporting herself on the cane that never left her grasp. María saw the old woman limping toward a group of Portillo men who were drinking coffee and talking.

"Want a little coffee to warm up, doña Maruca?" asked Rufelio.

"Does it have tequila in it?" she asked in her raspy voice.

"Only a little."

She waved her cane in front of him. "I don't want any."

"I can get you a cup without tequila, but this will really warm you."

"Maybe a young man like you, but this old body can only take it plain."

"I'll get you straight coffee, doña Maruca."

"I want straight tequila!"

Rufelio took a bottle of tequila from a picnic basket and served the old woman a glass. She drank a little, spit it out, and returned the glass to Rufelio. "Bah! You call this dirty water tequila? You don't know what real tequila tastes like."

María sat on the bench talking to Chuy. She could feel her brother's muscles tightening as Maruca limped toward them. "Here she comes, ready to attack me."

"Don't worry, Chuy, there's two of us."

Maruca raised her cane and dangled it in front of Chuy's face, but María knew that she wouldn't hit him, since she did so only when nobody was looking. Doña Maruca stood in front of him and shook her head. "How did an old devil like you get such a beautiful sister like this?" The old woman followed María around the park all morning. "That's a mean brother you have, full of bad habits."

"He doesn't have any more bad habits than the rest of us."

"Why is he always thinking of ways to kill me?"

"Don't worry, doña Maruca, you'll still be around long after most of us are gone."

"Where's your father? I don't see him anymore," asked the old woman who knew that don Severino was not invited to family reunions.

María tried to ignore her, but she persisted. "Why isn't your father here?"

"Maybe he has better things to do."

"I see . . . I see . . ." she said, leaning on her cane and surveying the park.

María thought of her father. "I should go see him, it's been a long time. I should take him a plate of soup, he likes that."

Valentín arrived and sat under a tree eating a plate of menudo. Doña Maruca limped toward him and with her cane she tousled his long hair. "You look like a girl, look at you, all you need is ribbons and flowers." Valentín smiled at doña Maruca as she limped away like a child.

After finishing three plates of menudo and half a dozen tortillas, Valentín stood up and viewed the park. Everyone had eaten and drunk, and gathered in

small groups. A few sat alone strumming guitars. They all looked relaxed to
Valentín. He walked toward a place in the park where he could reach the most
people. "Listen everybody, I just want to say a few words."

"That's all we're going to let you get away with," shouted Chuy. Doña
Maruca, who was standing next to him, waved her cane in front of his face and
said, "Let the boy speak or I'll break this on your head."

"All I want, all I am trying to do is to help you improve your lives."

"They should have named you Inocencio instead of Valentín," said Rufelio.

"That's right, said Chuy, who had moved away from doña Maruca. "Don't
you know yet that life is hopeless?"

"He's right, said Rufelio, "there's a cure for every ill, but no one has yet
found a cure for life." There was laughter, whistles and shouts. Chuy played his
guitar and sang his favorite song

> No vale nada la vida,
> la vida no vale nada...

Dr. Hernández arrived with his guitar. The Portillos looked at each other
and said, "Look who's here, the good doctor." They called to him, "Sing us one
of your songs, doctor, the way only you know how."

Doña Maruca squinted her cloudy eyes. "Bah! The brujo is here."

Ramón walked up to Chuy and whispered something to him. "Quiet, everybody," shouted Chuy."Ramón wants to talk to us. He has something important
to tell us."

There were shouts and hisses from the crowd. "Leave the preaching to your
son, Ramón. One's bad enough."

"All I want to say . . ." The singing and shouting drowned Ramón's voice,
and he walked away from the group and filled a paper cup with tequila.

Valentín's fast eyes followed Dr. Hernández and he stood up and surprised
the doctor at the entrance of the park's restroom. "Doctor!"

"Yes, camarada?"

"Do you think that life is hopeless?"

The doctor laughed hard. "There's no getting around it, camarada."

"Why can't I make these people see that it is possible to improve one's
life?"

"We are always more comfortable with our old clothes, even if the new
ones fit better."

"But change is necessary; don't you agree with me doctor?"

"Pues sí, camarada."

"Why can't they see it?"

"They're changing . . . they're changing . . . and their change is going to affect everybody." He saw Valentín's thoughtful face, laughed, and slapped him on the back. His feet were dancing. "Excuse me, camarada," he said walking into the restroom, "this is also urgent business."

It was late afternoon and María watched each group of relatives leave the park. She thought of her daughters and how they had left one by one. She thought of all that she had done for them and wondered if it had been enough. She looked at the sun and saw in its light the light of all the candles that she had lit. She thought of her father and wondered how many candles he had lit, and for how many saints, and for how many reasons. She could hear her father's words. "You can light many candles, María, say many prayers, but sometimes the saints act deaf."

María knocked on her father's door, but no one answered. She opened the door and walked in. She stood near the door and stared at her father and her two youngest brothers who were lying on the floor, surrounded by empty beer cans and wine bottles. She placed the bowl of soup she had made for her father on top of a small table and walked out of the room.

The following day, don Severino sat at the edge of the bed, staring at the plate of food, sighing, "María, poor María. She came and saw us like this." He massaged his thick grey hair forcefully, as he had done each morning, as if to exorcise all of the guilt, pain and misery of his life. "It's good for the hair, María, it wakes it up; and it clears the mind." He stood and walked into the kitchen and prepared himself a cup of coffee, then sat by the window and sipped it slowly, glancing at his two sons on the floor. He looked out of the window and felt that the lifeless streets looked like those of a ghost town. "Two more hours and life will appear . . . they'll crawl out of crevices like cockroaches . . . those who have lost hope . . ." He recalled her words. "No one who has lost hope keeps on living." Once again he glanced at his sons and saw their faces puffed and distorted by drink, wondering if they were hanging on by a thread of hope or if that delicate thread had broken. After finishing his coffee he stood slowly and walked into the kitchen to rinse his cup. He put on his faded gray coat, his worn felt hat, picked up his cane and walked out of the stale room.

The cool air hit his face and he buttoned his coat. "This kind of weather takes old men, María." The sound of church bells echoed in the empty streets—the last call for the first morning mass. "Ay, caray! It's later than I thought." He began the difficult climb up the steep stairs and walked into the dim church. When mass was over, he walked over to the candle stand and lit three candles.

He walked for several blocks until he stood in front of the city's main library. He sat on a bench outside of the building waiting for it to open, feeding the pigeons that gathered around him. María knew that her father was an avid reader, that he had a predilection for Spanish and French writers, and that when he found a book that he really liked he read it many times. "Any book worth reading once is worth reading twice, María." He walked out of the library with a copy of Victor Hugo's *Les Miserables*. He had lost count of how many times he had read it.

The streets were still empty except for a few drunks lying on the pavement. Don Severino knew that his sons were still asleep. He stopped at a small market and bought a dozen eggs, a quart of milk, three French rolls, and six pieces of sweet bread. He would prepare a good breakfast for his sons.

He entered the hotel room quietly so as not to wake his sons. He placed the groceries down, took off his hat and coat and with great difficulty, knelt on the floor and took out a statue of Saint Anthony from under his bed and placed it back on the altar. Rain suddenly pounded on the hotel window, jolting him. "Not even a warning; this is a bad sign." He sat in front of the rain-slapped window and watched undulating shadows pass by.

That night Chuy began to hemorrhage, and Lucas went out into the rainy street to call María. But when she arrived, Chuy had already died. She found her disheveled father and youngest brother kneeling on the floor beside Chuy, crying in spasms. "He coughed and sweated all day, María. I tried to give him soup but he refused to eat. I know the beer killed him."

"You killed him," shouted Lucas, "don't try to blame it on the beer."

María knelt next to her brother. The coldness of his hand traveled up her arm and made her shiver. He was only a few years older than her daughters. She had taken care of him as a boy and now she felt as if she had lost a brother and a son.

Don Severino and Lucas didn't attend the funeral. The old man told María that Lucas wouldn't stop drinking and that he couldn't leave him alone. "I must watch him every minute."

Lucas drank all of the tequila that don Severino had stacked in his cabinet and then took his father's pension money to buy himself more liquor. When the money ran out, he did what neither he nor anyone else in the family had ever done. Unshaven, his long hair uncombed, his eyes red and his face swollen from drinking and lack of sleep, he put on a torn shirt, stained trousers, his father's old coat, and with an affected quiver, he stood near a church on Sundays and near a market on weekdays and begged. He made enough for a few days supply of liquor and when the supply ran out he went out to beg again.

Four months later Lucas died. "He wouldn't eat no matter how hard I tried to feed him," said don Severino. "He just wouldn't take food into his mouth. I warned him, María, but he wouldn't listen. Stubbornness killed him, the way it kills all people."

"The old man killed him," said some Portillos, "the way he killed Chuy."

María found her father shaking, staring with anger and fright at the pieces of Saint Jude scattered on the floor. He had never broken a statue. He had stood them on their heads, hid them under the bed, threatened them, cursed them, but he had never broken one. "You deserved it!" he shouted at the broken statue. He had begun a novena to Saint Jude, praying faithfully every day for the recovery of his son, but the novena had been completed and his son lay dead.

"Don't blame yourself, papá, you were good to Lucas, offered him your house, tried to feed him . . ." Don Severino continued staring at the remains of the saint.

"This is no good," said the Portillos, "two funerals in four months . . . this is no good . . . they were young men, it wasn't their time yet."

"When your time has come, nothing can save you."

"But they were too young, why didn't the old man die instead of them?"

"Weeds don't die."

But only one month after Lucas's death, María walked into her father's hotel room and found him in his rocking chair, dead, clutching Saint Anthony in one hand and a rosary in the other.

"He died of old age."

"He died of guilt."

"He never felt guilt in his long miserable life."

All of the Portillos attended the wake. "A relative is a relative," said María, who as usual had taken care of the funeral arrangements and had urged everyone to attend.

Don Severino's wake was unusually quiet. Not even a whisper could be heard until don Severino's two sisters, Josefina and Consuelo walked in. They ran to the coffin and leaned over it, weeping in loud shrieking wails. Josefina grabbed her dead brother's hand. "My little brother! Poor little brother! He's dead . . . gone . . . gone from this world . . ."

Consuelo held his other hand. "I hope you found peace at last."

"Ay!" shrieked Josefina. "I know I'll be next. I can feel it in my old bones." The two sisters held each other. "I'm the next one, said Consuelo. "You can't die and leave me all alone."

One week after don Severino's funeral the hotel where he had lived for fifteen years burnt down.

"No one escaped. It was the worst hotel fire in the city's history."

"Their days were numbered. If the alcohol hadn't taken them, the fire would have."

The three consecutive deaths caused tension in the Portillo's family, and María knew that Ramón, because he was the oldest, was the most tense of all. After he had finished unpacking the cases of tequila at María's house, he sat across from her at the kitchen table. "A cup of coffee, Ramón?"

"How about a glass of tequila?"

"Tequila? What's the occasion?"

"Next week will be my last trip. No more. I'll let someone else take over. I am getting too old for so much excitement. I'll let someone else make the profit."

Ramón made a profit of one dollar for every bottle that he brought across the border. With a load of 500 bottles, and besides from what he earned from selling the cases, it was a good profit.

Some of the Portillos complained about the dollar that Ramón made on each bottle. "It's not right for him to make a profit with his own family."

But María told them,"You should try bringing the tequila yourselves, you'll think that you should charge two dollars per bottle.

A family meeting was held in order to choose a replacement for Ramón. "Do we have any volunteers?" asked Ramón.

"How about Rufelio?" said one Portillo.

"I'm too old," said Rufelio, "that's why Ramón is quitting."

"You probably think I am too young," said Valentín.

"Nobody asked you," said Ramón "You'd probably turn us all in."

One of Ramón's cousins volunteered.

"You're too honest," said Ramón. "When the border officer asks you 'Bringing anything from México?' you'll answer, 'Just tequila, officer.'"

"If you want a good liar," said Rufelio, "there's plenty to choose from."

"I nominate María," someone shouted.

"That's the best choice yet," said several Portillos.

"Leave me out of this."

"It's a great opportunity for you."

"I'll pass up this great opportunity."

"But you're the best one for the job."

"The best of a bad lot."

The matter was left undecided. Beer cans popped open, food appeared, guitars sprang out, people sang, and Valentín preached. "Listen, everybody, if no one wants the job, I'll take it. I think I could do a good job. This could be a big change for all of us . . . believe me, I'd do a good job . . ."

"A good job of smuggling dope."

"I would make a few changes."

"Leave the mass to the priests."

Valentín walked up to Dr. Hernández. "Doctor!"

"Sí, camarada."

"The more I try to figure these people out, the more confused I get."

Dr. Hernández laughed his strong laugh. "Listen, camarada, don't try so hard."

Ramón whistled as he loaded the tequila in his camper while Emilia prepared a plate of beans for him. He walked into her house, washed his hands and face and sat at the table.

"Ay Ramón, I'm going to miss you."

"Once I retire we will see each other more often."

"That's what you say, just to make me feel good."

"I'll always make time to see my little sister." He ate the beans, cupping them in small pieces of tortillas. "I couldn't stay away from your beans."

"I know, they're my magnet." She served Ramón a beer and he asked her for an extra glass. "Two at a time?"

Ramón placed one of the glasses in front of Emilia. "Come on, have a drink with me."

"You know I don't drink, Ramón, don't get me started, I have enough vices."

"Just a little, Emilia. Let's drink to my retirement."

"Okay, but only because it's a special day." She drank the glass of beer in gulps.

"Take it easy, you're supposed to drink it slowly, only drunks drink like that."

"See? Only one glass and I'm already drunk." Emilia opened another bottle of beer, refilled Ramón's glass, and served herself the rest.

"I thought you didn't like it."

"I didn't know how good it makes you feel. No wonder people drink."

"Just stay away from wine; it's bad stuff."

Emilia's eyes opened wider. "Listen, Ramón, how would you like to make a little extra money today since it's your last trip."

"No, Emilia, no dope."

"Wait, let me talk. It's not dope, it's a good deal. El Ronco made his fortune that way."

"If it's not dope, what is it?"

"Look, Ramón, wait for me a few minutes and I'll be back with your fortune."

"No, Emilia, it's getting late."

Emilia stood up and walked toward the door. "Wait here, Ramón, don't go, I'll be back in a few minutes, it'll be worth it, you'll see."

Ramón opened up another beer and sat on the sofa waiting for Emilia. About ten minutes later Emilia returned with her neighbor, La Loca Ramírez and her seven-year-old daughter. Each one was carrying a cage with two parrots inside.

Ramón jumped up. "What's this, Emilia?"

"This is your fortune."

"This is ridiculous. It's out of the question."

"But, Ramón, you can't pass up a good chance like this."

La Loca Ramírez spoke. "Señor Ramón, a lot of people make their fortune this way. Do you know that you can get more than two hundred dollars at the other side for one of these beauties? There's more than a thousand dollar profit for you here. And you can sell them real easy, people will grab them. Andele, Señor Ramón, buy the beautiful birds from me so my family can eat tonight. I'll give them to you real cheap, just because you're Emilia's brother. Ten dollars each; I'm almost giving them to you. Look how they talk. I trained them myself. They know every cuss word in Spanish and even a few in English."

"They talk real good," said Emilia, "just listen to them, they might teach you a word or two."

"That's the trouble, they talk too much. How can I take them across? They would give me away in no time at all. I'd have all the border officers surrounding the camper."

"That's no problem, Señor Ramón. I have it all figured out. We give them a little tequila and the birds will be passed out when you reach the border. You won't hear a peep out of them, they'll be as quiet as if they were dead."

"A thousand dollar profit," muttered Ramón. "That's good money."

"That's great money," said Emilia, "twice as much as you make on the tequila. Don't pass up a fortune, Ramón. If I could, I'd take the deal myself."

"A thousand dollars," sighed Ramón. "Okay, I'll take the birds."

Emilia embraced her brother. "Ay hermano, you're a good man."

La Loca Ramírez hugged her little girl who had been standing next to her looking desolate. "We'll have a good meal tonight, mi hijita." She took the money and handed Ramón the three cages. "Oh my little friends, how I hate to see you go. You were like my own little sons. But for Emilia's relative, I'll make the sacrifice." Ramón gave her an extra ten dollar bill. "Gracias, gracias." As she was leaving she said," Señor Ramón, don't forget to give them their taste of tequila before you leave."

"Don't worry," said Emilia. I'll take care of it myself."

As soon as La Loca Ramírez and her daughter left, Emilia took out a bottle of tequila from a kitchen cabinet, poured a little in a flat ceramic dish, then placed it in one of the cages. "Okay, lewd birds, your day has come. Let's see how well you can cuss when you wake up with a hangover." She repeated the same with the other birds.

Ramón looked on. "Get them good and drunk, I don't want them cursing the border officers."

"Don't worry, Ramón, these swearing birds will soon be in their ninth heaven."

Ramón placed the cages in the back of the camper and took off for the border.

The parrots were silent. "Dead to the world," thought Ramón. He thought about his retirement from the tequila and about the extra money. "A thousand extra . . . no, almost twelve hundred . . . maybe I can get more than two hundred for each bird . . ." He smiled at the police and the officer smiled back.

"Bringing anything from México?"

"Just this hat for my wife."

(Viejo cabrón)

"What was that?"

"What was what?"

"I thought I heard something."

"I didn't hear anything."

(Viejo cabrón)

"It sounds like a woman's voice."

(Viejo cabrón)

"It sounds like it's coming from the back of your camper, said the officer as he walked toward the back of Ramón's car.

(Viejo cabrón)

The officer stood in front of Ramón and asked him to unlock the back of the camper. Five of the parrots were completely passed out, but one of them was pacing his cage, drunk, repeating what was apparently his favorite curse.

The telephone rang and María answered it. "Ramón? Where are you? Oh, no, how did it happen? What? Are you joking? You're not joking? You were turned in by a parrot? Oh Ramón, and by a parrot!"

María hung up the receiver and sat down with her head bent. She soon stood up and squared her shoulders. She called all of her relatives and told them the bad news, then called Valentín and asked him to pick up his father at the border. Then she called Dr. Hernández. "Tell your friend, the lawyer, that he has work." She began to pray to all the saints. "Maybe one of them will listen."

Ramón's camper was confiscated, and he drove back to his house with Valentín. "I told you you would get caught," said Valentín, "and for what? Don't tell me it was worth it. If you're going to take these chances . . ."

Ramón looked at his son and shouted, "That's enough from you! I don't want to hear a single word coming out of your mouth!" They drove to their house in complete silence.

María sat tall as she observed her relatives entering the courthouse. Ramón sat next to his lawyer, occasionally glancing back at his family. He was perspiring heavily. The lawyer leaned toward him and whispered, Don't worry, we'll come out of this alive."

The judge walked in and Ramón felt a sudden headache coming on. He stared uneasily at the judge who turned out to be an attractive middle aged woman. His head began to pound. Hadn't a woman judge locked up his father? The next few minutes felt like a bad dream to Ramón. He turned to his lawyer. "How did we do?"

"Not bad. They're keeping the camper, as usual, and a thousand dollar fine."

"A thousand dollars?"

"They usually go easy on first offenders."

Ramón still felt dazed as he walked out of the courthouse. Someone shouted at him, "Hey, Ramón, where's the party going to be? Your house or María's?" María looked at Ramón. He looked older to her. She looked at Valentín, at Rufelio, and at all of her other relatives who stood in a circle outside of the courthouse trying to decide where to meet. She wondered if anyone would try to take up where Ramón had left off, or what other chamba they would find to supplement their incomes. She thought of herself, of her work, of the bundles of clothes that she sometimes took to sew in her house at night. She might start doing that regularly. Or maybe there was something else she could do. She looked at the sun; it looked like a host offering itself to her.

There Are No Madmen Here (San Diego: Maize Press, 1981). Revised in 1996. Used by permission of the author.